# The Vatican-Israel Accords

# The Vatican-Israel Accords

## Political, Legal, and Theological Contexts

## MARSHALL J. BREGER

*editor*

*University of Notre Dame Press*
*Notre Dame, Indiana*

Copyright © 2004 by University of Notre Dame
Notre Dame, Indiana 46556
www.undpress.nd.edu
All Rights Reserved

Manufactured in the United States of America

*Library of Congress Cataloging-in-Publication Data*
The Vatican-Israel accords : political, legal, and theological contexts /
edited by Marshall J. Breger.
    p.   cm.
Includes bibliographical references and index.
ISBN 0-268-04358-2 (cloth : alk. paper)
1. Catholic Church—Foreign relations—Israel.   2. Israel—Foreign
relations—Catholic Church.   I. Breger, Marshall J.
BX1628.V38   2004
327.456'3405694—dc22

                                         2003021192

I dedicate this book to my wife, Jennifer Anne Breger,
whose intellectual interests know no bounds and whose incisive
criticism significantly aided my efforts, and to our children,
Sarah Gavriella and Esther Meira,
who are the light of both our lives.

# CONTENTS

Acknowledgments                                                    xi

Contributors                                                      xiii


Introduction                                                        1
*Marshall J. Breger*


I  THE MAKING OF THE ACCORD

1  The Stages of Diplomatic Negotiations                           29
   *Lorenzo Cremonesi*


II  THE MEANING OF THE ACCORD

2  The Fundamental Agreement between the Holy See and the          51
   State of Israel: A New Legal Regime of Church-State Relations
   *David-Maria A. Jaeger, O.F.M.*

3  Israel's Understanding of the Fundamental Agreement with        67
   the Holy See
   *Leonard Hammer*

4    The Fundamental Agreement between the Holy See and Israel          96
     and the Conventions between States and the Church since
     the Vatican II Council
     *Silvio Ferrari*


III     VATICAN CONCORDATS AND THE ACCORD

5    The Fundamental Agreement between the Holy See and                 119
     the State of Israel and Church-State Agreements in Spain:
     Some Contrasts and Comparisons
     *Rafael Palomino*

6    The Position of the Catholic Church regarding Concordats           139
     from a Doctrinal and Pragmatic Perspective
     *Roland Minnerath*

7    The Holy See–PLO Basic Agreement in Light of the                   150
     Holy See–Israel Fundamental Agreement
     *Leonard Hammer*


IV     INTERNATIONAL LAW AND THE ACCORDS

8    Israel-Vatican Relations since the Signing of the Fundamental      167
     Agreement
     *David Rosen*

9    The Freedom of Proselytism under the Fundamental Agreement         183
     and International Law
     *Moshe Hirsch*

10   Progress for Pilgrims? An Analysis of the Holy See–Israel          203
     Fundamental Agreement
     *Geoffrey R. Watson*

11   Human Rights, the Foundation of Peace: The Teaching of the         235
     Catholic Church, with Special Reference to Religious Freedom
     *Giorgio Filibeck*

V   THE CHURCH IN THE HOLY LAND TODAY

12   Freedom of Religion and of Conscience in Israel          249
     *Ruth Lapidoth*

13   The Vatican and the Middle East during the Pontificate    276
     of John Paul II
     *Silvio Ferrari*

14   Palestinian Christians: Recent Developments               307
     *Drew Christiansen, S.J.*


VI   CATHOLIC-JEWISH RELATIONS AS
     BACKGROUND TO THE ACCORD

15   Jews and Catholics in the Last Half Century               343
     *Jack Bemporad*


     Appendix I
     Fundamental Agreement between the Holy See and the        359
     State of Israel

     Appendix II
     Agreement between the Holy See and the State of Israel     365
     Pursuant to Article 3§3 of the Fundamental Agreement between
     the Holy See and the State of Israel (also referred to as the
     Legal Personality Agreement)

     Appendix III
     The Basic Agreement between the Holy See and the           369
     Palestinian Liberation Organization

     Appendix IV                                                373
     Forerunner to the Accord: A Personal Recollection on
     Issues of Pilgrimage
     *Richard Mathes*


     Index                                                      379

# ACKNOWLEDGMENTS

I thank Interim Dean Robert Destro and Dean Douglas Kmiec of the Columbus School of Law, Catholic University of America, for their enthusiastic support of this project. I wish, as well, to thank Bernard Dobranski, formerly dean of the Columbus School of Law, for his support of a conference at the law school on the topic of this volume, entitled "Continuing the Dialogue: The Fundamental Agreement between the Holy See and the State of Israel: A Third Anniversary Perspective." Early versions of a number of the papers herein were first delivered at that conference. A number of those early versions were later published in volume 47 of the *Catholic University Law Review* in the Winter 1998 issue, and I thank the editors (former and present) for their assistance as well as for the requisite legal permissions. For this volume, the papers have been updated through early 2003.

Ms. Natalie Osterer rendered invaluable and incisive research assistance and Ms. Julie Kendrick cheerful yet assiduous assistance on the typescript.

I wish, as well, to acknowledge the financial support from the Bradley Foundation, Milwaukee, Wisconsin, that made this publication possible.

Earlier versions of various chapters appeared in the *Catholic University Law Review*, vol. 47 (Winter 1998), as noted below:

"The Fundamental Agreement between the Holy See and the State of Israel: A New Legal Regime of Church-State Relations," Father David-Maria A. Jaeger.

"The Fundamental Agreement between the Holy See and Israel and the Conventions between States and the Church since the Vatican II Council," Silvio Ferrari.

"The Fundamental Agreement between the Holy See and the State of Israel and Church-State Agreements in Spain: Some Contrasts and Comparisons," Rafael Palomino.

"The Position of the Catholic Church Regarding Concordats from a Doctrinal and Pragmatic Perspective," Monsignor Roland Minnerath.

"The Freedom of Proselytism under the Fundamental Agreement and International Law," Moshe Hirsch.

"Progress for Pilgrims? An Analysis of the Holy See–Israel Fundamental Agreement," Geoffrey R. Watson.

"Freedom of Religion and of Conscience in Israel," Ruth Lapidoth.

In a volume such as this it is appropriate to acknowledge the pioneering efforts of the late Yaacov Herzog *z'l* in laying the early foundations for Israel's diplomatic relationship with the Vatican.

# CONTRIBUTORS

### Jack Bemporad

Rabbi Jack Bemporad earned a B.A. with honors in philosophy from Tulane University and an M.A. with honors in philosophy from Hebrew Union College. He was a Fulbright Scholar at the University of Rome. He was ordained a rabbi in 1959 and received an honorary doctor of divinity from Hebrew Union College in 1984. Rabbi Bemporad has taught at Southern Methodist University, the University of Rome, the New School of Social Research, and the University of Pennsylvania. He is a former chairman of the Interreligious Affairs Committee of the Synagogue Council of America (SCA), and former director of the Commissions on Worship and Adult Education of the Union of American Hebrew Congregation's National Organization of Reform Judiasm. He represented the International Jewish Committee on Interreligious Consultations at the Vatican to negotiate the Prague meeting, and headed the Synagogue Council of America's Delegation to Prague. In 1995, Rabbi Bemporad received the prestigious Luminosa Award of the Focolare Movement, and in 1996, the Raoul Wallenberg Humanitarian Leadership Award of the Center for Holocaust and Genocide Studies of Ramapo College. He is currently director of the Center for Christian-Jewish Understanding of Sacred Heart University in Fairfield, Connecticut.

Rabbi Bemporad has edited three books and has written numerous articles and theological papers that have appeared in the *Handbook of American Psychiatry*, *The Encyclopedia of Religion*, and other periodicals, journals, and publications. Recent works include *Stupid Ways, Smart Ways to Think about God*, with Michael Shevack (1999), and *Our Age* (1996).

### *Marshall J. Breger*

Marshall J. Breger is a professor of law at the Columbus School of Law, Catholic University of America. In fall 2002 he was Lady Davis Visiting Professor of Law at the Hebrew University in Jerusalem. From 1997 to 1999 he was an adjunct fellow for the Center for Strategic and International Studies (CSIS). He also serves as vice president of the Jewish Policy Center, a public policy think tank in Washington, D.C. During the George H. W. Bush administration, he served as solicitor of labor, the chief lawyer of the Labor Department. From 1985 to 1991 Breger was chairman of the Administrative Conference of the United States. From 1983 to 1985 he was a special assistant to President Reagan and his liaison with the Jewish community. He writes a regular column for *Moment* magazine.

Breger writes and speaks regularly on both legal issues and issues of Jewish public policy and has published in numerous law reviews as well as in periodicals such as the *Middle East Quarterly*, the *Journal of International Affairs*, the *Los Angeles Times*, the *Washington Post*, the *Wall Street Journal*, and the *New York Times*. Among his most recent publications are *Jerusalem's Holy Places and the Peace Process*, with Thomas A. Indinopolos (1998), and *Jerusalem: A City and Its Future*, with Ora Ahemir (2002).

### *Drew Christiansen, S.J.*

Father Drew Christiansen, S.J., is associate editor of *America*, the national Catholic weekly. Previously he was senior fellow at the Woodstock Institute in Washington, D.C., and director of the Office of International Justice and Peace, United States Catholic Conference.

### *Lorenzo Cremonesi*

Lorenzo Cremonesi is senior correspondent, *Corriere Della Sera*, Milan. For fifteen years he was the paper's correspondent in Jerusalem.

### *Silvio Ferrari*

Silvio Ferrari is professor of ecclesiastical law at the University of Milan. He has served as editor of the *Quaderni di diritto e politica ecclesiastica* (Bologna), member of the editorial council of the *Journal of Church and State* (Waco), member of the executive committee of the European Consortium for Church and State Research (Milan), member of the board of directors of the International Academy for Freedom of Religion and Belief (Washington), and member of the research group on *droit* and religion (Conseil National de Recherche Scientifique, Strasbourg). He has written extensively on relations between church and state in Italy and Western Europe, on the Jerusalem question, and on relations between the Vatican and Israel.

### Giorgio Filibeck

Giorgio Filibeck received his doctor in jurisprudence from the State University of Rome in 1968. He has been a member of the executive staff of the Pontifical Council for Justice and Peace since 1969, Observer of the Holy See at the annual round table of the International Institute of Humanitarian Law since 1984, and Observer of the Holy See at the steering committee of the Council of Europe for Human Rights since 1992. He was a member of the delegation of the Holy See at the World Conference on Human Rights in Vienna in June 1993. He is author of *Human Rights in the Teaching of John Paul II* (1980), *The Theme of Violence in the Teaching of John Paul II* (1985), *The Right of Development—Conciliar and Pontifical Texts* (1991), and *Human Rights in the Teaching of the Church: From John XXIII to John Paul II* (1994).

### Leonard Hammer

Leonard Hammer teaches at the Academic Law College at Ramat-Gan. He received his Ph.D. from the University of London, working on the "International Human Right to Freedom of Conscience." He was law clerk to the Hon. Menachem Elon (retired), then deputy president of the Israel Supreme Court, in 1989–1990.

### Moshe Hirsch

Moshe Hirsch is a senior lecturer of international law at the Faculty of Law and at the Department of International Relations, the Hebrew University of Jerusalem, teaching international law, international trade law, and European Community law. He is also a member of the Think-Tank on the Future Status of Jerusalem, the Jerusalem Institute for Israel Studies. His recent publications focus on the future status of Jerusalem, international trade and European Union law, and international environmental law.

### David-Maria A. Jaeger, O.F.M.

Father David-Maria A. Jaeger, a Franciscan priest of the Custody of the Holy Land, is professor of canon law at the Pontifical "Athenaeum" Antonianum in Rome, and continues to serve on the delegation of the Holy See on the Bilateral Permanent Working Commission between the Holy See and the State of Israel. Among other appointments, he is a consultor of the Pontifical Council for the Interpretation of Legislative Texts and a judge of the appellate court for the dioceses of Texas. He was previously (1992–1998) the vicar judicial in the diocese of Austin, Texas.

### Ruth Lapidoth

Ruth Lapidoth is Greenblatt Professor Emeritus at the Hebrew University of Jerusalem, professor at the Law School of the College of Management, and senior researcher at the Jerusalem Institue for Israel Studies. In addition, she has taught and conducted research at various institutions in the United States and in Europe. She has served as a member of the Israeli delegation to the United Nations General Assembly and has been a delegate to various international conferences. She participated in the peace talks between Egypt and Israel and was legal adviser to the Ministry of Foreign Affairs from 1979 to 1981.

She was a member of the arbitration panel that dealt with a boundary dispute between Egypt and Israel (1988). Since 1989 she has been a member of the Permanent Court of Arbitration. In 2000 she received the Prominent Woman in International Law award from the WILIG group of the American Society of International Law.

### Richard Mathes

The Rev. Msgr. Richard Mathes studied philosophy and theology in Innsbruck, Paris, Cambridge, Bonn, and Rome, receiving his doctorate in philosophy at the Institut Catholique de Paris in 1968 and his doctorate in theology at the University of Bonn in 1974. From 1972 until the present, he has been lecturer in anthropology and philosophy of nature at the Angelicum in Rome. In 1977, he became chargé of the Holy See for the Notre Dame of Jerusalem Center. Msgr. Mathes was appointed cultural attaché to the apostolic delegation in Jerusalem, with CD status in 1978. He is presently rector of the Pontificio Istituto S. Maria dell'Anima, Rome, Italy. His major publications include *Evolution und Finalität-Versuch einer philosophischen Deutung* (1971), *Löwen und Rom: Zur Gründung der katholischen Universität Löwen unter besonderer Berücksichtigung der Kirchen- und Bildungspolitik Papst Gregors XVI* (1975), and *L'iniziatore di una scienza integrale, in Sant' Alberto Magno, l'umomo e il pensatore* (1982).

### Roland Minnerath

Rev. Roland Minnerath studied history at the Sorbonne, where he first published *Les chrétiens et le monde, 1er–2e siècle* (Paris, 1974). He also studied management, writing a dissertation on *Les organisations malades de la science: La rationalité du management* (Paris, 1982). After studies in theology and canon law in Strasbourg and Rome he was ordained a priest in 1978. His main publications at this time were *Le droit de l'Église à la liberté: Du Syllabus à Vatican II* (1982) and *L'Église et les États concordataires, 1846–1965* (1983). He entered the diplomatic service of the Holy See after attending the Pontifical Academy for Diplomacy in Rome. He served in the apostolic nunciatures in Brazil and Germany and the Secretariat of State of the Vatican. Since 1989 he has been a professor at the Catholic Theological Faculty of the University of Strasbourg, France. He also serves as a consultant to the Secretariat of State and member both of the Pontifical Academy for Social Sciences and the International Theological Commission. His most recent publications are *Jésus et le pouvoir* (1987), *De Jérusalem à Rome: Pierre et l'unité de l'Église apostolique* (1995), and *Histoire des conciles* (1996).

### Rafael Palomino

Rafael Palomino received his J.D. from the Universidad Autónoma de Madrid in 1989 and his Ph.D. from the Universidad Complutense de Madrid in 1993. In 1995 he received the Extraordinary Doctoral Dissertation Award from the Universidad Complutense School of Law. He is a member of the Center for Judeo-Christian Studies in Madrid and of the Consociatio Juris Canonici Studio Promovendo. He is author of, among other publications, *Las Objeciones de Conciencia: Conflictos entre Conciencia y Ley en el Derecho Norteamericano* (1994), *Derecho a la Intimidad y Religión: La Protección Jurídica del Secreto Religioso* (1999), and *Estado y Religión: Textos para una Reflexión Crítica* (2000). He is currently professor of law at Universidad Complutense de Madrid, research professor of the Human Rights Institute of Universidad Complutense, vice-director of *Anuario de Derecho Eclesiástico del Estado* (Church-State Law Spanish Yearbook), and secretary of the *Revista General de Derecho Canónico y Derecho Eclesiástico del Estado* (Church-State & Canon Law Review).

### David Rosen

Rabbi David Rosen is international director of interreligious affairs, American Jewish Committee. He was previously executive director, Israel office of the Anti-Defamation League. He is a former chief rabbi of Ireland and was a member of the Israeli negotiating team on the Vatican-Israel accord.

### Geoffrey R. Watson

Geoffrey R. Watson is a professor of law at the Catholic University of America's Columbus School of Law in Washington, D.C. Professor Watson received his B.A. from Yale in 1982 and his J.D. from Harvard in 1986. In 1986–1987 he clerked for the Hon. Harrison L. Winter, then-chief judge of the U.S. Court of Appeals for the Fourth Circuit. From 1987 to 1991 he served as an attorney-adviser in the Office of the Legal Adviser at the U.S. Department of State. From 1987 to 1989 he was assigned to the Office of Law Enforcement and Intelligence, and from 1989 to 1991 he was assigned to the Office of Near Eastern and South Asian Affairs, which deals with legal aspects of U.S. policy in the Middle East. From 1991 to 1995 he taught international law and related subjects at Seattle University School of Law. He has been teaching at the Catholic University of America since 1995. He is the author of *The Oslo Accords: International Law and the Israeli-Palestinian Peace Agreements* (2000).

# INTRODUCTION

*Marshall J. Breger*

The Fundamental Agreement between Israel and the Holy See was clearly a political document—one undertaken between two sovereign subjects of international law.[1] At the same time, there can be no doubt that the accord would not have been possible without significant change in the traditional theological approach of the Catholic Church toward the people of Israel. Any student of modern Christianity will understand immediately the extraordinary changes that have taken place in recent Vatican thinking toward Judaism and the Jewish people. Since the 1965 Vatican declaration *Nostra Aetate*[2] the Catholic Church has made a 180-degree turn in its view of Jews and Judaism. Moving beyond what Jules Isaac termed "the teaching of contempt,"[3] Catholics now teach that "the Jews still remain most dear to God."[4] In a 1985 statement, the Vatican told us that "Judaism is a living religion" and that the Hebrew Bible "retains its own value as revelation."[5] In a 2001 study, Cardinal Ratzinger, the Vatican's chief theologian, validated Judaism's interpretation of the Jewish Scriptures *for* Jews.[6]

### The Vatican and Israel

The Vatican view toward a Jewish state in Palestine has evolved together with its theological position toward Judaism.[7] In January 1904, Theodore Herzl, the founder of political Zionism, met with Pope Pius X to ask for his support for the Zionist enterprise.[8] The pope's reported response was swift and certain:

> We are unable to favor this movement. We cannot prevent the Jews from going to Jerusalem—but we could never sanction it. The ground of Jerusalem, if it were not always sacred, has been sanctified by the life of Jesus Christ. As the head of the Church I cannot answer you otherwise. The Jews have not recognized our Lord, therefore we cannot recognize the Jewish people.[9]

With the collapse of the Ottoman Empire and the entry of the British army, under Lord Edmund Allenby, into Jerusalem, the Holy See became increasingly concerned over the future status of the Holy Places[10] and made various efforts to ensure that its interests in the Holy Land would remain protected.[11] Its goal was to ensure control of Palestine by a Western power—preferably Catholic. First, the Vatican sought to have Italy or another Catholic state take the Palestine Mandate.[12] For a while it even championed the cause of Belgium.[13] Failing in such efforts the Vatican sought, at least, to keep the mandate in "Christian" hands.[14] As Cardinal Gasparri, the Vatican secretary of state, told the French attaché in Rome, "It is difficult to take a piece of our heart away from the Turks in order to give it to the Zionists."[15] Thus, fear of Zionism led the Holy See initially "to stir up opposition"[16] to Britain—a Protestant country—taking on the mandate.

During World War I, Britain had promulgated the Balfour Declaration, stating that it "view[ed] with favour" the development of a Jewish national home in Palestine.[17] By the time the League of Nations awarded the Palestine Mandate to Britain in 1922[18] (it actually took up the mandate in 1923), Britain had shifted ground, as it sought to navigate between its Balfour Declaration commitments and the interests of the local Arab population. The entire twenty-five years of British rule saw continuous Jewish immigration (legal and illegal) met by growing Arab resistance (violent and otherwise). By 1937, a royal commission (the Peel Report) called for the partition of Palestine to allow for the creation of independent Arab and Jewish states. At the same time it called for detaching Jerusalem, Bethlehem, Nazareth, and the Sea of Galilee as a *corpus separatum*, or a separate enclosure under international administration.[19] The commission's recommendations were shelved with the approach of world war. By the end of World War II, the intensity of Jewish commitment to Palestine grew and a war-weary Britain chose to "break camp" as part of its more general imperial retreat.[20]

In November 1947, the United Nations General Assembly voted in favor of partitioning Palestine into independent Arab and Jewish states after much hard lobbying by Zionists, who favored partition, and Arab leaders, who opposed it.[21] The Jerusalem-Bethlehem area (with a corridor to the Mediterranean Sea) was designated a *corpus separatum* to be administered by the United Nations itself.[22] Events on the ground, however, swiftly overtook diplomacy. The United Nations partition recommendation was not acted upon because of the outbreak of war in May 1948 between the newly declared State of Israel and five surrounding Arab nations.

Both at the time of the 1947 partition plan and afterwards, the Vatican supported the internationalization of the city of Jerusalem.[23] After the Six-Day War, however, Vatican policy on Jerusalem began to move away from its insistence on the creation of a separate legal jurisdiction or *corpus separatum* to accept the notion of international guarantees to safeguard the uniqueness of the city.[24] While the Vatican has never formally withdrawn its internationalization proposals, that option is simply not on the political agenda of any of the present "stakeholders" in the Jerusalem dispute.

### The Holy See–Israel Accord

In December 1993, the Holy See signed an accord with Israel that led to recognition and the exchange of ambassadors.[25] The bilateral agreement dealt with a variety of political issues, including taxation of churches and pilgrimage rights. The agreement committed both parties to promote religious freedom and ensure access to the Holy Places. As the accord stated, "[t]he State of Israel affirms its continuing commitment to maintain and respect the 'Status quo' in the Christian Holy Places to which it applies and the respective rights of the Christian communities there under."[26]

The 1993 accord called for the creation of a number of working groups to follow up in areas such as the taxation and the legal personality of the Catholic Church during a three-year period. Consistent with the Vatican's new approach toward the Jewish people, the agreement also stated that "[t]he Holy See and the State of Israel are committed to appropriate cooperation in combating all forms of antisemitism."[27]

Lorenzo Cremonesi's essay at the beginning of this volume provides a useful overview of the stages of negotiations that eventually resulted in the Fundamental Agreement—including an analysis of the various pitfalls that the parties encountered and how the Fundamental Agreement negotiations closely responded to the wider Middle East peace process.[28] In addition, the first of Leonard Hammer's two contributions to this volume provides an Israeli perspective on the Fundamental Agreement, offering a close technical analysis of the document.[29] For his part, Father David-Maria Jaeger provides a complementary analysis of the Fundamental Agreement from a Vatican perspective. Jaeger goes beyond the 1993 accord to discuss the 1997 agreement on legal personality as well.[30] Finally, Silvio Ferrari proffers an analysis of the Fundamental Agreement against the context of other Vatican agreements negotiated since Vatican II. This effort at comparative religious diplomacy sets the stage for understanding the diplomatic parameters within which the Vatican could operate in negotiating the Fundamental Agreement.

The Church expected the 1993 accord to begin a new day in Vatican-Israel relations. From 1993 to 1997, the hopes that the Fundamental Agreement would lead to a flowering of Vatican-Israeli relations were never consummated. Working group meetings on outstanding issues began auspiciously on July 4, 1994. Despite this initial effort, nothing was done to undertake the joint activity on anti-Semitism, and the taxation working group meetings petered out in early 1996. Most important, the agreement on legal personality, which had been assiduously negotiated by technical working groups throughout 1994 and 1995 and initialed by representatives of the negotiating team in May 1996, seemed to hit a deep freeze.

At first, delay was understandable. The election in May of Benjamin Netanyahu as prime minister was naturally going to create an interregnum until a new foreign policy team took over. The delay, however, had more deep-seated roots. Unlike the Peres government, which had an interest in matters European, the Netanyahu government expressed little interest in the Vatican "file." Indeed, Netanyahu visited Italy in February 1997 to meet with the pope at the Vatican,[31] and he conferred afterward with Cardinal Sodano, the Vatican secretary of state, and Vatican Foreign Minister Jean-Louis Tauran. Tauran asked about the Legal Personality Agreement and, to the Vatican's dismay, Netanyahu responded that this was the first he had heard of it.[32] For its part, the Vatican was extremely unhappy with this delay. In commenting on this lack of progress, Archbishop Claudio Celli in spring 1996 pointed out:

> In the name of the honesty and openness which has characterized the relations between the Holy See and the Israeli authorities, let me say at the outset and with great candor that we have recently arrived at a critical moment in our bilateral relationship: we cannot ignore the great need for a renewed commitment, lest the hope raised by the signing of the Fundamental Agreement should come to naught. For several months, the Holy See has not been able to convince its counterpart to take up the necessary work and, in particular, to proceed with the formalization of the sole concrete fruit of the efforts which followed the signing of the Fundamental Agreement.[33]

Following Celli's remarks at the Catholic University of America's Columbus School of Law, William Cardinal Keeler called a meeting on the need for progress with American Jewish leaders.[34] Shortly thereafter the Legal Personality Agreement was signed.

The delay in signing the Legal Personality Agreement was extremely frustrating for the Holy See. As one Vatican diplomat noted, it is necessary to bring "an awareness of the need to go forward with what the journey demands, otherwise there is the risk that everything that has already been done will be rendered void."[35]

From the Vatican perspective, recognition of the Church as a legal entity was of the utmost importance. For approximately 500 years, the Church had maintained an undefined legal status under the Ottoman Empire, the British Mandate, and Israeli rule. The Church and its institutions in Israel were recognized de facto under the Ottoman "Status Quo" agreements. Now, the Vatican had given away in the 1993 accord what it deemed to be its own best bargaining chip—recognition of the State of Israel. Some in the Roman Curia, who had urged caution in opening relations with Israel, were now suggesting "I told you so." The Church felt strongly the need to institutionalize its legal status.

From the Israeli perspective there was concern at the political level that an agreement with the Catholic Church might, in some way, offend the orthodox religious elements in Netanyahu's jostling governing coalition. The foreign minister, to some extent, was left to rely on the approval of the attorney general, a highly respected orthodox former jurist, not only for legal sufficiency, but for some element of political cover as well.

The agreement on the legal personality of the Catholic Church was approved by the Israeli cabinet on September 7, 1997, and signed by Israeli Foreign Minister David Levy and the Apostolic Nuncio Archbishop Montezemolo in Jerusalem on November 10, 1997.[36] The purpose of the agreement was to normalize the status and legal personality of the Catholic Church and its institutions. The agreement determined that the Catholic Church and many of its institutions would be assured legal personality (such as association or corporate status) under Israeli law. The institutions also would be included in a public registry and their interaction with non-Church bodies in Israel would be subject to Israeli law, including litigation in Israeli law courts.

On the other hand, Church institutions would maintain full internal autonomy in the administration of their institutions and assets in Israel. Adjudication of these matters would be left to the Church in accordance with canon law. Thus, Israel committed itself "not only to the de jure confirmation of those rights pertaining to the Catholic Church's educational and philanthropic institutions, but also to enshrine the authoritative structure of the Catholic Church's hierarchy and religious orders in Israeli law."[37]

The agreement also consists of directives, principles for implementation, and appendices. The appendices include the list of Church institutions that have been recognized as legal persons and are to be included in the state registry. Names of institutions may be added or removed from the list in the future.

It should be noted that during the negotiations the Israelis claimed that there was a need for positive legislation by the Israeli Knesset to implement the Legal Personality Agreement. Yet surprisingly, the "required" implementing legislation has not yet been submitted (and the extent to which such legislation is, in fact, "required," remains unclear).

It is important to note that the agreement concerns Catholic institutions with addresses in areas where Israeli legislation is in effect—which includes, of course, "East Jerusalem."[38] This resulted in the Palestinians calling the agreement "a stab in the back."[39] In early December 1997, the Palestinian legislature sent an "urgent message" to the Islamic summit in Teheran calling on Yasser Arafat to send a delegation to "inform the Pope of the dangerous consequences of this agreement."[40]

### Future Issues

We are entering the tenth year since the signing of the Fundamental Agreement. Despite the progress that has been made in Vatican-Israel relations, significant issues remain. The following are some of the most pressing issues.

#### Christians Living in the Holy Land

Christians face three practical problems which affect their relations with Israel. First, they are fractured and each group is concerned that another church might secure advantages that it does not have. Thus, they insist on the Ottoman "Status Quo" at all times even if doing so might hurt their individual interests. For example, the different denominations who claim possessory interests in the Church of the Holy Sepulcher jealously guard every inch of "title" and every presumption of customary privilege that they can. The Copts, an Egyptian Christian Church, and the Ethiopian Christians have argued for centuries over the monastery of Deir al-Sultan east of the Church of the Holy Sepulcher. The Copts were in possession until 1970, when on Easter night the Ethiopians entered and changed the locks while the Copts were at church. In protest, the Copts camped out for years in an encampment of "huts" by their old home. Efforts to remedy this reversal of fortune remain mired in the Israeli legal process.[41]

Even today, the Christian communities remain at odds over control of the Christian Holy Places. It has taken more than thirty years to create a consensus among the different denominations present at the Church of the Holy Sepulcher as to how to proceed with vital building repairs.[42] A consensus was only reached after Israeli officials, fearing a cave-in, threatened to make the repairs to the ceiling themselves. A dispute over the painting of the dome of the rotunda took more than twelve years to resolve.[43]

The Greek Orthodox have often indicated that maintenance of Israeli control of Christian Holy Places was preferable to revision of the Ottoman Status Quo.[44] The Greek Orthodox fear that, in any revision, they would lose out to the larger and more powerful Roman Catholic Church.[45] In speaking of the Holy Places, Metropolitan Timothy, secretary of the Greek Orthodox patriarch of Jerusalem, underscored that "[t]he Vatican does not represent us."[46] In late 1995, the Patriarch Diodoros I issued a call for a legally binding agreement with Israel that would not compromise the existing Status Quo.[47] Similar intramural tension might be expected among Muslim interests if they were to be handed the Muslim Holy Places to "govern."

Second, most of the lay Christians in the Jerusalem area are Palestinians and do not wish, out of either solidarity or fear, to isolate themselves from general Palestinian concerns. Many of the clergy, including the senior clergy, are from European countries and have interests that are not necessarily identical with the Palestinian laity.[48] This is particularly true for the Greek Orthodox, whose "parachuted" senior clergy (all Greek) are often at odds with the local Arab laity.

Third, there is a real concern with maintaining a sufficient Christian community in Jerusalem to serve as "witness" to Christian needs and concerns. This demographic problem may not be the fault of any specific party, but it is real. Since 1948, the Christian community of Jerusalem has dropped in size from thirty thousand to between ten and twelve thousand. Bethlehem, where Church tradition places Jesus' birth, no longer has a Christian majority.[49] Rev. Peter Vasko, a Franciscan priest and leader of the Holy Land Foundation, has warned, "If we don't do something now, within 60 to 70 years, there will be no Christian Churches in the Holy Land . . . Christian holy sites will be empty monuments."[50]

Rev. Drew Christiansen's essay in this volume[51] expands on the sociological history of the Palestinian Christians in their land. In so doing he provides, as well, a useful "church" history of the Palestinian Church in the last decade. His sensitivity to Palestinian Christian concerns reminds us that the Vatican-Israel relationship cannot ignore the Christian communities "on the ground."[52]

The Christian community never assumed that they need only be concerned with their relations with the Israeli government. In the mid-1990s the Palestinian Ministry of Religion appointed Ibrahim Kandallaf, a Greek Orthodox resident of East Jerusalem, to be adviser on Christian affairs. While Kandallaf's authority, so to speak, extended only to areas within the control of the Palestinian Authority, where there are presently few Christian holy sites, he operated de facto throughout eastern Jerusalem, joining Israeli officials on the dais at eastern Jerusalem Christian events.[53] His office was closed down by Israeli troops in April 1999 on grounds that he was representing the PA in Jerusalem in contravention of both the Oslo agreement and Israeli law.[54]

Further, in July 1997, the Palestinian Authority evicted a "White" Russian contingent from a church in Hebron (which it controls under the Oslo agreement) and presented it to representatives of the Russian patriarch in Moscow.[55] Thus, the Christian communities may have no choice but to negotiate with the Palestinians.

Indeed, in 1996, Israeli officials raised concerns over the fate of a Christian holy site, Jesus' Cradle, which is located on the Temple Mount, suggesting that the Muslim authorities might be planning to tear down that Christian site.[56] For their part, the *waqf* denied the charge.

The now seemingly failed discussions over Jerusalem's "final status" has given rise to serious Christian-Jewish fissure. The so-called Abu Mazen–Beilin "non-paper" on final status issues, including Jerusalem, purportedly called for the Church of the Holy Sepulcher to be placed under extraterritorial Palestinian jurisdiction.[57] And, indeed, at the July 2000 Camp David negotiations it was rumored that this was on offer. Throughout the negotiations the Church feared the consequences of their exclusion from the talks. They desperately wanted a "place at the table."[58]

The negotiations had indeed covered vital Christian concerns. According to one account, President Clinton's proposals to breach the "log jam" on Jerusalem included placing the Christian quarter under Palestinian sovereignty. It was Yasser Arafat who refused, insisting "that the Armenian quarter must fall under Palestinian sovereignty as well."[59] The Vatican responded harshly to these reports, telling the Israelis they felt betrayed.[60]

The patriarchs of the Greek Orthodox, Catholic, and Armenian Orthodox churches sent a letter to President Bill Clinton, Prime Minister Ehud Barak, and Palestinian Leader Yasser Arafat asking for the right to send representatives to the Camp David peace talks and any future forums dealing with the status of Jerusalem.[61] Reports suggest that these overtures were rebuffed, although then-Secretary of State Madeline Albright traveled to Rome shortly after to brief the Holy See on the Jerusalem dossier.[62]

It should have been no surprise, then, that shortly after signing the 1993 Vatican-Israel accord the Vatican moved toward establishing official links with the Palestinian Liberation Organization (PLO). In October 1994, following several months of negotiations, the Vatican and the PLO announced the establishment of official links. The PLO opened an office at the Vatican and the papal nuncio in Tunis became responsible for the Vatican's contacts with PLO leaders. In a joint statement issued by the Vatican, the parties announced that the official links would "open channels for communication" to "jointly . . . search for peace and justice . . . in the Middle East" with a view toward "preserving the religious and cultural values which mark the Peoples of the region, and which properly belong to the Holy Land and especially to the Holy City of Jerusalem."[63] By 1997 the Vatican had signed an agreement with the PLO.[64] A more detailed analysis of the Vatican/PLO agreement appears in the second contribution of Leonard Hammer to this volume.[65] His analysis includes a comparison to the Fundamental Agreement between the Vatican and Israel and explores the possible political consequences that could arise from perceived differences in the two agreements.[66]

### The Status of the Holy Places

Having recognized both the State of Israel and the PLO, the Vatican hoped to have a "seat" at the table when final status issues were discussed.[67] As noted previously, this does not seem to have occurred.[68] Still the Vatican has asserted its position in the Jerusalem question as not only a matter of right but "a right which it exercises—to express a moral judgment on the situation."[69] However described, this right does not extend to such "technical aspects" as the territorial boundaries of the city or its form of governance.[70] Rather, Vatican concerns center around three objectives.

First, the Vatican consistently has promoted the adoption of an "internationally guaranteed special statute" to resolve the issue of Jerusalem.[71] The goals of such a statute would be to (1) safeguard the global character of Jerusalem as a sacred heritage common to the three monotheistic religions; (2) preserve religious freedom in all aspects; (3) protect the "Status Quo"; (4) assure permanence and the development of religious, educational, and social activities proper to each community; (5) ensure equality of treatment to all three religions; and (6) establish an appropriate juridical safeguard that does not reflect the will of only one of the interested parties involved.[72]

As a matter of principle, the Vatican adheres to the view that the issues surrounding Jerusalem are of concern to more than the two parties involved, and that there is a unique international interest in what happens to the Holy City. As one authoritative Vatican source has noted, "When it comes to Jerusalem, the voice of others (besides Israelis and Palestinians), the presence of additional subjects legitimized by international law, and the appropriate contribution of religious and cultural institutions . . . cannot be considered purely superfluous, or worse, unsuitable."[73]

Second, the Vatican cares about more than the "simple extraterritoriality" of the Holy Places. Its focus is on what we moderns might call the environmental and cultural character of the Jerusalem it cares about most—the Old City. It wants the surrounds of the Holy Places to reflect their august majesty (no McDonalds, perhaps), and it needs a living community of the faithful to breathe life into what would otherwise be holy relics. More than anything, it is this demographic concern that keeps the Vatican from limiting its concerns to the Holy Places themselves.

Finally, the Vatican believes that religious rights of freedom of religion and conscience must be preserved and protected. Optimally, the Vatican is insistent on an international statutory instrument to achieve this goal. Yet to a nuanced observer, it appears that the specific modalities of "bilateral-plus" are open to discussion. We must remember that most of this work has already been resolved in the Fundamental Agreement.[74] In this area at least, there is little untethered ground for a new international agreement to cover.

Indeed, some have suggested that were Israel to affirm existing international instruments (many of which it already has committed itself to), the required bow to the notion of international guarantees might well be met. Several of these instruments include the United Nations Declaration on the Elimination of All Forms of Intolerance and of Discrimination Based on Religion or Belief,[75] the 1972 UNESCO Convention Concerning the Protection of the World Cultural and Natural Heritage,[76] and the 1976 Recommendation Concerning the Safeguarding and Contemporary Role of Historic Areas (which Israel signed onto in January 2000).[77]

The exact modalities of such an arrangement to protect religious rights, if any, will likely depend in large measure on the general state of Vatican-Israel relations at the time. To the extent that the Vatican's concerns regarding Jerusalem and the Holy Places are met through the Fundamental Agreement, the Vatican's need to "internationalize" these issues likely will lessen. Silvio Ferrari's earlier work[78] and his more recent study in this volume on religious freedom as a component of concordat agreements[79] help us understand the various nuances involved in the Vatican position.

### Catholic-Jewish Relations

As has been suggested earlier, Vatican-Israel relations will always be affected by the broader historical context of Catholic-Jewish relations.

These relations face considerable tension. Issues related to the canonization of Pius IX[80] and Pius XII[81] and the Church's historical record in World War II[82] have been the cause of unease between the communities. Recent Catholic theological statements such as *Dominus Iesus*[83] have also created controversy. On the other hand, the 2001 Pontifical Biblical Commission report on the place of Jewish scripture in the Hebrew Bible is a significant theological document expressing equality and respect for the two differing religious narratives.[84] Rabbi Jack Bemporad's essay in this volume lays out in great detail the changes in theological understanding between Jews and Catholics that have occurred in the last half century.[85] His analysis of the relevant religious texts shows how their reinterpretation was a *sine qua non* of the political reevaluation of recent years.

### Middle East Politics

The failure of the July 2000 Camp David negotiations and the resultant al-Aqsa intifada led to a collapse of the Oslo peace process.

Obviously the general geopolitics of the Middle East will affect the contours of future Vatican-Israel relations. However one views the final resolution, the "standoff" at the Church of the Nativity in Bethlehem clearly has had an effect on the Vatican's diplomatic position toward Israel's ability to "protect" the Holy Places. So has the long (and for the Church) dispiriting dispute with the Israeli government over the placement of a mosque in the forecourt of the Church of the Annunciation in Nazareth.[86] Both these events will surely energize the Vatican's desire for "international guarantees" for the Holy Places.

Silvio Ferrari's essay on Vatican–Middle East diplomacy in recent years[87] assists in offering a larger perspective from which to view recent diplomatic developments. He makes clear how the Vatican deals with the general problem of Christians in Muslim lands focusing on the formal and informal position of Christians in Palestine, Lebanon, and Jordan.

At some future time, however, negotiations will almost certainly recommence with issues surrounding Jerusalem at the center of the negotiation.[88] There can be little doubt that the experience of Vatican-Israel diplomacy will serve the parties in good stead when they move again into the phase of negotiations that affect religion and the Holy City.

### *Taxes*

A financial agreement regarding tax-exempt status between the two parties is still being negotiated. Three broad issues are being discussed in this so-called economic agreement: fiscal questions (i.e., taxation and immunity or exemption from taxation); questions regarding ecclesiastical property; and state participation in covering the cost of educational and social services provided by the Church to the residents of the state.

Issues concerning the tax status of clergy and tax exemption for religious property are based on a 1948 understanding Israel reached with France, as the then-interlocutor for the Catholic community.[89] The Fischer-Chouvel agreement, as the exchange of letters is called, "exempts from customs and local taxes all goods—religious and other kinds—imported for the use of French and Italian churches, hospitals, hostels, and other affiliated institutions."[90] The heads of these churches are further exempted from customs on vehicles imported for official use.

In the matter of taxation, the Church claims recourse to the Ottoman Status Quo agreements that gave it preferential rights regarding taxation. Three kinds of taxes are at issue: national taxes (such as income taxes), municipal property taxes or *arnona,* and certain limited exemptions from import duties, for example, on items for which there is no locally produced substitute (e.g., motor vehicles) and specific items that must be imported for use in worship and religious observances (e.g., sacred vessels, vestments, books).

Generally, the heads of churches do not pay import duties for cars. The government of Israel does not accept this in principle, but to avoid conflict the Ministry of Religion transfers funds to the Treasury as an internal budgeting matter from a so-called "special fund" sufficient to meet these duties. The churches further generally claim exemption from land taxes. At least, they do not pay.[91]

The question of municipal property taxes or *arnona* is a more difficult matter. Again, the Church claims exemption, pointing to a 1938 mandatory ordinance which the Vatican would like to more or less codify.[92] The spanner in the works is recent government legislation that reduced tax exemptions for church property, other than houses of worship, which still receive full exemption.[93]

A second issue revolves around the return of church property. More than twenty specific properties are in dispute, the most important of which is the Cenacle on Mt. Zion. The Shrine of the Cenacle, commemorating the Last Supper, was taken away by the Ottoman Turks in the mid-sixteenth century and is now in the possession of the successor State of Israel. Other cases include property in Haifa now used by the army, a chapel in Caesarea, and a convent in Jerusalem occupied by the Hebrew University.

A more theoretical issue turns on the proper interpretation of the 1924 Order in Council (promulgated by Britain as the mandatory power at the time, and inherited by the State of Israel), which removes jurisdiction from the courts in disputes over Holy Places and religious buildings, establishing the exclusive jurisdiction in these matters with the executive.[94] However, the formulation of the Order in Council is sufficiently broad that it has been held to apply to any property of some religious significance or character. Indeed, in one recent case the courts, relying on the Order in Council, refused to issue an injunction against private persons who had claimed a Church cemetery in the town of Ramleh. Accordingly, the matter was removed to a government department, which appointed an official with no legal qualifications to decide and whose very first decision was that he would not be bound by the rules of evidence. The matter dragged on for several years, until another official decided it. The decision was in favor of the Church, but the Vatican has consequently taken the position that it should not be deprived of access to the judicial courts in defense of its property, and that removal of jurisdiction to the executive should apply only to the handful of shrines subject to the internationally sanctioned legal regime of the Status Quo. This, of course, is not the present judicial understanding of the Order in Council.[95]

With reference to the issue of state participation in paying for educational and social services provided by the Church, it must be borne in mind that in practice, the state has been offering a degree of financing for Church schools for some time now, but that this has been discretionary and not based on agreed norms and criteria. No major controversy appears to exist in this area, but still, even though there may be agreement on the governing principles, putting them into practice requires careful formulation.

Negotiations have moved forward sluggishly with the Israeli Treasury maintaining a strong "watching brief" on fiscal issues. The fact that the Bahai religious organization had succeeded in hammering out their own tax agreement with the Israelis through an exchange of letters dated April 22, 1987, provided succor to the Vatican negotiators.[96] Pre-negotiations on the "economic agreement" started at the subcommission level on July 4, 1994, and the actual negotiations were taken up by the Bilateral Commission on March 11, 1999. The rhythm of these negotiations has varied greatly over time. Between November 2002 and early April 2003, Israel's government suspended talks because, it said, of the impending early general elections. The negotiations started anew on April 10, 2003, with follow-up meetings over the summer. In late August, however, the Israeli government cancelled the meetings set for September and failed to suggest dates for the resumption of talks. What this means for the future of negotiations remains unclear.

### The Benefits of a "Hot Line" between Rome and Jerusalem

The frenetic diplomacy surrounding Camp David II led to great frustration among Church officials, who felt that issues vital to them were being raised without any opportunity for their involvement, if not comment. This led to criticism by many in the Church of Israel's intentions regarding Jerusalem and the Old City. In response, "Officials at the Vatican . . . propose[d] that a permanent mechanism for consultations between the Vatican and Israel be set in place to examine in advance decisions that might arouse emotional responses on the part of one side or the other."[97] This notion is worth exploring and expanding to broader issues of dispute between the Church and the Jewish community. If such a "hot line" had been in place it could likely have played a constructive role in the dispute over the mosque in Nazareth and the more recent standoff in Bethlehem.[98]

### Conclusion: Religion and the State

Both the Vatican and the State of Israel present unique vantage points from which to examine how religion and religious identity interact with the state and, in particular, the democratic state. The Church, of course, historically viewed, and indeed still views, itself as in possession of unalloyed universal truth. Historically, Catholic countries were never responsive to theories of toleration and religious pluralism. The 1492 expulsion averred to in Rafael Palomino's essay on the concordat in Spain stands as mute testimony to this religious exclusivity.[99] Only after Vatican II have countries who view themselves as Catholic in national identity had to wrestle seriously with issues of religious freedom and pluralism. Giorgio Filibeck's essay in this volume explores the relationship of human rights to the quest for peace in the context of the Holy See's evolving view of human rights and religious tolerance.[100]

Issues of religious toleration and pluralism in Judaism were of theoretical interest only until the creation of the State of Israel in 1948. While an effort was made by some religious parties to institutionalize Jewish (religious) law in the new Jewish state,[101] it did not succeed. The Knesset, in 1980, did ordain that any lacunae in legal interpretation should be answered by recourse to the principles of "Israel's Heritage," a more elusive—and perhaps more flexible—reed than *halacha* or Jewish law.[102]

While Israel today, with an almost 20 percent Arab minority, is an explicitly democratic state, it is one which seeks, at least in the eyes of most citizens, to maintain a specifically Jewish character. During the last Labor government the issue arose both in matters small—should the national anthem, "Hatikva," speak exclusively of a homeland for Jews—and large—should a majority of specifically Jewish voters be required to elect a government that agrees to give up national territory.

The signing of the Vatican-Israel accord opened a new chapter in both the bilateral relations between Israel and the Holy See and the relations between the Catholic Church and the Jewish people. It also offered a unique opportunity to explore principles of religious freedom and toleration in a state that maintains a particular religious character. As such, developments which flow from the accord are of interest not only to students of Israel and the Vatican, but also to comparativists in the theory of church and state in the modern age.

The essays in this volume offer insight into how domestic issues of church and state can play out over a transnational and international context. Father Jaeger's analysis of the accord, noted above, offers insights into church-state issues from a Vatican perspective.[103] The international implications of some of these issues are developed by Moshe Hirsch in his study of the right of conversion in international law,[104] and by Geoffrey Watson in his paper on the international legal issues associated with the religious duty of pilgrimage.[105] In contrast, Ruth Lapidoth discusses church-state relations in the domestic law of Israel, the country where the accord must be effectuated and where the promise of freedom of religious expression must be fulfilled.[106]

Because the accord is only one of many bilateral Vatican agreements which address the position of the Holy See and the Catholic Church as to respective states, the inclusion of the comparative studies of Silvio Ferrari,[107] Rafael Palomino (already cited),[108] and Msgr. Roland Minnerath[109] on concordats—those official agreements that govern the Roman Catholic Church in its relations with specific nation-states—add a unique dimension to our understanding of the context within which the Fundamental Accord was negotiated. While the accord is in specific terms not a concordat, but rather an agreement regulating a political relationship that has been integrated into a document of political recognition, the comparative study of concordats provides useful background against which to better understand the accord.

The unique contribution of this volume is its treatment of a bilateral treaty on religious issues from domestic, comparative, and international law perspectives. It allows, I believe, for a deeper contextual understanding of the issues involved. One can hope that future studies of religious liberty abroad take advantage of this approach, which is far more suited to the study of law and religion than purely doctrinal analysis.

More specifically, one can hope that this volume will encourage further comparative study of Vatican concordats in their political and cultural context, such as those in France and Poland, as well as the study of religious liberty abroad in areas including Asia, Africa, China, and the Muslim world. This said, the Vatican-Israel Agreement remains *sui generis,* as must any agreement that deals with religion in what so many view as the Holy Land. Future agreements with the Greek Orthodox and other Christian groups will surely come, as well as agreements, formal and informal, with both Palestinian and Muslim authorities regarding the Muslim holy sites.

We must admit that the experience of both parties under the Fundamental Agreement has been fitful at best. As David Rosen's contribution to this volume points out, in the dispute over the appointment of the successor to the Greek Catholic archbishop of Galilee the Fundamental Agreement was ignored,[110] as it was in the siege at the Church of the Nativity in Bethlehem. For the Vatican the standoff proved especially painful, as they were forced to watch the continued desecration of one of their most holy sites.[111] Indeed, Vatican officials have suggested that the experience underscores the need for an "international statute" on Jerusalem.[112]

Certainly, Vatican-Israel relations have suffered during the last few years. Vatican complaints about Israeli conduct throughout the al-Aqsa intifada and Operation Defensive Shield have taken on a steady drumbeat.[113] For their part, Israelis remain concerned over the lack of Vatican understanding of their restraint at the Church of the Nativity in Bethlehem and at the failure of the Vatican to place dispositive weight on the fact that the Palestinian "militia" and accused terrorists invaded the church, breaking locks to do so.[114]

In fairness, we should note that the Vatican perspective has not differed markedly from those of the European countries generally. And little use was made of the accord in bilateral issues that arose in the last few years. Still, the experience of Israel and the Holy See in drafting the Fundamental Agreement will remain the starting point for further negotiated solutions for religion and religious values in the Arab-Israeli conflict.

## NOTES

1. The question of whether the Vatican should be treated as a sovereign state has been fully reviewed by scholars. The references are well arrayed in Yasmin Abdullah, "The Holy See at United Nations Conferences: State or Church?" 96 *Colum. L. Rev.* 1835, 1835 n.3 (1996).

2. The Second Vatican Council, Declaration on the Relationship of the Church to Non-Christian Religions, *Nostra Aetate*, no. 4, Oct. 28, 1965 [hereinafter Declaration], reprinted in Eugene J. Fisher, *Faith Without Prejudice: Rebuilding Christian Attitudes Toward Judaism* 131 (1993).

3. Jules Isaac, *The Teaching of Contempt: Christian Roots of Anti- Semitism* 17 (Helen Weaver trans., Holt, Rinehart and Winston, 1964) (1962).

4. Declaration, *supra* note 2, at 132.

5. Commission for Religious Relations with the Jews, Guidelines and Suggestions for Implementing the Conciliar Declaration, *Nostra Aetate*, no. 4, Dec. 1, 1974, reprinted in Fisher, *supra* note 2, at 133, 134. These themes were further explicated in the commission's 1985 statement, Notes on the Correct Way to Present the Jews and Judaism in Roman Catholic Preaching and Catechesis (Vatican City, June 24, 1985).

6. Pontifical Biblical Commission, *The Jewish People and Their Sacred Scriptures in the Christian Bible* (Liberia Editrice Vaticana, Vatican, 2002).

7. The literature on the Vatican-Israel relationship is limited, yet growing. See Silvio Ferrari, "The Vatican, Israel and the Jerusalem Question (1943–1984)" 39 *Middle East J.* 316, 316–31 (1985); see also George Emile Irani, *The Papacy and the Middle East: The Role of the Holy See in the Arab-Israeli Conflict, 1962–1984*, at 13–30 (1986); Andrej Kreutz, *Vatican Policy on the Palestinian-Israeli Conflict: The Struggle for the Holy Land* 93–94 (1990). See generally Sergio I. Minerbi, *The Vatican and Zionism: Conflict in the Holy Land, 1895–1925* (Arnold Schwarz trans., 1990); Livia Rokach, *The Catholic Church and the Question of Palestine* (1987).

8. See *The Diaries of Theodor Herzl* 427 (Marvin Lowenthal ed. & trans., 1956).

9. Id. at 428. Earlier, Herzl met with the Vatican secretary of state, Cardinal Merry del Val, who informed him that "in order that we should come out for the Jewish people in the way you desire, they would first have to accept conversion." Id. at 421; see also Alex Bein, *Theodore Herzl: A Biography* 490 (Maurice Samuel trans., 1941).

10. See Kreutz, *supra* note 7, at 36 ; see also Fred J. Khouri, "The Jerusalem Question and the Vatican," in *The Vatican, Islam, and the Middle East*, at 143–44 (Kail C. Ellis ed., 1987).

11. See Khouri, *supra* note 10, at 144; see also Kreutz, *supra* note 7, at 36–43.

12. See Silvio Ferrari & Francesco Margiotta Broglio, "The Vatican, the European Community, and the Status of Jerusalem," 3 *Studi in Memoria di Mario Condorelli* 571, 573–74 (Dott. A. Giuffrè ed., 1988).

13 . See Minerbi, *supra* note 7, at 23–24. At a different point the Vatican also bruited about the notion of a Belgian serving as chair of an international condominium to control the Holy Places, should Britain retain the remainder of Palestine under a "mandate." Id. at 19.

14. This desire was not mitigated by the tragedy of World War II. By this time, "[s]uch a solution it well knew, however, was unattainable, and in the actual circum-

stances it preferred the Arabs to the Jews." Id. at 574 (citing the comments of John Victor Perowne, British plenipotentiary minister to the Holy See, in the summer of 1949).

15. Kreutz, *supra* note 7, at 36.

16. See Kreutz, *supra* note 7, at 42 and nn. 81–82 (attributing the phrase to Lord Arthur James Balfour, British foreign secretary).

17. See the Balfour Declaration (Nov. 2, 1917), reprinted in *The Arab-Israel Conflict and Its Resolution: Selected Documents,* at 20 (Ruth Lapidoth & Moshe Hirsch eds., 1992) [hereinafter *Arab-Israel Conflict Documents*].

18. See Minerbi, *supra* note 7, at 178–95 (describing in detail the Vatican's objection and opposition to the mandate).

19. See *Palestine Royal Commission Report,* Cmd. 5479 (London, H. M. S. O., 1937).

20. See generally, Tom Segev, *One Palestine Complete: Jews and Arabs Under the British Mandate* (2000); A. J. Sherman, *Mandate Days: British Life in Palestine* (1998).

21. See G. A. Res. 181(II), U. N. GAOR, 2d Sess., 1947, at 146–50, U. N. Doc A/64 (1947), reprinted in *The Jerusalem Question and Its Resolution: Selected Documents,* at 6–10 (Ruth Lapidoth & Moshe Hirsch eds., 1994).

22. See id. at 131. This tracked the views of the 1937 royal (Peel) commission report, which called for the partition of Palestine to allow for the creation of independent Arab and Jewish states. See *Palestine Royal Commission Report,* 1937, Cmd. 5479, at 382–83; see also *Palestine Statement of Policy by His Majesty's Government in the United Kingdom,* 1937, Cmd. 5513. Concerning Jerusalem and its Holy Places, the report stated: "The partition of Palestine is subject to the overriding necessity of keeping the sanctity of Jerusalem and Bethlehem inviolate and of ensuring free and safe access to them for all the world." *Palestine Royal Commission Report, supra,* at 381. Safeguarding the Holy Places was considered, in the words of the mandate, "a sacred trust of civili[z]ation." League of Nations Covenant art. 22, para. 1, reprinted in *Arab-Israel Conflict Documents, supra* note 17, at 15, 23–24. Accordingly, the members of the royal commission proposed that Jerusalem, Bethlehem, Nazareth, and the Sea of Galilee (Lake Tiberias) be made a *corpus separatum,* and thus be detached from the proposed Arab and Jewish states. With a designated road access to the sea, the Christian holy areas would have the status of a separate enclave under international administration. See *Palestine Royal Commission Report, supra,* at 381–84, and accompanying map no. 8.

23. See Ferrari & Broglio, *supra* note 12, at 579–80. For a useful presentment of the past Vatican discussion on Jerusalem (internationalization of the whole city) and present position ("special status" and "international guarantees") see generally Silvio Ferrari, "The Religious Significance of Jerusalem in the Middle East Peace Process: Some Legal Implications," 45 *Cath. U. L. Rev.* 7–33 (1998); Silvio Ferrari, "The Struggle for Jerusalem," 11 *Eur. J. Int'l Aff.* 22–39 (1991); Ferrari, *supra* note 7, at 316–31.

24. See Ferrari & Broglio, *supra* note 12, at 583.

25. See Fundamental Agreement Between the Holy See and the State of Israel, Dec. 30, 1993, Vatican-Isr., 33 I. L. M. 153 (1994) [hereinafter Fundamental Agreement].

26. Id. art. 4, para. 1, at 155.

27. Id. art. 2, para. 1, at 155.

28. See Lorenzo Cremonesi, "The Stages of Diplomatic Negotiations," this volume.

29. See Leonard Hammer, "Israel's Understanding of the Fundamental Agreement with the Holy See," this volume.

30. Msgr. Richard Mathes also touches on the difficulties encountered in formulating such agreements between sovereign states in his firsthand account in this volume of how the Holy See and Israel dealt with the issue of allowing pilgrimages to the Holy Land and the parallels and lessons to be taken from that experience and applied to the negotiations leading to the Fundamental Agreement.

31. See Beatrice Bretonniere, "Netanyahu Faces Tough Issues on First Meeting with Pope," *Agence France Presse*, Feb. 3, 1997; "Israel's Netanyahu in Rome to Meet Pope, Italians," *Reuters*, Feb. 3, 1997.

32. Personal communication with author.

33. See the Most Rev. Claudio Maria Celli, The Holy See, "The Catholic Church and the State of Israel," remarks delivered Apr. 8, 1997, at a symposium entitled "Continuing the Dialogue: The Fundamental Agreement Between the Holy See and the State of Israel: A Third Anniversary Perspective," and cosponsored with the Embassy of Israel. Early drafts of a number of the chapters in this volume were first delivered at the symposium. At the conference Eliahu Ben-Elissar, then Israel's ambassador to the United States, announced that "[t]he legal agreement, already initialed by the two sides, will be brought before the government for ratification in the very, very near future." Larry Witham, "Catholic Church Frustrated with Israel: Diplomacy Stalled Despite Recognition," *Washington Times*, Apr. 9, 1997, at A12.

34. Others gave credit to importunements to the Israeli government by the Conference of Presidents of Major Jewish American Organizations. See Haim Shapiro, "Agreement with Vatican to be Signed This Month," *Jerusalem Post*, Sept. 15, 1997.

35. See *supra* note 33 (quoting the remarks of Archbishop Claudio Maria Celli).

36. See Agreement Between the Holy See and the State of Israel Pursuant to Article 3 § 3 of the Fundamental Agreement Between the Holy See and the State of Israel (hereinafter Legal Personality Agreement), June 4, 1999, 91 *Acta Apostolicae Sedis* 490 (1999).

37. David Rosen, "New Agreement Between Vatican and Israel Yet Another Step on the Journey of Reconciliation," *Irish Times*, Nov. 18, 1997, at 14, available in 1997 WL 12035986.

38. See Legal Personality Agreement, *supra* note 36, at 490.

39. "Palestinians Call Vatican-Israeli Accord a 'Stab in the Back,'" *Agence France-Presse*, Nov. 11, 1997, available in 1997 WL 13431992.

40. "Palestinians Ask Islamic Summit to Counter Vatican-Israel Agreement," *Agence France-Presse*, Dec. 9, 1997, available in 1997 WL 13450716.

41. In *The Coptic Patriarchate v. The Minister of Police* (1971), 25(1), P. D., 225, the Copts secured an order of eviction. Enforcement was postponed to allow the government to make determinations as to substantive rights under the 1924 Order in Council. See "Palestine (Holy Places) Order in Council," in Lionel G. A. Cust, *The Status Quo in the Holy Places of Christendom* 65 (1971). The committee has met once since 1971, but a second petition in 1977 based on grounds that the court was waiting for the government to act failed. See *The Coptic Patriarchate v. The Government of Israel* (1979), 33(1), P. D., 225. At dif-

ferent times, both the Egyptian and the Ethiopian governments have intervened on behalf of their "charges." See generally Walter Zander, "Jurisdiction and Holiness: Reflections on the Coptic-Ethiopian Case," 17 *Israel L. Rev.* 245 (1982).

42. See Lisa Pevtzow, "Holy Squabbles," *Jerusalem Post Magazine,* Apr. 1, 1994, at 6 (describing the territorial battles among the six religious denominations housed in the church).

43. See Mary Curtius, "Holy Sepulcher Church Paint Job an Act of Faiths," *Los Angeles Times,* Apr. 15, 1995, at A1; see also Michael Krikorian, "A Simple Cross Ends Decades of Division," *Los Angeles Times,* Dec. 30, 1995, at B4. A Roman Catholic investment banker from Rye, New York, George Doty, who provided the funding, "stressed that all the work had taken place within the framework of the status quo." Haim Shapiro, "Holy Sepulcher Cupola Unveiled After 68 Years Under Wraps," *Jerusalem Post,* Jan. 3, 1997, at 15, 20. Only after seeking the assistance of the Pontifical Mission for Palestine, a social services organization, was Doty able to secure the agreement of all the religious "stakeholders" to begin the restoration. See Graziano Motta, "Jerusalem Basilica's Dome Is Restored," *L'Osservatore Romano,* weekly ed., Feb. 8–19, 1997, at 8.

44. See Haim Shapiro, "Greek Orthodox: Consult Us on Status of Holy Places," *Jerusalem Post,* July 20, 1994, at 1.

45. Thus, the Greek Orthodox Church, together with eleven other church leaders, signed a memorandum calling for the maintenance of the Status Quo in regard to Christian Holy Places. See generally memorandum "The Significance of Jerusalem for Christians," Nov. 14, 1994 (on file with author). But note that the Catholic Church already adopted this position in its 1993 accord with Israel. See Fundamental Agreement, *supra* note 25, art. 4, para. 1, at 155.

46. Shapiro, *supra* note 44, at 1.

47. See Haim Shapiro, "Patriarch Wants Agreement Between Non-Catholic Church and Israel," *Jerusalem Post,* Dec. 29, 1995, at 24.

48. Indeed, the only senior Christian clergy who is a "local" (other than the Armenians, who only recently have had an independent "home" country) is the Latin Patriarchate, His Excellency Michel Sabbah, the first Palestinian Christian to hold that office. See Michel Sabbah, "The Church of Jerusalem: Living with Conflict, Working for Peace," *Commonweal,* Jan. 12, 1996, at 14 (presenting the views of Michel Sabbah).

49. It is unclear what, if anything, can be done to resolve this problem. It may be necessary for the municipality to consider providing housing assistance for Christians in the Old City, where most of them live, in the same way that the government of Israel provides incentives for building new areas for Jewish settlement. While this may cause problems for Israel, which historically has not distinguished between Palestinian Christians and Muslims, some focus on this issue may be needed to preserve Christian life in the Holy Land.

50. David Gibson, "Holy Land's Christians in Need of Miracle," *The Record* (Bergen County, N.J.), Dec. 26, 1996, at A1, available in 1996 WL 6124127.

51. See Rev. Drew Christiansen, "Palestinian Christians: Recent Developments," this volume.

52. Id.

53. See Bill Hutman, "Olmert: PA Official Liaising with Churches," *Jerusalem Post*, Nov. 28, 1996, at 2.

54. Id.; "Israeli Police Closes Palestinian Adviser's Office in East Jerusalem," *BBC World Wide Monitoring* (citing Voice of Israel), Apr. 13, 1999.

55. See Serge Schmemann, "Arafat Enters into a New Fray, Over a Russian Church," *New York Times*, July 11, 1997, at A3.

56. See Karin Laub, "Foreign Minister Asks Policy to Monitor Christian Holy Site," *Assoc. Press*, Dec. 3, 1996, available in 1996 WL 4452274.

57. The Abu Mazen–Beilin "non-paper" was concluded and initialed in November 1996, but was never accepted by either Yasser Arafat or then-Prime Minister Shimon Peres. See Ze'ev Schiff, "Beilin and Abu Mazen Drafted a Document on Final Status; Agreed to Establish a Palestinian State," *Ha'aretz*, Feb. 22, 1996, at 1; see also David Makovsky, "Time for Beilin to Disclose Agreement in Full," *Jerusalem Post*, Feb. 25, 1996, at 2; Yossi Beilin, "The Past, Present and Future of the Oslo Process: View from the Labor Party," *Peacewatch* No. 112 (Was. Inst. for Near East Policy, Washington, D.C.), Dec. 11, 1996, at 1 (summarizing a Beilin speech). The exact text of the Abu Mazen–Beilin plan was not leaked to the press until fall 2000 and was made available in *Newsweek*. See Michael Hirsch, "The Last Peace Plan: The 1995 Document that Paved the Way to Camp David," *Newsweek*, Sept. 25, 2000, at 46.

58. Larry Kaplow, "Christians Want in on Middle East Talks," *Atlanta Constitution*, July 21, 2000.

59. Bernard Wasserstein, *Divided Jerusalem: The Struggle for the Holy City*, 315–16 (2001). For reports that Arafat in fact does not want control of the Armenian quarter of Jerusalem, see "Jerusalem Continues to Hold Up Summit Deal, Israeli Official Says," *Deutche Presse-Agentur*, July 19, 2000 (stating that Israeli radio reported that "Arafat has rejected all compromise proposals regarding Jerusalem, and demands full Palestinian sovereignty over East Jerusalem, with the exception of the Western, or Wailing Wall, the holiest site in Jerusalem, and the Jewish and Armenian Quarters in the Old City").

60. Personal communication with member of Vatican negotiating team, July 2002.

61. Eric Silver, "Pope Says Holy City Sites Need Protection," *The Independent* (London), July 24, 2000, at 12.

62. "Albright Sees Vatican as Critical to Agreements in Jerusalem," *Agence France-Press*, July 31, 2000, found in 2000 WL 24682134.

63. "PLO, Vatican Establish Links, but No Full Diplomatic Recognition," *Deutsche Presse-Agentur*, Oct. 25, 1994, available in LEXIS, Nexis Library, Allnews File.

64. See appendix III of this volume.

65. See Leonard Hammer, "The Holy See–PLO Basic Agreement in Light of the Holy See–Israel Fundamental Agreement," this volume.

66. Id.

67. The Vatican secretary of state for foreign affairs, Archbishop Jean-Louis Tauran, has pointed out that "[t]he religious aspect of Jerusalem must be discussed in a multilateral forum, and we want to be involved in it." "Vatican Official: Nobody Can Claim Exclu-

sive Rights to Holy Places," *Jerusalem Post,* Dec. 19, 1995, at 1. See also Ross Dunn, "Leaders: Do Not Divide Us," *Sydney Morning Herald,* July 22, 2000, at 17; Lamia Lahoud, "Jerusalem Patriarchates Want Voice at Camp David," *Jerusalem Post,* July 20, 2000, at 3; Charles M. Sennott, "Christian Leaders Request a Voice in Talks about Jerusalem," *Boston Globe,* July 21, 2000, at A4.

68. See Mark Matthews, "Christians Hope for a Presence in a Peaceful New Jerusalem, Muslims and Jews Dominate Negotiating," *Baltimore Sun,* Sept. 6, 2000, at 1A.

69. "Vatican Note: Jerusalem: Considerations of the Secretariat of State," 26 *Origins* 250, 250 (1996) [hereinafter "Vatican Note"]. Indeed, this right is contained in Article 11 of the Fundamental Agreement between the Holy See and the State of Israel, which provides that the Holy See maintains the right, in every case, to exercise its moral and spiritual teaching office. See Fundamental Agreement, *supra* note 25, art. 11, para. 2, at 157.

70. See "Vatican Note," *supra* note 69, at 253. The Holy See "is not concerned with the question of how many square meters or kilometers constitute the disputed territory." Id. at 251. Still, it is important to underscore its view that "a political solution will not be valid unless it takes into account in a profound and just manner the religious needs present in the city." Id. at 253.

71. See Angelo Macchi & Giovanni Rulli, "The Future of Jerusalem," *La Civiltà Cattolica* (Rome), June 15, 1996, reprinted in 26 *Origins* 254, 256 (1996).

72. See *Gerusalemme nei Documenti Pontifici,* at 215–16 (Edmond Farhat ed., Libreria Editrice Vaticana, 1987).

73. Macchi & Rulli, *supra* note 71, at 254.

74. Freedom of religion and conscience are protected in Article 1, sections 1 and 2. See Fundamental Agreement, *supra* note 25, art. 1, paras. 1–2, at 154–55.

75. See Nov. 25, 1981, G. A. Res. 36/55, U. N. GAOR, 36th Sess., Supp. No. 51, U. N. Doc. A/36/51 (1982).

76. See UNESCO Convention Concerning the Protection of the World Cultural and Natural Heritage, Nov. 16, 1972, 6 UNESCO Doc. 17/C/106 (1972), reprinted in 11 I. L. M. 1358 (1973). Israel accepted the 1972 convention on June 10, 1999. See United Nations Educational, Scientific and Cultural Organization Convention Concerning the Protection of the World Cultural and National Heritage, *Ratification Status,* to be found at http://www.uhc.unesco.org./wldrati.htm.

77. The convention and the recommendation are reprinted in *Conventions & Recommendations of UNESCO Concerning the Protection of the Cultural Heritage* (1985). See discussion in *Jerusalem Post,* "News in Brief," Dec. 19, 2001.

78. Silvio Ferrari, "The Holy See and the Postwar Palestine Issue: The Internationalization of Jerusalem and the Protection of the Holy Places," 60(2) *International Affairs,* 261–83 (1984); Silvio Ferrari, "The Vatican and the Jerusalem Question (1943–1984)," 39(2), *The Middle East Journal* 316–31 (1985); Silvio Ferrari, *The Vatican, The European Community and the Status of Jerusalem* (1988); Silvio Ferrari, *Vaticano E Israele* (1991); Silvio Ferrari, "The Vatican, the Palestine Question and the Internationalization of Jerusalem

(1918–1948)," Anno LX(240) *Rivista di Studi Politici Internazionali* 550–68 (1993); Silvio Ferrari & F. M. Broglio, *supra* note 12.

79.  Silvio Ferrari, "The Fundamental Agreement between the Holy See and Israel and the Conventions between States and the Church since the Vatican II Council," this volume.

80.  See Waveney Ann Moore, "Bridging the Chasm between Catholics, Jews" (Religion Series), *St. Petersburg Times*, Jan. 27, 2001 (discussing the recent beatification of Pius IX and the strong feelings some Jews have on the issue); Gary Wills, "Move to canonize Pius IX Insults Jews," *Chicago Sun-Times*, July 2, 2000 (citing Jewish protest of the move to canonize Pius IX).

81.  See Albert Friedlander, "The Tragedy of Pius XII," *The Tablet*, Jan. 2, 1999 (discussing the views of Catholic priests and Jewish rabbis on the issue of canonization of Pius XII); Tom Tugend, "Jewish Group Protests Proposed Pius XII Canonization," *Jerusalem Post*, Feb. 21, 1993 (describing the views of Rabbi Marvin Hier of the Simon Wiesenthal Center against canonization and explaining the beatification/canonization process).

82.  See generally John Cornwell, *Hitler's Pope* (1999); Carlo Falconi, *The Silence of Pius XII* (trans. Bernard Wall, Boston: Little Brown, 1970); Guenter Lewy, *The Catholic Church and Nazi Germany* (1964); Anthony Rhodes, *The Vatican in the Age of Dictators, 1922–1945* (1973) (for general sources criticizing Pius XII's actions during World War II; cf. Pierre Blet, S. J., *Pius XII and the Second World War: According to the Archives of the Vatican* [trans. Lawrence J. Johnson, New York: Paulist Press, 1999]); Robert A. Graham, S. J., "How to Manufacture a Legend" and "Pius XII's Defense of Jews and Others: 1944–45," in *Pius XII and the Holocaust: A Reader* 15–89 (for sources which defend the Church's actions).

83.  Congregation for the Doctrine of the Faith, *Dominus Iesus: On the Unicity and Salvific Universality of Jesus Christ and the Church* (2000), available at http://www.vatican.va/roman_curia/congregcfaith_doc_20000806_dominus-iesus_en.html. For articles discussing the controversy surrounding the *Dominus Iesus* see Douglas Davis, "Furor over Cardinal's Comment on Converting Israel," *Jerusalem Post*, Sept. 12, 2000, at 3; Edmund Doogue and Stephen Brown, "*Dominus Iesus* a 'Public Relations Disaster' for Ecumenism, Say Critics," *Christianity Today*, Sept. 13, 2000, available at http://www.christianitytoday.com/ct/2000/137/34.0.html; Gary Greenebaum & Robert Guffey Ellenson, "The Nation/Religion: Salvation that Reopens the Door to Intolerance," *Los Angeles Times*, Sept. 17, 2000, at 2.

84.  Pontifical Biblical Commission, *supra* note 6.

85.  See Jack Bemporad, "Jews and Catholics in the Last Half Century," this volume.

86.  See Leora Even Frucht, "Between Cross and Crescent," *Jerusalem Post*, Jan. 22, 2002. The extent to which the Muslim "side" was fueled by Islamic fundamentalism is perceptively analyzed in Uzi Benjamin, "Critical State," *Ha'aretz*, Mar. 10, 2002; the extent which the Nazareth crisis was triggered by Likud efforts to create a "conservative" Arab constituency which got out of hand is detailed in Charles M. Sennott's *The Body and the Blood: The Holy Land's Christians at the Turn of a New Millennium*, 208–14 (Public Affairs, New York, 2001). See also David Rosen, "Israel-Vatican Relations since the Signing of the Fundamental Agreement," this volume.

87. Silvio Ferrari, "The Vatican and the Middle East during the Pontificate of John Paul II," this volume.

88. Bernard Wasserstein reminds us that "Jerusalem was the core issue that was discussed at Camp David and Jerusalem was what ultimately prevented an agreement." Wasserstein, *supra* note 59, at 313.

89. A 1948 exchange of letters between the representative of the Jewish Agency in Paris and the director-general of the French Foreign Ministry led to a continuing dispute as to whether the exchange constituted an agreement by Israel to continue the privileges and exemptions for French Catholic institutions as enumerated in the Ottoman Status Quo. Israeli authorities viewed the exchange as merely an agreement to conduct negotiations as to whether the historical arrangements were to continue to have effect. See Eitan Margalit, "Comments on the Fundamental Agreement Between the Holy See and the State of Israel," *Justice*, June 1994, at 24, 25.

90. Asher Maoz, "Religious Human Rights in the State of Israel," in *Religious Freedom in Global Perspective*, at 372–73 (J. D. ven der Vyver & J. Wilte, Jr. eds., Kluwer, Hague, 1996). The exchange of letters is considered "highly classified." Id.

91. On several occasions, local authorities threatened to shut down electricity and on one occasion placed a lien on convent furniture.

92 See the Rates and Taxes (Exemption) Ordinance, No. 18, of 1938, *Palestine Gazette*, June 30, 1938. The text is based on the draft ordinance published in *The Palestinian Gazette*, Sept. 30, 1937.

93. Arrangement of State Budget Law of 2002, sec. 2 (Dec. 29, 2002).

94. Palestine (Holy Places) Order in Council, July 25, 1924, in 3 Drayton, Laws of Palestine 2825 (1934).

95. See Ruth Lapidoth, "Freedom of Religion and of Conscience in Israel," this volume.

96. Letter from Deputy Secretary-General of the Bahai World Centre M. R. Smith to Marshall Breger, dated June 24, 2002. See Charlotte Halle, "Bahai Feel Bashed by Local Media," available at www.bahaindex.com/news/archive/2001–09–02.html. The Israeli Treasury Department had held up renewal, claiming that more Israeli citizens should be hired by the Bahai world headquarters in place of the present system of religious volunteers. Gavin Rabinowitz, "Treasury Tells Bahai to Have More Israelis if Status Pact Is to Be Renewed," *Ha'aretz*, Apr. 2, 2002. As of July 2002 these problems have apparently been resolved. Conversation with head, Bahai Washington office, July 10, 2002.

97. Dalia Shehori, "Vatican Proposes Open Channel for Talks with Israel," *Ha'aretz*, June 30, 2000.

98. In fact, the Israelis chose not to use the Catholic Church as interlocutors in this conflict. Instead they sought assistance from the Americans and the British, as well as the Anglican church, which had sent a special envoy of the archbishop of Canterbury, Canon Andrew White. Gavin Rabinowitz, "Bethlehem Standoff Tests Mettle of Interfaith Leaders," *Ha'aretz*, Apr. 26, 2002. It has been suggested that it was British observers to the EU Middle East negotiating team that brought about the agreed-on compromise. Hannah Kim, "Between Lives/Liquidating an Initiative," *Ha'aretz*, July 26, 2002.

99. See Rafael Palomino, "The Fundamental Agreement between the Holy See and the State of Israel and Church-State Agreements in Spain: Some Contrasts and Comparisons," this volume.

100. Giorgio Filibeck, "Human Rights, the Foundation of Peace: The Teaching of the Catholic Church, with Special Reference to Religious Freedom," this volume.

101. See Emanuel Rackman, *Israel's Emerging Constitution 1948–1951,* at 31–32, 45–49 (1954). The argument for institutionalizing religious law in the Israel legal system is developed in K. Kahana, *The Case for Jewish Civil Law in the Jewish State* 109–13 (1960).

102. See "The Foundation of Law Act," 1980, 34 *I.S.I.* 5740 (1980). A criticism of the effectiveness of the act can be found in Ya'akov Meron, "Practical Application of the Foundations of Law Act," 8 *Jewish Law Annual* 159 (1989).

103. See David-Maria A. Jaeger, "The Fundamental Agreement between the Holy See and the State of Israel: A New Legal Regime of Church-State Relations," this volume.

104. See Moshe Hirsch, "The Freedom of Proselytism under the Fundamental Agreement and International Law," this volume.

105. See Geoffrey R. Watson, "Progress for Pilgrims? An Analysis of the Holy See–Israel Fundamental Agreement," this volume.

106. See Ruth Lapidoth, "Freedom of Religion and of Conscience in Israel," this volume.

107. See Silvio Ferrari, "The Fundamental Agreement between the Holy See and Israel and the Conventions between States and the Church since the Vatican II Council," this volume.

108. See Palomino, *supra* note 93.

109. See Roland Minnerath, "The Position of the Catholic Church Regarding Concordats from a Doctrinal and Pragmatic Perspective," this volume.

110. David Rosen, "Israel-Vatican Relations since the Signing of the Fundamental Agreement," this volume.

111. See Haim Shapiro, "Church of the Nativity Back to Normal," *Jerusalem Post,* May 13, 2002; Ibrahim Hazboun, "Rival Clergy Join in Prayer at Jesus' Birth Grotto," *Jerusalem Post,* May 12, 2002, at 2; Arieh O'Sullivan et al., "Church of the Nativity Agreement Reached," *Jerusalem Post,* May 10, 2002; Margot Dudkevitch, "Bethlehem Agreement (Still) Close," *Jerusalem Post,* May 9, 2002.

112. Concern was expressed that as the Israelis had classified the clerics in the church as "hostages," military efforts might be made to "rescue" them. See "Vatican Makes Proposal to End Bethlehem Standoff," *Reuters,* Apr. 7, 2002, at 3. In the midst of the impasse Pope John Paul sent a special envoy, Cardinal Roger Etchegaray, to Jerusalem to seek a solution. See Haim Shapiro, "Papal Envoy to Visit," *Jerusalem Post,* May 1, 2002, at 3; Greer Fay Cashman, "Papal Envoy Expresses Concern over Bethlehem Standoff," *Jerusalem Post,* May 3, 2002, at 4A.

113. John L. Allen, Jr., "In Paul's Footsteps, Pope Shows Will for Unity," *National Catholic Reporter,* May 18, 2001; "Vatican Urges International Observers in the Holy Land," *America Press,* Feb. 11, 2002; "Vatican Blasts Israeli Vote Rejecting Palestinian State," *Agence France Presse,* May 13, 2002.

114. Indeed, the Catholic "narrative" differs considerably whether it is recited by representatives of the Latin patriarch (who tracks the PA view that the armed men were invited in) or by representatives of the Custos (the Franciscan order charged with protection of the holy sites, which has denied these assertions). At the same time, representatives of the Custos, including Fr. David Jaeger, were alleged to have "hyped" fears of starvation, although initial observations after the siege reported "seeing large amounts of spilled and half-eaten meals" (John L. Allen, Jr., "Bethlehem Standoff Exposed Weaknesses of Vatican Diplomacy," *National Catholic Reporter*, May 24, 2002). The former Israeli ambassador to the Holy See has complained of a "cacophony of voices on the Catholic side, many singing different tunes" (John L. Allen, Jr., "Farewell Interview with Israel's Ambassador to the Holy See," *National Catholic Reporter*, May 2, 2003). This view was rejected outright by Franciscan spokesman Fr. David Jaeger. See Fr. David Jaeger, "Response to Ambassador Neville Lamden Interview on April 30, 2003," in National Catholic Reporter Online, Special Documents, May 15, 2003, at http://natcath.org/NCR_Online/documents/jaeger_response051503.htm. Whoever is correct in this specific matter, the perception of multiple spokesmen representing Vatican "interests" is a clear weakness in Vatican diplomacy in the region.

# I

# THE MAKING OF
# THE ACCORD

# 1

# THE STAGES OF DIPLOMATIC
# NEGOTIATIONS

*Lorenzo Cremonesi*

## The Difficulties of Dialogue

When, in early 1992, diplomats representing Israel and the Holy See had their first contacts with the intention of drafting a bilateral agreement, the difference between their respective starting positions appeared enormous. Not only did they have different and often completely opposing positions, but the very nature of the agreement was perceived in completely different ways.

Israel repeated in no uncertain terms that the final goal of all negotiations must be first and foremost the establishment of full diplomatic relations, after which any issues put forward by the Church could be discussed. The Vatican, on the other hand, sought immediate contacts in order to resolve bilateral issues (such as the fiscal and legal status of the Church in the Holy Land, freedom of education for local Catholic schools, and freedom of movement for pilgrims and members of the clergy), and above all to ensure its presence at Mideast peace talks. The Vatican expressed willingness to consider the possibility of a gradual normalization of diplomatic relations, but did not however show any inclination toward making a specific commitment at this stage. As Eitan Margalit, the Israeli diplomat in charge of negotiations with the Vatican from October 1992, put it: "We Israelis demanded the normalization of diplomatic relations. This had been our main goal since 1948, and the Secretariat of State was well aware of this. The Holy See considered it a matter of great importance to be openly accepted as a party to the peace process between us and the Arabs, especially with regard to the issue of Jerusalem. The agreement became possible only when these two demands converged. It was a long process of mutual accommodation, aimed at creating a confluence of interests, which at the beginning indeed appeared quite divergent."[1]

The real point of departure of negotiations was the beginning of the Arab-Israeli peace process. From that moment, it would seem that talks between Israel and the Vatican mirrored, often astonishingly, those engendered by the mechanisms established at the Madrid Conference in the fall of 1991, which unfolded in the following months. It was the success of the Israeli-Palestinian track in particular that pushed the Holy See to seek a seat at the negotiating table. Israel responded that this request would be granted only after the complete normalization of relations. The Israeli government looked to the recent normalization of relations with Russia (still the Soviet Union at the time) as an appropriate model for the Vatican as well. Just as Moscow was recognized as cosponsor of the peace conference only after the reopening of embassies, so the bid by the Holy See for "observer status" in both the Madrid forum and the multilateral talks, held nearly three months later in the Russian capital, would have been acceptable to the Israelis under the same conditions. It was then that the decision to seek a compromise reached maturity in the Vatican. On the other hand, the beginning of direct negotiations between the Arabs and the Israelis, and especially the consent by the PLO to be represented at Madrid by a joint Palestinian-Jordanian delegation, provided the Secretariat of State with a suitable response to traditional pressure from the Arab world against opening dialogue with Israel. "The Arabs could not ask us to be more Catholic than the Pope. If they had chosen to negotiate directly with Israel, and even Yasser Arafat was doing so, there was absolutely no reason the Holy See could not do the same," Vatican officials repeatedly explained.[2]

The first steps were taken over difficult terrain, fraught with reticence, prejudice, and mutual suspicion. It seemed as if the recent dispute over the Carmelite monastery inside the former concentration camp of Auschwitz,[3] and the more distant incident of 25 June 1987, when the pope received Kurt Waldheim in the Vatican,[4] would even overshadow the pope's historic visit of 13 April 1986 to the Rome synagogue. On top of everything came the misunderstandings that had arisen during the 1990–91 gulf crisis, when Jewish demonstrations in Saint Peter's Square brought the Holy See to issue a "Declaration" on 25 January 1991, clarifying the state of relations with Israel, as perceived by the Secretariat of State. The document stated that the lack of diplomatic ties did not indicate a lack of recognition. On the contrary: "[I]t must be clear that the Holy See never questioned the existence of the State of Israel."[5] A detailed list of important Vatican events to which Israeli representatives had been openly invited was offered as proof of this: from the funeral of Pius XII and the numerous pontifical audiences granted to various members of the Israeli government, to the many references to Israel in papal addresses.

Also mentioned, however, were the continued existence of "certain legal difficulties regarding the establishment of formal diplomatic relations."[6] First of all, there was the question of Palestinians in the Occupied Territories, from which ensued the issues of the Vatican's opposition to the annexation of the part of Jerusalem conquered in June 1967, and the state of the Catholic Church in Israel and areas under Israeli military administration. The document underscored a factor, later reiterated during diplomatic negotiations: the necessity to make a clear distinction "between the religious and the political, between the Church's attitude toward Judaism on the one hand, and relations between the Holy See and the State of Israel on the other."[7] In support of this theory, the document cited a fundamental passage from the Notes on the Correct Way to Present the Jews and Judaism in Preaching and Catechesis in the Roman Catholic Church, published by the Committee for Religious Relations with the Jews on 24 June 1985, which still represents the essence of Catholic doctrine on the subject.[8] The passage reads as follows: "Christians are invited to understand their attachment (of the Jews to the land of their fathers), which has its roots in biblical tradition, without however drawing any religious conclusions from this connection." The document also included the central declaration: "The existence of the State of Israel and the political choices it makes, should be considered not from a religious perspective, but in terms of the common principles of international law." A clear distinction was thus made between politics and religion, relations between the two states and interfaith dialogue. This theme was to be present beneath the surface throughout the entire period of negotiations, finally demonstrating its great significance at the moment of signing the Fundamental Agreement on 30 December 1993, when it would be presented and interpreted in a completely different way by each party.

Two key figures during the stages of preliminary contacts were Avi Pazner,[9] ambassador to Rome, newly appointed at the direct instigation of then-Prime Minister Yitzhak Shamir; and Monsignor Andrea Cordero Lanza di Montezemolo, appointed apostolic delegate in Jerusalem on 28 April 1990. Pazner had an important advantage, having been personal adviser and press secretary to Shamir for nearly a decade. The two had a long-standing friendship, which allowed Pazner to maintain a direct and exclusive channel of communications with the prime minister. It was no secret that he aspired to achieve the greatest ambition of every Israeli ambassador to Italy. "From the moment I arrived in Rome, I always had the goal of ending my term with the success of having established diplomatic relations with the Vatican. I felt that this was possible, and that the time was ripe," he said enthusiastically.[10]

He treated it as a personal mission, and did everything he could to convince Shamir of its importance. He was to play a significant role during the initial steps, when he succeeded in convincing Shamir, as well as his foreign minister, David Levy, to be more flexible on the issue of diplomatic relations, and to accept the Vatican strategy of gradual negotiations. The fall of the Shamir government in the elections of 23 June 1992, and the victory of Yitzhak Rabin's Labour coalition, were to sever the direct link between the embassy in Rome and the prime minister's office. By this point however, Pazner's role had become far less relevant.[11] On 29 July, thirty-six days after the election, Israel and the Vatican in fact announced the formation of a bilateral commission charged with studying the unresolved issues between the Church and the Jewish state. The Labour government furthermore promised to expedite the peace process—soon to begin were secret direct negotiations with the PLO, based on the principle of "land for peace." Rabin, in September of that year, also professed assent to territorial compromise in the Golan Heights, for the sake of negotiations with the Syrians. Simultaneously, the mechanism of Israeli-Vatican relations had by this time been irreversibly set in motion.

Montezemolo too had a special rapport with his superiors. The Secretariat of State had chosen one of its best diplomats to serve in Jerusalem. Born in Torino on 27 August 1925, he studied architecture, and was ordained on 13 March 1954. Immediately thereafter, he entered the diplomatic corps of the Holy See as secretary to the nunciature in Mexico, Japan, and Kenya, and then as head of the mission to Papua New Guinea and the Solomon Islands. His talents as a gifted negotiator emerged, however, when—as nuncio, between 1980 and 1986—he managed to develop excellent ties with the Sandinista government, and successfully mediated some aspects of the conflict between Honduras and Nicaragua. He then served in Uruguay, from 1986 to 1990. In 1994, while serving in Jerusalem, he was promoted to nuncio.[12] "A diplomat before a theologian, more concerned with politics and international relations than with religious or doctrinal implications, it was almost as if he had been purposely chosen with the intention of paving the road to diplomatic negotiations," said Rabbi David Rosen, member of the Israeli delegation (in the initial period of talks, considered very close to the minister of religious affairs, and chosen to counterbalance the influence of the Foreign Ministry), then-director of the Anti-Defamation League in Jerusalem, and ardent advocate of interfaith dialogue.[13]

It was Montezemolo who, with the explicit consent of the Secretariat of State, initiated the first contacts with Israeli leaders. He took up his position in Jerusalem in June 1990, and already on 16 October, he met privately with President Chaim Herzog in the president's office. Dialogue was not easy, and first concerned finding appropriate channels of communication. The gulf crisis and the opposing positions adopted by the Vatican and by Israel in this matter made any improvement in relations nearly impossible. "Upon my arrival in Jerusalem, I encountered a state of impasse. Our relations with the Israelis were rather cold. There was mutual respect, but extreme alienation. There was no communication or any form of dialogue. Above all, no normalization process was underway, and nothing was being done to begin such a process. No action was being taken to improve and formalize our relations," explains Montezemolo.[14] Furthermore, the Israeli side showed no desire to improve ties. "In my many conversations with Church leaders, from late 1988 to September 1991, never was I instructed by my superiors to offer improvement in relations. Our position was clear: We are always ready. If you truly wish to normalize relations, you have only to say the word. Our address is the same as it was 2,000 years ago," recalls Yitzhak Shoham, then attaché to the embassy in Rome for relations with the Holy See.[15]

Mordechai Drori, ambassador to Rome from December 1986 to October 1991, described the situation as follows: "Personally, Prime Minister Shamir had little interest in the Vatican or in meeting with the pope. When he visited Rome in February 1988, he did not request an audience at the Vatican, and I myself advised against a meeting with the pontiff, because in fact there was nothing to be said. Nonetheless, Monsignor Luigi Gatti from the Secretariat of State telephoned regarding the opportunity for a meeting, which in the end never took place."[16] These two Israeli diplomats make no secret of the friction created by the First Gulf War.[17] "The serious crisis between Israel and the Vatican exploded in January 1991. We didn't speak to each other for nearly four months," admits Shoham. "Things began to improve slowly, in April. It was then that the Holy See clearly explained that their main concern had been the fate of Christian communities in the Middle East. Up until that point, they had always cited three reasons for the absence of diplomatic relations: the fact that Israel's borders had not yet been determined by a peace treaty and were not internationally recognized; opposition to our annexation of East Jerusalem; and the persisting Palestinian question."

The diplomatic offensive launched by Montezemolo and Pazner in late 1991 was aimed first of all at dispelling the ill feelings aroused by the latest disputes. They were assisted by an element of great importance: by the spring, American efforts were already under way to exploit the window of opportunity created by the war for the resolution of the Arab-Israeli conflict. The shuttle diplomacy of Secretary of State James Baker had successfully led to the Madrid International Peace Conference, notwithstanding the politics of intensification maintained by Jewish settlement activity in the Occupied Territories—a policy intentionally pursued by the ultranationalist government of Yitzhak Shamir, with the clear intention of making the occupation of the West Bank and Gaza irreversible.

### The Peace Process and the Vatican Track

The turning point in relations between the Holy See and Israel came between October 1991 and April 1992. As noted earlier, the Vatican track closely paralleled the peace process. Looking back, we can infer that the Vatican's desire to take part in the process was so great that it was prepared to comply with Israel's prerequisite of full diplomatic relations. A cursory glance at the principal stages of negotiations between Israel and the Holy See suffices to convey how very close the correlation with the peace process was. As already pointed out, the establishment of the Bilateral Commission was announced nine months after the Madrid Conference. Furthermore, the crisis in Israeli-Vatican talks coincided with the impasse in the peace process that followed the expulsion to Lebanon of four hundred activists of the Islamic fundamentalist organization Hamas from the Occupied Territories on 17 December 1992, and with the decrease in American diplomatic efforts in the Middle East, due to elections in the United States. Likewise, talks resumed on both tracks in March-April 1993, and finally, in late August of the same year—immediately after the completion of the Oslo Accords between Israel and the PLO concerning autonomy in the West Bank and Gaza—the agreement between the Church and the Jewish state was signed.[18]

Vatican diplomats tend to downplay these facts, dismissing them as mere "coincidences." Montezemolo often said simply: "It is a mistake to bind together two processes that are so fundamentally different. They undoubtedly possess a common base, a single source—the historical need for resolution and general normalization in the Middle East. Both processes are part of the same series of events that unfolded on the stage of changing reality. They followed different paths, however, and the development of the Vatican-Israeli accords was certainly never contingent upon that of the peace process."[19] For the Israelis on the other hand, the political significance of such "coincidences" was clear. In their opinion, these were so obvious and politically motivated by the desire "not to miss the boat on the peace process" that they criticized the Secretariat of State for acting "in a purely temporal and unscrupulously pragmatic fashion, constantly being dragged along by events, and in no way seeking to pre-empt them."[20] Justice Minister Yossi Beilin, then head of the Israeli delegation to negotiations with the Holy See on 29 July 1992, noted: "One could say that were it not for the Madrid Conference and subsequently the Oslo Accords—in short, without the presence of the peace process—the agreement with the Vatican would have been signed much later. Vatican officials would certainly have preferred to await some change in direction on the road to Arab recognition of Israel before taking any steps. Without Oslo, the agreement might have been signed anyway, but everything would have been more difficult. Witness the fact that until early September 1993, it was not yet clear when full diplomatic relations would be achieved. Instead, immediately after the announcement of our agreement with the PLO, we were much more adamant in our insistence, and the Vatican much more flexible in accommodating us."[21]

The opening of dialogue in the spring of 1992 found the two parties inclined to make important initial concessions. Israel, for the first time, agreed to begin formal discussions without insisting upon its customary stipulation regarding full diplomatic relations. The Vatican principle of "gradual process" had won the day. The Church had maintained that the exchange of ambassador and nuncio should only come at the end of a long series of partial agreements geared toward the normalization of relations in all areas. The Holy See, for its part, was willing to recognize—albeit in a very hypothetical fashion—that the beginning of negotiations must, by virtue of circumstances, lead to full diplomatic relations. On 27 April, Montezemolo and Ambassador Moshe Gilboa—the Foreign Ministry official in charge of relations with the various churches—came up with the idea of a "Bilateral Permanent Working Commission" to meet periodically until an agreement was drawn up. On the following day, Montezemolo met again with President Herzog and took the opportunity to personally inform him of the latest developments.

It was during the course of a semisecret meeting on 20 May, at the Foreign Ministry in Jerusalem, that the two parties appeared ready to formalize their contacts. Montezemolo was accompanied by legal expert Father David Jaeger, Secretary of the Apostolic Delegation Monsignor Antonio Arcari, and financial expert on Church property Florent Arnaud. On the Israeli side were Moshe Gilboa, who was to be replaced in September by Eitan Margalit, his deputy Eli Yerushalmi, and Esther Efrat Smilg of the Foreign Ministry legal department, who was to be replaced a few months later by Chemda Golan, and Tel-Aviv lawyer Zvi Terlo, an expert on relations with the Church and canon law. Montezemolo had no further doubts, from this meeting on, that matters could truly be set in motion: "I made it clear that ours was no longer an academic discussion, but a working meeting intended to achieve a final accord or treaty."[22] "We were finally moving from form to substance. We could begin to negotiate the legal status of the Church in the Holy Land, keeping well in mind that the normalization of relations would inevitably be achieved, as a natural stage of the negotiations," encapsulated David Jaeger.[23] In the dispatch sent that same day to the Secretariat of State, Montezemolo thus stated that he had expressed the desire "to strengthen reciprocal relations," adding—in English—the exact phrase he had used in speaking with the Israelis: "without excluding possible normalization or mutual diplomatic relations, at a proper time, maybe step by step."[24] Montezemolo also requested "complete confidentiality," at least until the official announcement of the establishment of the Bilateral Commission. The Israelis, however, felt that news of their contacts would in some way reach the media, and believed that it would be rather difficult to keep the entire affair secret. In fact, the constant leaks concerning the course of the negotiations were a source of serious resentment on the part of the Vatican.[25]

It was agreed that all decisions taken by the "experts" comprising the Bilateral Commission would be subject to the final approval of the Secretariat of State and the officials of the Israeli Foreign Ministry. The final arbiters were to be Yossi Beilin and Monsignor Claudio Maria Celli, undersecretary for relations with states and head of the Vatican committee.

### Lengthy Negotiations concerning the "Agenda"

On 15 July 1992, the agenda for negotiations was set and immediately received the go-ahead from Celli and Beilin. It consisted of eleven points, of which seven had been submitted by the Holy See and four by Israel. The points submitted by the Vatican were the following:

- Freedom of Religion and Conscience: was approved in November 1992, but was only adopted in its final form—as Article 1 of the fifteen which appeared in the final document—on 10 June 1993.
- Legal Matters: were partially resolved at the meeting held on 19 April 1993. It was decided, however, that disputed issues would be settled by the subcommission on legal matters—as per the agreement—by June 1996. The subcommission was to be headed by Auxiliary Latin Bishop Giacinto Marcuzzo and Zvi Terlo.
- Pilgrimage and Holy Places: was based upon the codification of the Status Quo, approved in late November 1992.
- Education: was the object of heated debate in November-December 1992, above all due to the expressed wish of the Israeli police and security services to be allowed to interfere in the activities of the Catholic schools. According to the Israelis, the issue of free education was "used" by the Holy See "as a pretext" to freeze talks from 17 December 1992 (concomitant with the expulsion to Lebanon of over 400 Palestinian Hamas activists) until late March 1993, when the peace process recommenced, and the PLO—having obtained Israeli consent to the presence of a contingent of international observers in Hebron—agreed to resume negotiations for the implementation of autonomy in Gaza and Jericho. The final text on education, as it appears in Article 6 of the agreement, was approved only on 10 June, 1993.
- Communications Media: was approved on 19 April 1993 and established in Article 8 of the agreement, concerning the right of the local Church to own mass media "in harmony with the rights of the State," and Catholic access to the Israeli media.

- Social Welfare: was approved on 21 April 1993 and appeared in Article 9 of the agreement.
- Economic and Fiscal Matters: deals with one of the most controversial and sensitive issues in all of the negotiations. The Holy See wanted to preserve and extend the privileges and fiscal exemptions obtained over the years since the days of the Ottoman Empire. In particular, the representatives of local Church institutions—led by Notre Dame representative Richard Mathes, and Florent Arnaud—pressed for maximum extensions, knowing full well that a victory in this sense would help them make the agreement acceptable to the leaders of the Palestinian Church (first and foremost the Latin patriarch of Jerusalem, Monsignor Michel Sabbah), who did not look kindly upon the negotiations with Israel. The other churches—especially the Greek and the Armenian—also feared that a separate agreement between Israel and the Vatican would shatter the old coalition, which had de facto created a single Christian front on fiscal issues, and would thus weaken their bargaining position in disputes with Israel. The issue was debated on several occasions.

    Officials of the Ministry for Religious Affairs—which was in the hands of the Sephardic orthodox Shas party at the time—made matters even more complicated, seeking to undermine the spirit of compromise that characterised Foreign Ministry politics. In the end, it was decided not to decide, and at the meeting of 10 June they produced Article 10 of the agreement, in which (as in the case of the legal matters) they provided for the establishment of a subcommission charged with the task of reaching an agreement on financial matters by June 1996, to be headed by Palestinian Bishop Kamal Bathish and Ehud Kaufman, who was in charge of international relations at the Finance Ministry.

The four points submitted by the Israelis in effect all revolved around the primary issue of full diplomatic relations with a view toward the exchange of nuncio and ambassador. They were as follows:

- Normalization of Diplomatic Relations: the issue has already been discussed. It is interesting, however, to try and briefly reconstruct the content and terms of implementation of Article 14 of the agreement, which has the greatest political implications of any article in the entire document. This article in fact addresses such a delicate area that it is the only one to have an "additional protocol" and a final "mutually accepted interpretation" (the latter was supposed to have remained secret, but had reached the media even before the official signing), which stated that the exchange between Israel and the Holy See would take place immediately at the level of "special representatives," having "respectively, the personal rank of Apostolic Nuncio and Ambassador," and enjoying "all the rights, privileges and immunities granted to heads of diplomatic missions." This was an obvious last-minute compromise between the Vatican desire to proceed in a gradual manner and the assurance of full normalization sought by the Israelis. The latter were afraid that every impasse in the peace process with the Arabs could hold up negotiations with the Church. The "Additional Protocol" thus clearly stated that full diplomatic relations would be established in any case, four months from the date of the agreement's ratification.

For the "special representatives," the Vatican looked toward two major models employed in recent years.[26] The first was the case of Myron C. Taylor, President Franklin D. Roosevelt's "personal representative" to Pius XII during the Second World War,[27] and the second was that of the progressive restoration of Vatican relations with the countries of Eastern Europe. These comprised three basic options: *(a)* exchange of "personal representatives" between leaders; *(b)* the Yugoslavian precedent of the 1960s—representatives between governments; and *(c)* representatives between "sovereign entities," as in the case of the USSR, and later the Russian Federation, where an exchange of ambassador and nuncio took place, but without officially announcing the establishment of full diplomatic relations.[28] The first formal discussion of this issue took place in March 1993. It was only between the second half of November and 10 December, however, that they arrived at the final formula, whereby it was established that by January 1994, the "special representatives" would be appointed—to remain in office until the establishment of full diplomatic relations. As mentioned earlier, the latter was to occur no later than four months from the date of ratification of the agreement by the Holy See and the Israeli government. Upon normalization, the two subcommissions, established to deal with unresolved legal and financial issues, were also to begin operating.

All of this was carried out to the letter. On 19 January 1994, Israel appointed Shmuel Haddas, an experienced ambassador close to retirement, as "special representative" to the Holy See. The Secretariat of State appointed Montezemolo. On 10 March came the ratification of the agreement. At ten A.M. on 15 June, full diplomatic relations were declared (twenty-five days before the four-month deadline), accompanied by the inauguration of the nunciature in the old Franciscan monastery of Saint Peter in Jaffa, and the opening of the Israeli embassy in the Vatican (henceforth distinct from the embassy already operating in Rome). On 4 July, the two subcommissions convened for the first time. Montezemolo presented his credentials to Israeli President Ezer Weizmann at the president's office in Jerusalem on 16 August.

- Cooperation in Combating Anti-Semitism: this was explicitly requested by the Israelis, and encountered no particular opposition from the Church. Article 2 of the agreement was thus completed by November 1992, employing a number of phrases taken from the many papal documents condemning anti-Semitism and all other forms of racism.

- Matters of Pilgrimage and Tourism: once the mutual desire for cooperation had been defined in general terms in Article 5, it was—as in the agreement of January 1993—left up to the two subcommissions to work out the legal and financial details. It was not an easy task. Often in the past, there had been tensions between Jewish and Christian tour guides over the custom of tourists and pilgrims in the region.
- Cultural Exchanges: adopted in March 1993. One of the first examples of such exchanges was the exhibition in the Vatican Museums of the Dead Sea Scrolls, on loan from the Israel Museum in Jerusalem, in June of the following year.

### From the Bilateral Commission to the Fundamental Agreement

The announcement of the establishment of the Bilateral Commission on 29 July 1992 was followed by a long period of preparations. In September, Eitan Margalit replaced Moshe Gilboa and requested time to familiarize himself with the subject. The Israeli committee was built around a small group of experts: Zvi Terlo, already mentioned; Tamara Golan of the Justice Ministry was replaced at this time by Esther Efrat Smilg (perceived by the other side as being too rigid, and thus a serious obstacle during the talks); Avraham Talmon, representing Finance Ministry interests; Uri Mor, representing those of the Ministry of Religious Affairs; and Naomi Tisdale, representing the Jerusalem Municipality as the mayor's adviser on relations with the churches. They were joined by the aforementioned David Rosen. Also present, although not an official member of the delegation, was Shlomo Gur, a young and very able diplomat who was the right-hand man of Yossi Beilin, and who on numerous occasions was to conduct secret direct talks with David Jaeger in order to resolve various crises. Montezemolo was accompanied by Jaeger, Mathes, Arnaud, and Arcari (later replaced by the apostolic delegation's new secretary, Thomas Gullickson), as well as by Auxiliary Bishop Hannah Kaldani, the vicar of the Latin Patriarchate, resident in Nazareth, and Pierre Grech, secretary general of the Latin Bishops Conference in the Arabic Regions and of the Assembly of the Catholic Ordinaries in the Holy Land.

On 23 October, Israeli Foreign Minister Shimon Peres was received by the pope, whom he invited to visit Jerusalem, and later met with Monsignor Jean-Luis Tauran for about half an hour.[29] It was only on 2 November, however, that the Bilateral Commission truly came to life. Disagreements arose immediately. The Israelis saw the negotiations as a series of separate issues, to be resolved empirically, case by case, in order to pave the way to diplomatic normalization, as quickly as possible. The Holy See, on the other hand, sought a comprehensive legal construct governing not only relations between the two parties, but above all providing a clear definition of the status of the Catholic Church and its rights in the region. "There is no specific legislation in Israel regarding religious minorities and the Churches. Everything is done in a haphazard fashion, at the discretion of the respective military and civilian authorities. The Catholic Church is entirely at the mercy of the authorities," Montezemolo would often protest.[30] Privately, the officials of the Foreign Ministry sometimes admitted that he was right.[31] The ongoing exodus of Christians from the Middle East, and especially the shrinking of the Catholic community in Jerusalem and near the Holy Places, was another major source of concern to the Church.[32]

In order to remedy the situation, Vatican officials envisioned a kind of concordat, and on numerous occasions mentioned the Lateran Treaty as a possible model for accords with the State of Israel.[33] The Israelis, however, reacted in a confused manner, taking their time, requesting instructions from the foreign minister's office, in order to contend with the elaborate proposals constantly put forth by the other side. "The talks proceeded too slowly. The main problem was that the Israelis were unable to fit the negotiations into the framework of their normal working patterns. They were unfamiliar with the Church, and had no knowledge of concordats or canon law. It was always a clash between two different legal approaches. We had to build from scratch an alphabet of communication between two nearly opposite ways of thinking," lamented David Jaeger after the November 2 meeting.[34]

The impasse in negotiations was exacerbated on 17 December 1992 by the political crisis that followed the aforementioned expulsion to Lebanon of the four hundred or so Palestinian Hamas activists. An editorial appearing in *L'Osservatore Romano* at the time criticized the Israeli move and urged the Rabin government to rescind its decision.[35] However, this did not interfere with the visit—scheduled in advance—of Celli in Jerusalem on 19 December, and in Amman on the following day, which in any event did not contribute to removing the deep-seated obstacles. "We understood that the Israelis were having difficulty in determining exactly what the Catholic Church was. They refused to accept international legal classifications alien to their own legal system, and above all they rejected the principle that the Holy See can be recognized as an independent actor on the stage of the community of nations. We asked that they reformulate their principles—which were limited to relegating the Catholic Church to the status of 'non-profit organization'—and guarantee the status of religious institution endowed with its own sovereignty," observed Montezemolo.[36]

The search for compromise turned into a fierce duel—especially between Terlo and Jaeger—fought over legal definitions and scholarly dissertations on the rudiments of international law. Inevitably, the specific bilateral issues were laid aside.

The entire strategy of negotiation had changed. If at first each point was dealt with down to its specific applications, the two parties now sought out a common denominator, referring back to very general principles, such as freedom of conscience, education, and religion, or the ethical and philosophical ideas expressed in the UN Universal Declaration of Human Rights. This was, in a sense, a victory for the Vatican delegation, which had insisted on resolving matters of principle, once it realized the extent of the differences between the two sides. Indicative of this atmosphere of mutual lack of understanding were the harsh exchanges that took place at a meeting in late December, described by Montezemolo as follows: "Having seen that the Israelis refused to recognize the independent legal status of the Church, we therefore asked them to define that of Israel. We insisted that the date of Israel's founding was that of Resolution 181 for the partition of Palestine, approved by the United Nations on 29 November 1947. They responded angrily, that the Jewish State was not founded by UN concession, but by virtue of the free desire for self-determination of its inhabitants, who took up arms on 15 May 1948, but immediately added: 'This land was given [to us] by God in biblical times.' I then observed: 'If you say that this land was obtained by virtue of your will, and then you assert that it was by the will of God, isn't this a contradiction?' In the end, we settled on 15 May 1948—which was useful as an indirect affirmation of the fact that the agreement did not include East Jerusalem, the West Bank, or Gaza, occupied by Israel in June 1967. Henceforth, we also agreed that we should stick to very general principles, in order to avoid pointless debates."[37]

The height of the crisis came between 26 and 27 December, while debating the Israeli proposal that the Church must be "subject to the authority of the land." Montezemolo replied that it could be nothing but "independent of the authority of the land." It was at this stage of virtual impasse of the official negotiations that the secret channel between Jaeger and Gur was opened. "We jokingly called this channel our 'second Oslo'," Yossi Beilin later confirmed.[38] The initiative came from Jaeger, who was considered instrumental to the successful resumption of negotiations in the eyes of the press and the Israeli diplomats. An Israeli Jew by birth, converted to Christianity and ordained a priest, a scholar of canon law and expert on the question of the Holy Places in the Holy Land, he frequently served as a veritable bridge between the two parties—thanks to his "Jewish-Christian" identity—in the search for dialogue at all costs.[39] His knowledge of Hebrew and of Israeli society was to be indispensable to the Holy See. The Israelis, too, often turned to him for clarifications regarding the style and workings of Vatican diplomacy.[40]

Only in late March 1993, after a long hiatus requested by the Holy See on 6 January, was a compromise reached, adopting the intentionally vague wording "in harmony with the rights of the State," open to various interpretations. This formula was employed in Articles 6, 8, and 9 of the Fundamental Agreement, concerning, respectively, Catholic scholastic and educational activity in Israel (and in the Occupied Territories as long as they remain in Israeli hands), freedom of information for the local Church, and charity and good works.

Yossi Beilin summarized the conflict and the path adopted for its resolution as follows: "At the heart of the main difficulties was the clash between two legal systems—that of the State of Israel, and canon law. It was essential for us to make it clear that the Church is not above our laws. Negotiations on this point were dedicated to seeking out a formula that would be sufficiently vague to satisfy the expectations of both sides, without necessarily providing full and detailed answers. This was the case, for example, regarding the matter of education. Establishing that the Catholic educational system must be 'in harmony with the rights of the State in the field of education' meant that it could not contravene Israeli laws, without our having to resolve the issue of exactly who has the upper hand. It was upon this constructive ambiguity that we based the agreement, convinced that it was possible to agree on some very general principles, relying on mutual flexibility with regard to the difficulties that were bound to arise in everyday life."[41]

In late August, the road to the accord was basically open, lacking only the green light from the Vatican to seek agreement on the issue of diplomatic relations. An article in the Israeli daily *Ha'aretz* on 28 August reported a creeping fear in the Foreign Ministry: "It is now widely believed that the Vatican will not normalize diplomatic relations until there is progress on the road to peace." Then, all of a sudden, came the turning point. The Bilateral Commission reconvened in Jerusalem on 13 September. That same day, Yitzhak Rabin and Yasser Arafat shook hands in Washington. On 20 September, during an audience in the Vatican, the pope personally congratulated Ashkenazi Chief Rabbi of Israel Yisrael Meir Lau on the developments in negotiations between Israel and the PLO.

According to the timetable set by Rabin and Arafat (which turned out to be unrealistic), the autonomy process could begin as soon as 13 December 1993. In mid-October, translation of the Fundamental Agreement from English into Hebrew was begun. On 10 December the document was complete, and it was decided that it would be signed on 30 December, following a final meeting in the Vatican at the highest level on the preceding day.

There was no lack of last-minute difficulties. The most serious of these arose during the meeting in the Vatican on 29 December, when Celli told Beilin that they wanted a professional diplomat as ambassador to the Holy See. The Israelis had in principle considered appointing Rabbi David Rosen. The move created a moment of disorientation among the Israeli delegation, followed by serious tension between the Ministry of Religious Affairs and the Foreign Ministry. In the end, Israel decided to comply with the request.[42]

Even during the signing ceremony at the Foreign Ministry in Jerusalem, the differences that had characterised relations between the two sides since the negotiations' earliest exchanges resurfaced. Especially evident were the two fundamentally different conceptions of the agreement. For the Israelis, it had a symbolic value, well beyond its technical and diplomatic aspects. Above all it represented the advent of a completely new era of relations between Judaism and Christianity. It was treated almost as if it were primarily a theological rather than a political document. The Holy See, on the other hand, sought to limit its capacity to the field of international politics. This explains the extremely different tones evident in the speeches made by the respective heads of the two delegations. Beilin spoke emphatically, stressing the historic value of the event. "Formally, the accord that we are signing today is between a small state and an even smaller one. Its repercussions, however, go well beyond geographical boundaries, touching the hearts of millions of Jews and over a billion Christians. Behind this document are thousands of years of history characterised by hatred, fear, ignorance, and scant dialogue. There have been only a few years of understanding, and too many of darkness," he said, finally donning a skullcap and reciting in Hebrew the prayer for peace.[43] Celli's words were far drier and more factual, recalling the principal stages of the Bilateral Commission's work, briefly summarizing the articles of the agreement, lingering on Article 2, reiterating the Church's condemnation of anti-Semitism.

In any case, both sides had reason to be satisfied. Through the agreement with the Church, Israel could now hope to improve dialogue with the Arab-Christian community in the Middle East, and above all to combat that which Yossi Beilin called "the vestiges of Christian anti-Semitism." The Foreign Ministry believed that its effects would be felt in the long term. Beilin was convinced of this: "Many believing Catholics are convinced to this day that there is something evil about Jews," he said. "The move by the Holy See can contribute to changing this way of thinking. This is why the agreement has value that transcends the world of politics, touching upon religion, education, and psychology."[44]

For the Holy See, the results of the agreement were much more tangible and immediate. Apart from the legal and financial effects, which would benefit the everyday life of the Catholic community in the region, Vatican diplomacy now found itself in a better position vis-à-vis negotiations on the future of Jerusalem than it was prior to December 1993. The city is never mentioned by name in the agreement, but in a communiqué issued in the Vatican on the day after the signing ceremony, the Secretariat of State continued to reiterate that its position on Jerusalem had not changed. The communiqué reads as follows: "The Holy See feels the duty and the right to continue to demand—as it always has—some guarantees in the international arena. It asks that whoever exercises sovereignty—whether alone or together with others—adhere to a special internationally guaranteed statute, concerning guardianship over the great religious and cultural values present in this area."[45] The agreement with Israel did not mean the legitimization of the political or religious status quo prevailing in Jerusalem since 1967. It was a message intended to reassure the Arab world, the eastern churches, and above all, the Palestinians. Montezemolo has since repeated on many occasions that when the time comes to negotiate the final status of the city, the Holy See will also want to have a say in the matter. Clearly, the establishment of full diplomatic relations offers no guarantee against renewed political and religious tensions between Israel and the Vatican over one of the most complex issues of the entire Arab-Israeli peace process.

## NOTES

An earlier (albeit much shorter) version of this chapter first appeared as "Le tappe del negoziato diplomatico," in *Quaderni di diritto politica ecclesiastica*, trans. Shmuel Sermoneta-Gertel (Milan, 1995).

1. Interview with Eitan Margalit in his office at the Foreign Ministry in Jerusalem, Nov. 28, 1993.

2. This same sentence was repeated to me many times in 1992 and 1993 by Father David Jaeger and Monsignor Andrea Cordero Lanza di Montezemolo. The latter is also quoted on the subject by Henri Tinq, *L'Etoile et la Croix. Jean-Paul II—Israel: l'explication* (Paris: Editions Jean-Claude Lattès, 1993), 253–54.

3. On file with author.

4. George Weigel, *Witness to Hope* (New York: Cliff Street Books, 1999), 667.

5. Id., at 548.

6. Clare Pedrick, "Pope Rejects Pacifism, Calls for 'Just Peace' in Persian Gulf," *Washington Post*, Feb. 19, 1991, A8.

7. Cf. the text of the "Declaration" issued by Holy See Press Office Director Joaquin Navarro-Valls, Jan. 25, 1991.

8. Id.

9. On Pazner's role, cf. Tad Szulc, *Pope John Paul II—The Biography* (New York: Scribner, 1995), 449–55.

10. From an interview granted to me by Avi Pazner in his office at the Israeli embassy in Rome, May 6, 1993.

11. Id.

12. On Montezemolo, cf. Emanuele Orsi, "L'accordo fondamentale tra la Santa Sede e lo Stato di Israele," unpublished dissertation, Università Cattolica del Sacro Cuore di Milano, 1996–97 academic year.

13. Interview in Jerusalem with Rabbi David Rosen, member of the Israeli delegation, Dec. 26, 1993.

14. Interview with Monsignor Andrea Cordero Lanza di Montezemolo in his office at the apostolic delegation in Jerusalem, June 4, 1994.

15. Interview with Yitzhak Shoham in his office at the Foreign Ministry in Jerusalem, July 12, 1994.

16. Interview with Ambassador Mordechai Drori in Jerusalem, May 30, 1994.

17. Concerning tension between the Vatican and Israel during the Gulf War, cf. Silvio Ferrari, *Vaticano e Israele dal secondo conflitto mondiale alla guerra del Golfo* (Florence: Sansoni, 1991), 189–90.

18. Among the growing number of works on the Oslo Accords and the peace process, cf. Avi Shlaim, *War and Peace in the Middle East: A Critique of American Policy* (New York: Whittle Books, 1994), 104–42; Harvey Sicherman, *Palestinian Autonomy, Self-Government and Peace* (Boulder, Colo.: Westview Press, 1993); *The Palestinian-Israeli Peace Agreement: A Documentary Record* (Washington, D.C.: Institute for Palestine Studies, 1994); Shimon Peres, *The New Middle East* (New York: Henry Holt and Company, 1993); Jane Corbin, *Gaza First: The Secret Norway Channel to Peace between Israel and the PLO* (London: Bloomsbury, 1994); Hanan Ashrawi, *This Side of Peace* (New York: Simon & Schuster, 1995); Mahmoud Abbas (Abu Mazen), *Through Secret Channels* (London: Garnet Publishing, 1995); David Makovsky, *Making Peace with the PLO: The Rabin Government's Road to the Oslo Accord* (Boulder, Colo.: Westview Press, 1996); Ruth Lapidoth, *Autonomy: Flexible Solutions to Ethnic Conflicts* (Washington, D.C.: United States Institute of Peace, 1997); Uri Savir, *The Process: 1,100 Days that Changed the Middle East* (New York: Random House, 1998); Yossi Beilin, *Touching Peace: From the Oslo Accord to a Final Agreement* (London: Weidenfeld & Nicolson, 1999).

19. Interview with Montezemolo in Jerusalem, June 16, 1994.

20. Interview with Mordechai Drori, May 30, 1994.

21. Interview with Yossi Beilin in his office at the Foreign Ministry in Jerusalem, June 19, 1994.

22. Interview with Montezemolo, June 4, 1994.

23. Interview with David Jaeger in Jerusalem, July 8, 1994.

24. Interview with Montezemolo, June 4, 1994.

25. News of the first secret contacts appeared in the *Jerusalem Post* on May 21, 1992. On July 28, *Corriere della Sera* anticipated the Israeli-Vatican announcement regarding the Bilateral Commission by one day. The first excerpts from the "Fundamental Agreement" were published by *Corriere della Sera* on December 30, 1993, and more extensively five days later in the Israeli daily *Yedioth Ahronoth*. Cf. also Lorenzo Cremonesi, "L'accordo tra Santa Sede e Israele," *Vita e Pensiero* (Feb. 1994): 88–97.

26. Conversation with David Jaeger in Jerusalem, Oct. 18, 1993.

27. On the role and function of Myron Taylor, cf. Ennio Di Nolfo, *Vaticani e Stati Uniti, 1939–1952: Dalle carte di Myron C. Taylor* (Milano: Franco Angeli, 1978).

28. Regarding renewal of relations between the Vatican and the former countries of the Iron Curtain, cf. Andrea Ricardi, *Il Vaticano e Mosca* (Rome-Bari: Laterza, 1992), 365–77; and Owen Chadwick, "The Christian Church in the Cold War," in *Penguin History of the Church Series* 7 (1993): 199–218.

29. Cf. interview with Shimon Peres following his audience with the pope, published in *Corriere della Sera,* Oct. 23, 1992.

30. Repeated to me by Jaeger and Montezemolo on numerous occasions during the course of negotiations.

31. "Montezemolo was right when he maintained that our legislation concerning the Christian churches in Israel is confused. We will not change it, however, during negotiations with the Vatican. We will see what can be done in the coming years," said Eitan Margalit in an interview in his office at the Foreign Ministry in Jerusalem, June 12, 1994.

32. Among the growing body of literature on the subject of the Christian exodus from the Middle East and particularly from Jerusalem and the Occupied Territories, cf. Youssef Courbage and Philippe Fargues, eds., *Christians and Jews under Islam* (London: I. B. Tauris, 1998), 153 *et seq.;* "Les communautés chrétiennes dans le monde musulman arabe," *Proche Orient Chrétien* 47 (1997); Michael Prior and William Taylor, eds., *Christians in the Holy Land* (London: Scorpion, 1994), esp. Bernard Sabella, "Socio-Economic Characteristics and the Challenges to Palestinian Christians in the Holy Land," 31–44, and Sami F. Geraisy, "Socio-Demographic Characteristics: Reality, Problems and Aspirations within Israel," 45–55; Jean-Pierre Valognes, *Vie et Mort des Chrétiens d'Orient: Des Origines à nos jours* (Paris: Fayard, 1994), 566–613; Daphne Tsimhoni, *Christian Communities in Jerusalem and the West Bank Since 1948: An Historical, Social and Political Study* (Westport-London: Praeger, 1993); Lorenzo Cremonesi, "Cristiani in Medio Oriente: Tra la denuncia dell'intolleranza e la necessità del compromesso," *Vita e Pensiero* (July-Aug. 1992): 482–90.

33. Notwithstanding the fact that the concordat format is only used in agreements between the Holy See and Catholic countries, a number of principles from the Lateran Treaty are explicitly mentioned in a working document of the Holy See delegation, *Towards an Agreement between the Holy See and the State of Israel,* which was used as an initial platform for the proposal of topics for negotiation in the summer of 1992.

34. Interview with David Jaeger on that day.

35. Cf. *L'Osservatore Romano,* Dec. 22, 1992.

36. From the interview with Montezemolo, June 4, 1994.

37. Ibid. The same idea is briefly explained by Montezemolo in an interview published in *Corriere della Sera,* Dec. 30, 1993.

38. Cf. interview with Yossi Beilin in *Corriere della Sera,* Dec. 30, 1993.

39. On Father David Jaeger, cf. the Israeli daily *Hadashot* of April 7, 1993, as well as interviews with him that appeared in *Yedioth Ahronoth* on January 3, 1994, and in *Corriere della Sera* on the following day. See also Jaeger's doctoral dissertation (unpublished), discussed in the 1989 edition of *Pontificium Athenaeum "Antonianum" di Roma:* "The Roman Pontiffs in Defense of Christian Rights in the Holy Land: From 'Causa Nobis' to Redemptionis Annos" (1921–1984)."

40. Yossi Beilin said of him, during an interview on June 19, 1994: "He undoubtedly cut an unusual figure in this context. His story is incredible in its own right. At first, we did not know what to make of him, nor were we able to predict the ramifications of his involvement in this endeavor, assuming in principle that someone like him would try to show that he is more Catholic than the pope. But then we had to admit that he was of great help to both sides. Of course, he had his own inhibitions, psychological barriers, and

doubts. Nevertheless, he proved to be a natural bridge, without fear and without complexes. I am sure that he was indispensable to the Catholic delegation, thanks to his profound knowledge of Israel. In our dealings, he always sought to explain and to reassure."

41. Ibid.

42. Recounted in *Corriere della Sera,* Dec. 31, 1993.

43. The English text of Beilin's speech was distributed to the press by the Israeli Foreign Ministry.

44. Interview of June 19, 1994.

45. From the original text distributed at 4 P.M. on December 30, 1993, by the Holy See Press Office.

**II**

# THE MEANING OF
# THE ACCORD

2

# THE FUNDAMENTAL AGREEMENT BETWEEN THE HOLY SEE AND THE STATE OF ISRAEL

## A New Legal Regime of Church-State Relations

*David-Maria A. Jaeger, O.F.M.*

As a participant in the negotiations that produced the Fundamental Agreement between the Holy See and the State of Israel, and in the follow-up negotiations, which have produced the Legal Personality Agreement and are ongoing on other matters, it is my purpose especially to bear witness on this occasion to certain aspects of the larger significance and legal impact of the Fundamental Agreement. Notwithstanding actual statements of fact, my testimony reflects strictly my own understanding of the guiding principles and larger purpose of the agreement and is not given on behalf of any other person or institution.

Accordingly, this is no more than a preliminary—and, therefore, perforce somewhat superficial—treatment of a number of serious questions. Historical, constitutional, political, and even religious questions are touched upon in some manner or other by the Fundamental Agreement. Inevitably, recourse has to be made to overbroad generalizations and excessive simplifications of deep and complex issues. This is, in fact, only an outline for a much larger study already in progress, which will amount to a history of, and a commentary on, the Fundamental Agreement.

## Introduction

On December 11, 1993, Pope John Paul II delivered an address that traced in bold, imaginative lines a new vision for the future of the Christian presence in a renewed Middle East.[1] Speaking to a convention of experts in Roman and canon law that was being held at the Pontifical Lateran University in Rome, the supreme pontiff reviewed the Church's centuries-long search for a legally secure existence in a region which saw the birth, successively, of the three great monotheistic religions. The holy father spoke of the ways pursued in the past to assure the Christian religious minorities a necessary autonomous space, which have borne fruit in legal and social institutions that deserve recognition and esteem. However, the pontiff emphasized that "the profound social changes" of our times render "insufficient the sole safeguards traditionally accorded to personal situations or to individually construed aspects of worship."[2] Rather, he states:

> [T]he freedom of religion cannot, in fact, be reduced to the sole freedom of worship, but includes also the right to non-discrimination in the exercise of the other rights and of the freedom that are proper to every human person, considered both in its individual and in its communitarian dimension.[3]

This contemporary insight into the exigencies intrinsic to the dignity of the human person poses a challenge and a task to every state. Quoting a decision issued by the United Nations Human Rights Committee, the holy father said that each state is called to examine its own legal order and to modify and perfect it accordingly.[4] "A mature conception of the State and of its legal order," the pontiff proceeds, inspired by that which the common conscience of humanity has expressed in the rules of the international community, demands the effort to ensure equality of treatment to every person, irrespective of his ethnic, linguistic, cultural, and religious origin.[5] He concludes that it is in societies that are built or refashioned in accordance with these principles that "it will be possible to guarantee, increasingly better, also to the Christians of the Eastern Mediterranean, a future that will preserve their special identity and will be respectful of the human person and his fundamental rights."[6]

The supreme pontiff is calling here, in effect, for a paradigm shift in the church-state relationship that became the norm in the Middle East in the seventh century, and that the State of Israel also inherited upon its creation in 1948. Fewer than three weeks after the pontiff's address, on December 30, 1993, the Holy See and the State of Israel signed their Fundamental Agreement, which represents the first concrete application of the new paradigm and creates a new and different kind of legal relationship between the Church and the state in that region.

## The *Ancien Régime*

The modern problems of church-state relations in the Holy Land originated with the Muslim conquest in 638.[7] To be sure, there had been earlier problems in this region. For instance, problems in church-state relations existed in the period beginning at Pentecost and ending in the fourth century with a series of legal dispositions that first assured the Church its freedom and then Christianized the Roman Empire itself. With the freedom of the Church, and even more with the Christian confessionalization of the Roman Empire, which included the Holy Land, the previous problems ended except for some episodic recrudescence, such as those occurring under Julian the Apostate (362–365). This momentous transformation did not necessarily and at all times ensure the full liberty of the Catholic Church in relation to the state. Subsequent conflicts took place within Christendom and were thus internal to the Christian *Res publica*. Even the Persian occupation of 614, while certainly destructive, did not alter the situation definitively. However, the conquest of 638 did alter the situation. A different, very definite legal order was thereby established, which would only be interrupted (with no lasting effect) by the Crusades.

Having been governed between 639 and 1099 by the Muslim Arabs, the Holy Land, after the withdrawal of the Crusaders, came under Muslim Mameluk rule. In 1516–17, the Holy Land passed into the hands of the Muslim Ottoman Turks, thus remaining subject to the Muslim legal system, which determined, among other things, the legal condition of the Church and Christians.[8] While the political rulers, dynasties, and empires changed, the meta-constitutional fundamentals of the Islamic *Res publica*, rooted in their shared religion, remained constant.

The Islamic commonwealth is based on an absolute monism, which consists of maintaining the unity of the spiritual and the temporal juridical spheres. It is, therefore, a pure theocracy, *sensu pleno*.[9] The intentional sphere of the Islamic legal order, or juridical universe, knows no limit at all, either territorial or personal, given that it is destined to be extended to the whole world.[10] In terms of the actual situation, however, the legal order draws a distinction between territory in which the Islamic *imperium* already has been established effectively, namely the *dar-al-islam* or "homestead of Islam," and territory that is still outside its rule and is yet to make its "submission," which is what the word *islam* means. This latter territory, called *dar-al-harb* or "home of war," is the object of the believers' all-out efforts, designated *jihad* or "holy war," to ensure its submission.[11]

Comprised geographically within *dar-al-islam,* there may be unbelievers who, while not yet ready to surrender to Islam in matters of religious belief and practice, are prepared to submit to the Islamic *imperium* politically. These unbelievers, provided they belong to the "People of the Book" or *ahl-al-kitab,* a designation applicable principally to Jews and Christians, may be spared the sword and may obtain the condition of *religio tolerata* for their beliefs and practices. To achieve this condition, unbelievers must accept the status of *ahl al-dhimma,* which means substantially "people under protection."[12] Such a status is formalized through the payment of a special poll tax and is construed as a status of perpetual humiliation, which is due to their obstinate persistence in unbelieving, and lasting for as long as this resistance to Islam perdures.

Given the monistic nature of the Islamic *Res publica,* the status of *dhimma* leads to the effective exclusion from it of those consigned to this status. Moreover, it brings with it multiple public law disqualifications, as well as many civil law and penal law restrictions and inequalities, while the very *toleratio* of the religion itself is clearly circumscribed.[13] Even the "autonomous" personal jurisdiction granted to the respective hierarchies or religious authorities of *dhimma* communities is a concession that by its nature does not empower its beneficiaries to claim or vindicate any rights over the Islamic empire, within which they are meant to operate. The absolute theocracy of the Islamic *Res publica* and the intrinsic anomalousness of the *dhimma* status in relation to this seamless religious-political continuum, or whole, do not allow for adequate ground on which to take a stand in defense of the rights of those consigned to *dhimma* status vis-à-vis the Islamic empire itself.[14]

The circumscribed "autonomy" granted the *dhimma* communities in matters that go well beyond the intrinsic exigencies of proper religious governance is itself a potent double-edged sword. Superficially, this "autonomy" could be presented, and has been presented by its apologists, as the expression of an enlightened tolerance, but in reality, it is even more an expression, a cause, and an instrument of the effective isolation of those considered to belong to those communities.

Given the seamless religious-political whole of the surrounding society, Christians, under these conditions, were not even second-class citizens. Rather, *qua* Christians, they were effectively excluded from a society and a state that professed to be integrally Islamic. When considered in the context of their Christian identity, they were forced to exist only within the confines of socio-juridical enclaves, or "ghettoes." Christian churches thereupon became "ghettoes" legally, and would perforce become sociologically and psychologically as well. Indeed, the allied combination of the prohibition and corresponding renunciation of evangelization, and the socio-juridical confinement of Christians within their own partly and forcibly "autonomous" enclaves, operated a profound distortion in the image of the Christian community. The community was forced into the alien mold of an ethnic or tribal society, which only properly survives through natural procreation, with membership determined by natural descent, and with a role in the life of its members and a share of their overall social, political, and legal identity far in excess of that proper to the Church.[15]

The application of this fundamental meta-constitutional conception of the Islamic *Res publica* "with its consequences for the Christians under its rule" was not, of course, always consistent. Far-reaching constitutional developments within the Ottoman Empire in its last century, as well as the welcome emergence of a secular Arab national consciousness in which Christians and Muslims could share in perfect equality, served as powerful agents of change, even as the Ottoman Empire was collapsing. Later, there were a variety of developments in the several Arab states with their different, evolving political and legal regimes. However, at the time Ottoman rule in Palestine ended (1917–18), the legal regime in force was still fundamentally premised on the monistic nature of the political-religious Islamic *Res publica* and the consequent constitutional-legal confinement of the tolerated minority religions within their partly and really forcibly "autonomous" ghettoes. Under the Ottomans, the "autonomous" ghettoes were known as "*millets*." It was a system in which the Muslim religious community was numerically identical with the political community, and so not properly existent as such, while those not belonging to it were contained in the socio-juridical ghettoes of the *millets*.[16]

Following its liberation-occupation of Palestine in 1917–18, Great Britain, both as belligerent occupant and later as the mandatory power on behalf of the League of Nations, essentially was committed to upholding the legal regime of church-state relations already in place in Palestine. Pending final disposition of the Palestine issue, Great Britain perfected, adapted, and consolidated these relations.

With its founding in May 1948 the State of Israel inherited this state of affairs. It was in direct contradiction with Israel's Declaration of Independence, which envisaged a completely different kind of political society, namely, a modern democracy, predicated on the equality of all its citizens before the law. Israel's vision is evident from its unconditional promise that the state

> will be based on freedom, justice and peace by the prophets of Israel; it will ensure complete *equality of social and political rights* to all its inhabitants *irrespective of religion*, race or sex; it will guarantee freedom of religion, conscience, language, education and culture.[17]

The original vision of the modern Jewish national movement, or Zionism, like the Declaration of Independence, envisaged a lay modern democracy, in which citizens would be equal before the law, regardless of their various choices of religious beliefs. The Zionists anticipated a state in which the Church would not have to play a role in the lives of its members beyond that proper to it, and where the Church would be able to re-emerge as a spiritual and religious society based on a shared faith. The Zionists desired to remove the Church from the focus of not necessarily voluntary quasi-ethnic identification in a context where everyone else was so identified. Ideally, the Zionists envisioned a state that would be more like the United States, contemporary England, or post-1984 Italy rather than Lebanon, the Balkans, or even Northern Ireland.

Although it would have been entirely natural for the new state to draw the consequences from its proclaimed self-understanding and formally abolish the *millet* regime as incompatible with its democratic aspirations, this did not happen. In fact, the abolition of the Jewish religious community (Knesset Israel) in the next decade only strengthened that regime by putting the Jewish community in the same position previously occupied by the Muslims. The Muslim community, indeed, has suffered the most paradoxical fate under this dispensation. Having lost its identification with the ruling political community, the Muslim community has not been able to acquire any communal or institutional structure of its own, and to that extent still does not have a communal or institutional existence of its own apart from the state that services it. For the Christian churches, on the other hand, this turn of events meant that they were to remain exactly where they had been all along, within sociological, legal, and civic enclaves that were outside the mainstream of national life. To this extent, Christian churches were *millets*, called "Recognized Religious Communities" under the Israeli system.[18]

Briefly, this system assigns each citizen a religion, which then becomes part of his civil identity. The state establishes criteria for religious classification, which in most circumstances broadly correspond to those religions concerned. However, discrepancies and contradictions still remain. If the particular religion to which a citizen is assigned corresponds to one of the several Recognized Religious Communities, the state leaves the citizen to the operation of the laws and courts of that "community" with respect to specific matters, notably certain areas of marriage and family law. Normally, a citizen may not opt out of the religion assigned to him or her except by formal conversion to another religion. In any case, there are no provisions for religionless persons or any others who so choose to contract marriage, for example, or to be buried. The system of religious classification as part of the citizen's civil identity vis-à-vis the state and society both expresses and powerfully reinforces present ethnic distinctions in society. It acts as a guarantor of enforced "group identity," which is a powerful barrier against assimilation. Above all, however, it distorts the process and meaning of assuming a religious identity of making choices of faith. By inextricably and perversely tying faith to belonging (or not belonging) to a given ethnic group, nationality, or tribe, the system of religious classification distorts religious faith itself.[19] Nowhere is this more unnatural than in the case of Christianity and the Church.

Indeed, it cannot be said that under this system the churches themselves are accorded recognition of their proper identity. Rather, the Recognized Religious Communities are a creation of the state and, as such, a construct of the civil law. This is brought out clearly by the 1926 Religious Communities Ordinance,[20] the substance of which still appears to be in effect. The ordinance recognizes the non-Jewish religious community as only a substratum of sorts, having no more than a certain *potentia oboedientialis,* or a mere radical capacity for legal personality and legally recognized organization. For the religious community to acquire legal capacity and a legally recognized organization, it must petition the Minister of Religious Affairs, a figure that is a relic from an earlier, very different kind of constitutional regime. If the minister accepts the petition, he may enact regulations for that religious community, bestowing legal recognition upon it, pursuant to his own authority and the authority of the state under the ordinance, its statutes, or bylaws. Obviously, Catholic churches, recognized for the purpose of the operation of personal status laws and the tribunals that administer them, never petitioned the minister to organize them in this manner and were therefore repeatedly subjected to court challenges as to their legal personality in the State of Israel.[21]

While the courts of the Catholic Church, *sui iuris,* have functioned fully, under the different statutes that govern the operation of the personal status laws, independent of formal legal organization and religious community status, the vaunted "autonomy" that this independence gives the churches might itself, in the last analysis, turn out to be something quite different. Any possible benefits of the churches' independence surely are outweighed by such results of this system as the deleterious "balkanization" of society and the inequality of citizens before the law. It could be argued that the state, far from recognizing the independence of the canonical legal order, co-opts it materially, and makes it formally part of its own law, with a variety of possible consequences, such as the possible ability of the civil courts to treat questions of canon law arising before them as questions of law coming within judicial notice, as in *iura novit curia,* rather than questions of fact as would presumably be the case with any independent legal order.[22] In addition, the tribunals of the churches, put in the false position of servicing the civil legal construct of the Recognized Religious Community, may find themselves having to hear cases and decide questions that fall distinctly outside the proper, or at least appropriate, reach of ecclesiastical or spiritual law, and to regulate issues for which no body of canonical norms actually may exist. Hence, a body of norms or "personal status" code may have to be invented to deal with matters more appropriately and expertly dealt with by the civil legislature and judiciary, such as matters in which all citizens should be equal before a body of enlightened law made by their democratically elected representatives "without distinction of religion, race or sex."[23]

Finally, the *millet*, or the system of Recognized Religious Communities, does not recognize the Catholic Church at all. It only makes reference to the several churches *sui iuris* that are endowed with distinct regional and local hierarchies and particular laws. These churches consist of the several Eastern Catholic churches and the Latin Church. The system effectively has disregarded the fact that these several churches are in reality "parts" or "manifestations" of a single body of religious believers, the Catholic Church.

### The Emergence of the New Regime

All of the tensions, indeed, the contradictions inherent in the survival of the *millet* regime of the modern State of Israel became instantly visible in the negotiations over the Fundamental Agreement between the Holy See and the State of Israel. The chief purpose of these negotiations was to lay the foundations for the normalization of church-state relations. The revelation of these contradictions would not in itself have been a problem if the delegation of the State of Israel had not assumed that the Fundamental Agreement could be crafted in such a way as to reflect, in essence, the *status quo ante* with respect to church-state relations, without any substantial change in the relationship itself and, in part, by using rather than disregarding the previously discussed 1926 Religious Communities Ordinance. For its part, however, the delegation of the Holy See was bound to insist that in the fundamental legal relationship between the Church and the state, there had to be a precise determination that the active subject (the titular or holder) of rights and obligations vis-à-vis the state would be the Catholic Church,[24] not simply the several Recognized Religious Communities, or even their aggregate, or any other fragmentary institutional expression of the Church.

Because there was so much at stake for either side, the confrontation between the differing approaches and expectations of the two delegations was intense. In the end, Israel yielded by acknowledging that the negotiations could not go forward at all unless it was prepared to depart radically from its inherited and incongruously preserved regime of state-church relations. This meant recognizing the Catholic Church as a juridical subject. In other words, the Catholic Church would be the active subject of rights and duties vis-à-vis the state, which is another term for the church-state relationship. It was this courageous, farsighted, and revolutionary decision on the part of Israel that made it possible for the negotiations to proceed and for the Fundamental Agreement to take shape.

The delegation of the Holy See never intended to demand the abolition, *hic et nunc,* of the Recognized Religious Communities regime. The delegation assured the State of Israel that it understood that the curious survival of this old regime was tied to internal needs and debates within the majority Jewish population, and that its continued applicability to the state's Christian citizens was simply incident to these factors. For this reason, the Church had not taken any public position or initiative on the matter, but would simply await the eventual resolution of the internal Jewish debate, at times, almost a Kulturkampf, in the confident hope that ultimately the inherent logic and dynamic integrity of the Declaration of Independence would prevail, leading to the quiet abandonment of the Recognized Religious Communities regime. The delegations of the Holy See and of the State of Israel converged on this matter, laying the foundations for a totally new legal regime of church-state relations. This new regime under the Fundamental Agreement would operate in conjunction with the old *millet* or Recognized Religious Communities regime. While utterly incompatible in their assumptions, principles, and essential purposes, the two regimes are destined to live side by side for the foreseeable future and need not clash much in practice. The Recognized Religious Communities regime needs to extend to a very narrow and specialized area, mostly certain parts of family law, while the vast expanse of church-state relations is left without competition to the terms of the Fundamental Agreement.

Still, some of the legal experts taking part in the negotiations insisted on the need to create some link between the old and the new regime. Accordingly, the legal experts identified this new, hitherto unheard of subject, the Catholic Church, in terms of the several bodies that were considered to be known to the law under the old regime as the new subject of the Fundamental Agreement. These complex, delicate, and arduous negotiations ultimately became Article 13, paragraph 1 of the agreement.

Initially, the delegation of the Holy See entertained some doubt as to whether there was really a need to link the two regimes. In the end, it agreed that some transitional language between the old and the new order could be devised, provided it was absolutely clear that this entirely "new" active subject, the Catholic Church, was in no way reducible to the aggregate of the bodies "recognized" by the old regime. Hence, the all-important "*inter alia*" language in Article 13, paragraph 1(a) was created. This transitional norm can be said to represent a distinct advantage to the Church. While the language makes it clear that the Church's rights and freedoms proclaimed and recognized in the Fundamental Agreement apply to all of the recognized bodies, it by no means confines these rights and freedoms to previously recognized bodies, but extends them to the Catholic Church as such.

As the compromise formulation also suggests, the delegation of the Holy See was able to maintain the integrity of its position that the Church "does not know" the Recognized Religious Communities, as such an autonomous creation of the civil law, but only "knows" the church *sui iuris:* those bodies that belong to it, are legislated by it, and are subject exclusively to its own laws. The attentive reader of the treaty norm will see clearly that the Holy See does not refer directly to the Recognized Religious Communities. Instead, it provides that the Holy See "knows" the Church *sui iuris* and the state "knows" the Recognized Religious Communities. The assumption is made that these are two formalities under which the same material reality is found. Although this is not an entirely accurate assumption, there is enough truth to it to serve the present purpose.[25]

The Fundamental Agreement's creation of a whole new conceptual framework for church-state legal relations necessarily reaches far beyond the agreement itself, providing the entire dynamic for the process set in motion by the Fundamental Agreement.[26] The Fundamental Agreement gives broad recognition to the Catholic Church's "subjecthood," the independence and sovereignty of its supreme authority, and the Church's coordinate, rather than subordinate, status with the state.[27] This recognition receives detailed, concrete, and practical expression in the first treaty after the creation of the Fundamental Agreement to be produced by the Bilateral Commission between the Holy See and the State of Israel—the Legal Personality Agreement. The commission concluded the treaty for the purpose of completing and implementing the Fundamental Agreement.

Significantly, the Legal Personality Agreement drafted pursuant to Article 3, paragraph 3 of the Fundamental Agreement established[28] that in the forum of the state, questions of canon law shall be considered questions of fact, as are, in Israel, all questions concerning the law of other independent legal orders, such as foreign states. Thus, the treaty sweepingly ends any possibility of the appropriation of canon law by the state, which might have resulted from the *millet* or Recognized Religious Community regime. More importantly, the treaty recognizes the canonical legal order as being as complete, independent, and sovereign within the sphere of competence proper to the Church as that of the state itself, or any state. This advance does, in turn, involve assumptions, implications, and consequences that are the exact opposite of those characterizing the attitude to the Church of the *millet* or Recognized Religious Communities regime.

More profoundly, the Fundamental Agreement and the Legal Personality Agreement[29] put an end definitively and irrevocably to any possible applicability to the Catholic Church or any of its church *sui iuris* of the model of religious community organization legislated in the 1926 Religious Communities Ordinance, otherwise still in force. Instead of being an amorphous substratum that needs to be organized by government edict, the Catholic Church is now fully recognized as a whole and in its diverse formations and expressions. The Church has solidified its status as an organic, sovereign, and independent society, with its own primary legal order, sovereign authority, and administrative, judicial, and legislative apparatus.

Thirteen centuries of legal history have come to an end. A new legal regime of relations between the Catholic Church and the state has been put in place in the heart of the Middle East. Both as a testimony to some other states in the region, where salutary secularization, democratization, and legal modernization are still to reach analogous levels, and as a milestone on Israel's long road to achieving more fully the vision articulated in its own Declaration of Independence, the new legal regime built on the foundation of the Fundamental Agreement is at once a notable achievement and solemn promise, a solid realization, and a beacon of hope.

### After the Fundamental Agreement: Going Forward

On 11 May 1994, the delegations of the Holy See and of the State of Israel signed a memorandum spelling out first steps for the negotiations on the further, detailed agreements mandated by the Fundamental Agreement. They created two subcommissions "to study and report" on the issues involved: Juridical subcommission charged first of all with the implementation of Article 3, paragraph 3 of the Fundamental Agreement, and an economic subcommission charged with implementing Article 10, paragraph 2. Both subcommissions held their inaugural meetings on 4 July 1994, and then began their working sessions in October of the same year.

In the late summer of 1995 the juridical subcommission, having gone as far as it was able, turned in its report to the commission, which then brought the negotiations—pursuant to Article 3, paragraph 3 of the Fundamental Agreement—to a successful conclusion. This second treaty between the Holy See and the State of Israel was signed on 10 November 1997 and entered into force (in accordance with its Article 13) on 3 February 1999. It bears the title Agreement between the Holy See and the State of Israel Pursuant to Article 3, par. 3, of the Fundamental Agreement between the Holy See and the State of Israel (also referred to as the Legal Personality Agreement).[30] By means of this agreement the State of Israel assures full recognition of the legal personality of the Catholic Church and of the public legal persons in the Church that are present and active, at least to some degree, in the State of Israel and in all Israeli-governed territory, both those now existing and those yet to be created. The agreement likewise contains detailed legal provisions for the recognition of dissolution by the Church of an ecclesiastical legal person, for the law governing them (the canon law), for the proper forum for dispute resolution, and allied matters. In a significant provision likely to have an even broader impact in Israeli law, the agreement establishes (in its Article 9) that questions of canon law are to be regarded, in the Israeli forum, as questions of fact, thus resolving a potential ambiguity on this score.

The economic subcommission wrapped up its work in January 1995, reporting modest though not insignificant results. The commission itself took up the negotiations on 11 March 1999, and at the time of writing is continuing them, with a view to fashioning an agreement pursuant to Article 10, paragraph 2 of the Fundamental Agreement. At stake are rules for the protection of ecclesiastical property, the restitution to the Church of certain properties, the fiscal status of the Church in Israel (immunities or exemptions that, in the view of the Holy See, are both to consolidate the rights acquired through the centuries and to mirror the enlightened rules of societies such as the United States and the several states), and state budgetary participation in the educational and charitable works of the Church for the benefit of residents of the state. Obviously the stakes are very high, and the negotiations are very complex.

The financial status negotiations take place (as they did on the Fundamental Agreement) mostly at the "working level" (the "level of experts"), headed, as before, respectively, by the apostolic nuncio to Israel and by the head of the Foreign Ministry unit charged with relations with the Holy See. The plenary commission, headed respectively by the undersecretary for relations with states at the Holy See's Secretariat of State and by Israel's deputy foreign minister, has also met since the conclusion of the Fundamental Agreement—most recently in spring 2002, to help expedite the current negotiations, which may be said to have been proceeding at a very slow pace, considering that the agreement that the parties had aimed to achieve by 1996 is by now long overdue.

Either before or shortly after the conclusion of these negotiations, it is essential that negotiations be started pursuant to Article 12 of the Fundamental Agreement. On a number of occasions, the delegation of the Holy See gave notice to the other party of issues it considers a priority. These include religious and spiritual assistance to persons in circumstances that restrict their freedom to move around, such as members of the military, hospital patients, and prisoners; the issuing of residence permits to ecclesiastical and religious personnel; and the review of official educational materials for the purpose of ensuring that their contents offer a fair presentation of the Christian religion and Church, promoting mutual respect and favoring dialogue and equality. Among other issues already specifically identified in the talks so far are found the application of labor laws (the Church, a strong defender of the rights of labor, would seek recognition of the specificity of working for—and therefore, in some sense, representing—the Church), as well as social security, national health care, and fiscal provisions as they apply to individual persons.

## Final Remarks

The Fundamental Agreement represents a determined, visionary attempt by the sovereign authority of the Catholic Church to transform radically the relationship between the Church and society in the Middle East, starting with a potentially new and different kind of Middle Eastern polity, which is—at least intentionally—committed to the principles of secular (in the sense of nontheocratic, not necessarily militantly secularist), modern democracy, however imperfectly realized to date. By now it has been followed by one more treaty of a similar nature and composition—with Israel's immediate neighbor, which shares with it the Holy Land.[31] While these agreements are in themselves prominent new and ineradicable "facts" on the historical-legal landscape of the region, their fruitfulness may not be automatic or immediate in every respect. Their implementation may—and does—undergo delays and even setbacks, arising both within the bilateral relationship and in the larger regional context. Thus, there can be no doubt that a pall has been cast over the Holy Land as a whole by the interruption of the Palestinian-Israeli peace negotiations since the start of the al-Aqsa intifada in September 2000, and the allied eruption of reciprocal violence, with grave consequences for the life of both nations. Among other things, this turn of events has inevitably resulted in disruption of the process whereby the Palestinian nation had been assembling and developing the elements of independent national life—a process intended to be influenced by the Basic Agreement.

In the bilateral realm, the entire relationship between Israel and the Catholic Church was severely challenged by the initial decision of the government of Israel to build a mosque on public land right in front of the Basilica of the Annunciation in Nazareth, in spite of the continuing entreaties and protests of the Holy See, of all the Christian churches in the Holy Land, and of Christian leaders and believers worldwide, all demanding that the government of Israel revoke this decision and create there instead the public square that had been originally planned for that space. Happily, in spring 2002 the government of Israel reversed the odd position it had staked out and revoked its decision to build that particular mosque. Nonetheless, the damage to bilateral relations has been considerable.

While this issue—one of truly unprecedented gravity in the history of relations between the Catholic Church and the State of Israel—does not, of its nature, belong in the deliberations of the Bilateral Permanent Working Commission between the Holy See and the State of Israel (the forum for the ongoing negotiations on the further treaties required by the Fundamental Agreement), it is impossible to imagine that its impact could be isolated from every (or indeed, any) other facet of the bilateral relationship.

We are entering the tenth year since the signing of the Fundamental Agreement in 1993. One must hope that the tenth year after its signing will see the conclusion of the various agreements still necessary for its full implementation.

## NOTES

This is a revised text of the paper prepared for delivery at the April 8, 1997, symposium at the Catholic University of America, Columbus School of Law, and first published in 47 *Catholic University Law Review*, 427–40 (1998).

1. John Paul II, "Discorso ai partecipanti al IX Colloquio Internazionale Romanistico-Canonistico organizzato dalla Pontificia Università Lateranense," in *L'Osservatore Romano*, Dec. 12, 1993; reproduced in *Il diritto romano canonico quale diritto proprio delle Comunita' cristiane dell'Oriente mediterraneo: IX Colloquio internazionale romanistico canonistico* ("Utrumque Ius": Collectio Pontificiae Universitatis Lateranensis, 26), at ix–xii (Vatican City, 1994).

2. Id.

3. Id.

4. See id.

5. Id.

6. Id.

7. See A. O. Issa, *Les minorités chrétiennes de Palestine à travers les siècles* 22–65 (1977) (describing the events and developments concerning the juridical condition of the Church in the period between Pentecost and the Constantinian Peace of the Church).

8. Anything that is said here of Islamic legislation or political organization is not meant to apply to any Muslim-majority political society existing today. Additionally, this discussion is not intended to give any sort of illustration of Islamic religion and law. References to these realities are made only with respect to their incidental effect on the previously observable legal condition of the Church and its members in the region that currently corresponds to the territory of the State of Israel. For the general reader, a reasonably brief, judiciously balanced view of the laws of Islam is offered by Y. Linant de Bellefonds, "Law," in 2 *Religion in the Middle East: Three Religions in Concord and Conflict* 413–58 (A. J. Arberry ed., 1969).

9. See Sami Awad Aldeeb Abu-Sahlieh, *L'Impact de la religion sur l'ordre juridique cas de l'Egypte non-musulmans en pays d'Islam* 45 (1979). Abu-Sahlieh observes that Muhammad "a établit à Médine le noyau du premier Etat islamique, un Etat-religion, basé sur une loi révélée et sur un critère de distinction religieux." Id. This is entirely different from the phenomenon of a state religion in Christendom. The Christian confessional state is predicated on the ultimately irreducible duality of the state and religion, no less than on their deliberate joining together.

10. Cf. N. Armanazi, *L'Islam et le droit international* 98, 100 (1929).

11. Cf. Abu-Sahlieh, *supra* note 9, at 48–49; N. Armanazi, *supra* note 10, at 69.

12. For the historical origins and early development of this status, in law as well as in fact, see generally A. S. Tritton, *The Caliphs and Their Non-Muslim Subjects: A Critical Study of the Covenant of Umar* (1970). For a detailed historical-juridical study of Islam from the very beginning to the fall of the Ottoman Empire, see Antoine Fattal, *Le Statut Légal des Non-Musulmans en Pays d'Islam* (1958). For an unusual and somewhat idiosyncratic treatment, see Bat-Ye'or, *The Dhimmi: Jews and Christians Under Islam* (David Maisel et al. trans., 1985). See also the collection of contributions to the study of the *dhimmi* specifically in the Ottoman Empire in *Christians and Jews in the Ottoman Empire: The Functioning of a Plural Society* (Benjamin Braude & Bernard Lewis eds., vols. I, II, 1982).

13. Cf. Abu-Sahlieh, *supra* note 9, at 52–58.

14. On the *dhimma* system, and the autonomous role of the communities subject to it, see Richard B. Rose, "Islam and the Development of Personal Status Laws Among Christian Dhimmis: Motives, Sources, Consequences," 72 *Muslim World* 159 (1982).

15. See D.-M. A. Jaeger, "Christianity in the Holy Land: The Main Issues," in *Papers Read at the 1979 Tantur Conference on Christianity in the Holy Land* 74–78 (D.-M. A. Jaeger ed., 1981).

16. See generally Anton Odeh Issa, *Les Minorites Chretiennes de Palestine: A Travers les Siecles* 101–226 (1976) (providing vicissitudes occurring during the approximately thirteen centuries from the first Muslim conquest to the end of the Ottoman rule in the Holy Land); Charles A. Frazee, *Catholics and Sultans: The Church and the Ottoman Empire 1453–1923*, at 59–64, 145–50, 214–20, 304–11 (1983) (providing an overview of the relationship between the Catholic Church and the Ottoman Empire and its resulting impact on the Holy Land).

17. Declaration of the Establishment of the State of Israel, 1948, 1 L. S. I. 3, 4 (1948) (emphasis added).

18. See Silvio Ferrari, "Libertà Religiosa e Pluralismo Confessinale: Il Caso di Israele," in *Raccoltà di Scritti in Onore di Pio Fedele* 890–902 (1984) (providing an understanding view of how Israel has handled its difficult legacy in this area).

19. Among other things, the system traps in the Recognized Religious Community all the children and grandchildren of members of that church, and effectively compels them to maintain an institutional affiliation with that same church or another such church. Members must abide by this system in order to be able to exercise such fundamental civil rights as contracting marriage or burial. This renders largely meaningless the basic statistics of church membership.

20. Religious Communities Organization Ordinance (no. 19 of 1926) (Moses Doukham ed.); *Laws of Palestine 1926–1931*, vol. 4 at 1303–5 (Tel Aviv, Palestine: L. M. Rotenberg, 1933).

21. See "The Greek Patriarchate v. Ramle Municipality," 36(3) *Israel Law Reports* 670 (exemplifying the Israeli Supreme Court's rejection of such challenges). The Israeli Court's landmark decisions, such as *Greek Patriarchate*, came to play an important role in shaping the favorable position assumed by the delegation of the State of Israel, which made it possible to adopt art. 3, para. 3 of the Fundamental Agreement, as well as the

agreement's further implementation by means of the Legal Personality Agreement (currently awaiting signature).

22. This is, of course, not a simple matter. For a profound, masterly exposition of the interaction between state law and religious law in Israel, at least under the "*ancien régime,*" see Izhak Englard, *Religious Law in the Israel Legal System* 49–77 (1975).

23. Declaration of the Establishment of the State of Israel, 1948, 1 L. S. I. 3 (1948).

24. Cf. "Fundamental Agreement Between the Holy See and the State of Israel, Dec. 30, 1993," 86 *Acta Apostolicae Sedis* 716–29 (1994), art. 3, para. 2 (recognizing the rights of the Catholic Church).

25. Art. 13, para. 1(c) was added both to respect the principle of reciprocity and to prevent any claims (of which the Vatican delegation was warned in the course of the negotiations) by Israel's local authorities that they were not bound by the state's treaty. See "Fundamental Agreement," *supra* note 25, art. 13, para. 1(c), at 158.

26. See id. art. 12; id. art. 3, para. 3; id. art. 10, para. 2.

27. See id. art. 3, paras. 1–2.

28. See id. art. 9.

29. The Legal Personality Agreement was made pursuant to art. 3, para. 3 of the Fundamental Agreement. See "Fundamental Agreement," *supra* note 25, art. 3, para. 3, at 155.

30. 91 *Acta Apostolicae Sedis* 490–574 (1999).

31. "Basic Agreement between the Holy See and the Palestine Liberation Organization, Feb. 15, 2000," *L'Osservatore Romano,* Feb. 16, 2000; cf. D.-M. A. Jaeger, "L'Accordo di base tra la Santa Sede e l'Olp," 12 *Ius Ecclesiae* 262–69 (2000).

3

# ISRAEL'S UNDERSTANDING OF
# THE FUNDAMENTAL AGREEMENT
# WITH THE HOLY SEE

*Leonard Hammer*

*Interpretation of texts in international law is an art, not a science—
but one that tends to disguise itself in science.*[1]

### Introduction

Although subject to some uncertainty,[2] the approach of the Vienna Convention towards treaty interpretation is essentially a textual-based approach.[3] The treaty text is deemed to encompass an authentic expression of the intentions of the parties with the goal being to elucidate the meaning of the text.[4] Of course, given the imprecise nature of language, attempting to comprehend a particular treaty term can regress to relative applications by the respective parties to the treaty.[5] Merely drafting a lucid treaty text does not definitively indicate in any practical sense the scope or manner in which to define the terms.[6]

This problem regarding a textual interpretation is even graver for a multilateral treaty that involves a host of parties. The parties to the treaty might maintain a unique view and understanding of the treaty terms. Although the exterior intentions of the various treaty parties might have been to draft a treaty, it is difficult to derive the actual intentions from the text when accounting for the diverse political interests involved in the making of the treaty.[7] The atmosphere of acceptance among multilateral treaty parties tends to obscure possible internal divisions among the treaty parties, as well as other misgivings that might have been over-looked in the attempt to reach a compromise.[8] The problem is complicated further upon considering the particular meaning that might be accorded to a treaty and its terms due to the different cultural and legal approaches of the treaty parties. For example, various terms and phrases of the UN Convention on the Privileges and Immunities of the United Nations[9] had not been adequately defined by the treaty drafters nor was there any indication in the *travaux preparatoires* as to the meaning of the terms. In an advisory opinion, the International Court of Justice (ICJ) re-sorted to its understanding of the practical purpose of the treaty, the informal practice of the UN, and the current meaning accorded to the treaty terms.[10] While the ICJ might have adequately interpreted the treaty, the approach of the ICJ ap-pears to be a subjective attempt to consequentially discern the meaning of a treaty's terms.[11]

While many of the problems associated with the interpretation of treaties are difficult to avoid, a bilateral treaty presents an easier medium for discerning the meaning of the text as well as the underlying and overlying intentions of the states to the treaties.[12] The language of the text generally does not result from a group of committees or experts, who might only issue statements and views that represent a select number of states. Rather the parties to a bilateral treaty tend to shape and form the treaty between themselves and their representatives. Hence, in analyzing a bilateral treaty and in attempting to manifest a proper meaning, the task is some-what easier, although of course not wholly perfect. Furthermore, the *travaux pre-paratoires* and other ancillary sources might play a different role in interpreting a bilateral treaty. For example, prior versions leading up to the treaty have a dimin-ished significance since the textual changes reflect a clear bilateral intention to alter the text. Further, the object and purpose for entering into a bilateral treaty can take on an added importance given the proximity of the parties to the reasons for engaging in a treaty and the ensuing document that results.[13]

Thus, while understanding the specific text of the treaty is imperative, one also is to read the treaty as a unitary document and not as a singular expression of a specific term. What is required is a form of commingling the approaches towards treaty interpretation,[14] with a view towards defining the text. Therefore, in deter-mining the authentic expression of the parties' intentions as derived from the treaty text, one could consider the object and purpose of the parties in using spe-cific language, consider the circumstances surrounding the treaty, and expand upon the meaning of the text by accounting for the reasons why the parties desired to enter into a treaty.[15]

### The Agreement between Israel and the Holy See

The Holy See–Israel Fundamental Agreement from 1993[16] serves as a characteristic example of an exercise in bilateral treaty interpretation. The importance in discerning the intentions of the parties is a key element to understanding the Fundamental Agreement, given the historical significance of the document and the delicate issues that the Fundamental Agreement raises. Furthermore, a cloud of religious issues that are inherent in agreements with the Holy See[17] also pertain to this Fundamental Agreement. Israel's position as the Jewish state, and the fact that it controls or has sovereignty over significant structures and areas that are sacred both to Jews and to the Church, places the Fundamental Agreement in a context that is something more than just a treaty: the Fundamental Agreement also is a testament to the changing attitude of the Church towards the Jewish religion and its people,[18] as well as the Israeli government's policy towards other religions in Israel.[19]

The focused analysis on Israel's understanding of the Fundamental Agreement will further serve to elucidate the text by providing a specific understanding of one of the parties to the agreement. While the Holy See and Israel might maintain different interpretations to the text, especially when considering the intentional ambiguities placed therein,[20] providing a sharper understanding of the Fundamental Agreement can better serve future applications and expansions of the agreement, such as the Legal Personality Agreement of 1997[21] and the Financial Status Agreement currently being negotiated.[22] Hence while the Fundamental Agreement might at times come across as vague[23] or too general,[24] understanding the issues surrounding the drafting will clarify the terms and assist the future negotiations that the drafters of the agreement envisioned.[25]

### Brief Background

Following the Oslo Accords between Israel and the Palestine Liberation Organization, Israel's relations with countries that had previously either ignored Israel, or reacted coolly to its overtures, changed dramatically.[26] Israel desired to reap the fruits of the peace process by initiating relations with as many state entities as possible.[27]

For the Israeli side, negotiating the Fundamental Agreement with the Holy See was a prudent political move that also would incorporate taking small steps to rectify the prior two thousand years of misunderstanding between the Jewish people and the Catholic Church.[28] Because Israel now had an opportunity to make order with a number of important religious bodies, it was willing to concede the treatment of the Holy See as a sovereign state and grant the Catholic Church a form of autonomous status in Israel. Israel desired to remove the issues surrounding the negotiations from a religious context and approach the negotiations from within a political framework.

The State of Israel did not desire solely to establish a *sui generis* relationship between the parties, but also wanted to engage in formal diplomatic relations with the Holy See. Such relations would ensure for an ongoing relationship with a specific sovereign body. The issues surrounding the Church and the Holy See's religious representation in Israel therefore were low-key and peripheral, relative to the possible political gains for Israel. Of course, Israel could not ignore that it also felt duty bound to address the prior history between Catholicism and Judaism, as well as protect current Jewish interests worldwide. Further, from a domestic standpoint, it was more beneficial to Israel to negotiate with a single body, namely, the Holy See, than with all the Roman Catholic institutions located in Israel. Although it did not maintain a presence in Israel before the Fundamental Agreement, the Holy See in essence represented not only itself as a sovereign state but also the variety of religious bodies affiliated with the Catholic Church in Israel that might be subject to the terms of the Fundamental Agreement.[29] This approach makes it easier for Israel in future negotiations, such as in the current Financial Agreement, in that Israel only need negotiate with one unit in working out issues such as collection of social security tax or the breadth and scope of financial benefits to be accorded to the Church.

From a "realpolitik" perspective, the Catholic Church desired to assert its presence in Israel with a view towards improving its rights and status under international law.[30] It is important to recall that the Holy See is a sovereign body that also represents a variety of Catholic interests worldwide.[31] Because the Catholic Church views itself as an autonomous body distinct from the state, the Fundamental Agreement provided the opportunity to the Church to assert its autonomous role in Israel while also guaranteeing the variety of rights that are noted in the Fundamental Agreement.[32] The Holy See therefore wanted to strengthen its position among its flock in Israel[33] and entrench its interests in the Holy Places and other important property interests it holds in Israel. Entering into the Fundamental Agreement further provided the Church with the possibility of rectifying various negative perceptions of Israelis vis-à-vis the Catholic Church and Christianity, and bolster the Church's influence in the Muslim world through its presence in Israel.[34]

Recognizing the reality that the Palestinians and Israelis will eventually initiate final status talks that affect Jerusalem and a variety of other sacred places, the Holy See desired to assert its position on these matters and attempt to directly participate in the Palestinian-Israeli negotiations.[35] Hence the Church also was looking to the future, when the Palestinian Authority will maintain some form of control over a variety of Christian Holy Places or serve as the authority on deciding such matters.[36] Such an objective was partially realized in the Holy See–PLO Basic Agreement of February 2000.[37]

Upon accounting for these political considerations, it is impossible to ignore the dual character of the ongoing relationship between the Holy See and Israel. There is the historical and religious nature of the relationship, as well as the usual political nature of relations between states. The Fundamental Agreement establishes a system for addressing these multifaceted issues through diplomatic channels and in a more formal manner,[38] without sacrificing the surrounding religious character of the issue.

One therefore may characterize the Fundamental Agreement from three different frameworks. First, there is the formal state-state relationship between Israel and the Holy See. This is signified by the envisioned relationship between the two parties, as for example pertaining to upholding international human rights obligations.[39] Second, there is the relationship between the State of Israel and the Catholic Church (of which the Holy See is the representative body). The Fundamental Agreement envisions not only communication by way of the Holy See between Israel and the Catholic Churches found therein but also establishing ongoing arrangements and understandings,[40] such as the Financial Agreement currently being negotiated. Third, there is a historic aspect to the Fundamental Agreement, whereby the State of Israel represents the Jewish people worldwide with a view towards rectifying and maintaining relations between Jews and Christians in a broader sense, such as found in Article 2 of the Fundamental Agreement regarding anti-Semitism.

Of course, these categories are not mutually exclusive, nor did the parties desire that they be. Clearly, upholding a state's human rights obligations as noted in Article 1 also is to apply to the Christians located in Israel. Indeed, the multifaceted nature of the Fundamental Agreement is what allowed for its creation, given the crosscutting cleavages in certain areas where state interests are served for one party while nationalistic interests are served for the other. For example, the application of domestic law to the Holy See is a problematic notion,[41] given the different systems and understanding of the status and roles of law within society. A balance had to be created between the Israeli focus on the legal relationship between the state and the religious communities therein and the Holy See's responsibility towards its religious constituents worldwide.[42] Hence the language of the Fundamental Agreement is intentionally open-ended and somewhat amorphous. Article 3(1),[43] for instance, uses language such as "committing" the parties to respect the principle that both sides are free to exercise their rights, given the difficulties in structuring a section that was agreeable to both parties.

In analyzing the Fundamental Agreement, the three approaches will be referred to because certain sections that relate solely to the historic position of the Catholic

Church and the Jews, or to the relationship between Christians and Jews, maintain a different normative status than other sections that might pertain to state-state relations. Additionally, the different approaches demonstrate the intentions of the parties when drafting the sections, thereby assisting to provide for a more definitive understanding of the text.

### The Preamble

The preamble to the Fundamental Agreement is significant[44] because it focuses on the broader historic dimension of the relationship between the Holy See and Israel and demonstrates that the agreement applies to matters that have unique religious significance for each party. Hence the second sentence designates Israel as the "Holy Land." The terms are clearly referring to the territory of the State of Israel, yet within a religious context that demonstrates the importance of the land to both the Jews and the Catholic Church.[45] As indicated in other sections of the Fundamental Agreement, the Israeli side adhered to the practical position that what was important was to agree with another political entity without fully delving into the problems of semantics or the religious significance of certain terms for the Catholic Church. At times, especially where no political ground was lost, the Israeli negotiators tended to bend towards the demands of the Holy See, given Israel's key goal in effectuating a political agreement. By contrast, for the Holy See it was imperative to stress the religious aspect of the relationship and the ongoing importance of Israel, the Holy Land, to its religion. Hence the preamble provides a certain sense of the approach of each side given their underlying political interests and their overlying goal in reaching a fruitful agreement.

The third paragraph of the preamble also is of consequence, in that it refers to the Jews as a "people," an important development for the Israeli drafters. The significance of this term will be considered later, in the discussion regarding Article 2 of the Fundamental Agreement, where the drafters used similar language.

### Article 1

The importance of Article 1 is that it represents a formal declaration by both parties to uphold the international human right to freedom of religion and conscience. This human right is treated as an absolute right and is referred to in a general manner, such that it refers to all religions and their human right to freedom of religion and conscience. In a sense, this article sets the tone for the remainder of the Fundamental Agreement, which in certain instances expands upon and defines the human right to freedom of religion.[46] The article then provides the context for subsequent articles that are based on the freedom of religion by integrating the human right to freedom of religion and specifying the manner in which the parties intend to implement that right.[47]

The key difference is that compared to the Holy See, Israel is a party to a greater number of human rights treaties, namely, the International Covenant on Civil and Political Rights (ICCPR) and the International Covenant on Economic, Social and Cultural Rights (ICESCR).[48] Israel is therefore bound to a comprehensive set of delineated rights. For example, Article 27 of the ICCPR might provide grounds for the Church to assert its rights as a religious minority group located within the state or to claim the right to educate its followers pursuant to the ICESCR.[49]

By contrast, the Holy See made a formal affirmation in Article 1(2) regarding the right to respect other religions and their followers. Israel did not make such a declaration, possibly because it had already committed itself to upholding the ratified international human rights instruments.

Note as well the different language used when referring to the state's obligations under the human rights instruments. Regarding Israel, the language is the more binding to "uphold and observe," whereas for the Church it is to "uphold." This demonstrates the different approach of the Holy See towards the law, whereby there is a certain sense of coexistence with the law rather than a commingling with the legal system. The Holy See is ultimately bound to its canon law even for entities located in other states, with a view towards upholding the laws of the state where there is no conflict with the moral and spiritual sphere. Hence throughout the Fundamental Agreement, the purpose of language such as "uphold" also can be the Holy See's assertion of its autonomous existence within the state. For example, in Article 1, the idea is to indicate that the Holy See will promote religious freedom, but within the limit that its own believers will not be swayed to observe different religious practices.[50]

## Article 2

In drafting Article 2, the Israeli representatives referred to statements made by the pope regarding Israel and the Jews in the Vatican II Council of 1965 (the *Nostra Aetate*),[51] as well as subsequent guidelines to Vatican II issued in 1974 and 1985 by the Vatican Commission for Religious Relations with the Jews.[52] The significance of Vatican II was that the Church recognized the existence of the Jewish religion and how the Jews also can fall under the will of God. Further elaboration of Vatican II in 1974 and 1985 addressed the importance of condemning all forms of anti-Semitism and discrimination. For the first time, the 1974 Guideline refers to the

"Jewish people" in a religious context, and the 1985 Guideline attempts to conciliate the notion of the Christians as the chosen people by delineating the Jews as the chosen people of God of the Old Covenant that has never been revoked.[53] Furthermore, the 1985 Guideline refers to the importance of the awareness of faith and religious life of the Jewish people as they are professed and practiced still today.[54]

These developments in the Catholic Church were not lost upon the Israeli drafters. They recognized the sea change in the attitude of the Church towards Judaism and other religions following Vatican II, such that the Fundamental Agreement presented the drafters with an opportunity to begin to rectify Catholic-Jewish relations and present Israel, and the Jewish people, in a proper light. Hence the Israeli drafters based the language used in this section on specific statements made by the pope and the subsequent interpretations accorded to these statements in the guidelines to Vatican II.[55] The article then represents a binding commitment for the Catholic Church, given the source of the language and the importance of the 1974 and 1985 Guidelines, whose purpose is to interpret the words of the pope.

As a result, the first paragraph, Article 2(1), addresses the importance of combating anti-Semitism. Granted, the terms used in the paragraph are not those ordinarily found in international documents relating to freedom of religion.[56] Indeed, the notion of "commitment" implies a pledge to undertake a specific policy rather than a more formalized, and binding, legal commitment. The parties used this language to avoid an ongoing and probably endless debate regarding the required form of commitment and future cooperation. Hence, "appropriate cooperation" in this context is a rather loose phrase that can be interpreted to mean nonabsolute cooperation, with the terms to be interpreted pursuant to their common, ordinary usage. It is an example of a constructive ambiguity that the parties intentionally left as is to avoid a breakdown of the negotiations. As a result, the first paragraph pertains to the broader Catholic-Jewish relationship as understood by the Holy See, and does not operate in a strictly legal sense. This is indicated, for example, by the commitment to promote tolerance that is to apply worldwide and not solely to Christian institutions in Israel. Indeed, the reference to teaching tolerance to all "communities" applies to both social and religious communities. It remains to be seen, however, how the parties intend to implement this section both in Israel[57] and in other communities.

Note as well that the term "racism" is in the modern notion of the term pursuant to the International Convention on the Elimination of All Forms of Racial Discrimination, thus including apartheid or Nazism. "Religious intolerance," despite being a phrase used in the 1981 Declaration on the Elimination of All Forms of Intolerance and of Discrimination Based on Religion or Belief,[58] is a nontechnical term that, given the difficulty in defining it,[59] is meant to have an ordinary definition in this case.

The significance of the second paragraph is the reference made to the "Jewish people." The condemnation of anti-Semitism refers not only to discrimination against Jews as a religious sect but also to discrimination against the Jewish people. In essence, the Jews are viewed as something more than a religious group, also as a national ethnic group with their own state and subject to their own sovereignty. Hence this section is important not only for historic reasons surrounding the relationship between Christians and Jews, but also because it relates to the broader notion of the State of Israel as a representative of the Jewish people.

### Article 3

Article 3 encompasses the approach and understanding of the parties when considering the rights of the state and the position of the Holy See within the framework of Israeli domestic law. First, regarding the term "rights and powers," the Holy See and Israel maintain a different comprehension when accounting for state's rights. State's rights are a secular concept that refers to the broader, statutory rights accorded to the state by law. For the Holy See this presented a problem given its basis of law on canon law and its assertion that it operates as an autonomous entity within the state. While one may analogize to a state structure in according the Holy See sovereign, state-like, international status while subjecting the Roman Catholic churches to the "domestic" canon law,[60] the domestic status of the Church's worldwide bodies is a different matter.

More particularly concerning Israel, the parties have already reached an agreement regarding the legal status of the local entities in the 1997 Agreement between the State of Israel and the Holy See Pursuant to Article 3(3) of the Fundamental Agreement between the State of Israel and the Holy See[61] (aka, the Legal Personality Agreement). The question is, are the rights in the Fundamental Agreement held by the local churches in Israel or by the Holy See? If the Holy See, then the status of the local churches is similar to that of an alien, with the sovereign body acting on behalf of its charges to assert its rights. However, this also would tend to diminish the autonomous status of the local churches. If, however, the local churches are the rights holders, then one must ask what is the purpose of the Legal Personality Agreement given that the local churches had essentially acted in an autonomous fashion until now? Furthermore, the role of the Holy See in relating to its Israeli churches merits consideration. For its part, Israel desired not to grant the Church a singular representative status but rather treat it as a nonprofit organization pursuant to its domestic laws.[62]

Given the difficulty in resolving the different approaches, Article 3(1) is rather open-ended and must be read within the proper context as creating a common ground between the parties. In essence, this "valise" paragraph is more like an introductory statement noting that the powers of the state activate the relevant rights for each party, with a view towards maintaining a mutual relationship and adequate cooperation. The parties made a pragmatic attempt to resolve their differences in a concrete manner by using the language "respective rights and powers," implying an independent status for each party when exercising their rights and powers.[63]

Article 3(2) is a continuation of such an approach by delineating the specific spheres within which each party is to operate.[64] Note the deference of Israel towards the Catholic Church as the paragraph is structured in a manner that reflects the Church's understanding of the role of the state vis-à-vis the Church. The Church is to carry out the services that it deems imperative, with a view towards allowing for some form of necessary state intervention. The state is not ignored but is understood to perform a secular role that is removed from a religious context.[65] For example, the Church would adhere to basic state requirements regarding education, but the Church is to decide upon the content of their educational activities, with the state intervening when considering fiscal matters or other secular issues.

The underlying purpose is that the Church can demonstrate to other entities, both in Israel and abroad, that Israel recognizes the Church and its function as a provider of specific services, such as education and charity, to its believers in a semi-autonomous manner. For Israel, this form of recognition was not a difficulty given that the Catholic Church already conducts these activities within the state. Nonetheless, the call for "dialogue and cooperation" indicates that there is no automatic operation of the paragraph. For example, the state may legally deny a work permit to a particular individual who has entered Israel for purposes of education, but the parties also are to attempt to reach a settlement in case of dispute.

### Article 3(3) and the Legal Personality Agreement

The parties have already implemented Article 3(3), as confirmed by the ratified Legal Personality Agreement.[66] Yet it is important again to note that the Fundamental Agreement calls for giving effect to the "Catholic legal personality at canon law." Israel did not desire to create a state within a state by granting full autonomy to the Catholic Church. On the other hand, the Holy See desired that the Catholic churches in Israel would maintain a *sui generis* position independent of the state[67] so that canon law may be upheld. The parties therefore agreed that the churches would still be subject to canon law, yet would maintain a separate legal status in Israel. This tends to reflect the reality of the situation in that a variety of Catholic churches already existed in Israel as autonomous entities. Given that Israel desired to apply the Fundamental Agreement to these local bodies, via the Holy See, to simplify its dealings with the local churches, and the Holy See desired that the benefits of the Fundamental Agreement accrue to the Catholic churches in Israel, both sides did not have much to lose and everything to gain by approaching the legal personality as such.

The approach to the issue of legal status is indicated in Article 2 of the Legal Personality Agreement, where a distinction is created between the Holy See as the sovereign authority over the Catholic Church, and the Catholic Church as acquiring legal personality in domestic Israeli law. The point of Article 2 of the Legal Personality Agreement was to remove ambiguities since the entity being accorded legal personality in Israeli domestic law for purposes of the Fundamental Agreement is the local Catholic Church. Yet, pursuant to canon law, the Catholic Church is of course subject to the determinations of the Holy See. Furthermore, given the international personality of the Holy See, the embassy of the Holy See is for the benefit of the Holy See qua state and not for the Catholic Church. Nonetheless, the Catholic Church maintains a singular status for issues pertaining to domestic Israeli law, such as ecclesiastic property or implementing education rights.

This is a rather unique arrangement for the Catholic Church since it does not have any formalized charter creating status under domestic law, but rather the Church's status is created by and subject to canon law. Despite the lack of any legal status, the Church need not apply for legal personality status as a nonprofit organization or particular religious body. Rather, the Legal Personality Agreement automatically accords the entities listed in the agreement as acquiring legal status.[68] Israel, as a sovereign state, can now operate directly with the relevant church bodies rather than be subject to the internal chain of command, and the Catholic Church acquires legal status without tainting its unique relationship with the Holy See based on canon law.

Articles 3, 4,[69] and 5[70] of the Legal Personality Agreement entrench this notion of legal status by mentioning the variety of Catholic legal orders established by the Holy See along with other important religious entities in Israel. What is significant is that while the Holy See maintains its overarching status over these entities pursuant to the relevant canon law,[71] the variety of church orders also can maintain direct relations with the government of Israel. Hence Article 6 of the Legal Personality Agreement states that the relevant entities in the Fundamental Agreement were founded by the Holy See pursuant to canon law, to be considered as if the Holy See founded the legal entities in its sovereign capacity.[72] On the other hand, Israel will apply its domestic law for all domestic legal actions that are to be taken by the local churches in their transactions with other domestic legal entities.[73] Article 6(4)(a) therefore provides that, given the right circumstances, Israel's domestic court system is the proper legal venue.

In essence the Holy See and Israel agreed to a legal fiction that upholds the link created by canon law between the local church bodies and the Holy See while providing Israel with the opportunity for legal relations with the local churches. The cutoff point in the Legal Personality Agreement for Israel's controlling legal capacity appears to be for issues pertaining to internal jurisdictional or administrative matters, whereby the Holy See's control via canon law would apply.[74]

Article 6(2)(c) also creates a special relationship for immovable property, a major concern for the Holy See.[75] Recognizing the autonomous status of the local churches, the parties desired this provision regarding immovable property to avoid pressure from the state, such as forced land sales, and to prevent corruption from within, like sales below market value. As a result, legal action taken on such property requires prior written approval by the Holy See.[76]

### Article 4

Article 4 addresses two different aspects regarding the places deemed sacred by the Catholic Church. The first relates to what is commonly referred to as the Status Quo. This is a system established by Sultan Abdul Mejid through an 1852 *firman* to freeze the positions of the various religious parties that had been present in the Holy Land[77] back to 1757.[78] The normative position of the arrangement developed with time given the repeated references to it, as exemplified in the 1878 Treaty of Berlin.[79] The purpose of the Status Quo arrangement was not necessarily to decide upon the absolute possession of sacred places by one religion or church over another, but to maintain a form of working order to provide all the parties with access to the principal holy sites. Hence for the Christians, the Catholic Church, by way of France, and the Greek Orthodox Church, through Russia, continued (and continue) to attempt to exert pressure and changes to the Status Quo,[80] since it related not only to possession and worship rights but also to details pertaining to the hanging of pictures, the form of worship or the language that is to be used during worship, and the carrying out of repairs.[81]

The relevant aspects of the Status Quo for the Catholic Church, at the very least as intended by the Fundamental Agreement, is that the Status Quo applies to the Church of the Holy Sepulcher, the Church of the Nativity in Bethlehem, the Sanctuary of the Ascension, and the Tomb of the Virgin (Mare Nostrum).[82] Pursuant to the Status Quo as it existed in the early part of the twentieth century, the Catholic Church maintained a right to conduct services in the Holy Sepulcher and the Sanctuary of the Ascension, whereas the Church of the Nativity and the Mare Nostrum were subject to claims by the Catholic Church, although the Church did not maintain any form of control.[83]

The post–World War I mandate period under British rule saw a continuation of the Status Quo as applied during Ottoman rule. The key development was the Palestinian (Holy Places) Order in Council of 1924, Article 13, which removed the jurisdiction of the Holy Places from the civil courts, save for procedural matters,[84] and placed such issues in the hands of the high commissioner.[85] During Jordanian rule, the government essentially adhered to the Status Quo, although one commentator has noted that there existed a certain amount of favoritism towards the Arab religions.[86]

It is important to recognize that the Status Quo is not a firm and fast rule of law but is an attempt to accommodate all the religious interests and their conflicting claims. The Status Quo has been subject to change, and continues to evolve, depending on the influence of the authorities and the relevant religious parties. For example, the Gregorians lost certain rights in the Holy Sepulcher due to an inability to pay a fee demanded by the Turks during the rule of the Ottoman Empire.[87] Similarly, following Israeli rule of Jerusalem after 1967, the government altered the manner of prayer at the Western Wall, thereby allowing Jews to pray at that site throughout the year as well as use chairs or benches.[88] The Israeli government also mandated that the Church could undertake repairs to the Holy Sepulcher. Israel made further alterations to the Status Quo by the Holy Places Law of 1967[89] and the Basic Law: Jerusalem Capital of Israel in 1980.[90] These laws applied to all Holy Places,[91] along with the areas subject to the 1852 *firman* that devised the Status Quo, with a view towards preventing desecration of the Holy Places and providing for free access to these areas.[92] When confronted with an issue pertaining to the interpretation of these laws, the key criterion for the Israeli judiciary appears to be a preservation of public order, with a view towards providing for the right to worship, where possible.[93] Yet it should be noted that the judiciary considers any substantive change to the rights of the parties at the sacred places, including those within the Status Quo, to be a matter for the government and not for the courts.[94]

Recognizing the ability to play a role in the ongoing changes, and considering the possibility of working with another entity such as the Palestinian Authority, which eventually might control certain sacred places, the Catholic Church desired to entrench its position in the matter of the Status Quo and the sacred places. Seeing an opportunity to protect its interests, the Fundamental Agreement states in Article 4(1) that the Status Quo is to be maintained for the Holy Places "to which it applies." The implication of this language is to the Status Quo as it applies in the present, thereby incorporating the changes that have occurred under Israeli rule. Nonetheless, the "respective" rights is meant as a limiting factor to be construed as solely applying to the parties to the Fundamental Agreement. The Israeli government made it clear to the other religious interests in Israel that the Fundamental Agreement would not create any alterations to the current Status Quo nor serve as a basis for changing the positions of the various religious parties who have an interest in the Holy Places.

Note, however, that the language of respective rights of the "Christian communities" is broader language than merely the Catholic Church, as it applies to all the Christian communities. This reflects the multi-tiered level of the Fundamental Agreement, as the Holy See is not only serving in its capacity as a sovereign entity, but also as a representative of the various Christian communities that might maintain a claim to a variety of properties both from a legal standpoint[95] as well as from a metaphysical, spiritual standpoint.

Article 4(2) encompasses the cautious approach of Israel by according to the arrangement of the Status Quo a normative preference over other articles of the Fundamental Agreement. In essence, the Fundamental Agreement cannot provide the Holy See with an advantage over other religious interests. Further, the paragraph implicitly indicates the Holy See's recognition of other religious interests and rights to the Holy Places given its commitment to uphold the Status Quo, as is, within the Christian Holy Places.

Article 4(3) reiterates the Israeli policy towards scared places, taking into consideration the domestic law[96] to prevent any desecration and provide for free access to the sacred places. Consequently, the use of the term "continuing respect" and protection, thereby implying an obligation that had already existed. By contrast, the notion of Israel "agreeing" with the Holy See seems inclined towards the Church's understanding of a sacred site, especially given the Church's role of deeming the proper "character" for such sites. While the "continuing respect" might counterbalance such an understanding, it does not address future occurrences that might entail a conflict between the state and what the Church considers to be proper respect and protection.

Additionally, there is no official or accepted list that designates what is considered to be a sacred place.[97] The Israeli courts rely on the mandate law that had adopted a rather subjective approach to deeming something sacred pursuant to the interests and claims of the specific party.[98] It would seem that the majority of items listed in the Fundamental Agreement as sacred, such as convents and cemeteries, would be considered sacred in domestic law as well.

Article 4(4) also uses the language of "continuing," yet this paragraph requires further elaboration given that it is addressing worship, an action that also relates to the Status Quo. That is, considering Article 4(2), it would be inconceivable to provide for automatic right of worship even in places that the Status Quo clearly does not provide for same.[99] The Holy See desired that the right to worship be granted as an express norm, but that presented problems for the Status Quo as well as for other religions whose interests the Israeli government had guaranteed.[100] Further, as noted earlier, Israeli law provides for free access to all Holy Places, but that does not mean an automatic right to worship.[101] Yet considering Article 1 of the Fundamental Agreement, whereby Israel affirmed its international human rights obligations that specifically provide for the right of worship as a form of manifestation of the right to freedom of religion,[102] along with the realization that guaranteeing access to a scared place without worship seems somewhat odd,[103] the two parties came to a meeting of the wills whereby Israel "agrees" with the Holy See regarding the "continuing" right of worship. The implication is that the right to worship implicitly exists according to the demands and laws of a democratic state. It remains to be seen whether the Holy See will rely on this guarantee as a means of changing the current position of worship rights or the Status Quo.

### Article 5

Unlike the right to freedom of worship, the right to pilgrimage is not an inherent human right under the international human rights treaties noted in Article 1 of the Fundamental Agreement. While one can possibly infer an emerging customary norm to provide for religious pilgrimage[104] certainly when mandated by the specific religious belief in question,[105] there is no clear directive from international human rights treaties such as the Universal Declaration of Human Rights (UDHR) and the ICCPR that the right to freedom of religion also incorporates the right of pilgrimage.[106]

Reflecting this status of pilgrimage in human rights law, Article 5 of the Fundamental Agreement tends to use the rather nonbinding language of having an "interest in favoring" Christian pilgrimages. Similarly, Article 5(2) uses general language to "express the hope" that pilgrimages will increase understanding between the religions in Israel. This article does not seem to create any binding duty on the respective parties to provide for automatic pilgrimage or promote it.[107] Further, the article centers on Christian pilgrimage, thereby not affecting other arrangements made between the parties with other states or other religions.[108]

Nonetheless, the article notes the dual "interest" in favoring pilgrimage. The parties desired to demonstrate that pilgrimage is an important issue. Hence Article 5(1) mandates that the parties "consult and cooperate" whenever possible problems arise. This is a rather significant directive given the importance of pilgrimage to the Holy Land and the possibility that restrictions imposed on pilgrims can be abused or applied in a discriminatory fashion. Indeed, it is certain to be an important issue in future negotiations, following the talks pertaining to the Financial Agreement. Given the equivocal nature of the right under international human rights law, it would seem that the Church can assert a right of pilgrimage when the religion specifically mandates such action, in a manner similar to the Muslim journey to Mecca, or where the pilgrimage serves a specific goal of furthering a particular religious practice or belief.

### Article 6

The next few articles of the Fundamental Agreement essentially reiterate what Article 3(2) had generally noted regarding the Church's moral, educational, and charitable functions. The purpose in expanding on these functions in a more specific manner was to provide them with greater normative strength, as well as create an opportunity for further modification, where necessary.

Article 6 espouses a similar notion to Article 3(2), yet Article 6 uses the more specific language to "establish, maintain, and direct schools and institutes." These are more concrete terms that provide the Church with the opportunity to maintain an internal school system. Indeed, this has proved to be a rather important aspect of the Financial Agreement given the Church's current presence in Israel as a provider of education services even for some of the non-Christian populace.

The proviso of exercising the right "in harmony with the rights of the State" is again a reflection of the Church's approach towards the separation of church and state. That is, the Church maintains its autonomous status exclusive of the sovereign's law, while deferring towards the state's regulations regarding secular aspects of education. Yet the article does not address the more difficult issues regarding the composition of assistance and extent of support that the state is to accord to Catholic schools, and it seems to gloss over the potential conflict that is raised by operating an exclusive Catholic school system without determining its social and fiscal position within the state.

### Article 7

Article 7 is an expansion of Article 2(1) to promote mutual understanding between the parties. The first part of the Article relates to worldwide promotion, meaning the more general relationship between Jews and the Church and not solely between Israel and the Church. The article's last phrase requires the parties to act "in conformity" with the laws and regulations rather than the more usual phrase of "in harmony." Apparently, the Church also desired to include in this article their canon law along with Israeli law when considering who has access to historical documents.

## Article 8

Article 8 differs from the previous three articles in that it places the onus on Israel to uphold the right of the Church to free expression. This is significant given that there is no provision in the Fundamental Agreement pertaining to the issue of proselytizing. While proselytizing might not be a major problem between the Holy See and Israel due to changing policies towards the relationship between the Church and Judaism,[109] instances might occur whereby limiting proselytizing curtails an individual's ability to espouse a belief. The right therefore can emanate from an assertion of freedom of expression, a right that this article specifically upholds. Hence even if one is to avoid invading another individual's personal sphere of liberty when engaging in proselytizing,[110] it is possible that one may assert a free expression right as a basis for communicating proselytizing information through the Church's communications media.

While the Church's activities are subject to be "in harmony" with the state, the Fundamental Agreement confines this limitation to the "field of communications media." The meaning is again to reflect the distinction between the Church and state. The state's sphere of activity relates to specific areas of communication laws applicable to all other forms of communications media, with the Church operating in its own sphere when considering what to broadcast and in what format.

## Article 9

Article 9 also relates to the role of the Church within the state and its ability to operate in an autonomous manner. Similar to the previous articles, this particular article relates to issues that affect the Financial Agreement given the significant charitable services provided by the Church in the field of health and social welfare. Hence the meaning of "in harmony with the rights of the State" is that the Church is operating according to domestic codes and regulations, such as upholding basic hygiene laws and the like.

Articles 6, 7, 8, and 9 essentially pertain to activities that are usually reserved for the state. The question then is, what arrangements should be made between the Church and the state? Must the state reimburse the Church for activities that it has undertaken in place of the state? Is such reimbursement required, considering the charitable nature of the activities? Can the Church instead demand that the state provide access for all its believers in an equal manner to that provided to other religions in Israel or do these articles sanction a different form of relationship, given the Church's desire for a more autonomous status?

The answers partially depend on how one defines the notion of being "in harmony" with the laws of the state and what is the meaning of the "right" accorded to the Church. Every article notes that in essence it is a "right" of the Church to undertake the activities relevant to the article, such that one must ascertain what form of right is being discussed.[111] Given that the context is between the state and a specific body located within the state (i.e., the Catholic Church rather than the Holy See), it is possible that the Church can assert these rights against the state in a positive manner, such as demanding financial recompense or some sort of benefit due to the reduced fiscal allocations that result for the state. The Church's autonomous legal status recognized under the Legal Personality Agreement possibly entitles the Church to make such claims against the state. On the other hand, it seems that the Catholic Church has a narrow right that both parties either affirm or recognize within the framework of the specific article. The term "reaffirm" implies a previous existing regime of institutions or activities. The implication is that the Church has conducted such activities until this point, and the Church and Israel are merely restating their understanding that such activity will continue. It will be interesting to see how the parties address these matters both for the Financial Agreement and in future negotiations on other matters.

### Article 10

Considering the Financial Agreement currently subject to negotiations, it is imperative to read sections (1) and (2) as a unit to understand Article 10. The first paragraph is a "valise" paragraph restating the notion that both parties recognize the Catholic Church's right to property. Of course, this paragraph is operating within the context of the Status Quo[112] and, similar to the prior articles, is a reaffirmation of the right. This language thereby avoids the implication that further or additional rights to property are being granted to the Church.

Article 10(2) makes use of another constructive ambiguity. Accounting for the delicate issue of church property, the notion of a "comprehensive agreement" is rather amorphous language and difficult to define. In essence the parties desire to attain a settlement regarding property and other financial issues, but recognize that it will take time and further negotiations, as indicated by the ongoing negotiations for the Financial Agreement. In one fell swoop, the article also is attempting to tackle a host of thorny issues relating to the financial status not only of the Church, but also "specific Catholic Communities or institutions." While the term "Catholic Church" also includes its communities and institutions,[113] the term "specific" implies that the Church foresees the Financial Agreement as applying to specific institutions.

Part of the problem is that specific institutions could make demands that are contrary to Israeli domestic law. Although its status is unclear, Israel had made an arrangement with France in 1948 that accorded tax privileges to the clergy and exempted taxes on religious property.[114] Yet international law does not mandate such financial arrangements like tax exemptions for Church bodies, nor are they considered automatic "rights" to be granted to the Church (or any other religious bodies).[115] Similarly, it is unclear whether the Status Quo arrangements provide for some form of tax exemptions.[116]

Unlike the delineated and specific rights noted in Articles 6, 7, 8, and 9, the notion of property and economic rights are uncertain given the controversy surrounding crucial fiscal issues and other property matters. Hence Article 10(2)(b) proposes the formation of a specific working commission to address these matters. Further, the parties did not adhere to the timetable of Article 10(2)(c), given the need for additional refinement and ongoing negotiation. It therefore seems that both Articles 10(2)(c) and (d) are declarations of intent, with a view towards reaching a final settlement, rather than creating binding normative sections.

### Article 11

This article falls within the broader Israel–Holy See political relationship between two sovereigns and relates to a political, rather than religious, context. Note the terminology of "States and nations" rather than merely "States," since one could have a number of nations located within a state. The reasons for this language are obvious given the current developments in Israel and demonstrate the Holy See's future goal of negotiating with the Palestinian Authority. Further, the terms "violence and terror" imply acts against civilians. This phrase was used rather than "terrorism" because certain acts of terrorism could be legitimized if the terrorists are acting as a liberation movement.

Article 11(2) provides the Holy See with the opportunity to act as a moral or spiritual representative for given issues, such as refugee problems or human rights violations. However, when acting in its sovereign capacity,[117] the Holy See will not involve itself with secular issues. This results from the internal composition of the Holy See, such that it is to remain a stranger to temporal, or secular, conflicts. Yet the drafters further refined the article by noting that this neutral stance applies to unsettled border conflicts and disputed territory. The idea was based on a desire to keep the relationship neutral and not to become entangled with political issues.

### Article 12

Article 12 represents a glance into the future, whereby the parties agree to good-faith negotiations. The general language of the second sentence indicates that the parties intend to negotiate issues that are not specifically mentioned in the Fundamental Agreement. The obligation of good-faith negotiations also would be binding on the parties in such circumstances.

### Article 13

Article 13 is interesting, as it brings to the fore the political approach of the parties. It is, however, unclear why the parties placed this section towards the end of the document. Usually, important clarification of terms such as the relevant parties to a treaty are placed at the beginning of the treaty. It is possible that the definitions in Article 13 reflect the positions of the parties, for example the Church as an autonomous body overseeing the variety of Catholic institutions located in Israel.

For the Holy See, all divisions of the Catholic Church are subject to its jurisdiction. Hence Article 13(a) includes church communities and institutions. This essentially links all aspects of the Fundamental Agreement between the Holy See and Israel to the domestic relationship between Israel and the Church. Furthermore, it indicates the approach of the Church as imposing its hierarchical structure even on institutions located within Israel. The Holy See desired to cling to the position that the Catholic Church itself is a rights holder and not merely a provider of services to its believers. Hence the communities and institutions are also under its authority in a manner that differs from the other religious communities located in Israel.[118] Nonetheless, Article 13(b) also states that while "communities" of the Church are subject to its authority, church institutions located in Israel also must be "Recognized Religious Communities," meaning subject to the system of domestic Israeli law. The Holy See then desired to create a coordinate status with the state for its institutions located in Israel, rather than a subordinate status that would conflict with its canon law.[119] As noted earlier, Israel desired to forge ahead with the Fundamental Agreement and treated the religious structure of the Church as a peripheral issue by essentially replacing the recognized communities under domestic law with the Catholic Church. Furthermore, Article 13(1)(b) maintained intact the present structure for the local religious institutions, such that acknowledging the role of the Holy See as an overlying authority was not a major problem for Israel.

It is significant that Article 13(2) refers to the proviso that the Fundamental Agreement does not detract "from the generality of any applicable rule of law with reference to treaties." The implication is that the parties agree to enter into a treaty pursuant to international law, despite potential doubts pertaining to the legal status of the Holy See.[120]

## Articles 14 and 15

These articles are essentially procedural paragraphs. The goal is to initiate the Fundamental Agreement following its ratification by the respective parties. As noted earlier, the parties have already negotiated and ratified the Legal Personality Agreement referred to in Article 3(3). Current negotiations are under way to create a Financial Agreement. Although progress has been made, there is no ensuing document and the current negotiations are being conducted in secrecy. The parties will probably engage in future agreements to encompass issues that either were not considered by the parties or that relate to additional matters requiring a formal agreement.

## Conclusion

Because the Fundamental Agreement between Israel and the Holy See is a bilateral treaty, it is easier to detect the ambiguities and differences when interpreting the Fundamental Agreement. Such differences are at times intentional, since the parties desired to forge ahead with the Fundamental Agreement rather than get mired in the intricacies of interpretation. The advantage in interpreting a bilateral treaty, however, is that one could account for the particular approach of the parties and the interests that they were asserting. While these approaches might result in an awkward use of language, it provides the interpreter with the ability to focus on the intentions of the parties in using a specific terminology and in explaining the meaning of an awkward phrase.

Granted, ambiguities and misunderstandings abound in the Fundamental Agreement, especially when considering the radically different approach of the parties concerning the position of the Church within a formal state construct. Even if subject to different interpretations, the nature of the treaty is such that discrepancies can be ironed out and disagreements can be addressed.[121] It is to the credit of the representatives from Israel and the Holy See that they managed to forge a document agreeable to both parties.[122] The religious issues that were raised by the Fundamental Agreement and the importance accorded to the Holy Land by both parties no doubt placed a difficult gloss over the negotiations. All too often through the ages, religion has served as a basis for strife and source for conflict. The Fundamental Agreement is not only a political triumph, but also represents a willingness to create an amicable and realistic atmosphere for future negotiations and an enduring relationship.

## NOTES

This chapter would not have been possible without the assistance of certain individuals from the Israeli Foreign Ministry, notably Ariel Kenet, director of the Department of Religions and Religious Movements and Communities, as well as Inspector General Eitan Margalit. In particular, however, I must acknowledge Advocate Tzvi Terlo, who proved to be not only a valuable and rich source of information, but also a wonderful and varied individual. His time and efforts on my behalf are greatly appreciated and shall not be forgotten.

1. C. F. Amerasinghe, "Interpretation of Texts in Open International Organisations," 65 *Brit. Ybk. Int'l. L.* 175, at 182 (1994).

2. See, e.g., M. Villiger, *Customary International Law and Treaties: A Study of Their Interactions and Interrelations with Special Consideration of the 1969 Vienna Convention on the Law of Treaties* 333–35 (1985), noting a tendency towards the textual approach despite initial misunderstandings when drafting Article 31. The doubts regarding reliance on the text emanate from the debates during the drafting of the Vienna Convention where some states asserted an intention-oriented approach. See I. Sinclair, *The Vienna Convention on the Law of Treaties* (1984) and the subsequent practice of certain states, such as the United States, that tend to refer to the *travaux preparatoires*. See, e.g., M. Van Alstine, "Dynamic Treaty Interpretation," 146 *U. of Penn. L. R.* 687 (1998); M. Halberstam, "The Use of Legislative History in Treaty Interpretation: The Dual Treaty Approach," 12 *Card. L. R.* 1645 (1991) (criticizing U.S. courts for referring to domestic legislative history).

3. Article 31 of the Vienna Convention on the Law of Treaties states: "A treaty shall be interpreted in good faith in accordance with the ordinary meaning to be given to the terms of the treaty in their context and in the light of the object and purpose." Vienna Convention on the Law of Treaties, May 23, 1969, 1155 U. N. T. S. 331 [hereinafter Vienna Convention]. Note that the object and purpose has been understood as operating within the context of a textual interpretation, such that the goal is to expand on the meaning of the text. Sinclair, *supra* note 2, at 130–31.

4. Id. at 115, referring to the approach of the International Law Commission.

5. C. Kuner, "The Interpretation of Multilingual Treaties: Comparison of Texts Versus the Presumption of Similar Meaning," 40 *Int'l. and Comp. L. Q.* 953 (1991). See generally R. Rorty, *Contingency, Irony, and Solidarity* (1989).

6. See also C. Lim & O. Elias, "The Role of Treaties in the Contemporary International Legal Order," 66 *Nordic J. Int'l. L.* 1 (1997), discussing the distinction proposed by Wittgenstein between a rule and its application, such that even if a rule, or in this context a treaty text, is clear, its application or interpretation in a practical sense could lead to a result that differs from the intentions of the parties.

7. Id. at 13–14, noting that the consensus might only be an illusion.

8. B. Simma, "Consent: Strains in the Treaty System," in *The Structure and Process of International Law: Essays in Legal Philosophy Doctrine and Theory* 487 (noting the problems of consensus voting) and 495 (noting that the objectives of treaty parties change over the course of time) (R. MacDonald & D. Johnston eds., 1986).

9. UN Convention on the Privileges and Immunities of the United Nations, Apr. 12, 1946, U. N. T. S., sec. 22 of the treaty, particularly the phrases "experts on missions" and "during the course of their missions."

10. Applicability of Article VI, Section 22, of the Convention on the Privileges and Immunities of the United Nations, advisory opinion of Dec. 15, 1989, at sec. 5, paras. 40–52.

11. Id. Note that the separate opinion of Judge Evenson even suggested that the term "expert" should extend to the expert's family as well.

12. See, e.g., *Case Concerning Kasikil/Sedudu Island (Botswana/Namibia)*, Dec. 13, 1999, www.icj-cig.org/icjwww/idocket/ibona/ibonaframe.htm, visited on June 28, 2002, at para. 30, 43–45, where the ICJ, in adopting the textual approach, interpreted the terms pursuant to the object and purpose of the particular parties and their understanding of the terms over time.

13. See, e.g., *Case Concerning the Gabc'ikovo-Nagymaros Project (Hungary/Slovakia)*, Sept. 25, 1997, www.icj-cij.org/icjwww/idecisions/isummaries/ihssummary19970925.html, visited on June 28, 2002, at para. 142, where the ICJ, relying on the *pacta sunt servanda* rule, focused on the purpose of the treaty and the intentions of the parties rather than proposing a literal application of the treaty.

14. See, e.g., D. Harris, *Cases and Materials on International Law*, at 814–16 (1998).

15 Vienna Convention, *supra* note 3, at art. 31 (3) and 32, referring a would-be interpreter of a treaty respectively to subsequent agreements and practice along with supporting material such as the *travaux preparatoires* to understand the text further and to confirm the meaning of the text.

16. Fundamental Agreement Between the Holy See and the State of Israel, Dec. 30, 1993, Vatican-Isr., 33 I. L. M. 153 (1994)[hereinafter Fundamental Agreement].

17. Y. Abdullah, "The Holy See at United Nations Conferences: State or Church?" 96 *Colum. L. R.* 1835 (1996) (noting that the Holy See is a religious organization pursuant to its stance at international conferences); M. Van Der Molen, "Diplomatic Relations Between the United States and the Holy See: Another Brick from the Wall," 19 *Val. U. L. R.* 197 (1984) (discussing the Vatican as a spiritual authority due to representative status of Catholic Church).

18. See, e.g., *In Our Time: The Flowering of Jewish-Catholic Dialogue* (E. Fisher & L. Klenicki eds., 1990).

19. See David-Maria A. Jaeger, "The Fundamental Agreement between the Holy See and the State of Israel: A New Legal Regime of Church-State Relations," this volume.

20. See, e.g., Fundamental Agreement, *supra* note 16, at art. 10(2), regarding the future creation of a "comprehensive" settlement.

21. Agreement Between the State of Israel and the Holy See Pursuant to Article 3(3) of the Fundamental Agreement Between the State of Israel and the Holy See, June 4, 1999, 91 *Acta Apostolicae Sedis* 490 (1999) [hereinafter Legal Personality Agreement].

22. Fundamental Agreement, *supra* note 16, art. 10.

23. See, e.g., id. at art. 10(1), noting the Church's right to property.

24. See, e.g., id. at art. 1, pertaining to Israel's obligation to uphold its human rights commitments pursuant to ratified treaties.

25. Future negotiations mentioned in the Fundamental Agreement, *supra* note 16, include the Legal Personality Agreement, *supra* note 21, at art. 3, and the Financial Status Agreement, *supra* note 16, art. 10 and 10(2)(a), pertaining to other issues that the parties may desire to address, for example, education.

26. See, e.g., *Regional Security Regimes: Israel and Its Neighbors* (E. Inbar ed., 1995), noting a greater acceptance of Israel among the Arab states following the Madrid peace process, such as to create a change in the deterrence policy of Israel's national security system.

27. M. Perko, "Towards a 'Sound and Lasting Basis': Relations between the Holy See, the Zionist Movement and Israel, 1896–1996," 2 *Israel Studies* 1 (1997).

28. The Israeli side recognizes that one agreement cannot rectify the prior problems between the Catholic and Jewish religions.

29. See Fundamental Agreement, *supra* note 16, art. 13, and the Legal Personality Agreement, *supra* note 21.

30. See, e.g., Marshall J. Breger & Thomas A. Idinopulos, *Jerusalem's Holy Places and the Peace Process* 27 (1998), noting the importance accorded by the Church to such recognition.

31. G. Arangio-Ruiz, "On the Nature of the International Personality of the Holy See," *Revue Belge De Droit Int'l.* 354 (1996) (according broad international status for the Holy See as incorporating both the Vatican City and the Roman Catholic Church); H. Cardinale, *The Holy See and the International Order* 84–86 (1976) (noting how the Holy See is the supreme organ of the Catholic Church, such that the entities operate as a state and government but in a broader spiritual context); Van Der Molen, *supra* note 17.

32. See, e.g., Fundamental Agreement, *supra* note 16, arts. 6, 7, 8, and 9.

33. Breger & Idinopulos, *supra* note 30, also point out the communication problems associated with a European clergy serving an Arabic population.

34. Perko, *supra* note 27, notes that a key goal of the Holy See was to assure the Church's freedom and security in Israel.

35. Breger & Idinopulos, *supra* note 30, at 33–34, noting that one of the Holy See's key goals is to ensure equal treatment of all religious interests.

36. See, e.g., Fundamental Agreement, *supra* note 16, art. 4, where the Church is considering the future position of sacred places that might not be within the control of the State of Israel. See also id. at 32, referring to an informal agreement between the Holy See and the Palestinian Authority.

37. See, e.g., "Document A4," 29 *J. Palestinian Studies* 143 (2000) and discussion *infra*.

38. See, e.g., Fundamental Agreement, *supra* note 16, art. 2(2).

39. Id., art. 1.

40. See, e.g., id., art. 10.

41. See discussion, *supra* note 16, regarding Article 3 of the agreement.

42. Arangio-Ruiz, *supra* note 31, at 365 (distinguishing between the relationship of the Holy See to the Roman Catholic Church as an internal matter and the Holy See's

diplomatic relations as an international matter); Perko, *supra* note 27 (referring to the dual and intermingled role of the Holy See as a vehicle for representing Catholic interests worldwide as well as a sovereign, state-like entity).

43. See discussion *infra*.

44. Note as well that the preamble constitutes an important aspect of the treaty by providing grounds for establishing the object and purpose of the treaty. Sinclair, *supra* note 2, at 118.

45. Cf. Note on the Correct Way to Present the Jews and Judaism in Preaching and Catechisms in the Roman Catholic Church, at sec. VI, 25 (June 24, 1985) (Vatican Commission for Religious Relations with the Jews) [hereinafter 1985 Guideline], where the Holy See specifically recognizes the right of the State of Israel to exist pursuant to international law, but on a secular level separate from a religious viewpoint.

46. S. Ferrari, "The Fundamental Agreement Between the Holy See and Israel and the Conventions Between States and the Church since the Vatican II Council," 47 *Cath. U. L. R.* 385, 400 (1998).

47. Id.

48. M. Hirsh, "The Freedom of Proselytism Under the Fundamental Agreement and International Law," 47 *Cath. U. L. R.* 407, 411 (1998).

49. Ferrari, *supra* note 46, at 399. See also Hirsh, *supra* note 48, at 424, noting that Article 1 is the grounds for upholding the practice of proselytizing given the absence of any mention of this right in other parts of the agreement.

50. Ferrari, *supra* note 46, at 397. This understanding of course relates to the ongoing debate regarding the interpretation of Article 18 of the International Covenant on Civil and Political Rights and whether it provides for a right to change one's religion. While the drafters of Article 18 were equivocal on this issue, the general comment to Article 18 of the Human Rights Committee appears to uphold the notion that one maintains the right to change one's religion. See also Hirsh, *supra* note 48, at 411–15, and sources cited therein.

51. Declaration on the Relationship of the Church to Non-Christian Religions, 4 *Nostra Aetate* (Oct. 28, 1965) (Ecumenical Council Vatican II) [hereinafter Vatican II].

52. Guidelines and Suggestions for Implementing the Conciliator Declaration, 4 *Nostra Aetate* (Dec. 1, 1974) (Vatican Commission for Religious Relations with the Jews) [hereinafter 1974 Guideline]; 1985 Guideline, *supra* note 45.

53. 1985 Guideline, *supra* note 45, art. 1, sec. 3, citing statements made by Pope John Paul II.

54. Id., and art. 4, sec. 25.

55. See, e.g., Vatican II, *supra* note 51, and 1974 Guideline, *supra* note 52. See also 1985 Guideline, *supra* note 45, at sec. VI, noting the importance in remembering the Holocaust and the significance of that event for the Jewish people.

56. Cf. International Covenant on Civil and Political Rights, Dec. 19, 1966, art. 18, 999 U. N. T. S. 171 [hereinafter ICCPR].

57. Implementation in Israeli schools also presents a difficulty given inherent political struggles, such as problems relating to educating Israeli children about the significance to other religions of the millennium celebrations.

58. GA Res. 36/55, U. N. GAOR, 36th Sess., Supp. No. 51, at 171, U. N. Doc. A/36/51 (1982) [hereinafter 1981 Declaration].

59. N. Lerner, *Group Rights and Discrimination in International Law* (1991), noting a subjective understanding of the term "intolerance" and the difficulty in providing a legal definition. Cf. id., art. 2, sec. 2 (describing intolerance as restricting with intent to impair a religion or belief ).

60. See, e.g., Arangio-Ruiz, *supra* note 31.

61. Legal Personality Agreement, *supra* note 21.

62. Ferrari, *supra* note 46, at 402.

63. Id.

64. Id.

65. The 1985 Guideline, *supra* note 45, hints at such an understanding by recognizing the existence of Israel as a state pursuant to international law and in a manner that is removed from any specific religious framework. See 1985 Guideline, sec. 6(25).

66. The relevance of the Legal Personality Agreement, *supra* note 21, for interpreting this agreement is important given Article 31(3) of the Vienna Convention, which notes that subsequent agreements further assist to clarify a treaty. See generally *Case Concerning Maritime Delimitation and Territorial Questions Between Qatar and Bahrain—Jurisdiction and Admissibility*, I. C. J. Reports 112 (1994) (official minutes of a post-agreement meeting of the Council of Arab States constituted part of binding instruments).

67. Ferrari, *supra* note 46, at 403.

68. See Legal Personality Agreement, *supra* note 21, art. 11, and the appendices listing the various legal personalities that fall under the agreement.

69. Referring to the *Custodia Terra Sancta,* which derived from the fourteenth-century practice of the French Mamaluks.

70. Legal Personality Agreement, *supra* note 21, art. 5, provides the Holy See with the opportunity to change the recognized orders if, for example, they fall into disuse or are internally altered.

71. But cf. id., art. 5(a), where only pontifical orders can acquire legal status, and not those of a bishop's order, in contrast to the canon law.

72. Id., art. 6(1).

73. Id., art. 6(2)(a).

74. See generally id., art. 6(2) and 6(3).

75. See, e.g., A. Pacini, "Socio-Political and Community Dynamics of Arab Christians in Jordan, Israel, and the Autonomous Palestinian Territories," in *Christian Communities in the Arab Middle East: The Challenge of the Future* 283 (A. Pacini ed., 1998).

76. Note that the Legal Personality Agreement, *supra* note 21, art. 7, upholds any prior rights that an entity might have acquired.

77. L. Cust, *The Status Quo in the Holy Places* (Ariel Publishing House, 1980) (1929) notes that the Status Quo was implemented to ease the internal strife between the Roman Catholic Church and the Greek Orthodox Church. This conflict was played out historically principally between France and Russia, whereby each asserted its own interest in the

Holy Land by way of support for the respective churches and depending on the balance of power. See also W. Zander, *Israel and the Holy Places of Christendom* (1971).

78. Note that the Catholics claim a broader right to a variety of Church property on the basis of a treaty from 1740, with the contention being that a 1757 *firman* had violated the treaty. See, e.g., Y. Englard, "Legal Status of the Holy Places in Jerusalem," 28 *Isr. L. R.* 589, at n.7 (1994).

79. See, e.g., R. Lapidoth, "Freedom of Religion and of Conscience in Israel," 47 *Cath. U. L. R.* 441, at 450 at n.36 (1998), referring to Article 62 of the Treaty for the Settlement of Affairs in the East, 13 July 1878, 153 Consol. T. S 172, 190 (1878).

80. Zander, *supra* note 77, at 77–80.

81. Cust, *supra* note 77, at 10–11.

82. See, e.g., Lapidoth, *supra* note 79, at 449. The Cenaculum on Mount Zion is not included in the Status Quo arrangement due to an imperial decree in 1552 that ejected the Franciscans from the Cenacle and placed the area under the control of the *waqf* of Nebi Daud. See id. at 7, n.*

83. Cust, *supra* note 77, at 15, 35–34. The Armenians and Greek Orthodox Church also maintain a controlling capacity.

84. W. Zander, "Jurisdiction and Holiness: Reflections on the Coptic-Ethiopian Case," 17 *Isr. L. R.* 245 (1982).

85. Palestinian (Holy Places) Order in Council of 1924; art. 14 of the order envisioned the creation of a formal body under the high commissioner, but it was never implemented. Cust, *supra* note 77, at 11. Note that in 1965 the Jordanians, contrary to a 1961 decision that gave Deir al-Sultan to the control of the Ethiopians, interpreted Article 14 only as providing the high commissioner with the ability to declare a spot a Holy Place but not to make changes to the Status Quo, such that Deir al-Sultan was returned to the Coptics. Zander, *supra* note 84 (analyzing the Israel Supreme Court case where the Supreme Court deferred to jurisdiction of the government rather than decide the issue). It therefore seems that pursuant to practice, issues regarding the Status Quo are to be left in the hands of the ruling authority. R. Lapidoth, *The Basic Law: Jerusalem Capital of Israel* 17 (1999).

86. Zander, *supra* note 77, at 87–89.

87. See, e.g., Cust, *supra* note 77, at 14 n.*

88. Essentially, the Israel Supreme Court deemed the British Order in Council (Western Wall) of 1931 to be discriminatory towards the Jews and the order was treated as invalid.

89. Holy Places Law 1967 (Seifer Chukim) 75. Note that the law specifically states that it is not to be understood as detracting from any previous law.

90. Basic Law: Jerusalem Capital of Israel 1980 (Seifer Chukim 5740) 186. See generally Lapidoth, *supra* note 85, for a complete analysis of this Basic Law. Note that the Basic Laws are to eventually serve as a basis for an Israeli constitution.

91. Id., including the sacred places mentioned in art. 4(3).

92. Englard, *supra* note 78, at 593 notes that the context of the law maintains a secular gloss, such that no desecration occurs if one has access to a site, even if from a religious standpoint such access is equivalent to a desecration. Note as well that the courts

have continued to rely on the mandate law that forbids intervention of the court into these matters (see Lapidoth, *supra* note 85, at 17 n.10), although deference is given to the Israeli law in the case of conflict for matters relating to the domestic law, such as desecration or access. Id. at 88 and 91, referring to 222/68 *Chugim Leumiyiim Aguda Reshuma et al. v. Minister of Police* 24(ii) P. D. 141 (1970). See also Law to Revoke Outdated Laws, 4 Dinim 2177 (1984), at sec. 3, revoking the 1931 Mandate Law regarding the Western Wall.

93.  England, *supra* note 78, at 595; Lapidoth, *supra* note 85, at 91. Lapidoth notes that the Status Quo is a form of *lex specialis* that still applies despite any domestic law to the contrary.

94.  Lapidoth, *supra* note 85, at 89, citing 267/88 *Reshet Koleli Haidra et al. v. Court for Matters Relating to et al.* 43(iii) P. D. 728 (1989). See also 188/77 *Coptic Orthodox Church et al. v. Government of Israel* 33(i) P. D. 225 (1979), noting a similar position regarding the Deir al-Sultan that is under the Status Quo; Zander, *supra* note 77 (critical analysis of the decision). Note as well that the court will alter the Status Quo for the sake of public safety. See, e.g., 512/00 *Etziyon v. Israel* (decided Feb. 24, 2000) (appellant's arrest for loudly praying on the Temple Mount and refusing evacuation was upheld given dangers he posed to public safety).

95.  See Fundamental Agreement, *supra* note 16, at art. 10.

96.  See Holy Places Law, *supra* note 89.

97.  Lapidoth, *supra* note 85, at 85, referring to a UN secretariat list prepared in 1950. See The Holy Places, Working Paper Prepared by the Secretariat, UN Doc. T/L 49, July 3, 1950.

98.  See, e.g., Lapidoth, *supra* note 85, at 86–87, quoting a variety of Israeli cases.

99.  For example, in the Church of the Ascension.

100.  See Breger & Idinopulos, *supra* note 30, at 28, referring to an agreement with the Greek Orthodox Church and other church leaders.

101.  Lapidoth, *supra* note 85, at 90 also notes the hesitation by the courts to get involved in issues involving worship.

102.  See, e.g., ICCPR, *supra* note 56.

103.  See England, *supra* note 78.

104.  Zander, *supra* note 77, at 120 notes that states have generally not limited the right to pilgrimage, given the financial benefits that accrue to the state.

105.  P. Mason, "Pilgrimage to Religious Shrines: An Essential Element in the Human Right to Freedom of Thought, Conscience and Religion," 25 *Case W. Res. J. Int'l. L.* 619 (1993).

106.  G. Watson, "Progress for Pilgrims? An Analysis of the Holy See–Israel Fundamental Agreement," 47 *Cath. U. L. R.* 497 at 518–25 (1998), noting a possible emergence of state practice in Arab states that provide for the ability of pilgrimage.

107.  Id. at 498 and 507, referring to an address by M. Hirsh.

108.  Id. at 507, referring to the peace treaty between Israel and Jordan and the Interim Agreement with the PLO that provide for pilgrimage of Muslims.

109.  Hirsh, *supra* note 48, at 409.

110.  See id.

111.  Id. The "right" of the state is understood as the legal right granted to the state under its local laws. The right granted to the Church, however, seems to be of a more Hohlfeldian variety in the form of an entitlement.

112.  See id., regarding art. 4(2), which is a normative section subjecting the rest of the Fundamental Agreement to the conditions imposed by the Status Quo.

113.  See Fundamental Agreement, *supra* note 16, at art. 13(1)(a).

114.  Breger & Idinopulos, *supra* note 30, at 31.

115.  It is possible that certain states provide for such tax exemptions out of a deference to the religion.

116.  Given that the 1757 *firman* served as a source for the 1852 *firman,* it is interesting to note that the 1757 *firman* does not mention any form of exemption. But see Zander, *supra* note 77, at 139–40, referring to a Palestinian Conciliation Commission draft that included, among the more common rights, the freedom from taxation, describing it as a "usual and generally accepted point."

117.  See Watson, *supra* note 106, at 503, discussing the distinction between the Holy See and the Vatican.

118.  Jaeger, *supra* note 19 (comparing the current situation in Israel that designates recognized religious communities with the former *millet* system under Muslim rule).

119.  Id. at 436–38.

120.  Watson, *supra* note 106, at 500, concluding that the majority of evidence based on state practice and the *travaux preparatoires* of the Vienna Convention indicates that the Holy See maintains a treaty-making capacity.

121.  Note as well subsequent delays due to domestic issues, such as delaying official publication of the Fundamental Agreement until it had been ratified by the Israeli Knesset or not publishing the Legal Personality Agreement due to technical delays.

122.  In discussions with representatives from both the Holy See and Israel, each party noted a deep respect and admiration for the other.

# 4

# THE FUNDAMENTAL AGREEMENT BETWEEN THE HOLY SEE AND ISRAEL AND THE CONVENTIONS BETWEEN STATES AND THE CHURCH SINCE THE VATICAN II COUNCIL

*Silvio Ferrari*

Since the conclusion of the Vatican II Council, the Holy See has signed more than sixty conventions of various titles with twenty-eight different countries.[1] Most of these have been with European and Latin American countries where Catholicism, or at least Christianity, has had, and continues to have, considerable influence. One convention was signed with the Muslim state of Morocco, another with Israel, and one with a very specific scope with the Ivory Coast.

Many of these conventions regard particular, though sometimes very important, questions such as the appointment of bishops, the definition of diocese boundaries, and religious assistance to the armed forces. About ten conventions[2] contain a general, or at least broad, regulatory discipline concerning church-state relations. Because the Fundamental Agreement between the Holy See and Israel falls in this latter group, this chapter will focus on these broader conventions.

## Freedom of the Church and Cooperation with the State in Conventions since the Vatican II Council

The Vatican II Council documents define the relationship between the Church and states in terms of reciprocal independence and autonomy on the one hand and cooperation on the other.[3] Since the Vatican II Council, however, these concepts have been translated into different forms in the conventions.

### European Conventions
The affirmation of the reciprocal independence of the Church and states and the consequent necessity of their mutual cooperation is a clearly identifiable theme in these conventions. This trend began with the Spanish Agreement of 1976 and continued with subsequent refinement through conventions with Italy, Poland, and Croatia.

The July 28, 1976, agreement between the Holy See and Spain declares that:

The Holy See and the Spanish Government . . . considering that the Vatican II Council, in its turn, has established as fundamental principles, to which the relations between the political community and the Church must conform, both the mutual independence of both Parties, in their order, and a healthy cooperation between them . . . deem it necessary to regulate with distinct Agreements the subjects of common interest that, in the new circumstances which have emerged since the signing of the Concordat of August 27, 1953, require a new set of regulations.[4]

The above statement is contained in the preamble of the agreement and regards only the *independence* of the state and the Church. Moreover, it refers to the principles of the Vatican II Council as the foundation of this independence. These principles are certainly important to the Church, but they may not be held in equal regard by the state.

The agreement between the Holy See and Italy of February 18, 1984, introduced important new elements. It declares that:

The Italian Republic and the Holy See reaffirm that the State and the Catholic Church are, each in its own order, independent and sovereign and commit themselves to the full respect of this principle in their mutual relations and to reciprocal collaboration for the promotion of man and the common good of the Country.[5]

This provision, no longer contained in the preamble of the agreement, but in Article 1, refers to the foundation of the principle of reciprocal independence and sovereignty as being not only the declaration of the Vatican II Council but also Italian constitutional law. In the preamble it is stated that the Holy See and the Italian Republic, "bearing in mind, on the part of the Italian Republic, the principles proclaimed in its Constitution and on the part of the Holy See, the Second Ecumenical Council's declarations . . . have recognized the opportunity of entering into the following mutually agreed amendments to the Lateran Concordat." The provision thus provides the argument with a broader and more solid foundation.

The concordat with Poland in 1993 and the agreements with Croatia in 1996 continued this trend with just one variation. The term "sovereign," which in the Italian case is justified by the mention of the sovereignty of the Church contained in Article VII of the Italian Constitution,[6] is replaced by the word "autonomous," thus reinstating the language used in the constitution *Gaudium et Spes*.[7] Apart from this change, the Italian model has been followed virtually to the letter.[8]

This brief examination illustrates that the aforesaid principles of the Vatican II Council, which were adopted to regulate relations between the Church and the state, have been transposed practically in full into these conventions. Consequently, this has led to a radical departure from the formula used prior to the Vatican II Council. The Spanish Concordat of 1953 offers a final example of that formula by affirming that "the Spanish State recognizes the Catholic Church's character of a perfect society and guarantees it the free and full exercise of its spiritual powers and of its jurisdiction, as well as the free and public exercise of worship."[9]

Some experts have pointed out, correctly in my opinion, that the progression from the pre–Vatican II Council formula to those in use in the last thirty years does not imply any alteration in the central nucleus of ecclesiastical doctrine on relationships with states. In both cases, before and after the council, the intention was to claim the original and autonomous character of the legal system of the Church.[10] To declare that the Church is a perfect legal society is no different from declaring that it is an original and autonomous society analogous to those that legal science defines as primary legal systems. Nevertheless, the progression from a formula centered on the "perfect society" category to one which hinges on concepts of independence and autonomy has not been unimportant. Under a historical and political profile, this progression has marked the break with the concordats stipulated, between the two world wars, with the totalitarian German or authoritarian Italian, Spanish, and Portuguese regimes. It has smoothed the way for the liberal democracies that have emerged in Europe during the last fifty years to conclude new conventions with the Catholic Church. The very substitution, in Spain and Italy, of the term "concordat" with "agreement" also has been adopted to mark this break with the past. In the field of law, this same progression has made it possible to reopen dialogue with "secular" legal science that the insistence on nineteenth-century notions risked rendering impossible.

Indeed, the principles of independence and autonomy of the Church and cooperation with the state have been acknowledged without problems in the laws of the European states because these same principles, albeit with different breadth and significance, had already found autonomous citizenship.[11] Various factors were responsible for this development. One is the process of secularization, which has influenced the legal systems of these states and indirectly favored the recognition of the independence of the Catholic Church and of other religious communities.

Additionally, the development of the rights of freedom, extended to guarantee the Church's collective manifestations and beliefs, has allowed the guarantees of religious freedom to the individual to be extended to institutions, thus providing an important support to the principle of the autonomy of religious confessions. Furthermore, recourse throughout Europe to a concerted policy between the state and the most important social organizations, such as trade unions, parties, and pressure groups, also has created a favorable climate for cooperation between the state and religious confessions.

The agreements and pacts of various types between certain states, including Germany, Italy, Spain, Poland, and in the future probably Portugal,[12] and certain religious organizations, not only the Catholic Church, are the most evident manifestations of this evolution in European law. The aims of these agreements are to recognize the autonomy and independence that, by nature, distinguish the religious groups and then to translate them into state laws in different ways, depending on the particular characteristics of each religious community.

In particular, as far as the Catholic Church is concerned, the evolution of the European legal culture has made it possible to transpose the principles expressed in the Vatican II Council documents on the subject of relations between the Church and states into state law through conventions. In this way, the particular intensity and specificity that characterize the Catholic Church's independence and autonomy have been acknowledged by many states' legal systems, without encountering the difficulties that would probably have emerged had the notion of "perfect society" been maintained.

### *The Latin American Conventions*

This last conclusion is only partly valid for the Latin American conventions. The agreements and conventions concluded after the Vatican II Council with Argentina,

Colombia, and Peru are in fact significantly different from the European model, and in some cases maintain formulae that recall the concordats stipulated in Europe between the two world wars.[13]

The Argentine Agreement of 1966, for example, does not contain any explicit reference to the principles of independence, autonomy, and cooperation. Similar to the Italian Concordat of 1929, it opens with the statement that "[t]he Argentinean State recognizes and guarantees the Roman Catholic Apostolic Church the free and full exercise of its spiritual power, the free and public exercise of its worship, and likewise of its jurisdiction in the field of its competence, in order to achieve its specific ends."[14] Although the preamble references the principles of the Vatican II Council, the wording still is indebted strongly to classical ecclesiastical public law and implicitly to the doctrine of the Church as a "perfect society."[15]

With respect to this point of departure, the 1973 concordat with Colombia marks a step forward. After mentioning in the preamble the purpose of assuring a fruitful cooperation[16] between state and Church, the agreement declares, in Article II, that "[t]he Catholic Church shall keep its full freedom and independence from the civil power and consequently may exercise freely and wholly its spiritual authority and its ecclesiastical jurisdiction, governing itself and administrating itself according to its own laws."[17] Moreover, Article III confirms that "canon law is independent from civil law and is not a part of it, but it shall be respected by the Authorities of the Republic."[18] The 1980 agreement with Peru follows the fundamental lines of this model. For example, the preamble mentions the cooperation between church and state, Article I recognizes the full independence and autonomy of the Church, and Article II recognizes the Church's legal personality.[19]

Despite the significant innovations contained in these two texts, the Latin American conventions diverge from the European models on one important point: they do not contain any reference to the distinct order of the Church and of the state. In the absence of this specification, the very acknowledgment of the independence and autonomy of the Church could be viewed as a state concession and may lead to the idea of a sort of self-imposed limitation by the state on its sovereignty. Though this is more evident in the wording used in Article I of the Argentine Agreement, it is also valid for the Columbian and Peruvian conventions. Indeed, in all of these conventions, recognition of the independence and autonomy of the Church is disconnected from any premise serving to make such recognition explicit and serving to provide a justification for it; therefore, it is attributable to an act of free self-determination by the state. In the European conventions, such recognition is instead expressed in terms that make it contingent upon the acknowledgment, as much by the Church as by the state, of the existence of two distinct orders, spiritual and temporal. Both church and state admit their own incompetence in the order belonging to the other, with the exception of what regards the development of the human person and the promotion of the common good, which are explicitly identified as areas of reciprocal cooperation.

This difference probably is attributable to a different degree of evolution within the respective political and legal systems. The democratic tradition of many Latin American countries has been more fragile. Recall that the Argentinean and Peruvian concordats were concluded with military governments, and, likewise, the Colombian concordat was concluded while the country was under a state of siege. This has stifled the development of a legal culture able to set the independence and autonomy of the Church in a context of independence and autonomy extended to a plurality of social organizations. Additionally, it stifled the interpretation of the notion of "*libertas Ecclesiae*" as the more intense specification of freedom rights due to organized groups. Proof of this, by the way, is the absence of pacts with minority religious confessions. In this context, the traditional model, linked to the concept of the Church as "*societas perfecta,*" does not appear to have been completely overcome. In its turn, the absence of a break of proportions similar to the European model, where very few concordats were concluded from the middle of the nineteenth century until the outbreak of the First World War, has probably contributed to developing the Latin American model in a more markedly consistent and linear fashion.

### Conventions with Islamic Countries

The conventions with Morocco and Tunisia present a completely different picture from those discussed so far. It is not difficult to understand why. The Moroccan convention was stipulated with a country where the distinction between the spiritual and temporal orders is extremely weak. Consequently, it cannot supply a sufficient basis for affirming the independence and autonomy of the Church. This basis must therefore be sought elsewhere and precisely in the principle of tolerance that, as is declared explicitly in the letter from King Hassan of Morocco, "characterizes Islam and has always presided over Our relations between the Moroccan State and the Catholic Church."[20] The legal status of the Catholic Church in Morocco is consistent with this premise. It is, at least formally, a status granted by the king in the exercise of his right of sovereignty,[21] even if, de facto, it was defined through negotiations between representatives of the two parties.

The convention with Tunisia, the most "secular" country of the Islamic world and a country where the French cultural influence has been strongest, presents a completely different picture. In a certain sense, it is a more "Western" one. Yet even in this convention, there is no room for notions of independence and autonomy of the Church, nor cooperation with the state. The convention limits itself to declaring that the government of the Tunisian Republic "protects the free exercise of the Catholic religion in Tunisia,[22] accepts that the Catholic Church in Tunisia, . . . provides, in compliance with the general laws of the country, for its internal organization,"[23] and "shall not hinder the exercise of the spiritual authority of the Prelate of Tunis over the Catholic believers in Tunisia."[24] The freedom that the Church enjoys in Tunisia does not flow from any recognition by the Tunisian state of the original and autonomous character of the ecclesiastical legal system.[25]

Considered as a whole, these conventions are not very satisfactory from the Holy See's point of view. For decades, the Catholic Church acted in many Islamic countries through the good offices of the colonial powers, especially France, Italy, and Spain. The era of decolonization forced the Catholic Church to act in the first person. In the Western world, the Church worked within a context of legal and sociopolitical categories that it had helped to forge. In the Islamic world, however, that context did not exist, and thus the instrument of the concordat has revealed evident limitations.

### Brief Summary

From this schematic examination emerges indications that the Vatican II Council's views on church-state relations have been almost fully acknowledged in the conventions with European countries. In the conventions with Latin American countries, the principles of the independence and autonomy of the Church and cooperation with the state are likewise affirmed, but with different and perhaps less satisfactory wording. The differences in the political and legal situations of Europe and Latin America help us to understand why the same principles have not been translated into a univocal formula on both continents.

Our examination also shows how these same principles have been unable to find acknowledgment in two conventions stipulated with countries without a Christian tradition. In these nations, either the traditional Islamic model has prevailed, which is based on the principle of tolerance (Morocco), or there is a more secular model that is, nonetheless, unwilling to accept the independence and autonomy of the Church (Tunisia).

Does this conclusion mean that the notions of independence and autonomy of the Church and of cooperation with the state are not "exportable" to conventions with states with a non-Christian tradition? Is the process of adaptation to the particular local circumstances contained in the European and Latin American conventions impossible with such countries? Or, after examining the Fundamental Agreement between the Holy See and Israel, is a different conclusion possible?

### The Fundamental Agreement between Israel and the Holy See

Before examining the contents of the agreement, it is useful to remember that the State of Israel was born from the intersection of two different roots. One is more secular, connected to eighteenth-century Zionism and its intention to put an end to the persecution of the Jews by guaranteeing them a state in which to live. The other is more religious, based on the idea of the realization of the divine promise to provide a land to the people elect. These two traditions coexist in the State of Israel, though not without problems. Israel cannot be considered a fully secular state, though it is not a confessional state either, because the religious element is intimately connected to the national element.[26] Indeed, the secular-confessional dialectic, which is of typically Western origin, may be applied to Israel with difficulty, as from a certain standpoint Israel is to be found halfway between the East and the West. From this point of view, Israel is a good test case to determine how far the conceptual categories born in the West, with the determining contribution of Christianity, as in the case of the distinction between spiritual and temporal order, can be applied in countries where this contribution is a minority compared to other cultural traditions, such as the Islamic, or in the case under discussion here, the Jewish tradition, and where such a distinction consequently is less established.[27]

This peculiar characteristic of Israel is reflected in the two articles that are the foundation on which the entire Fundamental Agreement rests, namely, Articles 1 and 3.

#### Article 1 of the Fundamental Agreement

Article 1 obligates both parties to uphold "the human right to freedom of religion and conscience."[28] This is a new wording that does not appear with the same breadth of meaning in the other conventions with the Holy See. References to the right to religious freedom are not absent in other conventions, but normally these references serve to reaffirm the principle of the independence and autonomy of the Church, which is usually stated in a more specific form, or they regard the exercise of specific rights, for example, the right of parents to educate their children.[29] There is not otherwise a general commitment with respect to religious freedom, which is instead found in Article 1 of the Fundamental Agreement. It is therefore necessary to assess carefully the causes and scope of this innovation.[30]

With respect to the clauses, the request to insert a clause guaranteeing the freedom of religion and of conscience in the Fundamental Agreement appears to have been put forward by the Holy See during the negotiations.[31] It is possible that the Holy See was concerned with protecting the Israeli Catholic community, a small minority of the Israeli population principally composed of Arabs, from possible discrimination. The Israeli government, sensitive to these issues due to the historical experience of the Jewish people, raised no objections. This was also due to the fact that the reference to religious freedom served to give a solid basis to a commitment which Israel holds particularly dear, namely, fighting anti-Semitism.[32]

The commitment to uphold religious freedom made in Article 1 of the Fundamental Agreement goes beyond these important but contingent motives. From the Holy See's point of view, it appears as the first full realization in concordat law of the Vatican II Council's declaration, *Dignitatis Humanae,* which states that every "human person has a right to religious freedom" and requires this right to be "given such recognition . . . as will make it a civil right."[33] In this document, the right to religious freedom is conceived as a natural right. In other words, every person has the right to religious freedom simply because he or she is a human being. This principle is expressed in Article 1 with the formula "human right to freedom of religion and conscience,"[34] which is more consonant to the language of international law. In any case, this "absolute" nature of the right to religious freedom involves a legal obligation of general scope. The Catholic Church and the State of Israel committed themselves to upholding religious freedom not only of their own believers and citizens, but also those of any other entity. The rights and freedoms recognized by the Catholic Church must not become the reason for even indirect limitations on the rights and freedoms of other individuals and groups.

Examining the letter of the law, the commitments undertaken by the two parties in Article 1 of the agreement are not identical, either in content or scope. With respect to content, Israel agrees to "uphold and observe" the right to religious freedom, while the Catholic Church is bound only to "uphold" religious freedom.[35] The different nature of the two subjects probably explains the disparity of their obligations. The Catholic Church must promote the right to religious freedom, but it is not obliged to observe the same if this means, for example, "to accept that, within itself, other faiths are embraced by its believers even if they are different from its own and that different rites from its own are celebrated."[36] With regard to scope, the agreement refers to the international conventions signed by Israel and the Holy See to determine the rights to religious freedom that the parties agree to honor. This reference confers a different scope to the obligation assumed by the two parties. In particular, Israel (but not the Holy See) signed the International Covenant on Civil and Political Rights (ICCPR) and the International Agreement on Economic, Social and Cultural Rights, which contain important provisions on the subject of freedom of religion.[37]

Article 1 binds the parties to respect the human right to religious freedom.[38] This explicit qualification of religious freedom as a human right, the significance of which has already been seen in relation to the Vatican II Council's documents, fulfills various functions. First, this article should be considered in the context of

Israel's legal tradition, which in the absence of a written constitution has broadly utilized the international conventions on human rights to make up for the absence of a law on religious freedom at the constitutional level.[39] The reference to human rights contained in Article 1, moreover, serves to stress the importance of the right to religious freedom and, finally, to place its interpretation in the light of what has been acquired during the last fifty years, in terms of doctrine and jurisprudence, on the subject of human rights.

These acquisitions tend to highlight a dual-dimension of the individual and collective right to religious freedom. In the individual dimension, the right to religious freedom is substantiated through a series of rights belonging to each human being. The common reference, as much by the Holy See as by Israel, to the Universal Declaration of Human Rights supplies an initial catalog of these rights, including the individual right to change one's religion,[40] which has not been reaffirmed explicitly in all subsequent international instruments. It is possible to develop this catalog through reference to the other conventions to which Israel and the Holy See are parties.

The group dimension of the right to religious freedom does not find such an explicit reference in the provisions of international law. However, the nearly unanimous opinion of the doctrine[41] and, more timidly, the jurisprudence of the international bodies[42] has stressed the need to recognize entitlement to the right to religious freedom not only of individuals, but also of communities. The observation that often "individuals are discriminated against because of their membership in some specific group"[43] created a broad consensus for the proposal to draft "a more general notion of *rights* inherent to the condition of some specific and well-defined groups,"[44] among which the religious communities maintain an important position. From this perspective, it is easy to see the increasing intersections between the reflections of the most recent international doctrine and the principles of the freedom due to the religious communities as set out in the Vatican II Council documents: the catalog of the freedoms that are the competence of the religious communities, as written in the declaration *Dignitatis Humanae,* is substantially identical to the one that lawyers draw from the international provisions protecting religious freedom.[45]

A closer examination of the contents of Article 1 of the Fundamental Agreement, from the point of view of group rights to religious freedom, reveals that here, too, the obligations assumed by the parties are not identical. For instance, Israel, which is party to the ICCPR, is bound to respect Article 27 thereunder, which provides that "[i]n those States in which ethnic, religious, or linguistic minorities exist, persons belonging to such minorities shall not be denied the right, in community with the other members of their group, to enjoy their own culture, to profess and practice their own religion, or to use their own language."[46] The Catholic population in Israel certainly qualifies as a religious minority.[47] As such, the Holy

See could, if necessary, ask that this provision be respected. Its scope, according to prevailing doctrine, encompasses not only the "collective human rights of religious minorities . . . to found and operate the communal institutions required for the perpetuation of the minority's religion,"[48] but also the cultural dimension connected to the religious experience. Indeed, authoritative experts maintain that "even when we consider a strictly religious minority, namely, a group differing from the majority only in its religious belief, e.g., Catholics in England—we must not lose sight of the link between religion and culture."[49] The reference in Article 27 of the ICCPR to "the right . . . to enjoy their own culture" may be interpreted to apply not only to ethnic minorities, but also to religious minorities.[50]

With respect to this picture defined by the reference to the "human right to freedom of religion and conscience,"[51] the character of many of the provisions contained in the Fundamental Agreement is essentially one of integration and specification. For instance, the commitment undertaken by Israel and the Holy See to "respect the 'Status quo' in the Christian Holy Places to which it applies and the respective rights of the Christian communities there under"[52] is a particular application of the right to observe and practice one's own religion, which is guaranteed by Article 18 of the ICCPR.[53] Article 6, which reaffirms "the right of the Catholic Church to establish, maintain and direct schools and institutes of study at all levels,"[54] is a development and specification of Article 13 of the International Covenant on Economic, Social and Cultural Rights. These two provisions, together with Article 8[55] and Article 10 of the Fundamental Agreement, also may be considered specifications of Article 27 of the ICCPR.

Article 1 of the Fundamental Agreement therefore seems to have dual functions. On the one hand, it binds the parties to a series of obligations that may be defined summarily by the expression "human right to freedom of religion and conscience,"[56] and more analytically identified through the Universal Declaration of Human Rights and the other international conventions already mentioned. On the other hand, it supplies the context in which the subsequent provisions of the agreement are to be set forth and interpreted. Indeed, these provisions interact in several respects with the provisions contained in the international instruments on human rights. For example, Article 6 of the Fundamental Agreement declares the right of the Catholic Church in Israel to "establish, maintain and direct schools and institutes of study at all levels; this right being exercised in harmony with the rights of the State in the field of education."[57] This provision might be read, forcing its interpretation a little, in the sense that the right of the Catholic Church to establish schools remains subordinate to the existence of a state law that provides for this possibility. However, Article 13 of the International Covenant on Economic, Social and Cultural Rights declares "the liberty of parents . . . to choose for their children schools, other than those established by the public authorities, which conform to such minimum educational standards as may be laid down or approved by the State. . . ."[58] This provision obligates the state to provide for the possibility of creating private schools, otherwise the right of the parents would be frustrated, and limits its power to the determination of the educational requirements to which these schools must conform.[59]

### Article 3 of the Fundamental Agreement

The recognition of "group rights" or "community rights" raises several delicate issues. One is that not all groups are equal and, therefore, all groups are not entitled to the same rights. It is at this point that, in my opinion, the connection between Article 1 and Article 3 of the Fundamental Agreement resides. Until now, we have discussed only the sphere of Article 1, which establishes a common platform for the rights of individuals and also of religious communities. Article 3 specifies these rights in relation to a particular community, the Catholic Church.

The first commentators on the Fundamental Agreement did not devote much attention to Article 3, which was mainly read in light of Article 1.[60] The legal status of the Catholic Church in Israel, as defined in Article 3, would therefore find its foundation in the commitment to respect religious freedom assumed by the State of Israel in Article 1 of the agreement. More precisely, it would be a consequence of the collective right to religious freedom due to the members of the Church itself. This interpretation, although confirmed in the conclusions reached by the part of canon law doctrine reflecting on the relations between religious freedom and *libertas Ecclesiae,*[61] does not appear to be supported by Article 3 of the Fundamental Agreement.

It is well known that the status of the Catholic Church in Israel was one of the thorniest points of the negotiations. The Israeli government, following the United States model, tended to consider ecclesiastical organizations in the broader category of nonprofit organizations. Moreover, they were willing to recognize the legal personality of only single church institutions, but not the Catholic Church as such. Instead, the delegates of the Holy See asked that the Catholic Church be granted an independent legal personality.[62] Important practical consequences were at stake, though it was above all a clash between two antithetical legal concepts that are the fruit of two distinct cultural traditions.

Article 3 of the Fundamental Agreement is the result of this clash, and it can be considered from two angles: structural and linguistic. From the structural angle, an analogy emerges with the European convention[63] since the Vatican II Council, examined earlier: the identification of two distinct orders, the "respective rights and powers"[64] that depend on the Holy See and Israel, the independence and autonomy of each of the parties in their respective orders, where it is stated that both parties "are free in the exercise of their respective rights and powers,"[65] and the commitment to "co-operation for the good of the people."[66] The second paragraph of

Article 3 further specifies the principle of distinction between the orders, delimiting them by indicating the functions belonging to one sphere or the other. Specifically, the "religious, moral, educational and charitable functions" are delegated to the Church's authority, while "functions such as promoting and protecting the welfare and the safety of the people"[67] are delegated to the state. The second paragraph of Article 3 reaffirms the autonomy of the Church in regulating its own internal organization and in carrying out the activities connected to the functions that are recognized as its own. The Church retains the right "to have its own institutions, and to train, appoint and deploy its own personnel in the said institutions or for the said functions to these ends."[68] From this angle, the Fundamental Agreement is far more comparable to the European conventions than to those between the Holy See and Morocco or Tunisia.

If the structure of Article 3 closely follows that of the corresponding articles of the European conventions, from the language angle it is certainly different. The terms "autonomous" and "independent" have been replaced by the word "free," and whereas the European conventions employ the term "own order" in referring to state and church, Article 3 incorporates the phrase "respective rights and powers."[69] This difference in language may be explained in two ways. First, the spiritual-secular distinction is less important in the Jewish tradition, and it is therefore difficult to theorize about the distinction of an order of the Church and an order of the state. Second, the common-law tradition, in particular the North American tradition, has exercised and continues to exercise influence on the Israeli legal culture, which has inherited the Anglo-Saxon lawyers' wariness of wording based on general and abstract concepts, namely, independence and autonomy, and the preference for concrete and pragmatic solutions founded on the recognition of rights and powers to specific subjects.

In any case, to understand correctly the legal position of the Catholic Church within the Israeli legal system, it appears to me that the last paragraph of Article 3 is decisive. Article 3 states that "[c]oncerning Catholic legal personality at canon law the Holy See and the State of Israel will negotiate on giving it full effect in Israeli law."[70] Although the expression "Catholic legal personality at canon law" is not totally self-evident, the meaning of the provision is sufficiently clear. The commitment by Israel and the Holy See to carry out negotiations does not simply regard the attribution of legal personality, meaning "any" form of legal personality, to the Catholic Church and its organizations, but it also regards the attribution of full effect in Israeli law to legal personality as it is recognized by canon law. The code of canon law clearly states that: (1) the Church, as such, enjoys legal personality, and that (2) such personality is enjoyed "*ex ipsa ordinatione divina.*" First, under this construction the legal personality of the Catholic Church can neither be confused with nor exhausted in the legal personalities of other organizations that are a part of the Church. This conclusion is confirmed by Article 2 of the agreement between the Holy See and the State of Israel, November 10, 1997, where "the State of Israel agrees to assure full effect in Israeli law to the legal personality of the Catholic Church itself." Second, the legal personality of the Church derives from an original source, and does not depend in any way upon the state. The characteristics of originality and independence are constitutive parts of the notion of legal personality articulated under canon law. Consequently, these same characteristics of legal personality must be mirrored in the form of legal personality that will be granted to the Church under Israeli law.[71] Therefore, Article 3 of the Fundamental Agreement is an autonomous base, independent of Article 1 and competing with it for the legal status of the Church under Israeli law.

### *Religious Freedom and Freedom of the Church in the Fundamental Agreement*
The remarks made in the two previous paragraphs allow us to reach a conclusion which, starting with the Fundamental Agreement, regards more general relations between the state and religious communities. The commitment to respect the collective right to religious freedom is a legal platform valid for all religious communities. Consequently, religious communities can enjoy a series of rights, ranging from organizing themselves autonomously to teaching their doctrine freely, which the state is obliged to guarantee.

From this common platform it is possible to further specify the rights due to the religious communities by means of bilateral agreements between the state and these communities. This is what has happened in many European countries, as we have seen. These further specifications integrate the general law, which derives from the right to religious freedom, by adapting it to the peculiar characteristics of each religious community.

With respect to the Fundamental Agreement, Article 1 supplies the common platform. Thereafter, Article 3 and, in relation to more specific sectors, Articles 6, 8, 9, and 10 adapt and integrate Article 1 to mold it to the requirements of the Catholic Church, just as a different agreement might do for the requirements of another religious confession.

Generally, this system suitably protects both individual and group religious freedom, as long as two conditions are respected. First, the specification of rights to religious freedom through agreements must not contradict the common platform guaranteed to individuals and groups by the human right to religious freedom. Second, there should be correspondence between the agreements of the different religious communities and between these agreements as a whole and the unilateral state discipline of the religious communities that have not stipulated agreements, to avoid inequality which could adversely impact religious freedom. The "equal freedom"[72] of all religious communities, with or without agreements with the state, is the insuperable limit of any agreement system.

### The Fundamental Agreement as a Model for Conventions with Non-Christian Countries

The Fundamental Agreement undoubtedly marks an important step forward compared to the other conventions concluded with non-Christian countries. In this context, three elements are particularly worthy of consideration. First, the right to religious freedom is a fundamental meeting point and an important point of departure for cooperation between the Catholic Church and states. The Vatican II Council delineates "the right to religious freedom in analogous terms to those of modern legal doctrine, for which it takes shape as a subjective, individual and collective public right."[73] The Fundamental Agreement, however, with its reference to the Universal Declaration of Human Rights, allows us to broaden this intersection from the structure of the right to religious freedom to its contents, identifying a catalog of rights that both the Church and the state undertake to support. The Catholic Church's interest in obtaining, especially in countries where it is a minority religion, precise guarantees of religious autonomy and freedom could coincide with the interests of states. Even where states are not spontaneously inclined to protect rights to religious freedom, they may have a measurable interest in demonstrating to the international community their respect for one of the fundamental human rights. As such, the reciprocal commitment to develop the right to religious freedom could be the starting point of a policy of agreements extended to states, which have so far remained extraneous to any type of conventions with the Holy See.[74]

Second, the Fundamental Agreement demonstrates that it is possible to translate the principles of the independence and autonomy of the Church and of the distinct orders of the state and of the Church into legal categories unrelated to the Western legal tradition, as was unsuccessful in the conventions with Morocco and Tunisia. It is an inevitable step if we do not wish to limit the field of application of the conventions between the Church and states to countries with a Christian tradition. The Fundamental Agreement hinges on the freedom of the Church and of the state in the exercise of their respective rights and powers. It is a formula that could be used in very different legal systems, provided we succeed in clarifying the margin of ambiguity which still may be inherent in it. From this point of view it is important to take into consideration the agreement recently concluded by the Holy See and Kazakhstan.[75] Its Article 1 commits the parties to acknowledge and respect "mutual freedom in the exercise of their rights and powers" and to cooperate for the good of the people. The structure and the wording of this article have no precedent in the conventions with other Islamic states (Morocco and Tunisia), but recall closely Article 3 of the Fundamental Agreement with Israel. The model defined in this agreement has been "exported" to another non-Christian country, the Republic of Kazakhstan.

Finally, the importance of the human rights provision within the Fundamental Agreement must not be underestimated. This provision may be most useful in countries with no written constitution, such as in Israel, or where the constitution does not adequately protect religious freedom. In this case, the guarantees provided by international law on human rights are an alternative route which may compensate for the absence of similarly strong human rights guarantees in the internal law of a state.

It is too early to know for certain whether the Fundamental Agreement is a model that can be exported anywhere. For now, it is safe to say that the Fundamental Agreement provides some very interesting starting points for the development of a system of relationships based on agreements with states that do not belong to the cultural area of Christian tradition.

## NOTES

1. Cf. Jośe T. Martin de Agar, *Raccolta di Comcondati 1950–1999* (Libreria Editrice Vaticana, Vatican, 2000).

2. I refer to the following conventions: Accord Between the Holy See and Croatia on Legal Questions, 1996, 83 *Acta Apostolicae Sedis* 977 (1997) [hereinafter Croatia]; Fundamental Agreement Between the Holy See and the State of Israel, Dec. 30, 1993, Vatican-Isr., 33 I. L. M. 153 (1994) art. 1 [hereinafter Fundamental Agreement]; Accord Between the Holy See and the Republic of San Marino, Apr. 2, 1992, 85 *Acta Apostolicae Sedis* 324 (1993); Convention Between the Holy See and the Republic of Malta Concerning Catholic Schools, Nov. 28, 1991, 85 *Acta Apostolicae Sedis* 569 (1993); Convention Between the Holy See and the Republic of Malta Concerning Immovable Church Property, Nov. 28, 1991, 85 *Acta Apostolicae Sedis* 588 (1993); Agreement to Amend the 1929 Lateran Concordat, Feb. 18, 1984, Holy See–Italy, 24 I. L. M. 1589 (1985) [hereinafter Lateran Concordat]; Letter from Pope John Paul II to King Hassan II of Morocco, Feb. 5, 1984, 76 *Acta Apostolicae Sedis* 712 (1984) [hereinafter Morocco I]; Letter from King Hassan II of Morocco to Pope John Paul II, Dec. 30, 1983, 76 *Acta Apostolicae Sedis* 712 (1984) [hereinafter Morocco II]; Agreement Between the Holy See and the Republic of Peru, July 19, 1980, 72 *Acta Apostolicae Sedis* 807 (1980) [hereinafter Peru]; Instrumento de Ratificación de 4 de diciembre de 1979, Acuerdo Entre el Estado Español y la Santa Sede, Sobre Asistencia Religiosa a las Fuerzas Armadas y servicio Militar de Clérigos y Religiosos de 3 de enero de 1979 (B. O. E. 1979, 300) [Agreement Between Spain and the Holy See Concerning Religious Assistance to the Armed Forces and the Military Assistance of Clergy and Religious Persons] [hereinafter Spain I]; Instrumento de Ratificación de 4 de diciembre de 1979, Acuerdo Sobre

Asuntos Económicos, de 3 de enero de 1979 (B. O. E. 1979, 300) [Agreement Between Spain and the Holy See Concerning Economic Matters][hereinafter Spain II]; Instrumento de Ratificación de 4 de diciembre de 1979, Acuerdo Entre el Estado Español y la Santa Sede, Sobre Asuntos Jurídicos, de 3 de enero de 1979 (B. O. E. 1979, 300) [Agreement Between Spain and the Holy See Concerning Juridical Matters] [hereinafter Spain III]; Instrumento de Ratificación de 4 de diciembre de 1979, Acuerdo Entre el Estado Español y la Santa Sede, Sobre Enseñanza y Asuntos Culturales, de 3 de enero de 1979 (B. O. E. 1979, 300) [Agreement Between Spain and the Holy See Concerning Education and Cultural Matters] [hereinafter Spain IV]; Instrumento de Ratificación de España al Acuerdo Entre la Santa Sede y el Estado Español de 28 de julio de 1976 (B. O. E. 1976, 230) [Agreement Between Spain and the Holy See] [hereinafter Spain V]; Concordat Between the Holy See and the Republic of Colombia, July 12, 1973, 67 *Acta Apostolicae Sedis* 421 (1975) [hereinafter Colombia]; Agreement Between the Holy See and Argentina, Jan. 28, 1966, 59 *Acta Apostolicae Sedis* 127 (1967) [hereinafter Argentina]. Additionally, I refer to the convention with Tunisia (1964), although it was stipulated a year before the conclusion of Vatican II. See Convention Between the Holy See and the Republic of Tunisia, June 27, 1964, 56 *Acta Apostolicae Sedis* 917 (1964) [hereinafter Tunisia].

3.  See Vatican II Council, *Gaudium et Spes* (Dec. 7, 1965), reprinted in *Vatican Council II: The Conciliar and Post Conciliar Documents*, para. 76, at 984–85 (Austin Flannery ed. & Ambrose McNicholl trans., 1975): "The political community and the Church are autonomous and independent of each other in their own fields. Nevertheless, both are devoted to the personal vocation of man, though under different titles. This service will redound the more effectively to the welfare of all insofar as both institutions practice better cooperation according to the local and prevailing situation." Id. para. 76, at 984.

4.  Spain V, *supra* note 2.

5.  Lateran Concordat, *supra* note 2.

6.  The Italian Constitution mentions the sovereignty of the Church in Article VII. See Costituzione [Cost.], art. VII ("The State and the Catholic Church are, each within its own order, independent and sovereign.").

7.  Vatican II Council, *supra* note 3, para. 76, at 984.

8.  See the purely formal changes in Croatia, *supra* note 2, and the Concordat Between the Holy See and the Republic of Poland, art. I, July 28, 1993, *Acta Apostolicae Sedis* 310 (1998) [hereinafter Poland].

9.  Concordat Between the Holy See and Spain, Aug. 27, 1953, art. II, para. 1, 45 *Acta Apostolicae Sedis* 625, 626 (1953).

10.  See Giorgio Feliciani, "Droit Canonique des Relations de l'Eglise Catholique avec les Etats Depuis 1917," *Le Supplément*, Dec. 1996, at 100–2.

11.  See *supra* note 6 (quoting Article VII of the Italian Constitution); See also Grundgesetz [GC] [constitution], art. 137 (Germany) ("Each religious body regulates and administers its affairs independently within the limits of general laws."); Constitucion [C. E.], ch. II, sec. 1, art. 16, para. 3 (Spain) (obligating the public powers to maintain the appropriate "relations of cooperation with the Catholic Church and other denominations").

12. On April 26, 2001, the Portuguese Parliament approved a new law on religious liberty which makes possible the conclusion of agreements with different religious communities.

13. See Antonio Ingoglia, "L'Istituto Concordatario Nei Paesi Ispano Americani," in *10 Lo Studio del Diritto Eclesiástico: Actualitá e Prospettive* 201–6 (Valerio Tozzi ed., 1997) (discussing these Latin American conventions).

14. Argentina, *supra* note 2.

15. See Ronald Minnerath, *L'Eglise et les Etats Concordataires (1846–1981)* 93 (1983). Regarding this agreement, also compare the contributions published in 3 *Anuario Argentino de Derecho Canonico* 347 (1996).

16. Colombia, *supra* note 2.

17. Id. art. II, at 422.

18. Id. art. III, at 422.

19. Peru, *supra* note 2; id. art. I, at 807; id. art. II, at 807.

20. The convention with Morocco was concluded through an exchange of letters. In the first letter, the king of Morocco expressed the fundamental principles of the legal status conceded to the Catholic Church. Morocco I, *supra* note 2. In the second, the pope gave his "agreement that the Church and the Catholics in the Kingdom of Morocco should conform everything to the rules agreed upon." Morocco II, *supra* note 2.

21. Both King Hassan's letter and Pope John Paul II's reply refer to "le statut ainsi octroyé à l'Eglise." Morocco I & II, *supra* note 2.

22. Tunisia, *supra* note 2.

23. Id. art. 4, at 918.

24. Id.

25. See Minnerath, *supra* note 15, at 87.

26. See Ariel Rosen-Zvi, "Freedom of Religion: The Israeli Experience," 46 *Zeitschrift fur Ausländisches Öffentliches Recht und Völkerrecht* 215 (1986) ("The Jewish religion, throughout the generations, has been identified with the Jewish nation."); see also Claude Klein, "Stato, Ebraismo e Confessioni Religiose in Israele," in *Il Mediterraneo nel Novecento: Religioni e Stati* 110–25 (Andrea Riccardi ed., 1994) (discussing the debated question of the religious qualification of the Israeli state).

27. Cf. Rosen-Zvi, *supra* note 26, at 215 ("The Jewish national tradition, as opposed to the tradition of the Christian peoples, desists from giving to Caesar what belongs to him: rather, it demands from its adherents to give to the religion their all.").

28. Fundamental Agreement, *supra* note 2, art. 1, para. 1, at 154.

29. Freedom of religion is referred to in the preambles of many agreements, but these references do not have any further developments in the text of the agreements unless it is to reaffirm the principle of the freedom of the Church which is already included in that of independence and autonomy. See Croatia, *supra* note 2; Poland, *supra* note 8; Lateran Concordat, *supra* note 2; Spain V, *supra* note 2. In this sense, for example, Article 4 of the agreement with Croatia on legal questions declares: "In the respect of the right to religious freedom, the Republic of Croatia recognizes to the Catholic Church, and to its

communities of any rite, the free exercise of its apostolic mission, in particular with regard to divine worship, government, teaching and the activity of the associations disciplined in Art. 14." Croatia, *supra* note 2. In other cases, the same reference to the freedom of religion has the function to specify the scope of specific provisions. For an example of this, see the agreement with Croatia on cooperation in the fields of education and culture: "The Republic of Croatia, in the light of the principle of religious freedom, respects the fundamental rights of parents to the religious education of their children." See Croatia, *supra* note 2. Another example is art. 12 of the same agreement, which provides:

> On account of the service that the Catholic Church provides to society, and in respect of religious freedom, the Republic of Croatia allows the Church to have suitable access to the State means of social communication, in particular to the radio and to the television. . . . In respect of the principles of religious freedom in a pluralist society, the Republic of Croatia shall vigil with consistency so that in the means of social communication the feelings of Catholics shall be respected, and likewise the fundamental human rights, of ethical and religious order. (Id. art. 12.)

30. Cf. Natan Lerner, "The 1992 UN Declaration on Minorities," 23 *Isr. Y.B. on Hum. Rts.* 111, 111–24 (1993) (stressing the utility of the conventions stipulated between states and religious confessions to reinforce the protection of religious freedom, and to integrate the provisions, which are not always satisfactory, contained into the instruments of international law).

31. See Lorenzo Cremonesi, "Le Tappe del Negoziato Diplomatico," *Quaderni di Diritto e Politica Eclesiástica*, Apr. 1995, at 165.

32. See Fundamental Agreement, *supra* note 2, art. 2, at 155 (providing a commitment to combat anti-Semitism).

33. Vatican II Council, *Dignitatis Humanae* (Dec. 7, 1965), reprinted in *Vatican Council II: The Conciliar and Post Conciliar Documents* 799, 800 (Austin Flannery ed. & Laurence Ryan trans., 1975).

34. Fundamental Agreement, *supra* note 2, art. 1, at 154.

35. Id.

36. Tullio Scovazzi, "L'Accordo Fondamentale tra la Santa Sede e Israele: Aspetti di Diritto Internazionale dei Trattati," *Quaderni di Diritto e Politica Eclesiástica*, Apr. 1995, at 163.

37. See International Covenant on Civil and Political Rights, Dec. 19, 1966, art. 18, 999 U. N. T. S. 171, 178 [hereinafter ICCPR]; International Covenant on Economic, Social and Cultural Rights, Dec. 19, 1966, art. 13, 993 U. N. T. S. 3, 8; see also Scovazzi, *supra* note 36, at 161–62. On the other hand, Article 1 of the Fundamental Agreement contains a declaration to respect "other religions and their followers" that is binding only for the Holy See. Fundamental Agreement, *supra* note 2, art. 1, para. 2, at 154.

38. See Fundamental Agreement, *supra* note 2, art. 1, at 154.

39. See Rosen-Zvi, *supra* note 26, at 219–20; Shimon Shetreet, "Some Reflections on Freedom of Conscience and Religion in Israel," 4 *Isr. Y.B. on Hum. Rts.* 194, 196 (1974); see also Eyal Benvenisti, "The Influence of International Human Rights Law on the Israeli Legal System: Present and Future," 28 *Isr. L. Rev.* 136–53 (1994).

40. See Universal Declaration of Human Rights, Dec. 10, 1948, G. A. Res. 217 A(III), U. N. GAOR, 3d Sess., U. N. Doc. A/810, at 71 (1948).

41. See Yoram Dinstein, "Freedom of Religion and the Protection of Religious Minorities," 20 *Isr. Y.B. on Hum. Rts.* 155, 178 (1990); Alessandro Pizzorusso, "Libertà Religiosa e Confessioni di Minoranza," *Quaderni di Diritto e Politica Eclesiástica,* Apr. 1997, at 49.

42. On the evolution in this direction of the jurisprudence of the European Commission on Human Rights, see Javier Martinez Torrín, "La Giurisprudenza degli Organi di Strasburgo sulla Libertà Religiosa," 1 *Rivista Internazionale Dei Diritto* 338–39 (1993).

43. Natan Lerner, Group Rights and Discrimination in International Law 169 (1991).

44. Id. at 17.

45. See id. at 80–84.

46. ICCPR, *supra* note 37, art. 27, at 179.

47. See Dinstein, *supra* note 41, at 164–70 (discussing the characteristics of religious minorities).

48. Id. at 168.

49. Id. at 169.

50. Id. Moreover, this provision should be interpreted broadly, consistent with Article 1 of the Declaration on the Rights of Persons Belonging to National or Ethnic, Religious and Linguistic Minorities, which ensures: "States shall protect the existence and the national or ethnic, cultural, religious and linguistic identity of minorities within their respective territories and shall encourage conditions for the promotion of that identity." Declaration on the Rights of Persons Belonging to National or Ethnic, Religious and Linguistic Minorities, art. 1, para. 1, G. A. Res. 47/135, U. N. GAOR, 47th Sess., Agenda Item 97(b), at 4, U. N. Doc. A/RES/47/135 (1993); see also Lerner, *supra* note 30, at 111–24.

51. Fundamental Agreement, *supra* note 2, art. 1, para. 1, at 154.

52. Id. art. 4, para. 1, at 155.

53. ICCPR, *supra* note 37, art. 18, at 178.

54. Fundamental Agreement, *supra* note 2, art. 6, at 156.

55. Article 8 of the Fundamental Agreement affirms that the "right of the Catholic Church to freedom of expression in the carrying out of its functions is exercised also through the Church's own communications media." Id. art. 8, at 156.

56. Id. art. 1, at 154. The utility of the conventions stipulated between the Holy See and states, considered "alternative ways of action" compared to the "global and regional instruments" existing in this sector, to reinforce the protection of the right to religious freedom is stressed by Natan Lerner, "The Holy See and Israel: Protecting Human Rights by Bilateral Agreements," *Anuario de Derecho Eclesiastico del Estado,* 1997, at 139.

57. Fundamental Agreement, *supra* note 2, art. 6, at 156.

58. International Covenant on Economic, Social and Cultural Rights, *supra* note 37, art. 13(3), at 8.

59. See Yoram Dinstein, "Cultural Rights," 9 *Isr. Y.B. on Hum. Rts.* 58, 68–73 (1979).

60. See David-Maria A. Jaeger, "In Margine all' 'Accordo Fondamentale' tra la Santa Sede e lo Stato di Israele," in *La Porta D'Oriente* 21 (1995); Francesco Lozupone, "Stato e

Confessioni Religiose in Israele," in *Minoranze, Laicità, Fattore Religioso* 198 (R. Coppola & L. Troccoli eds., 1997).

61.  See Luigi Mistó, *"Libertas Religiosa" and "Libertas Ecclesias: Il Fondamento della Relazione Chiesa-Comunità Politica nel Quadro del Dibattito Postconciliare in Italia* 179–87 (1982).

62.  See Cremonesi, *supra* note 31, at 177–81.

63.  An analogy with Article 1 of the Italian Agreement (which on this point is substantially identical, as we have seen, to the other European conventions) has been picked up by Francesco Margiotta Broglio, "L'Accordo 'Fondamentale' tra la Santa Sede e lo Stato d'Israele (30 Dicembre 1993)," *Nuova Antologia*, Apr.-June 1994, at 157.

64.  Fundamental Agreement, *supra* note 2, art. 3, para. 1, at 155.

65.  Id.

66.  Id. art. 3, para. 1, at 155. An application of this principle may be found in Article 11 of the Fundamental Agreement, where the Holy See declares that "owing to its own character, it is solemnly committed to remaining a stranger to all merely temporal conflicts." Id. art. 11, para. 2, at 157. The extraneousness of the Holy See to temporal questions is affirmed on account of the nature itself of the Holy See, which presupposes the existence of an order to which the Holy See is by its very nature extraneous.

67.  Id. art. 3, para. 2, at 155.

68.  Id.

69.  Id. art. 3, para. 1, at 155.

70.  Id. art. 3, para. 3, at 155.

71.  1983 Code of Canon Law c.113, sec. 1 (providing that the Church's legal personality is enjoyed *"ex ipsa ordinatione divina"*). Other canons define the prerogatives of the Church by emphasizing their original character. See id. c.129, sec. 1 (*"Potestas regiminis . . . ex divina institutione est in Ecclesia"*); id. c.747, sec. 1 (*"Ecclesiae . . . officium est et ius nativum . . . a qualibet humana potestate independens, omnibus gentibus Evangelium praedicandi"*).

72.  In this perspective, it is useful to remember the first section of Article VIII of the Italian Constitution, even if its potential does not appear to be fully exploited: "[a]ll religious denominations are equally free before the law." Costituzione [Cost.], art. VIII.

73.  Giuseppe dalla Torre, *La Citta' Sul Monte* 79 (1996).

74.  Naturally, this is not possible with everybody, nor with everybody in the same way. Rights to religious freedom could turn out to be infertile ground for starting concordat relations with Islamic countries, for example.

75.  The agreement, signed on September 21, 1998, is printed in Agar, *supra* note 1.

**III**

# VATICAN CONCORDATS
# AND THE ACCORD

# 5

## THE FUNDAMENTAL AGREEMENT BETWEEN THE HOLY SEE AND THE STATE OF ISRAEL AND CHURCH-STATE AGREEMENTS IN SPAIN

Some Contrasts and Comparisons

*Rafael Palomino*

There can be no doubt that one of the most important church-state agreements of the last century is the Fundamental Agreement between the Vatican and Israel. I hope to discuss this agreement by contrasting it with the Spanish experience of official relations with the Vatican.

In order to provide a contrasting perspective, a comparative law method must develop an approach in which two legal systems, or two different topics from two or more legal systems, are compared. Obviously, setting forth a comparison requires a common feature or characteristic. One might wonder whether the Israeli system of church-state legal relationships has features or aspects in common with the Spanish one. In fact, the history, origins, and legal traditions of the two systems are different. Only two common features can be found: both signed agreements with the Holy See and both are currently democracies. These common aspects are enough to offer a useful comparative study. Moreover, nothing more is necessary since the differences between both legal systems, even in sharp contrast, could offer us new ideas and original results to enrich the legal environment in which we live. This analysis does not intend to provide our own legal systems with some foreign "solution which, like a new electrical appliance, can be fitted with an adaptor and plugged into the system back home. . . . The hope is that the experiences of countries at comparable stages of social and economic development will give us insight into our own situation."[1] But certainly this comparison will help us to understand better the Fundamental Agreement's significance, extent, and prospects.

Common features aside, religious liberty is another relevant topic that stimulates comparative analysis. Religious liberty is a common struggle for many countries and can be seen today as an expression of the effort to recognize and protect a basic need of human beings. The specific expressions of religious liberty vary from one state to another and between cultures. Behind these differences, however, it is possible to identify a common basic content, which is often proclaimed in international legal declarations. In recent years, religious liberty has become the key point for comparative studies on church-state legal affairs both abroad and in our own legal systems.[2] The practical dimension of the comparative approach to religious freedom is clear: furnishing recent democracies—particularly, but not exclusively, Eastern European countries—with pluralistic societies' legal experiences in church-state affairs.

From these three starting points (a church-state agreement, democracy, and religious liberty in both countries) I shall analyze the current Spanish legal system on church-state agreement[3] along with short comparative references to the Holy See–Israel Fundamental Agreement. Before beginning the analysis it is necessary to briefly discuss the sociological and historical conditions of the Spanish system.

### Historical, Legal, and Sociological Background

Spanish state unification began in the fifteenth century. In the unification process, religion was one of the most important underpinnings. Catholic religion defined a part of the new political identity. Consolidating a new kingdom required fortification of the Catholic religion at the expense of other religious groups: the Muslims and Jews. Muslims were expelled from Spain, first as enemies of the Christian kingdoms, and later as insurgents and insincere converts to the Christian religion.

The matter of Jews was different from that of Muslims. During the Middle Ages, Jews lived in Spanish territories, Christian and Muslim, as a separate community. For a long time Christian kings protected Jews because, among other reasons, the Jewish communities provided the Crown with tax-collection funds. However, when the unification process became stronger, along with factors such as popular pressure and hostility from nobility, the Jewish people were faced with a dilemma: conversion or expulsion. The Crown struck several bargains to avoid this dilemma. One of the best arrangements was the Taqqanot (ordinances, rulings) of Valladolid of 1432.[4] Abraham Bienveniste summoned representatives from the Jewish communities in Valladolid, and together they drafted special regulations concerning the social life of these communities. The regulations were based on Abraham Benveniste's serious effort to return religious life and traditions to the Sephardim (the Jews who inhabited Sepharad, Spain in Hebrew). The Taqqanot was approved by the political power as a law of the courts of Castile, and could be regarded as the precedent of modern legal agreements with religious minorities.[5]

Notwithstanding these efforts, the disastrous final solution put the Jewish communities' members in a terrible dilemma: conversion or expulsion. Many of the Sephardim converted to Christianity, some sincerely, others in a nominal way. The latter, despite their conversion, preserved their own religious tradition secretly. Many others departed from their cherished land, Sepharad, homeland of Jewish Diaspora poetry and thought. The Spanish Inquisition added to the effect of these regulations by preserving Catholic religious identity as a pillar of the modern state. Protestantism did not grow in Spanish land. In fact, for Spanish rulers, as for other European countries, Protestantism was a heresy against the Catholic Church and simultaneously a serious menace to the state. As a result of that unification process, neither Judaism, Islam, nor Protestantism flourished freely in Spain. Even today, Judaism, Islam, and Protestantism are strange to Spanish society. Although there are no official reports on religious affiliation,[6] these religions are real minorities[7] in Spain's population.[8]

Centuries of popular literature created this equation: to be Spanish is to be Catholic. This equation isolated the religious history of Spain from that of the rest of Europe, in which no such formulation existed. In Europe, many countries were devastated by wars of religion. By contrast, in Spain the wars came later[9] and in a different fashion, because Spanish religious uniformity subtly bore a problem of important dimensions: the competition for domination in public policy and affairs of religious groups against nonreligious groups. This problem arose in the nineteenth century, when the king dissolved the Jesuit order and when the state secularized church property. Later, open hostility toward religion developed during the Second Spanish Republic (1931–1939).

The Second Republic's hostility toward religion explains, in part, why the military party that won the civil war (1936–1939) adopted religion as a central rule of its regime. For example, the Principles of the National Movement Law, one of the fundamental laws of the regime, established that "[t]he Spanish Nation assumes as a touchstone the submission to the Law of God, according to the Doctrine of the Holy Roman, Catholic and Apostolic Church, the Sole true faith undivided from the national conscience, which will inspire the national law."[10]

Such a provision is strange, bearing in mind the historical European context. In fact, post–Second World War European democracies relinquished the religious definition of the state some time ago, and have embraced religious liberty.

In 1953 the Spanish government signed a concordat with the Catholic Church (Concordat between the Holy See and Spain of 1953) that complied with the characteristics of a Catholic-state agreement. In the middle of the twentieth century, the explicit new trends that the Catholic doctrine assumed in the Second Vatican Council declaration, *Dignitatis Humanae*,[11] changed in part prior Spanish legislation. Indeed, the Spanish Religious Liberty Law of 1967[12] was a timid attempt to meet the theoretical requirements of the revised Catholic doctrine.

In the 1970s, three conflicting movements arose. First, the Church in Spain requested a new system of church-state relations in which the Church would not be so joined to the state. Second, the state demanded a new concordat. In addition, in the public ecclesiastical law (part of the canon law system) some scholars argued that concordats were redundant in modern democratic states.[13] These three movements created a rare environment for church-state relations in the last years of Franco's regime.[14]

At the end of Franco's authoritarian regime, the path to democracy was possible through continuity rather than through rupture. This is what is called transition in Spain—that is, some sort of measured evolution toward democracy, starting from the institutions of the previous regime—and its landmark was the Law of the Political Reform of 1977.

### Democratic Church-State Legal System and Agreements

It is worth noting that adopting transition as the political mechanism or attitude for change implicitly justified the presence of church-state agreements.[15] Transition itself required strong commitments and dialogue between social groups and the government. Social and political pluralism that a democracy embraces calls for the negotiation of legislation concerning a wide range of matters, including church-state affairs.[16] Consequently, the new legal system of church-state relations followed the principles of the political transition: formal continuity through agreements instead of rupture. But these agreements meant something different. They were tokens of religious liberty, in the organizational dimension, instead of privileges bestowed upon a single religious group.

The Spanish government and the Catholic Church canceled the old system. However, this cancellation was transitional, since the concordat of 1953 was not repealed completely, but revisited[17] with a new agreement in 1976.[18] In this transitional agreement, the state relinquished the bishops' nomination privilege. Additionally, the Church renounced exclusive canon law jurisdiction over the clergy.

It seems to be useful to contrast the 1976 Spanish transitional agreement with the Vatican-Israeli one. The preamble to the 1976 Spanish Agreement proclaimed religious liberty a right that the state must recognize. This assertion is consistent with the right to religious liberty that the Second Vatican Council proclaimed.[19] However, religious freedom is not the main topic of the Spanish Agreement. In contrast, the Fundamental Agreement is grounded mainly upon religious freedom that appears in the first article.[20] This is significant: religious freedom is not only an implicit reason for the Fundamental Agreement, but is a specific part of it. The Fundamental Agreement lists a series of institutional and individual religious rights, generally acknowledged today, albeit not specifically listed in obligatory positive law.[21] In this sense, it is clear that the Fundamental Agreement goes further than the Spanish one and constitutes a great development in the relations between Israel and the Catholic Church, and also in international law.[22] In comparing these agreements, it is clear that both the 1976 Spanish Agreement and the Fundamental Agreement could be called "symbolic agreements,"[23] that is, texts crafted in broad terms that require further development to achieve real efficiency and meaning.

After the ratification of the 1976 Spanish Agreement, a constituent assembly drafted a new constitution that was submitted to a referendum and approved in 1978. The Spanish Constitution of 1978 established a new system of church-state relationships. Concerning regulation of religious freedom, Article 16 provides:

1. Freedom of ideology, religion, and worship of individuals and communities is guaranteed, with no other restriction on their expression than may be necessary to maintain public order as protected by law.

2. Nobody may be compelled to make statements regarding his religion, beliefs, or ideology.

3. There shall be no State religion. The public authorities shall take the religious beliefs of Spanish society into account and shall in consequence maintain appropriate co-operation with the Catholic Church and the other denominations.[24]

For a broad overview of the constitutional system, this article must be connected with other constitutional provisions, such as Article 14,[25] Article 9(2),[26] Article 10(2),[27] Article 27,[28] and Article 32.[29]

The 1978 Constitution sought a middle ground between the aggressive separatism proclaimed by the Second Spanish Republic and the Catholic state of

Franco's regime, therefore taking into account historical experience.[30] To that aim, the Constitution implicitly embraces four principles which guide church-state legal relations. The Spanish Constitutional Court (highest legal interpreter of the Constitution) has defined and recognized these principles.[31] The first principle is the religious liberty principle. The basic content of this principle is that religious liberty is understood not only as a fundamental freedom proclaimed in the Constitution, but also as the basic attitude of the state toward religion. The state does not intend to treat one particular religious group specially; rather, the government promotes religion as a right of each citizen. According to the religious liberty principle, the best way to protect religious freedom is to avoid the legal establishment of any official religion.

The second principle is the secularity or laicity principle. In accordance with this principle, the state is impartial toward the various individual religious subjects. Professing one's faith is a right which belongs to human beings and is not a freedom or right the state could exercise. This principle, however, does not promote a system of strict separation between religion and the state.

The third principle is the equality/nondiscrimination principle. According to Article 14 of the Constitution, nondiscrimination is a basic human right and should be entirely applied to individuals and in a relative fashion to religious groups. In other words, nondiscrimination is employed in relations between the state and religious groups. It is not so clear, however, if the principle is exercised between religious and nonreligious groups, because religious bodies constitute a different category under Spanish law.

The last principle is the cooperation principle. According to this principle, the government and religious bodies are viewed as different entities with different goals and are not subordinate to each other. Churches and the state operate in the same society and are not isolated from each other as in France. This coexistence may be understood in two ways: the first, a separationist model, in which the government avoids as far as it could promoting relationships with religious groups *as religious*. The second, a cooperationalist model, in which the government facilitates legal relationships with religious groups in their religious character. At the same time, the cooperationalist model is not a system of "established church."

State and religious groups have common fields of interest because the state promotes religious freedom and religious groups are institutional or organizational channels of religious liberty. These entities share a cooperative relationship, which is evidenced through the legal dialogue that thwarts possible clashes between secular legislation and religious conduct. A cooperationalist approach may be useful for transitional periods in those countries in which churches and religious groups have in the past suffered persecution and wrongful confiscation, democracy begins to settle, and restoration is required for a peaceful corrective justice application.[32]

Pondering these four principles as a whole shows that the Spanish church-state system fulfills the characteristics of the European model of church-state relations. This European model could be identified by three main features: (1) state neutrality or impartiality toward religion; (2) a special religious sector that operates in the legal system within the public sector; and (3) narrow intervention of the state in the religious area, and state respect for religious autonomy.[33]

Along with the aforementioned principles are two other relevant topics essential to understanding the new Spanish system. First, in 1979, Spain entered an international system of regional human rights protection when it signed the European Convention on Human Rights of 1950. The legal framework of the European Convention has provided an effective tool for the protection of individual freedoms in Europe. Especially from 1993 (the *Kokkinakis* case on freedom of proselytism) onwards, European Court of Human Rights decisions have contributed to the uniform legal understanding of religious freedom in Europe, and have played a major role as a corrective device against legal practices contrary to religious freedom of individuals and communities in European countries.[34]

It is also meaningful to note the new territorial structure upon which the Spanish Constitution settled. The Constitution decentralized the state and created regional units, several of them based upon historical nations within Spain. These entities are called "Autonomous Communities," and they enjoy broad powers on various matters. The legislation that they enact will grow in importance and effect on legal regulation of religious matters.

Let us now consider specifically the role of agreements in this new system, whether it is compulsory for the state to conclude these arrangements and what the criteria are for signing agreements with religious groups. According to the Constitution, the state is not required to facilitate church-state agreements. Article 16 of the Constitution mandates cooperation with religious groups. Indeed, cooperation could be achieved through different devices. The Religious Liberty Law of 1980[35] developed the constitutional provisions concerning religious liberty. This law contains different tools to achieve cooperation between the state and religious entities.

The first of these legal devices for cooperation is the Spanish *Religious Entities Register Book*.[36] Registration in this special book, after compliance with several conditions, endows religious groups with a special legal rank or position in the Spanish legal system, the category of religious confession. Registration cannot be used as a tool for keeping under control legality or even authenticity of religious beliefs, as the Spanish Constitutional Court recently held.[37] The second tool is the Commission of Advisors on Religious Liberty,[38] which comprises representatives of religious groups, of the government, and experts on religious liberty. The aim of the commission is to counsel the government on religious legal matters. The third tool is the agreements with the Spanish government.[39] Legal agreements convey special meaning concerning cooperation with religious groups and accommodation of religious needs, though these agreements are not necessarily special privileges.

Scholars still discuss the legal nature of agreements, that is, whether they belong to an intermediate law situated between the internal state law and religious norms, or whether they belong to the internal state law. The controversy is not meaningless because the nature of agreements determines the legitimacy of unilateral governmental changes made in them.[40]

To perform these agreements, two conditions are required. The first condition is registration in the Spanish *Religious Entities Register Book.* The second condition is a "notorious settlement" (*notorio arraigo*) in Spain. This "notorious settlement" is an obscure clause with no clear meaning. Scholars have thoroughly studied this clause, and have contrasted it with similar clauses from the Italian and German agreements systems. This attempt has proven futile because the Spanish government has interpreted the clause with discretion. In fact, the government has not chosen a numerical interpretation of "notorious settlement," but rather a historical interpretation. This explains why Spain has signed agreements with Muslims and with Jews. However, it has not signed any agreement with Jehovah's Witnesses, who are more numerous in Spain. The Catholic Church is a different case concerning the "notorious settlement" clause, as it is supposed to be implicit (Article 16(3)) in the text of the Spanish Constitution.

According to the Constitution, but prior to the Religious Liberty Law of 1980, the Catholic Church entered into four agreements. The concordatary system, a system in which a single legal agreement collects all the topics of common interest, was relinquished and partial agreements on specific matters were established instead.[41] This split method can be justified as a way of efficient negotiation. Additionally, it is also the consequence of the concordat crisis mentioned earlier. The agreements signed in 1979 deal with four main issues. The first of these agreements of 1979 covers legal matters, including marriage, legal personality recognition according to canon law, protection of religious sites and religious archives, and observance of religious days.[42] The second agreement covers financial matters, such as tax exemptions and governmental funds.[43] The third agreement deals with religion and culture, including religious education in public schools, Church-monitored education facilities, and ecclesiastical properties with cultural or historical value.[44] Finally, the fourth agreement deals with chaplaincy and military service of the clergy and members of religious orders.[45]

In addition, in 1992 Spain entered into agreements with three other religious groups: the Evangelical entities,[46] the Jewish communities,[47] and the Muslim Commission.[48] These agreements work in the legal system as ordinary laws and contain provisions similar to those in the agreements with the Catholic Church, including more specific norms concerning dietary religious rules and places of burial. These three agreements marked the real end of the Catholic state. With them, Spain canceled its debt with the religious minorities proscribed and expelled from Spain long ago.

The agreement system operates both between the Spanish state and religious groups as single entities established in the country and at different levels. For instance, the regional units, or Autonomous Communities, are able to sign agreements. In fact, these entities have signed agreements with the Catholic bishops concerning religious places, lands, and goods with artistic significance.[49] In 1995, the Evangelical Church also signed the Collaboration Agreement between the Community of Madrid and the Evangelical Council of Madrid. This agreement is configured as a framework to be used in future agreements by various sectors. It stresses collaboration in the areas of culture and social work with the hope of building an institutional relationship between the two participants. Consequently, Spain follows the model of regional church-state agreements already well established in Germany and Italy.

Another example of this model of regional church-state agreements is reflected in agreements signed between the Spanish government or governmental agencies and representatives of religious groups concerning matters of common interest, such as chaplaincy assistance in prisons and public hospitals.[50]

From the agreements described, we can foresee a legal system in which different types of pacts exist, namely, agreements between churches or religious groups and the state, between churches or religious regional groups and Autonomous Communities, and between special religious representatives and the state or Autonomous Communities. This is a complex but practical system, close to the legal system prevailing in other areas, for example, labor law, tax law, and environmental law. In these legal areas, the dialogue between the state and the representatives of social groups makes the law more efficient and real.[51]

Turning to a comparison of the Vatican-Israel Fundamental Agreement with the Spanish model of church and state agreements, two topics should be noted: first, the agreements system in general, and second, agreements with the Catholic Church. From a global perspective, it is clear that Israel has not reached a full legal development of agreements as a system of church-state legal relations. Furthermore, this specific legal mechanism is not mandatory in the Israeli legal system. Precedents of accommodation of religious personal law and jurisdiction in religious-related matters already exist.[52] However, this accommodation is derived from the Ottoman legal tradition rather than the right to religious freedom pattern. In this sense, Israel is still in the beginning of modern church-state relations. Israel lacks a written constitutional text from which basic principles of the church-state legal relationship can be drawn. Moreover, the Human Dignity and Liberty Law of 1992[53] does not explicitly include the right to religious freedom. Notwithstanding this, the Israeli Declaration of Independence of 1948, as an interpretatory guiding principle,[54] shows Israel's commitment to religious freedom. This is a sound basis for considering these covenants as legal instruments to develop special aspects of religious freedom.

It is neither feasible nor reasonable to transpose the framework of the Fundamental Agreement into other religious groups as long as basic prerequisites for signing a treaty, such as international legal personality and complete legal structure of the religious body, are not available for many religious groups. It is important to note that the agreements system serves to recognize religious identity as it is defined by the religious group itself.[55] Recognizing religious identity purports to recognize the religious freedom of groups and individuals. In other words, such agreements provide a legal translation to a common language—which governmental officials can recognize, even if they are not believers—of the religious needs and demands of individuals and communities, avoiding legal clashes or practical misunderstandings.

Comparing the Spanish system with the Fundamental Agreement, it is clear that the Fundamental Agreement contains the basis of a full legal structure of church-state relations in its initial stage, financial matters, legal personality, educational matters, mass media, and church property, and that it is similar to the Spanish system. Nonetheless, the topics the Fundamental Agreement contains must be further developed. To achieve this progress, the Fundamental Agreement provides for bilateral subcommissions in Article 3(3)[56] and Article 10(2)(b).[57] These commissions are not permanent entities of cooperation and coordination like those supplied in the Spanish legal system by the different agreements and legal texts,[58] but rather they are the first step of real implementation.

### Some Relevant Aspects

To depict briefly some significant aspects of the Spanish agreement system, I have selected those that can serve as a useful foreign sample for the development of the Fundamental Agreement: legal personality recognition and financial matters. In this section, references to the agreements system will be circumscribed as much as possible to the legal treatment accorded the Catholic Church.

The Spanish legal system provides special legal personality to religious groups. This special personality is called a "religious confession." Religious groups obtain this categorization from inscription in the *Religious Entities Register Book*. Religious confessions enjoy full organizational autonomy, freedom to enact internal rules, and the ability to sign agreements with the state. Thus, a religious confession is the basic and specific organizational category in the Spanish church-state system. However, not every religious group is automatically classified as a religious confession. According to the Religious Liberty Law, admission to the *Register Book* has formal requisites: a historical foundation in Spain, identification details, representatives,[59] and a substantial condition as well. The substantial condition is a religious purpose, a term that is not defined in the Religious Liberty Law.[60] Instead, Article 3(2) of the Religious Liberty Law states that "[a]ctivities, purposes and Entities relating to or engaging in the study of and experimentation with psychic or parapsychological phenomena or the dissemination of humanistic or spiritualistic values or other similar non-religious aims do not qualify for the protection in this Act." This indirect control over religious character has been strongly criticized[61] because somehow it encourages a three-tier church-state legal system, that is, religious confessions with agreement, religious confessions without agreement, and religious groups without registration, as in Italy.[62] In fact, the problems arising from the formulation of a legal concept of religion are common to other legal systems because a legal concept of religion arbitrarily discriminates between religion and other phenomena.[63] In order to obtain the advantages that the law grants to religious confessions, religious entities and religious associations must be registered in the *Religious Entities Register Book.*

The Spanish legal system respects the highly complex legal personality of the Catholic Church and recognizes the Holy See. In fact, the Constitution recognizes the Catholic Church explicitly. The 1979 Agreement on Legal Matters acknowledges the territorial divisions of the Catholic Church in Spain: dioceses and parishes. Article 1(2) of this agreement provides that legal recognition of these territorial entities is achieved by providing the state with notification of the entity's existence.[64] The reason for the notification recognition system, rather than new registration of a religious entity inside a religious confession, rests in the structural and organic character of dioceses and parishes, which represent the inward legal dimension of the Church.

The Catholic Church's presence in a land, territory, or nation is inconceivable without these or similar entities. It should be noted that the Spanish Assembly of Catholic Bishops is recognized automatically in the Agreement on Legal Matters.[65] For the legal recognition of other entities of the Catholic Church, registration is required. In order to determine the faculty of acquiring, renting, purchasing, or performing other legal acts, canon law operates as a special rule to determine the legal capacity.

The Fundamental Agreement between the State of Israel and the Holy See demands full legal recognition of the Catholic Church's legal personality in Israeli law. This was the first step for enhancing the legal relationship, just as it was necessary for the Catholic Church to recognize the State of Israel. Recognition of the Catholic Church in Israel required an enormous effort by the Israeli government to understand a complex entity foreign to the Israeli legal system. In my view, it was a complicated task. This complexity was not due to the experts' capacity to work or negotiate, but to the politicians' ability to understand something completely new, especially if this topic is considered under the religious view and not according to an international law outlook. At any rate, the parties finally reached a new agreement in 1997, entitled Agreement between the State of Israel and the Holy See Pursuant to Article 3(3) of the Fundamental Agreement between the State of Israel and the Holy See (also referred to as the Legal Personality Agreement).[66] The new agreement is a good example of deference toward the Catholic Church's legal and religious autonomy. In fact, the Israeli government does not require special legal requirements (aside from those of canonical legal nature) to recognize the legal personality of Catholic institutions. In addition, the agreement guarantees regular development of economic and legal transactions according to Israeli law, with the very few limitations which the canon law entails concerning certain kinds of transactions. A special schedule[67] provides rules for merger and dissolution of legal persons, and for the official registry set up for recording documents related to the agreement. From my point of view, this system of legal recognition of personality complies with the needs of the Catholic Church adequately.

On financial matters[68] the Spanish legal system provides for direct and indirect financial aid to the Catholic Church. Concerning indirect aid, the Church is under the regulation of nonprofit corporations. The Church also enjoys tax-free status for religious activities such as collections, religious literature distribution, and religious education for clergy. The Church is exempt from real estate taxes on Church properties such as churches, places of worship and their annexed facilities used as offices, clergy residences, and seminaries, as well as transfer tax on goods destined for worship or charity.

According to the Agreement on Financial Matters, direct aid consists of a special assignment in the state budget (that diminishes) and an income tax return assignment that follows the Italian pattern. In addition, the Agreement on Financial Matters provides that the Catholic Church will discontinue using direct aid as soon as it achieves self-sufficiency.[69]

Article 10 of the Fundamental Agreement provides the basic platform for solving the difficult issue of tax exemption.[70] This question concerns not only the Catholic Church, but also other Christian denominations. No legal basis for exemption exists in the Israeli legal system because none existed in the Ottoman tradition. Exemptions, however, are essential to the economic survival of many Christian entities in Israel.

In fewer than twenty years, the Spanish legal system has evolved from a Catholic state to a system grounded on religious liberty. Furnished with a new sense, agreements serve to develop the institutional dimension of religious liberty: promoting religious liberty respecting religious identity of the groups. Spanish legal background and experience cannot be applied as a whole to the Israeli legal system. However, the Israeli legal system can discern from the Spanish experience that agreements on religious matters are more than a tool for establishing mutual relationships with a religious group.

It is important to stress that the Fundamental Agreement embraces religious liberty as an essential element of the common commitment between its signatory entities. Religious liberty is not the only reason or motive for this agreement; it is the core of it. Religious liberty and the Fundamental Agreement run together. As an Israeli scholar recently pointed out, the future development of religious human rights in Israel will be influenced by, among other things, the agreement signed between the Holy See and the State of Israel.[71]

Furthering the Fundamental Agreement means promoting religious freedom in Israel, because the development of the agreement means the recognition of religious identity and religious needs. All the efforts to complete the success of the Fundamental Agreement will be efforts to ensure a first human freedom, religious freedom.

## NOTES

1. Mary Ann Glendon et al., *Comparative Legal Traditions*, 2d ed. (St. Paul, Minn.: West Publishing Co., 1994), 10.

2. W. Cole Durham, "Perspectives on Religious Liberty: A Comparative Framework," *Religious Human Rights in Global Perspective: Legal Perspectives*, ed. Johan D. van der Vyver & John Witte (The Hague: Martinus Nijhoff Publishers, 1996), 1–3.

3. Church-state agreements may be defined broadly as contracts signed by the political power and the religious groups concerning matters of common interest with national or international legal value. For further information about the Spanish system of church-state relationships, see generally Iván C. Ibán, "State and Church in Spain," *State and Church in the European Union*, ed. Gerhard Robbers (Baden-Baden: Nomos Verlagsgesellschaft, 1996), 93–117. The Spanish section of the *European Journal for Church-State Research*, ed. R. Torfs (Leuven: Peeters), also might be useful.

4. Yolanda Moreno Koch, *Fontes Iudaeorum Regni Castellae, De Iure Hispano-Hebraico, Las Taqqanot de Valladolid de 1432: Un Estatuto Comunal Renovador* (Salamanca: Universidad Pontificia de Salamanca, 1987), provides the text of the Taqqanot.

5. Luis Suárez Fernández, *Judíos Españoles en la Edad Media*, 2d ed. (Madrid: Rialp, 1980), 242–45.

6. There is no official data of religious affiliation in Spain due to a constitutional provision concerning religious liberty that protects citizens from being compelled to disclose their religion. See Article 16(2) of the Constitution of 1978. However, the Spanish Ministry of Justice has published a report of registered religious groups, churches, and denominations: *Guía de Entidades Religiosas de España (Iglesias, Confesiones y Comunidades Minoritarias)* (Madrid: Ministerio de Justicia, Secretaría General Técnica, 1998).

7. Natan Lerner, *Group Rights and Discrimination in International Law* (Dordrecht: Nijhoff, 1991), 75. Minorities are nondenominative groups, small in number in the context of the whole population, with their own religious, ethnic, or linguistic features that are different from the majority of the population and with a sense of solidarity that serves to preserve their own identities.

8. Francisco Azcona Sanmartín, "El Empuje de un Catolicismo más Auténtico," in *Alfa & Omega* (Madrid: F. San Agustín), Feb. 22, 1997, 3. The following data of religious affiliation of the adult Spanish population are from an unofficial poll of Cires: Affirms her/his religion is Catholic: 88.1% in 1990; 89.3% in 1991; 91.1% in 1992; 91.5% in 1993; 91.2% in 1994; 90.7% in 1995; 90.3% in 1996. Declares his/her religion is other than Catholic: 1.23% in 1990; 1.09% in 1991; 0.98% in 1992; 1.34% in 1993; 1.36% in 1994; 1.7% in 1995; 1.8% in 1996. Declares no religion: 9.73% in 1990; 8.63% in 1991; 7.38% in 1992; 7.11% in 1993; 7.43% in 1994; 7.64% in 1995; 7.83% in 1996.

9. Claudio Sánchez-Albornoz, *España: Un Enigma Histórico* (Barcelona: Edhasa, 1991), 2:563.

10. Artículo 2 de la Ley de los Principios del Movimiento Nacional, 17 de Mayo de 1958, reprinted in Jorge de Esteban, ed., *Las Constituciones de España* (Madrid: Taurus, 1981). English translations are not official. The Spanish language version of this provision is *La Nación española considera como timbre de honor el acatamiento a la Ley de Dios, según la doctrina de la Santa Iglesia Católica, Apostólica y Romana, única verdadera y fe inseparable de la conciencia nacional, que inspirará su legislación.*

11. Amadeo de Fuenmayor, *La Libertad Religiosa* (Pamplona: Eunsa, 1974). I agree with this author. Religious liberty proclaimed in the Second Vatican Council could be seen not as a drastic change in Catholic doctrine, but rather as the necessary consequence of the Catholic doctrine on human rights in the postwar era, applied to church-state relations.

12. For a comparative study of the Religious Liberty Law of 1967 and the Religious Liberty Law of 1980, see Iván C. Ibán, "Dos Regulaciones de la Libertad Religiosa en España," in *Tratado de Derecho Eclesiástico del Estado* (Pamplona: Eunsa, 1994), 379–427.

13. The echo of this argument in Spain appeared in an interview reported in Pedro Lombardía, "Concordato Sí, Concordato No," in *Escritos de Derecho Canónico* (Pamplona: Eunsa, 1974), 3:423–46.

14. Pedro Lombardía, "Chiesa e Stato Nella Spagna Odierna," *Il Diritto Ecclesiastico* 84 (1973): 148–50.

15. Pedro Lombardía, "Opciones Políticas y Ciencia del Derecho Eclesiástico Español," in *Anuario de Derecho Eclesiástico* 1 (1985): 31.

16. Agustín Motilla, "Notas sobre Problemas Fundamentales del Derecho Eclesiástico Contemporáneo (en torno a la Concepción y Metodología de la Ciencia del Derecho Eclesiástico)," *Anuario de Derecho Eclesiástico del Estado* 5 (1989): 218–19.

17. Pedro Lombardía, "Los Acuerdos entre el Estado y las confesiones religiosas en el nuevo Derecho eclesiástico español," in *Escritos de Derecho Canónico y de Derecho Eclesiástico del Estado* (Pamplona: Eunsa, 1991), 481.

18. Instrument of Ratification, Dated 19 August 1976, of the Agreement of 28 July 1976 between the Holy See and the Spanish State (B. O. E., 1976, 230). Alberto de la Hera and Rosa M. Martínez de Codes, *Spanish Legislation on Religious Affairs* [hereinafter *Spanish Legislation*] (Madrid: Ministerio de Justicia, Centro de Publicaciones, 1998), 47–49.

19. "The Holy See and the Spanish Government, in view of the profound process of transformation experienced by the Spanish society in recent years concerning relations between the political community and religious faiths, and between the Catholic Church and the State, [and] taking into account that on its part Vatican Council II . . . asserted religious freedom as a right that should be recognized in society's legal code . . . deem it necessary to regulate by means of specific Agreements those subjects of common interest that, under the new circumstances arising after the signing of the Concordat of 27 August 1953, require new regulation." Instrument of Ratification, Dated 19 August 1976, of the Agreement of 28 July 1976 between the Holy See and the Spanish State, Preamble (B. O. E. 230, 1976). *Spanish Legislation*, 47.

20. The first article of the Fundamental Agreement provides:

1. The State of Israel, recalling its Declaration of Independence, affirms its continuing commitment to uphold and observe the human right to freedom of religion and conscience, as set forth in the Universal Declaration of Human Rights and in other international instruments to which it is party.

2. The Holy See, recalling the Declaration on Religious Freedom of the Second Vatican Ecumenical Council "Dignitatis Humanae," affirms the Catholic Church's commitment to uphold the human right to freedom of religion and conscience, as set forth in the Universal Declaration of Human Rights and in other international instruments to which it is a party. The Holy See wishes to affirm as well the Catholic Church's respect for other religions and their followers as solemnly stated by the Second Vatican Ecumenical Council in its Declaration on the Relation of Church to Non-Christian religions, "Nostra Aetate."

Fundamental Agreement between the Holy See and the State of Israel, Dec. 30, 1993, art. 1, Vatican-Isr., 33 I. L. M. 153, 154 (1994) [hereinafter Fundamental Agreement].

21. Natan Lerner, "The Holy See and Israel: Protecting Human Rights by Bilateral Agreements," *Anuario de Derecho Eclesiástico del Estado* 13 (1997): 145.

22. Shmuel Haddas, "Diplomatic Relations between the Holy See and the State of Israel," in *A Challenge Long Delayed: The Diplomatic Exchange between the Holy See and the State of Israel*, ed. Eugene J. Fisher and Leon Klenicki (New York: Anti-Defamation League, 1996), 29–32.

23. Lombardía, "Opciones Políticas y Ciencia del Derecho Eclesiástico Español," 34.

24. *Spanish Legislation,* 28. The Spanish text of Article 16 of the Constitution of 1978 reads as follows:

1. Se garantiza la libertad ideológica, religiosa y de culto de los individuos y las comunidades sin más limitación, en sus manifestaciones, que la necesaria para el mantenimiento del orden público protegido por la ley.

2. Nadie podrá ser obligado a declarar sobre su ideología, religión o creencias.

3. Ninguna confesión tendrá carácter estatal. Los poderes públicos tendrán en cuenta las creencias religiosas de la sociedad española y mantendrán las consiguientes relaciones de cooperación con la Iglesia Católica y las demás confesiones.

25. *Spanish Legislation,* 27. Article 14 of the Constitution of 1978 provides: "Spaniards are equal before the law and may not in any way be discriminated against on account of birth, race, sex, religion, opinion or any other condition or personal or social circumstances" (Spanish text: Los españoles son iguales ante la ley, sin que pueda prevalecer discriminación alguna por razón de nacimiento, raza, sexo, religión, opinión o cualquier otra condición o circunstancia personal o social).

26. *Spanish Legislation,* 26. Article 9(2) of the Constitution of 1978 provides: "It is incumbent upon the public authorities to promote conditions which ensure that the freedom and equility of individuals and of the groups to which they belong may be real and effective, to remove the obstacles which prevent or hinder their full enjoyment, and to facilitate participation of all citizens in political, economic, cultural and social life" (Spanish text: Corresponde a los poderes públicos promover las condiciones para que la libertad y la igualdad del individuo y de los grupos en que se integra sean reales y efectivas; remover los obstáculos que impidan o dificulten su plenitud y facilitar la participación de todos los ciudadanos en la vida política, económica, cultural y social).

27. *Spanish Legislation,* 26. Article 10(2) of the Constitution of 1978 provides: "The rules relating to the fundamental rights and liberties recognized by the Constitution shall be interpreted in conformity with the Universal Declaration of Human Rights and the international treaties and agreements thereon ratified by Spain" (Spanish text: Las normas relativas a los derechos fundamentales y a las libertades que la Constitución reconoce se interpretarán de conformidad con la Declaración Universal de Derechos Humanos y los tratados y acuerdos internacionales sobre las materias ratificados por España).

28. *Spanish Legislation,* 30. Article 27(3) of the Constitution of 1978 provides: "The public authorities guarantee the right of parents to ensure that their children receive religious and moral instruction that is in accordance with their own convictions" (Spanish text: Los poderes públicos garantizan el derecho que asiste a los padres para que sus hijos reciban la formación religiosa y moral que esté de acuerdo con sus propias convicciones).

29. *Spanish Legislation,* 31. Article 32 of the Constitution of 1978 provides: "1. Men and women are entitled to marry on a basis of full legal equality. 2. The law shall regulate

the forms of marriage, the age at which it may be entered into and the required capacity therefor, the rights and duties of the spouses, the grounds for separation and dissolution, and the consequences thereof" (Spanish text: 1. El hombre y la mujer tienen derecho a contraer matrimonio con plena igualdad jurídica. 2. La ley regulará las formas de matrimonio, la edad y capacidad para contraerlo, los derechos y deberes de los cónyuges, las causas de separación y disolución y sus efectos).

30.  Lombardía, "Opciones Políticas y Ciencia del Derecho Eclesiástico Español," 16.

31.  Pedro-Juan Viladrich, "Los Principios Informadores del Derecho Eclesiástico Español," *Derecho Eclesiástico del Estado Español*, 2d ed. (Pamplona: Eunsa, 1983), 169–261.

32.  Durham, "Perspectives on Religious Liberty: A Comparative Framework," 21.

33.  Silvio Ferrari, "The New Wine and the Old Cask: Tolerance, Religion and the Law in Contemporary Europe," *Ratio Iuris* 10 (1997): 77–78.

34.  Javier Martínez-Torrón and Rafael Navarro-Valls, "The Protection of Religious Freedom in the System of the European Convention on Human Rights," *Helsinki Monitor* 9, no. 3 (1998): 25–37.

35.  General Act 7/1980 of 5 July of Religious Liberty (B. O. E., 1980, 177). *Spanish Legislation*, 41–46.

36.  Ibid., Article 5. See also Royal Decree 142/1981, Dated 9 January, concerning the Organization and Functioning of the Registry of Religious Entities (B. O. E., 1981, 27). *Spanish Legislation*, 123–26.

37.  See Spanish Constitutional Court Decision of February 15, 2001, STC 46/2001, asserting that the Ministry of Justice cannot deny registration to the Unification Church on the basis inter alia of foreign reports concerning Unification Church illegal activities in other countries.

38.  Article 8, General Act 7/1980 of 5 July of Religious Liberty (B. O. E., 1980, 177): "An Advisory Committee on Freedom of Religion is created in the Ministry of Justice whose membership, which shall be stable, shall be divided equally between the representatives of the Central Government and of the corresponding Churches, Faiths and Religious Communities or their Federations including, in any case, those that have a long-established influence in Spain, with the participation as well of persons of renowned competence whose counsel is considered to be of interest in matters related to this Act." *Spanish Legislation*, 44.

39.  Article 7(1), General Act 7/1980 of 5 July of Religious Liberty (B. O. E., 1980, 177): "The State, taking into account the religious beliefs existing in Spanish society, shall establish, as appropriate, cooperation agreements or conventions with the Churches, Faiths or Religious Communities enrolled in the Registry where warranted by their traditional acceptance in Spanish society, due to their area of influence or number of followers." *Spanish Legislation*, 44.

40.  For details concerning the nature of the agreements, see Agustín Motilla, "Algunas consideraciones en torno a la Naturaleza Jurídica y Eficacia Normativa de los Acuerdos Aprobados según el Artículo 7 de la Ley Orgánica de Libertad Religiosa," *Anuario de Derecho Eclesiástico del Estado* 10 (1994): 345–68.

41. For many scholars, however, the four 1979 agreements, along with the 1976 agreement, could be understood as a whole concordat. See Pedro Lombardía and Juan Fornés, "Las Fuentes del Derecho Eclesiástico Español," in *Tratado de Derecho Eclesiástico del Estado* (Pamplona: Eunsa, 1994), 321–76.

42. Instrument of Ratification, Dated 4 December 1979, of the Agreement of 3 January 1979 between the Spanish Government and the Holy See concerning Legal Affairs (B. O. E., 1979, 300). *Spanish Legislation*, 51–55.

43. Instrument of Ratification, Dated 4 December 1979, of the Agreement of 3 January 1979 between the Spanish Government and the Holy See concerning Economic Affairs (B. O. E., 1979, 300). *Spanish Legislation*, 63–67.

44. Instrument of Ratification, Dated 4 December 1979, of the Agreement of 3 January 1979 between the Spanish Government and the Holy See concerning Education and Cultural Affairs (B. O. E., 1979, 300). *Spanish Legislation*, 57–62.

45. Instrument of Ratification, Dated 4 December 1979, of the Agreement of 3 January 1979 between the Holy See and the Spanish Government concerning Religious Attendance of the Armed Forces and Military Service of Clergymen and Members of Religious Orders (B. O. E., 1979, 300). *Spanish Legislation*, 69–74.

46. Law 24/1992, of 10 November, Approving the Agreement of Cooperation between the Spanish Government and the Federation of Evangelical Entities of Spain (B. O. E., 1992, 272). *Spanish Legislation*, 75–85.

47. Law 25/1992, of 10 November, Approving the Agreement of Cooperation between the Spanish Government and the Jewish Communities of Spain (B. O. E., 1992, 272). *Spanish Legislation*, 87–99.

48. Law 26/1992, of 10 November, Approving the Agreement of Cooperation between the Spanish Government and the Islamic Commission of Spain (B. O. E., 1992, 272). *Spanish Legislation*, 101–13.

49. See Agustín Motilla, "Fuentes Pacticias del Derecho Eclesiástico Español," *Anuario de Derecho Eclesiástico del Estado* 3 (1987): 188.

50. "Orden de 24 de noviembre de 1993 por la que se dispone la publicación del Acuerdo sobre Asistencia religiosa católica en los establecimientos penitenciarios" (B. O. E., 1993, 298), reported in Antonio Molina and Maria Elena Olmos, *Legislación Eclesiástica*, 12th ed. (Madrid: Civitas, 2000), 272–76. "Orden de 20 de diciembre de 1985 por la que se dispone la publicación del Acuerdo sobre asistencia religiosa católica en centros hospitalarios públicos" (B. O. E., 1985, 305), reported in ibid., 234–37.

51. Rafael Navarro-Valls, "Los Estados Frente a la Iglesia," *Anuario de Derecho Eclesiástico del Estado* 9 (1993): 43–51.

52. Asher Maoz, "Religious Human Rights in the State of Israel," in *Religious Human Rights in Global Perspective: Legal Perspectives,* ed. Johan D. van der Vyver & John Witte (The Hague: Martinus Nijhoff Publishers, 1996), 349.

53. Yaffa Zilbershatz, "Highlighting Constitutional Changes in the Israeli Legal System," *Justice,* December 1995, 28–32.

54. Ariel Rosen-Zvi, "Freedom of Religion: The Israeli Experience," *Zeitschrift für ausländisches öffentliches Recht und Völkerrecht* 46/2 (1986): 215.

55. Antonio Vitale, *Corso di Diritto Ecclesiastico: Ordinamento Giuridico e Interessi Religiosi*, 6th ed. (Milano: Giuffrè, 1992), 158.

56. Article 3, para. 3: "Concerning Catholic legal personality in canon law the Holy See and the State of Israel will negotiate on giving it full effect in Israeli law, following a report from a joint subcommission of experts." Fundamental Agreement, 33 I. L. M. 153, 155 (1994).

57. Article 10, para. 2(b): "For the purpose of the said negotiations, the permanent bilateral working commission will appoint one or more bilateral subcommissions of experts to study the issues and make proposals." Fundamental Agreement, 33 I. L. M. 153, 157 (1994).

58. Indeed, the Fundamental Agreement is itself a result of the Permanent Bilateral Working Commission created on July 1992. See Rafael Palomino, "El Acuerdo Fundamental entre la Santa Sede y el Estado de Israel," *Anuario de Derecho Eclesiástico del Estado* 11 (1995): 353–55.

59. Article 5(2), General Act 7/1980 of 5 July of Religious Liberty (B. O. E., 1980, 177): "Registration shall be granted by virtue of an application together with an authentic document containing notice of the foundation or establishment of the organization in Spain, declaration of religious purpose, denomination, and other particulars of identity, rules of procedure, and representative bodies, including such body's power and requisites for valid designation thereof." *Spanish Legislation*, 43.

60. *Spanish Legislation*, 42–43.

61. Gloria Morán, "The Legal Status of Religious Minorities in Spain," *Journal of Church and State* 36 (1994): 579.

62. Silvio Ferrari, "State and Church in Italy," in *State and Church in the European Union*, ed. Gerhard Robbers (Baden-Baden: Nomos Verlagsgesellschaft, 1996), 173.

63. Kent Greenawalt, "Religion as a Concept in Constitutional Law," *California Law Review* 72 (1984): 755–57; Stangley Ingber, "Religion or Ideology: A Needed Clarification of the Religion Clauses," *Stanford Law Review* 41 (1989): 234.

64. "The Church is free to establish its own organization. In particular, it may create, modify, or suppress dioceses, parishes and other territorial circumscriptions, which shall be considered as having legal personality under State law at the time they acquire legality under canon law, and this is made known to the State's competent agencies." Article 1(2), Instrument of Ratification, Dated 4 December 1979, of the Agreement of 3 January 1979 between the Spanish Government and the Holy See concerning Legal Affairs (B. O. E., 1979, 300). *Spanish Legislation*, 51.

65. "The State recognizes the civil legal nature of the Spanish Conference of Bishops, in accordance with the Statutes approved by the Holy See." Article 1(3), Instrument of Ratification, Dated 4 December 1979, of the Agreement of 3 January 1979 between the Spanish Government and the Holy See concerning Legal Affairs (B. O. E., 1979, 300). *Spanish Legislation*, 52.

66. *Acta Apostolicae Sedis* (1999): 490–574. R. Palomino, "L'Accordo sulla personalità giuridica tra Israele e la Santa Sede," *Quaderni di Diritto e Politica Ecclesiastica* no. 2 (1998): 419–27.

67.  See J. Martín de Agar, *Raccolta di Concordati* (1950–1999) (Città del Vaticano: Librería Editrice Vaticana, 2000), 543–48.

68.  José María González del Valle, "Régimen Económico, Patrimonial y Fiscal," in *Derecho Eclesiástico del Estado Español*, 2d ed. (Pamplona: Eunsa, 1983), 265.

69.  "The Catholic Church declares its intention of obtaining sufficient resources for its needs of its own accord. Once this has been achieved, both parties shall agree to substitute the system of financial collaboration described in the preceding paragraphs of this article, in other areas and by other means of economic collaboration between the Catholic Church and the State." Article 2(5), Instrument of Ratification, Dated 4 December 1979, of the Agreement of 3 January 1979 between the Spanish Government and the Holy See concerning Economic Affairs (B. O. E., 1979, 300). *Spanish Legislation*, 64.

70.  Asher Maoz, "Religious Human Rights in the State of Israel," 372–73.

71.  Ibid., 385.

# 6

## THE POSITION OF
## THE CATHOLIC CHURCH
## REGARDING CONCORDATS
## FROM A DOCTRINAL AND
## PRAGMATIC PERSPECTIVE

*Roland Minnerath*

In the last thirty years concordats, conventions, or agreements between states and the Holy See, against all predictions, have increased in number and variety of types.[1] The ongoing practice of signing concordats witnesses the legal nature of the Catholic Church in its relationship with states, and the common principles it shares with secular powers.[2] Currently the word *concordat* is used for encompassing covenants dealing possibly with all aspects of church life. But those are rare today. The Holy See prefers more concise instruments dealing with specific questions, which are easier to elaborate and eventually to modify. They may be called conventions, agreements, *modus vivendi*, or protocols. But whatever the designation—from now on the word *concordat* will be used as a generic term for any kind of international agreement with the Holy See—these instruments have all the same legal force: they are treaties between two subjects of international law, each one sovereign in its own sphere, either spiritual or political. They are negotiated, signed, and ratified according to current international practice. Under the regime of the League of Nations some concordats were even registered in the *Record Book of International Treaties* in Geneva.[3]

The first element of doctrine inherent in concordats is precisely that the Catholic Church through the Holy See, understood as the organ of its supreme government, is qualified as a subject enjoying sovereignty equal to the state. The history of concordats is parallel to the history of the reappropriation of the sovereignty of the Church in her internal affairs. Not without reason was the first concordat ever, that of Worms in 1122, negotiated at the end of the long-lasting struggle for free investitures in the medieval church, thanks to the Gregorian Reform. Only where two subjects of equal legal capacity decide to settle their common interests is a concordat possible.

Agreements entered into between a state and a national conference of bishops or other national church authorities are not concordats. They are internal settlements according to state law. With concordats we have two subjects of independent primary or original legal systems which decide to conclude a specific covenant. This feature of the Catholic Church is unique among religious communities in world history. It is the result of a specific development of the Catholic Church in the West, where papacy was recognized as the supreme authority of the Church over political, national, and cultural borders. It also results from the self-understanding of the Catholic Church, different from the Byzantine or Protestant model, which steadily defended through the second millennium the principle of its inner autonomy with respect to the control of secular law and political power. From that time on the relationship between church and state was conceived as one of distinction between two orders and at the same time of cooperation between both.

Concordats implicitly mean that religion as such on the one hand, and the community of faithful on the other, cannot be treated as purely private issues. If church and state must be distinguished in their organization, legal structures, and aims, they cannot ignore each other. Religion is not a matter of pure individual conscience.[4] By its very nature it implies community, organized structure, and social visibility. As such the political community or state cannot but be interested in it. State and church must be legally separated. But in society, all communities, religious, philosophical, or whatever, coexist in mutual respect. As such the state has the responsibility to ensure that they behave according to law and that public order is preserved.

Obviously, the relationship of both powers, spiritual and temporal, shifted continuously according to circumstances. In the Catholic experience, the supreme spiritual authority, however, never claimed to absorb the political domain, even in the two-swords theory of Boniface VIII. The political authority also did not dare to exercise the spiritual direction of the whole church as in Byzantine "cesaropapistic" theory and practice. "The emperor is in the Church," said Saint Ambrose in the fourth century, "not over the Church," and this statement remained a leading principle of Catholic understanding.

After the rise of national states and the period of absolute monarchies, until 1914, it was not unusual that concordats signed with Catholic sovereigns intended to limit the inner autonomy of the Church. Most monarchs wanted to appoint their bishops themselves and prohibited them from having any free contact with the Roman Curia. This was the case of the concordat of 1516 between the pope and the king of France, which was in force until the revolution. Still worse for the independence of the Church were concordats with Spain (1753) and Portugal (1857), by which the pope had to give up all his ecclesiastical jurisdiction to the monarchs in Latin America and India. Even after the independence of Latin American states, the concordats signed with most of them between 1851 and 1887 maintained the so-called right of *padronado*, exercised by the new republics.[5]

Induced by the control of the state on inner-church affairs, a new doctrine emerged in the eighteenth century among the lawyers and jurists of Würzburg, Germany. They developed the concept that the church, like the state, is a "perfect society." This expression, often misunderstood, has no moral or theological connotation.[6] It only meant that church and state, each one in its own sphere, spiritual and temporal, enjoy all the means needed to achieve their respective aims, including a legal system which is not derived one from the other. Through this doctrine the visibility and the social aspect of the church were highlighted. With the help of this doctrine, the Catholic Church endeavored to win back those original rights which the absolutist regimes had confiscated during the former centuries.

In many ways the French Concordat signed in 1801 between Pius VII and Napoleon Bonaparte extended the Gallican ideology of the former royal concordat of 1516, as the state maintained its control over the Church by continuing to appoint bishops and prohibiting free communication with Rome. The only important innovation was a new understanding of the state in relation to the Church. Catholic faith was no longer the official religion of the state, but that of the majority of its citizens. State law also introduced new concepts as it granted the Lutheran, Reformed, and Jewish minority religious communities equal legal recognition and rights.[7]

Between 1850 and 1960, the doctrine of the two perfect societies became official in concordatarian negotiations with most so-called Catholic states.[8] The Church considered that it had to win back its freedom by directly confronting its rights with those of the modern state. There was no question of religious freedom of the individual, but only corporate freedom of the Church. Thus, the doctrine elaborated a whole set of principles based on natural law which helped to clearly establish the respective competencies of spiritual and temporal power. Competencies were drawn according to the final aim of both societies: the temporal aim of peace and justice among citizens was subordinated to the spiritual aim of leading believers to eternal life.

The Church claimed not only to be recognized in its structures and institutions, for example, dioceses, parishes, seminaries, and schools, but it also concluded that it had a primary right to legislate, for instance, on marriage and religious education of Catholics. As the same men and women were both citizens and believers, the state with a Catholic majority was supposed to follow the social and moral teachings of the Church and eventually tolerate minority religions but not grant them the same rights.[9] These theories were not unusual in other confessional backgrounds in the nineteenth century, when states with established churches prohibited the very existence of minorities on their soil.

From World War I to the Second Vatican Council (1962–1965) the doctrine of the two perfect societies began to bring some fruits. The concordats of Pius XI and Pius XII are among the most accurately elaborated treaties of the kind. Most of them have survived the war, like the concordats with Germany (1933) and Austria (1933) that are still in force without any change. The Italian Concordat of 1929 and the Spanish one of 1953 belong also to that period.

Most of these concordats had been eagerly desired by both parties. With Italy, the settlement of the "Roman question" had been desired by the popes ever since 1870. The compromise reached in 1929 was satisfactory for both sides, as the concordat was signed together with the Lateran Treaty creating the Vatican state and giving to the Holy See the territorial independence it needed to guarantee its specific sovereignty in church matters.

It has often been said that the Church signed the Reich Concordat of 1933 under the pressure of the Nazi regime.[10] Under the circumstances there was no other reasonable means to try to safeguard the corporate rights of Catholics in the area of youth education and associations, as well as religious teaching. One must not forget that concordats had already been signed with many of the Länder of the Weimar Republic: Bavaria (1924), Prussia (1929), and Baden (1932).

The Second Vatican Council developed Catholic doctrine on social issues. At the same time the culture of human rights, spreading worldwide since the end of World War II, was given full consideration in papal documents such as the encyclical *Pacem in Terris* (1963). Two documents of that council would have a deep impact on principles regulating church-state relations. These are the constitution *Gaudium et Spes* on the Church and the world, and the declaration *Dignitatis Humanae* on religious freedom. The latter appeared as a revolution of Copernican dimension in respect to the previous theory of the "two perfect societies." In fact, the council shifted from the traditional approach of the corporate right of the Catholic

Church to the basic right of each human person to have or not to have a religion, to exercise it privately and publicly under legal guarantees.

The state was now meant to be neutral in questions of religion. Its specific duty was to effectively promote the right to religious freedom by protecting the rights of others and safeguarding public order, public health, and public morality. The state would not identify itself with a given religion. Nevertheless, it was admitted that a religion having historical links with a people could receive special legal protection, under the condition that the fundamental rights of all other communities would be recognized.[11]

It is important to notice that the Church from that time on implicitly wished to deal with states governed according to the rule of law. This implies that a state does not place itself above citizens, but rather acts at the service of their fundamental rights and tries to promote the common good, identified through the democratic process. Promoting the freedom of the Church was no longer understood as winning recognition from the political power, but rather such freedom was enshrined in the very concept of the dignity of each human being. Therefore, the new approach of the Church converged in a way with the international instruments elaborated since 1948, where freedom of religion is based on an individual right, while the corporate rights of communities are considered to be derived from the rights of individuals to enter into community with others for worship, teaching, and living their faith. It is precisely in the field of the corporate right of the Church as a community that concordats fill a gap.

Concordats in the post–Vatican II era until now can no more be misused to justify state jurisdiction over religious matters. Now concordats are concluded with constitutional states. They do not imply privileges for Catholics. Since the Spanish Agreement of 1976, the habit has been introduced to dedicate the preambles to the statements of both parties. Often, doctrinal principles are enunciated in these preambles. The Spanish Agreement clearly referred to Vatican II as it stressed that "fundamental principles [for the] relations between the political community and the Church are the mutual independence of both parties in their own field and a healthy collaboration between both." It also recalled the double approach of Vatican II toward religious freedom, which is at the same time individual, as set forth in paragraphs 2 and 13 of *Dignitatis Humanae,* and corporate, remembering that "the freedom of the Church is the fundamental principle of the relations between church and public authorities and the whole civil order," as stated in *Gaudium et Spes* in paragraph 76, 3.

The Italian Concordat of 1984 recalls, on the side of the Church, the changes introduced with the doctrine of religious freedom, and, on the part of the state, the principles of the Constitution of 1947. The Italian Concordat gives a concise doctrinal definition in Article 1: "Church and state are each in its own realm independent and sovereign." This wording, which fits perfectly with Catholic doctrine, is actually drawn from Article 7 of the Constitution. It will be repeated in many concordats after 1984.[12] The mutual independence of both partners is now the key concept of concordatarian law. Thus the Italian state no longer automatically recognizes the effects of canonical marriage and judgments of ecclesiastical courts, as in 1929, but preserves its right to judge their conformity with civil law. Religious teaching is offered at school, but pupils or their parents may freely choose if they wish to avail themselves of it. An additional agreement on financial questions sealed the mode in which the state collaborates in the financing of the Catholic Church. In the Polish and the Israeli preambles, specific considerations appear. The first stresses the historical moment of the fall of communism and the significance of the pontificate of Pope John Paul II for the nation. The Israeli preamble underlines the singular character of the Holy Land for both partners and the "unique nature of the relationship between the Catholic Church and the Jewish people."

A classification of the post–Vatican II concordats could be suggested. Significant steps have been undertaken by the Holy See with countries which named Catholicism as the state religion in their constitutions or concordats, such as Spain, Italy, Colombia, Argentina, Monaco, Peru, and Malta. The mention of state religion disappeared from all new concordats signed after 1964. It was the wish of the Holy See to avoid these statements, which looked like privileges and were incompatible with the doctrine of the confessional neutrality of the state.

At the same time the Holy See strongly expressed its desire to review those concordats which still allowed to secular powers specific ecclesiastical rights like the appointment of bishops. This objective was achieved with Argentina abolishing the secular right of patronage in 1966, Spain in 1976, Monaco in 1981, and Haiti and Italy in 1984. Also, San Marino renounced its policy of intervening in ecclesiastical appointments in 1992. While Franco refused in 1967 to renounce unilaterally his right of intervention in the appointment of bishops, the Haitian president decided to do so in 1984. Only the right to object, for general political reasons, to the appointment of bishops was conceded to governments. As for Spain, political changes also introduced changes in the legal treatment of minority religions.

The concordats of the 1930s and 1940s with Germany, Austria, and Portugal were maintained thanks to accommodations and readjustments. In Germany, several partial agreements have been signed since 1960 with the different Länder. It was a requirement of the German Concordat of 1933 and the Prussian Concordat of 1929 that any revision of the diocesan circumscriptions needed the agreement of the respective governments. So the important modification introduced in 1994 with the creation of two new ecclesiastical provinces and three new dioceses was carried out with appropriate conventions with the Länder involved. Moreover, new general conventions were signed between 1994 and 1998 with Länder like Thüringen, Saxen, Mecklenburg-Vorpommern, and Saxen-Anhalt. In Portugal, Article 24 of the 1940 concordat prohibiting Catholics who had contracted canonical marriage from resorting to the civil law of divorce was abolished in 1975.[13]

Only the new Colombian Concordat of 1973 did not follow the general evolution. It maintained a broader state control over the appointment of bishops and some judicial privileges for the clergy. The constitutional court declared unconstitutional some articles of the concordat. Finally, an agreement on the revision of the concordat of 1973 was reached in 1992, recognizing with more consequence the autonomy of each partner in its own sphere.

In the past, it was rare for non-Catholic countries to sign concordats with the Holy See. Diplomatic relations with non-Catholic governments were first established in 1806 with Prussia, in 1848 with the United States (until 1868), in 1894 with Russia, and even with China after 1880. In the nineteenth century, the first concordats ever signed with a non-Catholic state, namely, Orthodox Russia in 1847, 1882, and 1907, were aimed at protecting the Polish Catholic population of the empire. There were also concordats with Montenegro in 1886 and Serbia in 1914, both Orthodox countries, which had the goal of protecting the rights of the Catholic minorities as requested by the Congress of Berlin in 1878. Under Pius XI, Lutheran Prussia in 1929 and the kingdom of Yugoslavia in 1935 drew up concordats. While the former is still in force over seventy years after the dissolution of Prussia, the latter never reached the step of ratification because of the opposition of the Orthodox hierarchy. It never was applied, although bilateral local agreements between the state and the Orthodox, Protestant, Muslim, and Jewish communities were in force.

During the communist era, only two Eastern European states with strong Catholic populations concluded agreements with the Holy See: Hungary concluded a secret partial accord in 1964, and Yugoslavia concluded a protocol in 1966. These emergency agreements, a result of the so-called "Ostpolitik" of the "little steps" undertaken during the Cold War, at least allowed Catholics to have some religious life and to survive in a hostile environment.[14] Moreover, under political pressure, an agreement without international character was signed in 1957 by the Polish government and the primate acting in the name of the Polish bishops.

A total innovation was the *modus vivendi* negotiated with Tunisia in 1964. Tunisia is, according to its constitution, a country with Islam as the state religion, although one of the most moderate ones. This agreement created the conditions for the Catholic minority, most of them foreigners, to live in Tunisia in harmony with other citizens. The norm referred to in Article 1 is exclusively the Tunisian Constitution's guarantee of freedom of conscience and religion.

With Morocco, an unusual kind of agreement was reached in 1983–84. Formally, it consists of an exchange of letters between the pope and the king. The human right to religious freedom is not invoked, but the king grants freedom of religion to Catholics in virtue of "the spirit of extreme tolerance which characterizes Islam." Here we face a different political philosophy, unparalleled in other concordats, and an exception to international standards and Catholic principles as well. In this agreement pragmatism precedes doctrine, as the aim obtained seems more desirable than its doctrinal justification.

The agreement with the State of Israel carefully insists on common international standards as the reference for religious freedom and cooperation between church and state.[15] The agreement with Israel is a unique case in which the Holy See stresses its commitment to comply with international instruments to which it is a party. Implicitly meant are the Convention on the Elimination of All Forms of Racial Discrimination to which it acceded in 1969, and the Declaration on the Elimination of All Forms of Intolerance and of Discrimination Based on Religion or Belief of 1981. Also unique is Article 2, in which both partners commit themselves to combat anti-Semitism. Upon opening negotiations in 1992 with the Holy See, Israel's priority was the establishment of diplomatic relations, while the Holy See preferred to solve bilateral problems. Israel had at that time no experience dealing with the Holy See, its legal nature, and its claim to enjoy a proper legal independence in its own sphere. The fundamental principle that "both are free in the exercise of their respective rights and powers" was finally admitted after long negotiating. The Legal Personality Agreement pursuant to Article 3 of the Fundamental Agreement was signed in November 1997. It assures full effect in Israeli law to the legal personality of the Catholic Church and its local institutions.

A further category of concordats could be identified, namely, those concluded after Vatican II with states having no concordatarian tradition or resuming such a tradition after the end of communist rule.[16] This is presently the case with respect to Malta (1985–1995), Poland (1993), San Marino (1898, 1992), Croatia (1996–1998), Hungary (1990–1997), Estonia (1998), Lithuania (2000), Latvia (2000), and Slovakia (2000). An interesting parallel could be drawn between Central Europe after World War I and after 1990, when nearly all new states created out of the central empires established diplomatic relations with the Holy See, for example Latvia in 1922, Poland in 1925, Lithuania in 1927, Czechoslovakia in 1927, and Yugoslavia in 1935.

Poland and Croatia recall in their concordats that they have a Catholic majority population. They both strongly underline the "historic and present role" of the Church in educating the people and promoting their culture. Coming from former communist regimes, they wish to repair some injustices of the past. The main problems at stake are the legal recognition of the Catholic Church and its institutions, and the restitution of confiscated properties. It is interesting to note, as it was recently confirmed by a symposium held in Budapest in March 1997, that all Central and Eastern European states contemplate cooperation with the churches in financing arrangements.[17] This is a remarkable achievement due in part to the new Italian model set forth by the revision of 1984. Again political changes and the legal settlement of religious rights are related.

Difficulties were raised at the moment of ratifying the Polish Concordat and the third Maltese Agreement. The respective oppositions in parliaments thought the autonomy of the state was not fully respected in some specific items. In Malta, two agreements, one on religious education in schools and the other on church properties, were signed in 1991 and ratified in 1993. A third one on marriage was blocked for two years by the opposition before finally being ratified in Parliament. The objection was against the automatic equivalence of canonical marriage and civil effects. In Poland, similar objections were raised, arguing that the rights assured to the Church in canonical marriages and school education conflict with state competencies. The objection suggests that the fundamental criteria of mutual independence of both legal orders should be in all ways carefully respected.

Particularly significant is the Basic Agreement negotiated with the Palestine Liberation Organization and signed in 2000. In many aspects it is parallel to the Fundamental Agreement with Israel. Among other similarities, it mentions the commitment of both parties to maintain and observe the regime of the Status Quo in the Christian Holy Places. It appears clearly that more and more states without a Catholic background are interested in signing conventions with the Holy See. Among those should be mentioned Gabon (1997), Kazakhstan (1998), and even a regional organization of states, namely, the Organization of African Unity (2000).

In conclusion, it should be remembered that concordats exist within the most diverse categories of church-state patterns, even systems of total separation like France, which has agreements running from 1801 through 1921 to 1974. Systems of separation with institutional cooperation like Germany and Austria have the strongest concordatarian tradition. In the Eastern European countries, the model of legal distinction with cooperation of church and state is being adopted. By establishing concordats with all types of states, common principles have arisen and are being enforced as conforming to the self-understanding of the Church and the demands of states under the rule of law. There is no question anymore of privileges, but strictly of human rights. Thus the international character of the Holy See indirectly confers to the parallel agreements concluded between states and other religious communities the support of an international treaty, as it is the first duty of the state to treat all its citizens equally.

## NOTES

An earlier version of this paper was delivered during the April 8, 1997, symposium at the Catholic University of America, Columbus School of Law.

1. For a recent collection of concordats and agreements see J.T. Martin de Agar, *Raccolta di concordati 1950–1999* (Vaticano: Libreria editrice vaticana, 2000); followed by J.T. Martin de Agar, *I condordati del 2000* (Vaticano: Libreria Editrice Vaticana, 2001). Former concordats are to be found in: A. Mercati, *Raccolta di concordati su materie ecclesiastiche tra la Santa Sede e le Aurotità civili,* vol. 1, 1108–1914; vol. 2, 1915–1954 (Vaticano: Tipografia Poliglotta Vaticana, 1919 & 1954). On the subject see R. Minnerath, *L'Eglise et les Etats concordataires, (1846–1978) La souveraineté spirituelle* (Paris: Cerf, 1983); J.B. d'Onorio, "Concordats et conventions post-conciliaires" in *Le Saint-Siège dans les relations internationals,* ed. J.B. d'Onorio (Paris: Cerf-Cujas, 1989), 193–246; "La diplomatie concordataire de Jean-Paul II" in *La diplomatie de Jean Paul II,* ed. J.B. d'Onorio (Paris: Cerf, 2000), 251–302; J.P. Durand, ed., "Quand le Saint-Siège signe des concordats," *Revue d'éthique et de théologie morale "Le Supplément"* 199 (1996): 7–146.

2. On the legal nature of the Catholic Church and the Holy See: H.H. Köck, *Die völkerrechtliche Stellung des Heiligen Stuhls* (Berlin: Duncker & Humbolt, 1975).

3. With reference to Article 18 of the League of Nations Covenant, the concordat with Latvia of May 30, 1922, was registered under Nr. 443 by the secretary general of the League of Nations. The Missionary Agreement between the Holy See and Colombia of May 5, 1928, was registered under Nr. 1808.

4. The community dimension of religion is recognized by international law: Universal Declaration of Human Rights (1948), Article 18; International Covenant on Civil and Political Rights (1966), Article 18.

5. See R. Minnerath, *L'Eglise et les Etats concordataires,* 281–92.

6. See. R. Minnerath, *Le droit de L'Eglise à la liberté. Du Syllabus à Vatican II* (Paris: Beauchesne, 1982), 19–80; and "Le droit public ecclésiastique. Une doctrine des relations de l'Eglise et de l'Etat," *Lumière et Vie* 37 (1988): 63–77.

7. On the modern period, see J. F. Maclear, ed., *Church and State in the Modern Age, A Documentary History* (New York, Oxford: Oxford University Press, 1995).

8. R. Minnerath, *L'Eglise et les Etats concordataires,* 57–63.

9. See R. Minnerath, *Le droit de L'Eglise à la liberté,* 81–119.

10. Cf. F. Margiotta-Broglio, "La politique concordataire du Vatican vis-à-vis des Etats totalitaires," *Relations internationales* 27 (1981): 319–42; F.J. Coppa, ed., *Controversial Concordats: The Vatican's Relations with Napoleon, Mussolini and Hitler* (Washington, D.C.: The Catholic University of America Press, 1999).

11. R. Minnerath, *Le droit de L'Eglise à la liberté,* 121–60; "La libertà dell'atto di fede" in *Il Concilio Vaticano II, Recezione e attualità alla luce del Giubileo,* ed. R. Fisichella (Torino: San Paolo, 2000), 631–37.

12. The Italian Revision Accord has been studied, for example, by G. Dalla Torre, ed., *La revisione de Concordato* (Città del Vaticano: Libreria Editrice Vaticana, 1985), and

R. Coppola, ed., *Atti del convegno italiano di studio sul nuovo Accordo tra Italia e Santa Sede* (Milano: Giuffrè, 1987).

13.  On church-state relations in the European Union, see A. Robbers, ed., *Staat und Kirche in der Europäischen Union* (Baden-Baden: Nomos, 1995).

14.  See H. Stehle, *Die Ostpolitik des Vatikans* (Bergisch Gladbach: Gustav Lübbe, 1983).

15.  See, for instance, F. Margiotta-Broglio, "Israel-Vatican: un accord historique entre espoirs et craintes," *Géopolitique* 45 (1994): 43–47; S. Ferrari, "L'Accordo Fondamentale tra S. Sede e Israele e le convenzioni post-conciliari tra Chiesa e Stati," in *Winfried Schulz in Memoriam*, ed. C. Mirabelli, vol. 1 (Frankfurt: Lang, 1999), 249–68.

16.  See O. Luchterhandt, *Die Neuordnung des Verhältnisses von Staat und Kirche in Mittel- und Osteuropa* (Münster: Aschendorff, 1995).

17.  Cf. Budapest Symposium, *The Role of the Churches in the Renewing Societies, Lectures and Documents, March 3–5, 1997* (Budapest: International Religious Liberty Association, European Section, 1998).

# 7

## THE HOLY SEE–PLO BASIC
## AGREEMENT IN LIGHT OF
## THE HOLY SEE–ISRAEL
## FUNDAMENTAL AGREEMENT

*Leonard Hammer*

### Introduction

While the Fundamental Agreement between Israel and the Holy See emerged following the peace process between Israel and the Palestinians, the peace process itself also created another important player that implicates the Holy See's interests in the Holy Land, namely, the Palestinian Authority (PA). Included within the limited capacity of the PA is responsibility over religious sites within the Palestinian Authority's civilian control. The Church of the Nativity located in Bethlehem is already subject to some form of PA authority. It is conceivable that the PA also will eventually assert sovereignty over other important sites, especially those located in East Jerusalem.[1] Furthermore, should a final peace plan between Israel and the PA include some form of partition of the Old City, then the PA also might be responsible for the Church of the Holy Sepulcher. Hence, the Holy See felt compelled to form some type of arrangement with the PA that protected the Holy See's interests, especially considering its previous unequivocal support for the creation of an independent Palestinian state.[2]

There also are broader issues that concern the Holy See that compel it to enter into an agreement with the PA. Treatment of Palestinian Christians both in the PA's area and beyond, and the possibility that the PA eventually might fall under Islamic rule,[3] are pressing concerns for the Holy See. Other issues concerning the Holy See that drive it to maintain some form of relationship with the PA are the decreasing Christian population in the Holy Land, the increasing sales of Church land, lack of unity among the local church institutions (thereby further decreasing the Holy See's influence), and the sociocultural gap between European-trained Church leaders and their Arabic believers.[4]

The Holy See therefore realized an important goal in entering into the Basic Agreement between the Holy See and the Palestinian Liberation Organization of 16 February 2000.[5] For the Holy See, it does not matter which party it is dealing with as long as its goal of maintaining some form of religious influence in the Middle East is being met. Recognizing the limited capacities of the PA however, the Holy See sought to narrow the scope of the Basic Agreement to areas pertaining to religious issues. Such a focused approach undergirds the Holy See's underlying pragmatic objectives to uphold a Christian presence in the Holy Land and entrench its foothold and control over the local Christian faithful.

From the PA's side, considering the general significance for an autonomous entity to enhance its foreign relations capacity, the ability to engage in foreign relations is a major concern for the Palestinian Authority. In striving towards legitimacy and eventual statehood, the Palestinian Authority attempts to assert its international relations ability by engaging in diplomatic meetings,[6] participating in international fora,[7] and expanding upon its limited treaty-making capacities.

The resultant document therefore merits consideration to determine the guarantees that the Holy See has received from the PA and how the Basic Agreement compares to the Fundamental Agreement between Israel and the Holy See. Additionally, recognizing the importance of the Israel–Holy See Fundamental Agreement and the possibility for potential overlap of rights and responsibilities among the three parties that could result from eventual land exchanges, one also must consider whether the Holy See overstepped its self-defined boundaries for nonintervention into Middle East affairs as agreed to in the Israel–Holy See agreement of 1993.[8] This chapter will also consider whether the Palestinian Authority has breached any understandings it may have had with Israel regarding its foreign relations capacity.

### The PA's Capacity for Foreign Relations

Regarding the Palestinian Authority, it is significant that initially the Palestinian Authority had no right to engage in foreign relations pursuant to the original 1992 Declaration of Principles between the PLO and Israel.[9] In the subsequent Cairo Agreement, Article IV(2)(a) continues with the prevention of any foreign relations, although Annex IX recognizes the possibility that the PLO will conduct negotiations with other states or international organizations for the benefit of the Palestinian Authority's economic viability and development of an infrastructure, as well as for cultural, scientific, and educational arrangements. The PA then can engage in cultural exchanges, ensure the maintenance of peace and safety for the benefit of the local population within its area of control, and uphold the general rights of its population.[10] Article IX(5) of the 1995 Interim Agreement extended the PLO's foreign relations power to include the West Bank, although the agreement clearly noted that the ability to conduct foreign relations is of limited capacity that does not accord the Palestinian Authority any sovereign, state-like status.[11]

Israel in essence had to acknowledge the reality that some form of intergovernmental contacts will and must take place to uphold the Palestinian Authority's existence and viability.[12] Note however that the agreements between Israel and the PLO state that the role of the PLO is to act "for the benefit of" the Palestinian Authority and not "on behalf of" the Palestinian Authority. The purpose of such language is to provide a more limited form of representation by the PLO due to Israel's contention that the Palestinian Authority does not have any intrinsic ability or authority to enter into international agreements. The foreign relations powers in the areas of economic development or cultural exchanges are more of a functional capacity accorded to the PLO to provide for intergovernmental arrangements with the Palestinian Authority, without according it the full capacity of a sovereign state.

One of the interesting factors regarding the arrangement between Israel and the PLO is that the understanding does provide the Palestinian Authority with the ability to maintain the classic elements of statehood. The Palestinian Authority controls a territory, a population, and has a government with limited foreign relations capacity. Yet the limited foreign relations capacity does not seem sufficient to accord the Palestinian Authority an elevated state status, such as to grant it state sovereign immunity. Rather, the foreign relations powers in the areas of economic development or cultural exchanges are more of a functional capacity accorded to the PLO to provide for intergovernmental arrangements with the Palestinian Authority,[13] without according it the full capacity of a sovereign state.[14] This is typical of an autonomous arrangement given the understanding of an autonomous entity as one that has not yet achieved independent statehood.[15]

That the PLO can however maintain some form of limited international relations with other states[16] merits further examination. In particular, it seems that the Palestinian Authority can engage in cultural exchanges,[17] ensure the maintenance of peace and safety for the benefit of the local population within its area of control, and uphold the general rights of its population.[18] Included within the limited foreign relations capacity is responsibility over religious sites within the Palestinian Authority's civilian control, given the transfer of power over these areas from Israel to the Palestinian Authority in the 1995 Interim Agreement. Hence *prima facie* the Basic Agreement does not appear to breach any understanding between the PLO and Israel since it pertains to religious interests of a segment of the PA's population that relate to cultural matters.

Nonetheless, certain provisions of the Basic Agreement merit further examination given the broad scope of the language and the clear deviation from religious or cultural themes. The agreement therefore will be examined to assess its significance for Israel and whether the agreement altered Israel's position vis-à-vis the Holy See or the PA.

### The Holy See–PLO Basic Agreement

The preamble to the Basic Agreement uses rather strong language in entrenching the interests of the Holy See within the PA's area of control. The preamble refers to the Holy See's strong ties to the Palestinian people and the desire for a peaceful solution of the Palestinian-Israel conflict "which would realize the inalienable national legitimate rights and aspirations of the Palestinian people" pursuant to, among other things, relevant United Nations and Security Council resolutions. The first paragraph of the preamble also refers to the status of each party. In particular, one is to consider the PLO as working for the benefit "and on behalf" of the Palestinian Authority, language that is directly conflicting with the Israel-PLO peace agreements. In essence, Israeli fears pertaining to the possible growth in stature of the Palestinian Authority, especially regarding foreign relations, have proved correct given that the PLO is serving a more executive foreign relations function for the Palestinian Authority by acting on its behalf and not only for its benefit.

The second paragraph of the preamble uses rather interesting language, deeming the Holy Land "a privileged space for inter-religious dialogue." Such language tends to solidify the Holy See's position within the Holy Land and provides groundwork for placing the Basic Agreement within a cultural and religious context rather than a formalized state-to-state agreement. Furthermore, it is possible that the Holy See's understanding of "dialogue" here includes the ability to proselytize.

In the following paragraphs, particularly the seventh paragraph, there is rather strong language regarding the fundamental importance of an equitable solution for Jerusalem "based on international resolutions" and, in a veiled reference to establishing Israeli settlements, that "unilateral decisions and actions altering the specific character and status of Jerusalem are morally and legally unacceptable." Indeed the paragraph goes on essentially to mirror the UN Security Council's initial plan to internationalize Jerusalem, a recommendation that is supported by the Holy See.[19] Similarly, the fifth preambulary paragraph reaffirms the need for a "just and comprehensive" peace, and the sixth paragraph calls for a peaceful solution "which would realize the inalienable national legitimate rights and aspirations of the Palestinian people" on the basis of international law and relevant UN and Security Council resolutions.

The preamble therefore could be understood as an attempt by the Holy See to involve itself with the Israel-PA peace process. Furthermore, the aforementioned paragraphs broaden the scope of the Basic Agreement by encroaching upon political matters that for the PA do not address cultural exchanges with the Holy See but relate to policy decisions regarding issues subject to negotiation. Indeed, the official Israeli Foreign Ministry reaction was to express great displeasure at what it considered to be an intervention into the Israeli-Palestinian negotiations. The preamble clearly supports the international position regarding Jerusalem, serving as a launching point for the Holy See and the PA to assert their political views rather than staying within the confines of the stated policy to address solely religious or cultural issues and, regarding the Holy See, to deal with the protection of Christian Holy Places.

It is important to recall that pursuant to the Fundamental Agreement between the Holy See and Israel, the Holy See had, in Article 11(2), "solemnly committed itself to remaining a stranger to all merely temporal conflicts." Article 11(1) of the Holy See–Israel agreement does provide the Holy See with the opportunity to act as a moral or spiritual representative for given issues, such as refugee problems or human rights violations, but the Holy See is not to get involved with secular issues. Indeed, the drafters of the Holy See–Israel Fundamental Agreement further refined Article 11 by noting that the neutral stance adopted by the Holy See applies to unsettled border conflicts and disputed territory, thereby clearly enunciating the boundaries for the Holy See's activities. The idea was based on a desire to keep the relationship between the Holy See and Israel neutral and not to become entangled with political issues. Hence the preamble to the Holy See–PLO Basic Agreement appears to violate such a commitment by delineating the principles and extent for the peace negotiations, by summarizing the political stance of the Holy See regarding certain issues like Jerusalem and by making statements that relate to secular, temporal issues.

Concerning the substantive articles of the Basic Agreement, Article 1(1) is significant simply because it recognizes the PLO's commitment to uphold Article 18 of the Universal Declaration of Human Rights and other international instruments regarding the right to freedom of religion and conscience. Similar language is used in the Holy See–Israel Fundamental Agreement,[20] save for the fact that Israel already is a party to the human rights instruments referred to in the article.

Given that the PLO is not a signatory to international human rights treaties, the reference to "other international instruments relative to its application" is presumably referring either to treaties that the PA eventually will sign or to the customary norms pertaining to the human right to freedom of religion and conscience. Such customary norms might apply to the Palestinian Authority because of its existence as a governmental authority over a particular territory. Such an application of human rights norms to the Palestinian Authority derives either from the passage of control over the Occupied Territories from the Israeli military to the PLO, which would include *inter alia* the right to freedom of religion and conscience subject to specific limitations, or because the Palestinian Authority effectively controls and governs an area whereby part of its responsibilities as the effective governing presence would include the application of various human rights norms.[21]

By contrast, Article 1(2) of the Basic Agreement only "affirms" the Holy See's commitment to uphold the right to freedom of religion, again similar operative language to that used in the Holy See–Israel Fundamental Agreement.[22] In this article, the Holy See seems to have adopted a strategy similar to that taken in its agreement with Israel. In the Holy See–Israel agreement, Israel took on a broader responsibility vis-à-vis its human rights obligation given that Israel is a party to a greater number of human rights treaties than the Holy See. Similarly, in the Holy See–PLO agreement, the Holy See is not bound to any specific human rights treaty since no reference is made to any particular treaty, unlike the PLO, which consented to the standards noted in the Universal Declaration.

It is noteworthy that PLO Chairman Yasser Arafat hesitated to sign the Basic Agreement because of its reference to freedom of conscience.[23] Apparently, the concern for Arafat was internal Islamic opposition due to the broad scope accorded by the right to other belief systems. He nevertheless consented to its inclusion when the Holy See noted that surrounding Arabic countries use such a formula and that it conforms to the human rights standards created by the United Nations.[24]

What might not have been explained to Chairman Arafat, and what could prove to be a future problem, is that the general Muslim opposition to the right to freedom of religion and conscience was not necessarily due to the existence or recognition of other forms of beliefs, such as another religious or even a conscientious belief. Rather, the problem centers on the ability to change one's belief, particularly when derived from a proselytizing religion. The relevance of this distinction is that out of all the human rights treaties dealing with the right to freedom of religion, the Universal Declaration of Human Rights is the most specific document that clearly upholds the right to change one's belief. Note that during the drafting of the international human rights treaties, some states pointed out a conflict with their internal laws if the right to freedom of religion also was to provide for a change of religion, especially when associated with missionaries and possible fraudulent changes of religion.[25] Other states objected to the right to change a belief, reasoning that it supported improper missionary work, caused greater long-term damage to society,[26] and that the broad provision for the right to freedom of religion already implies a right to change one's religion as well.[27] Because many Arabic states objected to the language of the Universal Declaration due to the inherent right to change one's religion, resulting in some countries abstaining from the final vote on this article in the General Assembly,[28] the drafters of the International Covenant on Civil and Political Rights attempted to replace the direct reference to the right to change one's religion or belief.[29] Indeed, the issue regarding the right to change a belief persisted until the end of the General Assembly's fifteenth session, when initially the phrase "to have a religion or belief of one's choice" was proposed and rejected as being too static, followed by the present language that provides for the right "to adopt" a religion or belief.

Hence it is possible to interpret the International Covenant on Civil and Political Rights as not providing a right to change one's religion when compared to the unequivocal language of the Universal Declaration.[30] It therefore is possible that Arafat's hesitation resulted from concerns regarding the ability to change one's religion, particularly due to proselytizing, but in the end the Palestinian Authority adopted the broader standards of the Universal Declaration.

The significance in this different application of standards is the effect it might have on the Holy See's ability to proselytize. Clearly the ability to proselytize is an important right for the Holy See, yet, similar to the Holy See–Israel Fundamental Agreement, there is no provision in the Basic Agreement with the PLO that pertains specifically to the issue of proselytizing. Furthermore, unlike the Holy See–Israel agreement, which refers to a host of other human rights from which one may derive the right to proselytize,[31] the Holy See–PLO agreement makes no further mention of free expression or other human rights associated with proselytizing. This could derive from the Holy See feeling comfortable relying on the standards of the Universal Declaration, in which there is no imposition of specific limitations on the freedom of religion or belief,[32] with the result that the Holy See arguably has free reign when asserting the ability to change a belief by way of proselytizing.[33]

Furthermore, the subsequent articles of the Basic Agreement outline the basis for implementing the human rights of each party to the agreement, such as to provide sufficient protection to the Holy See's rights and meet its specific policy goals. Hence although Article 2(1) relates to a rather general prohibition to prevent discrimination,[34] the remaining provisions go on to provide for specific rights of the Holy See within the areas controlled by the PA. The Holy See seems to have taken advantage of the PA's desire to enter into an agreement, and thereby enhance the PA's legitimacy, by drafting the rights provided in the remaining articles to the favor of the Holy See and its interests. For example, Article 3 upholds equality for all religious affiliations under Palestinian law, including freedom from discrimination due to religious affiliation. The agreement uses rather strong language ("including specifically") to entrench protection to the individual members of the Church located in the Palestinian Authority's territory or subject to the PA's control. This is supported by the inclusion of "affiliation, belief or practice" as grounds for preventing discrimination, again rather broad categories that include a host of church activities.

In a rather interesting contrast to the Holy See–Israel Fundamental Agreement, the agreement between the Holy See and the PLO refers to the protection of human and civil rights "of all citizens."[35] While the PA might have favored language that tends to legitimize its position as an independent sovereign, the language also limits the scope of application of the rights, such as not applying to overseas Christians engaged in a pilgrimage to the holy sites located in the PA's region of control. By contrast, the Holy See–Israel agreement uses a more general reference to "people"[36] regarding the rights surrounding the freedom of religion, thereby not limiting the rights being granted to a specific protected group whose definition is subject to the existing political powers of the state.[37]

Article 4 of the Basic Agreement entrenches the Status Quo regime for the Christian Holy Places. In particular, the Status Quo applies to the Church of the Nativity in Bethlehem, which is subject to PA control. Additional sites under the Status Quo that are important to the Holy See and that could eventually fall under the PA's control are two sites in East Jerusalem, the Tomb of the Virgin[38] and the Sanctuary of the Ascension,[39] as well as the Church of the Holy Sepulcher, located in the Old City of Jerusalem.

Clearly entrenching the Status Quo is an important element for the Holy See because of the uncertain future status of the PA and the form of government that will be instituted in the long term. Given Arafat's recognition of the Christians as an important potential ally both politically and economically, the current PA does not wish to alienate the Holy See in any way. Therefore, the PA has demonstrated a great deal of respect for the Status Quo, particularly in upholding its directives.

Nonetheless, the Status Quo regime is subject to constant change and evolution depending on the political powers that maintain sovereignty over the area. Under Israeli rule, for example, the right of due process and ability for free expression and freedom of religion have contributed to the capacity of the various religious bodies to attempt to institute changes to the Status Quo. A religious order may turn to the justice system or petition the government with a view towards defending its interests and upholding its right to freedom of religion.[40] Similarly, should the PA undergo a radical shift towards instituting a fundamentally Islamic state, it is possible that the Status Quo could be subject to alterations that would effect Christian interests in the holy sites.

The Holy See therefore desired a specific article in the Basic Agreement that would protect the Status Quo of the Christian Holy Places. Even with an internal political change of the controlling civilian authority, the substantive rights of the religious orders are largely determined by reference to the Status Quo. Hence the Status Quo is referred to as a "regime,"[41] indicating some form of normative status. No mention is made, however, of the other Christian sacred places that might be located in the PA's area. In the Holy See–Israel Fundamental Agreement, Israel pledged to continue its respect for such places,[42] again indicating the existence of some form of legal construct that served to uphold the rights of the Christians in Israel. It is interesting that no reference is made of such sacred places in the Holy See–PLO agreement.

Article 4 of the Basic Agreement also seems contrary to the broader approach adopted in the preamble regarding the status of Jerusalem and the desire to safeguard the regime of the Status Quo in "those Holy Places where it applies."[43] It is possible that the PA did not desire to refer to the Status Quo in the substantive provisions of the agreement because that could affect its bargaining position with Israel over Jerusalem. Yet the Holy See no doubt desired to entrench its own interests, such that the language of the article focuses on the Christian Holy Places without infringing any future claims by the PA to other areas under the Status Quo. The result is that the Holy See–Israel agreement evinces a stronger desire by Israel to ensure the prevention of any alterations to the Status Quo for the other religious interests to which it applies. Article 4(2) of the Holy See–Israel agreement therefore accords the Status Quo a normative preference over the other articles of the Fundamental Agreement, thereby preventing the Holy See from receiving an advantage over other religious interests. By contrast, the Holy See–PLO agreement does not fully entrench the position of the Status Quo, despite such issues arguably falling within the domain of foreign affairs power that have been accorded to the Palestinian Authority by Israel. Rather, the focus is solely on the Holy See's interests in protecting the Christian Holy Places.

Article 5 recognizes the ability of the Catholic Church to carry out necessary functions and traditions, "such as those that are spiritual, religious, moral, charitable, educational and cultural." This rather broad provision refers to a number of important operations conducted by the Church to benefit their believers and entrench their position in society. The Holy See–Israel Fundamental Agreement addresses these aspects in Articles 6, 7, 8, and 9 in a more absolute manner. The divergence reflects the different positions of the parties given that Israel is a sovereign state and the PA has yet to achieve independent-state status.

By contrast, when referring to economic, legal, and fiscal matters, the Basic Agreement utilizes language that mirrors the Holy See–Israel agreement. Article 6 therefore recognizes the Catholic Church's rights in economic, legal, and fiscal matters, but such rights are to be exercised "in harmony" with the rights of the PA. Similar language is used in the Holy See–Israel agreement whenever it addresses matters that overlap between the civilian authority of the state and the religious authority of the Church by way of its canon law.

The basic approach of the Church is that it is to carry out services that it deems imperative, with a view towards providing for some form of necessary external intervention. The state or other authority is not ignored, but is understood to perform a secular role that is removed from a religious context. Hence the Church must act pursuant to the rights of the PA, a method that recognizes and entrenches the Palestinian Authority's abilities as an autonomous entity while still respecting the Catholic Church's understanding of its spiritual position. In the matter of fiscal issues, the spiritual sphere is less defined when compared to matters relating to education and culture, where the religious domain of the Church is more apparent, such that the Basic Agreement uses the phrase "in harmony" to demonstrate the overriding state interests of the PA.

Article 7 accords full legal personality to the Catholic Church. Thus, Articles 6 and 7 make a direct reference to the envisioned relationship between the PA and the Catholic Church, a relationship analogous to that between Israel and the Catholic Church. It is the canon law that ultimately binds the Holy See, even for entities located in other states, with a view towards upholding the laws of the state where there is no conflict with the moral and spiritual sphere. The Catholic Church in essence has some form of autonomous status under canon law while also maintaining a separate legal status in Israel. Hence in the 1997 Legal Personality Agreement between Israel and the Holy See,[44] Articles 2 and 3 assure for "full effect" in Israeli law of the Catholic Church as well as a variety of other religious orders.

In the PLO Basic Agreement, the actual activities provided to the domain of the Catholic Church are not as clearly defined. While the Palestinian Authority is an emerging autonomous entity, it clearly can control fields relating to internal matters, such as education and culture. Yet, it chose not to assert these issues and demonstrate its autonomous authority by delineating more specifically the role of the Palestinian Authority and the role of the Church. Again this indicates the Holy See's upper hand because it was dealing with an autonomous entity whose final status was still subject to negotiation.

Article 8 offers a rather broad proviso that the Basic Agreement shall not prejudice any other agreement between the parties and any other party. This catch-all article provides the grounds for limiting the application of various aspects of the agreement that contravene previous agreements with Israel both between Israel and the PLO and between Israel and the Holy See.

## Conclusion

Given the broad language of Article 8 that the Basic Agreement is "without prejudice" to other previous agreements between the parties, one must wonder what exactly is the consequence of this agreement for Israel? Do the negative references to political issues and to the question of Jerusalem remove any obligations between Israel and the Holy See? Has the PA usurped its autonomy powers such as to throw the agreement into doubt?

The issue regarding the status of relations and the agreements among these three actors is somewhat unique. In each instance, Israel maintains a separate relationship with the other two actors, such that the deviant aspects of the agreement affect Israel's understanding with each party on a singular basis due to prior, separate treaties with each entity. In analogous circumstances, international law raises a presumption that if there is no direct conflict between the different agreements that relates to the subject matter of the treaties, then there is no conflict and the agreements may stand.[45] In this instance, there is no serious, substantive conflict between the Holy See–PLO Basic Agreement and either Israel's Fundamental Agreement with the Holy See or Israel's understandings with the PLO. Rather, the agreement between the Holy See and the PLO refers to a number of issues in permissive provisions of the agreement that should not have been addressed, namely, Jerusalem and the overall peace process, but there is no infringement of the mandatory, substantive provisions that had been reached with Israel.

What did seem to occur was a divergence by the Holy See and the PLO from their previous, separate agreements with Israel. In such a case, if the divergence defeats the object of one or both of the instruments that are at issue, then the benefits to the parties can be nullified. Yet even by a divergence, one must consider, among other things, the entire complex of relevant legal provisions and the overall factual circumstances.[46]

Focusing on the relevant legal provisions and surrounding factual circumstances, it seems that all of the agreements make a distinction between the political aspects of the agreements and the substantive provisions contained in the articles.

For example, the preamble to the Basic Agreement oversteps the authority of the parties by addressing aspects that are outside the domain of the Holy See and the PLO pursuant to their respective agreements with Israel. From a policy standpoint, these issues were rather important to Israel both in its negotiations with the PLO and with the Holy See. Hence the focus on the preamble as laying the groundwork for the object and purpose of each treaty, because the political policy and underlying reasons for creating an agreement are stated by the parties.

Nonetheless, the operative aspects of the agreements encompass broader issues external to the political framework. Clearly the focus of both the Fundamental Agreement and the Basic Agreement is to forge a relationship with the Holy See, with a view towards ameliorating its rights with those of the state or autonomous entity. The agreements are not solely addressing political interests per se, nor are they preventing each party from developing their respective relations. Upon analyzing treaties, and recognizing the inherent assumption that they are to be upheld, one must distinguish between the spirit of good relations as opposed to a concrete conflict or actual divergence by another party. The result is that there does not seem to be a significant divergence by the PLO or the Holy See that would call into question the status of their relationships with Israel. Indeed, the political references in the preamble are subject to ongoing negotiations and political developments,[47] while the substantive aspects pertaining to the rights of worship or the Status Quo are meant to reflect a finalized understanding.

While Israel might be politically slighted by the Holy See–PLO Basic Agreement, Israel also has achieved some benefits. For example, upon comparing the Basic Agreement to the Holy See–Israel Fundamental Agreement, it is clear that the latter is a sharper instrument that has attempted to address a variety of issues. The Holy See–PLO agreement is a different form of document when considering the broad language, the general nature of the commitments, and the lack of any explicit delineation of the articles and their implementation. One can maintain that the Basic Agreement merely is a framework that has not really accorded much to either party, save for generating political goodwill between the signatories and raising the ire of Israel.

Furthermore, it would seem beneficial for Israel that the Holy See maintains some form of ties with the Palestinian Authority. Such relations could serve to stabilize the internal government of the PA by having the Holy See lurking in the background to ensure the protection of its interests and those of the Christian minority. Having an external influence working to shore up the democratic nature of a newly formed government can only serve to benefit Israel in the long run, despite the non-substantive, albeit politically troubling, rhetoric in the preamble of the Basic Agreement.

## NOTES

1. The sites include the Tomb of the Virgin and the Sanctuary of the Ascension. See discussion *infra.*

2. E. Evans, "The Vatican and Israel," 158 *World Affairs* 88 (1995) at 89, referring to A. Kreutz, *Vatican Policy on the Palestinian-Israeli Conflict* (New York: Greenwood Press, 1990), 29.

3. A. Pacini, "Socio-Political and Community Dynamics of Arab Christians in Jordan, Israel, and the Autonomous Palestinian Territories," 259, in A. Pacini, ed., *Christian Communities in the Arab Middle East: The Challenge of the Future* (Oxford: Clarendon Press, 1998), at 280.

4. Pacini, "Socio-Political and Community Dynamics," 282–85.

5. The Basic Agreement is reprinted in 29(3) *J. Pal. Studies* 143 (2000).

6. In particular, the Palestinian Authority attempts to assert its presence in Jerusalem by arranging diplomatic meetings in East Jerusalem's Orient House.

7. For example, the Palestinian Authority, by way of the PLO, maintains observer status in the United Nations.

8. See Article 11(2) of the Fundamental Agreement and discussion *infra.*

9. 32 ILM 1525 (1993). See also F. Kirgis, "Admission of 'Palestine' as a Member of a Specialized Agency and Withholding the Payments of Assessments as a Response," 84 *Am. J. Int'l. L.* 218 (1990), concluding in a pre-Oslo analysis that the PLO lacked any attributes of statehood due to the lack of control over a particular territory or an identifiable population.

10. J. Singer, "Aspects of Foreign Relations," 28 *Isr. L. R.* 268 (1994), basing his conclusion on the transfer of power from Israel to the PA in the Occupied Territories that could only have been of a limited capacity up to the actual control of the military, whose forces were bound to peace and security in a rather narrow manner; O. Dajani, "Stalled Between Seasons: The International Legal Status of Palestine During the Interim Period," 26 *Denver J. Int'l L.* 27 (1997).

11. See, e.g., Singer (1994) (no sovereign immunity for the PA); C. Fassberg, "Israel and the Palestinian Authority: Jurisdiction and Legal Assistance," 28 *Isr. L. R.* 318 (1994) (no sovereign immunity since not a state).

12. Singer (1994) notes as well the PA's contention that Israel never had foreign relations power over the Occupied Territories and it should not automatically assume such powers at this juncture.

13. Lapidoth (1997; 162).

14. Cf. D. Tunis "Caglar v. H. M. Inspector of Taxes," 92 *Am. J. Int'l. L.* 305 (1998), discussing UK tax case whereby the UK tax authorities did not consider employees of the Northern Cyprus authority to be governmental employees. These employees therefore were excluded from claiming a tax refund. While the situation is factually different, the outcome indicates that limited international recognition and limited foreign relations capacity diminishes the entity's claim for state-like status and other benefits, such as sovereign immunity.

15. See Lapidoth (1997; 46–47), noting the possibilities for using an autonomy model when considering the possibility of shared sovereign powers between the central, state government and the autonomous entity.

16. Singer (1994), referring to M. Hannum and R. Lillich, "The Concept of Autonomy in International Law," 74 *Am. J. Int'l. L.* 858–89 (1980); Dajani (1997).

17. Singer (1994) notes that particular UNESCO arrangements had been made.

18. Singer (1994), basing his conclusion on the transfer of power from Israel to the PA in the Occupied Territories that could only have been of a limited capacity up to the actual control of the military, whose forces were bound to peace and security in a rather narrow manner.

19. M. Perko, "Towards a 'Sound and Lasting Basis': Relations Between the Holy See, the Zionist Movement and Israel, 1896–1996," 2 *Israel Studies* 1 (1997).

20. Article 1(1) of the Fundamental Agreement.

21. E. Benvenisti, "The Influence of International Human Rights Law on the Israeli Legal System: Present and Future," 28 *Isr. L. R.* 136 (1994).

22. See Article 1(2) of the Fundamental Agreement.

23. L. Cremonesi, "More Catholic Than the Pope," *Ha'aretz* papal pilgrimage supplement, March 2000.

24. Cremonesi (2000), quoting Vatican officials regarding this matter.

25. E/CN.4/SR.161 (1950). A memo drafted by the UN secretary general highlighted this problem as troubling many states that disallow one to change religions. E/CN.4/528 (1951).

26. UN General Assembly Third Committee, Fifth Session, meeting 288 (1950). Saudi Arabia echoed this argument at the next GA Third Committee meeting (GA Third Committee, Sixth Session, meeting 367 (1951)).

27. E/CN.4/SR.319 (1952). See also E/CN.4/528 (1951). Memo by the secretary general, who outlined Saudi Arabia's and Egypt's position on this matter.

28. UN General Assembly Third Committee, L.876.

29. UN General Assembly Third Committee, Fifteenth Session, meetings 1021–1028 (1960).

30. Note that the Human Rights Committee's 1992 general comment to Article 18 interprets the phrase in paragraph 5 as "the right to replace one's current religion or belief."

31. For example, freedom of expression that is specifically upheld in Article 8 of the Holy See–Israel agreement.

32. Save for the general statements of Article 29.

33. Note as well Article 5 of the Holy See–PLO agreement, discussed *infra*.

34. Note that Article 2(2) relates to encouraging inter-religious dialogue, an arrangement that, from a methodical basis, appears better suited to Article 1.

35. Article 3 of the Basic Agreement.

36. See, e.g., Article 5(2).

37. Note that this was a common problem with the variety of treaties that had been created following the Congress of Vienna in the nineteenth century, as states would guarantee the freedom of religion to their citizens and then impose a rather stringent and narrow

classification as to whom the state considered to be its citizens, usually excluding followers of minority religions who merited such protection.

38. The Tomb of the Virgin is not used by the Roman Catholic Church for services, although it originally had a right to do so under the *firman* that established the Status Quo. Yet, the Church lays claim to a right of possession. L. Cust, *The Status Quo in the Holy Places,* (1929; reprint, Jerusalem: Ariel Publishing House, 1980) 34–36.

39. The Sanctuary of the Ascension is located on the Mount of Olives.

40. See discussion *supra* in this chapter regarding the Holy See–Israel Fundamental Agreement.

41. Cf. Article 4 of the Holy See–Israel Fundamental Agreement, where no mention is made of this term.

42. Article 4(3) of the Fundamental Agreement.

43. Article 3 of the Basic Agreement.

44. See discussion *supra* regarding the Holy See–Israel Fundamental Agreement.

45. See, e.g., Jenks, "The Conflict of Law-Making Treaties," 30 *Brit. Ybk. Intl. L.* 401 (1953) at 425–27, noting by lawmaking treaties that a conflict arises if one party cannot comply with a previous agreed-to treaty due to a conflict in a subsequent treaty with another party.

46. T. Meron, *Human Rights Law Making in the United Nations* (Oxford: Oxford University Press, 1984) at 143 makes this point by human rights treaties.

47. See "Vatican will not interfere with determination of sovereignty in Jerusalem," *Ha'aretz,* Sept. 8, 2000, 3A, noting that the Holy See declares that it will not interfere in the final status negotiations; "Abu Mazan: We Will Not Agree to 'the Sovereignty of God'," *Ha'aretz,* Sept. 20, 2000, 2A, noting the PA's stance that it will (currently) not accept international or religious supervision over the Temple Mount.

**IV**

# INTERNATIONAL LAW
# AND THE ACCORDS

# 8

## ISRAEL-VATICAN RELATIONS SINCE THE SIGNING OF THE FUNDAMENTAL AGREEMENT

*David Rosen*

The historic Fundamental Agreement between the State of Israel and the Holy See, concluded at the end of 1993, involved three relationships. The immediate result of the agreement was the normalization of relations between the Holy See and the State of Israel that led to the exchange of ambassadors four months later. Second, as the preamble of the agreement indicates,[1] the accord took place within the wider context of Catholic-Jewish reconciliation, on which it undoubtedly had a profoundly positive impact in turn. Indeed, for many Jews, especially in Israel, the diplomatic normalization served as testimony and proof of the genuineness of the transformation in theological attitudes and teaching that had taken place over the previous thirty years.[2] The third relationship addressed by the majority of the articles in the Fundamental Agreement is that between the Catholic Church in Israel and the state.

While Israel's goal was essentially the first of these relationships,[3] the Holy See's primary interest concerned the third.[4] Indeed, this difference reflects the divergent perceptions of the principle purpose of the bilateral relations, which as I will indicate below often continues to be at the root of tensions that have emerged in the relationship.

It also naturally affected the negotiations themselves and was the major internal factor (as opposed to external political factors)[5] that delayed the pace of the negotiations, until a creative formula was produced that could satisfy the contradictory assumptions of the parties.

For the Holy See, the rights of the Catholic Church and its communities in Israel were the subject of the overwhelming bulk of the negotiations, concerned institutions and persons subject to two equal and independent sovereign legal systems, namely, Church canon law on the one hand and the laws of the State of Israel on the other. The Vatican's negotiating team thus proposed the use of language that would reflect such parity.

The State of Israel, however, like any other sovereign state, sees itself as the exclusive authority in the borders of its jurisdiction. Accordingly it saw these negotiations as a process of regularization of the rights of a particular community and its members, subject to the rights of the state—the phrase that the Israeli team sought to incorporate into the text of the agreement.[6]

The inability to bridge this gulf of perception caused a substantial hiatus in the negotiations until language was found that creatively allowed both sides to interpret the agreement in accordance with their different assumptions. Accordingly the Fundamental Agreement talks of the exercise of the rights of the Catholic Church "in harmony with the rights of the State" of Israel.[7]

It was precisely this divergency in perception of the primary purpose of the accord that also lay behind the final hurdle that delayed the signing of the agreement.[8]

The Holy See's primary concerns—to resolve outstanding questions concerning the Catholic Church's status in Israel and to enshrine its traditional privileges as de jure rights recognized as such by the state—meant that it was in no hurry to concede to Israel the latter's chief goal of full diplomatic relations as long as these concerns had not been completely resolved.

While Israel faced little difficulty in guaranteeing or reaffirming its commitment to the freedom of religion and conscience; the protection of the Status Quo regarding holy sites; and rights of education, media, and charitable organizations, etc., the questions of regularizing the legal standing of church personnel and institutions, and transforming its traditional taxation and excise privileges from de facto into de jure, were not simple matters.

The Holy See would have liked to have been considered as an extraterritorial entity, enjoying the same privileges granted to foreign delegations and their properties. There was no way that Israel was going to grant such status, especially not for a community overwhelmingly made up of Israeli citizens. Moreover, aside from the principle, to have done so for the Catholic community without doing so for other Christian denominations would have posed substantial difficulties for Israel. Furthermore, to provide for the latter but not to grant the same rights for the much larger Muslim minority, or even to do so for Muslims as well but to continue to deny such to the Jewish majority in a Jewish state, is not something that could be achieved lightly, even if this were to be considered acceptable and/or necessary.

As the resolution of such matters would inevitably involve further deliberations, the State of Israel wished to go ahead with its primary objective—the establishment of full diplomatic relations, and to then subsequently resolve these outstanding issues. In the Vatican's Secretariat of State there was concern that to agree to such would be to forfeit the leverage on Israel's full compliance. Probably, there was also concern that to accede to Israel's position would precisely overemphasize the significance of the diplomatic aspect and dwarf the dimension of the Church's interests concerning its communities in Israel, to the point where the latter would be diminished if not lost altogether in the eyes of the world at large and the Arab world in particular. It should be recalled in this regard that straight after the establishment of the Bilateral Commission to negotiate an agreement between the parties, Archbishop Jean Louis Tauran, the Holy See's secretary for relations with states (i.e., its minister of foreign affairs), set out on a tour of Arab countries to explain the purpose of these bilateral negotiations.[9] In his talks with Arab leaders, he sought to impress upon them the value of such negotiations for the Church's interests and its communities in Israel, as well as to minimize their political significance!

The Holy See proposed a compromise formula in which full diplomatic relations would be established, but representation would not be at the ambassadorial level until these issues were resolved.[10] This was also not acceptable to Israel. It was only through indirect intervention at the highest level that the Vatican Secretariat of State reluctantly withdrew its insistence on this condition and agreed to go ahead and conclude the Fundamental Agreement,[11] in which Israel gave its commitment (together with the Holy See), to "negotiate in good faith" with the "aim to reach agreement within two years"[12] on these outstanding issues. To this end, juridical and fiscal subcommittees of experts were established.[13] However, it took the State of Israel much longer to conclude an agreement with the Holy See over the juridical matter, and it has still not yet concluded negotiations on the economic issues.

The reasons for these delays were not due to any ill will, but rather the result of bureaucratic factors (see below), even though there have been those in the Vatican who have viewed such prevarications as proof of their original suspicions. I do believe, however, that it is not incorrect to say that because Israel sees these matters as so very secondary to the primary goal that it has already achieved, it does not share the Holy See's sense of importance, let alone urgency, concerning these issues.

Notwithstanding, during the year and a half following the signing of the Fundamental Agreement much progress was actually made by the Juridical Committee. However, matters were overtaken by political upheavals in Israel. The assassination of Yitzhak Rabin led to a reshuffling of political responsibilities, including within the Israel Ministry of Foreign Affairs, which naturally affected the work of the committees. By the time new personalities had assumed the reins of leadership, Israel was in the throes of early elections which resulted in the defeat of the Labor-led government and the ascent to power of Benjamin Netanyahu.

Netanyahu's newly formed coalition was immediately caught up in crisis after crisis, and the new minister of foreign affairs, David Levi, had his own priorities which did not affect the ministry kindly. In fact, many aspects of the work of the Ministry of Foreign Affairs remained in limbo without leadership, including matters relating to Israel-Vatican relations. As opposed to the Rabin government, in which there were a minister and deputy minister of foreign affairs—namely, Shimon Peres and Yossi Beilin—who deeply appreciated the moral and political value of promoting Vatican-Israel relations,[14] there was no one in the Netanyahu government who saw this as a priority. It has even been suggested that the latter sought precisely to court evangelical fundamentalist Christian support at the expense of the traditional churches[15]—in this case the Catholic Church—which are perceived as less positively inclined towards Israel, especially as their local constituencies are Palestinian. Only after much nagging from within the Vatican, from interested Israelis (especially members of the Bilateral Commission), and from Diaspora Jewish leaders egged on by Catholic counterparts[16] did the minister of foreign affairs get around to signing a second agreement with the Holy See,[17] containing the formula devised by the juridical subcommittee.

As indicated, it was a complicated task to find an appropriate designation under Israeli law for the legal status of the Catholic Church, its structure and institutions, which would be acceptable to both parties. While the Church's institutions and communities in Israel are indeed subject to the laws of the state, they nevertheless derive their internal authority and structure from Rome. The Vatican sought to have this structure and its authority recognized as such by the State of Israel—something that is arguably without parallel or precedent. However, the juridical agreement did just that and gave legal recognition to the Church's internal structure, strengthening its control of its own institutions in Israel.[18] This is undoubtedly a historic achievement for the Catholic Church, as no ruling authority in the Holy Land—in particular a non-Christian one—has ever granted any church such de jure recognition. In effect, this agreement concerning the Church's legal status is recognition on the part of the State of Israel of the Holy See's historic standing and inherent stake in the Holy Land.

At the same time, the agreement was a significant achievement for the State of Israel in both historic and political terms, as the Catholic Church thereby not only reaffirmed its recognition of the sovereignty of the Jewish people in their historic homeland,[19] but also registered and placed its institutions under Israel's legal authority and protection. An examination of the list of these religious institutions reveals a variety throughout Israel, many of which are located in East Jerusalem. (No less fascinating is the fact that some of these institutions are part of larger organizations whose place of regional authority is to be found in neighboring Arab countries!)[20] The Vatican insists that nothing in its agreements with Israel should be interpreted as taking a position on unresolved borders, let alone on the future of Jerusalem, which is a matter of dispute between Israel and the Palestinians.[21] Yet one cannot but be struck by the significance of it registering these institutions under Israeli law and sovereignty.

The very fact that the Holy See has done so raises questions about some of the other positions of the Vatican, not least of all its call for "international guarantees"[22] concerning the future of religious rights and freedoms in Jerusalem. This itself is a change from the former position of the Holy See supporting the internationalization of the city.[23] However, especially after having signed the Fundamental Agreement with Israel, normalizing relations between the two and confirming Israel's commitment to religious freedom, the protection of the holy sites, and the legal "Status Quo" governing them, an obvious question occurs: What is behind the call for international guarantees? If Israel is a trustworthy partner and for that reason the Holy See entered into the bilateral accord between them, then why does it need international guarantees at all? On the other hand, if Israel is not trustworthy in the Vatican's eyes, then we may not only ask what value is the Fundamental Agreement itself, but also why should international guarantees provide any greater security whatsoever? The answer, I believe, is that the Vatican's call for international guarantees is not at all the result of a lack of trust in Israel, but the very contrary.

As noted earlier, the Vatican has obtained a significant achievement in Israel's acknowledgment of its inherent status and stake in the Holy Land. To obtain such acknowledgment from an Islamic political entity or one embracing a significant Islamic influence would be far more problematic.[24]

Of course, if the Holy See would have tried to negotiate with those in Israel who advocate theocracy, it would have faced the same problem.[25] Fortunately, Israel is a modern democracy and was able to negotiate freely. However, even if the Vatican might not have been able to gain such an explicit recognition of its inherent stake in the Holy Land from any of the other political entities in the Muslim world that lay claim to Jerusalem, it could use its agreement with Israel as leverage. This was evident in the Vatican's agreement with the PLO—significantly only agreed upon and signed just five weeks before the papal visit to the Holy Land.[26] Similarly, some kind of international charter ("guarantees") based upon the accord with Israel could probably obtain the signatures of all parties with a possible interest in Jerusalem to a document affirming the principle of religious freedom and respect for the aforementioned Status Quo. This would provide the Vatican with extra international legal protection for its own interests, regardless of who would assume political control of any part of Jerusalem.

The difference in the perception of the State of Israel and the Holy See of the character of their bilateral relationship was revealed most vividly in the controversy regarding the appointment of the successor to Maximus Saloum, the Greek Catholic archbishop of the Galilee.[27] The Greek Catholic (Melkite) community, which happens to be the largest Christian denomination within the green line (the borders of the State of Israel prior to June 4, 1967), is in communion with Rome. Accordingly, the Church's appointments require Vatican authorization. Usual procedure involves the recommendation of the local church and then of the synod, which in this case is convened by the Patriarchate of Antioch. The Vatican may or may not endorse the recommendation. However, regarding the succession of Archbishop Saloum, there was an internal struggle between two competing groups within the local church itself. The candidate of one of these groups was considered to be close to the Israeli security authorities and arguably was preferred for that reason. However, his candidature was not endorsed by the Holy See, which explained its actions on two main grounds. To begin with, it is usual for the candidate for archbishop to already be a bishop, which was not the case. Perhaps more significantly, the Vatican wanted an appointee who would not perpetuate the internal division within the local community and thus sought an outside appointment in the person of Bishop Boutros Mouallem, who had been serving as Melkite bishop in Brazil.[28]

Persons close to the Israeli minister of foreign affairs, Ariel Sharon, were convinced that more sinister motives lay behind the appointment, especially as Mouallem is originally Palestinian. Accordingly, Sharon was persuaded that Mouallem was preferred over the local candidate, who was viewed as very friendly towards Israel, because of interference from representatives of the Palestinian Authority and even radical Palestinian personages close to the Vatican who had interceded against the local candidate and on behalf of Mouallem. Against the advice of professional officials in the Ministry of Foreign Affairs, Sharon sought to prevent the appointment. Prime Minister Netanyahu's government was at one of its numerous vulnerable moments, and his dependency upon Ariel Sharon was increasing. The latter had no difficulty in persuading Netanyahu to react very strongly to the Vatican's decision, even to the extent of threatening to refuse the new archbishop's entry into Israel (a strange threat, as Mouallem had regularly visited his family and community in Israel in the course of recent years without encountering any unusual problems from any Israeli security quarters).[29]

While the Israeli government's attitude revealed poor intelligence and even poorer tactics, it also revealed the distance in perception of the nature of the bilateral relationship between Israel and the Holy See. Precisely because Israel understands the relationship in purely diplomatic terms, the appointment of the head of a church in communion with Rome was viewed and interpreted in a political manner. Accordingly, Israel saw the decision as reflecting "bad faith" on the part of the Holy See. The latter saw precisely Israel's reaction as the act of "bad faith," not just because of what it saw as the misinterpretation of its motives, but above all because it contravened Israel's commitment to the free exercise of religious institutional life of the Church given in the Fundamental Agreement.[30] Moreover, the apparatus designed for bilateral issues and even normal diplomatic discretion were ignored, in what the Vatican saw as reckless disregard. The end was Israel's inevitable and foreseeable embarrassing climb down and the enthronement of Boutrous Mouallem as Greek Catholic archbishop in accordance with the Holy See's decision.[31] However, the episode left a bad taste for Israel-Vatican relations and above all reflected the continued disparity in attitude toward the bilateral relationship.

The ongoing controversy between Muslim and Christian interests in Nazareth[32] has also had a negative impact on Israel-Vatican relations. The controversy related to the preparation of a plaza next to the Church of the Annunciation, in anticipation of the hundreds of thousands of Christian pilgrims who were expected in the year 2000.[33] However, certain Muslim elements (led by the Islamic Movement in Israel) claimed that the plaza would encroach on Muslim religious trust (*waqf*) land, where they were accordingly determined to erect a mosque (or rebuild, according to their claims).

The local Christian communities were not only concerned about making adequate preparations for the millennial year, but were above all fearful that compromise of any kind in this controversy would only encourage a process of Islamicist attrition against Christian communities and properties. Accordingly, the Holy See was enlisted by its community to impress upon Israel the deleterious consequences of capitulating to Islamicist interests. Officials were informed that these consequences could involve the closure of churches and the cancellation of celebrations planned for the year 2000. With amazing indiscretion, the Israeli officials concerned revealed the content of these confidences to the press, which in turn elicited a rather convoluted semi-denial from the Vatican's spokesperson.[34] Naturally, this episode hardly enhanced Vatican confidence in Israel's reliability and responsibility, which was not improved by what was perceived at the time as a general inadequacy in preparing for the "jubilee" year.[35]

In contrast, the Catholic Church and other Christian communities were encouraged by the successful parliamentary and government opposition to attempts to extend the provisions of what is known as the Missionary Law (in fact, this 1977 law does not prohibit proselytizing, but only the offer of material incentive for the purpose of changing one's religious affiliation).[36] The proposals first put forth by Knesset members Gafni and Zvili, and then subsequently reintroduced by M. K. Pinhassi, would have made it an offense not only to disseminate but even possess materials for the purpose of proselytization.[37]

In response to concern expressed from various Christian (including Catholic) and Jewish quarters regarding the implications and consequences of such regulations for the freedom of religious speech in Israel, Prime Minister Netanyahu personally gave verbal and written assurances that his government would oppose and prevent such legislation.[38]

Other positive developments since the Fundamental Agreement were to be seen in the first comprehensive translations into Hebrew and wide dissemination of the major Catholic documents dealing with Jews, Judaism, and Israel since *Nostra Aetate*.[39] There was also a definite improvement in Jewish-Israeli attitudes, including within the rabbinic establishment, towards contacts with the Catholic world in particular and the Christian world in general. This was evidenced in the increasing number of leading Israeli rabbis that began to meet with Christian leaders and theologians.[40]

The Vatican agreement with the PLO caused something of a flurry in Vatican-Israel relations. At the time of concluding the Fundamental Agreement with Israel, the Vatican had announced its intention to pursue parallel agreements with other relevant parties.[41]

The Palestinian Authority, however, had sought to mollify the Islamicist elements within Palestinian society and was concerned that a bilateral agreement with the Vatican might face opposition from those quarters.

However, Chairman Arafat was very conscious of the public relations potential of the papal visit and, recognizing the value of a bilateral accord in preparation for the visit, concluded an agreement with the Holy See on February 15, 2000.[42]

The Israeli minister of foreign affairs at the time, David Levi, and his director general, Eytan Bentsur, reacted very negatively to the agreement, particularly as it contained an implicit criticism of Israel describing "unilateral decisions" concerning Jerusalem as "morally and legally unacceptable."[43]

However, Vatican representatives were not too perturbed by his reaction, as it actually mitigated Islamic Palestinian nationalist criticism by suggesting that the PLO agreement with Israel was in conflict with Israel's interest.[44]

Notwithstanding, a more insightful view of the agreement than that of Mr. Levi was articulated by editorial comment in the leading Israeli daily *Ha'aretz*,[45] which pointed out that this agreement recognized all previous agreements as binding and that accordingly Israel could challenge anything in it that could be considered an infringement of the Oslo Accords. Moreover, *Ha'aretz* even suggested that those who reacted negatively had not read the accord very well. The piece quoted Dr. Menachem Klein of Bar Ilan University and the Jerusalem Center for Israeli Studies. "We have here nothing less than an historic document," Klein stated. "The agreement with the Vatican upgrades . . . the official Palestinian position . . . agree[ing] to confer special status to Jerusalem's holy areas and to have special arrangements in the city."

Israeli concern over the Holy See's agreement with the PLO was nevertheless quickly forgotten in the weeks ahead as preparations for the papal visit built up to a frenzy.

Indeed, the historic visit of Pope John Paul II was to a very large degree a climax of the Fundamental Agreement itself. The establishment of the Permanent Bilateral Commission of the Holy See and the State of Israel that led to the accord had been facilitated substantially by external political developments, that is, the Madrid Peace Conference.[46]

Moreover, the issues that were to be under discussion as a result also involved matters of direct interest to the church—not least of all, the future of Jerusalem.

However, the process was greatly galvanized by Pope John Paul II's personal commitment to Catholic-Jewish reconciliation,[47] and above all his plans for the year 2000, which was designated as the Great Jubilee.

In the Vatican document *Tertio Millenio Adveniente*, which laid out the pope's vision for religious activities for the years leading up to and culminating with the Great Jubilee, his intention to visit the Holy Land in the year 2000 was already evident. Indeed, he had spoken of this many times before.[48]

However, even if a papal visit might have been possible in the absence of diplomatic relations between Israel and the Holy See, it certainly would have proved to be extremely problematic.

Moreover, the visit of Pope Paul VI in January 1963 had left a bitter taste that had not been forgotten in Israel.[49] Despite the extensive efforts at the time to facilitate his entry into Israel to visit Christian holy sites (a special road was laid on Mt. Zion) and provide hospitality, Pope Paul VI refused to meet with any of Israel's elected officials in Jerusalem, and while he invited them to meet with him at Megiddo, he made no mention and thus expressed no recognition of the State of Israel as such, neither at the time nor even at his departure. Israel had been willing to endure the snub, in the hope that the visit would be an initial stage towards warming the bilateral relationship and eventual diplomatic ties. These, however, were not forthcoming and thus the visit was generally seen in retrospect in a negative light.

Israel was not likely to allow such an experience to repeat itself and would insist that the state and its highest elected officials be shown the honor of their status accordingly. A state visit of the pope to a country with which the Vatican did not have diplomatic relations would have posed substantial if not unsurmountable political and diplomatic hurdles. Accordingly, the anticipated papal visit to the Holy Land proved to be a significant incentive in galvanizing the normalization of bilateral relations leading to the exchange of ambassadors.[50]

In its own inimitable style, Israel was late in preparing the logistics for the visit, but when preparations finally got under way, they were handled with great speed and efficiency.

On March 21, Pope John Paul II descended the ramp onto the tarmac at the Ben Gurion Airport to be received by the State of Israel's leaders with all the pomp and ceremony accorded to a visiting head of state.

The moment was one of enormous historical significance, embodying the transformation in the Catholic Church's teaching not only towards Jews and Judaism, but also towards the very idea of a sovereign Jewish state in the Holy Land.[51]

The papal visit was first and foremost a personal pilgrimage as well as a great morale booster to Christianity in the region. The visit also purposefully set out to advance relations not only between the Catholic Church and Jewry, but also with Islam. However, the pope was entering into a very volatile political context where even though the peace process was still alive, there was still much acrimony and tension between Israelis and the Palestinians together with competition for entitlement and legitimation.

Pope John Paul II evidenced masterful diplomacy in displaying empathy for Palestinian suffering without pointing an accusing finger at Israel specifically. Similarly, he was able to convey to both Israel and the Palestinians a message of support for their respective aspirations.[52]

However, the impact of the papal visit upon the Israeli Jewish public was quite astounding. In order to appreciate this, one needs to bear in mind that Israeli Jews do not live in a Christian environment and do not meet modern Christians. Even when they travel abroad, their encounters are overwhelmingly with non-Jews rather than with Christians. As Christianity is predominantly irrelevant to the vast majority of them, the images that they carry with them have primarily been taken from the tragic past. Precisely because Israelis had such little knowledge of the changes that had occurred in the previous thirty-five years since the promulgation of *Nostra Aetate,* the papal visit startled many when they discovered that the Catholic Church is not only no longer hostile towards the Jewish people, but that it seeks a positive relationship of mutual respect and cooperation with the people that John Paul II has described as "the [Church's] dearly beloved elder brother . . . of the original covenant never revoked by God."[53]

Pope John Paul II has shown himself to be a master of the use of symbols and images, and this was never more evident than during his visit to Israel.

Two such moments stand out in particular. First at Yad Vashem—the Holocaust memorial center—where the pope stood in profound tearful solidarity with Jewish suffering and where he was reunited with survivor friends and those whose lives he helped save.

No less impressive was the moment when John Paul II stood alone at the Western Wall—the remnant of the Temple Mount destroyed by the Romans—in prayerful respect for Jewish tradition. Moreover, the Israeli public was greatly impressed when the pope placed at the wall the text of the prayer from the liturgy of repentance that had been recited in St. Peter's two weeks beforehand, beseeching Divine Forgiveness for sins committed by Christians against Jews down through the ages.[54]

One of the immediate positive consequences of the pope's visit was the willingness of Israel's Ministry of Education to begin to address the Church and its teaching in the classroom. For the first time a circular went out from the director of the ministry (on March 29, 2000) to head teachers in all Israeli state schools, providing textual sources showing the changes in Catholic teaching towards Jews, Judaism, and Israel, and recommending that these be taught and discussed in their classrooms.

In light of how far the Catholic-Jewish dialogue has progressed in the West, especially in the United States, this step of the Israeli Ministry of Education appears rather basic. However, in terms of how most Israeli Jews have perceived the Christian world, it is a most significant development and positive testimony of the impact of the papal visit upon the Jewish people, in Israel in particular.

However, as attitudes towards Christianity are still conditioned to varying degrees by the tragic Jewish experience of the past, the process of Jewish-Catholic reconciliation—especially where Jews do not encounter modern tolerant Christians—still has a very long way to go. Pope John Paul II has made a unique contribution to this endeavor, in which his visit to the synagogue in Rome in 1986, his forthright condemnations of anti-Semitism as a sin against God and man,[55] the normalization of relations between the Holy See and Israel, and his visit to the Holy Land have stood out as highlights. Although all this has certainly led to a far more positive attitude towards the Vatican in Israel, there have also been a number of controversies that have had a negative impact. These have included the question of Christian symbols at Auschwitz and other sites of the Shoah that Jews find offensive,[56] the canonization of Edith Stein[57] (and to a lesser degree, the beatification of Pope Pius IX[58]), and the question of Pope Pius XII's role during the period of the Shoah and his own proposed beatification.[59] Similarly, the Vatican's institutional reticence regarding transparency and making archival material accessible, as well as continuing "revelations" regarding the use of Vatican channels for Nazi criminals and their plunder,[60] have likewise acted to reinforce historic negative images. There was also great disappointment and consternation within Jewry—and in Israel in particular—over the political exploitation of the pope's visit to Syria by President Bashar Assad and the latter's anti-Semitic utterances, which did not elicit any rebuke from the pope or Vatican spokespersons.[61] Notwithstanding, Jewish attitudes in Israel toward Christianity appear to have generally shifted in a favorable direction and are reflected in increasing academic interest in Christianity.[62]

One of the most important ways in which this change will be further advanced is through the bilateral cooperation between the Holy See and the State of Israel that the Fundamental Agreement envisaged.[63] While there has been some of this on a cultural level, little has been done in terms of the impressive commitment of the Holy See in the Fundamental Agreement to join with the State of Israel in the actual combat of anti-Semitism as well as other bigotry throughout the world.[64]

Yet the moral undertakings of the Fundamental Agreement are precisely what Pope John Paul II has recognized and pointed out as the central challenge ahead for the Christian-Jewish relationship. He has referred to this as the "third dimension" of the dialogue and a "sacred duty." In this regard, the pope stated that "Jews and Christians, as children of Abraham, are called to be a blessing for the world [Gen. 12:2], by committing themselves to work together for peace and justice among all people."[65]

Indeed, precisely the achievements of the Fundamental Agreement, and that which it symbolizes, render the shared bilateral challenge all the more compelling, "to promote mutual understanding among nations, tolerance and respect for human life and dignity."[66]

## NOTES

1. See Eugene Fisher and Leon Klenicki, eds., *"A Challenge Long Delayed": The Diplomatic Exchange Between the Holy See and the State of Israel* (New York: Anti-Defamation League, 1996).

2. See author's address to the International Jewish-Catholic Liaison Committee (ILC) meeting in Jerusalem, Mar. 1994, ICCI, Jerusalem.

3. See F. Michael Perko, "Toward a Sound and Lasting Basis—Relations between the Holy See, the Zionist Movement and Israel, 1896–1996," *Israel Studies* 2, no. 1.

4. Statement of Vatican spokesperson Joachin Navarro Valls, Dec. 30, 1993, quoted extensively in the international media the following day. See also the text of the "Introductory Intervention" of Archbishop Msgr. Claudio Maria Celli at the meeting of the Bilateral Commission in Jerusalem, Nov. 13, 1995, in the course of which he stated: "The Holy See . . . considers the establishment of official relations . . . not as an end in itself, but as a means—principally for the communities of the Catholic faithful. In fact, a significant portion of the agreement is devoted to the Catholic Church and her institutions located

in the State of Israel" (page 6). He furthermore reiterated that "the Fundamental Agreement . . . is an agreement concerning principles and fundamental norms . . . to inspire and regulate relations and cooperation between the State of Israel and the Holy See between the Authorities of Israel and the Catholic Church which is present in the territory of the State and wishes to take part actively and loyally in the life of the country" (page 4).

5. E.g., Israel's expulsion of Hamas activists. See *Jerusalem Post,* Sept. 20, 1993.

6. Draft proposals submitted at the meeting of the Bilateral Commission's Committee of Experts, convened at the Israeli Ministry of Foreign Affairs on January 6, 1993.

7. Articles 6, 8, and 9 of the Fundamental Agreement.

8. *Jerusalem Post,* Jan. 8, 1993.

9. See Thomas F. Stansky, "Vatican-Israel Diplomatic Relations," *America* 169, no. 14 (Nov. 6, 1993): 9; and *Corriere della Sera,* Sept. 1992.

10. Reported in the *Jerusalem Post,* Sept. 24, 1993.

11. "Israel Dossier—A secret meeting," *Inside the Vatican,* Jan. 1994, 52. See also Shaike Ben Porat, *Conversations with Yossi Beilin* (Tel Aviv: HaKibbutz Hameuchad, 1996), 119.

12. Fundamental Agreement, Article 10, 2a and 2c.

13. The initial meetings of these subcommittees took place on July 4, 1994, when the Juridical Committee met at the Ratisbonne Monastery in Jerusalem. However, substantive meetings only took place on October 11 and 12, after the hiatus of the summer vacations and the Jewish festivals in early autumn.

14. Ben Porat, op. cit. p. 188, and dinner speech of Shimon Peres following the signing of the Fundamental Agreement quoted in the *Jerusalem Post,* Dec. 31, 1993.

15. See Labib Kopti, "Christian Zionism Defined," Catholic Information Network, Aug. 26, 1997, at http://www.ciri.org; and Sabeel statement, "A Vision for Peace," presented by Patriarch Michel Sabbah at Sabeel Conference at Tantur on February 14, 1998.

16. See *The Jewish Week,* New York, Apr. 11, 1997. Also, the author was party to a variety of direct communications on the subject both representing ADL directly and as part of the Presidents' Conference and IJCIC.

17. The Legal Personality Agreement was signed on November 10, 1997; see the Vatican Information Service and *Jerusalem Post,* Nov. 10, 1997.

18. See David Rosen, "Rome and Jerusalem, the Latest Landmark," at http://www.israel.org.mfa/holysart.html. Also in French in *'Sens' Les Racines de L'Antijudaisme Chrétien,* no. 2, 1998.

19. See Pope John Paul II's apostolic letter of April 20, 1984, *Redemptionis Anno,* in *Spiritual Pilgrimage—Texts on Jews and Judaism, 1979–1995,* ed. E. J. Fisher and L. Klenicki, (New York: Crossroad, 1996).

20. The text of the Fundamental Agreement specifies the Eastern Catholic Patriarchates; the Greek Melkite Catholic (based in Latkia, Syria); the Syrian Catholic (based in Damascus); the Maronite (based in Lebanon); the Chaldean (based in Baghdad); and the Armenian Catholic Patriarchates; as well as the Latin Patriarchate of Jerusalem.

21. The original text submitted by the Holy See's negotiators to the Committee of Experts, which sought to specify these, was rejected by the Israeli team. As a result, the

Vatican agreed to excise these specific references and suffice with a general statement which serves as the second clause of Article 11 of the Fundamental Agreement.

22. *New York Times,* Jan. 7, 1992; *Jerusalem Post,* May 14, 1998. Address of Msgr. Jean Louis Tauran, New York, Oct. 25, 1998; *Ha'aretz* and *Jerusalem Post,* Oct. 27, 1998.

23. See Livia Rokach, *The Catholic Church and the Question of Palestine* (Atlantic Highlands, N. J.: Sage Books, 1987), 166; also Ruth Lapidoth and Moshe Hirsch, *The Jerusalem Question and Its Resolutions* (Dordrecht-Boston, London: Martinus Nijhoff, 1994).

24. Territory which has been at any time under Islamic control is seen as Islamic inheritance (see E. Sivan, "Le Caractère Sacre de Jerusalem dans L'Islam," *Studia Islamica* 28 (1967): 148–82; also C. D. Matthews, *Palestine—Mohammedan Holy Land* (New Haven: Yale University Press, 1949). While it is certainly possible from an Islamic perspective to reach an accommodation with a non-Islamic power—especially with "People of the Book"—a formal legal acknowledgment that another religious community has an accepted inherent stake in what is seen as part and parcel of the Islamic world is quite another matter.

25. See "Rabbi Shach—It Is Forbidden to Establish Diplomatic Relations with the Vatican," *Davar,* Aug. 10, 1992.

26. The Basic Agreement between the Holy See and the Palestinian Liberation Organization, Feb. 15, 2000.

27. See Michael S. Arnold, "Test of Faiths," *Jerusalem Post Magazine,* Aug. 28, 1998; and Akiva Eldar, *Ha'aretz,* Aug. 6, 1998.

28. Arnold, loc. cit., and conversation of the author with the apostolic nuncio Msgr. Pietro Sambi.

29. Associated Press, Aug. 6, 1998; *Jerusalem Post,* Aug. 7, 1998.

30. *Ma'ariv,* Aug. 6, 1998.

31. Reuters and Associated Press, Aug. 17, 1998; *Ha'aretz,* Aug. 18, 1998; and *Jerusalem Post,* Oct. 16 and 18, 1998.

32. *Jerusalem Post,* Mar. 16, 1998; *Yediot Ahronot,* Jan. 22, 1999; AP, Apr. 8, 1999.

33. *Jerusalem Post,* Oct. 19, 1997; *Yediot Ahronot,* Jan. 5, 1999; *Ha'aretz,* Feb. 22, 1999.

34. *Yediot Ahronot,* Apr. 13, 1999.

35. *Jerusalem Post,* Feb. 19, Mar. 16, and Apr. 12, 1999.

36. Knesset Penal Law, 5737–1977 (P/950).

37. *Jerusalem Post,* May 21 and May 28, 1997, and Jan. 22, 1998; CNN World News, July 8, 1997; *Ha'aretz,* July 18, 1997; *Dispatch from Jerusalem,* a bimonthly newspaper published by Bridges For Peace, Jerusalem vol. 22, no. 5, Sept. and Oct., 1997, http://www.bridgesforpeace.com.

38. Letter from Prime Minister Benjamin Netanyahu to Abraham H. Foxman, June 3, 1998. See also *Christians in Israel* VII, nos. 1 and 2 (1997–1998 and 1998) and the paid advertisement of Christian leaders in the *Jewish Voice,* Sivan 5758.

39. Yisrael Lippel and David Rosen, eds., *Hakenesiah Hakatolit, Haam HeYehudi u Medinat Yisrael,* Jerusalem Institute for Interreligious Research and Relations (Jerusalem: Gefen, 1996); *Kovetz Mismachim Nozriim Bnei Zemanenu al Yahasim bein Yehudim ve Nozrim,* ICCI and IJCIR, Sept. 1996.

40. Cf. meetings of chief rabbis with patriarchs (June 1998) and leading cardinals, and participation of chief rabbis and other leading rabbis in Annual Interfaith Meetings of Sant Egidio. Also see *Yediot Ahronot* and *Ma'ariv* of April 12, 1999, regarding the meeting of the nuncio with Rabbi Ovadiah Yossef.

41. "Vatican pact answers prayers, not questions," *Jerusalem Post*, Dec. 31, 1993.

42. The Basic Agreement between the Holy See and the Palestine Liberation Organization.

43. *Jerusalem Post*, Feb. 16, 2000.

44. Personal conversation of the author with the papal nuncio, Msgr. Pietro Sambi, following his meeting with Minister Levi.

45. *Ha'aretz*, Feb. 16, 2000.

46. Archbishop Jean-Louis Tauran, "The Holy See and the Middle East" (address delivered by the Holy See's secretary for relations with states at the Catholic University of America, Mar. 9, 1999).

47. Fisher and Klenicki, *Spiritual Pilgrimage*, particularly the text of the papal address at the Vatican concert commemorating the Shoah, Apr. 7, 1994 (p. 188); also, the interview in *Parade Magazine*, Apr. 3, 1994.

48. E.g., "Jerusalem Rabbi meets with Pope," *Jerusalem Post*, Jan. 11, 1993.

49. A. Gilbert, *The Vatican Council and the Jews*, (Cleveland: The World Publishing Company, 1968), chap. 7. Cf. A. Rabinovich, "Real Presence," *Jerusalem Post*, Mar. 19, 2000; and Y. Klein Halevi, "Pilgrimage in the Lions' Den," *Jerusalem Report*, Mar. 27, 2000.

50. "Vatican grants Israel full recognition," *Chicago Tribune*, Dec. 16, 1993.

51. David Rosen, "A history of reconciliation," *Jerusalem Post*, Dec. 31, 1999; David Rosen, "A symbolic act of transformation," *Jerusalem Post*, Mar. 21, 2000.

52. Papal address at the Dehaishe refugee camp, Mar. 22, 2000.

53. Papal address at the Great Synagogue, Rome, Apr. 13, 1986; and papal address to the Jewish community in West Germany, Nov. 17, 1980; published in Fisher and Klenicki, eds., *Spiritual Pilgrimage*.

54. *Yediot Ahronot* and *Ma'ariv*, Mar. 24 and 27, 2000.

55. *Vatican Information Service*, bulletin no. 75.4: 172–78.

56. John Pawlikowski, "The Auschwitz-Birkenau Controversy: Towards a Permanent Resolution of the Current Crisis," published by the Bernadin Center, Chicago, Jan. 1999; see also *The Tablet*, Aug. 22, 1998.

57. Feature by Douglas David on Edith Stein, *Jerusalem Post*, Oct. 9, 1998.

58. "Beatification of Pope causes embarrassment and regrets," National Association Press Agency, Rome, Dec. 21, 1999.

59. *Zenit*, Sept. 10, 1998; Albert Friedlander, "The tragedy of Pius XII," *The Tablet*, Jan. 2, 1999.

60. *International Herald Tribune*, July 23, 1997. See also Eliahu Salpeter, *Ha'aretz*, Sept. 23, 1998.

61. "Assad strikes an anti-Semitic note, but Pope bears the brunt of criticism," Jewish Telegraphic Agency, May 8, 2001; Shlomo Avineri, "The Pope's Silence," *Jerusalem Post*, May 9, 2001.

62. Geoffrey Wigoder, report to the ILC meeting on education, Jerusalem, Mar. 1994.

63. Articles 2 and 3.

64. Article 2, clause 1.

65. Papal address in Mainz, Nov. 17, 1980, quoted in Fisher and Klenicki, eds., *Spiritual Pilgrimage*.

66. Article 2, clause 1.

9

# THE FREEDOM OF PROSELYTISM UNDER THE FUNDAMENTAL AGREEMENT AND INTERNATIONAL LAW

*Moshe Hirsch*

Religions interact with one another in various ways, but proselytism unquestionably is one of the most sensitive topics in inter-religious affairs. With respect to the relationship between Jews and Christians, Eugene Fisher described proselytism as "[o]ne of the most ancient and disastrous . . . tensions between the Jewish and Christian communities."[1] Conflicting views regarding proselytism have also given rise to considerable tensions between other religions.[2] In light of these opposing perspectives, it is not surprising that the shaping of international norms in this sphere has become a contentious issue in the international arena.

## Conversion and Proselytism: Inter-Religious and Interpersonal Dimensions

The processes of proselytism and conversion may be examined on two levels: (1) the inter-religious level, in other words, the interaction between two religious groups, and (2) the interpersonal level, that is, the interaction between the prose-lytizer and the potential proselyte. These inexorably linked dimensions present difficult questions concerning international human rights.

Conversion constitutes a dynamic dimension of every religion. Through this pro-cess, religions acquire new believers and lose existing ones. Generally, "[E]very reli-gion strives to increase the number of its adherents, while concomitantly avoiding, as much as possible, conversions of its believers to other religions." The motivation un-derlying these concurrent aims derives from several sources, the most prominent of which is the metaphysical moral conception of contemporary world religions.[3] This moral vision engenders the "desire to bring about the universal acceptance and ap-plication of the vision, which it holds to be universally true in principle."[4]

The substance of international legal rules pertaining to proselytism are contro-versial between states and religions because they are designed to regulate activity in a competitive environment. The basic setting in which the process of conversion takes place closely resembles a zero-sum game. In a zero-sum game, whatever one player wins, the other player loses.[5] Likewise, in inter-religious conversions every new convert to a religion is an apostate to another religion. The religions' prefer-ences are opposed and they are considered rivals.[6]

Different religions develop distinct attitudes with respect to conversion and proselytism that evolve over time. The difference between the basic approaches of the major contemporary religions toward proselytism, particularly between Ju-daism and Christianity, is remarkable. Historically, proselytism has been central to Christianity,[7] while the Jewish faith generally has refrained from proselytic efforts.[8] Notably, although the Catholic Church discontinued missionary campaigns that target Jews,[9] other Christian denominations still engage in such proselytism. The disparate missionary approaches of different religions have greatly influenced their positions concerning the legal question of whether proselytism should be al-lowed or prohibited.

Under international law, proselytism is viewed as interpersonal in nature and governed by human rights law. The freedom to proselytize implicates two distinct, but related, notions of freedom: the freedom of the proselytizers to conduct prose-lytizing activities and the freedom of the potential proselyte not to be interfered with by such activities. This distinction is made in pursuance to Sir Isaiah Berlin's seminal essay "Two Concepts of Liberty."[10] Berlin distinguished between the "nega-tive" and the "positive" senses of freedom. According to Berlin, the negative sense refers to the freedom to be free of unwanted interference.[11] Berlin argues that "[t]he wider the area of non-interference the wider my freedom."[12] In contrast, the positive sense refers to individual autonomy to exercise religious freedom without external constraints or coercion.[13] Thus, the positive sense embodies the view that "I am free if, and only if, I plan my life in accordance with my own will."[14]

When we turn to international human rights law, and particularly to the freedom of religion, the distinction between Berlin's notions of freedom corresponds to the freedom to maintain a religion without interference and the freedom to persuade another person to abandon his or her religion in favor of another. Undoubtedly, these two aspects of proselytic freedom frequently clash. The legal system is assigned the task of reconciling these competing interests. Naturally, the legal equilibrium is dynamic and influenced by various religious and geopolitical factors.

### Freedom of Religion under the Fundamental Agreement: Asymmetric Obligations

The provisions of the 1993 Fundamental Agreement between the Holy See and the State of Israel[15] (1993 Fundamental Agreement) obligate both parties to respect the human right to freedom of religion. However, the 1993 Fundamental Agreement does not precisely define this important obligation. Instead, the agreement incorporates specific rules pertaining to the freedom of religion that were set out in other international instruments. Surprisingly, the parties' obligations regarding the freedom of religion are defined in separate provisions and are not necessarily symmetrical.

Israel's obligations in this regard are enumerated in Article 1(1) of the 1993 Fundamental Agreement, which provides that "[t]he State of Israel . . . affirms its continuing commitment to uphold and observe the human right to freedom of religion and conscience, as set forth in the Universal Declaration of Human Rights and in other international instruments *to which it is a party.*"[16] Likewise, the Holy See's obligations appear in Article 1(2) stating that "[t]he Holy See . . . affirms the Catholic Church's commitment to uphold the human right to freedom of religion and conscience, as set forth in the Universal Declaration of Human Rights and in other international instruments *to which it is a party.*"[17]

These provisions clearly bind both parties to protect the freedom of religion as provided under the 1948 Universal Declaration of Human Rights.[18] Yet the application of additional international rules depends upon whether a particular party, and not both, is a party to a certain international instrument. Thus, apart from the mutual obligations established by the 1948 Universal Declaration, each party to the 1993 Fundamental Agreement is bound to protect the freedom of religion only to the extent that it is a party to another international instrument. Therefore, beyond the mutual obligations under the 1948 Universal Declaration, the parties' duties regarding the freedom of religion are not necessarily symmetrical.

The primary international instruments which define the freedom of religion are the 1948 Universal Declaration,[19] the 1966 International Covenant on Civil and Political Rights (ICCPR),[20] and the 1981 Declaration on the Elimination of All Forms of Intolerance and of Discrimination Based on Religion or Belief (1981 Declaration).[21] Israel has joined the ICCPR and is a member of the United Nations, where the 1981 Declaration was adopted by consensus. The Holy See, on the other hand, has neither joined the ICCPR nor is it a member of the United Nations. As a result, although Israel is bound under the 1993 Fundamental Agreement to observe the freedom of religion vis-à-vis the Holy See, in accordance with the above international instruments, the Holy See is bound to observe this freedom vis-à-vis Israel, in accordance with the 1948 Universal Declaration alone.

The following sections examine the evolution of the freedom to proselytize as part of the freedom of religion. Undoubtedly, the subject of proselytism aroused much controversy during the deliberations of the major global documents that defined freedom of religion under international law.[22] Finally, this chapter draws its conclusions regarding the scope of the freedom of proselytism in Holy See–Israel relations.

### The Evolution of the Freedoms to Maintain and Change a Religion

The first arena of the inter-religious controversy regarding conversion and proselytism was the UN General Assembly's Third Committee. The draft Article 18 of the 1948 Universal Declaration, as submitted to the General Assembly, provided that "[e]veryone has the right to freedom of thought, conscience and religion; this right includes freedom to change his religion or belief, and freedom, either alone or in community with others and in public or private, to manifest his religion or belief in teaching, practice, worship and observance."[23]

The representative of Saudi Arabia objected to the language contained in the second portion of draft Article 18 that recognized "the right to change one's religion or belief."[24] Although the objection concerned the freedom of individuals to change religions, the explanation provided by the Saudi Arabian representative, as well as those of other Muslim states, indicated that the objection was aimed at avoiding foreign mission and political intervention.[25] The Third Committee rejected the Saudi Arabian proposal to delete the second part of the draft article. Draft Article 18 was ultimately adopted by twenty-seven states with five Islamic states against and twelve abstentions.[26] The final version of the 1948 Universal Declaration included the original formulation.[27]

The issue of conversion re-emerged during the drafting stages of the ICCPR. The text submitted to the General Assembly provided, in part, as follows:

(1) Everyone shall have the right to freedom of thought, conscience and religion. This right shall include freedom to maintain or to change his religion or belief, and freedom, either individually or in community with others and in

public or private, to manifest his religion or belief in worship, observance, practice and teaching.[28]

When the Third Committee of the General Assembly considered this text, the representative of Saudi Arabia objected to the formulation because it could be construed to favor missionary activities.[29] Following the proposed amendments by Brazil, the Philippines, and the United Kingdom, the Third Committee compromised between the conflicting proposals. Under an amendment that was later incorporated into the final version of the ICCPR, the phrase "to maintain or to change his religion or belief" was replaced by the words "to have or to adopt a religion or belief of his choice."[30] The final text of Article 18 reads as follows:

(1) Everyone shall have the right to freedom of thought, conscience and religion. This right shall include freedom to have or to adopt a religion or belief of his choice, and freedom, either individually or in community with others and in public or private, to manifest his religion or belief in worship, observance, practice and teaching.[31]

The second paragraph of Article 18 was adopted as amended by the General Assembly, providing that "[n]o one shall be subject to coercion which would impair his freedom to have or to adopt a religion or belief of his choice."[32] Article 18(3) provides that "[f]reedom to manifest one's religion or belief may be subject only to such limitations as are prescribed by law and are necessary to protect public safety, order, health, or morals or the fundamental rights and freedoms of others."[33]

The main difference between the text of Article 18 of the Universal Declaration and that of the 1966 ICCPR is that the explicit freedom "to change his religion" in the Universal Declaration was replaced by more vague words of "to have or to adopt a religion . . . of his choice."

The third global instrument concerning the freedom of religion, the 1981 Declaration, is not a binding treaty like the ICCPR, but is considered as a guide for interpreting international norms that define the freedom of religion.[34] In light of the former debates, it is not surprising that the right to change a religion was fiercely debated during the deliberations over the 1981 Declaration.[35] The trend toward the exclusion, or at least the erosion, of any explicit reference to the right to change a religion has continued and even intensified.

The text of draft Article 1 of the 1981 Declaration, submitted to the General Assembly by the Commission of Human Rights and the Economic and Social Council, was identical to Article 18 of the ICCPR. The language regarding the individual's freedom "to have or to adopt a religion or belief of his choice" was opposed by forty Muslim states.[36] Again, the desire to avoid tacit approval of proselytism was one of the primary reasons that motivated the Muslim states to propose the dele-tion of these words.[37] The Western states realized that the allegiance of the Muslim states held the key to the adoption of the 1981 Declaration. To garner universal ap-proval, the Western states acquiesced to the inclusion of the Muslim states' pro-posal contingent upon the adoption of a new article in order not to derogate from the Universal Declaration and the international covenants.[38]

The final version of Article 1 which emerged from these negotiations provides that:

1. Everyone shall have the right to freedom of thought, conscience and religion. This right shall include freedom to have a religion or whatever belief of his choice, and freedom, either individually or in community with others and in public or private, to manifest his religion or belief in worship, observance, prac-tice and teaching.
2. No one shall be subject to coercion which would impair his freedom to have a religion or belief of his choice.
3. Freedom to manifest one's religion or belief may be subject only to such limita-tions as are prescribed by law and are necessary to protect public safety, order, health or morals or the fundamental rights and freedoms of others.[39]

Article 8 embodies the compromise that paved the road for the adoption of the 1981 Declaration, providing that "[n]othing in the present Declaration shall be con-strued as restricting or derogating from any right defined in the Universal Decla-ration on Human Rights and the International Covenants on Human Rights."[40]

### The Freedom of Proselytism under Contemporary International Law

The examination of the aforementioned international documents raises the question of whether the freedom of religion includes the freedom to proselytize. First, it is important to distinguish between the internal and the external aspects of the freedom of religion. The internal aspect embraces the internal (autonomous) freedom to believe in a religion or to change it without interference. The external aspect refers to the freedom to manifest one's religion either alone or in a commu-nity.[41] When analyzing the evolution of the freedom of religion under these global instruments, it becomes apparent that while the debate between Muslim and Western states focused on text regarding the internal aspect of the freedom of in-dividuals to change religion, the apparent motive underlying the Muslim states' position concerned the external aspect, or the freedom of proselytism.

Under general international law, the individual's freedom to change a religion, that is, the internal aspect, is hardly disputed.[42] Consequently, national laws that proscribe apostasy are inconsistent with contemporary international law.[43] The question regarding the freedom of proselytism, however, is still unsettled. This question, as elaborated earlier, involves two distinct freedoms: the freedom of the proselytizer to conduct proselytizing activities (the "positive" sense of freedom) and the freedom of the potential convert/proselyte not to be interfered with in his faith by proselytizing activities (the "negative" sense of freedom).[44] The elements constituting the freedom to proselytize, the negative and positive aspects, are expressed in international human rights law as the freedom to maintain a religion and the freedom to change someone else's religion respectively. We shall first examine the freedom to conduct proselytizing activities. Next, we will consider the relationship between the two freedoms under contemporary international law.

Whether an individual has the (positive) freedom to proselytize is derived from the external dimension of the freedom of religion. Although the freedom of proselytism is not explicitly mentioned in international agreements, the external aspect of the freedom is commonly described as the "freedom, either individually or in community with others . . . to manifest his religion or belief in worship, observance, practice, and teaching."[45] Article 6 of the 1981 Declaration elaborates further and provides a list of nine specific freedoms included in the freedom of religion, some of which may be relevant to proselytism. Article 6(d) of the 1981 Declaration provides for the freedom "[t]o write, issue and disseminate relevant publications," and Article 6(e) refers to the freedom "[t]o teach a religion or belief in places suitable for these purposes.[46] Additionally, the freedom of expression may protect other proselytic activities.[47]

In light of these international agreements, it is clear that where proselytism is part of "manifesting a religion with others," proselytism is *prima facie* included with the freedom of religion. This is clearly the case with some religions like Christianity, for whose adherents the mission is an essential duty.[48] In opposition stands the freedom of adherents of other faiths to practice their religion without interference. The ICCPR and the 1981 Declaration describe this autonomy as the "freedom to have a religion." The relationship between the freedom to maintain a religion and the freedom to change a religion contained in international agreements warrants careful scrutiny.

The evolution of the texts of the universal documents shows that the emphasis has shifted from the freedom to change a religion toward an emphasis on the individual freedom to retain a religion without interference. Article 18 of the 1948 Universal Declaration explicitly refers to the freedom to change a religion, but does not mention the freedom to maintain a religion. Article 18 of the 1966 ICCPR refers to the freedom "to have a religion," but obscures the freedom to change a religion, "freedom to adopt a religion . . . of his choice."[49] Article 1 of the 1981 Declaration mentions the "freedom to have a religion," but the reference to freedom to change a religion was deliberately deleted from the final text.[50]

This shift does not indicate that the freedom to change one's religion on the internal level is not protected under international law, or that proselytism is not included within the freedom of religion on the external level.[51] However, the tendency to emphasize the freedom to maintain a religion and to weaken, or obscure, the freedom to change a religion should not be underestimated. Rather, this trend should be given due weight when delineating the border between the freedom of proselytism and the individual's freedom to maintain a religion without interference.

The boundary between the freedom of proselytism and the freedom to maintain a religion without interference may be drawn in various locations alongside a continuum. At one end of the continuum, the freedom to maintain a religion is completely protected by the prohibition against proselytism, at the other, an absolute protection is accorded to the freedom of proselytism by a norm that prohibits any restriction on such activities.

Two intermediate positions may reconcile the disparity between these extremes. Closer to the position assigning maximum protection to the freedom to maintain a religion, it is possible to consider a religious belief as a "restricted-access domain." This "semiprivate" religious[52] realm should be protected from certain intrusive acts, including some proselytism activities.[53] Closer to the position assigning maximum protection to the freedom of proselytism, it is possible to set a rule permitting proselytism with an exception prohibiting coercive acts that impair free choice.[54]

| Maximum protection to the freedom to maintain a religion (complete prohibition of proselytism). | Restricted-access religious domain (proselytism activities penetrating the "semiprivate" realm are prohibited). | Only coercive acts are prohibited. | Maximum protection to the freedom to change a religion (absolute freedom of proselytism). |
|---|---|---|---|

The difference between the two intermediate positions on the continuum is the degree of limitation imposed on proselytic activities. Whereas only coercive acts are prohibited under the second formulation, additional proselytic activities which invade the semiprivate domain are prohibited under the first formulation. Thus, both intermediate models prohibit forced conversion or exerting improper pressure, for example, by material inducements.[55] However, actively approaching other persons in order to persuade them to indicate or discuss their religious beliefs would be permissible under the second intermediate position, but could be prohibited under the first intermediate position protecting the semiprivate domain.[56]

Having defined the alternative locations on the continuum, the unsettled question is which position reflects prevailing principles under international law. First, in light of the aforementioned global instruments, it is clear that the two extreme positions on the scale are illegal under international law. The freedom to proselytize, as a component of the freedom to manifest a religion, is protected under international law, and consequently a sweeping prohibition on proselytism is unlawful. On the other hand, the freedom to maintain a religion is also protected under international law, and an absolute freedom of proselytism without limitation is unquestionably also illegal.

The two intermediate positions, which restrict proselytism to a different degree, are central to the dilemma regarding the freedom to proselytize under international law. The intermediate position which prohibits only coercive acts is more consistent with the freedom to change a religion. On the other hand, the "semiprivate" position is more in line with the freedom to maintain a religion. The previous analysis of the evolution of international law regarding the relationship between the freedoms to maintain and to change a religion demonstrates that the recent trend in international law emphasizes the freedom to maintain a religion, thus obscuring the freedom to change a religion. This trend suggests that the intermediate position representing the restricted-access realm is more consistent with contemporary international law.

Accordingly, this analysis of the evolution of the freedom of religion leads to the conclusion that present international law permits proselytism to the extent that it does not traverse the "limited-access religious realm" of individuals. One may suggest that Article 8 of the 1981 Declaration preserves completely the previous equilibrium between the clashing freedoms as it existed under the 1966 ICCPR and the 1948 Universal Declaration. This view, however, overlooks the explicit and deliberate change in the main provision in the 1981 Declaration (Article 1) that was made following adamant opposition of forty Muslim states to the former treaty provisions.[57]

The theme underlying the "semiprivate" religious domain is that persons should not be asked to reveal or discuss their religious preference, either explicitly or implicitly through a request to participate in a religious activity, unless they have previously expressed a desire to do so. Thus, for example, operating a religious center that provides religious articles or services to persons who indicate their will to receive them is permitted under this principle.[58] Approaching a person without a prior invitation in order to persuade him/her to discuss his/her religion, whether privately or publicly, constitutes a trespass upon the "semiprivate" religious realm and should be prohibited.

## The Case Law of the European Court of Human Rights and General International Law

It would be useful to examine the judgments rendered by the European Court of Human Rights in light of the principles of general international law regarding the freedom of proselytism. In *Kokkinakis v. Greece*,[59] the applicants visited the home of Mrs. Kyriaki, a member of the Greek Orthodox Church, to discuss with her possible conversion to the Jehovah's Witnesses. Mr. Kokkinakis was subsequently found guilty and prosecuted under a Greek law that proscribed proselytism.[60] His initial sentence was four months imprisonment, which was later converted into a pecuniary penalty.[61] In his application to the European Court of Human Rights, Mr. Kokkinakis argued, *inter alia,* that the Greek criminal proceedings infringed his freedom of religion under Article 9 of the 1950 European Convention for the Protection of Human Rights and Fundamental Freedoms (ECHR),[62] which is very similar to Article 18 of the 1948 Universal Declaration.[63]

The European Commission and the Court of Human Rights ruled that proselytism is included within the freedom to manifest one's religion, a right protected by Article 9 of the ECHR.[64] Consequently, the Greek statute constituted an interference with Mr. Kokkinakis's exercise of his right under the article.[65] Next, the court considered whether the Greek law was justified under the permitted restrictions on the freedom of religion provided under Article 9(2) of the ECHR.[66] Greece contended that the law aimed at prohibiting proselytism in order to protect the freedom of religion of other people maintaining a different religion from that of Mr. Kokkinakis.[67] Both the commission and the court agreed that the law has been "in pursuit of a legitimate aim under Article 9 para. 2 [of the ECHR]: namely, the protection of the rights and freedoms of others, relied on by the Government."[68]

The next question examined by the court was whether the Greek legislation was necessary in a democratic society. The court made a distinction between

> bearing Christian witness and improper proselytism. The former corresponds to true evangelism, which a report drawn up in 1956 under the auspices of the World Council of Churches describes as an essential mission and responsibility of every Christian and every church. [T]he latter represent[s] a corruption or deformation of it . . . [and] is not compatible with respect for the freedom of thought, conscience and religion of others.[69]

The court observed that the Greek courts established Mr. Kokkinakis's liability by merely citing the Greek legislation without specifying in what way he had attempted to convince his neighbor by improper means.[70] Consequently, the court held that Mr. Kokkinakis's conviction was unjustified by a pressing social need.[71]

Moreover, the court concluded that the conviction was disproportionate to the legitimate legislative aim and, as a consequence, was not necessary in a democratic society.[72] The court held that the Greek law, as applied to Mr. Kokkinakis, violated Article 9 of the ECHR.[73]

The judgment rendered by the European Court of Human Rights in *Larissis v. Greece*[74] is largely based upon the *Kokkinakis* case and further elaborates on the concept of improper proselytism. The applicants in the *Larissis* case were followers of the Pentecostal Church and officers in the Greek air force.[75] The three applicants attempted to convince several soldiers under their command, as well as civilians, to accept the beliefs of the Pentecostal Church. They were indicted and found guilty by several Greek courts for violating the local law regarding proselytism. The applicants argued before the European Court that their prosecution, conviction, and punishment amounted to a violation of Article 9 (and other provisions) of the European Convention.[76] The court considered that it was not disputed that these acts by Greece constituted interference with the exercise of the applicants' rights to freedom of religion under Article 9(1) of the Convention.[77] Consequently, the court proceeded to examine whether these acts were consistent with requirements set out in Article 9(2) of the Convention. The court found that the above measures were "prescribed by law" and essentially purused the legitimate aim of protecting the rights and freedoms of others.[78] Citing the *Kokkinakis* decision, the court affirmed that the freedom to manifest religion includes the right to try to convince others to change their religion and that Article 9 does not protect "improper proselytism."[79]

The European Court made an important distinction between the proselytism of the involved members of the air force and that of the civilians. As to the airmen, the court pronounced that

> [T]he hierarchical structures which are a feature of life in the armed forces may colour every aspect of the relations between military and personnel, making it difficult for a subordinate to rebuff the approaches of an individual of superior rank or to withdraw from a conversation initiated by him. Thus, what would in the civilian world be seen as an innocuous exchange of ideas which the recipient is free to accept or object, may, within the confines of military life, be viewed as a form of harassment or the application of undue pressure in abuse of power.[80]

Implementing this distinction, and following the examination of the evidence in each case, the court found that the Greek measures relating to the airmen did not violate Article 9 of the Convention.[81] The court, however, found that the civilians whom the applicants attempted to convert were not subject to pressure and constraints of the same kind as the airmen. Consequently, the Greek measures regarding these attempts to proselytize civilians were considered by the court as violating Article 9 of the Convention.[82]

By evaluating the European Court's decisions in light of general principles of international law, it is clear that the different legal rules prevailing in the different systems lead to different conclusions regarding the freedom to proselytize. First, it is important to examine similar legal principles recognized in both the European and global frameworks. The court in *Kokkinakis* and *Larissis* recognized that the proselytism issue involves both the freedom to manifest a religion through proselytism and the freedom of the potential convert to maintain his or her religion. This was the basis for the intermediate ruling accepting that the Greek prohibition on proselytism was "in pursuit of a legitimate aim": protecting the freedoms of others.[83] This ruling is certainly consistent with the global principles regarding proselytism.

Confronted with divergent aspects of the rival freedoms to proselytize and to maintain a religion, the court distinguished between "bearing Christian witness" and "improper proselytism,"[84] and held that the latter is unlawful. Although the court did not define "improper proselytism," it cited the report drawn under the auspices of the World Council of Churches noting that proselytism may include violence, brainwashing, offering material or social advantages, or exerting improper influence on people in distress.[85] This description suggests that the court drew the line separating lawful and unlawful proselytism in a way similar to the prohibition of "coercion" established in the ICCPR and 1981 Declaration.[86]

The texts of Article 9 of the ECHR and Article 18 of the Universal Declaration are quite similar. It appears that the attempt by the European Court of Human Rights to balance the competing freedoms to maintain and to change religion through the limitation of coercion is compatible with the texts of these instruments. However, the court's equilibrium is not necessarily consistent with the significant changes that occurred on the global level following the conclusion of the ECHR in 1950. The developments in general international law, expressed in the different texts of the 1966 ICCPR and the 1981 Declaration, shifted the focus from the freedom to change a religion toward the freedom to maintain a religion without interference.[87] This process led to the current balance between these freedoms: the "semiprivate" religious realm.

Apart from the different legal principles that prevail in the different legal systems, the result also may have been influenced by the fact that the judges in the *Kokkinakis* and *Larissis* cases were European. The text of the judgments, including the crucial distinction made by the court between "bearing Christian witness" and "improper proselytism" (which was cited from a report drawn up under the auspices of the World Council of Churches), suggests that the judges that comprised a majority of the court were influenced by Christian beliefs. Christianity maintains starkly contrasting views regarding proselytism in comparison to some other religions.

## The Parties' Obligations regarding Proselytism
## under the Fundamental Agreement

The obligations undertaken by the parties to the 1993 Fundamental Agreement regarding the freedom of religion are asymmetrical: in addition to the Universal Declaration, each party is bound to observe this freedom in accordance with international instruments to which it is a party. An analysis of the international instruments shows that different principles that balance the freedom to maintain a religion without interference and the freedom to proselytize emerged from different instruments.

The Holy See is bound to observe the freedom of religion in accordance with the 1948 Universal Declaration.[88] The Universal Declaration emphasizes the freedom to change a religion but does not explicitly mention the freedom to maintain a religion. Thus, the principle that emerges from the Universal Declaration is similar to that which was adopted by the European Court of Human Rights in the *Kokkinakis* and *Larissis* cases, proselytism is permitted as long as it does not involve coercive acts impairing free choice.[89]

Israel is bound under the 1993 Fundamental Agreement to observe the freedom of religion in accordance with the Universal Declaration, the ICCPR, and the 1981 Declaration. The principle that emerges from these instruments creates a different balance between the competing freedoms: proselytic activities are allowed to the extent that they do not invade the "semiprivate" religious domain of others. Thus, the obligations regarding proselytism assigned to the Holy See and Israel under the Fundamental Agreement are asymmetrical.

### Conclusion

The obligations accepted by Israel and the Holy See under the Fundamental Agreement regarding freedom of religion are not the same. Apart from the Universal Declaration, both parties are bound to observe the international instruments to which they are parties. Because of their asymmetric legal postures, the parties are bound to comply with different duties concerning proselytic freedom. Although the Holy See is bound only to observe such freedom of proselytism with the narrow exception regarding coercive tactics, Israel is obligated to respect proselytic freedom to the extent that such efforts do not involve activities which intrude upon the "semiprivate" religious sphere.

The evolution of international law reveals that the freedom to proselytize is a source of tension not only between Jews and Christians but also among the other world religions. Developments in international human rights law demonstrate that norms in this sphere are affected by the religious beliefs of different religions and geopolitical influences of states backing these religions. Notwithstanding the global controversy concerning the breadth of proselytic freedom, certain rules have gained broad acceptance under modern international law.

The rules governing proselytism that are widely accepted in the international community today are threefold. First, everyone has the freedom to change his or her religion, and consequently, national laws that prohibit or punish "apostasy" are unlawful. Second, proselytism is included in the freedom to manifest a religion for some religions and, therefore, is protected to a certain extent under international law. Consequently, national laws prohibiting all proselytic activities are not consistent with international human rights law. Finally, it is accepted that coercive measures involved in proselytism that impair free choice are illegal.

The most controversial issue concerns the balance between the freedom to maintain a religion without interference and the freedom to proselytize. The evolution of general international law on the freedom of religion leads us to the conclusion that the border between these two competing freedoms should be drawn along the "semiprivate" religious realm of each person. Certain proselytic activities that penetrate this protective region should be prohibited under international law. The freedom of believers to be free from unwanted interference should not be overlooked. The specific rules derived from the concept of restricted-access religious domain are not yet fully clear. Future developments may further clarify this sensitive issue in international human rights law.

## NOTES

I am grateful to Professor Natan Lerner, Professor Ruth Lapidoth, Professor Eyal Benvenisti, and Dr. Leonard Hammer for their helpful comments on earlier drafts. Additionally, I would like to thank Mrs. Daniela Rothman for her valuable research assistance.

1. Eugene J. Fisher, "A New Maturity in Christian-Jewish Dialogue: An Annotated Bibliography 1975–89," in *In Our Time* 107, 136 (Eugene J. Fisher & Leon Klenicki eds., 1990). See, for example, the Israeli legislation prohibiting the provision or promise of material benefits as an inducement to change a religion, Penal Law Amendment (Enticement to Change Religion), 1977, 32 L. S. I. 62 (1977–78).

2. See Harold J. Berman, "Religious Rights in Russia at a Time of Tumultuous Transition: A Historical Theory," in *Religious Human Rights in Global Perspective: Legal Perspectives* 285, 301–3 (Johan D. van der Vyver & John Witte, Jr. eds., 1996) [hereinafter *Religious Human Rights*] (discussing the tensions stemming from the efforts of the Russian Orthodox Church to repel Western evangelical missionaries); W. Cole Durham, Jr., "Perspectives on Religious Liberty: A Comparative Framework," in *Religious Human Rights, supra,*

at 1, 4–5 (examining the emergence of proselytism as a source of tension and divisiveness among various religious denominations and its impact on international politics).

3. See Robert W. Hefner, "World Building and the Rationality of Conversion," in *Conversion to Christianity: Historical and Anthropological Perspectives on a Great Transformation* 3, 6–10 (Robert W. Hefner ed., 1993) (reviewing competing theories explaining the impetus behind proselytism among the various world religions).

4. Max L. Stackhouse, "Missionary Activity," in 9 *The Encyclopedia of Religion* 563, 563 (Mircea Eliade ed., 1987).

5. See Drew Fudenberg & Jean Tirole, *Game Theory* 4 (1991) (discussing the concept of zero-sum games); James D. Morrow, *Game Theory for Political Scientists* 74–75 (1994) (same).

6. For other settings in the international arena presenting strong features of zero-sum games, see Moshe Hirsch, "The Future Negotiations over Jerusalem, Strategical Factors and Game Theory," 45 *Cath. U. L. Rev.* 699, 700 (1996) (analyzing the status of Jerusalem according to the principles of game theory).

7. See William R. Hutchison, "Christianity, Culture, and Complications: Protestant Attitudes toward Missions," in *Pushing the Faith: Proselytism and Civility in a Pluralistic World* 78, 79–80 (Martin E. Marty & Frederick E. Greenspahn eds., 1988) [hereinafter *Pushing the Faith*] (discussing the roots of the Protestant mission); Stephen Neill, preface to *Christian Missions* 9 (1965) (commenting on the overwhelming breadth of history surrounding the expansion of Christianity); Robert J. Schreiter, "Changes in Roman Catholic Attitudes toward Proselytism and Mission," in *Pushing the Faith, supra*, at 93 (discussing Christian mission); John Witte, Jr., "A Primer on the Rights and Wrongs of Proselytism," 31 *Cumb. L. Rev.* 619, 622 (2000).

8. However, Jews actively proselytized in the late ancient and early medieval times. See Robert Goldenberg, "The Place of Other Religions in Ancient Jewish Thought, with Particular Reference to Early Rabbinic Judaism," in *Pushing the Faith, supra* note 7, at 27, 27–40 (tracing the development of proselytic attitudes in the Jewish faith); Robert M. Seltzer, "Joining the Jewish People from Biblical to Modern Times," in *Pushing the Faith, supra* note 7, at 41, 41–63 (same).

9. See Interview with Adv. Eitan Margalit, adviser to the Israeli minister of foreign affairs on inter-religious affairs, 2 *Justice* 24, 28 (June 1994).

10. Isaiah Berlin, *Four Essays on Liberty* 118 (Oxford: Oxford University Press, 1969).

11. See id. at 122 (discussing the notion of "negative" freedom).

12. Id. at 123.

13. See id. at 131–34 (discussing the notion of "positive" freedom).

14. Id. at 143–44.

15. See The Fundamental Agreement Between the Holy See and the State of Israel, Dec. 30, 1993, Vatican-Isr., art. 1, 33 I. L. M. 153, 154 (1994) [hereinafter Fundamental Agreement].

16. Id. art. 1, sec. 1 (emphasis added).

17. Id. art. 1, sec. 2 (emphasis added).

18. Dec. 10, 1948, G. A. Res. 217 A(III), U. N. GAOR, 3d Sess., U. N. Doc. A/810 (1948) [hereinafter 1948 Universal Declaration].

19. See id.

20. Dec. 19, 1966, 999 U. N. T. S. 171 (1967) [hereinafter ICCPR].

21. G. A. Res. 36/55, U. N. GAOR, 36th Sess., Supp. No. 51, at 171, U. N. Doc. A/36/51 (1982) [hereinafter 1981 Declaration].

22. On the evolution of the freedom of religion in international law, see Bahiyyih G. Tahzib, *Freedom of Religion or Belief: Ensuring Effective Inter-national Legal Protection* 63–121 (1996) (surveying the provisions from the major global documents from 1945 to the present); John P. Humphrey, "Political and Related Rights," in *Human Rights in International Law: Legal and Policy Issues* 171, 176–77 (Theodor Meron ed., 1988) (reviewing the historical development in the global recognition of religious freedom in international legal increments); Natan Lerner, "Religious Human Rights under the United Nations," in *Religious Human Rights, supra* note 2, at 79 (discussing the evolution of the freedom of religion under international law).

23. 1948 Universal Declaration, *supra* note 18, at 74. On the status of the Universal Declaration in international law, see Moshe Hirsch, "The Universal Declaration Rights: 40 Years Old," 29 *Int'l Probs. Soc. & Pol.* 49 (1990) (Hebrew with summary in English).

24. J. A. Walkate, "The Right of Everyone to Change His Religion or Belief: Some Observations," 30 *Netherlands Int'l L. Rev.* 146, 152 (1983).

25. See Tahzib, *supra* note 22, at 73–75 (citing statements of Saudi Arabia's representative in addressing the UN General Assembly's Third Committee).

26. See id. at 75.

27. See Walkate, *supra* note 24, at 152.

28. Id. at 153 (quoting draft Article 18, sec. 1 of the ICCPR); see also id. at 153–54 (discussing the negotiations of the Commission on Human Rights about this provision).

29. See Tahzib, *supra* note 22, at 84–85; see also Natan Lerner, "Proselytism, Change of Religion, and International Human Rights," 12 *Emory Int'l L. Rev.* 101, 119–21 (1998) (discussing the deliberations surrounding Article 18 of the ICCPR).

30. See Walkate, *supra* note 24, at 153; see also Brice Dickson, "The United Nations and Freedom of Religion," 44 *Int'l & Comp. L.Q.* 327, 342 (1995) (discussing the negotiations preceding the adoption of Article 18 under the ICCPR).

31. ICCPR, *supra* note 20, art. 18, sec. 1, at 178.

32. Id. art. 18, sec. 2, at 178.

33. Id. art. 18, sec. 3, at 178. Subsection 4 of Article 18 provides that: "The States Parties to the present Covenant undertake to have respect for the liberty of parents and, when applicable, legal guardians to ensure the religious and moral education of their children in conformity with their own convictions." Id. art. 18, sec. 4, at 178.

34. See Tazhib, *supra* note 22, at 186–88 (reviewing the legal status of the 1981 Declaration in the international arena); Dickson, *supra* note 30, at 344 (discussing the distinguishing features of the 1981 Declaration); Lerner, *supra* note 29, at 114 (characterizing the 1981 Declaration as "the most important international instrument regarding religious rights"); Donna J. Sullivan, "Advancing the Freedom of Religion or Belief through the UN Declaration on the Elimination of Religious Intolerance and Discrimination," 82 *Am. J.*

*Int'l L.* 487, 488 (1988) (asserting that because the 1981 Declaration was drafted in normative terms, it "gives specific content to the general statements of rights to freedom of religion . . . contained in the major human rights instruments").

35. See Myres S. McDougal et al., *Human Rights and World Public Order* 677–84 (1980) (discussing the history of the 1981 Declaration); Tahzib, *supra* note 22, at 164 (describing the road leading to the adoption of the 1981 Declaration as "long, arduous and full of obstacles"); Roger S. Clark, "The United Nations and Religious Freedom," 11 *N.Y.U. J. Int'l L. & Pol.* 197, 197 (1978) (examining the difficulty experienced by the United Nations in reaching an agreement to eliminate intolerance and discrimination based on religion or belief); Natan Lerner, "The Final Text of the UN Declaration Against Intolerance and Discrimination Based on Religion or Belief," 12 *Isr. Y.B. on Hum. Rts.* 185–88 (1982) (discussing the compromise regarding the "right to change a religion" that was adopted under the 1981 Declaration); Natan Lerner,"Toward a Draft Declaration Against Religious Intolerance and Discrimination," 11 *Isr. Y.B. on Hum. Rts.* 82–103 (1981) (providing a section-by-section analysis of the proposed draft that later became the 1981 Declaration).

36. See Walkate, *supra* note 24, at 148–50 (discussing the Islamic objections to the "right to change one's religion" provisions).

37. See Clark, *supra* note 35, at 197.

38. See Tahzib, *supra* note 22, at 167–68; Walkate, *supra* note 24, at 150.

39. 1981 Declaration, *supra* note 21, art. 1, at 171.

40. Id. art. 8, at 172.

41. The external freedom to manifest a religion is subject to certain limitations. See id. art. 1, sec. 3, at 171 (providing that the freedom to manifest a religion may be limited only when necessary "to protect public safety, order, health, or morals or the fundamental rights . . . of others"); ICCPR, *supra* note 20, art. 18, sec. 3, at 178 (same). The internal aspect of freedom of religion, however, is not similarly constrained.

42. See "UN Human Rights Committee: General Comment No. 22 on Article 18 of the International Covenant on Civil and Political Rights," 15 *Hum. Rts. L.J.* 233, 233 (1994) [hereinafter "Human Rights Committee"]; Tahzib, *supra* note 22, at 169; Karl Josef Partsch, "Freedom of Conscience and Expression, and Political Freedoms," in *The International Bill of Rights* 209, 211 (Louis Henkin ed., 1981); Sullivan, *supra* note 34, at 495; Walkate, *supra* note 24, at 154–55.

43. See Ann Elizabeth Mayer, *Islam and Human Rights: Tradition and Politics 141* (2d ed. 1995) (discussing the Shari'a rule that forbids Muslims from converting from Islam); Steven T. McFarland, "Missionaries and Indigenous Evangelists," *Cumb. L. Rev.* 599, 608 (2000).

44. See *supra* notes 10–14 and accompanying text (discussing these concepts).

45. 1981 Declaration, *supra* note 21, art. 1, sec. 1, at 171; see also ICCPR, *supra* note 20, art. 18, sec. 1, at 178; 1948 Universal Declaration, *supra* note 18, art. 18, at 74.

46. 1981 Declaration, *supra* note 21, art. 6, secs. d–e, at 172. Moreover, Article 6 also states that this list of freedoms does not constitute an exhaustive list. See id. (providing that "the right to freedom of . . . religion . . . shall include, *inter alia,* the following freedoms"); see

also Tahzib, *supra* note 22, at 183 (enumerating various freedoms that were excluded from Article 6 of the 1981 Declaration); "Human Rights Committee," *supra* note 42, at 233 (listing various acts that fall under the rubric of manifesting a religion or belief).

47. See ICCPR, *supra* note 20, art. 19, sec. 2, at 178 ("Everyone shall have the right to freedom of expression. . . ."); 1948 Universal Declaration, *supra* note 18, art. 19, at 74–75 (same); *infra* note 57 (discussing the relationship between the freedom of religion and the freedom of expression).

48. See *supra* note 7 and accompanying text (discussing the Christian mission).

49. ICCPR, *supra* note 20, art. 18, sec. 1, at 178.

50. See *supra* note 38 and accompanying text.

51. See text accompanying note 45.

52. See Ruth Gavison, "Privacy and the Limits of Law," 89 *Yale L.J.* 421, 428–30 (1980) (defining "privacy" as "a limitation of others' access to an individual"); see also Lerner, *supra* note 29 (asserting that a "zone of privacy" is tantamount to a "zone of freedom" comprised of various qualities and lifestyles every individual seeks to experience).

53. See *infra* text accompanying notes 55–58 for the question of which proselytism activities trespass the "semiprivate" religious realm.

54. The prohibition on coercion is explicitly mentioned in Article 18, subsection 2 of the ICCPR, and Article 1, subsection 2 of the 1981 Declaration. See ICCPR, *supra* note 20, art. 18, sec. 2, at 178; 1981 Declaration, *supra* note 21, art. 1, sec. 2, at 171. These provisions should certainly not dictate that all proselytic activities which do not involve coercion are permitted. Such a conclusion could have been justified if Article 18(1) of the covenant and Article 1(1) of the declaration would have protected only the freedom to proselytize and not the freedom to maintain a religion. Thus, the two competing freedoms are included in the first paragraph of these articles (though the freedom of proselytism only implicitly, as part of the freedom to manifest a religion), and the borderline between them should be drawn "within" the first paragraph, and not by a distinction between the main clause stating the freedom and the second clause dealing with coercion.

55. On the activities which are considered "coercive acts," see Acrot Krishmaswain, "Study of Discrimination in the Matters of Religious Rights and Practice," 11 *N.Y.U. J. Int'l L. & Pol.* 227, 230–33 (1978); see also Tahzib, *supra* note 22, at 127–28; Sullivan, *supra* note 34, at 494.

56. See *infra* note 58 and accompanying text for further elaboration on proselytism activities which are prohibited under the "semiprivate" religious concept.

57. Proselytism frequently involves freedom of expression, which is also protected under international human rights law. The above provisions regarding the freedom of religion *seem* to constitute *lex-specialist* norms which regulate the subject of proselytism. The motives underlying the freedom of expression do not necessarily apply to proselytism. Proselytism may be perceived as an instrument to preserve the basic freedom to change a religion. This, however, should not detract from the need to protect the corresponding freedom to maintain a religion without interference of proselytism. The concept of "semiprivate religious realm," it is submitted, leads to an adequate balance between the competing freedoms.

58. Similarly, the operation of religious television and radio channels, as well as mailing various documents, is permissible under this principle.

59. *Kokkinakis v. Greece,* 36 *Y.B. Eur. Conv. on H.R.* 181 (Eur. Ct. on H. R., 1993); see also T. Jeremy Gunn, "Adjudicating Rights of Conscience under the European Convention on Human Rights," in *Religious Human Rights, supra* note 2, at 305, 318–30 (discussing the *Kokkinakis* case).

60. See *Kokkinakis, supra* note 59, at 182 (discussing the provisions of the Greek statutes that define and punish proselytism). Proselytism is expressly forbidden under the Greek Constitution. See Greece Const. pt. II, art. 13, 2 ("Proselytism is prohibited"). Mrs. Kokkinkas was eventually acquitted. See id.

61. See *Kokkinakis, supra* note 59, at 182.

62. Nov. 4, 1950, 213 U. N. T. S. 221, 230 [hereinafter ECHR]. Article 9, section 1 of the ECHR provides: "A(1) Everyone has the right to freedom of thought, conscience and religion; this right includes freedom to change his religion or belief and freedom, either alone or in community with others and in public or private, to manifest his religion or belief, in worship, teaching, practice and observance." Id.

63. See 1948 Universal Declaration, *supra* note 18, art. 18, at 74.

64. See *Kokkinakis, supra* note 59, at 182–83.

65. See id. at 183.

66. See id. Article 9, sec. 2, of the ECHR provides that:

2. Freedom to manifest one's religion or belief shall be subject only to such limitations as are prescribed by law and are necessary in a democratic society in the interests of public safety, for the protection of public order, health or morals, or for the protection of the rights and freedoms of others.

67. See *Kokkinakis, supra* note 59, at 183.

68. Id.

69. Id.

70. See id.

71. See id.

72. See id.

73. See id.

74. *Larissis and Others v. Greece* (Case 140/1996/759/958–960), 24 February 1998.

75. Ibid., para. 7–8.

76. Ibid., para. 36.

77. Ibid., para. 38.

78. Ibid., paras. 42–44.

79. Ibid., para. 45.

80. Ibid., para. 51.

81. Ibid., para. 54.

82. Ibid., paras. 59–60.

83. *Kokkinakis, supra* note 59, at 183, and *Larissis, supra* note 74, paras. 43–44.

84. Id.

85. See "Cases: *Kokkinakis v. Greece*," 17 *E.H.R.R.* 397, 422 (1994); *Larissis* case, *supra* note 74, para. 45.

86. The 1981 Declaration and the ICCPR both prohibit coercive proselytic tactics that impair the freedom of religion. See 1981 Declaration, *supra* note 21, art. 1, sec. 2, at 171; ICCPR, *supra* note 20, art. 18, sec. 2, at 178.

87. See *supra* notes 50–51 and 54 and accompanying text (discussing the shift in focus toward maintaining a religion without interference under international agreements).

88. See *supra* note 18.

89. See *Kokkinakis, supra* note 59, at 183.

# 10

## PROGRESS FOR PILGRIMS?

An Analysis of the Holy See–Israel
Fundamental Agreement

*Geoffrey R. Watson*

The dawn of the new millennium drew unprecedented numbers of Christian pilgrims to the Holy Land. Pope John Paul II proclaimed the year 2000 a jubilee year, and he issued an apostolic letter encouraging Catholics to participate by making pilgrimages to Israel and Rome. During the jubilee year, record numbers of Christians made pilgrimages to Bethlehem, Nazareth, the Church of the Holy Sepulcher in Jerusalem, and other holy sites in Israel.[1] In March 2000, the pope himself visited Israel; it was the first official papal visit to the Jewish state.[2]

Yet, as Moshe Hirsch has noted,[3] the 1993 Fundamental Agreement[4] between the Holy See and Israel "stops short of formally recognizing a legal right of [religious] pilgrimage."[5] The agreement provides only that the Holy See and Israel "have an interest in favoring Christian pilgrimages to the Holy Land."[6] It does not explicitly acknowledge an individual right to pilgrimage, and it imposes no duty on the Holy See or Israel to admit pilgrims or to facilitate pilgrimage.

This chapter explores whether the Fundamental Agreement's provisions on pilgrimage are consistent with international law. In particular, it asks whether international human rights law obliges states to admit foreign pilgrims, and if so, whether the existence of such an obligation should influence interpretation of the Fundamental Agreement.

The first section of this chapter takes up a logically prior question: whether the Fundamental Agreement is a legally binding treaty, and whether it should be interpreted in accordance with treaty law. The analysis rejects recent suggestions that one or both parties lack the capacity to make treaties, and it concludes that the agreement is a binding treaty that should be interpreted in accordance with the Vienna Convention on the Law of Treaties.

The second section suggests that human rights instruments have been surprisingly slow to recognize a right of international pilgrimage. There is some state practice that might reflect the existence of a right of international pilgrimage and a correlative duty to accept foreign pilgrims, but it is not clear that this practice arises out of a sense of legal obligation. This section concludes that there is at most an emerging customary-law right of pilgrimage, and that this right would be subject to reasonable restrictions relating to health, safety, and security, as well as restrictions designed to protect holy places themselves. Because the background law on pilgrimage is not well settled, that law should not directly affect interpretation of the Fundamental Agreement.

Finally, the third section of this chapter observes that human rights law does not prevent states from undertaking an obligation to admit pilgrims. If pilgrimage continues to grow, states someday may have to establish rules and quotas regulating the flow of pilgrimage, similar to those established by Saudi Arabia to regulate the Muslim Hajj. Ironically, the regulation of pilgrimage itself may spur recognition of pilgrimage as a human right.

### The Nature of the Fundamental Agreement

Is the Fundamental Agreement a treaty? This question is important because the answer determines whether the instrument is legally binding and how it will be interpreted. The Vienna Convention on the Law of Treaties[7] defines a treaty as an international agreement "between States" that is "governed by international law."[8] The Fundamental Agreement clearly is "governed" by "law." The final clauses of the agreement provide for its "entry into force,"[9] and the operative provisions of the agreement contain terms of obligation such as "shall" and "affirms."[10] Moreover, the agreement appears to be governed by international law, not domestic law. As is typical of treaties, the agreement makes no reference to any governing domestic law. More significantly, the Fundamental Agreement is subject to ratification, which is a common characteristic of a treaty.[11] The parties' use of the term "fundamental agreement" rather than "treaty" is of little consequence; under the Vienna Convention, a treaty does not require any "particular designation."[12]

But is the Fundamental Agreement an agreement "between states"? The answer to this question seems to be obvious: both parties are widely recognized as states, and they participate in treaties and international organizations only open to states. Even so, each party's claim to statehood has been challenged in recent times. Some states still refuse to acknowledge the State of Israel. Up until the U.S. invasion of Iraq, Saddam Hussein's regime routinely referred to Israel as the "Zionist entity."[13] And some commentators still refuse to acknowledge the statehood of either the Holy See or the City of the Vatican.[14]

Israel is obviously a state. Israel clearly meets the traditional four-pronged test of statehood: a defined territory, a permanent population, a government, and the capacity to engage in foreign relations.[15] Israel's border disputes are not inconsistent with its statehood; dozens of states have long-standing border disputes with their neighbors.[16] Likewise, it is irrelevant that some states still have not recognized the State of Israel. Under the prevailing "declaratory" theory of statehood, recognition is not an element of statehood.[17] In any event, Israel is now recognized by dozens of states and by its old nemesis, the Palestine Liberation Organization.[18] Israel's membership in the United Nations is additional evidence of its statehood.[19] Israel is unquestionably a state.

The Holy See, for its part, clearly has the capacity to enter into treaties, regardless of whether it meets the technical definition of a state. The Holy See's treaty-making capacity clearly is recognized both in state practice and in the negotiating history of the Vienna Convention on the Law of Treaties. State practice on this question is quite compelling: the Holy See has become a party to dozens of treaties, bilateral and multilateral, and few, if any, states have objected to this practice. As for the Vienna Convention, its *travaux préparatoires* recognize that the Holy See is a "subject of international law" that "enters into treaties on the same basis as States."[20] An early draft of the Vienna Convention would have extended its definition of a "treaty" to any international agreement between states or "other subjects of international law,"[21] including the Holy See. The final draft of the convention instead provides that it does not apply to "other subjects of international law," but adds that it does not affect "the legal force of such agreements."[22] Thus, the convention does not maintain that agreements with "other subjects of international law" are nonbinding instruments; rather, by acknowledging the "legal force" of such agreements, the convention implies that they may be binding under the customary law of treaties.

The great weight of scholarly opinion also has concluded that the Holy See has treaty-making capacity, whether or not it is a state in the strict sense of the word. Even commentators who doubt the Holy See's statehood appear to stop short of concluding that it lacks treaty-making capacity.[23] Some older commentary questioned the Holy See's capacity to enter into treaties during the period after Italy's subjugation of the papal state in 1870 and before Italy's recognition of the State of the City of the Vatican in 1929.[24] But after 1929, most scholars have accepted that the Holy See has the capacity to make treaties, and that the Vatican, Holy See, or both are states under customary international law.[25] Insofar as scholarly commentary is a source of international law,[26] it supports the conclusion that the Holy See has the capacity to make treaties whether or not it fits the traditional definition of a state.

Because it is clear that the Holy See has the capacity to make treaties such as the Fundamental Agreement, it is not strictly necessary to determine whether the Holy See, the Vatican, or both are a state. In any event, there is abundant evidence that either the Holy See, the Vatican, or both constitute a state. The only difficulty is that the Vatican, which has a territory, population, and government, seems to fit the traditional legal definition of statehood more easily than the Holy See, which consists of the pope and central institutions of the Roman Curia. Yet it is the Holy See, and not the Vatican, that is a party to the Fundamental Agreement.

To appreciate this problem, one must understand the juridical difference between the Holy See and the Vatican. According to the Code of Canon Law, the term "Holy See" (or "Apostolic See") applies "not only to the Roman Pontiff but also to the Secretariat of State, the Council for the Public Affairs of the Church, and other institutions of the Roman Curia."[27] The Holy See, then, refers to the pope and other high organs of the Catholic Church; it is the institution through which the pope exercises "spiritual sovereignty" over the "Church universal."[28] The City of the Vatican, by contrast, is a physical territory, surrounded by Italy, that exists to ensure the independence of the Holy See, to support the work of the Church, and to provide a tangible symbol of the Church's sovereignty. It was established by the 1929 Treaty of the Lateran between Italy and the Holy See, in which Italy recognized a "State of the Vatican" over which the Holy See would have exclusive sovereignty.[29]

How is it, then, that the Vatican is the "state" but the Holy See is the party to the Fundamental Agreement and other treaties? Several theories have been advanced to explain this unique treaty-making arrangement. One theory is that both are states, or at least international personalities, acting in a "real union."[30] A second view is that the Vatican is the state and the Holy See is its government.[31] A third is that the Vatican is a "vassal state" of the Holy See.[32] These theories have a common point of departure: the proposition that the Vatican has at least some attributes of statehood.

That proposition is undeniable. The Vatican does in fact meet the traditional requirements of statehood as expressed in the 1933 Montevideo Convention, namely, that a state must have a defined territory, a permanent population, a government, and the capacity to engage in foreign relations.[33] The City of the Vatican has a defined, albeit small, territory that occupies less than half a square mile of land, a third the size of the next smallest state, Monaco. It is generally accepted that "no rule prescribes a minimum" amount of territory.[34] One commentator who argues that the Vatican is not a state nonetheless concedes that "[t]he size of the state . . . is not relevant to its claim to statehood."[35] As such, the Vatican is the world's smallest state.

Skeptics about the Vatican's claim to statehood focus more on the Vatican's supposed lack of a permanent population. They argue that the Vatican's population of more than one thousand people is not "permanent" because "citizens" of the Vatican are generally "Church officials and employees . . . [whose] citizenship is temporary."[36] But the Vatican does include at least *some* people whose citizenship is permanent. The pope himself, of course, is a permanent resident of the Vatican. The constitutional laws of the City of the Vatican also provide that cardinals living in Vatican City or in Rome are citizens of the City of the Vatican,[37] and their citizenship is lost only when "they cease to reside in the City of the Vatican or in Rome."[38] Other people who "reside in the City of the Vatican in a permanent fashion because of their rank, office, service or employment" are citizens.[39] This provision obviously contemplates that their residence may be "permanent."

In any event, the "permanent population" test of statehood is not whether citizens retain their citizenship indefinitely; after all, many states contain large numbers of people who are not citizens of the state, as well as people who voluntarily give up their citizenship to move abroad. Instead, the test is whether the population is permanent as opposed to transient. The Vatican clearly satisfies that test. In an increasingly interdependent and hectic world, it seems unlikely that the law will move to a more stringent definition of permanence. Indeed, statehood doctrine has long been criticized for being too narrow because it excludes nomadic peoples and national liberation movements from the definition of statehood.[40]

Those who doubt the Vatican's statehood also argue that it lacks a government in the traditional sense.[41] In one incarnation, this argument stresses that the government of the Holy See is "charged with overseeing a religion, rather than a nation."[42] But, of course, the Pontifical Commission does oversee the relatively mundane business of running a nation: it has jurisdiction over internal matters such as postal and telegraph services, security, personnel matters, technical services, medical services, the radio system, the Vatican Observatory, and tourist services.[43]

Opponents of the Vatican's statehood also emphasize that one arm of government, the Secretariat of State, handles international relations, whereas another, the Pontifical Commission, handles internal matters.[44] Thus, it is said that "[t]he Pontifical Commission is not, strictly speaking, the 'government' of the Vatican City, since it is mainly responsible for technical and other services, and does not maintain relations with foreign states or the United Nations."[45]

This argument also might imply that the Vatican lacks the capacity to engage in foreign relations, since such matters are handled by the Secretariat of State, not the "government" of the Vatican. Nonetheless, states routinely separate the powers of government, and in any event the sovereign pontiff has ultimate authority over both the spiritual and temporal activities of the Church, and over both domestic and international relations.[46] In any event, there exists clear evidence of the Vatican's capacity to engage in foreign relations, since it maintains diplomatic relations with more than 150 countries.[47]

In sum, the Vatican meets the traditional four tests of statehood. It has a defined territory, a permanent population, a government, and the capacity to engage in foreign relations. In addition, the Holy See clearly has treaty-making capacity. Because both the Holy See and Israel possess the capacity to make treaties, the Fundamental Agreement is a full-fledged treaty governed by treaty law.

A final question is whether the Fundamental Agreement is governed by the Vienna Convention on the Law of Treaties for purposes of interpretation. Is the Fundamental Agreement an agreement "between states" and therefore covered by the Vienna Convention, or is it an agreement between the State of Israel and a "subject of international law," and therefore governed by the customary law of treaty interpretation? As a practical matter, the answer may not matter much, since the Vienna Convention's provisions on interpretation, as on many other matters, reflect customary law.[48] Under both customary law and the Vienna Convention, the agreement should be interpreted "in good faith in accordance with the ordinary meaning to be given to the terms of the treaty in their context and in . . . light of its object and purpose," and, in cases of ambiguity, in accordance with any relevant *travaux préparatoires.*[49] More to the point, the Fundamental Agreement should be interpreted in accordance with "any relevant rules of international law applicable in the relations between the parties."[50] The question, then, is whether there are any "relevant rules" on international pilgrimage in human rights law. The next part of this chapter takes up that question.

### Pilgrimage under the Fundamental Agreement

Article 5 of the Fundamental Agreement deals with pilgrimage. It provides:

> 1. The Holy See and the State of Israel recognize that both have an interest in favoring Christian pilgrimages to the Holy Land. Whenever the need for coordination arises, the proper agencies of the Church and of the State will consult and cooperate as required.
> 2. The State of Israel and the Holy See express the hope that such pilgrimages will provide an occasion for better understanding between the pilgrims and the people and religions in Israel.[51]

At the outset, it is worth noting that the parties recognize an interest in favoring only Christian pilgrimages and not pilgrimages by members of other religions. This provision obviously is not intended to rule out pilgrimage by members of other religious groups; Israel, for example, surely has an interest in Jewish pilgrimage. Moreover, Israel has entered into separate agreements with the Palestinians and Jordan in respect of Muslim access to Muslim holy sites; those agreements do not contain any detailed provisions on Christian pilgrimage.[52]

A more interesting aspect of the provision is its limited character. As Moshe Hirsch has observed, Article 5 does not recognize an individual "right" to pilgrimage.[53] The provision does provide that the *parties,* Israel and the Holy See, "have an interest" in favoring pilgrimage to the Holy Land, but this provision does not explicitly recognize any *individual* interest in pilgrimage. Moreover, the provision speaks only of "favoring" pilgrimage, a more passive form of encouragement than "promoting" pilgrimage. Indeed, Article 5 fails to impose on the parties any affirmative duty to facilitate pilgrimage, much less subsidize it.

These limitations have potential significance because Article 5 must be construed in light of the human rights treaties to which Israel and the Holy See are parties. If human rights law requires the parties to recognize an individual right to pilgrimage, or even to take affirmative steps to promote it, then Article 5 cannot be construed as an effort to limit those rights and duties. Far from it: the Fundamental Agreement itself provides that it "does not prejudice rights and obligations arising from existing treaties between either Party and a State or States."[54] Similarly, human rights law provides that at least some rights of religious freedom are nonderogable.[55]

Is Article 5 consistent with international human rights law? It is not entirely clear that there is a right to international pilgrimage in human rights law, or that states have a duty to do anything more than "favor" pilgrimage. As Professor Hirsch has pointed out, the major human rights instruments speak only in general terms about freedom of religion and, separately, of freedom to travel; they generally do not provide explicitly that religious freedom includes a right of pilgrimage.[56]

Article 18 of the Universal Declaration of Human Rights, for example, provides in general terms that "[e]veryone has the right to freedom of thought, conscience and religion" and "to manifest his religion or belief in teaching, practice, worship and observance."[57] It is not made clear whether pilgrimage abroad is part of the right to "manifest" one's religious belief. It has been suggested that "when a pilgrimage is an essential part of a faith, any systematic prohibition or curtailment of the possibility for pilgrims . . . to enter a foreign country where the sacred place is located, would constitute a serious infringement of the right of the individual to manifest his religion or belief."[58] This view necessarily presupposes some right of pilgrims to enter foreign territory and some duty of states to admit foreign pilgrims.

The problem with this argument is that the Universal Declaration generally does not recognize a right of entry into foreign territory, or a duty of states to admit aliens; the Universal Declaration establishes such rights and duties only in respect to refugees. Article 13(2) of the Universal Declaration does recognize one's "right to leave any country, including his own, and to return to his country."[59] This provision, however, does not explicitly include a right to enter any country other than one's own, and it does not impose on states any obligation to admit tourists or travelers. By contrast, the Universal Declaration's provision on *internal* travel, Article 13(1), expressly provides that "[e]veryone has the right to freedom of movement and residence within the borders of each State."[60] Unlike Article 13(1), Article 13(2) refrains from establishing any generalized right of "movement" to, or residence in, other states.[61] That does not necessarily mean that one has a right to travel only to the high seas and uninhabited areas like Antarctica, but rather that one has a right to leave one's own country and visit or remain permanently in another country, if that country is amenable. As Professor Detlev Vagts has put it, there is a right to leave, but "[t]he right to enter a country does not . . . exist except in certain cases involving asylum seekers and, without that right to enter, the right to leave may be an empty one."[62]

Moreover, Article 14 of the Universal Declaration creates an explicit right of sojourn for refugees, but not for pilgrims. It states that "[e]veryone has the right to seek and to enjoy in other countries asylum from persecution."[63] Indeed, Article 14 has been read as providing "the only way of exercising"[64] the "right of immigration" set forth in Article 13(2). It seems doubtful that Article 14 reflects the *only* way to exercise the right set forth in Article 13(2). Article 13(2) does not merely establish a right of emigration or immigration; it establishes a right to leave and return, which implies that one has a right to make temporary visits to a willing recipient state. The 1986 UN Declaration on the Right to Leave and Return provides explicitly that the right to leave includes the right to leave temporarily.[65] Nonetheless, Article 14 does imply that a non-refugee has no right to seek asylum and, more generally, no right to enter a state that is not willing to accept visitors, tourists, pilgrims, or immigrants.

Indeed, it is often said that a state has an absolute or at least very broad right to exclude aliens[66] subject to obligations under refugee law.[67] That broad proposition has been criticized vigorously by some commentators as an inaccurate statement of the law and an ugly expression of nativism.[68] The World Tourism Organization even has suggested that "[t]ourism has become increasingly a basic need, a social necessity, a human right,"[69] a proposition that one commentator has dismissed as "frivolous."[70] But even one commentator who argues that states have a "qualified duty to admit aliens when they pose no danger to the public safety, security, general welfare, or essential institutions of a recipient state"[71] presses that case only for aliens seeking permanent residence, not visitors,[72] and he concedes that "a state has no duty to admit all aliens who might seek to enter its territory."[73]

In any event, even if the Universal Declaration does embrace a right to international travel, it is not directly binding on Israel or the Holy See because it is only a General Assembly resolution and not a treaty.[74] Of course, the Universal Declaration may have legal consequences anyway, either on the theory that it has become part of customary law,[75] or on the theory that it is an "authoritative interpretation" of the human rights provisions of the UN Charter.[76] Whatever the status of the declaration, it is appropriate to consult other human rights instruments that might contain a right of pilgrimage.

The International Covenant on Civil and Political Rights (ICCPR),[77] to which Israel but not the Holy See is a party, is of course a binding instrument, and it contains general language on religious freedom that is identical to that in the Universal Declaration.[78] The ICCPR also includes a paragraph providing that religious freedom "may be subject only to such limitations as are prescribed by law and are necessary to protect public safety, order, health, or morals or the fundamental rights and freedoms of others."[79] Interestingly, the right to return is phrased somewhat differently in the ICCPR than in the Universal Declaration. Like the Universal Declaration, the ICCPR provides that everyone "shall be free to leave any country, including his own,"[80] but while the Universal Declaration flatly provided for a "right . . . to return," the ICCPR provides only that "[n]o one shall be *arbitrarily* deprived of the right to enter his own country."[81] This equivocation on one's right to return to one's *own* country certainly raises questions about one's right to enter a *foreign* country.[82] Moreover, this provision on exit and entry is accompanied by a contrasting provision on internal travel: "Everyone lawfully within the territory of a State shall, within that territory, have the right to liberty of movement and freedom to choose his residence."[83] As with the Universal Declaration, the ICCPR provision on international travel is therefore more circumscribed than that on domestic travel. Finally, Article 13 of the ICCPR provides that aliens may be "expelled" from a state's territory "only in pursuance of a decision reached in accordance with law," implying that states have a right to expel, and presumably exclude, aliens.[84] Taken as a whole, the ICCPR does not appear to establish a general right to enter any foreign country.[85]

The 1981 UN Declaration on the Elimination of Religious Intolerance[86] contains somewhat more specific language relevant to pilgrimage. Article 6(a) of the declaration provides that religious freedom includes the freedom to "worship or assemble in connection with a religion or belief, and to establish and maintain places for these purposes."[87] But this provision says nothing about *international* travel for the purpose of assembling in connection with a religious belief. Article 6(i) recognizes a freedom to "establish and maintain communications with individuals and communities in matters of religion or belief at the national *and international* levels."[88] This provision does acknowledge an international dimension to religious observance, but it speaks of communication, not pilgrimage. Even if these provisions are intended to establish a right of international pilgrimage, they are not directly binding on states because the declaration is a nonbinding General Assembly resolution.[89] At most, such a resolution may serve as evidence of customary law.[90]

Other instruments speak more explicitly about pilgrimage, but like the Declaration on Religious Intolerance, they are not binding on Israel or the Holy See. In the mid-1960s, the UN Commission on Human Rights adopted the Draft Convention on the Elimination of All Forms of Religious Intolerance,[91] which obliged state parties to "ensure to everyone within their jurisdiction" the "freedom to make pilgrimages and other journeys in connexion with his religion or belief whether inside or outside his country."[92] The convention, however, proved controversial in the full General Assembly. India expressed doubts about the proposed provision on pilgrimage, and Turkey argued that recognition of a right of pilgrimage might compromise a state's effort to control the flight of capital.[93] In the end, the General Assembly failed to approve the draft convention.[94]

In 1989, the Conference on Security and Co-operation in Europe, (CSCE), now the Organization on Security and Cooperation in Europe (OSCE), adopted the Concluding Document from the Vienna Meeting of 1986–89,[95] a follow-up to the Helsinki Accords,[96] which set forth human rights standards for European states. The Holy See was one of the states participating in the Concluding Document; Israel and other "non-participating" Mediterranean states made "contributions" to the meeting.[97] The Concluding Document provided that:

> [Participating states] will allow believers, religious faiths and their representatives, in groups or on an individual basis, to establish and maintain direct personal contacts and communication with each other, in their own and other countries, *inter alia* through travel, pilgrimages and participation in assemblies and other religious events. In this context and commensurate with such contacts and events, those concerned will be allowed to acquire, receive and carry with them religious publications and objects related to the practice of their religion or belief.[98]

Like the Fundamental Agreement, this provision stops short of recognizing a "right" of pilgrimage. It provides only that states "will allow" pilgrimage, not that they are required to do so by international law. In any event, the Concluding Document, like the Helsinki Accords themselves, was not intended to be legally binding.[99]

Thus, while the major human rights instruments do recognize a generalized right of religious freedom and a right of international travel, few if any human rights treaties actually set forth a specific, binding norm on religious pilgrimage.

This surprising lack of specificity raises questions about the scope and even the existence of a right of pilgrimage in conventional human rights law. Some of those questions can be answered by reference to customary law.

There is significant state practice relating to religious pilgrimage. Saudi Arabian practice is especially instructive. Every year the Saudi government takes extraordinary steps to ensure a peaceful and orderly Hajj, or pilgrimage, to Muslim holy sites in Saudi Arabia. In Islam, unlike Christianity and some other religions, pilgrimage is obligatory: every able-bodied Muslim has a duty to perform the sacred journey at least once.[100] In the era of jet travel, this means that there are more pilgrims than Saudi Arabia possibly can accommodate in any given year. As a result, the Saudi government sets quotas on the number of pilgrims that may come from each state; each sending state is entitled to one pilgrim for every one thousand residents,[101] a limit that sometimes has led to complaints from people who think their country's quota is too small.[102] Other Islamic countries establish official Hajj ministries within Saudi Arabia to help coordinate the travel of their own nationals to the various pilgrimage sites.[103] The Saudi government also requires pilgrims to obtain meningitis and cholera vaccinations, a requirement that again has led to disputes with foreign pilgrims and sometimes their governments.[104] Administration of the Hajj is such an important and complex task that the Saudi government has established an entire ministry, the Ministry of Pilgrimage, to establish timetables for travel[105] and to promulgate regulations relating to health, safety, and welfare of pilgrims.[106]

Saudi Arabia's quota arrangements with other Islamic countries may not amount to formal international agreements, but they are consistent with the view that there is a "right" to make the sacred journey to Mecca and the other holy places. Indeed, the Muslim's duty to travel to Saudi Arabia would seem to be incomplete without a corresponding right to do so. Certainly there are many Muslims who regard the Hajj as a "right,"[107] and those dissatisfied with Saudi administration of the Hajj occasionally have called for international regulation of it.[108] The Organization of the Islamic Conference (OIC), for its part, repeatedly has expressed satisfaction with Saudi Arabia's management of the Hajj, and it has insisted on the need to respect both the "sovereignty" of Saudi Arabia and the pilgrimage rites themselves.[109] Despite this nod to Saudi sovereignty, the OIC surely would protest if the Saudi government severely restricted travel to Saudi Arabia for the Hajj.

Other states routinely encourage, or at least tolerate, pilgrimages to religious sites within their territories. There are a variety of Hindu, Buddhist, and Muslim sites in India, and the Indian government encourages tourists to visit many of these sites.[110] Buddhist pilgrims visit holy sites in a host of Asian states, including China, Japan, India, and states in southeast Asia.[111] Shinto pilgrims visit a variety of pilgrimage sites in Japan.[112] Christians make pilgrimages to Lourdes, France;[113] Fátima, Portugal;[114] Medjugorje, in Bosnia and Herzegovina;[115] and to a number of other sites around the world.[116] The Bible directs Jews to participate in three pilgrimage festivals—the Feast of Unleavened Bread, the Feast of Weeks, and the Feast of Tabernacles—every year.[117] Muslims, Jews, and Christians for centuries have made pilgrimages to religious sites in the Holy Land.[118] Israel has taken a variety of measures to ensure access to holy places in Jerusalem and elsewhere in the Holy Land.[119] The breakup of the Soviet Union has led to a revival of religious pilgrimage to sacred sites in the former Soviet republics, both from abroad and within.[120]

Still, states sometimes do restrict and even prohibit pilgrimage. Courts in the United States, for example, regularly have turned aside lawsuits by Native Americans seeking to enjoin governmental projects that would inhibit or prevent pilgrimage to sacred sites.[121] Russia's Parliament has proposed greater restrictions on religion in general, and on international pilgrimage in particular.[122] Although China has allowed some pilgrimage activity in territory it controls,[123] and it permits Muslims in China to make the Hajj to Saudi Arabia,[124] it also has a record of intolerance for religious freedom.[125] Israel welcomes millions of tourists a year, many of whom visit holy sites, but it also has restricted pilgrimage in some circumstances, for example by blockading Bethlehem, the birthplace of Jesus Christ,[126] and by forbidding Muslims under the age of thirty to make the Hajj.[127] Some states are particularly concerned with regulating the ingress of pilgrims: Saudi Arabia regulates the Hajj with pilgrim quotas, vaccination certificates, and the like. Other states seem more concerned with regulating the egress of pilgrims: Vietnam, for example, imposes special restrictions on those wishing to make the Hajj.[128]

There may be some reason to doubt, then, that there is a "general and consistent"[129] state practice of permitting, much less facilitating, religious pilgrimage. Still, the enormous volume of pilgrimage worldwide seems more impressive than individual states' restrictions, many of them partial, on pilgrimage. To constitute customary law, it is not necessary that this practice be universal or that states actively promote pilgrimage.[130] Moreover, there does appear to be a "general and consistent practice" of both permitting and actively promoting pilgrimage within the Islamic world.[131] The International Court of Justice has recognized the possibility of this sort of regional or special customary law.[132] In any event, whether or not there is a general and consistent practice of promoting pilgrimage, there clearly seems to be a general and consistent practice of permitting it, subject to restrictions designed to protect the health and safety of pilgrims and the security and territorial integrity of the state.

Even if there is a general and consistent state practice of permitting pilgrimage, there is more reason to doubt that this practice is accompanied by a sense of legal obligation, or *opinio juris*.[133] Customary law requires both practice and *opinio juris*.[134] States that admit pilgrims still require them to satisfy the same passport, visa, and vaccination requirements as any other visitors, and states routinely regard the issuance of a visa to a foreign national as a decision falling squarely within the discretion of the state, not a matter of right for the traveler.[135] On this view, an alien's entry into a state's territory is generally a privilege, not a right. Indeed, states even have been slow to implement the undisputed human right to leave one's own country, much less any right to enter another.[136] To be sure, Muslim states often do speak of the Hajj in terms of right, not privilege,[137] again raising the possibility that there is a regional or special customary-law rule for the Islamic world. Still, even Saudi Arabia's extensive preparations for the Hajj are probably motivated more by a sense of religious than legal obligation. Some states even have made explicit their view that there is no right of religious pilgrimage to foreign countries. Israel, for example, has taken the position that the Hajj is a "privilege and not a right," at least as long as Israel is in a state of war with Saudi Arabia.[138] Of course, Israel and other skeptics could be dismissed as persistent objectors to an existing, or emerging, right of religious pilgrimage.

On balance, it appears fair to conclude that most states continue to maintain a right to exclude aliens, including pilgrims. With the exception of Saudi Arabia, there are not many states that view visa applications from pilgrims more favorably than those from ordinary tourists. Within the Islamic world, there clearly is a sense of obligation attached to the Hajj that might suggest the formation of regional or special custom. Moreover, it is possible that a right of pilgrimage might emerge in customary law. The fact that pilgrimage is on the increase worldwide is likely to lead to more frequent claims of an individual right and corresponding state obligation.

Even if there is a right of pilgrimage in customary international law, it probably does not rise to the level of a peremptory norm, or *jus cogens*.[139] It is not likely that a very large majority of states recognizes such a norm, as is required of *jus cogens*.[140] States and international organizations sometimes have behaved as if no such norm exists. Most notably, the UN Security Council has imposed severe travel-related restrictions on Libya and Iraq, and those restrictions have prevented many residents of those states from participating in the Hajj.[141] Iraq has argued that such resolutions are illegal,[142] and Colonel Qadhafi has said that his people "have the right to make the pilgrimage," notwithstanding the sanctions.[143] While a growing number of commentators have weighed in on the existence and scope of the World Court's power to review the validity of Security Council resolutions,[144] and the court has arguably exercised such a power already,[145] the court thus far has declined to invalidate any Security Council resolution as a violation of *jus cogens*.[146] On the other hand, both Libya and Iraq have defied the Security Council's sanctions by sending pilgrims by air to Saudi Arabia,[147] and while the Security Council sometimes has condemned these acts,[148] it more recently has refrained from criticizing Iraqi pilgrimage flights.[149] Still, there is obvious disagreement, both inside and outside the Security Council, about the validity of the resolutions; this disagreement itself suggests that a *jus cogens* norm on pilgrimage has not yet emerged.[150] This reasoning is of course circular, but so is the concept of *jus cogens:* a norm is only peremptory if virtually all states treat it as such.

In sum, there does not appear to be a clear conventional or customary-law rule establishing a right of religious pilgrimage. The treaties and other instruments we have surveyed are, at best, inconclusive and, if anything, tend to support the view that no such rule exists. In human rights instruments, the right to religious freedom is usually cast in general terms, the right to leave a country is not accompanied by a right to enter another, and there is explicit provision for entry of refugees without making any such provision for pilgrims. If there is a right of pilgrimage, it is more likely found in customary law, and even then it seems most likely a regional or special rule, applicable foremost to the Islamic world. Whether or not there is such a right, it is clearly not a *jus cogens* norm, at least not yet.

### Conclusion

It would thus appear that the pilgrimage provisions of the Fundamental Agreement are quite consistent with human rights law. There may be a special customary rule establishing a right of Muslims to make the Hajj to the holy places in Saudi Arabia, but that rule would have no direct bearing on interpretation of the Fundamental Agreement because its terms are limited to Christian pilgrimage.

Human rights law does suggest, however, that the Fundamental Agreement should not be interpreted as affording fewer rights of pilgrimage to Muslims and members of other religions than to Christians. It may not be clear whether there is a right of international pilgrimage in human rights law, but there is clearly a rule forbidding discrimination on the basis of religion.[151]

Should human rights law require states to accept pilgrims? Certainly there is nothing in human rights law that *forbids* states to enter into bilateral or multilateral agreements requiring them to accept pilgrims for temporary visits to religious shrines. Such an obligation could, of course, be subject to restrictions designed to protect the health and safety of pilgrims and the security of the state. Israel itself has made useful steps in this direction in its agreements with the PLO and with Jordan.[152] Similarly, nothing in human rights law would forbid the Security Council from tailoring its sanctions resolutions more narrowly in the future to avoid interfering with religious pilgrimage.

By and large, it would appear that states have an interest in "favoring" pilgrimage, much as the Fundamental Agreement envisions. There are noble reasons to do so: pilgrimage is an important expression of religious devotion, and interaction between local nationals and foreign pilgrims may promote international understanding, though "understanding" itself does not always promote peace. There are also mundane reasons to favor pilgrimage: pilgrims, like ordinary tourists, are good for the economy of the receiving state. To be sure, pilgrimage carries increased risk of illegal immigration, capital flight, and, perhaps, degradation of religious shrines themselves. Still, these risks can be managed by controlling the volume and flow of pilgrimage, as some states do already.

Ironically, international pilgrimage may not be recognized as a human right until states band together to regulate it. As long as pilgrims have free access to holy sites in much of the world, they (and their governments) are unlikely to give much thought to the existence of a right to pilgrimage. If states become so overwhelmed by pilgrims that they cannot admit them all, then those pilgrims denied access (and their governments) are more likely to complain of a violation of a "right." The growing claims of right to make the Hajj demonstrate this point. If one looks for a right of pilgrimage today, one most likely finds a regional or special customary rule obliging the Saudi government to admit a limited number of Muslim pilgrims for the Hajj every year.

For the most part, international pilgrimage went smoothly during the jubilee year, thanks to careful planning by the Vatican, Israel, and other states hosting the massive influx of visitors.[153] But it is likely that sometime during the *next* millennium, the demand for pilgrimage will exceed the capacity of some states to host pilgrims. When that time arrives, more states will doubtless negotiate pilgrimage quotas resembling those already established by the Saudi government. Such quotas may or may not be coupled with an explicit acknowledgment of a "right of pilgrimage." Broader international regulation of pilgrimage will strengthen the argument that there is a general and consistent state practice of admitting pilgrims out of a sense of legal obligation. The law of religious pilgrimage is itself on a pilgrimage, on a journey into the corpus of human rights law. Like most pilgrimages, the voyage will be long, slow, and, ultimately, rewarding.

## NOTES

I would like to thank Professors Marshall Breger and Lucia Silecchia for their helpful comments on an earlier draft. An earlier version of this essay originally appeared in the *Catholic University Law Review*.

1. See Leora Eren Frucht, "Wish They Were Here," *Jerusalem Post*, Mar. 30, 2001, at 2B.

2. See Allesandra Stanley, "Pope Arrives in Israel and Gets Taste of Mideast Politics," New York *Times*, Mar. 22, 2000, at A8, col. 1.

3. See Moshe Hirsch, Address at Symposium, The Fundamental Agreement Between the Holy See and the State of Israel: A Third Anniversary Perspective (Apr. 8, 1997) (transcript on file with the *Catholic University Law Review*).

4. Fundamental Agreement Between the Holy See and the State of Israel, Dec. 30, 1993, Vatican-Isr., 33 I. L. M. 153 (1994) [hereinafter Fundamental Agreement].

5. Hirsch, *supra* note 3, at 14.

6. Fundamental Agreement, *supra* note 4, art. 5, para. 1, at 156.

7. Vienna Convention on the Law of Treaties, May 23, 1969, 1155 U. N. T. S. 331 [hereinafter Vienna Convention].

8. Id., art. 2, para. 1(a), at 333.

9. Fundamental Agreement, *supra* note 4, art. 15, at 158 (providing that the agreement will enter into force when ratified by both parties); id., art. 14, para. 2, at 158 (providing for exchange of diplomats after "entry into force" of the agreement).

10. See, e.g., id., art. 4, para. 1, at 155 (stating that Israel "affirms" its commitment to maintain the so-called "Status Quo" in the Christian Holy Places); id., art. 4, para. 2, at 155 (stating that the foregoing provision "shall" apply notwithstanding any inconsistent article in the agreement); id., art. 6, at 156 (stating that Israel and the Holy See "reaffirm" the Catholic Church's right to maintain schools).

11. See id., art. 15, at 158.

12. Vienna Convention, *supra* note 7, art. 2, para. 1(a), at 333.

13. Cf. Louis Rene Beres & Yoash Tsiddon-Chatto, "Osirak: 14 Years After," *Jerusalem Post,* June 7, 1995, at 6, available in 1995 WL 7558362 (stating that "Iraq has always insisted that a state of war exists with 'the Zionist entity'").

14. See, e.g., Yasmin Abdullah, "The Holy See at United Nations Conferences: State or Church?," 96 *Colum. L. Rev.* 1835, 1871–75 (1996) (arguing that the Holy See is not a state).

15. See Montevideo Convention on Rights and Duties of States, Dec. 26, 1933, art. 1, 49 Stat. 3097, 3100, 165 L. N. T. S. 19, 25 [hereinafter Montevideo Convention].

16. As Philip Jessup stated, "[T]here must be some portion of the earth's surface which its people inhabit and over which its Government exercises authority. No one can deny that the State of Israel responds to this requirement." U. N. SCOR, 3d Sess., 383d mtg., at 9–12 (1948), reprinted in Louis Henkin et al., *International Law* 247 (3d ed. 1993) (remarks of U.S. Permanent Representative Philip C. Jessup) (arguing that Israel is a state).

17. See Restatement (Third) of the Foreign Relations Law of the United States, sec. 202, reporters' note 1 (1987) [hereinafter Restatement] (discussing the preference for the theory of statehood).

18. See, e.g., Letter of Yasser Arafat to Yitzhak Rabin (Sept. 9, 1993) ("The PLO recognizes the right of the State of Israel to exist in peace and security."), in David Makovsky, *Making Peace with the PLO* 201 (1996).

19. Cf. U. N. Charter, art. 4, para. 1 (opening membership in the United Nations to peace-loving "states"); Hermann Mosler, *The International Society as a Legal Community* 60 (1980) ("[r]ecognition of a State . . . has now been substituted to a large extent, but not from all aspects, by admission to the United Nations.").

20. "Draft Articles on the Law of Treaties," art. 1, para. 8 [1962], 2 *Y.B. Int'l L. Comm'n.* 159, 162, U. N. Doc. A/Cn.4/Ser. A/1962/Add.1.

21. Id., art. 1, para. 1(a), at 161.

22. Vienna Convention, *supra* note 7, art. 3, para. (a), at 334.

23. See Abdullah, *supra* note 14, at 1874 (observing that "[t]he Holy See is party to numerous bilateral and multilateral treaties"); cf. id. at 1875 (arguing that the Holy See should be treated as a nongovernmental organization at international conferences and the United Nations, but avoiding comment on the Holy See's capacity to make treaties).

24. See Charles G. Fenwick, "The New City of the Vatican," 23 *Am. J. Int'l L.* 371, 371 (1929) (noting that some writers concluded that the Holy See "had since 1870 lost all international character whatever"); id. at 372 (noting that some publicists viewed concordats between the Holy See and Catholic states as "no more than domestic legislation on the part of the states concluding them with the Holy See"); cf. L. Oppenheim, 1 *International Law: A Treatise*, sec. 107, at 254 (H. Lauterpacht ed., 8th ed. 1955) (asserting that the Lateran Treaty of 1929 "marks the resumption of the formal membership, interrupted in 1871, of the Holy See in the society of States").

25. See, e.g., Oppenheim, *supra* note 24, 328 (Sir Robert Jennings & Sir Arthur Watts eds., 9th ed. 1992) ("The strict view ought probably to be that the Lateran Treaty created a new international state of the Vatican City, with the incumbent of the Holy See as its Head; but the practice of states does not always sharply distinguish between the two elements in that way. Nevertheless, it is accepted that in one form or the other there exists a state. . . ."); Fenwick, *supra* note 24, at 374 ("Technically speaking, a new state now enters the family of nations and, diminutive though it be, takes its place beside the other independent sovereignties. . . ."); Gordon Ireland, "The State of the City of the Vatican," 27 *Am. J. Int'l L.* 271, 273 (1933) ("By the cession of a small amount of territory, Italy has thus created a new temporal sovereign in the world. . . ."); id. (describing the Holy See as a "new state"); Josef L. Kunz, "The Status of the Holy See in International Law," 46 *Am. J. Int'l L.* 308, 310 (1952) (asserting that the Holy See has treaty-making capacity); Herbert Wright, "The Status of the Vatican City," 38 *Am. J. Int'l L.* 452, 452 (1944) (referring to the Vatican City as a "State").

26. See Statute of the International Court of Justice, June 26, 1945, art. 38, para. 1(d), 59 Stat. 1055, 1060 (providing that the ICJ shall apply "the teachings of the most highly qualified publicists" as "subsidiary means" for determining international law).

27. 1983 Code c.361 (Canon Law Society of America trans.); see also Hyginus Eugene Cardinale, *The Holy See and the International Order* 82 (1976) (providing a similar definition and noting that the Holy See also sometimes designates the pope in his role as "visible head of the Church," and sometimes refers more generally to the "spiritual organization of papal government").

28. See Cardinale, *supra* note 27, at 84.

29. "Treaty of the Lateran," Feb. 11, 1929, Vatican-Italy, art. 26, para. 2, 23 *Am. J. Int'l L.* 187, 195 (Supp. 1929) ("Italy . . . recognizes the State of the Vatican under the sovereignty of the Supreme Pontiff."); see also id., art. 2, at 187 ("Italy recognizes the sovereignty of the Holy See in the field of international relations. . . ."). The parties have recently reaffirmed their commitments. See Agreement to Amend the 1929 Lateran Concordat, Feb. 18, 1984, Vatican-Italy, art. 1, 24 I. L. M. 1589, 1591 (1985) ("The Italian Republic and the Holy See reaffirm that the State and the Catholic Church are, each in its own order, independent and sovereign. . . .").

30. Abdullah, *supra* note 14, at 1857–58. Another version of this theory reasons that:

> The Church and the Vatican State, remaining distinct persons in international law, are united, in virtue of a real union, in the person of the Pope. As Sovereign of both the Church and the State, the Pope uses the Holy See as the common supreme organ through which he exercises his sovereignty with regard to both these international bodies.

Cardinale, *supra* note 27, at 116.

31. Cf. Mark Thomas Van Der Molen, "Diplomatic Relations Between the United States and the Holy See: Another Brick from the Wall," 19 *Val. U. L. Rev.* 197, 198 (1984) ("The United States government asserts that [its] diplomatic relations with the Holy See concern only the Holy See's role as the authority of the secular Vatican City . . .").

The United States elevated its mission to the Holy See to a full-fledged embassy in 1984. See "Elevation of Mission to Holy See to Embassy," I *Cumulative Digest of U.S. Practice in International Law 1981–88*, at 894–96 (1993). Two lawsuits in U.S. courts challenged this decision on a violation of the Establishment Clause of the Constitution. Those lawsuits were turned aside on standing and political question grounds. See *Americans United for Separation of Church and State v. Reagan*, 607 F. Supp. 747 (D. Pa. 1985), aff'd, 786 F.2d 194 (3d Cir. 1986); *Phelps v. Reagan*, 812 F.2d 1293 (10th Cir. 1987).

32. Samuel W. Bettwy & Michael K. Sheehan, "United States Recognition Policy: The State of Vatican City," 11 *Cal. W. Int'l L. J.* 1, 9 (1981) ("Vatican City is but a vassal State of the Holy See.").

33. See Montevideo Convention, *supra* note 15, art. 1, 49 Stat. at 3100, 165 L. N. T. S. at 25.

34. Henkin et al., *supra* note 16, at 248.

35. Abdullah, *supra* note 14, at 1863.

36. Id. at 1862.

37. "Constitutional Law of the City of the Vatican," Law No. 3, art. 1, para. (a) (1929), reprinted in 3 *Constitutions of Nations* 666, 687 (Amos J. Peaslee, ed., 2d ed., 1956).

38. Id., art. 6, para. (a), at 687.

39. Id., art. 1, para. (b), at 687.

40. See S. James Anaya, "The Rights of Indigenous Peoples and International Law in Historical and Contemporary Perspective," 1989 *Harv. Indian L. Symp.* 191 (1990) (contrasting the writings of early natural-law writers, who held that indigenous peoples possessed certain characteristics of statehood, with the position of positivists and states, who denied the existence of such characteristics). As von Glahn put it:

> Indian tribes in North America and other tribes elsewhere were at one time held to be equivalent to international persons by a few writers. States, on the other hand, usually denied such status to tribes, and agreements made with them were subsequently (and often quite unfairly) denied the character of binding treaties.

Gerhard von Glahn, *Law Among Nations* 88 (2d ed., 1970). For more on the treaty-making capacity of indigenous peoples, see generally "Discrimination Against Indigenous Peoples:

Study on Treaties, Agreements and Other Constructive Arrangements Between States and Indigenous Populations," First Progress Report Submitted by Mr. Miguel Alfonso Martinez, Special Rapporteur, U. N. ESCOR, 44th Sess., Agenda Item 15, U. N. Doc. E/CN.4/Sub.2/1992/32 (1992); Ian Brownlie, *Treaties and Indigenous Peoples* (F. M. Brookfield ed., 1992).

Many commentators also have argued that statehood doctrine should make more allowance for national liberation movements. See, e.g., Anntonio Cassese, *International Law in a Divided World*, paras. 51–56, at 90–99 (1986) (arguing that national liberation movements have international personality); Helmut Freudenschuss, "Legal and Political Aspects of the Recognition of National Liberation Movements," 11 *J. Int'l Stud.* 115, 116 (1982) (arguing that such movements have a "limited" international personality); Malcolm Shaw, "The International Status of National Liberation Movements," 5 *Liverpool L. Rev.* 19 (1983) (arguing that national liberation movements are subjects of international law).

41. See Abdullah, *supra* note 14, at 1865–66.

42. Id. at 1865.

43. See id.

44. See id. (explaining the roles and structure of the administrative organs of the Catholic Church).

45. Id.

46. See Fundamental Law of the City of the Vatican, art. 1 (1929), reprinted in Peaslee, *supra* note 37, at 677 ("The Sovereign Pontiff, sovereign of the City of the Vatican, has full legislative, executive, and judicial powers."); id., art. 3, at 677 ("Reserved to the Sovereign Pontiff is the representation of the state of the Vatican, by the intermediary of the Secretary of State, for the conclusion of treaties and for diplomatic relations with foreign states."); id., art. 4, at 677 (providing that the pontiff may delegate legislative powers concerning the "government" of the City of the Vatican); id., art. 5, at 677 (reserving power to approve city budgets and accounts to the sovereign pontiff).

47. See 1996 *Catholic Almanac* 47 (Felician A. Foy & Rose M. Avato eds., 1995).

48. See Arbitral Award of 31 July 1989 (*Guinea-Bissau v. Sen.*), 1991 I. C. J. 53, 70, reprinted in 31 I. L. M. 32, 45 (1992) (noting that Articles 31 and 32 of the Vienna Convention "may in many respects be considered as a codification of existing customary international law"); Steven P. Croley & John H. Jackson, "WTO Dispute Procedures, Standard of Review, and Deference to National Governments," 90 *Am. J. Int'l L.* 193, 200 n.34 (1996) ("Articles 31 and 32 of the [Vienna] Convention, which cover the interpretation of treaties, are often considered to codify, or currently represent, customary international law.").

49. Vienna Convention, *supra* note 7, art. 31, para. 1, at 340; id., art. 32, at 340.

50. Id., art. 31, para. 3(c), at 340.

51. Fundamental Agreement, *supra* note 4, art. 5, at 156.

52. See, e.g., Treaty of Peace Between the State of Israel and the Hashemite Kingdom of Jordan, Oct. 26, 1994, art. 9, para. 1, 34 I. L. M. 43, 50 (1995) ("Each Party will provide freedom of access to places of religious and historical significance."); id., art. 9, para. 2, at 50 (providing that Israel "respects the present special role" of Jordan in Muslim holy shrines and that Israel "will give high priority to the Jordanian historic role in these

shrines" during peace negotiations); see also Interim Agreement on the West Bank and the Gaza Strip, Sept. 28, 1995, Isr.-PLO, Annex III, app. 1, art. 32, 36 I. L. M. 551, 619 (1997) (providing for access to, and protection of, holy sites in the West Bank and Gaza Strip); Protocol Concerning the Redeployment in Hebron, Jan. 17, 1997, Isr.-PLO, art. 6, 36 I. L. M. 650, 653 (1997) (making similar provision for holy sites in the Hebron area).

53. See Hirsch, *supra* note 3, at 12.

54. Fundamental Agreement, *supra* note 4, art. 13, para. 2, at 158.

55. See, e.g., International Covenant on Civil and Political Rights, Dec. 19, 1966, art. 4, para. 2, 999 U. N. T. S. 171, 174 [hereinafter ICCPR] (prohibiting any "derogation from" Article 18 of the ICCPR relating to religious freedom).

56. See Hirsch, *supra* note 3, at 12.

57. Universal Declaration of Human Rights, Dec. 10, 1948, art. 18, G. A. Res. 217 A(III), U. N. GAOR, 3d Sess., U. N. Doc. A/810, at 74 (1948) [hereinafter Universal Declaration].

58. Arcot Krishnaswami, "Study of Discrimination in the Matter of Religious Rights and Practices, U. N. Doc. E/CN.4/Sub.2/200/Rev.1 (1960)," reprinted in 11 *N.Y.U. J. Int'l L. & Pol.* 227, 247 (1978); see also Peter W. Mason, "Pilgrimage to Religious Shrines: An Essential Element in the Human Right to Freedom of Thought, Conscience, and Religion," 25 *Case W. Res. J. Int'l L.* 619, 638 (1993) ("[P]ilgrimage plays an important role in most of the world's religions. Therefore, it is necessary to recognize that the practice of pilgrimage must be protected as an essential part of the human right to freedom of thought, conscience, and religion.").

59. Universal Declaration, *supra* note 57, art. 13, para. 2, at 74.

60. Id., art. 13, para. 1, at 74 (emphasis added). Moreover, Article 29 of the *Universal Declaration* permits a restriction of rights if they are "determined by law" and meet the "just requirements of morality, public order and the general welfare." Id., art. 29, para. 2, at 77.

61. But cf. Warren Freedman, *The International Rights to Travel, Trade and Commerce* 25 (1993) (citing Article 13 and other provisions of human rights law as evidence that "the probabilities of . . . recognition of the human right to travel internationally have discernibly increased").

62. Detlev F. Vagts, "The Proposed Expatriation Tax, A Human Rights Violation?" 89 *Am. J. Int'l L.* 578, 579 n.13 (1995); see also Francis A. Gabor, "Reflections on the Freedom of Movement in Light of the Dismantled 'Iron Curtain,'" 65 *Tul. L. Rev.* 849, 851 (1991) ("Subsection 2 of article 13 clearly sets forth the right of free emigration from any country. This is, however, only a one-way freedom. Once individuals leave their native countries, they have to find a country that will admit them as aliens."). But cf. Daniel C. Turack, *The Passport in International Law* 12 (1972) (asserting that freedom to travel abroad "comprises the right to leave one's country, the right to gain ingress, travel within and egress from the country visited and the right to return to one's country"). For a summary of the negotiating history of Article 13 of the Universal Declaration, see Jeffrey Barist et al., "Who May Leave: A Review of Soviet Practice Restricting Emigration on Grounds of Knowledge of 'State Secrets' in Comparison with Standards of International Law and the Policies of Other States," 15 *Hofstra L. Rev.* 381, 385–87 (1987).

63. Universal Declaration, *supra* note 57, art. 14, at 74.

64. Gabor, *supra* note 62, at 851.

65. See Strasbourg Declaration on the Right to Leave and Return, Nov. 26, 1986, art. 1, reprinted in Hurst Hannum, Current Development, "The Strasbourg Declaration on the Right to Leave and Return," 81 *Am. J. Int'l L.* 432, 434 (1987) ("Everyone has the right to leave any country, including one's own, temporarily or permanently."). Representatives of eleven states, together with a UN special rapporteur on the right to leave and return, participated in the preparation of the Declaration on the Right to Leave and Return. See id. at 432.

66. See, e.g., *Kleindienst v. Mandel*, 408 U.S. 753, 765 (1972) (finding a right to exclude in "ancient principles" of international law); Nottebohm Case (Liech. v. Guat.), 1955 I. C. J. 4, 46–47 (Apr. 6) (Read, J., dissenting) (speaking of an "unfettered right" of states to refuse admission); Oppenheim, *supra* note 24, sec. 294, at 645–46 (discussing the ability of states to expel noncitizens); Guy S. Goodwin-Gill, *International Law and the Movement of Persons Between States* 160 (1978) ("States retain a wide margin of appreciation in the matter of entry to their territory."); Vagts, *supra* note 62, at 579 n.13 (noting that the right of entry does not exist "except in certain cases involving asylum seekers"); Georg Schwarzenberger, 1 *International Law* 361 (3d ed. 1957) (speaking of a "right of expulsion").

67. See Vagts, *supra* note 62, at 579 n.13 (discussing asylum). The Refugee Convention, of course, forbids states to expel or return (*refouler*) a refugee to a state where his or her life or freedom is jeopardized because of race, religion, nationality, or political belief. See Protocol to Convention on Status of Refugees, Jan. 31, 1967, 19 U. S. T. 6224, 606 U. N. T. S. 267; Convention Relating to the Status of Refugees, July 28, 1951, art. 33, para. 1, 189 U. N. T. S. 137, 176 (prohibiting, in these cases, expulsion or *refoulement* of refugees); cf. Convention Relating to the Status of Stateless Persons, Sept. 28, 1954, art. 31, para. 1, 360 U. N. T. S. 117, 152 ("The Contracting States shall not expel a stateless person lawfully in their territory save on grounds of national security or public order."); id., art. 32, 360 U. N. T. S. at 154 ("The Contracting States shall as far as possible facilitate the assimilation and naturalization of stateless persons.").

68. See, e.g., James A. R. Nafziger, "The General Admission of Aliens Under International Law," 77 *Am. J. Int'l L.* 804, 804–7 (1983) (arguing that states do not and should not have an unfettered right to exclude immigrants).

69. Promotion of Tourism, G. A. Res. 32/157, U. N. ESCOR, 2d Sess., Agenda Item 22, at para. 21, U. N. Doc. E/1978/98 (1978).

70. Philip Alston, "Conjuring Up New Human Rights: A Proposal for Quality Control," 78 *Am. J. Int'l L.* 607, 611 (1984); see also Christina M. Cerna, "Book Review," 79 *Am. J. Int'l L.* 817, 819 & n.2 (1985) (reviewing *Volkerrecht als rechtsordnung, Internationale Gerichtsbarkeit, Menschenrecht: Festschrift für Hermann Mosler* (Rudolf Bernhardt et al. eds., 1983)) (speaking of Sir Gerald Fitzmaurice, a former judge on the European Court of Human Rights, known for his skepticism about an overly expansive conception of human rights: "One can only imagine Fitzmaurice's reaction to such new human rights as the 'right to tourism' or the 'right to sleep.'") (citing Alston, *supra*).

71. Nafziger, *supra* note 68, at 805.

72. See id. at 806 ("[T]his article will focus on more or less permanent migration rather than on the admission of such transient classes of aliens as diplomats, temporary

workers, visitors, or students."); see also id. at 841 n.197 (noting Professor D'Amato's skepticism about a rule requiring admission of tourists, and implying that different equities might apply to more permanent visitors).

73. Id. at 804. There is extensive literature on the right to leave and return. See, e.g., J. L. Brierly, *The Law of Nations* 276–90 (Humphrey Waldock ed., 6th ed. 1963); Charles de Visscher, *Theory and Reality in Public International Law* 182 (P. E. Corbett trans., revised ed. 1968); Hurst Hannum, *The Right to Leave and Return in International Law and Practice* (1987); Rainer Hofman, *Die Ausreisefreiheit nach Völkerrecht und Staatlichem Recht* (1988); José D. Inglés, Study of Discrimination in Respect of the Right of Everyone to Leave Any Country, Including His Own, and to Return to His Country, U. N. Doc. E/CN.4/Sub.2/220/Rev.1, U. N. Sales No. 64 XIV. 2 (1963); *Liberté de Circulation des Personnes en Droit International* (Maurice Flory & Rosalyn Higgins eds., 1988) [hereinafter *Liberté de Circulation*]; Rona Aybay, "The Right to Leave and the Right to Return: The International Aspect of Freedom of Movement," 1 *Comp. L. Y. B.* 121 (1977).

74. As Eleanor Roosevelt noted at the time of the adoption of the Universal Declaration, the document "is not a treaty; it is not an international agreement. It is not and does not purport to be a statement of law or of legal obligation." Statement of Eleanor Roosevelt, Chairman of the Commission on Human Rights, 19 Dep't. St. Bull. 751 (1948), reprinted in Marjorie M. Whiteman, 5 *Digest of International Law* 243 (1965). Article 10 of the United Nations Charter provides the General Assembly may make only "recommendations" on matters within the scope of the United Nations Charter. See Josef L. Kunz, "The United Nations Declaration of Human Rights," 43 *Am. J. Int'l L.* 316, 318 (1949). But see Louis B. Sohn, "The Human Rights Law of the Charter," 12 *Tex. Int'l L. J.* 129, 133 (1977) (arguing that the Universal Declaration is a "binding instrument in its own right" as well as an authoritative interpretation of the United Nations Charter).

75. See, e.g., Namibia Case, 1971 I. C. J. 16, 76 (June 21) (separate opinion of Judge Ammoun) (noting that the Universal Declaration may have codified custom or "acquired the force of custom," and citing the right to equality as an example of a Universal Declaration norm that is a "preexisting binding customary norm"); Richard B. Lillich & Hurst Hannum, *International Human Rights* 134–36 (3d ed. 1995) (excerpting opinions of various states and scholars who maintain that some portions of the Universal Declaration now embody customary law); John P. Humphrey, "The International Bill of Rights: Scope and Implementation," 17 *Wm. & Mary L. Rev.* 527, 529 (1976) (noting that many authorities consider the Universal Declaration as "part of the customary law of nations"); Richard B. Lillich, "Invoking International Human Rights Law in Domestic Courts," 54 *U. Cin. L. Rev.* 367, 394–95 (1985) (same).

76. See Montreal Statement of the Assembly for Human Rights, Mar. 22–27, 1968, 9 J. Int'l. Comm'n. Jurists 94, 94–95 (1968), excerpted in Richard B. Lillich, *International Human Rights* 127, 128 (2d ed. 1991) [hereinafter Montreal Statement]; South West Africa (Eth. v. S. Afr., Liber. v. S. Afr.), 1966 I. C. J. 4, 293 (July 18) (dissenting opinion of Judge Tanaka) ("[T]he Universal Declaration of Human Rights . . . although not binding in itself, constitutes evidence of the interpretation and application of the relevant Charter

provisions."); Frank Newman, "Interpreting the Human Rights Clauses of the U. N. Charter," 1972 *Revue des Droits de l'Homme* 283.

77. ICCPR, *supra* note 55.

78. Id., art. 18, para. 1, at 178. Article 18 has been called "the most important provision on religious freedom in international law." T. Jeremy Gunn, "Book Review," 90 *Am. J. Int'l L.* 707, 708 (1996) (reviewing Bahiyyih G. Tahzib, *Freedom of Religion or Belief: Ensuring Effective International Legal Protection* [1996]). Indeed, the Human Rights Committee has said that the terms "religion" and "belief" in Article 18 should be "broadly construed." W. Cole Durham, Jr., et al., "The Future of Religious Liberty in Russia: Report of the De Burght Conference on Pending Russian Legislation Restricting Religious Liberty," 8 *Emory Int'l L. Rev.* 1, 15 (1994) (quoting General Comment Number 22(48) concerning Article 18). Nonetheless, the Human Rights Committee has been criticized for failing to find any violation of Article 18 in its decisions on petitions relating to religious freedom. See Gunn, *supra,* at 708.

79. ICCPR, *supra* note 55, art. 18, para. 3, at 178. On the other hand, the ICCPR also provides that "[n]o derogation" may be made from Article 18, the provision on religious freedom. Id., art. 4, para. 2, at 174.

Like other major human rights instruments, the ICCPR contains general norms forbidding discrimination based on religion. See id., art. 2, para. 1, at 173 (obliging parties to apply the ICCPR "without distinction of any kind, such as race, colour, sex, language, religion, political or other opinion, national or social origin, property, birth or other status"); id., art. 4, para. 1, at 174 (forbidding emergency measures that discriminate solely on the basis of religion); see also U. N. Charter, art. 1, para. 3 (providing that the United Nations should respect human rights "without distinction as to" religion); id., art. 55, para. (c) (stating that the United Nations "shall promote . . . universal respect for, and observance of, human rights and fundamental freedoms for all without distinction as to . . . religion"); International Covenant on Economic, Social and Cultural Rights, Dec. 16, 1966, art. 2, para. 2, 993 U. N. T. S. 3, 5 (providing that parties shall "guarantee" that rights will be "exercised without discrimination" as to religion). The Economic and Social Covenant also provides that parties should permit parents to choose schools that "ensure the religious and moral education of their children." Id., art. 13, para. 3, at 8. More generally, it provides that parties should recognize the right of everyone to "take part in cultural life." Id., art. 15, para. 1(a), at 9.

80. ICCPR, *supra* note 55, art. 12, para. 2, at 176.

81. Id., art. 12, para. 4, at 176 (emphasis added). The International Convention on the Elimination of All Forms of Racial Discrimination, to which both the Holy See and Israel are parties, speaks of the "right to leave any country, including one's own, and to return to one's country." Opened for signature Mar. 7, 1966, art. 5, para. (d)(ii), 660 U. N. T. S. 211, 220. Again, that convention contains a contrasting provision recognizing a "right to freedom of movement and residence within the border of the State." Id., art. 5, para. (d)(i), at 220. It also contains a general recognition of a "right to freedom of thought, conscience and religion." Id., art. 5, para. (d)(vii), at 222. Like the Economic and Social

Covenant, the Convention on Racial Discrimination seems to stop short of establishing a general right to enter any foreign country.

82. To be sure, there is a duty of states to admit their own nationals in ordinary circumstances. See, e.g., Goodwin-Gill, *supra* note 66, at 137 (citing Van Duyn v. Home Office, 1 C. M. L. R. 1, 18 (E. C. J. 1975) ("[I]t is a principle of international law . . . that a State is precluded from refusing to its own nationals the right of entry or residence.")). Even so, there has been debate over particular aspects of this duty, such as a state's obligation to receive its nationals when they have been expelled unlawfully from other states. See id. at 136–37.

83. ICCPR, *supra* note 55, art. 12, para. 1, at 176. Interestingly, the ICCPR does not list the right to leave and return as a non-derogable right. See id., art. 4, para. 2, at 174 (excluding Article 12 from the list of non-derogable provisions).

84. Id., art. 13, at 176. Moreover, this limitation on expulsion, like the right to leave and return, is apparently derogable. See id., art. 4, para. 2, at 174. Indeed, some states have taken reservations from Article 13 of the ICCPR. See Jorge A. Vargas, "NAFTA, the Chiapas Rebellion, and the Emergence of Mexican Ethnic Law," 25 *Cal. W. Int'l L. J.* 1, 58 n.351 (1994) (noting that Mexico took a reservation to Article 13 because its constitution gives it "absolute power" to deport aliens without formal proceedings) (citing Pacto Internacional de Derechos Civiles y Politicos, D. O. May 20, 1981, reprinted in *Legislacion Sobre Derechos Humanos* 161–86 (1993)).

85. Hannum, *supra* note 73, at 20 ("The Human Rights Committee has made clear that . . . there is no right in the Covenant to enter any Country except one's own. . . ."); Patrice Jean, "Le Contenu de la Liberté de Circulation," in *Liberté de Circulation, supra* note 73, at 21, 33 ("Il n'y a pas, semble-t-il, dans un monde de souveraineté juridique de l'Etat, de liberté fondamentale d'entrée."). But cf. id. at 34 ("[L]a plupart des pays respectent, plus ou moins, une sorte de droit de l'étranger à passage et brefs séjours innocents. Il en va autrement si la résidence se prolonge.").

86. Declaration on the Elimination of All Forms of Intolerance and of Discrimination Based on Religion or Belief, Nov. 25, 1981, G. A. Res. 36/55, U. N. GAOR, 36th Sess., Supp. No. 51, at 171, U. N. Doc. A/36/51 (1982).

87. Id., art. 6, para. (a), at 172.

88. Id., art. 6, para. (i), at 172 (emphasis added); cf. art. 6, para. (e), at 172 (recognizing the freedom to "teach a religion or belief in places suitable for these purposes").

89. See U. N. Charter, art. 10 (providing that the General Assembly may make "recommendations" on matters within the scope of the charter); id., art. 13, para. 1 (a)–(b) (providing that the assembly may make "recommendations" to encourage the "progressive development" and "codification" of international law and to promote cooperation in social fields); see also Roger S. Clark, "The United Nations and Religious Freedom," 11 *N.Y.U. J. Int'l L. & Pol.* 197, 208 (1978) (noting that the declaration would have "no enforcement procedures" and would not be "binding on any state").

90. See Oscar Schachter, "International Law in Theory and Practice," 178 *Recueil des Cours* 111–21 (1982–V), reprinted in Barry E. Carter & Philip R. Trimble, *International Law* 117 (1991) (arguing that law-declaring resolutions have legal effect as "evidence" of custom-

ary law). But cf. Montreal Statement, *supra* note 76, at 128 (asserting that the Universal Declaration of Human Rights is an "authoritative interpretation" of the U. N. Charter).

In 1986, the U. N. Human Rights Commission appointed a special rapporteur on religious intolerance and discrimination based on religion or belief. The special rapporteur's mandate covers "incidents and governmental actions" that are "inconsistent" with the Declaration on Religious Intolerance. C. H. R. Res. 1986/20, U. N. ESCOR, 42d Sess., Supp. No. 2, at 66–67, U. N. Doc. E/Cn.4/1986/65 (1986).

91. Report on the Twenty-Third Session, U. N. Commission on Human Rights, U. N. ESCOR, 42d Sess., Supp. No. 6, at 29, U. N. Doc. E/CN.4/940 (1967).

92. Id., art. 3, para. 2(e), at 33.

93. See U. N. GAOR 3d Comm., 22d Sess., 1487th mtg., at 119–20, U. N. Doc. A/C.3/SR.1487 (1967) (remarks of Turkey); U. N. GAOR 3d Comm., 22d Sess., 1486th mtg., at 116, U. N. Doc. A/C.3/SR.1486 (1967) (remarks of India). For a more comprehensive description of the debates over the draft convention, see Clark, *supra* note 89, at 211–14.

94. See generally U. N. GAOR 3d Comm., 22d Sess., 1486–1514th mtgs., at 113–257, U. N. Docs. A/C.3/SR.1486–1514 (1967) (discussing the history of and opposition to the draft convention).

95. See Conference on Security and Co-operation in Europe, Concluding Document from the Vienna Meeting, Jan. 17, 1989, 28 I. L. M. 527 (1989) [hereinafter Concluding Document].

96. Conference on Security and Co-operation in Europe, Final Act, Aug. 1, 1975, 14 I. L. M. 1292 (1975).

97. See Concluding Document, *supra* note 95, at 531.

98. Id., para. 32, at 545.

99. See Louis Henkin, *The Age of Rights* 57 (1990) ("Helsinki was not intended to be a legally binding agreement, and does not add legally binding human rights obligations. . . ."); Thomas Buergenthal, "Democratization and Europe's New Public Order," in *CSCE and the New Blueprint for Europe* 54 (Wyatt ed., 1991); Durham et al., *supra* note 78, at 20 n.41 ("ACSCE commitments, by their terms, do not constitute formal legal commitments in the same way that treaty obligations . . . do.").

The European Convention on Human Rights also speaks to freedom of conscience, but again it recognizes only a generalized right of religious freedom. See Convention for the Protection of Human Rights and Fundamental Freedoms, Nov. 4, 1950, art. 9, para. 1, E. T. S. 5, at 52 ("Everyone has the right to freedom of thought, conscience and religion; this right includes freedom . . . either alone or in community with others and in public or private, to manifest his religion or belief, in worship, teaching, practice and observance."). In any event, neither the Holy See nor Israel is a party to the European Convention, which provides that parties must be members of the Council of Europe. Id., art. 66, para. 1. Neither Israel nor the Holy See is a member of the council.

The European Court of Human Rights has not often found states in violation of Article 9. In one interesting case, the European Court found that Greece violated Article 9 by prosecuting and convicting a Jehovah's Witness for "proselytism." See "Kokkinakis v. Greece," 36 *Y.B. Eur. Conv. on H.R.* 181, 181 (Eur. Ct. on H. R. 1993).

General norms on religious tolerance also can be found in the 1993 Vienna Declaration and Programme of Action. See United Nations World Conference on Human Rights: Vienna Declaration and Programme of Action, June 25, 1993, U. N. Doc. A/Conf.157/24 (Part I) (1993); id., para. 22, at 34 (calling on states to "counter" religious intolerance, including desecration of religious sites, and inviting states "to put into practice" the U. N. declaration on religious tolerance); id., para. 30, at 35 (condemning religious intolerance); id., para. 33, at 36 (calling on states to provide education on religious tolerance).

100.  See *The Cow* 2:196 (The Koran, N. J. Dawood trans., 5th rev. ed. 1990) ("Make the pilgrimage and visit the Sacred House for His sake."); see also "Libya, Iraq Stand Firm Against UN Sanctions," *Jane's Def. Wkly.*, Apr. 23, 1997, at 18, available in 1997 WL 8211622 (quoting a Libyan diplomat's view that "[t]he Hajj pilgrimage is a religious duty for all Muslims, as explicitly stipulated in the Holy Koran").

101.  See, e.g., "Indonesia Will Not Apply for Haj Quota Increase," *Indonesian Nat'l News Agency*, Sept. 11, 1996, available in 1996 WL 12281711 [hereinafter "Haj Quota Increase"] (noting that Indonesia's quota is 1/1000th of its population, or about 200,000 people); Press Release, "Saudi Arabia Announces Regulations for Upcoming Hajj," para. 3 (Oct. 26, 1996), at http://www.saudi.net/press_release/96_spa/96_10.html#spa_10_26_Hajj [hereinafter Press Release] ("All Hajj missions must comply with the number of pilgrims agreed upon in the minutes of the meetings held with the Minister of Pilgrimage within the framework of the resolutions adopted by the 17th conference of foreign ministers of the Organization of the Islamic Conference.").

102.  Cf., e.g., "Haj Quota Increase," *supra* note 101, (reporting that Indonesia's president warned that the "irresponsible people" seeking a higher quota for Indonesia "were only interested in earning easy profits from haj pilgrims").

103.  See Press Release, *supra* note 101, para. 1 ("The Saudi Ministry of Foreign Affairs and the Saudi Ministry of Pilgrimage should be notified well in advance of the names of the members of official Hajj delegations.").

104.  See, e.g., Remi Oyo, "Nigeria/Saudi Arabia, Religion: Holier Than Thou," *Inter Press Service*, May 1, 1996, available in 1996 WL 9810351 (reporting that a "furor erupted" when Saudi Arabia barred 28,000 Nigerian pilgrims on health grounds, and quoting the administrator of the Nigerian state of Kaduna as saying that the Saudi government should not have "the exclusive right" to ban Muslims from the pilgrimage).

105.  See, e.g., Press Release, *supra* note 101, para. 8.

106.  See, e.g., "Hajj Regulations" (visited Mar. 14, 1998), at http://www.iad.org/books/HU-visa.html (setting forth rules on carrying money, travelers checks, and food); Islamic Aff. Dep't, "Safety Instructions" (visited Mar. 14, 1998), at http://www.iad.org/books/HU-visa.html (urging pilgrims to avoid walking under the sun without an umbrella, to keep valuables in certain safe places, to avoid accidents, and to respect the moral values and customs of Saudi society); see also Press Release, *supra* note 101, para. 4 (urging pilgrims to "take advantage of the facility of travelers checks in Saudi riyals sponsored by the Saudi Arabian Monetary Agency"); id., para. 5 (providing that men should be housed separately from "women who are not accompanied by a *muharram* (chaperon)").

107. See Oyo, *supra* note 104 (reporting that the administrator of the Nigerian state of Kaduna said that the Holy Places "belong, as a right to all Muslims of the world").

108. See id. (reporting that a local Nigerian official called for "a committee of world Muslims to take over the management of the Holy Places from the Saudi government").

109. See League of Arab States, Communiqués from Summit Meetings in Amman and Algiers, Nov. 11, 1987, June 9, 1988, 27 I. L. M. 1646, 1657 (1988). The Algiers communiqué stated:

> The Conference also expressed its solidarity with and support for the measures the Kingdom of Saudi Arabia might take in connection with the organization of the holy pilgrimage. . . . The summit insisted on the need to respect the holy places, the pilgrimage rites, the security and safety of pilgrims and the sovereignty of the Kingdom of Saudi Arabia. (Id.)

110. See Government of India, "Pilgrimage Sites" (visited Jan. 8, 1998), at http://www.meadev.gov.in/tourism/temples (containing links to tourist information on various pilgrimage sites).

111. See, e.g., Government of India, "Tourism in India—Pilgrimage Sites—Bodhgaya" (visited Jan. 8, 1998), at http://www.meadev.gov.in/tourism/temples/bodhgaya.htm (describing arrangements to visit Bodhgaya, "the most important Buddhist pilgrimage site in the world"); Pete Hessler, "Into the Past at China's Edge," *New York Times*, May 11, 1997, sec. 5, at 8 (reporting on the trek Buddhist pilgrims take to the top of Jizushar, or Chicken Foot Mountain, and stating that "it is, like all China's religious pilgrimages, a journey taken mostly by elderly women who silently nursed their faith through the dark years of the Cultural Revolution").

112. See, e.g., "Thousands Dazzled," *Daily Yomiuri*, Oct. 3, 1993, at 2 (describing a rite at the Ise Shrine, a major Shinto pilgrimage site); see also Steven R. Weisman, "Ise Journal: An Ancient Shrine Is Testing a Modern Emperor," *New York Times*, Oct. 9, 1989, at A4 (describing preparations for the pilgrimage of the emperor and empress of Japan to the Ise Shrine).

113. See Marlise Simons, "Pilgrims Crowding Europe's Catholic Shrines," *New York Times*, Oct. 12, 1993, at A1 (reporting on the growth of pilgrimage to Lourdes and other Catholic shrines).

114. See Christina Lamb, "Well-Trodden Pilgrim Path to Fátima," *Financial Times* (London), July 20, 1996, at 3 (reporting that Fátima, a "small town in central Portugal," is "fast becoming Europe's most popular pilgrimage site after Lourdes," and that 4 million people make their way to the shrine every year).

115. See Stacy Sullivan, "Peace Brings Pilgrims Back to Village of the Virgin," *The Times* (London), June 25, 1996, at 14 (reporting on renewed interest in pilgrimage to Medjugorje).

116. See Kenneth B. Noble, "Pope to Sanctify Mammoth Basilica," *New York Times*, Sept. 10, 1990, at A3 (reporting that the president of the Ivory Coast, Felix Houphouet-Boigny, built a huge basilica that he regarded as a "pilgrimage center for Africa's 100 million Catholics"); Anthony W. Robins, "The Stony Side of Costa Rica," *New York Times*,

Oct. 29, 1995, sec. 5, at 8 (describing the Basilica de Nuestra Senora de los Angeles in the city of Cartago, "a pilgrimage site that makes Cartago the Lourdes of Costa Rica"); Calvin Sims, "Buenos Aires Journal, a Saint Besieged: Heaven Knows Many Need Help," *New York Times,* Aug. 8, 1997, at A4 (reporting on a "vast pilgrimage" to pay homage to a statue of Saint Cayetano); Tom Utley, "Pilgrim's Progress in the Footsteps of a Saint," *Daily Telegraph* (London), June 9, 1997, at 6, available in 1997 WL 2315661 (describing a pilgrimage from Rome to Canterbury to Northern Ireland to "celebrate the coming of the Gospels to Britain"); cf. Daniel Johnson, "Mother of All Mothers," *The Times* (London), Aug. 21, 1997, at 21 ("The great Marian shrines, Walsingham, Guadalupe, Fátima, Lourdes, and now Medjugorje, have replaced those of other saints as the principal places of pilgrimage.").

117. See *Deuteronomy* 16:16–17; *Exodus* 23:14, 23:17, 34:23.

118. Cf. Adnan Abu Odeh, "Religious Inclusion, Political Inclusion: Jerusalem as an Undivided Capital," 45 *Cath. U. L. Rev.* 687, 692 (1996) ("[L]ocated within the Walled City are the sacred, holy shrines, revered by everyone, whether Christian, Muslim, or Jewish.").

119. See, e.g., Interim Agreement on the West Bank and the Gaza Strip, Sept. 28, 1995, Isr.-PLO, art. 32, para. 5, 36 I. L. M. 551, 619 (1997) ("During religious events that take place three times a year and other special occasions that shall be coordinated with the Israeli authorities, Palestinians shall have the right to religious pilgrimage to the Al-Maghtas under the Palestinian flag. Safe passage will be provided from the Jericho Area to Al-Maghtas for this purpose."); Treaty of Peace Between the State of Israel and the Hashemite Kingdom of Jordan, Oct. 26, 1994, Annex V, para. 18, 34 I. L. M. 43, 65 (1995) ("The existing arrangements for Muslim Israeli nationals who cross into Jordan in transit to Saudi Arabia for Muslim Pilgrimage, shall continue to be applicable."). See generally Uzi Benziman, "Israeli Policy in East Jerusalem After Reunification," in *Jerusalem: Problems and Prospects* 100, 112 (Joel Kraemer ed., 1980) (describing Israeli arrangements for Muslim and Christian access to holy places in Jerusalem); Ruth Lapidoth, "Religious Freedom in Israel," 47 *Cath. U. L. Rev.* 441 (1998).

120. One recent example took place in Ukraine:

> Reviving traditions long suppressed by Russian and Soviet rulers, thousands of Orthodox Jews descended on [Uman, a town in central Ukraine] today to celebrate the 5,758th New Year, Rosh ha-Shanah. Wearing black hats, prayer boxes and shawls, they came from as far away as Israel, the United States and France to visit the grave of Rabbi Nahman ben Simhah, the tsadik, or saint, who is the spiritual leader of the Hasidim from nearby Bratslav.

"Jews Make Pilgrimage to Ukraine," *New York Times,* Oct. 2, 1997, at A3; see also "In the Name of St. Nicholas, the Russian Faithful Walk," *New York Times,* June 10, 1997, at A3 (reporting on the recent revival of pilgrimage to the Russian village of Velikoretskoye, which once housed an icon of St. Nicholas the Miracle Worker).

121. See, e.g., *Wilson v. Block,* 708 F.2d 735 (D. C. Cir. 1983) (refusing to enjoin expansion of a ski area over a Navajo sacred site because the site was not sufficiently "central" to Navajo religious observance); *Sequoyah v. Tennessee Valley Auth.,* 480 F. Supp.

608 (E. D. Tenn. 1979) (refusing to enjoin the flooding of the Little Tennessee Valley because the sacred sites located there were not indispensable to Cherokee religious observance); see also *Tiano v. Dillard Dep't Stores, Inc.*, 139 F.3d 679 (9th Cir. 1998)(2=1 opinion) (upholding discharge of a seasonal employee who made a pilgrimage to Medjugorje in defiance of her employer, who had refused to grant her leave for the pilgrimage because it was the employer's busy season). See generally Mark S. Cohen, "American Indian Sacred Religious Sites and Government Development: A Conventional Analysis in an Unconventional Setting," 85 *Mich. L. R.* 771 (1987); Sarah B. Gordon, "Indian Religious Freedom and Governmental Development of Public Lands," 94 *Yale L.J.* 1447 (1985).

122. See, e.g., Proposed Law of the Russian Federation on Freedom of Conscience and Religious Belief, art. 21, reprinted in Durham et al., *supra* note 78, at 58–59 (providing that religious groups may "invite" foreigners to participate in "pilgrimages," but that entry may be refused if, *inter alia*, the foreigners' activities "contradict the standards of public morality in the Russian Federation"). The law was vetoed by President Yeltsin. See Harold J. Berman, "Religious Rights in Russia at a Time of Tumultuous Transition: A Historical Theory," in *Religious Human Rights in Global Perspective* 285, 297–300 (Johan D. van der Vyver & John Witte Jr. eds., 1996). More recently, however, President Yeltsin signed legislation imposing restrictions on "nontraditional" religions in Russia. See Daniel Williams, "Faith-Curbing Bill Becomes Law in Russia; Restrictions on Religion Enacted in Face of Global Criticism," *Washington Post*, Sept. 27, 1997, at A16.

123. See, e.g., Edward A. Gargan, "Chinese Are Said to Restore Shaky Calm in Tibet," *New York Times*, Feb. 4, 1988, at A15 (noting that China permitted a Buddhist festival that attracted many pilgrims).

124. See House Comm. on Foreign Affairs & Senate Comm. on Foreign Relations, 103rd Cong., *Country Reports on Human Rights Practices for 1993* 612 (Joint Comm. Print 1994). There are about 17 million Muslims in China. See id.

125. See, e.g., Secretary of State Madeleine K. Albright, U.S. Dep't of State, Special Press Briefing, Remarks on the *1996 Annual Reports on Human Rights Practices*, Jan. 30, 1997, at gopher://gopher.state.gov (asserting that religious persecution and intolerance has "increased" in China).

126. See Laurie Copans, "Updates with Lifting of Blockade," *Agence France-Presse*, Aug. 27, 1997, available in 1997 WL 13384537 (reporting that the Vatican called on Israel to lift the blockade).

127. See U.S. Dep't of State, *Country Reports on Human Rights Practices for 1996: Israel and the Occupied Territories*, sec. 2.d (1997), at http://www.state.gov/www/global/human_rights/1996_hrp_report/israel.html. The report stated:

> In 1996 the Government [of Israel] again permitted Muslim citizens over 30 years of age to perform the religious pilgrimage to Mecca, but it denied permission to Muslim citizens under 30 years of years [sic] of age on security grounds. The Government asserts that travel to Saudi Arabia, which is still in a state of war with Israel, is a privilege and not a right.

Id.; see also House Comm. on Foreign Affairs & Senate Comm. on Foreign Relations, 103rd Cong., *Country Reports on Human Rights Practices for 1993: Israel and the Occupied Territories*, sec. 2.c, at 1197 (1994) (reporting that the prohibition on the Hajj applied only to Muslim men under the age of thirty).

There also has been debate in Israel about whether to require pilgrimage groups to be accompanied by Israeli guides. According to one report, "Roman Catholic spokesmen have argued that it is spiritual leaders who should lead a group on a pilgrimage," while one Israeli official has argued that "Israel has abdicated its sovereignty over Christian holy places by allowing Christian groups to visit without Israeli guides." Haim Shapiro, PM Aide: "Sovereignty over Christian Holy Sites Lost," *Jerusalem Post*, Dec. 15, 1994, at 12, available in 1994 WL 9863638.

128. In Vietnam, "[b]oth law and regulation provide for the right of all citizens to obtain an exit permit," but the law makes an exception for "[m]embers of the small Muslim community seeking to make the [H]ajj" and certain other groups. U.S. Dep't of State, *Country Reports on Human Rights Practices: Vietnam*, sec. 2.d (1997), at http://www.state.gov/www/global/human_rights/1996_hrp_report/vietnam.html.

129. Restatement, *supra* note 17, sec. 102(2) (stating that "[c]ustomary international law results from a general and consistent practice of states followed by them from a sense of legal obligation").

130. See id., 102 cmt. b.

131. Cf. Mason, *supra* note 58, at 637 (describing the Hajj as the "clearest case for the protection of pilgrimage under the right to freedom of thought, conscience, and religion").

132. See Asylum (Colom. v. Peru), 1950 I. C. J. 266, 276–77 (Nov. 20).

133. See Restatement, *supra* note 17, at 102, cmt. c (maintaining that customary law requires both state practice and *opinio juris*).

134. See id.

135. Cf. Anthony A. D'Amato, *The Concept of Custom in Intenational Law* 77–78 (1971) (expressing skepticism that states' long-standing willingness to accept tourists reflects any sense of legal obligation to do so).

136. See Goodwin-Gill, *supra* note 66, at 29 (noting that while international law recognizes some right to travel, "State practice in the municipal sphere tends to reflect a claim of absolute discretion, rather than any restrictive rule of general international law"); cf. Freedman, *supra* note 61, at 17–25 (describing travel policies and restrictions of nine different states); Inglés, *supra* note 73, at 4 (finding that only a minority of states recognize a right to leave in their constitutional texts); Jean, *supra* note 85, at 33 (Il n'y a pas . . . de liberté fondamentale d'entrée.").

137. See, e.g., Paul Lewis, "U. N. Ignores U.S. Call to Rule that Iraqi Flight Broke Sanctions," *New York Times Abstracts*, Apr. 17, 1997, at A1, available in 1997 WL 7993452 (quoting Iraq's Saddam Hussein as asserting that Iraq had only "exercised its inherent right to use its civilian aircraft" when it flew Iraqi Muslims to Saudi Arabia for the Hajj, and reporting that Saddam Hussein warned that he "reserve[d] the right to fly planes again"); "Plane Flies to Jeddah," *APS Diplomat Recorder*, Apr. 20, 1996, available in 1996

WL 8934515 (quoting Libya's Qadhafi as saying his people "have the right to make the pilgrimage"); id. (quoting an Arab diplomat as saying that "Qadhafi has the religious right to send pilgrims on Libyan planes, but is wrong to defy the international community").

138.  See U.S. Dep't of State, *Country Reports on Human Rights Practices for 1996: Israel and the Occupied Territories* sec. 2.d (1997), at http://www.state.gov/www/global/human_rights/1996_hrp_report/israel.html.

139.  See Vienna Convention, *supra* note 7, art. 53, at 344 (defining a peremptory norm or *jus cogens* as one "accepted and recognized by the international community of States as a whole as a norm from which no derogation is permitted and which can be modified only by a subsequent norm of general international law having the same character").

140.  Cf. id. (providing that a *jus cogens* norm is one "accepted and recognized by the international community of states").

141.  See, e.g., S.C. Res. 748, U.N. SCOR, 3063d mtg., at 2, para. 4(a), U.N. Doc. S/Res/748 (1992) (deciding that all states shall "[d]eny permission to any aircraft to take off from, land in or overfly their territory if it is destined to land in or has taken off from the territory of Libya, unless the particular flight has been approved on grounds of significant humanitarian need" by a sanctions committee); S.C. Res. 670, U.N. SCOR, 2943d mtg., at 2–3, paras. 3–7, U.N. Doc. S/Res/670 (1990) (imposing aviation restrictions on Iraq).

142.  See Lewis, *supra* note 137, at A1 (reporting that Saddam Hussein described the restriction on Iraqi pilgrimage flights as "illegal").

143.  "Plane Flies to Jeddah," *supra* note 137.

144.  See, e.g., Jose E. Alvarez, "Judging the Security Council," 90 *Am. J. Int'l L.* 1 (1996); Thomas M. Franck, "The 'Powers of Appreciation': Who Is the Ultimate Guardian of UN Legality?," 86 *Am. J. Int'l L.* 519 (1992); Antonio F. Perez, "The Passive Virtues and the World Court: Pro-Dialogic Abstention by the International Court of Justice," 18 *Mich. J. Int'l L.* 399 (1997); W. Michael Reisman, "The Constitutional Crisis in the United Nations," 87 *Am. J. Int'l L.* 83 (1993); Geoffrey R. Watson, "Constitutionalism, Judicial Review, and the World Court," 34 *Harv. Int'l L. J.* 1 (1993).

145.  See Watson, *supra* note 144, at 14–28 (discussing three cases in which the World Court has exercised judicial review).

146.  See Questions of Interpretation and Application of the 1971 Montreal Convention Arising from the Aerial Incident at Lockerbie (Libya v. U.S.), 1992 I.C.J. 114, 126–27 (Provisional Measures Order of April 14).

147.  See Lewis, *supra* note 137, at A1; "Plane Flies to Jeddah," *supra* note 137.

148.  See, e.g., "Libya, Iraq Stand Firm Against UN Sanctions," *Jane's Def. Wkly.*, Apr. 23, 1997, at 18, available in 1997 WL 8211622 (noting that the Security Council accused Libya of four violations and Iraq of one violation, and that the "council's sanctions committee has reprimanded both countries and warned them against violations").

149.  See Lewis, *supra* note 137, at A1 (reporting that the Security Council refused to deliver "even the mildest rebuke to Iraq" after China and Egypt "took a firm stand against criticizing Baghdad").

150. Cf. Restatement, *supra* note 17, at 702 (omitting freedom of travel, religion, and pilgrimage from a list of norms of customary human rights law).

151. See *supra* notes 78–99 (describing nondiscrimination norms in various human rights instruments).

152. See *supra* note 119 (describing pilgrimage provisions in Israel's agreements with the PLO and Jordan).

153. Israel, the Vatican, and other states hosting pilgrims made extensive practical preparations for the extra visitors, and by and large pilgrimage went forward without incident. The Holy See also issued guidance on the spiritual dimensions of pilgrimage. One example was a Vatican document entitled "Pilgrimage in the Great Jubilee of the Year 2000." Among other things, the document was intended to "help all pilgrims and pastoral leaders of pilgrimages, so that in the light of the Word of God and the secular tradition of the Church, all may participate more fully in the spiritual riches of undertaking a pilgrimage." VIS Press Release, "Pilgrimage in the Great Jubilee Year 2000" (Apr. 28, 1998), at http://www.vatican.va/news_services/vis/dinamiche/e6_en.htm.

When presenting the document on pilgrimage, the president of the Pontifical Council, Cardinal Giovanni Cheli, said that "visits to shrines, particularly pilgrimages, constitute part of the vitality of the Church, a privileged place of evangelization, a truly efficient means of renewal in the sacraments and a driving force in the building of Church communities." Id. Archbishop Francesco Gioia, secretary of the council, added that pilgrimage is "a way towards a very symbolic objective. A way is made to the shrine which is considered 'the House of the Lord.'" Id. Underscoring the importance of the new document on pilgrimage, Vatican officials noted that it had been the "fruit of several years' effort" and that "the last Vatican paper dedicated to pilgrimages had been produced in 1936." Lynne Weil, "Vatican Document Explores Meaning of Pilgrimages," *Catholic Standard*, Apr. 30, 1998, at 5.

# 11

# HUMAN RIGHTS,
# THE FOUNDATION OF PEACE

## The Teaching of the Catholic Church,
## with Special Reference to Religious Freedom

*Giorgio Filibeck*

Some people may perhaps be surprised at the first part of the title I have chosen for this chapter: is it really true to say that human rights are the foundation of peace?

This is not an idle question. If we consider how the contemporary notion of "human rights" first came into being, we can see that it emerged against the background of strife and revolution. The main documents in which this notion was originally mentioned are the United States Declaration of Independence (1776) and the French Declaration of the Rights of Man and the Citizen (1789), which were drawn up in times of bitter struggle: they were written in blood.

Although recognition of human rights came about through war and violence, this does not mean that human rights are related to war. It is their violation which gives rise to conflict. In this sense, one might say that respect for human rights is a sure foundation for peace.

The appalling tragedy of the Second World War gave proof of the validity of this approach. It is neither a coincidence nor for rhetorical purposes that the founding Charter of the United Nations—which was drawn up at the end of that conflict—strongly emphasizes the importance of human rights. After affirming the commitment "to save succeeding generations from the scourge of wars," it stresses the importance of human rights: "We, the Peoples of the United Nations determined . . . to reaffirm faith in fundamental human rights, in the dignity and worth of the human person, in the equal rights of men and women and of nations large and small" (preamble to the Charter of the United Nations, para. 2).

Defending and promoting human rights was therefore one of the main objectives of this new organization, which resolved to draft a Universal Declaration of Human Rights that was destined to become one of the statutory benchmarks for the activity of the international community. The declaration, which was adopted by the United Nations General Assembly on 10 December 1948, contains a very important paragraph that supports our initial assumption: "Whereas it is essential, if man is not to be compelled to have recourse, as a last resort, to rebellion against tyranny and oppression, that human rights should be protected by the rule of law" (preamble, para. 3).

This wording once again brings up the age-old and complex question (*vexata quaestio*) of the legal basis of the right to resist injustice (*ius resistentiae*), which raises in different terms the classical yet still burning question: what are the legitimate ways of defending freedom? This is an issue which goes far beyond the legal sphere into the field of ethics, namely, that area in which conscience has the difficult task of discerning the issues and responsibly appraising the ways of supporting justice and opposing injustice. In the ultimate analysis, this is what is at issue when speaking about respect for or violation of human rights.

At this point, it is well to clarify that these rights can be vested not only in a person but also in a "collective" subject, such as the family (cf. Universal Declaration, art. 16.3) or a people (cf. Universal Declaration, art. 21.3).

In order to understand better the relationship between peace and human rights, peace must naturally be viewed positively and dynamically and not only as a negative and static concept. As it has already been authoritatively stated, peace cannot be reduced merely to the absence of war and cannot consist in a perfect balance of opposing forces. It can only be the result of an ongoing and constant development of an order in which the dignity of each individual person and every human community is given due recognition and promoted.

This is the way in which "peace with justice" is built up, with dialogue being the characteristic method of overcoming unavoidable tensions, and the use of force being placed solely at the service of the rule of law. This is certainly not the peace that the Roman historian Tacitus so vividly defined in reference to the Romans' expansionist policy, "where they make a desert, they call it peace" (*ubi solitudinem faciunt, pacem appellant*)!

One can now see more clearly that respect for human rights is the factor upon which peace depends. And this being so, individual human rights become so many fragments of that great mosaic of peace, constantly under restoration, the different colors of which stand for the various categories of these rights as defined in the international legal instruments that have sprung from the trunk of the Universal Declaration, such as civil, political, economic, social, and cultural rights. As we scan the list of human rights enshrined in the Universal Declaration, we become increasingly aware of how these rights contribute to determining the overarching framework of peace.

The Universal Declaration represents "a common standard of achievement for all peoples and all nations" (first paragraph after the preamble). Even though this proclamation has subsequently been challenged in the name of the diversity of cultures, at times in order to use this cultural "specificity" as a blanket to conceal "specific" human rights violations, its universal scope has served as a powerful factor for peace, pointing as it does to the fundamental principle of the unity of the human race. Although this principle has been savagely contradicted by history, it cannot be seen as a utopian vision, but remains the yardstick by which to measure the progress made by humanity.

The Universal Declaration is like a tapestry, woven from any number of threads, all originating in the concept of the dignity of the human person, which reinforces the social fabric to such a point that the figure of peace clearly emerges. The distinctive features of this figure always remain somewhat indistinct and need to be continually rewoven, because every violation of a human right breaks the thread that facilitates the identification of the attributes of peace.

The Universal Declaration is open to different interpretations: it is the sounding board of philosophical debate, but it is also the outcome of a political compromise. Although it is a legal instrument, it also has an ethical dimension. Perhaps it is this latter aspect which constitutes its greatest value, a treasure that deserves to be increasingly exploited.

To conclude this section, I should like to make the point that, in the first article of the Universal Declaration, the international community felt the need to draw attention to a duty of great relevance for peace: "All human beings are . . . endowed with reason and conscience and should act towards one another in a spirit of fraternity." The historical legacy of the French Revolution certainly influenced the choice of these words, but this indebtedness cannot diminish the universal value of fraternity and it cannot prevent us from recognizing it to be a deep-seated aspiration nurtured by every human conscience, beset as it may be by uncertainty and ambiguity, even if not always explicitly.

As the beginning of the preamble to the Universal Declaration explicitly states, we are all members of a "family."

I have deliberately refrained so far from any reference to the teaching of the Church, preferring to refer only to the paradigmatic document in which the international community, albeit limited to the members that it comprised in 1948, has expressed its consensus around the formulation of human rights.

The time has now come to show how the considerations I have made so far coincide substantially with the principles set out in the Church's magisterium, the origins of which are deeply rooted in a "Judeo-Christian" religious tradition which could not be shared within the context of the United Nations, but which nevertheless constitutes the *humus* in which the ideas of dignity and fraternity that inspired the Universal Declaration were able to germinate.

For the Christian, peace is a gift of God; it reflects the order of Creation, and is the effect of Redemption. The human person, created in the image and likeness of God and redeemed by the sacrifice of Jesus Christ, possesses a paramount dignity which forms the basis for establishing all of his or her fundamental rights, respect for which increasingly leads to the fulfillment of the order willed by God, and hence of peace. But it is a peace whose final realization forms part of an eschatological perspective.

These are the essential benchmarks that guide Christian thought and action, without any break between "faith" and "works": the annunciation of salvation is also the gospel of peace, because Christ himself "is the peace between us" (Eph. 2:14).

These are the premises underlying the Church's teaching on human rights, which has not, however, developed in a straight line, for initially it was marked by the Church's negative judgment of the French declaration mentioned earlier.

The controversy that was triggered by the historical framework in which the notion of human rights developed was subsequently overcome, thanks to the purification of their more contingent aspects and to a renewed perception of the theological basis of these rights, which were thereby enlightened to the gospel.

It is therefore not true that the Church has taken up human rights "late in the day," as some critics have seen fit to maintain. It is rather that the Church has taken a fresh look at the issue in order to apply age-old principles that are still very much alive in tradition, notwithstanding the errors and deviations of which even the history of the Church is not exempt.

As Pope John Paul II wrote in his apostolic letter *Tertio Millennio Adveniente* (10 November 1994), "[I]t is appropriate that, as the Second Millennium of Christianity draws to a close, the Church should become more fully conscious of the sinfulness of her children, recalling all those times in history when they departed from the spirit of Christ and his Gospel and, instead of offering to the world the witness of a life inspired by the values of faith, indulged in ways of thinking and acting which were truly forms of counter-witness and scandal" (no. 33).

In view of the scope of this chapter, I cannot possibly offer an adequate account of the progress made by the magisterium in this field, leading to a fully fledged corpus of teaching that constitutes one of the most important chapters in the Church's social teaching.

Looking back, in very broad outline, over the past hundred years, we can recall the Church's insistence on the conditions needed to create a political and economic system capable of ensuring respect for the dignity of the human person, with a special focus on workers' rights. Furthermore, the Church has often spoken out in denunciation of violations of fundamental rights perpetrated under dictatorial regimes and, during the Second World War, advocated the construction of a new social and international order in the wake of that war.

Although much can be said about the development of Church teaching, it might be useful to look closely at the attitude of recent popes toward the Universal Declaration.

The encyclical *Pacem in Terris* (11 April 1963) emphasized the connection between peace and human rights, referring to the Universal Declaration as "an important step on the path towards the juridical-political organization of the world community" (part IV).

Paul VI, in his message to celebrate the twenty-fifth anniversary of the Universal Declaration (10 December 1973) emphasized "the importance which is attributed to it as a sure path to peace."

John Paul II, in his address to the United Nations (New York, 2 October 1979) went still further, and defined the Universal Declaration as "a real milestone on the path of moral progress of humanity," adding that "this Declaration has struck a real blow against the many deep roots of war, since the spirit of war, in its basic primordial meaning, springs up and grows to maturity where the inalienable rights of man are violated."

In his first encyclical, *Redemptor Hominis* (4 March 1979), John Paul II had written: "After all, peace comes down to respect for man's inviolable rights—*opus iustitiae pax*—while war springs from the violation of these rights and brings with it still graver violation of them" (no. 17).

One might summarize, as in a sort of decalogue, the main elements that make up the Church's teaching on human rights, with one premise: justice is surpassed by love—the keynote of the Christian message—which may imply the need to waive the exercise of a given right (cf. 1 Cor. 6:7):

1. The dignity of the human person, created in the image and likeness of God, is the basis of human rights.
2. The defense and promotion of human rights form an integral part of the Church's mission.
3. The human person must be of paramount value in every political system or program.
4. Respect for human rights is the criterion by which to judge the legitimacy of all power.
5. There must exist a corresponding relationship between rights and duties.
6. The enjoyment of all categories of human rights is the condition for genuine development.
7. The right to life exists from the first instant of the conception until natural death.
8. Human communities, such as families, minorities, peoples, and nations, are also endowed with inalienable rights.
9. It is necessary for the Church to practice justice internally.
10. The protection of religious freedom is the yardstick by which to gauge progress in every society.

I should now like to focus on one of these principles, religious freedom, which is the most fundamental of all the fundamental rights in the Catholic Church's teaching because, for believers, it postulates the relationship between creatures and their Creator, going thus to the very root of human existence. In his encyclical *Centesimus Annus* (11 May 1991), John Paul II wrote: "In a certain sense, the source and synthesis of these rights is religious freedom, understood as the right to live in the truth of one's faith and in conformity with one's transcendent dignity as a person" (no. 47).

It is widely acknowledged that the Second Vatican Council marked a significant turn in the Church's teaching concerning religious freedom, because it clearly presented this freedom as a human right which must be guaranteed to every citizen, independently of his or her religious affiliation. This implies the recognition of the secular nature of the state.

The teaching is presented in the declaration *Dignitatis Humanae,* adopted by the council on 7 December 1965, a well-known document which is quite rightly referred to in Article 1 of the Fundamental Agreement between the Holy See and the State of Israel. This declaration begins by evoking the progressive awareness of human dignity and the growing aspiration to freedom which characterizes contemporary times, and solemnly affirms: "This Vatican Synod declares that the human person has a right to religious freedom" (no. 2). Moreover, it gives a definition of religious freedom: "Freedom of this kind means that all men should be immune from coercion on the part of individuals, social groups and every human power, so that, within due limits, nobody is forced to act against his convictions in religious matters in private or in public, alone or in association with others" (ibid.). The document also stresses the moral obligation of seeking the truth and conforming one's behavior accordingly, since the freedom of religion "has its foundation not in the subjective disposition of the person, but in his very nature" (ibid.).

The teaching of the council has been repeatedly and amply taken up by the magisterium of the popes. John Paul II, in particular, has strongly reiterated this teaching, from the time of his first encyclical, *Redemptor Hominis,* when he wrote that "the curtailment of the religious freedom of individuals and communities is not only a painful experience, but it is above all an attack on man's very dignity. . . . In this case we are undoubtedly confronted with a radical injustice with regard to what is particularly deep within man, to what is authentically human" (no. 17). He had personally experienced the dramatic situation of a believer in a regime which "gives only atheism the right of citizenship in public and social life," and he firmly addresses the responsible authorities: "No privilege is asked for, but only respect for an elementary right. Actuation of this right is one of the fundamental tests of man's authentic progress in any regime, in any society, system or milieu" (ibid.). In this regard, John Paul II's letter to the heads of state of the signatories to the Final Act of the Conference on European Security and Cooperation, of 1 May 1980, is particularly telling.

In it, he drew their attention to the different ways in which freedom of religion is exercised. I feel that it might be useful to quote verbatim from the relevant part of that letter:

(a)  at the personal level the following have to be taken into account:
— freedom to hold or not to hold a particular faith and to join the corresponding confessional community;
— freedom to perform acts of prayer and worship, individually and collectively, in private or in public, and to have churches or places of worship according to the needs of the believers;
— freedom for parents to educate their children in the religious convictions that inspire their own life, and to have them attend catechetical and religious instruction as provided by their faith community;
— freedom for families to choose the schools or other means which provide this sort of education for their children, without having to sustain directly or indirectly extra charges which would in fact deny them this freedom;
— freedom for individuals to receive religious assistance wherever they are, especially in public health institutions (clinics and hospitals), in military establishments, during compulsory public service, and in places of detention;

— freedom, at personal, civic or social levels, from any form of coercion to perform acts contrary to one's faith, or to receive an education or to join groups or associations with principles opposed to one's religious convictions;

— freedom not to be subjected, on religious grounds, to forms of restriction, and discrimination, vis-à-vis one's fellow citizens, in all aspects of life (in all matters concerning one's career, including study, employment or profession; one's participation in civic and social responsibilities, etc.).

(b)  at the community level, account has to be taken of the fact that religious denominations, in bringing together believers in a given faith, exist and act as social bodies organized according to their own doctrinal principles and institutional purposes. The Church as such, and confessional communities in general, need to enjoy specific liberties in order to conduct their life and to pursue their purposes: among such liberties the following are to be mentioned especially:

— freedom to have their own internal hierarchy or equivalent ministers freely chosen by the communities according to their constitutional norms;

— freedom for religious authorities (notably, in the Catholic Church, for bishops and other ecclesiastical superiors) to exercise their ministry freely, ordain priests or ministers, appoint to ecclesiastical offices, communicate and have contacts with those belonging to their religious denomination;

— freedom to have their own institutions for religious training and theological studies, where candidates for priesthood and religious consecration can be freely admitted;

— freedom to receive and publish religious books related to faith and worship, and to have free use of them;

— freedom to proclaim and communicate the teaching of the faith, whether by the spoken or the written word, inside as well as outside places of worship, and to make known their moral teaching on human activities and on the organization of the society; this being in accordance with the commitment, included in the Helsinki Final Act, to facilitate the spreading of information, of culture, of exchange of knowledge and experiences in the field of education, which corresponds moreover in the religious field to the church's mission of evangelization;

— freedom to use the media of social communication (press, radio, television) for the same purpose;

— freedom to carry out educational, charitable and social activities so as to put into practice the religious precept of love for neighbor, particularly for those most in need.

Furthermore:
- — with regard to religious communities which, like the Catholic Church, have a supreme Authority responsible at world level (in line with the directives of their faith) for the unity of communion that binds together all pastors and believers in the same confession (a responsibility exercised through magisterium and jurisdiction): freedom to maintain mutual relations of communication between that authority and the local pastors and religious communities; freedom to make known the documents and texts of the magisterium (encyclicals, instructions, etc.);
- — at the international level: freedom to free exchange in the field of communication, cooperation, religious solidarity, and more particularly the possibility of holding multinational or international meetings;
- — also at the international level, freedom for religious communities to exchange information and other contributions of a theological or religious nature.

Four elements make up religious freedom: (1) the right freely to seek the truth and to act accordingly, (2) freedom from all coercion in this area, (3) acknowledgment of this right in every national legal system, (4) the non-derogation of this right (as also provided for by the International Covenant on Civil and Political Rights, art. 4).

Following this extensive quotation, I will just add a reference to the message of the pope for the World Day of Peace (1 January 1991) on the theme: "If you want peace, respect the conscience of every person." After having mentioned the intolerance derived from fundamentalism and the danger of "forced conversions," John Paul II recalls "cases in which individuals are prevented—even through the imposition of severe penalties—from freely choosing a religion different from the one to which they presently belong." For the pope, such manifestations of intolerance "do not advance the cause of world peace."

Where discrimination is practiced within one and the same society between believers and nonbelievers, or between believers of different religions, the great energies that are released by religious faith are diminished and indeed rendered useless. This creates a group of second-class citizens who are incapable of offering their truly effective, because deeply motivated, contribution, which is necessary for the harmonious and peaceful advancement of society. This lays the foundation for deep divisions within one and the same national community, which unfortunately can also lead to bloodshed.

In our world, where major schools of philosophical thought are trying to show that the search for the meaning of human life is a futile and pointless exercise, religious faith is the only response that can fully satisfy the eternal and tormenting questions in every human mind: Who am I? Where did I come from? Where am I going? And it is also the only answer that can direct human conduct surely and motivate it positively to work for the common good. The desire for the transcendent makes it possible to recognize one's neighbor as a creature of God and to project onto human affairs, which are so often marked by pain and suffering, the light to understand their ultimate meaning. In that light, struggles for supremacy or to preserve privileges are properly relativised, because the true values of life belong to another dimension altogether, one to which all human acts are ordered.

Religious faith is a powerful factor for peace when it is lived authentically and is not ideologically contaminated. Religion can contribute to the construction of peace only if its transcendental specificity is acknowledged. And we can rightly attribute a transcendental nature to peace, in the sense that peace depends also on the religious attitude of human persons, and hence on the climate of religious freedom in which they live and work.

Unfortunately, there are many today who maintain that religion is a *factor of division*, the deepest division that exists, and that consequently the only way to prevent the religious strife that, particularly in the past, has caused so much bloodshed in the world, is to keep religious faith restricted to where it can do no harm to anyone, namely, within the individual conscience.

The historical reality of wars of religion is certainly deplorable, and all of us must humbly ask pardon of God for the part that our own religion has played in those conflicts. It is difficult to see how, even today, there are still cases in which restrictions on religious freedom seem to stem from the desire for one religion to dominate others.

Is religion, then, a source of conflict rather than of peace? Is the total freedom to practice religion, publicly and privately, therefore not a means of bringing about world peace? The truth is quite the contrary.

Religious tensions cease when religions recognize each other's right to exist without prejudice to their own profession of faith. The degree to which a country recognizes and protects religious freedom determines the level of peace it enjoys at home and abroad, for the germs of division and strife that fuel systems of oppression that are totally at odds with the dignity of the human person are thus rooted out.

Building up the Kingdom of God begins here and now (*hic et nunc*); this obliges all Christians to work to promote human rights, development, and peace, taking due account of the rightful autonomy of the political sphere, in a dialogue based on mutual respect with believers from other religions, and with those who hold other convictions.

This is not a question of "tolerance" as an end in itself, but rather a means of understanding that truth, which alone can bring us to the peace for which we all yearn, and which can only be achieved if there is full respect for religious freedom.

As Pope John Paul II pointed out in his message for World Peace Day, 1982:

And God does more than give creation to humanity to administer and develop jointly at the service of all human beings without any discrimination: he also inscribes *in the human conscience* the laws obliging us to respect in numerous ways the life and the whole person of our fellow human beings, created like us in the image and after the likeness of God. God is thus *the guarantor* of all these fundamental human rights. Yes indeed, God is the source of peace; he calls to peace, he safeguards it, and he grants it as the fruit of justice. (no. 4)

A gift of God, yes, but a gift entrusted to human beings. Such a high responsibility stems from the freedom which the Creator has given to his creature, that freedom which is an indelible sign impressed upon human nature, and which seems both to attract and to frighten us at the same time.

We are now living through a very special springtime in which, after a long harsh winter, the seeds of peace sown long ago in the Holy Land with the constant prayer and persevering commitment of believers and men and women of goodwill are finally ready to flower, unless the frost returns. . . .

Acknowledgment of the dignity of the human person and of peoples, together with the rights that flow from it, after decades of bloody violence of all kinds, has now opened up the path to peace through dialogue and negotiation. However, serious obstacles still remain, as the events of which we read every day tragically remind us. But what seems impossible in human terms can nevertheless become a reality by the grace of God. Will Christians be able to read the "signs of the times" and adapt their behavior to them? Will they be able to make the borders of the earthly Jerusalem and the heavenly Jerusalem, which are destined to coincide only at the end of time, come closer together? Will they, lastly, as disciples of the only Christ, be able to bear witness above all to unity and to show a humanity thirsting for hope and peace, the credible pledge of a reconciled presence of Christians in Jerusalem?

Peace, a gift of God, entrusted to humanity!

V

# THE CHURCH IN THE
# HOLY LAND TODAY

# 12

# FREEDOM OF RELIGION AND OF CONSCIENCE IN ISRAEL

*Ruth Lapidoth*

For almost two thousand years the Jews lived as a religious minority, sometimes tolerated and at other times persecuted in a great number of countries. Only in 1948 did they succeed in establishing a state in which they constitute the majority of the population. Moreover, this state was formally established as a "Jewish state." These circumstances explain the special interest in the question of how and to what extent Israel recognizes and implements the right to freedom of religion and of conscience.

Like all other human rights, this one as well has to be judged not simply by the general proclamation of the right but by the details of its implementation and by its limitations. It is therefore our intention to start, after a few preliminary remarks, with an examination of the Jewish character of the state, the principle of freedom of religion and of conscience, and the limitations of this freedom. The study of the implementation of the principle requires an analysis of certain details: the status of the Holy Places, equality of rights of members of different religions, the right to change one's religion, regulation of proselytizing activities, the right to a religious education, matters of personal status, and the situation of persons who do not belong to any religious group. The 1981 United Nations Declaration on the Elimination of All Forms of Intolerance and of Discrimination Based on Religion or Belief[1] also mentions most of these subjects as ingredients of freedom of religion.[2] Others are relevant only to few countries, including Israel, namely, the Holy Places and jurisdiction in matters of personal status.

### Some Preliminary Remarks

1. Israel has a rather heterogeneous population that belongs to various ethnic groups, adheres to different religions, speaks several languages, has different cultural and social traditions, and holds many different political allegiances and ideologies. Thus, religious affiliation is often connected with ethnic origin, language, culture, and political allegiance.

2. The land—or certain places in it—is also holy to four major faiths: Judaism, Christianity, Islam, and Baha'i. For the Baha'is it is not only the site of various sacred places but also of their spiritual and administrative world center.

3. About 80 percent of the population is Jewish, but the Jews are rather divided on matters of religion.

4. Israel has no written constitution. When the state was established, the Constituent Assembly decided not to draft a constitution, but instead resolved that basic laws on the various aspects of government and administration would be adopted gradually. Until 1992, human rights and civil rights were not codified in a basic law. Rather, they were guaranteed by the judiciary, which has gradually developed a voluminous case law on the subject (much like the situation in the United Kingdom). In 1992, however, the Basic Law: Freedom of Occupation and the Basic Law: Human Dignity and Liberty were adopted.[3] These laws do not deal specifically with freedom of religion, but they may have an impact on this subject, to be explained later.

5. Due to the system of government that prevails in Israel—a multiparty parliamentary democracy—Jewish orthodox religious parties have a considerable influence on the political life of the country.

6. Like many other Middle Eastern countries, Israel fears the spread of religious fundamentalism.

### The Jewish Character of the State

Although there is a Jewish majority in the country, Judaism has not been proclaimed the official religion of the state. Neither is Jewish law the applicable legal system, except in certain matters of personal status of Jews.

Some legal instruments, however, do refer to the Jewish character of the state. Thus, the 1948 Declaration on the Establishment of the State of Israel proclaimed "the establishment of a Jewish State in Eretz-Israel [the Land of Israel] . . . the State of Israel."[4] Similarly, the Basic Law: The Knesset, provides that:

A candidates' list shall not participate in elections to the Knesset and a person will not be a candidate for elections to the Knesset, if the objects or actions of the list or of the person, respectively, expressly or by implication, include one of the following:
  (1) negation of the existence of the State of Israel as a Jewish and democratic state;
  (2) incitement to racism;
  (3) support for an armed struggle of an enemy state or of a terrorist organization, against the State of Israel.[5]

The Jewishness of the state is also reflected in the fact that the Sabbath and the Jewish holidays have been declared to be the official days of rest for the Jews, that the flag and emblem express Jewish tradition, and that the army has to provide only kosher food to its soldiers.[6]

Another interesting Jewish-oriented provision has been included in the Law on the Foundations of Law, 5740–1980,[7] which deals with the filling of lacunae by the judges: "Where the court, faced with a legal question requiring decision, finds no answer ... in statute law or case-law or by analogy, it shall decide it in the light of the principles of freedom, justice, equity and peace of Israel's heritage."[8] The term "Israel," in this context, refers to Judaism, or the Jewish people.

Another relevant provision has been included in the two 1992 Basic Laws on human rights mentioned earlier: their express purpose is to protect the rights dealt with by these laws, namely, human dignity, liberty, as well as freedom of occupation, "in order to establish in a Basic Law the values of the State of Israel as a Jewish and democratic state."[9]

Several authors have discussed the compatibility of the Jewishness and the democratic character of the state.[10] According to Supreme Court Justice Itzhak Zamir, there is no contradiction if both terms are interpreted reasonably and moderately.[11] In no official text has the Jewish character of the state been defined.[12] It should, however, be remembered that the term "Jewish" has a religious as well as an ethnic connotation, and the two aspects are interwoven.[13] It is almost impossible to make a clear distinction between them.


## The Principle of Freedom of Religion and of Conscience

The basic attitude of the state toward religious freedom[14] and pluralism is reflected in the 1948 Declaration on the Establishment of the State of Israel: "The State of Israel ... will guarantee freedom of religion, conscience, language, education and culture; it will safeguard the Holy Places of all religions. ..."[15] The declaration is neither a constitution nor a statute, but the Supreme Court has decided that it "expresses the nation's vision and its credo," and should be taken into consideration "when [attempting] to interpret or clarify the laws of the State."[16] Moreover, the legislature has "upgraded" the relevance of the declaration by including in the two previously mentioned 1992 Basic Laws a provision which says that these fundamental human rights "shall be upheld in the spirit of the principles set forth in the Declaration on the Establishment of the State of Israel."[17]

In this context one should also refer to a legislative text enacted in 1922 at the time of the British Mandate, and which is still in force in Israel:

> All persons in Palestine [now Israel] shall enjoy full liberty of conscience, and the free exercise of their forms of worship subject only to the maintenance of public order and morals. Each religious community . . . shall enjoy autonomy for the internal affairs of the community, subject to the provisions of any Ordinance or Order issued by the High Commissioner [now the minister of religious affairs].[18]

As mentioned, the two 1992 Basic Laws deal specifically with "Human Dignity and Liberty" and certain rights which derive therefrom, and with "Freedom of Occupation." However, the general reference to "Fundamental Human Rights" in the context of "Basic Principles"[19] may perhaps be interpreted as a recognition of the validity of other fundamental human rights not expressly mentioned in the text, including freedom of religion. If this broad interpretation of the two 1992 Basic Laws is adopted by the Supreme Court, the result could be that freedom of religion would, to a certain extent, prevail over regular laws.[20]

Israel has also committed itself to freedom of belief and religion in various international instruments. Thus, it has ratified the 1966 International Covenant on Civil and Political Rights, which provides for religious freedom.[21] Similarly, under the 1993 Fundamental Agreement between the Holy See and Israel, the latter has committed itself to uphold and observe this freedom.[22] This text also gives legally binding effect, as between the two contracting parties, to the relevant provision of the 1948 Universal Declaration of Human Rights.[23]

Compliance with freedom of religion in Israel has been assured by criminal law, which made it a punishable offense to outrage religious sentiments, to disturb worship, or to desecrate places of worship.[24] The previously mentioned rights, and the protection by criminal law, have been granted to members of "all religions," without distinction.

The Supreme Court of Israel has recognized and implemented the principle of freedom of religion in various cases. In H. C. 292/83, *Faithful of the Temple Mount et al. v. Commander of Police in the Jerusalem Area*,[25] Justice Barak said:

Every person in Israel enjoys freedom of conscience, of belief, of religion, and of worship. This freedom is guaranteed to every person in every enlightened democratic regime, and therefore it is guaranteed to every person in Israel. It is one of the fundamental principles upon which the State of Israel is based. . . . This freedom is partly based on article 83 of the Palestine Order in Council of 1922, and partly it is one of those "fundamental rights which 'are not written in the book' but derive directly from the nature of our State as a peace-loving democratic State. . . ." On the basis of these rules, and in accordance with the Declaration of Independence, every law and every power will be interpreted as recognizing freedom of conscience, of belief, of religion and of worship. . . .[26]

However, freedom of religion is not an absolute right. It is subject to limitations and derogations. Thus, Israel's Supreme Court said that:

Freedom of conscience, belief, religion and worship is relative. It has to be balanced with other rights and interests which also deserve protection, like [the right to] private and public property, and freedom of movement. One of the interests to be taken into consideration is public order and security.[27]

However, not every concern for public order justifies a restriction on freedom of religion and of worship. Only if the danger to public order is very probable or almost certain may the authorities restrict this freedom.[28] The relevant case concerned the refusal of the police to allow a group of Jews to pray outside the Temple Mount near one of its gates on the anniversary of the unification of Jerusalem, because of an alleged danger to public order from certain Muslim groups. The Court rejected the police's argument and ordered the police to permit the holding of the prayers under certain conditions.

This limitation on the freedom of religion is in line with the provisions of the relevant international documents. Thus, Article 29(2) of the 1948 Universal Declaration of Human Rights provides that "[i]n the exercise of his rights and freedoms, everyone shall be subject only to such limitations as are determined by law solely for the purpose of . . . meeting the just requirements of morality, public order and the general welfare in a democratic society."[29]

Similarly, under the 1966 International Covenant on Civil and Political Rights, "[f]reedom to manifest one's religion or beliefs may be subject only to such limitations as are prescribed by law and are necessary to protect public safety, order, health, or morals or the fundamental rights and freedoms of others."[30] The Supreme Court of Israel has emphasized that it recognizes and sanctions not only freedom of religion, but also freedom from religion, namely, the freedom not to practice any religion.[31]

An interesting question concerning freedom of religion has been raised in several bigamy cases. In Israel bigamy is forbidden by penal law but it is permitted according to Islamic law and according to the custom of several Jewish communities. In some cases people accused of bigamy tried to defend themselves by claiming that the law against bigamy was contrary to the principle of freedom of worship. The Supreme Court has rejected this argument by making a distinction between what religion allows, on the one hand, and what it commands, on the other hand. Since bigamy is, at the most, allowed by the relevant religious laws and not commanded, its outlawing by the secular legislature is not contrary to the freedom of worship.[32]

### The Holy Places

Freedom of religion also implies certain rights with regard to the Holy Places, namely, freedom of access and of worship, as well as the protection of those places. The Holy Places have often been a source of conflicts.[33] In the nineteenth century a bitter controversy arose when certain European countries extended their protection over various Christian communities in Palestine, and over the places which were holy to them. In order to regulate the status of the different communities at the Holy Places, the Ottoman government promulgated a number of *firmans,* the most important one being that of 1852.[34] That *firman* dealt with certain Holy Places and determined the powers and rights of the various denominations in those places. That arrangement became known as the historical Status Quo.[35] The Status Quo has been applied to the Church of the Holy Sepulcher and its dependencies, the Deir [Convent] al-Sultan, the Sanctuary of the Ascension on the Mount of Olives, and the Tomb of the Virgin Mary near Gethsemane, all four in Jerusalem, as well as to the Church of the Nativity, the Milk Grotto, and the Shepherds' Field near Bethlehem. The British authorities tried to add two non-Christian places to the list of Holy Places subject to the Status Quo: the Western Wall and Rachel's Tomb, but these are not included.

The Status Quo obtained international recognition by the 1856 Conference of Paris after the Crimean War and by the 1878 Treaty of Berlin.[36] It has also been reconfirmed by the 1993 Fundamental Agreement between the Holy See and Israel,[37] and by the 2000 Basic Agreement between the Holy See and the PLO.

The 1922 terms of the British Mandate for Palestine,[38] approved by the Council of the League of Nations and by Great Britain, also dealt with the Holy Places. The mandatory power was requested to preserve "existing rights" in those places and to ensure free access and worship, subject to the requirements of public order and decorum. An international commission which was "to study, define and determine the rights and claims in connection with the Holy Places" was never established due to lack of agreement among the powers about its composition and procedure.[39]

In 1924 Britain adopted the Palestine (Holy Places) Order in Council, under which "no cause or matter in connection with the Holy Places or religious buildings or sites in Palestine or the rights or claims relating to the different religious communities in Palestine shall be heard or determined by any Court in Palestine."[40] Although the Order in Council does not say so expressly, it was assumed that these matters were to be handled by the British high commissioner (today the minister of religious affairs).[41]

The 1936 Criminal Law Ordinance,[42] by which the mandatory authorities codified the penal law in Palestine, includes several provisions on the protection of places of worship against desecration. These provisions are today included in Israel's Penal Law, 5737–1977.[43] In 1948 the State of Israel was established, and, as mentioned earlier, the declaration signed at that time by the leaders of the Jewish community included a provision on the safeguarding of the Holy Places of all religions.[44]

From 1948 until 1967 most of the Holy Places in the territory of former mandatory Palestine were under Jordanian control. However, as a result of the 1967 Six-Day War, they came under the administration of Israel. Immediately after the fighting ended, Prime Minister Levi Eshkol convened the spiritual leaders of the various communities and reassured them of Israel's intention to protect all the Holy Places and to permit free worship at them.[45] Soon the Knesset adopted the Protection of the Holy Places Law, 5727–1967,[46] which ensures protection of the Holy Places against desecration as well as freedom of access thereto. These principles were reconfirmed with regard to Holy Places situated in Jerusalem by the 1980 Basic Law: Jerusalem, Capital of Israel.[47] The details of the implementation with regard to some of the Jewish Holy Places were laid down by the regulations enacted by the minister of religious affairs in accordance with the Protection of the Holy Places Law of 1967.[48] In addition, one has to remember that there are certain provisions dealing with the Holy Places in various specific laws, such as the Mining Ordinance of 1925[49] and the Antiquities Law, 5738–1978.[50]

In order to complete the picture, one should mention certain international texts related to the Holy Places. We have already mentioned the 1993 Fundamental Agreement between the Holy See and Israel, which deals both with the preservation of the historical Status Quo in those Christian Holy Places to which it applies, and with the protection of freedom of Catholic worship at others.[51] In the 1994 Treaty of Peace between Israel and Jordan, Israel promised to "[respect] the present special role of . . . Jordan in Muslim Holy Shrines in Jerusalem," and "[w]hen negotiations on the permanent status will take place, Israel will give high priority to the Jordanian historic role in these shrines."[52]

With regard to the Palestinians, one should mention a letter sent by then-foreign minister of Israel Shimon Peres to the foreign minister of Norway in October 1993. The letter was kept secret for some time, and its discovery aroused much criticism in Israel. According to this letter, "all the Palestinian institutions of East Jerusalem, including the economic, social, educational, cultural, and the holy Christian and Moslem places, are performing an essential task for the Palestinian population . . ." and "will be preserved."[53] The meaning of this text and its effect raise difficult questions of interpretation.[54]

Freedom of access and of worship at the Holy Places in the West Bank and Gaza Strip, as well as the protection of those sites, have been dealt with by the 1994 Agreement on the Gaza Strip and the Jericho Area,[55] by the 1995 Israeli-Palestinian Interim Agreement on the West Bank and the Gaza Strip,[56] and by the 1997 Protocol Concerning the Redeployment in Hebron.[57]

How do courts in Israel deal with disputes in which Holy Places are involved? We have seen that the principles of freedom of religion and of worship are generally recognized. Moreover, only very few disputes have erupted with regard to freedom of access and of worship in places that are holy for only one religion or denomination. Though in recent years disputes—sometimes accompanied by violence— have occurred among various Jewish groups over prayer at the Western Wall,[58] most disputes concern places that are holy to two or more religions or denominations.

The attitude of the courts may be summarized as follows: the 1924 Palestine (Holy Places) Order in Council[59] is still in force except where it has been superseded by later Israeli legislation, like the 1967 Protection of the Holy Places Law.[60] Therefore, the courts will not rule on questions of substantive rights or claims to "Holy Places, religious buildings or sites."[61] Similarly, in principle, courts do not consider themselves authorized to adjudicate on matters related to the right to worship at Holy Places.[62] It is the government that is authorized to deal both with disputes about rights to Holy Places and with the modalities of worship. Thus, the Supreme Court has so far refused to intervene in order to ensure the right of Jews to pray in groups on the Temple Mount/Haram al-Sharif, which is holy to both Jews and Muslims, and is under the administrative control of the Muslim *waqf*.[63]

On the other hand, the courts consider themselves authorized to deal with all matters mentioned in the Protection of the Holy Places Law, 5727–1967,[64] namely, protection against desecration, against violation of freedom of access, and against the offending of the feelings of the members of a community with regard to the place that is sacred for them.[65] The courts are also authorized to deal with criminal offenses in order to preserve public order at the Holy Places.[66] Even where a dispute actually relates to claims or rights to a Holy Place, the courts may intervene in order to restore possession to a community if it had been deprived of this possession by a recent act.[67] The reason for this rule is that the courts have an obligation to preserve law and order.

This last consideration, the preservation of law and order, is so important that in some cases the Supreme Court has even refused to override a decision of the police to deny freedom of mere access (independent of worship) because of the fear that such access would jeopardize law and order. Thus, in certain cases individual Jews were denied access to the Temple Mount for reasons of public order.[68] Moreover, even a temporary complete prohibition for all Jews to ascend the Temple Mount may be lawful if needed for reasons of safety.[69]

An interesting question concerns the distinction between the right to worship at Holy Places, which according to the courts is not within their jurisdiction, and the right to access with which the courts are authorized to deal. The request of Jews for permission to pray in a group on the Temple Mount was considered a matter of worship,[70] but it seems that according to the Supreme Court the right of an individual to pray quietly alone is part of his or her right of access.[71]

An overall consideration of the courts has been that there is a presumption in favor of the courts having jurisdiction, and that "where there are two possible interpretations, the interpretation which should be chosen is the one which preserves jurisdiction and not the one which excludes it."[72]

Even in those cases where the courts do have jurisdiction, they exercise it with great caution:

> There are certain matters in the sphere of law which are also matters of society, faith, morals and policy. In such matters the Court is apt to decide not strictly according to the law, but it may interpret and implement the law flexibly, in accordance with non-legal considerations, if the public welfare requires it. Such are, usually, matters related to the Holy Places.[73]

The Holy Places in Israel are administered by members of the faith for whom those places are holy. In practice, Israel has been very careful to carry out the policy of respect for the Holy Places of all religions. At the entrance of each Holy Place the Ministry of Religious Affairs has posted an announcement in several languages requesting visitors not to desecrate the place, to be properly dressed, and to behave becomingly. In the few cases of violations of the sanctity of Holy Places, the police have acted diligently to apprehend the offenders and bring them to justice.

Sometimes it is difficult to strike the right balance between the granting of autonomy to the administrators of the Holy Places on the one hand, and assuring adequate protection on the other hand. Too much protection might be interpreted as interference.

### Equality of Civil and Political Rights of Members
### of Various Religions and Communities

Discrimination on grounds of religion or belief would certainly be contrary to religious freedom, and Israel's legislation and court decisions would not tolerate it. The Declaration on the Establishment of the State proclaimed that "[t]he State of Israel . . . will ensure complete equality of social and political rights to all its inhabitants, irrespective of religion, race or sex. . . ."[74] An interesting example demonstrating this equality is the provision in the Basic Law: The President of the State of 1964, which lays down only two conditions for a person to qualify as a candidate for this office: he must be a citizen and a resident of Israel.[75] An amendment proposed at the time, which would have reserved this office for Jews, was not adopted by the Knesset.

According to the Supreme Court, the general principle of equality is a basic value of the legal system of Israel. It is a central ingredient of the social consensus on which Israel's society is based.[76] This principle implies that any differentiation must be justified by the nature of the case and its circumstances.[77] Such differentiation exists, for instance, in matters of military service. Only Jewish and Druze residents are subject to compulsory service in the army, while others are not. The special treatment given to most non-Jews in this respect was designed to prevent a conflict of conscience, most of the non-Jews being Arabs, either Muslim or Christian, who may have close relatives in countries which are not yet at peace with Israel. This exemption, however considerate, brings about a material disadvantage for the residents who do not become soldiers, since the state grants certain benefits only to individuals who have served in the army. Incidentally, many non-Jewish youths serve in the Israeli army on a voluntary basis, after which they are qualified to receive the benefits.

Respect for religious pluralism and the wish to preserve the identity and traditions of different religious communities is the basis for laws that in certain areas reject indiscriminate equality for the entire population. Thus, the Law on Adoption of Children of 1981 prescribes that the adopting persons be of the same religion as the adoptee.[78] In the matter of weekly rest, the Hours of Work and Rest Law provides that non-Jews may choose Sunday or Friday instead of Saturday, which is the Jewish Sabbath.[79]

It is of course true that equality cannot be measured only by reference to the legal system, and some inequality on the economic and social level may exist despite the law. The lack of full social equality and intermingling in Israel is probably the result of the political situation. As mentioned, most of Israel's non-Jews are ethnically Arabs, and some suspicion or distrust may have resulted from their affinity with the people in certain neighboring areas who are still hostile toward Israel. However, Israel has to make great efforts to grant its Arab inhabitants more economic support, and to improve the infrastructure in Arab localities.

Among the specific provisions of Israel's laws which are intended to guarantee protection and equality to members of the various religions, let us mention the law on the Crime of Genocide (Prevention and Punishment), 5710-1950,[80] the Employment Service Law, 5719-1959,[81] the Succession Law, 5725-1965,[82] and the Defamation Law, 5725-1965.[83]

Equality among the members of various ethnic groups and faiths has to be supplemented by provisions against intolerance. But a prohibition of intolerance may easily be interpreted as a violation of the principle of freedom of opinion and of expression, which is the cornerstone of every democratic society. Therefore, intolerance is prohibited only when it reaches a certain level. Thus, under the Penal Law, 5737-1977,[84] the offense of sedition includes the promotion of feelings of ill-will and enmity between different segments of the population. The law also prohibits the publication or reproduction of publications of a seditious nature. Certain acts of sedition are considered serious offenses, for which the perpetrator may be imprisoned for up to five years.[85] Other provisions that deal with offending religious or traditional sentiments call for punishment of one to three years imprisonment. The punishment is doubled if the act is related to a racist motive.[86] In this context one should also refer to the exclusion from elections to the Knesset of parties whose objectives or actions entail incitement to racism, and to the general prohibition of incitement to racism.[87]

Despite these legal provisions, incitement to hatred on religious or ethnic grounds occurs among members of some extremist groups, and one may deplore that the state, despite its efforts, has not been more diligent in prosecuting the offenders.

It has been alleged that there is discrimination against non-Jews in the fields of immigration and nationality. The Declaration on the Establishment of the State states that "[t]he State of Israel will be open to Jewish immigration and the Ingathering of the Exiles. . . ."[88] Consequently, the Law of Return, 5710-1950, provides that "every Jew has the right to immigrate to the country,"[89] and according to the Nationality Law, 5712-1952, any Jews who immigrate to Israel may easily acquire Israeli nationality unless they do not wish to.[90] However, this privilege does not involve improper discrimination on religious grounds for several reasons:

1. When a people attains statehood in fulfillment of its aspiration for national liberation, it is common and natural that all members of that people are permitted and invited to come and live in that country.[91] From this point of view, Israel is no more discriminatory than most other new states. In fact, many states, new and old, have granted preference, in bestowing their nationality, to persons who have close social, cultural, or ethnic links with the nation. Examples include Greece, the Federal Republic of Germany, the former USSR, Italy, former

Czechoslovakia, Denmark, El Salvador, Guatemala, Honduras, Liberia, Mexico, Nicaragua, Poland, Venezuela, and Jordan.[92]

2. In 1965 the United Nations adopted the International Convention on the Elimination of All Forms of Racial Discrimination,[93] which has been in force among more than 160 states, including Israel. Although this document deals with racial discrimination,[94] it seems that by analogy one can draw some important conclusions with regard to restrictions or preferences on religious grounds as well. The convention has laid down that in matters of nationality, citizenship, and naturalization, states are free to prefer certain persons, on condition that there is no discrimination against any particular group (Article 1(3)). Since Israeli legislation does not impose restrictions on any particular group, it is within the letter and the spirit of the convention.

3. Moreover, the convention permits the granting of preferences, if necessary, to undo the effects of prior discrimination, namely, affirmative action (Article 1(4)). In the case of Israel, one has to remember that after 1939 the gates of mandatory Palestine had almost been closed to Jewish immigration, thus contributing to the perishing of millions of Jews in Europe during World War II. The wide opening of the gates for Jews on the establishment of Israel can thus be considered a lawful case of affirmative action.

4. It should be underlined that the law does not close the state's doors to anybody, but simply creates a preference in favor of Jews.[95] With regard to non-Jews, the applicable rules of immigration are quite similar to those that exist in other states. Anybody, including non-Jews, may apply for permission to enter Israel, and for naturalization. Just the automatic right to enter and the easy acquisition of nationality is reserved for Jews.

5. Moreover, not only do Jews enjoy those rights, but so do their family members, whether or not they are Jewish.[96]

In the matter of immigration and nationality, the dual nature of Judaism, as a religion and as an ethnic origin, is of particular relevance. Despite the semireligious definition of a Jew, the previously mentioned laws are basically concerned with the return of members of the Jewish people to their homeland. This right involves a continuing debate over the question "Who is a Jew?", a matter which is beyond the scope of this chapter.[97]

### The Right to Change One's Religion

Another aspect of religious freedom concerns the possibility to change one's religion. This right has been the subject of a special enactment adopted during the mandatory period, the Religious Community (Change) Ordinance of 1927,[98] which is still in force. Since—as will be seen later—belonging to a religious community has important consequences in matters of personal status and the jurisdiction of the courts, it was laid down that any change in a person's religion has to be registered. Thus, everyone is free to change his or her religion, but in order for that conversion to have legal consequences for the jurisdiction in family matters, and for that purpose only,[99] the change requires the consent of the new religious community which he or she joins. The head of this religious community will provide the convert with an appropriate certificate, which must be used to notify the Ministry of Religious Affairs of the change. The consent of the community that the person leaves is not needed.[100]

The religion of a minor shall not be changed unless both parents consent or unless a court approves the conversion. If the minor is above the age of ten, his or her consent is also required.[101]

### Proselytizing

It is doubtful whether a right to proselytize is included in the principle of freedom of religion. The previously mentioned international instruments provide for the right to manifest one's religion or belief "in teaching, practice, worship and observance,"[102] but proselytizing is not mentioned. Nevertheless, we will add a few clarifications on this matter.

Proselytizing is legal in Israel, but since 1977 it has been prohibited to promise money or other material advantages in order to induce someone to change his or her religion. Similarly, it is prohibited to receive material advantages in exchange for a promise to change one's religion.[103]

In short, missionary activity is allowed, but the buying of souls for money has been prohibited. This practice has also been condemned by various religions. The above-mentioned law applies equally to all religions. According to an instruction issued by the attorney general, no one shall be prosecuted under the 1977 law without prior authorization by the state attorney. In fact, the law has never been applied.

From time to time tensions rise as a result of overzealous attempts to proselytize, probably because of the differing attitudes of the various religions to proselytizing. For instance, the Jewish and the Druze religions do not encourage people to join their ranks, while some Christian groups consider proselytizing a holy mission. One can understand that members of a religion that does not try to influence others to join it can be irritated when members of other religions try to proselytize them.

## The Right to a Religious Education

The right to religious education is guaranteed by law.[104] It is essentially secured by governmental support and the recognition of the autonomy of the various religious communities. Parents may choose to send their children to a secular state school, to a religious state school, or to a private religious school.[105] The curriculum of schools in Arab areas is adapted to the environment and relevant traditions. In the eastern part of Jerusalem, children used to study in accordance with the Jordanian curriculum, but most schools have switched to the Palestinian one. In this context it should also be mentioned that since 1991 Israel is a party to the 1989 UN Convention on the Rights of the Child.[106]

## Matters of Personal Status

It is perhaps in matters of personal status that issues of religious freedom in Israel are most complicated and controversial. Under Ottoman rule (1517–1917), the recognized religious communities (*millets*) were granted autonomy in matters of personal status. This system was preserved with some modifications by the mandatory authorities[107] and later by the State of Israel. Today there are, in addition to the Jewish community, thirteen Recognized Religious Communities in Israel: the Muslim, Eastern Orthodox, Latin Catholic, Gregorian Armenian, Armenian Catholic, Syrian Catholic, Chaldean Uniate, Greek Catholic-Melkite, Maronite, Syrian Orthodox, Druze (since 1962), Episcopal-Evangelical (since 1970), and Baha'i (since 1971) communities. The last two do not have their own religious tribunals. The list of Recognized Religious Communities[108] does not include several Christian communities—such as Christian Monophysites (the Copts and the Ethiopian Orthodox Church), the Protestant-Lutheran, the Baptist, and the Quakers—nor does it include certain other religious communities within or outside the bounds of the Jewish community.

Priests of the various religious communities are in charge of conducting marriages and notifying governmental authorities for the purpose of registration.[109] Tribunals of recognized communities have jurisdiction in certain matters of personal status, sometimes to the exclusion of the jurisdiction of civil courts. There are differences in the scope of jurisdiction among the various communities. In certain matters the jurisdiction of the religious tribunals is exclusive, while in others it is concurrent and depends on the consent of all the parties involved.[110]

Both the religious tribunals and the civil courts apply mainly the religious laws of the parties concerned to questions of personal status,[111] in addition to relevant laws enacted by the Knesset.[112] The difference between the application of religious law by the civil courts on the one hand and the religious tribunals on the other hand is apparent in two matters. First, each of these jurisdictions applies its own rules of procedure and evidence. Second, the civil courts take into consideration rules of private international law (conflict of laws) whereas the religious tribunals disregard them.

Due to the jurisdiction and autonomy of the religious tribunals, Israel had to add to its 1991 ratification of the 1966 International Covenant on Civil and Political Rights a reservation that "to the extent that such law [the religious law of the relevant parties] is inconsistent with its obligations under the Covenant, Israel reserves its right to apply that law."[113]

Although, as mentioned, the religious tribunals are in principle autonomous and may apply their respective legal systems, Israel's Supreme Court has decided that these tribunals have to comply with certain laws of the state, such as the Succession Law, 5725-1965.[114] Moreover, they should also apply general legal principles derived from the basic values of Israel's legal system, including human rights. Thus, in view of the right to freedom of movement, the Supreme Court has limited the power of a Jewish religious tribunal to prohibit a party to leave the country.[115] Similarly, the Court has ruled that the tribunal must judge in conformity with the presumption of equal partnership of spouses in the property acquired by one of them.[116]

The jurisdiction of the rabbinical tribunals has given rise to considerable opposition from many Jews. This probably stems from three reasons. First, many nonreligious Jews resent the exclusive authority of the religious institutions and consider it to be a case of religious coercion.[117] Second, although Jewish law is quite liberal on certain matters, such as divorce by consent, it nevertheless includes some rather rigid rules and restrictions, as well as discrimination between the genders,[118] which may be considered outdated and may create unnecessary hardship. Third, the Jewish population in Israel is quite heterogeneous, but so far the state has in fact given the Orthodox establishment a monopoly over official activities, namely, the registration of marriages and jurisdiction in matters of personal status. This has engendered resentment from members of other movements, including the Conservative, Reform,[119] Kara'ites,[120] and Falashas (the Ethiopian Jews).[121]

It thus follows that nonbelievers and members of an unrecognized religious group are at a disadvantage in matters of personal status. No lay officials are authorized to celebrate and register marriages; there is no secular law on marriages; and civil courts have no jurisdiction in matters of marriage and divorce of Israelis. However, in order to alleviate the situation, in those matters of dissolution of marriage which are not within the exclusive jurisdiction of a religious tribunal (like mixed couples), the civil courts do have jurisdiction under certain circumstances.[122]

Similarly, since 1995 lay courts for family matters have been established but the law expressly provides that it does not restrict jurisdiction of the religious tribunals.[123]

## Conclusion

This survey has shown that under Israeli law, freedom of conscience, belief, religion, and worship is guaranteed in most spheres, in line with the state's international obligations. These freedoms are based both on legislative acts and on court decisions. They must, however, be balanced with other rights and interests and may be restricted for reasons of public order and security. They are protected *inter alia* by provisions of the penal law.

Israel also respects freedom of access to and of worship at the Holy Places and ensures the protection of these sites. However, in this sphere the powers of the courts are somewhat restricted in favor of the government, which is considered to be better suited to deal with certain matters concerning the Holy Places because of the international aspects of this sphere. An overriding consideration is the need to preserve law and order—a consideration which is of particular relevance with regard to the Temple Mount/Haram al-Sharif.

Freedom of religion requires equality of civil and political rights among members of different faiths. Equality for all citizens is a basic tenet of Israeli law, and distinctions are only permitted if they can be objectively justified by the nature and circumstances of the case. Such distinctions are sometimes necessary in order to respect the right of a religious group to be different and preserve its identity. Incitement, namely, severe intolerance, and the offending of religious feelings are outlawed by provisions of penal law.

Israel also recognizes the right to change one's religion. Proselytizing is permitted, but not for material gain. Every Israeli parent has the right to choose between a secular and a religious school for his or her children. Private religious schools are also recognized.

In matters of personal status, religious freedom is both particularly evident and problematic. The right of priests to celebrate and register marriages and the jurisdiction of the tribunals of the recognized religious communities in certain matters of personal status do enhance the religious freedom and autonomy of those communities. But on the other hand, since some of these powers are exclusive, people who do not belong to any religious group and those who are part of an unrecognized denomination may have grave difficulties. One way to overcome this hardship would be the introduction of an optional civil marriage law[124] as well as a secular law on matters of personal status that would be applied by the civil courts, which would have jurisdiction parallel to the religious tribunals.

# NOTES

This chapter is partly based on a lecture given at the Conference on the Fundamental Agreement between the Holy See and Israel held at the Columbus School of Law of the Catholic University of America in April 1997. The author wishes to express her thanks to Dr. Yaffa Zilbershats and to Mr. Rotem Giladi for their most valuable remarks. I also thank Ms. Mary Ann DeRosa, Ms. Cathy Strain, and Ms. Ricki Fishel for their patience and meticulous typing. An earlier, shorter version of this chapter was published in 47 *Catholic University Law Review* 441–65 (1998), and in *Freedom of Religion in Jerusalem* 3–46 (Ruth Lapidoth and Ora Ahimeir eds., 1999). The text has been updated through spring 2002.

1. G. A. Res. 36/55, Nov. 25, 1981, U. N. GAOR, 36th Sess., Supp. No. 51, at 171.

2. See id. However, due to the objection of some Muslim states, the declaration does not expressly mention the right to change one's religion. See Natan Lerner, "The Final Text of the U. N. Declaration against Intolerance and Discrimination Based on Religion or Belief," 12 *Isr. Y.B. on Hum. Rts.* 185, 185–89 (1982). It is, however, generally recognized that under international law freedom of religion includes the right to convert. See Universal Declaration of Human Rights, Dec. 10, 1948, art. 18, G. A. Res. 217 A(III), U. N. GAOR, 3d Sess., at 74 (1948) [hereinafter Universal Declaration]; International Covenant on Civil and Political Rights, Dec. 19, 1966, art. 18, 999 U. N. T. S. 172, 178 [hereinafter ICCPR]; see also Lerner, *supra*, 185–89.

3. Basic Law: Freedom of Occupation, 5752 (1991/92) S. H. 114, amended by Basic Law: Freedom of Occupation, 5754 (1993/94) S. H. 90, and 5758 (1997/98) S. H. 178; Basic Law: Human Dignity and Liberty, 5752 (1991/92) S. H. 150, amended by Basic Law: Human Dignity and Liberty, 5754 (1993/94) S. H. 90.

4. Declaration on the Establishment of the State of Israel, 1948, 1 L. S. I. 3, 4 (1948).

5. Basic Law: The Knesset (Amendment No. 35), 5762 (2001–02) S. H. 410, section 7A; see also Law on Political Parties, 5752-1992, 5752, (1991–92) S. H. 190, section 5(1), and Law on Political Parties (Amendment No. 13), 5762-2002, 5762 (2001–02) S. H. 410. For an interpretation of section 7A in its earlier version, see Amnon Rubinstein & Ra'anan Har-Zahav, *The Basic Law: The Knesset* 57–65 (1993) (Hebrew).

6. See Amnon Rubinstein & Barak Medina, *The Constitutional Law of the State of Israel* 109–11 (5th ed. 1996) (Hebrew) (stating other relevant statutory provisions as well as references).

7. Foundations of Law, 5740-1980, 34 L. S. I. 181 (1979–80).

8. Id.; see also Rubinstein & Medina, *supra* note 6, at 79–80.

9. *Supra* note 3.

10. See Aharon Barak, 3 *Interpretation in Law: Constitutional Interpretation* 328–47 (1994) (Hebrew); Claude Klein, *La Démocratic d'Israël* 286–94 (1997); Haim Cohn, "Values of a Jewish and Democratic State, Reflection on Basic Law: Human Dignity and Freedom," in *ha-Peraklit (Jubilee Book)* 9–52 (1993) (Hebrew); Menahem Elon, "Constitution by Legislation: The Values of a Jewish and Democratic State in Light of the Basic Law: Human Dignity and Personal Freedom," 17 *Tel Aviv U. L. Rev.* 659–88 (1993) (Hebrew); Ruth Gavison, "A Jewish and Democratic State—Political Identity, Ideology and Law," 19

*Tel Aviv U. L. Rev.* 631–82 (1995) (Hebrew); Ruth Gavison, *Israel as a Jewish and Democratic State: Tensions and Prospects* (1999)(Hebrew); Assa Kasher, "A Jewish and Democratic State—Philosophical Outline," 19 *Tel Aviv U. L. Rev.* 729–39 (1995) (Hebrew); *Israel as a Jewish and Democratic State* (Ron Margolin ed., 1999) (Hebrew); Yehuda Cohn, *Who's Afraid of a Jewish State: A Constitutional and Ideological Perspective* (2001) (Hebrew); Asher Maoz, "The Values of a Jewish and Democratic State," 19 *Tel Aviv U. L. Rev.* 547–630 (1995) (Hebrew); Binyamin Neuberger, *Religion and Democracy in Israel* (1997) (Hebrew); Ariel Rozen-Zvi, "A Jewish and Democratic State: Spiritual Parenthood, Alienation and Symbiosis—Can We Square the Circle?," 19 *Tel Aviv U. L. Rev.* 479–519 (1995) (Hebrew); Eliezer Schweid, "Israel as a Jewish Democratic State: Historical and Theoretical Aspects," in *Jerusalem City of Law and Justice* 125–45 (Nahum Rakover ed., 1998).

11.  See Itzhak Zamir, 1 *Administrative Power* 47–48 (1996) (Hebrew).

12.  As stated by Barak, *supra* note 10, at 332.

13.  See Claude Klein, *Le Caractère Juif de l'état d'Israël* 102 (1977).

14.  For background on freedom of religion in Israel, see generally S. Zalman Abramov, *Perpetual Dilemma: Jewish Religion in the Jewish State* (1976); Klein, *supra* note 10, at 229–64; Rubinstein & Medina, *supra* note 6, at 175–226; Zvi Berinson, "Freedom of Religion and Conscience in the State of Israel," 3 *Isr. Y.B. on Hum. Rts.* 223–32 (1973); Izhak Englard, "The Conflict between State and Religion in Israel, Its Historical and Ideological Background," 19 *Tel Aviv U. L. Rev.* 741 (1995); Izhak Englard, "The Conflict between State and Religion in Israel: Its Ideological Background," in *International Perspectives on Church and State* 219 (Menachem Mor ed., 1993) [hereinafter *International Perspectives*]; Izhak Englard, "Law and Religion in Israel," 35 *Am. J. Comp. L.* 185 (1987); Izhak Englard, "Religious Freedom and Jewish Tradition in Modern Israeli Law—A Clash of Ideologies," in *Religion and Law: Biblical-Judaic and Islamic Perspectives* 365–75 (Edwin B. Firmage et al. eds., 1990); Stephen Goldstein, "The Teaching of Religion in Government Funded Schools," 26 *Isr. L. Rev.* 36–64 (1992); Asher Maoz, "Religious Human Rights in the State of Israel," in *Religious Human Rights in Global Perspective: Legal Perspectives* 349–89 (Johan D. van der Vyver & John Witte eds., 1996); Asher Maoz, "State and Religion in Israel," in *International Perspectives, supra,* at 247; Simha Meron, "Freedom of Religion as Distinct from Freedom from Religion," 4 *Isr. Y.B. on Hum. Rts.* 219–40 (1974); Amnon Rubinstein, "State and Religion in Israel," in *J. Contemp. Hist.,* Oct. 1967, at 107; Chamman Shelach, "On Freedom of Conscience and Freedom of the Heart: Freedom of Conscience and of Religion in Israel and the Limitations on the Freedom to Marry," in *Civil Rights in Israel, Essays in Honour of Haim S. Cohn* (Ruth Gavison ed., 1982); Shimon Shetreet, "A Rejoinder," 4 *Isr. Y.B. on Hum. Rts.* 241–44 (1974); Shimon Shetreet, "Some Reflections on Freedom of Conscience and Religion in Israel," 4 *Isr. Y.B. on Hum. Rts.* 194–218 (1974); Frances Raday, "Religion, Multiculturalism and Equality: The Israeli Case," 25 *Isr. Y.B. on Hum. Rts.* 193–242 (1995); Shimon Shetreet, *The Good Land between Power and Religion* (1998) (Hebrew); Shimon Shetreet, *Between Three Branches of Government: The Balance of Rights in Matters of Religion in Israel* (1999) (Hebrew); Elyakim Rubinstein and N. Solberg, "Religion and State in Israel in Its Jubilee Year," 44 *Gesher* 7–20 (1998) (Hebrew); Amnon

Ramon, "Freedom of Religion and the Status of Christians in Jerusalem 1967–1997," in *Freedom of Religion in Jerusalem* 81–120 (Lapidoth and Ahimeir eds., 1999).

15. *Supra* note 4.

16. Election Appeal, 1/65, *Yardor v. Chairman of the Central Elections Committee for the Sixth Knesset*, 19(3) P. D. 365, 386 (by Agranat, J.). For an English summary, see *32 Justice* 38–42 (2002).

17. *Supra* note 3; *supra* note 9. The full text of section 1 common to both Basic Laws as amended reads: "Fundamental human rights in Israel are founded upon recognition of the value of the human being, the sanctity of human life, and the principle that all persons are free; these rights shall be upheld in the spirit of the principles set forth in the Declaration on the Establishment of the State of Israel."

18. Palestine Order in Council, 1922, 3 Drayton, Laws of Palestine 2587, section 83 (1934).

19. *Supra* note 3; *supra* note 9.

20. See id. This would be the consequence of the provision in section 8 of the Basic Law: Human Dignity and Liberty: "The rights according to this Basic Law shall not be violated except by a statute that befits the values of the State of Israel, and is enacted for a worthy purpose, and to an extent that does not exceed what is necessary, or by regulation enacted by virtue of express authorization in such a statute." Basic Law: Human Dignity and Liberty, 5754 (1993/94) S. H. 90. However, the law has no retroactive effect: "Nothing in this Basic Law affects the validity of any law (*din*) in force prior to the entry into force of this Basic Law." Basic Law: Human Dignity and Liberty, 5754 (1993/94) S. H. 90; see also Rubinstein & Medina, *supra* note 6, at 176; Hillel Sommer, "The Non-Enumerated Rights: On the Scope of the Constitutional Revolution," 28 *Mishpatim* 257, 324–26 (1997) (Hebrew); Rotem Giladi, "Freedom of Religion and the 'Constitutional Revolution,'" in *Freedom of Religion in Jerusalem* 61–80 (Lapidoth and Ahimeir eds., 1999). I wish to express my warm thanks to Dr. Barak Medina for having enlightened me on the various attitudes expressed by the Supreme Court on human rights not expressly enumerated in the Basic Law.

21. See ICCPR, *supra* note 2, art. 18. Israel ratified the covenant in 1991.

22. See Fundamental Agreement between the Holy See and the State of Israel, Dec. 30, 1993, 33 I. L. M. 153, 154 (1994) [hereinafter Fundamental Agreement]; see also Marie-Pierre Lafranchi, "L'Accord Fondamental du 30 décembre 1993 signé entre le Saint-Siège et Israël," 40 *Annuaire Français de Droit International* 326–55 (1994).

23. See Universal Declaration, *supra* note 2, art. 18. Originally, the United Nations General Assembly adopted the declaration "as a common standard of achievement" to which people should strive. Id. preamble. Opinions are divided on whether it has later acquired binding legal force. Its provision on religious freedom is referred to in the Fundamental Agreement as follows: "The State of Israel . . . affirms its continuing commitment to uphold and observe the human right to freedom of religion and conscience, as set forth in the Universal Declaration of Human Rights and in other international instruments to which it is a party." Fundamental Agreement, *supra* note 22, art. 1(1). For the parallel obligation of the Holy See, see Article 1(2).

24. See Offences against Sentiments of Religion and Tradition, 5737–1977, Penal Law, sections 170–74, Special Volume L. S. I. 54–55 (1977); see also Shmuel Berkovitz, *The Legal Status of the Holy Places in Jerusalem* 28–37 (1997) (Hebrew) (providing a detailed analysis of the relevant provisions).

25. H. C. 292/83, *Faithful of the Temple Mount v. Commander of Police*, 38(2) P. D. at 449, 454.

26. Id. (internal quotation from Landau J. in H. C. 243/62, 16 P. D. 2407); see also H. C. 7128/96, *Movement of the Faithful of the Temple Mount v. Government of Israel*, 97(1) Takdeen Elyon p. 480 (1997) ("Solomon's Stables" case).

27. H. C. 292/83, *Faithful of the Temple Mount*, 38(2) P. D. at 455.

28. See id. at 456.

29. Universal Declaration, *supra* note 2, art. 29(2).

30. ICCPR, *supra* note 2, art. 18(3), at 178.

31. See, e.g., H. C. 3872/93, *Meatrael Ltd. v. The Prime Minister and Minister of Religious Affairs*, 47(5) P. D. 485, 506; see also H. C. 5016/96, *Lior Horev et al. v. Minister of Transport et al.*, Takdeen Elyon 97(2), 5757/5758-1997, 611–48; ibid., 465 (1–36); ibid., 421 (1–40). In this case the Supreme Court looked for a balance between the right to freedom of movement and the need to respect religious feelings of the religious community. The dispute concerned traffic on the Sabbath in Bar Ilan St. Excerpts in English were published in 14 *Justice* 34–40 (1997).

32. See, e.g., Cr. A. 112/50, *Yossipoff v. Attorney General*, 5 P. D. 481; H. C. 49/54, *Malham v. Sharia Judge in Acre*, 8 P. D. 910; Cr. A. 338/74, *State of Israel v. Rubin*, 29(1) P. D. 166.

33. Shmuel Berkovitz, *The Battle for the Holy Places* 7–240 (2000) (Hebrew); see also Walter Zander, *Israel and the Holy Places of Christendom* (1971).

34. English translation reproduced in Zander, *supra* note 33, at 178–80.

35. See generally L. G. A. Cust, *The Status Quo in the Holy Places* (1929); Zander, *supra* note 33, at 53–54; Izhak Englard, "The Legal Status of the Holy Places in Jerusalem," 28 *Isr. L. Rev.* 589, 591–93 (1994); see also Berkovitz, *supra* note 33, at 19–20. The historical Status Quo should be distinguished from two other meanings of the term: the situation of all the various Holy Places and communities, and the relationship between secular and religious Jews in Israel. In this latter context, the term means compromise arrangements on matters concerning the Jewish faith, such as respect for the precepts of Judaism in public places and in the army, safeguarding the rights of the religious establishment, and application of religious law in marriage and divorce proceedings. See Eliezer Don-Yehiya, *The Politics of Accommodation: Settling Conflicts of State and Religion in Israel* 31–67 (1997) (Hebrew); H. C. 5016/96, *Lior Horev v. Minister of Transport*, English summary published in 14 *Justice* 34–40 (1997); and Cheshin, J. in H. C. 3872/93, *supra* n.31, at 506–7.

36. See 114 Consol. T. S. 406; Treaty for the Settlement of Affairs in the East, 13 July 1878, art. 62, 153 Consol. T. S. 172, 190 (1878).

37. See Fundamental Agreement, *supra* note 22, art. 4.

38. Terms of the British Mandate for Palestine Confirmed by the Council of the League of Nations, 24 July 1922, reprinted in *The Arab-Israel Conflict and Its Resolution: Selected Documents* 25–32 (Ruth Lapidoth & Moshe Hirsch eds., 1992).

39. Id. at 28; Zander, *supra* note 33, at 64–70.

40. The Palestine (Holy Places) Order in Council, 25 July 1924, 3 Drayton, Laws of Palestine 2625 (1934). In implementing this provision, the courts had to deal with the question of what is a Holy Place. The courts have generally held that, in the absence of a definition in the Order in Council, it may be presumed that the intention was that the holiness depends on the belief of members of the relevant group, namely, on their religion. See Berkovitz, *supra* note 24, chap. 4, 2nd ed. (2003); see also Haim Cohn, "The Status of Jerusalem in the Israel Legal System," in *Twenty Years in Jerusalem 1967–1987*, at 246, 258–61 (Joshua Prawer & Ora Ahimeir eds., 1988). The lack of a general definition or authorized list of Holy Places has led to an unreasonable increase in their number. While in 1950 a UN document enumerated thirty Holy Places in the Jerusalem area (UN Doc. T/L. 49, of 7 March 1950), according to a list prepared in 2000 by three authors—an Israeli Jew, an Armenian Christian, and a Palestinian Muslim—there were 328 (Yitzhak Reiter, Marlen Eordegian, and Marwan Abu Khalaf, "Between Divine and Human: The Complexity of Holy Places in Jerusalem," in *Jerusalem: Points of Friction and Beyond* 95–164, at 155–59 (Moshe Ma'oz and Sari Nusseibeh eds., 2000).

41. See Shmuel Berkovitz, "The Holy Places in Jerusalem: Legal Aspects (Part Two)," 12 *Justice* 17, 17–19 (1997) (discussing jurisdictional issues). According to Justice Agranat, the president of the Supreme Court, in H. C. 222/68, *National Groups, A Registered Association v. Minister of Police*, 24(2) P. D. 141, 203, 211, the authority of the mandatory power derived from the Terms of the British Mandate for Palestine, *supra* note 38, and from the purpose of the order in council. In Israel it is also based on Basic Law: The Government of 1968, section 29, which grants the government all powers not given to another organ. In the later, 2001 version of this Basic Law, the relevant provision is in section 32: 5761 (2000/1) S. H. 158.

42. See 1936 *Palestine Gazette* supp. 1, 285.

43. See Offences against Sentiments of Religion and Tradition, Penal Law, 5737-1977, sections 170–74, Special Volume L. S. I. 54 (1977); see also Shmuel Berkovitz, "The Holy Places in Jerusalem: Legal Aspects (Part One)," 11 *Justice* 4, 7–9 (1996) (analyzing the relevant provisions); Haim Cohn, *supra* note 40, at 252–53.

44. *Supra* note 4.

45. See Prime Minister Levi Eshkol's Address to the Spiritual Leaders of All Communities in Jerusalem (June 7, 1967), reprinted in 1 *Israel's Foreign Relations 1947–1974*, at 244–45 (Meron Medzini ed., 1976).

46. See the Protection of the Holy Places Law, 5727-1967, 21 L. S. I. 76 (1966–67).

47. See Basic Law: Jerusalem, Capital of Israel, of 1980, 34 L. S. I. 209 (1979–80).

48. See Regulations on the Protection of Places Holy for Jews, 5741-1981, K. T. 4252, 1212 (amended in 1989/90, K. T. 5237, 190).

49. See the Mining Ordinance of 1925, 2 Drayton, Laws of Palestine 938–39 (1934).

50. See the Antiquities Law, 5738–1978, section 29(c), 32 L. S. I. 93, 100 (1978); Berkovitz, *supra* note 43, at 6 (for additional provisions, and for an analysis); see also Berkovitz, *supra* note 24, at 27.

51. See Fundamental Agreement, *supra* note 22, art. 4.

52. Treaty of Peace between the State of Israel and the Hashemite Kingdom of Jordan, 26 Oct. 1994, art. 9, 34 I. L. M. 43 (1995). For analysis, see Reuven Merhav and Rotem Giladi, "The Role of the Hashamite Kingdom of Jordan in a Future Permanent-Status Settlement in Jerusalem," in *Jerusalem: A City and Its Future* 175–220, at 189–203 (Marshall Breger and Ora Ahimeir eds., 2002).

53. Full text reprinted in *Jerusalem Post,* June 7, 1994, at 1.

54. See Joel Singer, "Aspects of Foreign Relations under the Israeli-Palestinian Agreements on Interim Self-Government Arrangements for the West Bank and Gaza," 28 *Isr. L. Rev.* 268, at 292–93 (1994); Ruth Lapidoth, "Jerusalem and the Peace Process," 28 *Isr. L. Rev.* 402, 428–30 (1994) (analyzing the text of the letter); see also Sami F. Musallam, *The Struggle for Jerusalem: A Programme of Action for Peace* 37–48 (1996) (on the background to the sending of the letter).

55. See Agreement on the Gaza Strip and the Jericho Area between Israel and the Palestine Liberation Organization, 4 May 1994, U. N. Doc. A/49/180-S/1994/727 (Annex) of 20 June 1994, reprinted in 33 I. L. M. 622 (1994).

56. Israeli-Palestinian Interim Agreement on the West Bank and the Gaza Strip, K. A. 33, 1, reprinted in 36 I. L. M. 551 (1997) (excerpts).

57. See Protocol Concerning the Redeployment in Hebron and Note for the Record, 17 Jan. 1997, 36 I. L. M. 650 (1997); see also Berkovitz, *supra* note 33, at 215–23.

58. See, e.g., H. C. 257/89 and 2410/90, *Hoffman v. Custodian of the Western Wall,* 48(2) P. D. 256 and 54(2) P. D. 345 (considering disputes over the rights of worship and prayer at the Western Wall between Jews of different religious convictions). The issue was considered again by a nine-member panel of the Supreme Court. See H. C. 4128/00, *Director General of the Prime Minister's Office et al. v. Anat Hoffman et al.,* judgment of Apr. 6, 2003.

59. *Supra* note 40.

60. See Protection of the Holy Places Law, 5727-1967, 21 L. S. I. 76 (1966–67) (which *partly* superseded the Order in Council).

61. *Supra* note 40. For a famous interesting case, see H. C. 109/70, *Coptic Orthodox Mutteran of the Holy Seat in Jerusalem and the Near East v. Minister of Police,* 25(1) P. D. 225; H. C. 188/77, *Coptic Orthodox Mutteran of the Holy Seat in Jerusalem and the Near East v. Government of Israel,* 33(1) P. D. 225.

62. See, e.g., H. C. 222/68, *National Groups, A Registered Association v. Minister of Police,* 24(2) P. D. 141; H. C. 33/92, *Baruch Ben-Yosef v. Minister for Religious Affairs,* 46(1) P. D. 855; H. C. 537/81, *Hayim Stanger v. Government of Israel,* 35(4) P. D. 673. It seems, however, that in fact the Court's attitude has changed in this matter—see H. C. 2410/90, *Hoffman v. Custodian of the Western Wall,* 54(2) P. D. 345. In this case the Supreme Court discussed the right to pray at the wall without raising the question of jurisdiction.

63. The special difficulty with the Temple Mount is that it is not only holy for Jews as well as Muslims, but it has also become a national symbol for both communities. See Yitzhak Reiter, *The Temple Mount/Al-Haram Al-Sharif: Points of Agreement and Dispute* 2 (1997) (Hebrew); *Sovereignty of God and Man: Sanctity and Political Centrality on the Temple Mount* (Yitzhak Reiter ed., 2001) (Hebrew); Nadav Shragai, *The Temple Mount Conflict* (1995) (Hebrew).

64. See the Protection of the Holy Places Law, 5727-1967, 21 L. S. I. 76 (1966–67).

65. For an analysis of these notions, and the relations among them, see H. C. 7128/96, *Movement of the Faithful of the Temple Mount v. Government of Israel* (Justice I. Zamir) 97(1) Takdeen Elyon 480 (1997) ("Solomon's Stables" case).

66. See, e.g., Cr. Case (Jm.) 2986/87, *Government of Israel v. The Idra Institutions and Rabbi Goren*, 1988/89(2) P. M. 156 (Justice Proccacia), and the petition to the Supreme Court, H. C. 267/88, *The Idra Institutions and Rabbi Goren v. The Local Court in Jerusalem and the Government of Israel*, 43(3) P. D. 728 (Justice Barak); Cr. Case (Jm.) 203/84, *State of Israel v. Livni* 1989/90(3) P. M. 330 (the case of the Jewish underground); Cr. Case (Jm.) 51/76, *State of Israel v. Chanan*, 1976/77(1) P. M. 392. In principle, the courts may deal with criminal cases related to the Holy Places unless the offense is directly connected with the sanctity of the place where it was perpetrated. But so far in no criminal case have the courts abstained from assuming jurisdiction because of such a connection.

67. See, e.g., H. C. 109/70, *supra* note 61.

68. See, e.g., H. C. 2725/93, *Salomon v. Commander of the Police in Jerusalem*, 96(1) Takdeen Elyon 370; H. C. 4044/93, *Salomon v. Commander of the Police in Jerusalem*, 96(1) Takdeen Elyon 447. In both cases the Supreme Court decided by majority vote, and not unanimously.

69. See H. C. 1663/94, *Salomon v. Police Officer Givati*, 94(1) Takdeen Elyon 1078.

70. See, e.g., H. C. 222/68, *supra* note 62; H. C. 33/92, *supra* note 62; H. C. 537/81, *supra* note 62.

71. This was said in H. C. 99/76, *Cohn v. Minister of Police*, 30(2) P. D. 506. In H. C. 67/93, *"Kach" Movement v. The Minister for Religious Affairs*, 47(2) P. D. 1, 6, it was recognized that the right of an individual to pray alone is a part of his or her right of access, but the individual was not permitted to implement this right under the circumstances due to police fear that prayer with a prayer shawl may cause provocation; see also Itzhak England, "The Legal Status of the Holy Places in Jerusalem," 28 *Isr. L. Rev.* 595, 597 n.24 (1994) (stating that "freedom of access without freedom of worship is an absurdity").

72. H. C. 267/88, *supra* note 66, 742.

73. H. C. 7128/96, *supra* note 65.

74. *Supra* note 4.

75. See Basic Law: The President of the State of 1964, 18 L. S. I. 111 (1963–64).

76. See e.g., H. C. 721/94, *El-Al Israel Airlines Ltd. v. Danilevitz*, 48(5) P. D. 749, 759; H. C. 953/87 and 1/88, *Poraz v. Lahat, Mayor of Tel Aviv*, 42(2) P. D. 309, at 329–34. According to the Supreme Court in the El Al case, at 759–60, the principle of equality is also implied in Basic Law: Human Dignity and Liberty (*supra* note 3).

77. See the El Al case, at 761; see also the general comment on discrimination prepared by the Human Rights Committee established under the ICCPR, U. N. Doc. HRI/GEN/1/Rev3 (1997) 29, para. 13 (adopted in 1989).

78. Adoption of Children Law, 5741–1981, 35 L. S. I. 360 (1980–81). In December 1997 the law was amended in order to permit under certain circumstances adoption of children from abroad even if they are not of the same religion as the adopting parents: 5758 (1997/8) S. H. 20.

79. See Hours of Work and Rest Law, 5711-1951, 5 L. S. I. 125 (1950–51).

80. The Crime of Genocide (Prevention and Punishment) Law, 5710-1950, 4 L. S. I. 101 (1949–50).

81. Employment Service Law, 5719-1959, section 42(a), 13 L. S. I. 29 (1958–59).

82. Succession Law, 5725-1965, section 143, 19 L. S. I. 58 (1964–65).

83. Defamation Law, 5725-1965, section 1, 19 L. S. I. 254 (1964–65).

84. Penal Law, 5737-1977, sections 133–37, Special Volume L. S. I. 44–45 (1977).

85. See id. and sections 145, 170–74, 198 (including provisions on unlawful associations, public mischief, and offenses against sentiments of religion and tradition).

86. See, id., sections 144 D(1)(a) and 170–74. See, e.g., Cr. Ap. 697/98, *Tatiana Sozkin v. State of Israel*, Takdeen Elyon 98 (2), 5758/59–1998, 1. For a summary in English, see 19 *Justice* 50–54 (1998). The case dealt *inter alia* with offenses against sentiments of religion and tradition committed with a racist motive. The court tried to find the right balance between freedom of expression and the prohibition against hurting sentiments of religion.

87. See Penal Law (Amendment No. 20), 5746-1986, 40 L. S. I. 230 (1985–86) (adding sections 144a to 144e to the Penal Law). For the provision in the Law on Political Parties, see *supra*, text accompanying note 5.

88. 1 L. S. I. 4 (1948).

89. See 4 L. S. I. 114 (1949–50). This right may be refused to a person engaged in activity directed against the Jewish people, a person who endangers the public health, or a person with a criminal past liable to endanger public welfare.

90. See 6 L. S. I. 50 (1951–52); see also Claude Klein, "Nationalité et statut personnel dans le droit de la nationalité israélienne," in *Nationalité et statut personnel* 309–26 (Michel Verwilghen ed., 1984).

91. See Assa Kasher, "Justice and Affirmative Action: Naturalization and the Law of Return," 15 *Isr. Y.B. on Hum. Rts.* 101–12 (1985).

92. See Laws Concerning Nationality, U. N. Legislative Series, U. N. Doc ST/LEG/ SER. B/4 (1954), at 111, 123, 188, 198–99, 215–16, 217, 228, 288, 311, 351, 354, 387, 544–45 (referring to Czechoslovakia, Denmark, Greece, Guatemala, Honduras, Italy, Jordan, Liberia, Mexico, Nicaragua, Norway, Poland, and Venezuela, respectively); see also Federico De Castro y Bravo, "La Nationalité, la double nationalité et la supra-nationalité," 102 *R.C.A.D.I.* 521, at 565–68 (1961).

93. 660 U. N. T. S. 195.

94. The term "racial discrimination" has a very comprehensive meaning for the purpose of this convention: "[A]ny distinction, exclusion, restriction or preference based on race, color, descent, or national or ethnic origin. . . ." Id. at 195.

95. See Natan Lerner, *"Equality of Rights Under Israeli Law,"* 9 *Patterns of Prejudice* 1, 3 (1975); see also Klein, *supra* note 13, at 35.

96. Law of Return (Amendment No. 2), 5730-1970, adding section 4A, 24 L. S. I. 28 (1969–70).

97. See on this question, for example, Rubinstein & Medina, *supra* note 6, at 111–31; Avner H. Shaki, *Who Is a Jew in the Law of the State of Israel?* (1976–78) (two volumes) (He-

brew); Menashe Shava, "Comments on the Law of Return (Amendment no. 2), 5730-1970 (Who Is a Jew?)," 3 *Tel Aviv U. L. Rev.* 140 (1977) (Hebrew).

98.  2 Drayton, Laws of Palestine 1294 (1934).

99.  The Supreme Court has decided that the requirement of the consent of the head of the new religious community is relevant only for the purpose of the jurisdiction of the religious tribunals. See H. C. 1031/93, *Pesachu Goldstein v. Minister of the Interior,* 51(4) P. D. 661. The case arose because the authorized Orthodox rabbinate had not recognized a conversion to Judaism effected by the petitioner before a tribunal of the Conservative movement. An English summary of this decision was published in 15 *Justice* 43–48 (1997).

100.  See Pinhas Shifman, "Religious Affiliation in Israeli Interreligious Law," 15 *Isr. L. Rev.* 1, 15–40 (1980) (exploring issues of change in religious affiliation); Menashe Shava, "The Legal Aspects of Change of Religious Community in Israel," 3 *Isr. Y.B. on Hum. Rts.* 256–69 (1973); Asher Maoz, "Who Is a Convert?" 15 *Justice* 11–19 (1997).

101.  Capacity and Guardianship Law, 5722-1962, 16 L. S. I. 106, 108 (1961–62), as amended by Capacity and Guardianship (Amendment) Law, 5725-1965, 19 L. S. I. 113 (1964–65) (adding section 13A to the original statute).

102.  Universal Declaration, *supra* note 2, art. 18; see also ICCPR, *supra* note 2, at 172 (containing a similar provision: "to manifest his religion or belief in worship, observance, practice and teaching"); see Declaration on the Elimination of All Forms of Intolerance and of Discrimination Based on Religion or Belief, *supra* note 1, art. 6; The Document of the Copenhagen Meeting of the Conference on the Human Dimension of the Conference on Security and Cooperation in Europe (1990), art. 9(4), 29 I. L. M. 1306 (1990). The question may be raised: What is the difference, or what is the boundary, between teaching and proselytizing? See, however, the case of *Kokkinakis v. Greece* decided by the European Court of Human Rights in 1993, 260 Eur. Ct. H. R. (ser. A) 18 (1993), discussed in T. Jeremy Gunn, "Adjudicating Rights of Conscience Under the European Convention on Human Rights," in *Religious Human Rights in Global Perspective: Legal Perspectives* 305–30 (Johan D. van der Vyver & John Witte Jr. eds., 1996); see also Alain Garay, "Liberté Religieuse et Prosélytisme: l'expérience européenne," 17 *Revue Trimestrielle des Droits de l'Homme* 7–29 (1994); Moshe Hirsch, "The Freedom of Proselytism Under the Fundamental Agreement and International Law," 47 *Cath. U. L. Rev.* 407–25 (1998).

103.  See Penal Law Amendment (Enticement to Change Religion) Law, 5738-1977, 32 L. S. I. 62 (1977–78) (adding sections 174A and 174B); see also Ruth Levush, "Israel Status Report on the Anti-Proselytization Bill," 10 *Law Library Scope Topics,* June 1997.

104.  The main enactments in this field are Compulsory Education Law, 5709-1949, 3 L. S. I. 125 (1948–49); State Education Law, 5713-1953, 7 L. S. I. 113 (1952–53); Inspection of Schools Law, 5729-1969, 23 L. S. I. 195, 5729 (1968/69); Education Ordinance [New Version], 5778-1978, Law of Israel New Version, no. 31, at 607; see also Klein, *supra* note 13, at 133–34.

105.  See generally Goldstein, *supra* note 14; Claude Klein and Jonathan Kuttab, "Education as a Paradigm?" in *Jerusalem: Points of Friction and Beyond* 73–89 (Moshe Ma'oz and Sari Nusseibeh eds., 2000).

106.  U. N. Convention on the Rights of the Child, 1577 U. N. T. S. 3.

107. See generally Edoardo Vitta, *The Conflict of Laws in Matters of Personal Status in Palestine* (1947).

108. See Palestine (Amendment) Order in Council, 1939 *Palestine Gazette*, supp. 2, no. 898, 459 (section 16 added the Second Schedule to the Palestine Order in Council, 1922–1947); see also Rubinstein & Medina, *supra* note 6, at 149.

109. See Marriage and Divorce (Registration) Ordinance of 1919, 2 Drayton, Laws of Palestine 903 (1934).

110. See Palestine Order in Council, 1922, 2 Drayton, Laws of Palestine 2581 (1934), sections 47, 51–54; Rabbinical Tribunals Jurisdiction (Marriage and Divorce) Law, 5713-1953, 7 L. S. I. 139 (1952–53); Druze Religious Tribunals Law, 5723-1962, 17 L. S. I. 27 (1962–63); The Court for Family Matters (Amendment No. 5) Law, 5762-2001, 5761 (2001) S. H. 16 (2001–02), adding section 3 (B1). See also Pinhas Shifman, *Family Law in Israel* (Jerusalem, 1984) (Hebrew).

111. See Palestine Order in Council, 1922, *supra* note 110, sec. 47 (for the civil courts); Rabbinical Tribunals Jurisdiction (Marriage and Divorce) Law, 5713-1953, 7 L. S. I. 139, 5713 (1952–53), section 2 (for the Jewish religious tribunals).

112. See, e.g., the Succession Law, 5725-1965, 19 L. S. I. 58 (1964–65).

113. The International Covenant on Civil and Political Rights, 1966, was signed by Israel on December 19, 1966, and ratified in 1991 with the above reservation. Under an additional declaration, Israel's state of emergency constitutes a public emergency within the meaning of Article 4(1) of the covenant and, therefore, the state may derogate from some of its obligations under Article 9 of the covenant. The Family Court of Tel Aviv has hinted that perhaps a reservation not compatible with the object of a treaty might be disregarded by the Court (*L.S. v. L.S.*, of 30 January 2003, not yet published). The relevant text was the Convention on the Elimination of all Forms of Discrimination against Women, and the reservation was similar to the one added to Israel's ratification of the International Covenant on Civil and Political Rights.

114. The Succession Law, 5725-1965, 19 L. S. I. 58 (1964–65). If a religious tribunal disregards a provision of a law of the Knesset addressed also to the religious tribunals, its decision may be set aside by the Supreme Court because of excess of jurisdiction. However, the case law of the Court on this matter is not uniform. See Rubinstein & Medina, *supra* note 6, at 194.

115. See H. C. 3914/92, *Lev v. The Religious District Tribunal*, 48(2) P. D. 491. For an analysis of this judgment, see Ruth Halperin-Kaddari, "Rethinking Legal Pluralism in Israel: The Interaction Between the High Court of Justice and Rabbinical Courts," 20 *Tel Aviv U. L. Rev.* 683–747 (1997) (Hebrew).

116. See H. C. 1000/92, *Bavli v. The Supreme Rabbinical Tribunal*, 48(2) P. D. 221. For an analysis of this judgment, see Halperin-Kaddari, *supra* note 115.

117. See sources cited *supra* note 14.

118. See Ariel Rozen-Zvi, *Israeli Family Law: The Sacred and the Secular* 216 (1990) (Hebrew); Ariel Rozen-Zvi, "Rabbinical Courts, Halacha and the Public: A Very Narrow Bridge," 3 *Mishpat Umimshal* 173–220 (1995) (Hebrew). An additional area of concern is the status of an apostate. See Rabbi Yehuda Yisraeli, "The Marriage and Divorce Law in

Practice," 21–22 *Guevilin* 37 (1965) (Hebrew); Asher Maoz, "The Personal Status of the Apostate," 7 *Mishpatim* 442 (1977) (Hebrew).

119.  See Abramov, *supra* note 14, at 354–79.

120.  The chief rabbi of the Kara'ites in Israel is, however, recognized as a competent "Registering Authority" under the Marriage and Divorce (Registration) Ordinance of 1919. See *supra* note 109; see also Michael Corinaldi, *The Personal Status of the Kara'ites* (1984) (Hebrew); Ruth Lapidoth & Michael Corinaldi, "Freedom of Religion in Israel," in *Israeli Reports to the XIV International Congress of Comparative Law,* at 289–92 (A. M. Rabello ed., 1994).

121.  See Michael Corinaldi, *Ethiopian Jewry: Identity and Tradition* (1988) (Hebrew). See generally Baruch Bracha, "Personal Status of Persons Belonging to a Non-Recognized Religious Community," 5 *Isr. Y.B. on Hum. Rts.* 88 (1975).

122.  See Matters of Dissolution of Marriage (Jurisdiction in Special Cases) Law, 5729-1969, 23 L. S. I. 274 (1968–69).

123.  The Court for Family Matters Law, 5755-1995, 5755 (1995) S. H. 393 (1994–95). The law has already been amended several times.

124.  See Pinhas Shifman, *Civil Marriage in Israel: The Case for Reform* (1995) (Hebrew).

# 13

# THE VATICAN AND THE MIDDLE EAST DURING THE PONTIFICATE OF JOHN PAUL II

*Silvio Ferrari*

The Middle East policy of the Holy See can only be analyzed adequately by taking into account its particular transnational nature. This means that the Holy See's policy necessarily operates on three different but interconnecting levels.[1]

The first level, which may be called systemic, regards the place that the Middle East holds in the global strategy of the Holy See. From this angle the Middle East above all plays the role of meeting point between the three different cultural universes[2]—the Christian, Jewish, and Muslim communities—present and living together in the region. The subjects of dialogue between the different religions and of exchange between the different cultural systems are of fundamental importance. This is because the solutions adopted for the Middle East are to be projected onto a far greater backdrop involving all the other parts of the world, wherever the problem of developing a dialogue between different cultural models arises, with the aim of preventing the "clash between cultures" evoked by Samuel Huntington a few years ago. The Holy See and the Church hierarchy insist on the universal destiny of Jerusalem, on the need to find solutions which acknowledge the entire international community's interest in the Holy City and favor a mixed-religious society where

Christians, Jews, and Muslims coexist. At the same time, however, such solutions must not sacrifice the requirements of the local communities. This stance is a good example of the interaction between this first level of Vatican policy and the other two which follow.

The second level is regional and involves not only the Middle East but also the whole Mediterranean area. As there are strong Muslim communities in France, Italy, Spain, and other European countries, the existence of a significant Christian presence in the Middle East constitutes a balancing factor for the entire Mediterranean region.[3] In this light the Christian communities of the various Middle Eastern countries consider themselves, and are considered by the Holy See, as a single subject[4] in the dramatic awareness (often revealed by the Church authorities in the region) that "in the East either we shall be united Christians or we shall not be."[5] At this regional level Vatican diplomacy appears to be devoted above all to defining the overall lines of strategy and to assessing the implications that the choices made by one community may have on all the others. Its strenuous defense of the Lebanese model of *"convivialité,"* even when other solutions may have appeared more rewarding in the short term, should also be read in this light, which in political and diplomatic terms expresses the common thread that connects the various particular churches.

Finally, there is a local dimension where the national state element predominates. The quest for specific solutions suited to the political and social conditions in which the individual Christian communities live and act is to be found on this level. The "concordat" policy of the Holy See, which was inaugurated by the Fundamental Agreement with Israel and continued with the successful prosecution of an agreement with the Palestine Liberation Organization (PLO),[6] is an evident expression of the attention which is devoted to the specific requirements of each Christian community.

These examples clearly show the degree of complexity and dovetailing involved in the relations that run between these various levels. The Holy See and other subjects (patriarchs, bishops, national and regional bishops' conferences, nuncios, religious orders, and others besides) operating in the Middle East are all involved in this activity. Sometimes decisions made at the center have a determining influence on the choices made in the periphery, in other cases experience acquired in a specific situation takes on an increasingly wider significance. The Holy See's condemnation of the Iraq embargo, for example, originally arose from worries about the fate of the local Iraqi community (not only the Christian one). It later expanded, however, into a general feeling of suspicion of an instrument which, if applied for a long time and indiscriminately, causes the civilian population to suffer to an extent that is arguably out of all proportion to any political advantages it may be able to obtain.[7]

This complexity is further accentuated by the fact that the policy of the Holy See must be analyzed, in the Middle East or elsewhere, by adopting a tri-polar model which takes into account not only relations between the Holy See and states but also between the Holy See and local churches.[8] These two dimensions of Vatican policy are so closely interwoven that any historical analysis failing to take them adequately into account can only be dismissed as biased.

Finally, before closing these methodological premises, it is necessary to define the field of investigation.

In the geopolitical perspective of the Christian churches, the Middle East is crossed by a frontier which separates the Arabian peninsula from the rest of the region. That there are so few Christian places whose memory has reached us in this region, and that there are no autochthonous Christian communities in these countries of the Arabian peninsula, is indicative of the different nature of this geographical area. For reasons that go back to its limited Roman and Christian penetration, the historical and cultural evolution of the area was very different from that of the Arab countries facing onto the Mediterranean, which were more open to exchanges with the Western world. It is hardly surprising therefore that the Middle Eastern countries that have no diplomatic relations with the Holy See are to be found prevalently between the Red Sea and the Persian Gulf.[9] Here the development of Islam has often assumed such intransigent and illiberal forms as to render dialogue with the Christian, Western world rather difficult, and on more than one occasion it has been firmly condemned by the Holy See for the absence of the most elementary forms of religious freedom.[10]

These reasons explain why in the Middle East the attention of the Holy See has been directed above all towards those places where Christianity, through an uninterrupted chain of communities, has left its deepest mark. The following pages will be devoted to these countries, starting with an analysis of the main lines of the Holy See's Middle East policy. This is followed by a description of the developments involving in particular the papacy of Pope John Paul II, and finally by an examination of three specific situations—Lebanon, Israel and the Palestinian Territories, and Jordan—where the diplomatic activity of the Holy See has followed different but complementary strategies with the aim of guaranteeing the continuity of the Christian presence in the Middle East.

Throughout the twentieth century the Middle East policy of the Holy See appears to have been characterized by some lines of continuity.

Its first objective has been to maintain and consolidate the presence of Roman Catholic churches in those places where Christianity originated. The Holy Places scattered all over the region are reminders of the life of Christ and of the first Christian communities. It is therefore evident that the symbolic importance of this objective transcends the small numbers of Roman Catholics, observing the Latin or the Eastern rite, resident in the Middle East.[11]

The Middle East question occupies a central position in the policy of the Holy See. This is due to various factors, not least of which is the awareness that this part of the world is de facto unique. Here the Arab-Christian experience, which was uprooted from the north coast of Africa many centuries ago, has some chance of continuing to develop. This is an important ingredient in the dialogue between Christianity and Islam. It is also important to maintain a Roman Catholic presence in the region alongside the more numerous presence of other Christian churches. These considerations contribute towards keeping the Middle East question at the center of the Holy See's attention.[12]

Even before the crisis of the Ottoman Empire the conviction had formed in Vatican circles that the best means of maintaining a Catholic presence in the Holy Land was to develop a peaceful society where the Christian minority could coexist with the Muslim majority.[13] All other options (in particular one favoring the constitution of separate Christian states, which took shape just after the First World War) were considered scarcely realistic. This assessment was probably correct.[14]

Once the aims and the instruments of its Middle East policy had been defined, the Holy See concentrated its attention on the possible forms such a mixed religious society could assume.

The ideal model was identified in Lebanon, where at one time the numerical balance between Christians and Muslims guaranteed the equality of citizens belonging to the two communities and allowed for the establishment of a political system with more developed democratic components than those existing in any other country of the region. Elsewhere, where the Christians are a clear minority and the Lebanese model is not reproducible, the Holy See accepts the regime of *millet* but rejects—at least in principle—that of *dhimmitude* in the name of the equality of the civil rights and political rights due to every citizen.[15] There is a project, dear to an Arab minority of Western education, which aims to rethink the political systems of the Middle Eastern countries on the basis of the secular principle. However, this meets with little favor in papal diplomacy, which is convinced of the impracticability of transplanting from one shore of the Mediterranean to another a notion that the majority of the Arab population feels extraneous to its own history and culture.

A mixed Christian and Muslim society living side by side has been developed by using the opportunities offered as they arose through historical contingencies. Throughout all the nineteenth century and the first part of the twentieth the support of the European powers in particular was exploited, first through the regime of extraterritorial capitulations and then via the system of mandates.[16] Thanks to such support and to the work of the missionary religious orders, the basis of an educational system was created and from these schools emerged an Arab-Christian leadership group which was to play a crucial role in the political and cultural awakening of the Arab world between the nineteenth and twentieth centuries.[17] After the Second World War this group had a valuable function when the Christians had to organize their presence in the Middle East without the protective umbrella of the European powers. But right from the start the Holy See had always avoided relying too heavily on the support of the Western powers. Its experience of relations with France and Great Britain, both before and after the end of the Ottoman Empire, had taught it that the interests of Rome and the Middle Eastern communities often did not coincide with those of the Christian (or even Roman Catholic) states of the old continent. The farsighted approach of Vatican diplomacy was able to pick up the signals of the decline of the European colonial presence on the southern shores of the Mediterranean in time.[18]

After the Second World War the end of colonialism did not catch the Vatican Secretariat of State unawares. The swift development of diplomatic relations with the most important countries of the region is proof of this.[19] This is confirmed by the fact that these relations have survived undamaged through all the political upheavals involving Egypt, Iran, and Syria between the 1950s and 1960s.

The Holy See has been able to obtain these results through the development of a Middle East policy which shows clear signs of independence from that of the Western powers with which it was more in tune on other fronts, at least until the middle of the 1960s. On the occasion of the Israel-Palestine conflict, the Suez crisis and—in more recent times—the Gulf War,[20] the position of the Holy See has never lain along the political lines of the European countries, and even less so of the United States. The long absence of diplomatic relations between the Holy See and Israel, Washington's most faithful ally in the region, is the most evident example of this divergence. The principle of a mixed religious society where Christians and Muslims live alongside each other guides Vatican strategy. This is hardly reconcilable with the policy of confrontation which has led the United States (and, with some reluctance, its European allies) to take a hard stand first against Iran, then Libya, and finally Iraq, nor is it compatible with their unconditional support of Israel, the West's favored partner in the Middle East. These are not marginal differences. Indeed, they reflect two different interpretations of the sociopolitical processes in progress in the Arab countries. The first focuses on the elements of threat to the identity and economic interests of the West.[21] The second invests more (in the long-term view) in factors of integration, in the need for an overall economic balance between the north and the south of the world[22] and in the possibility of making the Mediterranean the meeting point between different cultures. These are no longer two cultures, but three. As a result of a long and tormented process of rapprochement, the Jewish component (and its state organization) has been fully inserted into the context of a mixed religious society which had originally been conceived for Christians and Muslims. In this way Vatican diplomacy has managed to give shape (within the limits that define political relations) to the papal "utopia" of the reconciliation of the three religions of Abraham.

This more strictly political work, whose interlocutors are the Middle Eastern states, is inextricably interwoven with the Holy See's activity in support of the local churches.

The relationship between Rome and the Middle East Roman Catholic communities has been neither simple nor linear. There is considerable correspondence, however, if it is considered synchronously with the evolution of political relations between the Holy See and the European states' hegemony in the Middle East.

The emancipation of the Near East from the religious protectorate of the European powers objectively favored the assumption of responsibilities and the maturation of the identities of the local Christian communities. These had already been active participants in the process of Arab reawakening that had developed in the second half of the last century.

The Holy See, aware of the provisional nature of the Western presence in the region, encouraged this evolution. The decisive turning point took place around the time of the First World War when some intentions that Pope Leo XIII had already expressed at the end of the nineteenth century were taken up again and brought to completion. These were the creation of the Sacred Congregation for the Oriental Church and of the Pontifical Institute for Oriental Studies in 1917, the boost provided by study of the Christian East with the encyclical *Rerum Orientalium* of 1928 and the decision, the following year, to supply the Eastern churches with their own code of canon law (but the latter would only see the light in 1990). Here were signals that the attempt to "Latinize" the Eastern churches—repeatedly criticized by Pope Pius IX and Pope Pius XII—was being abandoned, and that there was the will to value the diversity of rites and institutions of these churches.[23] For these reasons too the new importance acknowledged by the Second Vatican Council to the local churches, to their history and particular identity, found the Middle Eastern communities ready to develop reflection about the particular—and in a certain sense unique—characteristics of the Arab-Christian church and of its own specific role within the universal church.

Initially the accent fell mainly on the bridging function that this Arab-Christian church could provide, ensuring an exchange between the religious and cultural values of the Muslim East and Christian West. From the 1970s onwards, also in response to the growth of Islamic fundamentalism and to the escalation of the Israeli-Palestinian conflict, the accent was placed with greater emphasis on the Arab character of the Middle East Christian communities and on their mission to be "not only a church in the midst of Islam, but also a church for Islam."[24] The consequences implicit in this choice have been taken from the Latin patriarch of Jerusalem, who on several occasions has declared that "relations between Christians and Muslims are relations between the members of one single and same people, of the same nationality, but of different beliefs."[25] This has led some Arab-Christian communities (in particular the Palestinian and Iraqi communities, where the political situation has exasperated the burden of the psychological mechanisms governing the relationship between majority and minority) to leave the function of go-between between different religious and cultural worlds in the background. They have chosen to identify themselves fully with the sociopolitical objectives of the Arab-Muslim community, sometimes in forms and with modalities that have been judged as being excessively uncritical by papal diplomacy. It is not always easy to draw a boundary between the sociopolitical identity and the religious identity of the Arab-Christian churches. Nor is it always a simple matter to operate a synthesis between the positions of Rome and of these local churches. These difficulties are indicated by the reactions of the Arab-Christian communities to the approval of the Second Vatican Council's declaration *Nostra Aetate*[26] and more recently to the stipulation of the Fundamental Agreement and the establishment of diplomatic relations between the Holy See and Israel.[27] Equally significant is the demand for a specific role of the Middle Eastern communities in the dialogue between Christians and Jews.[28] Of course, these episodes may arise from normal center-periphery dialectics. However, it is clear that the Middle East churches, reinforced by the creation of connecting bodies such as the Council of the Eastern Catholic Patriarchs and the Assembly of the Ordinary Catholics of the Holy Land, are now an interlocutor endowed with a precise physiognomy. Papal diplomacy cannot afford to ignore them when outlining its strategy. For this very reason the absence of an interlocutor of similar importance in the State of Israel, where the Roman Catholic communities of Jewish expression are not able to sustain a similar role, is an increasingly significant element of imbalance.

To complete the reconnaissance of the context of the Holy See's Middle East policy it is necessary to take two other elements into account: relations with the Muslim community as a whole, and relations with the Christian, in particular the Orthodox, churches present in the region.

Vatican diplomacy has always borne in mind that the survival of the Eastern Christian communities depends not only on relations between the Holy See and the Arab states but also (and perhaps above all, at a moment and in a region where religion has reacquired such an important impact on politics) on social and religious relations between the local Christian and Muslim communities.

It is undeniable that at this level the difficulties are on the increase, both because of the crises which have violently struck the traditional places where these communities live alongside each other (from Cyprus to Lebanon, from Egypt to Jerusalem)[29] and on account of the growth of Islamic fundamentalism with the consequent tendency to "ghettoize" the non-Muslim communities of the Middle East.[30] These difficulties have only partly been balanced by progress in the dialogue between the Christian and Muslim religious authorities, which have considerably intensified since the Second Vatican Council. A common platform seems to have emerged here. Both religions reject individualism and secularization, and both recognize that living together in society is inconceivable without a moral law rooted in divine law. This very point of departure, however, which has allowed significant convergence on some themes (the defense of the family is one example) has signaled in other cases the limits of the dialogue, as from it Muslims often obtain implications (above all on the subject of religious freedom) which are unacceptable to Christians.[31]

This stalemate might perhaps be overcome by the growth of substantial Muslim communities in Europe and the maturation of a European Islam capable of uniting its own religious tradition with the inalienable values of Western civilization. Such a development might have an important effect on Middle Eastern and North African Islam. However, this will not happen in the near future even if it happens at all, and it is impossible as yet to predict what effects, if any, it may have.

The dialogue with the other Christian churches seems to have had more concrete results, and one of the most significant steps in this direction was taken during the meeting—in the Middle East—between Pope Paul VI and the patriarch Atenagora in 1964. These relations have also undoubtedly been affected by the problems which, in recent years, have slowed down every form of ecumenical collaboration. Nevertheless, perhaps also because of the "greater urgency"[32] to testify to the unity of Christians in Muslim lands, such problems have not prevented attaining objectives which have not been reached in other parts of the world. An example is the participation of the Roman Catholic churches (together with the Orthodox churches, pre-Chalcedonians, and Protestants) at the Council of Churches of the Middle East and the publication of some common declarations on delicate themes such as the status of Jerusalem and the human rights of Christians and Arabs.[33]

Relations with the Middle East Arab states, dialogue with the Muslim religious authorities, ecumenical commitment, support of the Roman Catholic communities: these are the four coordinates that have traditionally defined the Holy See's Middle East policy. Within these coordinates, what new events have characterized the papacy of Pope John Paul II?

### The Papacy of Pope John Paul II

In the course of Pope John Paul II's papacy, four events have modified the political and religious scenario of the Middle East. The first has been the growth of Islamic fundamentalism,[34] which was suddenly revealed (at least to the rather inattentive and short-sighted eyes of the West)[35] by the Iranian Revolution of 1979.

Studies conducted on this phenomenon allow us to define it as a movement seeking to recover an identity. Islamic fundamentalism was unleashed by the frustration caused by deep-rooted problems (from economic underdevelopment to the Israeli-Palestinian conflict) whose genesis and permanence were considered the responsibility of the West. The movement was further nourished by the failure of the processes of modernization and democratization inspired by the principles of the 1789 French Revolution or by the 1917 Russian Revolution, by the secular liberal model of the West or by the Marxist secular model of Eastern Europe.[36] Fundamentalist movements consider that the rebirth of the Arab countries of the Middle East can only take place through a return to the values of classical Islam and therefore also to the closely interwoven fabric of politics, society, and religion that is its distinguishing feature.

Legally speaking, the most evident expression of this is the reintroduction of the *shari'a* into the constitutions of some countries;[37] in some of these the entire state legislation has been subjected to a screening process to verify its conformity with the religious law (as happens in Iran, where it is submitted to a commission of wise men).

Although fundamentalism is neither confined to the Muslim religion nor to the Middle East,[38] its growth poses a serious threat to the Christian communities of the region.

The re-evaluation of classical Islamic law reduces the Christians (and the few Jews remaining in Arab countries) to the status of *dhimmi*, calling once more into question the principles of freedom and equality which after much effort had seemed to have at last conquered a place in the legal systems of some Middle Eastern states.[39] The growing resentment towards the United States and Europe, which are accused of wanting to keep the Middle East in a state of weakness and inferiority so as to better exploit it economically,[40] also has repercussions on the Christian churches (in particular on those of the Latin rite), which are identified, rightly or wrongly, with the West. The popular support enjoyed by governments (such as the Jordanian government) that are inspired by a liberal and moderate Islam able to welcome benevolently (though in respect of its own traditions) communities of different religious faiths has become progressively less certain, and a shadow of precariousness is thrown over their future.[41] In the countries where Islamic fundamentalism has gained power, such as Iran, the position of the Christian communities has worsened drastically.[42]

Besides the negative consequences which seem to have hit the Christian communities of the Middle East, the development of Islamic fundamentalism has also had an effect on the respect of the fundamental human rights of the individual. It has therefore affected one of the central distinguishing features of the teaching of

Pope John Paul II. In particular Islamic fundamentalism strikes at his approach to the issue of ecumenical dialogue, which is based on the acknowledgment of the "dignity of every human being created by God" and on respect of his or her fundamental rights.[43] For this reason, and out of concern about the deterioration in the conditions of life of the Christian communities of the Middle East, the Holy See has intensified and emphasized its declarations in favor of the rights of freedom and equality which every human being is entitled to enjoy regardless of his or her religious faith.[44] In open response to one of the most recurrent arguments of the doctrines inspired by Islamic fundamentalism, the Holy See points out that "there cannot be a 'holy war,' because the values of worship, brotherhood and peace, which spring from faith in God, summon us to meeting and dialogue."[45]

On the more general grounds of political and diplomatic strategy, the Vatican authorities attempt to defuse the elements which could provoke other fundamentalist outbreaks. They try in every way to prevent conflict and, where this is impossible, they take the utmost care to avoid providing any pretext that might lead Arab public opinion to confuse the action of the Holy See with that of the Western powers.

This strategy was put into practice during the First Gulf War. The Holy See tried in every way to avoid the outbreak of conflict, working right up until the last minute to find a diplomatic way out, even at the cost of risking a head-on collision with United States policy and of introducing new elements of tension into its already difficult relations with Israel.[46]

A decisive role in this choice was certainly the natural propensity of papal diplomacy to seek a peaceful solution to every controversy. This is borne out by the profound reflection on the traditional notion of "a just war," which was developed on the occasion of the First Gulf War.[47] Equally certainly, however, there remained the conviction that that particular conflict, on account of the times and means with which it was developed,[48] might have become charged with more general meanings. It could have had disastrous repercussions both on relations between the Arab world and the Western world and on the Christian presence in the Middle East.

The pope himself was the one to give voice to the full range of these worries a month after the beginning of the war:

> We know that the terrestrial globe is divided into different "worlds": the first, the second, the third and we are already speaking of a fourth. The worry is this: that war can create deeper chasms between these worlds. And this is our greatest worry, our fear for the future. The peoples, as a consequence of this war, can become even more divided, set against one another and become enemies. . . . This is the Church's fear. All my interventions, and all the interventions of my ministry in this subject, arise from this worry, which is the main worry.[49]

The directives drawn up during the Vatican summit of March 1991 were aimed at "rejecting every religious motivation or interpretation which might have been attributed to the war in the Gulf, in which there is to be seen neither a conflict between East and West, nor even less a conflict between Islam and Christianity."[50] These statements confirm that the Holy See's traditional aversion to any military solution of conflicts becomes even more acute when they assume the character of conflicts between cultures or religions in a way that upsets the design Pope John Paul II has drawn for his own papacy: to make common faith in God an element of reconciliation, rather than of division, among men.[51]

The intense diplomatic activity carried out by the Holy See on the occasion of the Gulf War closed with a fairly positive balance. Although it was impossible for it to prevent the war, the Vatican was substantially able to avoid negative repercussions on Christian communities and prevent the position of the Roman Catholic Church from being stamped, in the eyes of Muslim public opinion, onto that of the Western powers. Hence it was able to confirm the independence of the Vatican's Middle East policy and earn credit[52] in its relations with the Arab leadership. This credit was used shortly afterwards to proceed with normalizing diplomatic relations with Israel.[53]

All this must not, however, obscure the fact that these positive elements have only prevented the position of the Christian communities in the Middle East from worsening even further. After the Gulf War, Christians have continued to emigrate from the region, which confirms that the deep-rooted causes of their malaise are far from being removed.

Some observers consider this emigration to be an indicator of the failure of Vatican policy in the Middle East.[54] In reality it is proof of the objective limits that the action of the Holy See encounters in this region. This migratory phenomenon has developed since the Second World War, and Vatican authorities had already signaled the danger during the papacy of Pope Paul VI. The problem's complexity and dimensions largely escape the possibility of control either by Rome or by the local churches.[55] The web of economic, cultural, and social reasons that induce Christians to leave all the countries of the Middle East is such that any remedy served by Church authorities can be little more than a palliative, however right that remedy may be (greater internal cohesion of the local communities and greater support by the other churches).

The solution to the problem can only be in the long term and result from a conjuncture of situations, such as the pacification and economic development of the region, consolidation of the Muslim-Christian dialogue, and progress of the moderate and liberal components of the Muslim world, to indicate but a few. These might reverse the migratory trend, as has already happened once in the past.[56]

Of all the causes of the emigration problem, demographic research points to one culprit above all others: the Second World War, to which the increase in emigration is directly connected.[57] This observation confirms that the quest for peaceful solutions for the settlement of international disputes (which is one of the priorities of the entire policy of the Holy See)[58] becomes particularly pressing in the Middle East, as it is linked to the very survival of the Christian communities.

The most recent event to characterize the papacy of Pope John Paul II—the signing of the Fundamental Agreement and the opening of diplomatic relations with Israel—should be considered in this perspective.

### The Vatican and the Israeli-Palestinian Conflict

The policy of the Holy See towards Zionism first and the State of Israel second is too well known to examine it analytically here.[59] Rather than follow its stages step by step it is important to try to extrapolate the overall sense so as to find a common line.

Since the end of the last century the development of Zionism and the consequent increase in Jewish immigration into Palestine has posed a problem to the Holy See that was as much political as it was theological. Zionism's aspiration to bring about a Jewish state was an element of disturbance to the delicate balances that supported a Muslim and Christian society living alongside one another. It threatened to set in motion a conflict (as indeed happened) in which the Christian minority of Palestine and of the whole Middle East would have everything to lose.

This is the reason behind the concern with which the Holy See viewed the growth—in numbers and in means—of the Jewish communities in the Holy Land. It was with similar concern that the Vatican greeted Jewish efforts to provide themselves with a political organization and the recognition which they obtained, after the First World War, in international circles. Faced with these developments papal diplomacy aligned itself in favor of the proposals to entrust control of the region to international bodies able (or so the Vatican hoped) to avoid the outbreak of the war between the Jews and the Arabs. When war did break out the Holy See found itself closer to the Arab positions than to the Israeli ones on the crucial questions of the Palestinian refugees (among whom were a significant number of Christians) and on the status of Jerusalem. The same may be said of most of the religious orders present in the region and of the local Roman Catholic community, which (save for a few exceptions) had made a common front with the Palestinian Arabs in resisting the progress of the Zionist movements.

Vatican diplomacy has always taken care to prevent its choices being—or even just appearing to be—motivated by theological reasons. Independently from the success of these efforts, however, for a long time the position of the Holy See has experienced the same difficulty that the whole Christian community has had with understanding the meaning of the return of the Jews and, even more so, of the re-constitution of a Jewish state in Palestine. Through a slow process prompted by reflections by the French theology school of the 1930s, followed by the impact of the Shoah on the whole Christian world, and culminating in the Vatican Council declaration *Nostra Aetate,* these elements of incomprehension have gradually been overcome. As a consequence the way has been cleared for a more openly political consideration of the State of Israel and of the Israeli-Palestinian conflict.

In the course of Pope Paul VI's papacy the Holy See couched the Palestinian question in the same terms that characterize it even now. It sought, and seeks, a balance between the safety of the State of Israel and the right of the Palestinian people—who were deprived of their lands as a result of the conflict with Israel—to have a home. The Holy See has been subjected to contrasting pressures during this time: the United States insisted on the opening of diplomatic relations be-tween the Vatican and Israel; Israel periodically accused the Holy See of a pro-Arab bias, connecting this stance to prejudices of a religious nature which in reality had by then been overcome; and the Arab countries of the Middle East, with the tacit consent of their respective Roman Catholic communities, expressed dissatisfac-tion with Vatican policy and asked for more decisive support for the Palestinian cause. Despite all this, the Holy See has continued to adhere strictly to its position, upholding it in the meetings which have progressively intensified with both the Is-raeli and the Palestinian authorities.

The Vatican formulation of the question seems to be in agreement with the de-velopments that have characterized the Palestinian question since the Gulf War. The Holy See considered the Conference of Madrid and the negotiations following it to have made a positive contribution, though it regretted being kept at their mar-gins. In the messages he sent to Bush and Gorbachev, the pope stressed the impor-tance of that meeting, whose aim was to tackle contextually all the crises open in the Middle East (as the Holy See had more than once requested).[60] In this context the opening of negotiations between Israel, the PLO, and the Arab states offered for the first time concrete hopes of a peaceful solution to the conflict and led papal diplomacy to reconsider its own position in the light of the new balances which were emerging in the Middle East.

The conclusion of the Fundamental Agreement[61] and the opening of diplomatic relations between the Holy See and Israel (followed by the opening of diplomatic re-lations with Jordan and, in a legally different form, with the PLO) are the most im-portant outcomes of this process. The Holy See had already indicated that it was ready to establish diplomatic relations with the Jewish state and that it was waiting for the most favorable moment to do so.[62] The Vatican wished to offer a positive con-tribution to the peace process that was taking its first steps. At the same time there was the chance to do so without exposing the Middle Eastern Christian communities to the resentment of the states in which they lived (which had been the first to open negotiations with Israel). Moreover, there was a danger of remaining among the few which rejected any diplomatic relationship with the Jewish state. Finally, it was deemed opportune to be part of the negotiations that would touch questions dear to the Holy See (above all the status of the Holy City). The Vatican therefore revived Cardinal Tisserant's old idea[63] of tying recognition of the State of Israel to stipulation of a concordat with Israel which would safeguard the local Church.

The breakdown of the peace process following Rabin's assassination and the change of government in Israel soon froze all hopes. After months of inviting both sides to moderation and negotiation,[64] in the course of 1998 Vatican diplomacy voiced its dissatisfaction with the more rigid position of the government in Jerusalem.[65] The reasons for this change of direction were many and did not regard only the Israeli government's resistance to the actuation of the peace agreements. The Israeli religious right's ability to condition the Netanyahu government slowed the (already in itself complex) application of the Fundamental Agreement[66] and introduced new elements of tension, exemplified most recently by the archbishop of Akko[67] affair. The political weakening of Arafat, who had gambled more than any other on the success of the Oslo pacts, threatened to deprive the Holy See of a moderate interlocutor who was also open-minded towards the Christian component of the Palestinian people and to clear the way for more politically, and even religiously, radical elements.[68] The failure to conclude the peace has made the (already weak) hopes of resolving the problems of Lebanon and Jerusalem even fainter, creating a favorable climate for a revival of terrorism and the polarization that is rightly feared by the local churches.

Besides this political involution, the worsening of the Israeli-Palestinian conflict has had heavy repercussions on Pope John Paul II's more strictly religious and ecumenical strategy in the Middle East.

The framework of Pope John Paul II's overall design is reflected in his approach to the issue of Jerusalem, which is a microcosm of his general policy. Following in the footsteps of Pope Paul VI, the pope has repeatedly stated that the destiny of the Holy City is to be the point of reconciliation between Jews, Christians, and Muslims.[69] It would thus become, also from an institutional point of view, the concrete example that it is possible for the believers of these three religions to live together throughout the Middle East.[70] Vatican insistence on upholding the proposal of internationalization first and international guarantees[71] later with regard to Jerusalem indicates, besides the intrinsic merits of these solutions, the desire to testify to a value that goes beyond the boundaries of politics.[72] Equally revealing is the way Pope John Paul II conceived his trip to the Middle East: as a pilgrimage to the places of both the New and the Old Testament, in other words, the places of the book that unites the three religions of Abraham.[73] This attitude confirms that his approach to the Middle East question is not limited to defending the Christian presence. Taking the Christians as his point of departure, his purpose extends to promote the possibility of a mutual recognition of Christians, Jews, and Muslims, and he is fully aware of the significance that such an understanding might have on the fate of the region and of the whole world. The pilgrimage to Jerusalem that the pope was finally able to make is also part of this overall design. Indeed, it aimed to regenerate "with the Jewish, Christian and Muslim believers, this message and this prayer of peace which has already been addressed to the whole human family on 27th October 1986, at Assisi."[74]

To my mind this is the most significant step made by Vatican diplomacy during the papacy of Pope John Paul II. In short, it is the full translation, in the legal and political terms of the community of nations (and therefore outside any theological consideration),[75] of the affirmation that the Holy Land has a specific destiny in the history and geography of salvation as it represents the stable meeting point between Jews, Christians, and Muslims.

It is self-evident that any chance of developing the positive contents of such a meeting necessarily requires a context of peace. Therefore, the return to stalemate was suffered all the more keenly after the hopes which had been raised by the meetings of Madrid, Oslo, and Washington. Moreover, the breakdown of the peace process inevitably strengthens the spiral of conflict and suffering at the local and regional level, which is already a bad enough threat to the survival of the Christian communities.

In conclusion, the "stubborn" quest for a peaceful solution to the Israeli-Palestinian conflict appears to be a no-choice option. It is the only path that the Vatican can follow, for reasons that are both general and specific, not only political but also religious.

### Lebanon: Defense of *"Convivialité"*

The feature distinguishing Lebanon from the other Middle Eastern countries is the presence of a powerful Christian community with its own religious and cultural identity, an identity that is quite distinct from that of the Arab Muslims. The Christian community is fully integrated into the political and social structures of the state, and Christians for a long time were able to live peacefully alongside the other religious communities present in the country.

The National Pact of Community Coexistence of 1943 legally confirmed this society of mixed religions, which had existed for a long time. It was founded on a democratic system which assigned an important place to the religious communities through a delicate system of constitutional balances aimed at impeding the state from identifying with only one religious group. This model of interdenominational society was the basis of Lebanese national identity and independence, a right which was affirmed as much towards the West (personified at that time by the mandatory power, France) as towards the East (in particular with regard to Syria and its policy to annex Lebanon).[76]

A system of society and state developed from 1943 onwards which distinguished Lebanon from all the other countries of the Middle East. Culturally, Lebanon became the meeting place and point of exchange between Western values (mainly through the influence of French culture, followed later on by that of the United States) and Eastern ones. Politically, Lebanon developed an attempt to wed the secularity of the state with respect for the rights of the religious communities. In religion the country became the finest example of coexistence and Muslim-Christian dialogue.[77] For these reasons the Holy See regards the Lebanese "formula" with such favor, to some extent elevating it to the level of model for a Muslim-Christian mixed religious society in the Middle East and in other parts of the world. As Pope John Paul II has repeatedly declared, Lebanon "is something more than a country: it is a message of freedom and an example of pluralism for both the East and the West."[78]

In the mid-1970s, a series of internal and external factors (in particular the Israeli-Palestinian conflict and the rise of the Muslim fundamentalist movements) altered the balance between the religious communities and caused the whole Lebanese model to break down. The economic transformation of the country accentuated the corporative dynamics and degenerative factors already present in the political and legal structure of Lebanon.[79] The demographic balance changed, tipping in the favor of the Muslim community, which with increasing forcefulness claimed that the quotas of participation in the political and administrative power should be reviewed.[80] There were also powerful nuclei of Palestinian fighters settled in Lebanon, with the inevitable consequence of a serious deterioration of relations with Israel. Finally, after the Iranian Revolution there was an influx of Muslim fundamentalist movements which was to open, in 1970, a season of civil war that devastated the entire country.

In these circumstances the Holy See came down firmly in favor of the independence and unity of Lebanon, supporting the maintenance of the model of *convivialité* between the Christian and Muslim communities.

Even at the cost of entering into conflict with a part of the Lebanese Christians, who considered the *convivialité* experience to be irrevocably over,[81] Vatican diplomacy opposed the idea of dismembering the country into a Christian zone and a Muslim one. It rejected this design entertained on some occasions by Israel and the United States,[82] which partially came about through massacres aimed at provoking the territorial regrouping of the communities.[83]

A likely consequence of the creation of a "little Christian Lebanon" might have been an alliance between the Christians and the Israelis against the Palestinians and the Muslims. Both of these possibilities were judged by the Holy See to be disastrous, not only for the Lebanese Christian community and for the other Christian communities of the Middle East, but also for the future model of a mixed religious society of which the Middle East was a symbol. The common thread that linked all of Pope John Paul II's declarations during the Lebanese civil war was the invitation to "resist the temptation of separation"[84] and to prevent "the roots of social life and co-operation between the various groups in the Lebanon from being cut."

The conflict was concluded with the Taif Agreements. This was a "pax siriana . . . accepted without choice by the Maronite Patriarchate and the Vatican."[85] The agreements "revisited" the National Pact, increasing the power of the majority community (the Shiite Muslims) and an Arab foreign power (Syria). The overall context of this fragile peace was marked by the retreat of the Christian component, which was hit by "human and economic losses, demographically and in the field of education, which are greater than the national average"[86] compared to the Muslim population. The process of the "displacement of the Christians in Parliament, in the government, in the administration, in the army and in the internal security forces"[87] has generated the danger of the demotion of the Christians from a community to a minority. While its religious rights will be protected and guaranteed, however, the Christian community would no longer be able to participate in the social and political reconstruction with its own original project.[88] There is the risk of a "normalization" of Lebanon, reduced to the situation existing (as far as the position of the Christian community is concerned) in the other states of the Middle East.[89] In a broader perspective, the Holy See is deeply concerned about this eventuality, considering it to be a decisive step towards the consolidation of a "new order" in the Middle East which is based on religiously homogeneous states instead of on a model of a mixed religious society. The United States' acquiescence to Syrian control of Lebanon, which the Damascus government earned by participating in the anti-Iraq coalition, has made this fear even more concrete.

In the end the decisive step has to be taken by the Lebanese Christian community, which needs to overcome its own internal divisions[90] and reorganize itself socially and politically. It needs to eliminate the rigidity (for example, in the administration of Church properties) that has impeded the suitable employment of all its available resources. The decision to call a special synod for Lebanon should be considered in this sense. There is also the desire, which emerges from both synod and papal documents alike, to re-propose the traditional Lebanese model, which is still considered the best solution possible, both for its local value and because it would be a valid "signal" for the whole community of the Middle East.[91] This choice makes two objectives top priorities. The first is the full recovery of Lebanese independence, with the total withdrawal of Israeli and Syrian troops.[92] The second is the defense of the mixed religious society model,[93] whose vitality is confirmed both by its having survived the Lebanese civil war and in the Taif Agreements. The Holy See consequently rejects both the proportional type of electoral system, which would result in Muslim prevalence in the parliament,[94] and the proposal to have a nondenominational system of political representation, which would be difficult to practice in the present situation and would be unlikely to be advantageous to the Christian community.[95]

The reorganization of the Lebanese Christian communities—whose first, shy signals have already been picked up by some observers[96]—requires a favorable regional context.[97] The solution to the Lebanese problem is inextricably interwoven into and conditioned by three factors. First, there is the need to develop the Israeli-Palestinian peace process. Second, the Syrian army should leave the country. Third, there is the need to reduce the strength of Islamic fundamentalism, which is naturally averse to the experiment of inter-religious coexistence on an equal footing characteristic of Lebanon[98] and which is now represented by the Hezbollah party in Lebanese political life.[99]

In this context Vatican diplomacy has opted for a very cautious approach.[100] The Vatican's dissatisfaction over the Taif Agreements—above all for their incomplete and partial application[101]—can be better understood through the support it has given to Patriarch Sfeir's initiatives than any independent stand it has taken. Its reasons for being so cautious are probably twofold. One is the conviction that the external factors previously discussed require intervention on the regional scale, i.e., the Middle East, before local (Lebanese) issues can be solved. The other is the hope that time will work in the Christians' favor, giving them the chance to heal their war wounds and recover a religious, social, and political compactness. Failure to do so will make it hard for them to deal with the "post-Assad" period, an uncertain and potentially dangerous situation which will inevitably affect the future of Lebanon (and the region).

Besides these contingent choices, the diplomatic activity of the Holy See in the Lebanese crisis confirms some basic strategic lines that hold true for the entire Middle East region and whose origins can be traced right back to before the dissolution of the Ottoman Empire. First of all, the Vatican is convinced that the option of inter-religious coexistence between the Christian and Muslim communities within one state[102] is far more realistic than the formation of separate Christian states. Second, at least where any religious community is present in significant numbers, the Vatican stresses the need to guarantee effective equality in the enjoyment of the civil, social, and political rights due to citizens of different religious faiths. This may be attained through the construction of a secular and democratic state that respects (in the wake of Middle Eastern tradition) the role played by the religious communities, which also act as centers of sociopolitical organization.

### Jordan: The Moderate Option

Numerically speaking, Jordan stands at the opposite extreme compared to Lebanon. Its Christian community is a mere 4.2 percent of the total population and it is divided into many denominations.[103] Nevertheless, the general vicar of the Roman Catholics in Amman was able to declare that "setting aside Lebanon, we are the luckiest Christians in the East."[104]

This statement indicates that small numbers are not a determining factor for the fortunes of the Christian community when it is integrated in a political and social context that presents sufficient elements of safety.

From this standpoint the history of Jordan is exemplary. The persistence (longer than in other regions of the Middle East) of the tribal structure put a brake on the subordination of the Christians to the Muslims "according to the classic status of *dhimma* provided by Islamic culture." Instead it has allowed relations between these two communities to develop "on a plane tending towards equality on the basis of the force and influence that the various tribes were able to exercise."[105] Later on, the political orientation of the Hashemite dynasty has allowed the modernization of the country to come about within a legal framework where the principles of Western law have acted as a counterweight to the Islamic legal tradition, circumscribing its application to very precise sectors.[106]

In this context the Christian community was able to develop a network of schools and educational institutions. These allowed it to transmit its own religious and cultural values, which favored its cohesion. At the same time these schools guaranteed an educational service which was also open to Muslims.[107] Moreover, the course of events in the Middle East since the Second World War facilitated the development of constant and cordial relations between Jordan and the Holy See. After 1948 Jordan appreciated the Holy See's concern about the fate of the Palestinian refugees, while on the whole the Holy See was satisfied with Jordan's management of the Christian Holy Places in Jerusalem until 1967, with the stand King Hussein took on the issue of dialogue between Christians and Muslims,[108] and more recently with some of his statements about the destiny of the Holy City.[109]

It was therefore not surprising that a few months after his coronation King Hussein went to visit the Vatican (it was to be the first of a long series of visits).[110] Moreover, as soon as the political conditions of the region allowed it, diplomatic relations were established between the Holy See and Jordan.[111] Indeed Jordan also represented a model of inter-religious coexistence, albeit in a completely different sense from Lebanon, which was acceptable to the Holy See. A country with a large Muslim majority guided by a dynasty which is proud of descending in a direct line from Mohammed, Jordan is inspired by a liberal and moderate Islam which has been able to blend faith to its own religion with an opening up to modernity and, recently, respect for democracy.[112] Indeed the presence—in Parliament and, for a certain period, also in the government—of radical Islamic movements did not give rise to serious tensions with the non-Muslim religious communities (probably thanks to the vigilance and firmness of the government).[113] In this sense Jordan constitutes a model for all countries where the Christian community, in terms of numbers, can only aspire to a minority role.

Despite these positive elements, Jordanian Christians are as yet unable to rid themselves of the same feelings of uncertainty and precariousness (especially since King Hussein's death) that are felt by all the Christian communities of the Middle East. That this is so is substantiated by the continued exodus of Christians from Jordan even though they enjoy conditions of considerable political and social tranquillity. The Christians know that they can count on the support of the sovereign, but they also realize that he could not oppose a radical evolution of Jordanian public opinion. Hence their awareness that "even though it is enviable in relation to what exists in the rest of the Arab world, their condition is no less than that of a minority protected by an illuminated power and an illuminated Islam; it rests, not on rights recognized for all, but on a tolerant practice of the Koran, which is guaranteed by a political regime that can disappear at any moment."[114] This unsettled feeling, which is rooted not in the national situation but in a far wider context, can only raise the question as to whether it is possible to arrest a process of emigration that appears so far advanced that it cannot even be stopped where Christians can, with reason, define themselves as "the luckiest of the East."

### The Future of the Vatican Policy

Does the Holy See have a Middle East policy? This question is sometimes asked with a pinch of skepticism, comparing the Middle East to other regions of the world (such as Europe or Latin America) where the strategy of the Holy See is more evident. The answer is that it does.[115]

The analysis conducted in this chapter shows that the basic lines of this policy are the same as those that characterize the diplomatic activity of the Holy See everywhere: the defense of the Christian communities, respect for fundamental human rights, and the quest for peace, both for reasons of a general nature and because peace and human rights offer the best conditions for guaranteeing the permanence of Christians in the Middle East. Within these boundaries, the Middle East policy of the Holy See pursues the objective of safeguarding the chance for believers of different religions to live together, confirming that faith in God can be a factor of concord and not of conflict. This is the specific element that marks the Vatican's diplomatic activity in this region and distinguishes it from what it has done in other parts of the world. The concrete choices of papal diplomacy should be viewed in this context, in particular its insistence on Muslim-Christian coexistence and on full recognition of the presence of the Jewish people in the Holy Land. The exclusions also derive from this context: the Holy See rejects the fundamentalist prospect of a wholly and exclusively Muslim Middle East (and likewise an Israel that is wholly and exclusively Jewish), and it does not accept the constitution of separate Christian enclaves.[116]

The future of this policy and its chances of success depend on a number of variables that largely escape the control both of the Holy See and of the Middle East Christian communities. Among these variables are the peaceful solution of the conflicts still in progress (in particular the Israeli-Palestinian conflict), the economic growth of the Middle East region, the maturation of a liberal and moderate Islam, and the development of the dialogue between Christians, Jews, and Muslims. The uncertainty that dominates this scenario inevitably generates a sense of precariousness that feeds emigration. This can push those who remain (out of choice or necessity) towards "self-segregation" inside their own community or lead to uncritical identification with the political and cultural context in which the Christian minority is integrated. The efforts of the Holy See are designed to slow down the Christian exodus and correct its rudderless drifting, in the expectancy (or hope) that the general conditions of the region will allow the possibility of the coexistence of Jews, Christians, and Muslims. This hope is what has guided Vatican diplomacy throughout the papacy of Pope John Paul II.

## NOTES

1. Cf. J. Brian Hehir, "The Catholic Church and the Middle East: Policy and Diplomacy," in *The Vatican, Islam and the Middle East* 109–13 (Kail C. Ellis ed., 1987).

2. The meaning that the Middle East, "cradle of many civilizations and cross-roads of many religions" may have "for a peaceful coexistence and dialogue in reciprocal tolerance" in other parts of the world has recently been underlined in a meeting promoted by the Sacred Congregation for the Oriental Churches (see the Vatican press release, dated Apr. 18, 1998, available on website www.vatican.va/news_services/press/index.htm, visited on Oct. 24, 1998). For more in general on this subject, see M. Pacini, "Il dialogo fra gli

universi culturali. Alla ricerca di un nucleo di valori condivisi," in *Un'urgenza dei tempi moderni: il dialogo tra gli universi culturali* 5–18 (1997).

3. See in this regard the issue of Limes (1994) devoted to "Mediterraneo, l'Arabia vicina." The link between the situation of the Christian communities of the Middle East and that of the Muslim communities in Europe is signaled, for example, in a letter from the Eastern Catholic patriarchs, *Insieme davanti a Dio per il bene della persona umana e della società*, Dec. 29, 1994, at 2; cf. *Regno-att.* 2.1995.21.

4. This does not mean that each of them does not have its own individual character: on this point see J. Maïla, "Gli arabi cristiani: dalla questione d'Oriente alla recente geopolitica delle minoranze," in *Comunità cristiane nell'Islam arabo, La sfida del futuro* 31–33 (A. Pacini ed., 1996).

5. "Messaggio dei patriarchi cattolici d'Oriente, Aug. 24, 1991," cited in A. Filippi, "Sempre più Siria"; *Regno-att.* 18.1991.564. On this document see also *Avvenire*, Sept. 7, 1991.

6. On the constitution of a mixed commission between the Holy See and the PLO, directed at defining "a legal status of the Catholic Church in the Palestinian Territories," see the press release published in the *Bollettino* of the press office of the Holy See on Jan. 15, 1998, and *Regno-att.* 4.1998.131 (for previous contacts see the release published on Oct. 25, 1994): from then on the negotiations continued to a positive conclusion.

7. See the condemnation of the "merciless embargo" Iraq is subjected to contained in the pope's speech to the diplomatic corps on Jan. 10, 1998 (*Regno-doc.* 3.1998.81), and the more general one, "Economic embargoes are always to be condemned as they are detrimental to those who are most in need," pronounced during the journey to Cuba, Jan. 21–26, 1998 (L. Accattoli, "Testimonianza pubblica della fede"; *Regno-att.* 4.1998.80); see also, for some specifications, the interview with Mons. Tauran in *La Republica* on July 13, 1998.

8. See A. Riccardi, *Le politiche della chiesa* 5 (1997).

9. Only Kuwait (1968) and very recently Yemen (1998) have established diplomatic relations with the Holy See: the other states of the Arabian peninsula (Saudi Arabia, the United Arab Emirates, Bahrein, Qatar, Oman) have not yet done so. Anyway, the situation of the Christian communities is not the same in all these countries. See, for some outlines, M. Borrmans, "La politica mediorientale della Santa Sede," in *La politica internazionale della Santa Sede 1965–1990*, 91–101 (G. Barberini ed., 1992).

10. See in particular the speech by Pope John Paul II to the Middle East patriarchs of March 4, 1991 (which contains a direct reference to Saudi Arabia), the *Messaggio per la giornata della pace* dated Dec. 8, 1990, and the speeches to the diplomatic corps of 1990, 1991, and 1996, respectively, in *Regno-doc.* 7.1991.194; 1.1991.2 *et seq.;* 3.1990.72 and 3.1996.72; see also the speech made on Feb. 12, 1994, on the occasion of a congress on the Eastern Christian communities (*L'Osservatore romano* [hereinafter *OR*], weekly ed., Feb. 12, 1994).

11. It is enough to look through the pope's speeches to the diplomatic corps accredited to the Holy See to have confirmation of this. About 7 million Christians (of whom only a minority are Roman Catholics) live in the Middle East, which amounts to about 3% of the Christians (the vast majority of whom are Roman Catholics) that live in South America: despite this, in his speeches the pope devotes the same amount of attention to the Middle East as he does to South America.

12. For a discussion of the objectives of the Holy See's Middle East policy see A. Riccardi, "Il limes meridionale del Vaticano," 2 *Limes* 233–46 (1994).

13. On the centrality of the idea of coexistence between Muslims and Christians in the Middle East policy of the Vatican, see id. at 238.

14. For the same reason the Holy See does not encourage the hypothesis, aired before and after the Second World War, of an alliance between Maronites and Zionists: see L. Zitrain Eisenberg, "Desperate Diplomacy: The Zionist Maronite Treaty of 1946," 13 *Studies in Zionism* 2, 147–63 (1992).

15. In full harmony on this point with the representatives of the Middle East Roman Catholic churches; see the very firm declarations contained in the third pastoral letter (1994) of the Council of the Eastern Catholic patriarchs, cited by Borrmans, "Il contributo delle comunità arabo-cristiane al futuro delle società arabe del Medio Oriente: alcune prospettive" in Pacini, *supra* note 4, at 339–40.

16. See in this regard J. Hajjar, *Le Vatican, la France et le catholicisme oriental (1878–1914)* (1970), and on the period between the two world wars, id., *Le christianisme en Orient. Etudes d'Histoire contemporaine 1684–1968*, at 187–238 (1971).

17. See J. M. Billioud, *Histoire des chrétiens d'Orient* 115–25 (1995); A. Ferre, "Minoranze cristiane in Medio Oriente," in *Il Mediterraneo nel Novecento. Religioni e stati* 104–6 (A. Riccardi ed., 1994).

18. The Italian consul to Jerusalem reported in 1927 that Pope Pius XI had insisted, in a meeting with Mons. Robinson, on the necessity to "prepare native clergy ready to succeed the Europeans" in view of the "revolt of the Eastern peoples against all Western interference" (see S. Ferrari, "Pio XI, la Palestina e i luoghi santi," in *Achille Ratti Pape Pie XI*, at 921–22 (1996).

19. With Lebanon and Egypt in 1947, with Syria and Iran in 1953. Turkey follows in 1960, Iraq in 1966, Kuwait in 1968, and Cyprus in 1973. More recently, diplomatic relations have been established with Israel (1994), Jordan (1994), and Yemen (1998). In 1994 official (not diplomatic) relations were established with the Palestine Liberation Organization.

20. In confirmation of this it is possible to remember also the war of Algeria (see M. Impagliazzo, *Duval d'Algeria. Una chiesa tra Europa e il mondo arabo (1946–1988)* (1995)) and the recent re-establishment of diplomatic relations with Libya, which provoked the protests of the United States (see G. Arboit, *Le Saint-Siège et le nouvel ordre au Moyen-Orient* 133–34 (1996)); *La Republica* Mar. 12, 1997; see also the declarations of the director of the Vatican Press Office of Mar. 10, 1997, at the website www.vatican.va/news_services/press/index.htm, visited on Oct. 24, 1998.) The divergence between the Middle East policy of the Holy See and that of the United States is signaled, among others, by E. O. Hanson, *The Catholic Church in World Politics* 235 (1987).

21. For an analysis of this viewpoint see J. L. Eposito, *The Islamic Threat, Myth or Reality* (1992); for a different point of view see Bat Ye'or, *Juifs et chrétiens sous l'islam. Les dhimmis face au défi intégriste* (1994).

22. See *infra* note 40.

23. On these developments see J. Hajjar, "La chiesa e le chiese in Medio Oriente (1846–1965)," in *Storia della chiesa*, vol. XXIV, at 187 (A. Fliche & V. Martin, eds.),

*(Dalle missioni alle chiese locali (1886–1965)* (J. Metzler ed., 1990)); Billioud, *supra* note 17, at 134–41.

24. This expression was used by a Palestinian Roman Catholic priest, Rafiq Khoury, "L'insertion de nos Eglises dans le monde de l'Islam arabe," in *Le bullettin diocésain,* July-September 1993, at 223. An exception to this is a significant part of the Lebanese Christian community, which claims its own originality with regard to the surrounding Arab world.

25. This passage has been taken from a speech given in February 1997 (see 79 *La Documentation catholique* 645 (1997)); see also the speech given on May 24, 1995, in Chicago, id., Aug. 6–20, 1995, in particular pp. 750–51, and the declaration of June 16, 1996, to the Middle East Council of the Churches 687, id., July 21, 1996.

26. See M. L. Rossi, "La genesi della *Nostra aetate,*" in *Il Mediterraneo* 259–81.

27. See Arboit, *supra* note 20, at 167 and 174–75. See also *France Pays Arabes* no. 199, pp. 4–7 (Feb. 1994) and, more recently, the reservations expressed by Mons. Sabbah (*Regno-att.* 4.1998.129s).

28. Excessively dominated, in Mons. Sabbah's view, by the memory of the Holocaust:

> In the Middle East and in Israel Palestine, this dialogue has its own distinctive characteristic, in view of the historical events that serve as the reference and as the base of Jewish-Christian dialogue in the Western world. This reference in the Western world is past history during which the relationship between Christians and Jews was that of the persecutors and the persecuted. In the Middle East current history presents a reverse relationship. It is a relationship of conflict and oppression, in which the Palestinians are oppressed. . . . We say that local dialogue should have its own distinctive characteristic, and the universal Church to which the local Church belongs should therefore take this into consideration.

"Chrétiens en Terre Sainte," May 24, 1995, in *La Documentation catholique,* Aug. 6–20, 1995, at 751.

29. See S. Joseph, *Muslim-Christian Conflicts: Economic, Political and Social Origins* (B. L. K. Pillsburg, 1978).

30. See id.

31. On the Islam-Christian dialogue, see M. Borrmans, *Islam e cristianesimo, Le vie del dialogo* (1991); P. Rossano, "Percorsi religiosi tra conflitto e dialogo: ebrei, cristiani e musulmani," in *Il Mediterraneo,* 249–58; *Muslims in Dialogue: The Evolution of a Dialogue,* (L. Swindler ed., 1992); H. Goddard, *Christians & Muslims: From Double Standards to Mutual Understandings* (1995).

32. This expression is used by Pope John Paul II in a letter sent to the Latin patriarch of Jerusalem on Dec. 9, 1997, which can be found on the Vatican website www.vatican.va/news_services/press/index.htm, consulted on Oct. 24, 1998.

33. On the "substantially good" relations between Christian churches, albeit with some reserve by the Orthodox Church, Mons. Sabbah has recently spoken in an interview to *Regno-att.* 4.1998.130, where one can also find a synthesis of the most recent common declaration by the leaders of the Christian Churches, dated Jan. 24, 1998 (text in 80 *La Documentation catholique* 240–42 (1998)). For other common declarations see *Regno-doc.*

1.1995. 19–21; *La Documentation catholique* 197–98 (Feb. 21, 1993); 3 *Journal of Palestine Studies* 148–49 (spring 1992). For further references to the dialogue between the Christian Churches of the Middle East, see C. A. Kimball, *Angle of Vision: Christians and the Middle East* 40–45 (1992); Borrmans, "Il contributo delle comunità arabo-cristiane" 141–42, *supra* note 15; Billioud, *supra* note 17, at 239–40.

34. For a discussion of the exactness of this definition and of the impact of this phenomenon on the life of the Christian communities of the Middle East, see A. Wessels, *Arab and Christian? Christians in the Middle East* 188–222 (1995).

35. The ideological prejudices that delayed a timely and correct perception of the nature of the Khomeinist revolution have been pointed out by D. Johnston & C. Sampson, *Religion, the Missing Dimension of Statecraft* 12–14 (1994).

36. See R. Toscano, "Noi e loro: dieci tesi e una postilla," 2 *Limes* 247–50 (1994) and M. Jürgensmeyer, *The New Cold War? Religious Nationalism Confronts the Secular State* 1–8 (1993), which highlights the opposition of the fundamentalists to any social and political model of secular inspiration.

37. See A. E. Mayer, "Islam and the State," in 12 *Cardozo L. Rev.* 1015, 1015–56 (1990–91); id., *Islam and Human Rights, Traditions, and Politics* (Boulder, Colo.: Westminster Press 1999).

38. Besides Jürgensmeyer, *supra* note 36, see *Fundamentalism in Comparative Perspective* (L. Kaplan ed., 1993).

39. See Bat Ye'or, *supra* note 21, at 229 *et seq.*

40. Although it has never adhered to these arguments, the Holy See has repeatedly stressed the necessity that the international economic order should promote a fairer redistribution of the wealth deriving from the natural resources of the Middle East: see, for an example of this, the speech of March 4, 1991, addressed by the pope to the patriarchs and archbishops gathered at the Vatican after the Gulf War (*Regno-doc.* 7.1991.194). For more in general on this subject, which fits into the broader request for a redistribution of economic resources between the northern and southern regions of the world, see Bryan Heir, "Papal Foreign Policy," *Foreign Policy* 78 (1990).

41. Cf. id.

42. See J-P. Valognes, *Vie et mort des chrétiens d'Orient. Des origines à nos jours* 778–95 (1994).

43. *Discorso ai rappresentanti del mondo politico tunisino*, Feb. 22, 1997; *Regno-doc.* 9.1996.296.

44. Besides the declarations cited at note 10, see the speech addressed by the pope to the Muslim authorities of Nigeria (*Regno-doc.* 9.1998, in particular p. 266).

45. This passage is contained in Pope John Paul II's speech, *supra* note 40 (*Regno-doc.* 7.1991.194); the same concept has been reiterated in the speech to the Muslim authorities of Nigeria, *supra* note 44, in which it is affirmed that "every time violence is committed in the name of religion we must make it clear to everybody that, in such circumstances, we are not dealing with true religion." The absurdity of a war conducted in the name of God is recurrent in Pope John Paul II's declarations (see, for example, *OR*, Jan. 28–29, 1991).

46. See T. P. Melady, *The Ambassador's Story: The United States and the Vatican in World Affairs* 95–123 (1994) and S. Ferrari, *Vaticano e Israele. Dalla fine della seconda guerra mondiale alla guerra del Golfo* 189 *et seq.* (1991).

47. See the contributions collected in the volume *La pace sprecata. Il papa, la chiesa e la guerra nel Golfo* (D. Del Rio ed., 1991) and P. Hebblethwaite, *Pope John Paul II, the Gulf War and the Catholic Tradition* (1992).

48. Gérald Arboit wrote, "In the eyes of John Paul II this war is not a Gulf war but rather a World War," underlining the particular importance that this conflict held for the Holy See (*La Saint-Siège et le nouvel ordre au Moyen-Orient,* 43). The First Gulf War was generally considered to be the test bed of the new international balances after the end of bipolarism and of the traditional confrontation between Eastern countries guided by the Soviet Union and Western ones guided by the United States.

49. *Discorso al clero romano,* Feb. 14, 1991, in Del Rio, *supra* note 47, at 210–11.

50. *Comunicato conclusivo dei lavori,* at the end of the Meeting of the Patriarchs of the Catholic Churches of the Middle East and of the Presidents of the Episcopal Conferences of the countries involved in the Gulf War, May 5, 1991; *Regno-doc.* 7.1991.2–3.

51. "Faith in the same God," the pope stated, "must not be a source of conflict and rivalry, but of commitment to overcome contrasts existing in the dialogue and the negotiations," in *OR,* Jan. 28–29, 1991. Arboit refers to the centrality of the notion of reconciliation between the three religions of Abraham in Pope John Paul II's thinking in *supra* note 20, at 44 and 90.

52. See, in confirmation of the fact that the position of the Holy See did not escape the attention of the Arab leadership, the declarations by the leaders of the Lebanese Hezbollah cited in Wessels, *supra* note 34, at 224–25, and the letter by the general secretary of the Organization of the Islamic Conference cited in Arboit, *supra* note 20, at 45; *Regno.doc.* 7.1991.195; see also L. Accattoli, "Il papa," in Del Rio, *supra* note 47, at 71.

53. The downside of the Vatican's policy was instead the deterioration of its relations with the United States, which was to contribute towards excluding the Holy See from the Madrid Peace Conference.

54. See the references listed in note 116.

55. On the emigration of Christians from the Middle East, see Y. Courbage & Ph. Fargues, *Chrétiens et Juifs dans l'Islam arabe et turc* (1992), and Ph. Fargues, "I cristiani arabi dell'Oriente: una prospettiva demografica," in Pacini, *supra* note 4, at 55–74.

56. See Courbage & Fargues, *supra* note 55, at 143 *et seq.*

57. The importance of peace in arresting emigration is stressed by B. Sabella, "L'emigrazione degli arabi cristiani: dimensioni e cause dell'esodo," in Pacini, *supra* note 4, at 165.

58. See the declaration made by the Vatican secretary of state, Card. Angelo Sodano, on Oct. 2, 1990, on the occasion of the Holy See's manifestation of agreement to a project of declaration on the gulf crisis prepared by the ministers of foreign affairs of the countries adhering to the CSCE (see *OR,* Oct. 4, 1990).

59. See, for the period that goes up to the Gulf War, S. I. Minerbi, *Il Vaticano, La Terra Santa e il sionismo* (1988); Ferrari, *supra* note 46. For the subsequent years, besides the

references indicated in the following notes, see H. Tinqo, *L'Etoile et la Croix, Jean-Paul II–Israël: l'explication* (1993); S. I. Minerbi, "The Vatican and Israel," in *Papal Diplomacy in the Modern Age* 189–201 (P. C. Kent & J. F. Pollard eds., 1994); G. Rulli, *Lo Stato d'Israele* 383 *et seq.* (1998); A. Chouraqui, *La Reconnaissance. Le Saint-Siège, les Juifs et Israël* 225 *et seq.* (1992); F. M. Perko, "Towards a Sound and Lasting Basis: Relations between the Holy See, the Zionist Movement and Israel 1896–1996," 2 *Israel Studies* 1, 15–18 (1997).

60.  The messages were published in *L'Osservatore Romano*, Oct. 31, 1991. The need for a global regulation of the Middle East conflicts—the Iraqi, Palestinian, Lebanese, and Cypriot conflicts—is a recurrent theme in the declarations of the pope and the Vatican diplomacy: for some references see Arboit, *supra* note 20, at 34 *et seq.*

61.  On the Fundamental Agreement, see the contributions published by the 47 *Cath. U. L. Rev.* 2 (1998).

62.  See the declaration made by the director of the Vatican Press Office on Jan. 2, 1991, in which he affirmed that the Holy See recognized "implicitly" the State of Israel.

63.  On this idea, see Ferrari, *supra* note 46, at 291.

64.  Pope John Paul II's letters to Netanyahu and Arafat of June 16, 1997, in particular should be remembered; *Regno-doc.* 15.1997.497 *et seq.*

65.  See the interviews with Mons. Jean-Louis Tauran published in *Corriere della sera*, Apr. 17, 1998, at 8; *La Republica*, May 13, 1998, at 11.

66.  Above all the slow progress toward the stipulation of the Legal Personality Agreement concluded on Nov. 18, 1997 (for the text, see 2 *Quaderni di diritto e politica ecclesiastica* 521–27 (1998) and *Regno-doc.* 21.1997.706 and 1.1998.27): see "Catholic Church Frustrated with Israel Diplomacy Stalled Despite Recognition," *Washington Times*, Apr. 9, 1997, at A12.

67.  See *Regno-att.* 16.1999.560–61. Other signals of the deterioration in relations had already been registered in 1995 on the occasion of Card. Lustiger's visit to Israel (for more in general see the letter from Mons. Mathes, "Jerusalem, City of Peace," *Jerusalem Post*, Apr. 5, 1995, at 6), and in 1996 on the occasion of the presentation to the Knesset of a bill which punished every form of "enticement to change religion" (see 233 *France Pays Arabes* 13, June 1997): for other episodes of the same type see *Palestine Report*, Dec. 12, 1997, at 15.

68.  In this context it is important to remember the rumors, periodically recorded and denied in the press, regarding tensions between Christian and Muslim Palestinians; see *Jerusalem Times*, Oct. 13 and Dec. 12, 1997, and Jan. 12, 1998.

69.  See in particular the papal letter *Redemptionis Anno* of Apr. 20, 1984; 76 *Acta Apostolicae Sedis* 625–29 (1984); *Enchiridium Vaticanum* 9/776–782.

70.  The link between Jerusalem as the "symbol and instrument of peace and reconciliation" and the Holy Land as the "foremost place for the meeting and prayer of the peoples" is explicit in the speech to the diplomatic corps of Jan. 11, 1992 (*Regno-doc.* 3.1992.70), where there is also a reference to the "priority" nature of the "dialogue between Jews, Christians and Muslims" to ensure peace "in this region of the world and elsewhere." See also the letter sent by Pope John Paul II to the Latin patriarch of Jerusalem on Dec. 9, 1997 (at website www.vatican.va/news_services/press/index.htm, visited on Oct. 24, 1998).

71. On these proposals see Ferrari, *supra* note 46, at 100 *et seq.* and 191 *et seq.;* P. Pieraccini, *Gerusalemme, luoghi santi e comunità religiose nella politica internazionale* 437 *et seq.* (1996). The Vatican position has recently been summarized by Mons. Tauran in a speech given in Jerusalem on Oct. 26, 1998 (for the text, see *Regno-doc.* 1.1999.19). In relation to this speech a note by the Vatican information service (note 180 of Oct. 27, 1998) has stressed the request that "the Holy See participate in Israeli-Palestinian negotiations on the status of this city (Jerusalem)."

72. For the Holy See the question of Jerusalem "pertains rather to the domain of values than to that of territory" (Arboit, *supra* note 20, at 171).

73. See, for example, the apostolic letter *Tertio Millennio Adveniente,* Nov. 10, 1994, *Regno-doc.* 21.1994.646–47.

74. Giovanni Paolo II, *Udienza generale del 6.3.1991: OR,* Mar. 7, 1991. The statement that the possibility of making this journey is connected to the provision of international guarantees that allow the Holy City to recover its specific role, formulated by Mons. Tauran on the same day (see id.), confirms the thesis sustained by the text.

75. Already in 1985 the Holy See had invited those present to consider "the existence of the State of Israel and its political choices in a perspective that is not in itself religious, but which refers to the common principles of international law" (Segretariato per l'Unione Dei Cristiani, Commissione per I Rapporti Religiosi conl'Ebraismo, *Ebrei ed ebraismo nella predicazione e nella catechesi della chiesa cattolica. Sussidi per una corretta presentazione,* June 24, 1985; *OR,* June 24–25, 1985).

76. See F. Strazzari, "Alle radici dei cedri"; *Regno-att.* 6.1993.178.

77. Y. Moubarac, "The Lebanese Experience and Muslim-Christian Relations," in Ellis, *supra* note 1, at 226–28.

78. Giovanni Paolo II, *A tutti i vescovi della chiesa cattolica,* Sept. 7, 1989; *Regno-doc.* 19.1989.583. See also the *Messaggio del papa ai patriarchi, arcivescovi e vescovi cattolici del Libano,* June 20, 1992; *Regno-doc* 15.1992.460. For an indication about similar papal declarations, see Strazzari, *supra* note 76, at 180. See the document *Verso la pace in Medio-Oriente: prospettive, principi e speranze,* published by the Bishops Conference of the United States, Nov. 6–9, 1989; *Regno-doc.* 7.1990.211–12.

79. See B. Labaki, "Le comunità cristiane e la situazione economica e sociale in Libano," in Pacini, *supra* note 4, at 262–67.

80. See id. at 267–72.

81. "The Vatican," declared Bechir Gemayel in 1982, "has to understand that the Christians of the Lebanon are not the guinea-pigs of Muslim-Christian dialogue. The Lebanese mission as a bridge built between the West and the Arab world is over" (quoted by G. E. Irani, "La croix et le Liban," in 54 *Politique internationale* (1991/92), at 383.

82. See Wessels, *supra* note 34, at 117; Moubarac, *supra* note 77, at 231.

83. See G. Corm, "La crisi del sistema libanese," *Il Mediterraneo* 94.

84. This expression has been taken from the papal letter sent by Pope John Paul II to the bishops of all the world in May 1984 (cited in G. Rulli, *Libano. Dalla crisi alla "pax siriana"* 230 (1996).

85. Billioud, *supra* note 17, at 198.

86. Labaki, *supra* note 79, at 250.

87. Id. at 267.

88. See E. Piccard, "Le dinamiche dei cristiani libanesi: tra il paradigma delle 'ammiyyat e il paradigma Hwayyek," in Pacini, *supra* note 4, at 233–34; Rulli, *supra* note 84, at 357–58.

89. See Piccard, *supra* note 88, at 237.

90. See *Messaggio dei patriarchi cattolici d'Oriente*, Aug. 24, 1991, cited in Fillipi, *supra* note 5; 18 *Regno-att.*, 1991, at 564.

91. See the *Relatio ante disceptationem* published on Nov. 27, 1995; *Regno-doc.* 1.1996, in particular 9 and 14 and the sermon preached by Pope John Paul II on May 11, 1997; *Regno-doc.* 11.1997.339. See also the declarations by Mons. Bustros, who played a very important role in the preparation and development of the synod, in F. Strazzari, "Per il dialogo e per il Libano"; *Regno-att.* 6.1997.154–55.

92. See the communication published by the Lebanese bishops on May 8, 1991, cited in Rulli, *supra* note 84, at 347, the already mentioned message of the Eastern Catholic patriarchs of August of the same year (*Regno-att.* 18.1991.564), and the concluding message of the synod published on Dec. 14, 1995 (*Regno-doc.* 1.1996.19). More recently see the declarations by Mons. Bishara Rai, coordinator of the synod for Lebanon, reported in *Corriere della sera*, Apr. 7, 1994.

93. See the *Instrumentum laboris* of the synod, cited in L. Prezzi, "Rinnovamento spirituale rischio storico-civile"; *Regno-att.* 20.1995.587–588. See also the declarations by Mons. Tauran reported in Rulli, *supra* note 84, at 350.

94. See the declarations by the Maronite Patriarch Sfeir in Strazzari, *supra* note 76; *Regno-att.* 6.1993.178 and the *Messaggio conclusivo del sinodo*, Dec. 14, 1995; *Regno-doc.* 1.1996.17.

95. See *Messaggio conclusivo; Regno-doc.* 1.1996.16 *et seq.* On the question see the observations by J. Maila, "Gli arabi cristiani: dalla questione d'Oriente alla recente geopolitica delle minoranze," 31–35. For some voices in support of the development of political secularity in Lebanon, see M. Matté, "Indiretto non evasivo"; *Regno-att.* 2.1996.12 and Corm, *supra* note 83, at 97–98.

96. See Labaki, *supra* note 79, at 274–79. In this regard may also be interpreted the solid adhesion to the appeal by the Patriarch Sfeir to desert the elections of 1992: on this episode see M. E. Gandolfi, "Boicottaggio riuscito futuro islamico"; *Regno-att.* 18.1992.563–64. More recently it has been observed that in Lebanon "a climate of reconciliation, of reciprocal pardon and mutual acceptance is beginning, especially among the Christians" (Comunicato relativo alla quarta riunione del Consiglio postsinodale dell'Assemblea speciale per il Libano del sinodo dei vescovi, Sept. 26, 1998, in the website www.vatican.va/news_services/press/index.htm, visited on Oct. 29, 1998).

97. The fact that "the future of the Lebanese political system will depend, just as in the last century, on the evolution of the region" is stressed by Corm, *supra* note 83, at 97.

98. See in this sense Moubarac, *supra* note 77, at 233; Corm, *supra* note 83, at 94; Rulli, *supra* note 84, at 363–64; Wessels, *supra* note 34, at 120.

99.  Sheik Mohammed Hussein Fadlallah, spiritual guide of the Hezbollah party, declared in 1996 that he wanted to use Islam to "modify the pluralist structure of Lebanese society"(Billioud, *supra* note 17, at 198).

100.  The absence of any mention of Lebanon in the pope's speech to the diplomatic corps after 1998 is significant; equally significant is, in relation to the special synod on Lebanon, the prudence that characterizes the papal exhortation after the synod in comparison to the *Instrumentum laboris*, the *Relatio ante disceptationem*, and the message of the synod fathers.

101.  On the "unbalanced application to the detriment of the Christians" of the Taif Agreements, see Labaki, *supra* note 79, at 267.

102.  See Riccardi, *supra* note 12, at 238. It is also significant that two representatives of the Muslim community participated at the synod for Lebanon.

103.  For some data see Courbage & Fargues, *supra* note 55, in particular 325–28.

104.  This statement is cited by Billioud, *supra* note 17, at 221.

105.  A. Pacini, "Dinamiche comunitarie e sociopolitiche dei cristiani arabi in Giordania, in Israele e nei territori palestinesi autonomi," in Pacini, *supra* note 4, at 282. This finding is confirmed by the already cited declarations of the Latin vicar, according to whom "[w]e are not dhimmis, but full citizens"("Nous ne sommes pas des dhimmis, mais des citoyens à part entière").

106.  See id. at 288.

107.  See id. at 286–87 and Billioud, *supra* note 17, at 222.

108.  See J. L. Ryan, "The Holy See and Jordan," in Ellis, *supra* note 1, at 163 *et seq.*

109.  See, for example, the interview in *Corriere della sera* on Nov. 6, 1993. It is likely that the Vatican was not sorry about the cautious position taken by Jordan during the Gulf War.

110.  See id. at 164.

111.  On March, 13, 1994, after the signature of the Fundamental Agreement between the Holy See and Israel (Dec. 30, 1993) but before diplomatic relations were opened between them (June 15, 1994). On the negotiations that preceded the opening of diplomatic relations between Jordan and the Holy See, see Ryan, *supra* note 108, at 179, and Arboit, *supra* note 20, at 171.

112.  See Valognes, *supra* note 42, at 628–30.

113.  On these developments see Pacini, *supra* note 4, at 288–89.

114.  Valognes, *supra* note 42, at 632.

115.  The question probably arises from the fact that the efficacy of the Holy See's diplomatic action in the Middle East comes up against limits that are stronger than elsewhere: see in this regard Heir, *supra* note 40, at 48, and Billioud, *supra* note 17, at 238.

116.  One of the criticisms most frequently leveled at the Vatican's strategy in the Middle East is that it has neglected, in the name of a pro-Arab choice dictated by general considerations, the true interests of the local Christian communities, which have been sacrificed on the altar of Islam-Christian dialogue and opening to the third world (see Minerbi, *supra* note 59, at 189–201; Ye'or, *supra* note 21, at 269 *et seq.*). The continuous

emigration of Christians from the Middle East and the growth of Muslim radicalism are, in this perspective, the most evident symptoms of the failure of the policy pursued by the Holy See. It is difficult to evaluate how accurate these observations are as there is no proof that a different strategy would have led to better results. Had the conditions existed (which remains to be demonstrated), the creation of small Christian enclaves in the Middle East might have been the result of a different policy: but their capacity of survival in the long term, impact with the surrounding Arab countries and the fate of the Christian communities destined to remain outside the boundaries of these enclaves are questions which it is not possible to answer.

14

## PALESTINIAN CHRISTIANS

Recent Developments

*Drew Christiansen, S.J.*

### Introduction and Overview

Asked to supplement the essays of this volume with a survey article on Palestinian Christians today, I discovered to my dismay that there was scarcely any literature which examined in detail the events of the last two decades of Palestinian church history.[1] Yet, the past fifteen years, beginning with the first intifada (1987–1993), the mostly nonviolent Palestinian resistance to Israeli occupation begun in 1987, have witnessed dramatic changes in the consciousness, the activity, the leadership, and even the organization of the Church in the Holy Land. For this reason, I have proceeded with just a few paragraphs of historical background to provide instead an account of some developments in recent Palestinian Christian history with stress on the effect of the intifada and the troubled years following the Oslo Accords on Palestinian Christian self-awareness.[2] Here I have taken my lead from my Jesuit confrere, Peter Du Brul, whose "The Crisis of Palestinian Christians" is a thoughtful articulation of the impact of the intifada on the Christians of the Holy Land.[3]

While I am a Roman Catholic, I have tried to sum up currents in the broader Palestinian church scene, mainly from the point of view of the growing ecumenical interaction among the traditional Christian churches during the last decade. Viewed from the perspective of history, ecumenical coordination among the churches on issues of justice and peace, especially on matters affecting Jerusalem, is one of the great overlooked religious stories of the last decade. From the time of the Crusades there has been intense rivalry between the Greek Orthodox, Oriental, and Latin churches in the Holy Land. Their latest turn toward pragmatic ecumenism is as notable for the churches' prophetic advocacy on public issues, in a region where they were historically removed from public affairs, as it is for their unaccustomed unity in voicing their concerns. Both public advocacy and ecumenicity represent dramatic departures from the tense coexistence of the churches in past generations.

Because this volume centers on Catholic-Israeli and Catholic-Jewish relations, I have given extended treatment to developments in the Catholic Church in the Holy Land.[4] I have touched only lightly on specific developments internal to the Greek Orthodox Church, the largest Christian body in the Holy Land, the mainline Protestant churches, and Palestinian evangelicals.[5] Likewise, because my focus is Palestinian Christians, I do not examine the role of expatriate Christians, including the Christian Embassy, the controversial, evangelical supporters of the State of Israel.

The focus on the Catholic Church, I submit, is merited by more than the focus of this book. Though still perhaps second to the Greek Orthodox Church in total number of adherents, the Catholic Church has come out of the turmoil of the last years greatly strengthened and with increased public stature. The integration of the various Catholic churches under the Assembly of Bishops, the leadership of the Latin patriarch, Michel Sabbah, the renewal of the Latin Church in a multiyear synod, and the initiatives of the Holy See have all contributed to increasing the vitality of the Catholic Church, its mediating role among the churches, and its international stature.

This exposition primarily treats the contentious issues which the churches have had to address in response to the unresolved Israeli-Palestinian conflict and the partial peace which emerged after the 1993 Oslo Accords. These were also the issues that, in large measure, brought about a rapid maturation on the part of Palestinian Christians and their churches in the same period. They were likewise the issues of peace, justice, and human rights to which I had to respond on behalf of the United States Catholic bishops. As a result of attending to the events of the day, I fear I give too little sense of the faith life of the Palestinian Christians. I do not treat of their customs and devotions, nor do I relate at any length the joys and trials of their everyday lives. This is an omission I regret, and one I hope to remedy in the future.

In addition, my focus, like my work on behalf of the United States Catholic Conference (now the United States Conference of Catholic Bishops), focuses primarily, though not exclusively, on the work of the institutional, hierarchical Church.

I have been able to treat only briefly the faith-based initiatives of laypeople and clergy, and the numerous nongovernmental organizations led by Christian Palestinians. Like the faith life of the people, that is work for another, fuller, social history of these last, tumultuous years.

While some, especially among those strongly committed to Jewish-Catholic dialogue, may fear that this treatment centered on problems in the relationship between the Church and the Israeli polity (and to a lesser extent the Palestinian Authority) will be unsettling, I believe that learning how the churches experienced these years and how they responded to the issues that confronted them can itself be healing, if only for others to understand the perspective out of which Palestinian Christians have acted. I hope my reporting and interpretation of that history will contribute to such understanding. Furthermore, where points of difference may remain, as, for example, in the relation of Oriental Christians to the Western or so-called "international" Jewish-Christian dialogue, awareness of the distinctive position of the Holy Land's Christians can be a stimulus to further growth in Jewish-Catholic relations by the inclusion of an essential but largely ignored voice.

I write as a knowledgeable amateur. I am not a historian, but a social ethicist by training and expertise, and, by God's grace and the goodwill of the U.S. bishops, I have served for more than a decade as a liaison between the U.S. Church and the churches and governments of the region. First as director of the United States Catholic Conference Office of International Justice and Peace (1991–1998), and now as counselor for international affairs to the bishops (1998–present), I have been a privileged witness of Church life in the Holy Land. In that capacity, I have come to know many Palestinian Christians and hold them in affection. As a canon of the Holy Sepulcher, I also have special ties to the Latin Patriarchate of Jerusalem. I owe a profound debt of gratitude as well to the many Jewish and Muslim colleagues who have added to my understanding of the present situation of Christians in the Holy Land and who work with me on behalf of justice and peace in the Holy Land.

### *Analytical Summary*

In historical terms, the 1990s represent as significant an alteration in Christian life as did the imposition of the expanded *millet* (autonomous community) system by the Ottomans in the eighteenth century. The increased ecumenical collaboration among the churches of the Holy Land, their joint witness on behalf of justice and peace, and the adoption by many of a self-conscious Arab Christian identity mark the last two decades as a watershed in Christian Palestinian history. Prolonged political crisis was the occasion for evolution of the churches of the Holy Land away from the Ottoman model of minority religious existence toward a new, relatively ecumenical form of self-conscious Palestinian Christianity.

For Palestinian Christians generally, several developments are worth noting:

1. The first intifada stimulated an unprecedented level of practical ecumenical co-operation among church leaders, but unity in response to issues of justice yielded neither unity in prayer and doctrine nor greater cooperation in sharing the Holy Places.
2. The intifada also resulted in a flowering of Palestinian liberation theology, par-ticularly among Protestants, and, for Catholics, in searching pastoral teaching on the part of the Latin patriarch.
3. Jerusalem, the foremost among Christian Holy Places, became the focus of nu-merous initiatives by the three patriarchs and heads of churches resident in the city, and at a very late stage their concerns and ideas played a significant role in deliberations on the future of the Holy City.
4. The churches' advocacy on behalf of justice, peace, and human rights for Pales-tinians created points of tension with Israeli government officials, and more re-cently with the Palestinian Authority, and led to accusations that the church leaders were meddling in politics.
5. Tension also exists within the Arab community between Christians and mili-tant Muslims as a result of militants' harassment of Christians and provocative acts such as demands for construction of a mosque in Nazareth.

For the Catholic Church, a number of additional points may be made:

1. The establishment of the Assembly of Catholic Bishops of the Holy Land con-tributed to uniting the Latin and Eastern Catholic churches in both pastoral and social action.
2. The appointment of a native Palestinian, Michel Sabbah, as Latin patriarch provided the Church with an exceptional leader at a time of enormous change.
3. The universal Church has provided important support for Palestinian Chris-tians through the visit of Pope John Paul II (2000), the Fundamental Agree-ment with Israel (1993), the Basic Agreement with the PLO (2000), and with various initiatives addressing the future of Jerusalem.
4. While, with the whole church in the Middle East, the church in the Holy Land has been concerned with its identity as an Arab church in a Muslim culture, the Catholic, and particularly the Latin, Church in the Holy Land has also taken ini-tiatives to open up a "local" dialogue with Judaism.

### Overview

The survey proceeds in four stages. The first section highlights the principal de-velopments of the last decade and a half. The second treats the growing ecumenism that has marked this period, and the third reviews the evolution of the Catholic Church. The fourth and last section looks at the relations between the churches and their neighbors: Muslims and Jews, the State of Israel, and the Palestinian Authority. I conclude with some brief observations on the prospects for the future of Christianity in the Holy Land.

## The Intifada and the Churches of the Holy Land

### The Churches of the Holy Land

Historically, the churches of the Holy Land have been divided according to their ecclesiastical and geographic origin. The first Christians gathered in Jerusalem after Jesus' ascension and a community formed on Mount Zion near the Cenacle, led by James, "the brother of the Lord." After the destruction of the city by Hadrian in the year 70, the Christians were permitted to resettle in the ruined city, again in the vicinity of Mount Zion.[6] While Jerusalem is "the mother church" and was honored by the Council of Nicaea (325), in Roman times metropolitan sees were established along the lines of political jurisdiction, so for more than four centuries Jerusalem was subordinate to the bishop of the Roman provincial center at Caesarea and the regional capital at Antioch.[7] As a formal church institution, therefore, the patriarchate of Jerusalem dates only to the tenure of Bishop Juvenal in the fifth century.[8]

After the split of the Eastern Church from the Western Church in 1054, Jerusalem became part of the Orthodox East. The Latin Patriarchate was founded after the flight of the Orthodox patriarch and the crusaders' conquest of Jerusalem in 1099. After the Muslim reconquest of the city, the title of Latin patriarch was preserved in Rome until the patriarchate was formally re-established in 1847. In the interim, the Western Christian presence at the Holy Places was preserved, with papal approval, by the Franciscan Custody of the Holy Land. Under the Status Quo established by the Ottomans in the nineteenth century, Franciscan friars continue to administer activities in most of the Catholic Holy Places.

The first Christian nation, the Armenians are also the oldest foreign Christian settlement in the Holy City, dating from the fourth century. Other ancient churches in the Holy Land include the Syrian Orthodox Church, the Coptic Orthodox Church, and the Ethiopian Orthodox Church. Other churches of west European origin, including the Anglican and Lutheran churches, arrived with the missionary expansions of the nineteenth century. The same period brought the establishment of national church institutions, such as Augusta Victoria Hospital, Dormition Abbey, and the Church of the Resurrection, all German foundations of Kaiser Wilhelm II. Through their consulates general in Jerusalem, the traditional Catholic powers (France, Belgium, Italy, and Austria) continue to exercise patronage toward institutions such as schools, hospitals, and orphanages that have historic ties to their home countries.[9]

### Intifada

The first intifada (1987–1993) marked a major transition in the evolution of Palestinian Christianity. Popular pressure drew the churches into the struggle of the Palestinian people. Christians did not want to be left out of the struggle of their people for liberation. The Palestinians' "shaking off" Israeli occupation, moreover, coincided with the appointment in 1987 of a Palestinian, Michel Sabbah, a native of Nazareth, as the Latin or Roman Catholic patriarch. Sabbah's appointment meant that for the first time in hundreds of years a Palestinian was leader of one of the principal churches in Jerusalem. Under local Palestinian leadership, the Catholic, Anglican, and Lutheran churches became advocates for their people. At critical moments, they joined other church leaders in Jerusalem in speaking out on behalf of their people's rights, the pursuit of peace, and Christian rights and interests in the Holy Land.

Another unintended consequence of the intifada was to foster grassroots ecumenism among the churches of the Holy Land. Identifying themselves as Palestinians, the Christian laity and clergy tended to put aside the traditional denominational badges that had divided them and to refer to themselves simply as "Christians." Political solidarity gave rise to signs of church unity. For example, outside the major centers, in the villages, Latins (Roman Catholics) adopted the Orthodox calendar for major feasts. (In Nazareth, Bethlehem, and Jerusalem, where pilgrims and international audiences expected the observance of the Western calendar, the churches continued to meet those expectations.) While the Greek hierarchy, at least, continued to spurn pastoral collaboration at the local level, the Arab laity and some of the parish clergy came to regard it as natural.

Despite its positive influence on ecumenical cooperation, the intifada exacted a high price from the Palestinian people. An uprising of young people, the movement disrupted the traditional authority of fathers over their families, spawning a variety of social ills, including incidents of family violence. Curfews and school closings interrupted and sometimes ended educational careers. Unemployment, confinement, and other factors contributed to drug problems that had previously been unknown. Closures, restrictive housing policies, demolitions, and confiscations led to late marriages and emigration by young people. These and other social ills created a demand for pastoral care and for social interventions on the part of the churches to stabilize the Christian presence in the Holy Land. But, even as church-based aid gave relief to the Palestinian poor and assisted economic development in hard times, some observers believed that the need for Christians to rely on church institutions for support reinforced older relationships of dependency and sometimes resulted in resentment on the part of the laity toward the institutional church.[10]

Tension between the Arab faithful and the hierarchy was particularly strong in the Greek Orthodox community. The Greek Orthodox Patriarchate's often secret sales of church-owned property to the Israelis infuriated Palestinians. Furthermore, while the Western churches (Latin, Anglican, and Lutheran) had local Palestinian leadership, which represented a decolonization of nineteenth-century church foundations, the Greek Orthodox Patriarchate remained firmly in the hands of a confraternity of Greek monks. Since only celibates may be ordained bishops in the Orthodox tradition, the married Arab parish clergy, with very few exceptions, were excluded from advancement. Protest grew to schism in 1998 when dissident clergy and laity, gathering in Amman, Jordan, announced the formation of an independent Arab Orthodox Church.

### Liberation Theology

Since the intifada was a popular liberation movement, it was natural that Palestinian Christians began to explore their own brand of liberation theology. Naim Ateek, an Anglican canon of Saint George's Cathedral, broke ground with the publication of his *Justice and Only Justice: A Palestinian Theology of Liberation* (1989). "A theology of liberation," he wrote, "is a way of speaking prophetically to a particular situation, especially where oppression, suffering and injustice have long reigned. God has something very relevant and very important to say to both the oppressed and the oppressors in the Middle East."[11] In the absence of a real opportunity to establish a binational state for Jews and Palestinians in the area that was Mandate Palestine, Ateek supported the establishment of a Palestinian state on the West Bank and in Gaza.

With the founding of Sabeel, an ecumenical liberation theology center, Ateek and his collaborators began to develop an international following for the Palestinian cause and the rights of Palestinian Christians. Church people from abroad attended the center's annual conference, and a network of supporters, the Friends of Sabeel, extended its work into Europe and North America. Sabeel's international connections also contributed to intellectual ferment in Western intellectual circles. Into its orbit came feminist theologian Rosemary Radford Ruether, independent Jewish "theologian" Marc Ellis, nonviolent activist Jim Douglass, and the Irish priest and scripture scholar Michael Prior.[12] In a contrast with a more narrowly construed liberationist style, Father Elias Chacour, a Melkite (Greek Catholic) pastor, offered a consistent message of reconciliation as the only route out of the Palestinian-Israeli conflict, the same lesson taught at the intergroup school he founded at Ibillin in the Galilee.[13]

The Roman Catholic contribution to this liberation theology came in the form of pastoral letters from the Latin patriarch (see "The Catholic Church in the Holy Land" below) and statements from the Justice and Peace Commission of the patriarchate.[14] Less overtly liberationist, these letters and statements nonetheless carried an agenda of liberation informed by biblical theology and Catholic social teaching. They addressed vital issues such as violence and nonviolence, the relation between justice and true peace, the defense of human rights, the Palestinian connection to the land, the relation of Oriental Christians to Judaism and the State of Israel, their relations with Islam, and the place of Christianity in Arab culture.

The practical face of the Catholic Church's commitment to the human rights for Palestinians may be found in the Society of Saint Yves, a legal aid society. Established with the support of the Latin Patriarchate in 1990 and headed by the outspoken Israeli advocate Lynda Brayer, Saint Yves first came to public attention during the 1991 Persian Gulf War when the Israeli Supreme Court ordered the government to distribute gas masks to Palestinians as well as to Jewish Israelis. Subsequently, Saint Yves made a name for itself in appeals against house demolition orders and the forced removal of Bedouins from their encampments.

### After Oslo (1993–2000)

The Oslo Accords, signed on September 13, 1993, marked an end to the intifada and the opening of an uncertain period of Palestinian history. Even as cooperation grew between the Palestinian Authority and the State of Israel, an uncertain half-peace bred occasions for confrontation. This period of protracted trouble and recurring crises was the matrix in which Palestinian Christian identity continued to evolve. The churches' advocacy on behalf of justice for Palestinians and their common ecclesiastical interests led to collective action. Twice in seven months, for example, church leaders took the unprecedented step of closing places of worship in protest of Israeli government policy. In April 1999, to protest inaction by Israeli police against Islamic fundamentalist violence against Christians in Nazareth, all churches were closed for two days; in November 1999, to manifest their objection to the laying of a cornerstone for a disputed mosque in Nazareth, the patriarchs and the Franciscan Custos closed the shrines of the Holy Land to pilgrims. The first action prompted the police to end the violence; the second had no apparent result.

Some of the most significant events for Palestinian Christians in the period after Oslo, however, came about as a result of outside initiatives by the Holy See. These were the Fundamental Agreement between the Holy See and the State of Israel, the Basic Agreement between the Holy See and the Palestine Liberation Organization, and advocacy on the future of Jerusalem in which the heads of churches in Jerusalem worked in tandem with initiatives from the Vatican. (For treatment of the pilgrimage of Pope John Paul II, see "The Great Jubilee and Papal Visit" below.)

### Fundamental Agreement

Little more than three months after the Oslo agreements were sealed, on December 30, 1993, the Holy See and the State of Israel signed a "Fundamental Agreement" as a framework for regularizing the Church's relation with the Jewish state. Within six months, the two parties had established diplomatic relations and exchanged ambassadors. The agreement affirmed common commitments to religious liberty, freedom of conscience, and the struggle against prejudice and anti-Semitism. It also affirmed the Catholic Church's institutional rights to conduct its own activities in worship, communications, education, social services, and health care.

The Fundamental Agreement was to be followed by two additional concordats, one providing "legal personality" to church bodies and institutions in Israel, the other determining fiscal rights and responsibilities. The first has been completed and ratified; the second is still under negotiation.

In the view of the Holy See, the Oslo Accords had overcome the mutual non-recognition of Israel and the Palestinians, a situation which until then had prevented the Holy See's full diplomatic engagement with Israel, a goal the world Jewish community had vigorously pursued. In addition to firming up the Church's rights in Israel, the establishment of relations offered an improved position from which to enter into discussion on the future of Jerusalem and the Holy Places when Israelis and Palestinians undertook final status talks.

Palestinian reactions to the agreement were hardly enthusiastic. Some felt recognition of the State of Israel gave too much too early to the Israelis. Non-Catholics feared that the agreement established a special relation between the Catholic Church and Israel to the disadvantage of other Christian churches. Orthodox critics worried that the agreement would undermine "the Status Quo" in the Holy Places, the arrangements governing the sharing of Christian shrines by several churches imposed by the Ottomans in the mid-nineteenth century. Israeli and Palestinian Catholics murmured that the agreement had been drafted at the international level over the heads of the local church. Nonetheless, the Fundamental Agreement advanced the legal standing of the Church in Israel, though, as events proved, much more slowly than it would have appeared at the time of the signing. (See "Implementing the Fundamental Agreement" below.)

### Holy See–PLO Basic Agreement

On February 15, 2000, five weeks before Pope John Paul II's pilgrimage to the Holy Land, the Vatican and the PLO announced the signing of a "Basic Agreement" with the Palestinians which in many respects paralleled the 1993 Fundamental Agreement with Israel.[15] Before dealing with protections for the Church itself, the accord affirmed freedom of religion and conscience. Though the phrase "freedom of religion and conscience" is enshrined in international law, rights of conscience had been a source of prolonged hesitation on the part of the Palestinian Authority because some Muslims regarded freedom of conscience as an opening for individual conversion, a possibility rejected by Islamic law. In a response to reactions of other churches to the 1993 Israeli accord, the agreement gave priority to the maintenance of the Status Quo in the Holy Places. The remainder of the document established guarantees for the freedom of believers and of Catholic institutions.

The major source of controversy over the agreement was the support in its preamble for Palestinian national goals and especially for the advancement of a common position on Jerusalem. The preamble of the agreement affirmed the signatories' hope for the realization of "the inalienable national aspirations of the Palestinian people." What stirred heated reaction on the part of the Israeli government and some Jewish commentators, however, was the document's expressed concern for "an equitable solution for Jerusalem" and denunciation of unilateral Israeli actions affecting the Holy City.

Critics seemed to forget that for thirty years the Vatican had pursued "an internationally guaranteed special statute" for Jerusalem (see "Jerusalem" immediately below) and adhered to the view of the international community that East Jerusalem was illegally occupied. In a 1998 address, the Vatican Foreign Minister, Archbishop Jean-Louis Tauran, had underscored this point, declaring the existing situation of the city "a case of manifest international injustice . . . brought about and . . . maintained by force."[16] While technically the preambular language of the Vatican-PLO agreement was not legally binding, it brought the Vatican to the Palestinian side on the larger issue. It also associated one of the future negotiating partners, the Palestinians, with the Vatican's plea for a special internationally guaranteed statute for the city.

### Jerusalem

Throughout the 1990s, Jerusalem had been a source of contention between the government of Israel and the churches. Repeatedly the local churches and churches abroad protested Israeli annexation and confiscation of land in and around Jerusalem as violations of international law and the expectation set by the Oslo Accords that matters relating to Jerusalem would be settled in a final status agreement. Furthermore, the closure of the city to local Palestinian pilgrims and the denial of freedom of movement to clergy and church officials from the West Bank to Jerusalem was a constant irritant. In addition, the Municipality of Jerusalem and the national Finance Ministry attempted to collect taxes and assess penalties for alleged past nonpayment from Catholic shrines and Christian nongovernmental organizations (NGOs) in the city, in defiance of historical immunities and, in the case of Catholic institutions, a "freeze," under terms of the Fundamental Agreement, on changes in tax status until a new treaty on financial matters had been concluded.

In November 1994, the patriarchs and heads of churches published a memorandum, "On the Significance of Jerusalem for Christians" (see "Memorandum on Jerusalem" below). The memorandum affirmed the universal religious significance of Jerusalem, rejected the proposition that Jerusalem belonged to just one people or one religion, and asked for a special statute with international guarantees to secure the attachment of Jews, Christians, and Muslims to the Holy City.

In response, a group of U.S. church leaders, including William Cardinal Keeler, then president of the National Conference of Catholic Bishops and U.S. Catholic Conference, wrote President Bill Clinton in March 1995 supporting the memorandum and asking the president to use his influence to oppose unilateral Israeli actions intended to affect facts on the ground in Jerusalem. Subsequently, Churches for Middle East Peace (CMEP), a Washington-based coalition of church offices working on Mideast peace issues, published an ad in the *New York Times* promoting a "shared Jerusalem," and local groups replicated the ad in several regional papers around the United States. In July 2000, as the Camp David II talks took place, CMEP placed a second series of advertisements in U.S. denominational journals around the "shared Jerusalem" theme.

In April 1996 the Holy See authorized the apostolic delegate in Jerusalem and the nuncio to Israel, Archbishop Andrea Cordero Lanza di Montezemolo, to discuss the future of Jerusalem with White House and State Department officials and members of Congress during a visit to Washington. Later that spring, in keeping with the anticipated opening of final status negotiations, the Vatican Secretariat of State published an unprecedented public paper titled "Considerations of the Secretariat of State on Jerusalem," delineating the Church's thinking on the question.[17]

"Considerations" enumerated the concerns Israeli and Palestinian negotiators should include in an internationally guaranteed special statute: (1) recognition of the universal significance and uniqueness of Jerusalem; (2) preservation of the historical, cultural, and environmental heritage of the city; (3) equality of rights for all its citizens whatever their faith; (4) freedom for the three religious communities to operate in all their institutional expressions; and (5) freedom of access for local (Palestinian) as well as international pilgrims to the Holy Places. "Considerations" was followed in June by an authoritative commentary in the Jesuit journal *Civiltà Cattolica*.[18]

The "special statute," sometimes confusingly translated as "special status," was repeatedly misrepresented in the media, sometimes by diplomats, and even occasionally by scholars, as a call for "internationalization" of the city. First proposed by Pope Paul VI following the 1967 Six-Day War, the statute was offered as an alternative to internationalization as represented by the *corpus separatum* envisaged in the 1947 United Nations Partition Plan for Palestine. According to that proposal, Jerusalem and much of the surrounding area would have been under international administration. By contrast, the statute only proposes a set of binding treaty provisions drafted, negotiated, and approved by the signatories of an Israeli-Palestinian peace agreement. It would require "international guarantees" to provide a court of appeal in the event of noncompliance by the sovereign government(s) charged with its implementation. With the Vatican position clearly articulated in "Considerations," Vatican and United States Catholic Conference staff undertook consultations with U.S., Israeli, Palestinian, and European diplomats to make the Church's views known in preparation for discussion of the religious dimensions of the Jerusalem question in the final status talks.

In October 1998, Latin Patriarch of Jerusalem Michel Sabbah convoked a symposium for heads of episcopal conferences and their representatives on the future of Jerusalem. The feature event of the symposium was an opening address by Archbishop Jean-Louis Tauran, the Holy See's foreign minister. Tauran attempted to dispel the mistaken impression that all that concerned the Holy See was access to the Holy Places. "The distinction made between 'the question of the holy places and the question of Jerusalem,'" he declared, "is unacceptable to the Holy See." He went on to affirm that "the Holy See is indeed interested in [the political] aspect [of the Jerusalem question] and has a right and duty to be, especially in so far as the matter remains unresolved and is the cause of conflict, injustice, human rights violations, restrictions of religious freedom and conscience, fear and personal insecurity."[19] The archbishop identified with "the majority in the international community" as expressed in the pertinent U.N. resolutions.[20] Tauran concluded his address by urging the participants to be "ambassadors of Jerusalem. . . ."[21] In line with Archbishop Tauran's request, European, North American, and Latin American bishops' conference presidents convened separately at the time of the symposium to begin their own informal coordination in support of the Church of Jerusalem.

### Ecumenical Interaction

#### Ecumenical Initiatives

As we have seen, the intifada forced the Christian churches to overcome their traditional rivalries in support of the Christian Palestinian people. (See "Intifada" above.) As the struggle against Israeli occupation grew, the laity identified less with denominational adherence and more with simply being Palestinian Christians. In response, the hierarchs of the Jerusalem churches found it necessary to come together to address the issues of pressing concern to their peoples. Together they published pastoral statements and took initiatives on common problems. They continue to meet regularly to discuss common business, and they convene on an emergency basis to address crises like the opening of the Hasmonean Tunnel and the final status talks at Camp David.

## *Memorandum on Jerusalem*

In the period after Oslo, cooperative efforts among the patriarchs and heads of churches grew in visibility. In November 1994, the patriarchs and heads of churches published a joint memorandum entitled "On The Significance of Jerusalem for Christians." (Also, see "Jerusalem" above.) They wrote, "[T]he experience of history teaches us that in order for Jerusalem to be a city of peace . . . it cannot belong exclusively to one people or to only one religion. Jerusalem should be open to all, shared by all."[22] The document went on to affirm the rights of the Christians of Jerusalem as well as the rights of Jews and Muslims in the city. It also proposed "a special statute for Jerusalem . . . in order to satisfy the national aspirations of all its inhabitants, and in order that Jews, Christians and Muslims can be 'at home' with one another. . . ."[23] Like the Holy See, the Jerusalem church leaders called for international guarantees to help implement the statute. "Jerusalem," they wrote, "is too precious to be dependent solely on municipal or national political authorities, whoever they may be."[24]

## *Hasmonean Tunnel*

In a highly provocative move, in 1996 the government of Israeli Prime Minister Benjamin Netanyahu opened the Hasmonean Tunnel under the Haram al-Sharif or Temple Mount, a site theretofore accessible only to archaeologists, to the public. The heads of churches joined Muslim leaders in protesting the government's action as a stimulus to incitement. They also censured the move as a unilateral change in Jerusalem contrary to the Oslo Accords. Latin Patriarch Michel Sabbah led a silent, candlelit procession of Christians of all denominations through the Old City in prayer for peace. Responding to the procession, Mr. Uri Mor, director of Christian Communities Affairs in the Israeli Ministry of Religion, charged Patriarch Sabbah with meddling in politics. The United States Catholic Conference defended the patriarch, as it had done before, affirming the duty of bishops to defend human rights, and to promote justice and peace.

## *Denial of Jerusalem Residency*

Israel's withdrawal of Jerusalem residency from Palestinians who claimed Jerusalem as their home was another issue which pitted the patriarchs and heads of churches against the Israeli government. The Likud government of Benjamin Netanyahu had been confiscating residency permits from Palestinians who, according to Israeli authorities, no longer made Jerusalem "the center of their lives." Couples who had to move to have space to raise a family due to the prohibitive housing conditions created for Arab Jerusalemites by the government, those who had married spouses from the West Bank, those who had to move abroad to find remunerative work, even graduate students out of the country for more than a couple of years, all were denied the right to make Jerusalem their home.[25]

For church leaders in Jerusalem, the denial of residency was a pastoral and ecclesial issue as well as a political one. As pastors, they were committed both to promoting a strong family life for their people and to maintaining "the living Christian presence in the Holy Land." The lack of housing deliberately created by Israeli policies resulted in overcrowded homes and family tensions. Most of all, it forced young people to delay marriage, frequently to their mid- and late thirties, and, when couples planned to marry, it built pressures for emigration. Subsequent Israeli government policies denied marriages celebrated in Palestinian territories recognition in Israel, forcing spouses to leave the city to take up family residence on the West Bank. In an effort to relieve these pressures, the churches had built hundreds of units of housing for young families, but these church-sponsored projects could only meet a small part of the need.

In a recent survey, more than a third of respondents on the West Bank and in Jerusalem, and a quarter of the respondents in Israel, agreed with the statement, "If I could, I would emigrate myself."[26] Among Christians in Israel more than 40 percent thought "Israeli restrictions" were the primary motive for emigration, with lack of employment and Islamization as the next most important factors. For West Bank and Jerusalem residents, lack of employment was the number one factor, followed by Israeli restrictions and lack of housing.[27]

Together, the withdrawal of residency permits and adverse Israeli housing policies for Palestinians were a principal cause of the emigration of Christians from the Holy Land. From the point of view of the churches, the crisis of emigration was particularly acute in Jerusalem, the site of Jesus' ministry, passion, death, resurrection, and ascension, and, therefore, Christianity's foremost Holy Place. By the year 2000, there were only about 5,000 Palestinian Christians (perhaps as few as 4,500) living in Jerusalem, down from 10,000 in 1967, and from more than 30,000 in 1948. Without a "living Christian presence," as Church officials did not tire of repeating, the Christian Holy Places in Jerusalem were threatened with becoming mere museums and tourist stops. After a dramatic increase in the rate of confiscations, the patriarchs and heads of churches wrote in 1999 to Israeli Interior Minister Eli Suissa, protesting the policy. Subsequently the heads of corresponding churches in the United States, including Bishop Joseph Fiorenza, president of the National Conference of Catholic Bishops and United States Catholic Conference, wrote a joint letter in support of the Jerusalem church leaders.

In the spring of 2000, then Israeli Justice Minister Yossi Beilin and then Infrastructure Minister Natan Sharansky announced the confiscation policy would be rescinded and thousands of canceled permits would be reissued. Church officials report, however, that at the bureaucratic level little has happened to reverse the policy. Confiscations continue, but at a slower pace, and there has been no progress on restoration of the invalidated papers.

### Final Status Talks

During the failed July 2000 final status talks between Palestinian President Yasser Arafat and Israeli Prime Minister Ehud Barak at Camp David, Maryland, the leaders of the Jerusalem churches again came together in the hope that joint action might make their concerns heard. After first writing the negotiators to offer their prayers for the success of the talks, the three patriarchs sent an urgent message to Barak, Arafat, and U.S. President Bill Clinton on July 20, opposing a well-reported proposal for annexation of the Armenian Quarter to Israel. They also requested a consultative status in the talks. According to several sources, the Palestinian side had already agreed in negotiation to the annexation in discussions over the future of Jerusalem.

Days after, as the talks themselves were about to collapse, Palestinian and Israeli officials met separately with the three churchmen. They were assured that Christian concerns would be taken into account in future negotiations, that they or their representatives would be consulted in discussions over Jerusalem and particularly the disposition of the Old City, and that international guarantees as part of arrangements for Jerusalem were admissible. Progress had been made, it appears, in placing Christian concerns on the agenda. Following the collapse of the Camp David talks, U.S., Palestinian, and Israeli representatives visited Rome to consult with Vatican officials and promised further consultations with the churches.

### The Great Jubilee and Papal Visit

For the Christian churches, and especially for the Roman Catholic Church, the year 2000 marked the Great Jubilee of the Birth of Jesus Christ. Pope John Paul II in a 1994 apostolic exhortation, *Tertio Millennio Adveniente,* made the preparation for the jubilee a major effort in church renewal.[28] He exhorted the whole church to self-examination and reconciliation, especially in relation to offenses against other churches and other world religions. He himself led the way with a special service of pardon at Saint Peter's on the first Sunday of Lent 2000, which included a "confession of sins committed against the people of Israel" and for "sins committed in the service of truth," i.e., religious intolerance.[29] This followed a controverted 1998 reflection from the Vatican's Commission for Relations with the Jews on the Shoah or Holocaust entitled "We Remember."[30] At a meeting of the International Catholic-Jewish Liaison Committee, the Jewish cochair, Dr. Gerhard Riegner, had expressed serious disappointment that the document "[avoided] taking a clear position on the direct relation between the teaching of contempt and the political and cultural climate that made the Shoah possible."[31]

The pope made public his desire to be a pilgrim to the Holy Land as part of his observance of the jubilee. Explicit commitment for the visit, however, was a matter of on-again, off-again talks between the Holy See and the government of Israel, with a firm decision being taken only late in 1999. The visit became one of the great successes of Pope John Paul's pontificate. His meetings with Israeli leaders, his visit to Yad Vashem, the Israeli Holocaust memorial, and his prayer at the Western Wall won over the Israeli public and politicians, and Jews abroad. Suspicions raised by "We Remember," the service of pardon, the proposed canonization of Pius XII, and other issues were mooted. Jewish-Catholic relations entered a new era of good feeling with a higher level of mutual confidence. "Here, right now," Israeli Prime Minister Ehud Barak told the holy father at Yad Vashem, "time itself has come to a standstill." The prime minister also noted that "the righteous gentiles" who risked their lives to save Jews from the Holocaust were "mostly children of your faith."[32]

The first full day of the pilgrimage took place in the Palestinian Self-Rule Area of Bethlehem. It included a papal mass in Manger Square, a visit with Palestinian President Yasser Arafat, and an appearance at the Deheisheh refugee camp in the vicinity of Bethlehem. Local Christians took pride in the celebration of parts of several multilingual liturgies in Arabic. They were delighted too that the largest public event ever held in Israel was a mass for youth at Tabghe near the Mount of Beatitudes where 150,000 pilgrims from around the world joined with them in prayer. In addition, at Nazareth, the pope received the *acta* of the recently concluded synod of the Latin Church, thereby approving plans for renewal of the local church.

In accepting the welcome of Palestinian National Authority President Yasser Arafat, the pope acknowledged the suffering of the Palestinian people: "No one can ignore how much the Palestinian people have had to suffer in recent decades. Your torment is before the eyes of the world. And it has gone on too long."[33] The holy father went on to affirm the right of the Palestinians to a national homeland and the right of Palestinian refugees to homes of their own.

### Elusive Ecumenical Concord

On the Christian ecumenical front, the jubilee was only a modest success. The restoration of the dome of the Holy Sepulcher, completed in 1997, with the help of the Pontifical Mission (and Catholic Near East Welfare Association), seemed to open an auspicious period of cooperation among the churches which had to agree to the work plan for the restoration. But similar cooperation was not forthcoming for the restoration, or even the cleaning, of either the Church of the Holy Sepulcher, known in the East as the Church of the Resurrection, or the Church of the Nativity in Bethlehem.

With a vision of throngs of pilgrims crowding the Holy Sepulcher for the jubilee, Uri Mor of Israel's Department for Christian Community Affairs pressed the churches to agree to the opening of an emergency exit to the church. For centuries, there has been only one door to the church, and during the Orthodox Holy Fire ceremony on Holy Saturday the door is barred shut. During the 1998 ceremony, Israeli police had to intervene to break up a melee between Greeks and Syrians over questions of precedence at the holy site, creating very reasonable apprehension of a conflagration. But, after two years of negotiation, no agreement could be reached over opening the exit. Old ecclesiastical rivalries continued to rule.

Jerusalem church leaders did come together to mark the opening of the jubilee in Manger Square on December 4, 1999. They could not agree, however, to recite the Lord's Prayer together. Furthermore, in welcoming Pope John Paul II, Greek Orthodox Patriarch Diodoros I warned Catholics against proselytizing through their work in education and social service. For his part, the pope urged that "in the Holy Land where Christians live side by side with the followers of Judaism and Islam, where there are almost daily tensions and conflicts, it is essential to overcome the scandalous impression given by our disagreements and arguments."[34]

### The Catholic Church in the Holy Land

The Catholic Church in the Holy Land consists of five Eastern Catholic churches and the Western Latin (or Roman) Catholic Church. The most numerous of these is the Melkite or Greek Catholic Church, concentrated in Galilee with a patriarchal vicar in Jerusalem. The second in size is the Latin Church, whose patriarchal seat is Jerusalem. Both jurisdictions, besides Israel proper, embrace Jerusalem, the Palestinian Territories, and Jordan. (The Latin and Maronite jurisdictions also include Cyprus.) In addition, there are some 5,000 Maronite Christians, and smaller groups of Armenian, Syrian, and Chaldaean Catholics. The Latin patriarch also serves as ordinary for the Community of Saint James, an association of Hebrew-speaking Christians. (The diocesan synod of 1996–2000 recommended that the Holy See assign this community its own "ordinary," i.e., ecclesiastical superior, from its own number, and in August 2003 Pope John Paul II named Benedictine abbot Jean-Baptiste Garion auxilliary bishop of the Latin Patriarchate of Jerusalem with responsibility for the Hebrew-speaking Catholic community in Israel.) According to the 1999 edition of the *Annuaire de l'Eglise Catholique en Terre Sainte,* there are some 72,000 Latin Catholics, 94,000 Melkites (Greek Catholics), and 13,000 Maronites in the Holy Land, with Armenian, Syrian, Chaldaean, and Hebrew-speaking Catholics each numbering only in the hundreds, for a total of approximately 180,000.[35] These figures do not reflect large numbers of Catholic, especially Filipino, guest workers or of Russian immigrants to Israel who have recently sought pastoral care from the Catholic Church.

### *The Assembly of Catholic Bishops*
The 1990s saw major changes strengthening the Catholic Church in the Holy Land. During the first half of the decade the apostolic delegate, Archbishop Andrea Cordero Lanza de Montezemolo, oversaw the establishment of the Assembly

of Catholic Ordinaries of the Holy Land. The Assembly brought into coordination the Latin or Roman Catholic Church and the Eastern churches (Melkite, Maronite, Syrian, Armenian, Chaldaean) in communion with Rome as well as the Franciscan Custos or Guardian of the Holy Land.

Because the Eastern churches are independent units within the universal Church, an inter-ritual structure, respecting the patriarchal autonomy of the Oriental churches, was needed to differentiate the assembly from the national episcopal structures found in most other countries. All the same, the Latin patriarch, not one of the prelates of the Oriental churches, was named *ex officio* as president of the assembly. The assembly permits the bishops to coordinate strategy on pastoral matters, such as catechetics, marriage, and the liturgical calendar, and to cooperate in preparation of special events, such as the Great Jubilee and the papal pilgrimage. It also has provided a forum for interaction with Israeli government officials and political leaders. Overall, the assembly has promoted integrated action by the Catholic Church in Israel and the Palestinian Territories.

### A Palestinian Patriarch

Pope John Paul II's 1987 appointment of Michel Sabbah as patriarch of Jerusalem for the Latins was a watershed for the history of the Catholic Church in the region. For the first time in eight hundred years a Palestinian had been named to the See of Saint James. A native of Nazareth and a priest of the Latin Patriarchate, until his appointment Sabbah served as a professor of Arabic literature and a village pastor. The pride of his flock in Sabbah's position may be seen in the annual Palm Sunday procession from Bethpage on the Mount of Olives to Saint Ann's Church near Saint Stephen's Gate. The procession, with the patriarch and ranking clerics in the position of honor, has become a symbol of Christian solidarity, with thousands of Palestinians marching, watching along the procession's path, and crowding the grounds of Saint Ann's to hear the patriarch's message and to receive his blessing at the end of the march.

### Pastoral Teaching and Witness

An important aspect of Patriarch Sabbah's ministry has been his public teaching through pastoral letters, public statements, homilies, and messages, particularly at Christmas and Easter. He has employed his pastoral letters to bolster the identity of his people, to nourish their consciousness as Oriental, Arab Christians, to address the injustices suffered by the Palestinians generally, and to witness the requirements of a just peace that requires more than the mere cessation of conflict.

In a 1993 pastoral letter entitled "Reading the Bible in the Land of the Bible," Sabbah took up the problems of biblical interpretation presented to Palestinian Christianity by Zionist claims to the land of Israel, made by both Jews and some

American evangelicals such as the Christian Embassy.[36] He refused to let the terms of Jewish and Christian relations be set by post-Holocaust Christians in the West, proposing that the Jewish-Christian dialogue in the Holy Land must begin with local history and local circumstances, particularly the century-long Palestinian-Israeli struggle. He meditated on the long history of suffering and subjugation the Palestinian Christians had endured, and, invoking the mystery of the cross, he admonished his people to accept their difficult vocation to witness to the gospel in the land where it was first preached.

Patriarch Sabbah also penned the introduction to a 1998 text, "Seek Peace and Pursue It," a short catechism on the Christian approach to peace and justice in the Holy Land, published by the Latin Patriarchate.[37] In his introduction, Sabbah affirmed the right and the duty of church leaders to speak out against injustice. The text itself opposed political stands which imposed on oppressed people the duty to remain silent and refrain from demanding their rights.

"Seek Peace" also warned against the resort to violence in the defense of human rights as conducive of still greater violence against the oppressed themselves, and, in keeping with Catholic teaching, opposed terrorism as a "criminal" act. Legitimate recourse to force, it taught, is a last resort after all other means have been tried without success. At the same time, the peace catechism concluded that "for Israelis as for Palestinians, justice means mutual recognition of the human dignity and of all the rights of the other, political, civil and religious."[38] Rejecting the radicalization of religion for the sake of political struggle, the catechism identifies the Church's role as the defense of humanity. "Although her members belong to one or another group or people in conflict," the catechism affirms, "[the Church] has concern for the good of both parties. For she is at the service of the human person as such, thus at the service of all."[39]

### Relations with Jews

While he accepts the course set by the Second Vatican Council for Catholic relations with Jews, including the rejection of the so-called "teaching of contempt" and the medieval charge of "deicide" against the Jewish people, Patriarch Sabbah has expressed reservations about the applicability of the conclusions of the Euro-American Jewish-Catholic dialogue for Oriental Christians. The history of Christianity in the Orient after the Islamic conquest is different than that of Western Europe. For centuries, like Jews, Christians had lived as *dhimmi*, or members of a protected minority, under Muslim domination. Also, like Jews, the Holy Land's Christians had suffered as victims of Western aggression and imperialism. During the Crusades, they were killed and abused along with Muslims and Jews. During the last century, they continued to suffer from Western meddling in Palestine and from the injustice worked on the Palestinian people by many Zionists and Israelis with

Western encouragement. These injustices as much as the European Holocaust, as Sabbah sees it, need to inform the context of the Jewish-Christian dialogue in the Holy Land. Indirectly, they should also color the international dialogue as well.

These reservations notwithstanding, Patriarch Sabbah has endeavored to open a dialogue with Israeli Jews. In the Christian environment of Jerusalem, where the Oriental Orthodox and Greek Orthodox churches, based on the anti-Judaism of some church fathers, continue to refuse to adopt new attitudes toward the Jews, making progress in the Jewish-Christian dialogue is a struggle. Patriarch Sabbah has taken a number of initiatives to jump-start the conversation. In two meetings with Israel's chief rabbis, for example, he has underscored the need for the two re-ligions to join in dialogue, to bring Muslims into their conversation, and to collab-orate in the cause of peace. The first of these encounters was a personal victory of sorts in that only weeks before Ashkenazi Chief Rabbi Meir Lau had publicly pro-fessed ignorance that there was a Latin patriarch of Jerusalem. In these first, tenta-tive efforts, the Latin Church has functioned as a bridge between the wider Chris-tian community and the observant Jews in Israel.

### International Role

Patriarch Sabbah's leadership skills have been recognized far beyond the Holy Land. He has served as president of the Council of Catholic Patriarchs of the East, and from 1994 to 1998 as co-president of the Middle East Council of Churches. He is president of the Conference of Latin Bishops in the Arab World. In 1999, he was elected international president of Pax Christi International, a broad-based Catholic peace movement. In an exceptional appointment, Pope John Paul II in 2000 named him a member of the council of cardinals supervising Vatican finances.

## Christians and Their Neighbors

### Christian and Muslim in the Arab World

As Palestinians and Arab Israelis, Palestinian Christians feel a kinship with Mus-lims and a pride in their Arab culture. Christians led the Arab Awakening of the late nineteenth and early twentieth century. They were among the founders of secu-lar Arab political movements.[40] At the beginning of the twenty-first century, faced with the success of Zionism and rise of "political Islam," Middle East Christians have reaffirmed their bonds with their Muslim neighbors and their attachment to a common Arab culture.

The Church's attitude to Islam must be taken in the context of the unique reli-gious circumstances of the Middle East as the birthplace of the three Abrahamic religions. Recalling the golden age of Islamic culture, for example, the Catholic patriarchs of the East have noted in a pastoral letter, entitled "Together Before God for the Common Good of the Person and Society: The Co-existence of Muslims and Christians in the Arab World" (1994), that in addition to historic conflicts, the great monotheistic religions have also "lived through centuries of communication, interaction and collaboration."[41] They contended, moreover, that the coexistence of Christians and Muslims is "fundamental to the identity of our churches in the design of the universal Church."[42] Acting on recommendations of the 1999 First Congress of Patriarchs and Bishops of the East, the patriarchs counseled that the three religions "ought to make the effort to surmount present difficulties and create the conditions required for frank and constructive encounter for the good of the [Middle East] and of the world."[43] In the same spirit, the patriarchs also endorsed the development of "a dialogue with Judaism [rooted] in present circumstances taking into account the demands of justice, peace and reconciliation and points of religious convergence."[44]

Middle Eastern Christians continue to see themselves as a bridge between Islam and Christianity, between the Arab world and the West (including Israel). Citing "Together Before God," the Catholic patriarchs observed, "Our life in common over the course of long centuries represents a fundamental and incomparable experience. It partakes of the will of God for [Christians] and for [Muslims]."[45] Addressing the religious revival in the Arab world and elsewhere, they wrote, "A healthy religious attitude could be a positive element in guiding contemporary history if religion returns to its pure sources, apart from sectarian and aggressive tendencies."[46] The pastoral letter goes on to relinquish the nineteenth-century strategy of seeking special privileges for the Church and its members, and urges the faithful to assume, alongside Muslims (and Jews), the responsibilities of full and equal citizenship in the societies to which they belong. The letter exposes the trap of confessionalism, pleads for dialogue to overcome mutual ignorance and prejudice, and endorses religious pluralism.

The relations of Christian and Muslim Palestinians in the Holy Land must be understood in the context of this mediating role of Christians in the Middle East. It is commonly said that in the place of formal inter-religious dialogue with Muslims, Palestinian Christians carry out a dialogue of daily life. Muslims, for example, are frequently enrolled in greater numbers than Christians in Catholic schools, and they often outnumber Christians as the recipients of aid from Catholic donor agencies. Still, some tensions are apparent.

### Demography

The first tension is a demographic one. Muslim couples tend to have larger families than Christians do. With more family connections overseas and higher levels of educational attainment, moreover, Christians are inclined to emigrate at higher rates than Muslims. Accordingly, Muslims have begun to outnumber Christians even in such traditional Christian strongholds as Bethlehem and Nazareth. In the Old City of Jerusalem, Christians have sold so many properties and businesses that the majority of residents and business proprietors in the Christian Quarter today are said to be Muslim. This shift in the demographic balance is a constant source of anxiety for those Christians who remain.

### Fundamentalism

A second source of tension is the growth of Islamic fundamentalism. The causes and degree of anti-Christian activity on the part of the Islamists are hard to assess. For example, David Bar-Ilan, spokesman of former Prime Minister Benjamin Netanyahu, greatly exaggerated the scope of anti-Christian activity by Muslim fundamentalists, and he wrongly attributed it to conspiracy organized by the PLO. Church officials admitted there had been some incidents of harassment, sometimes by low-level Palestinian officials acting on their own, but they denied that there was any systematic discrimination or persecution. Their repudiation of the charges was corroborated by the Palestinian Human Rights Monitoring Group.[47]

Nonetheless, provocative acts against Christians seem to be on the rise in all parts of the Holy Land, in both Israel and the Palestinian Territories. With the success of the Islamic Movement, a militant Muslim political party in Israel, Christian fear of radical Islam is especially acute. Opinion research shows that Israeli Christians see Islamization as the number two threat to Arab Christians, just behind economic deterioration and unemployment.[48] The three-year occupation until spring 2002 of land adjacent to the Church of the Annunciation in Nazareth is the most conspicuous incident of anti-Christian provocation to date. The Nazareth episode illustrates how complicated it can be to assess what the sources of anti-Christian activity may be.[49]

### The Nazareth Mosque Controversy

In the fall of 1997, militants from the Islamic Movement occupied land adjacent to the Church of the Annunciation, Nazareth's foremost Christian shrine. The property had been designated by the Nazareth Municipality at the prompting of the Israeli Ministry of Tourism for construction of a square and a bus parking area to accommodate the influx of pilgrims anticipated for the Great Jubilee in 2000. The protestors claimed that the property was *waqf* (Muslim trust) land because a small memorial to Shehab al-Din, an Islamic scholar and nephew of the Saladin, stood on a corner of the space.

The dispute was quickly entangled in politics. It became an opportunity for the Islamic Movement, a fundamentalist Muslim party, to win enough votes to control the municipal council by a one-vote majority. The Islamic Movement, in turn, functioned as the vehicle for disempowered Arabs who had come to Nazareth in 1948 to express their discontent with the Christian-Muslim alliance, Hadash, the party of the urban elite, which had ruled Nazareth for decades. With a Christian as incumbent mayor and a Muslim majority in the council, the municipal government became deadlocked.

Initially the Israeli government promised church officials that the issue would be resolved in court. During the spring 1999 elections, however, government ministers from three right-wing Israeli parties, including Likud, sought votes among Israeli Arabs with promises of aiding the construction of a mosque on the site. The outgoing Likud government announced a compromise in which a modest building for a shrine to Shehab al-Din, but not a mosque, could be constructed. In September 1999, the Israeli District Court decided against the Islamic Movement, ruling that the property was state land. Within days, however, the new government of Prime Minister Ehud Barak announced a further "compromise" in which a mosque of larger proportions would be constructed on part of the site as well as on adjoining land to be purchased from private owners. The projected square would be built on the land immediately adjacent to the basilica and a wall constructed to divide the two.

The Holy See, the U.S. bishops' conference, and other Catholic groups denounced the decision as provocative. United States Catholic Conference president Bishop Joseph Fiorenza suggested the Israeli government's action pointed to its inability to serve as guardian of the Holy Places. Locally, the patriarchs and heads of churches along with the Franciscan Custos closed all the Christian shrines for two days in protest. International pressure came from the Arab world as well, with Muslim authorities in several countries condemning the provocative gesture as an attempt to divide the Arab Israeli community. The government of Saudi Arabia offered to pay for construction of the mosque but only on condition that it would be erected at another site.

During his jubilee pilgrimage, Pope John Paul II and Vatican Secretary of State Angelo Sodano requested that the Israeli government revoke its decision. Meanwhile, Minister Haim Ramon wrote to leaders of the Islamic Movement in July 2000 to say that the mosque would be built as agreed at government expense. Nonetheless, protest leaders attempted to goad the government into action by unloading building supplies at the site, preempting the government's announced one-year delay in construction out of respect for the jubilee.

In response to international pressure, the Sharon government set up a special committee under Housing Minister Natan Scharansky to reconsider its previous decision. The Scharansky Commission proposed a number of alternative sites for the mosque,[50] and in March 2002 the Sharon government voted to terminate the project. The Muslim activists rejected all alternatives,[51] with one local leader claiming "we will stay here and continue building."[52] By March 2003 the mosque was half-complete, as a result of nighttime building by the activists and the absence of police enforcement, and a district court ordered its full demolition. While the immediate threat to the Church of the Annunciation has been forestalled, harsh feelings remain.

The effort to construct the Nazareth mosque, especially in the absence of any other moves to reassure Israeli Christians of the government's goodwill, unnerved Galilee's Christians and diminished their trust in the national government. The unprecedented police tolerance of the Islamic Movement's demonstrations, their inaction during anti-Christian rioting at Easter 1998, and exceptional travel permits granted Muslim demonstrators from the West Bank and Gaza had already created deep suspicion of Israeli collusion in the affair and increased fear for the future of the Christian presence in Israel. Public opinion research shows that, by a two-to-one margin, Christians see the Israeli government as the principal source of the tensions in Nazareth.[53] (Respondents, it is worth noting, attribute Muslim-Christian tensions in the Bethlehem area almost equally to Islamic fundamentalism and Israeli government instigation.)[54]

### State of Israel

Interaction between the Catholic Church and the State of Israel takes place at least at two levels. One consists in relations with the Vatican and the international church. The other is with the local, mostly Palestinian church. It often appears as if Israeli officials prefer to work with the Holy See rather than deal with the local church. Such triangulation may also be found in relations between the Israeli government and other local churches. The most egregious case of this sort is government openness to the so-called Christian Embassy, a group of American evangelicals with Zionist leanings used to counter the indigenous (and international) Christian sentiment critical of Israeli policies or sympathetic to the Palestinians. Many pilgrim and study groups as well as ecumenical delegations of visiting Catholic prelates and Protestant church leaders, either sponsored or hosted by the government of Israel, are used to bolster support for Israel and to blunt the influence of local Christians on the worldwide Christian opinion. Of course, such triangulation works both ways, and the local church, for its part, gets aid and considerable clout from its Vatican and other international Catholic, Protestant, and Orthodox ties as well.

### Implementing the Fundamental Agreement

The 1993 Fundamental Agreement between Israel and the Holy See was justly hailed as a major development in the relations between the Catholic Church and the State of Israel, and was warmly received by Catholics and Jews worldwide (see "Fundamental Agreement" above). Implementation of the agreement, however, proved very slow. More than three years after the agreement was signed the Vatican signatory, Monsignor Claudio Maria Celli, told an audience at the Catholic University of America that on nearly every point the agreement was still to be executed. In the interim, there had been numerous incidents of bureaucratic tension between Israeli government officials and the local church, international church bodies, and the Vatican. As director of the Office of International Justice and Peace of the United States Catholic Conference, I observed in a November 1996 presentation at the Israeli Embassy to the United States that the agreement seemed to be treated as a landmark in Jewish-Catholic relations rather than as a binding international agreement.

Five and a half years after the signing, the treaty was finally published in the official gazette of the Israeli government, placing government bureaus under obligation to observe its provisions. Under Ehud Barak's premiership, moreover, the Israeli government took additional initiatives to prevent problems from arising and to better manage relations with the Church. The prime minister's office, for example, set up a special subcommittee tied to final status talks on the churches and Jerusalem, and the more tactful Foreign Ministry won out over the Finance Ministry to conduct negotiations with the Holy See on the fiscal treaty mandated by the 1993 Fundamental Agreement. As of spring 2003, talks under the government of Prime Minister Ariel Sharon are grinding on with no apparent result.

### Religious Freedoms

Despite the Oslo Accords and the Fundamental Agreement, Palestinian Christians have seen their freedoms denied on the grounds of security. From the point of view of religious freedom, the most important violation has been the denial of freedom of movement of Palestinian Christians in and out of Jerusalem and with it the lack of access to Jerusalem's Holy Places. For Palestinian Christians, unlike most of their co-religionists elsewhere, praying at the shrines is an integral part of their religious life, and so lack of access to Jerusalem has been a special burden. While closure of Jerusalem has affected Palestinians generally, it has also interfered with the functioning of the church, preventing clergy and church workers from coming to Jerusalem and in some cases, as with professors at Bethlehem University, hindering personnel from entering the Palestinian Self-Rule Area.

Christian leaders have also come under criticism from government officials for advocacy on behalf of justice and human rights of Palestinians or for finding fault with Israeli policy. Church leaders, several of whom are Palestinian themselves, have been wrongly accused by government officials of being spokesmen for the Palestinian Authority. The Latin patriarch has been the most frequent target of such accusations. But Uri Mor, director of the Israeli Department of Christian Community Affairs, has reserved the harshest action for Greek Orthodox Archimandrite Attala Hanna, threatening to review the government's entire relation with the Orthodox Church unless the priest ceased speaking out on so-called political issues.

Under the first Sharon government (2001–2003), the ultra-Orthodox Shas party controlled the Interior Ministry. In a campaign of exclusion, begun by bureaucrats of the ministry alarmed at the number of foreign workers in the country, the Interior Ministry began to deny visas and residency permits to foreign nationals and to refuse or delay the renewal of visas of those already there. Many thousands were affected, including Jews from abroad. The Catholic Church, and particularly the Latin Patriarchate with about a third of its clergy and many of its seminarians from Jordan, was adversely affected by the ban. In March 2003 an ad-hoc committee presented Archbishop Pietro Sambi, the apostolic nuncio to Israel, with a report on more than eighty priests, religious, and seminarians adversely affected by the visa policy. The report identified the denials as violations of religious liberty under the Fundamental Agreement. Within the government, the Israeli Ministry of Foreign Affairs had for some time represented the problem as a grave issue in need of remedy. Within days of release of the report, the new minister of the interior, Avraham Poraz, announced a solution. Requests for visas and permits approved and submitted by religious authorities to the Ministry of Religious Affairs would be granted.

### Mouallem Controversy

After the Nazareth mosque dispute, the most contentious issue between the Catholic Church and Israel was the 1998 appointment of Bishop Boutros Mouallem as Melkite (Greek Catholic) archbishop of Akko (Galilee). While in the past sovereigns and governments sometimes had a say in episcopal appointments, that has not been the case as the Vatican, especially in the last half of the twentieth century, has more and more centralized the appointment of bishops. Thus, when the Vatican named Mouallem, an expatriate Palestinian from Brazil, as Melkite archbishop for the Holy Land, the strong public objection by the government of Prime Minister Benjamin Netanyahu created a major crisis in relations between the Church and the State of Israel. The government went so far as to recommend the appointment of Father Emile Shoufani, a Melkite priest from the Galilee, as its favored candidate, and to threaten denying Bishop Mouallem a visa to enter the country.

So grave was the perceived interference in an internal church matter that Fr. David-Maria Jaeger, O. F. M., a canonist and a key Vatican adviser on relations with Israel, hinted publicly that Israel was threatened with being added to a short list of nations where the Church was openly persecuted. After weeks of acrimonious public controversy, the government relented, and Archbishop Mouallem was able to take charge of his see.[55]

### The Palestinian Authority

Relations between the churches and the Palestinian Authority (PA) have on the whole been positive. In part, these affirmative relations derive from shared nationality, the indigenous, local leadership of the Western churches, and their support for Palestinian rights and independence. In the case of the Vatican, positive attitudes toward the Palestinian people come from its "Mediterranean policy" toward Arab nations, and most of all from its special interest in the preservation of "the living Christian presence" in "the cradle of Christianity," that is, the lands of the Middle East where Christianity first flourished. From the Palestinian side, the ties of the local Christian communities to the world church have elicited international concern for injustices suffered by Palestinians and support for Palestinian national aspirations.

The Holy See–PLO Basic Agreement (see above) may be seen as the single most important outcome in this relationship to date. Generally, the PA has been favorable to the small (1.8 percent) Christian population. It has proved itself quick to contain anti-Christian incitement. During the Nazareth mosque controversy, it opposed the demands of the demonstrators, and it worked successfully to bring Muslim authorities and Arab governments to join the opposition. Internally, in the Self-Rule Areas it has maintained a secular approach to politics.

Despite generally positive relations, tensions remain. On taking possession of Bethlehem at Christmas 1996, Palestinian President Yasser Arafat and his wife assumed the position of honor at the Latin Christmas Mass in the Church of the Nativity. Since Ottoman times, it had been customary for the government to send a lesser ranking, local Christian official to sit in its place. The British and the Israelis had maintained the same practice. So, when Mr. Arafat, a Muslim, broke with long-standing custom, a short-lived controversy ensued.

Local church officials have not spared Mr. Arafat and his administration from criticism. For example, in his 1999 Christmas homily, delivered with Mr. Arafat seated in the place of honor, Latin Patriarch Michel Sabbah criticized the PA for its violations of human rights and its arbitrary style of government. In voicing such a public rebuke, the patriarch put to rest Israeli accusations that his pronouncements on issues of justice were merely partisan political exercises.

## Conclusion

### *The Future of Palestinian Christianity*

The future of Palestinian Christianity remains in question. The next decade will be crucial in determining whether Palestinian Christianity has a future in the land of its birth. The Christian presence may not be reduced to the ecclesiastic's nightmare of a cluster of museums bereft of local worshipers and attended by internationals with no ties to the land or its Oriental Christian heritage. Yet, if something approximating that nightmare is to be avoided, action will have to be taken, both in Israel and in the Palestinian areas, to prevent the further diminution of the Christian population and to secure a viable future for the Church in the Holy Land.

In Israel, where the Christian population grew fourfold between 1948 and 1990, Christian discontent is the greatest. Resentful of second-class treatment, fearful of an Islamic resurgence that is abetted by Israeli officials, Israel's Christians are showing a lack of faith in the future and a corresponding readiness to emigrate.

For Catholics, at least, the legal basis for securing the Christian presence has been secured with the Fundamental Agreement between Israel and the Holy See. Institutionally, the Catholic Church has also been strengthened by the united leadership provided by the Assembly of Ordinaries, the appointment of a Palestinian to head the local church, and the renewal of the Latin Church through its synod. These are formidable resources, but whether these developments are enough to preserve a sizable lay presence in the face of economic disadvantage, Islamist agitation, and the political tensions inherent in the situation is very hard to predict.

The probability of success at preserving a Christian presence in the Holy Land would be greater were the Orthodox Church more united internally. The mutual disaffection of the Arab laity and the Greek hierarchy will continue to be a serious liability for the entire Christian community. The survival of Christianity in the Holy Land demands that both of the major churches to which Palestinians belong be strong and internally united. After the death of the long-ailing Patriarch Diodoros in 2001, there seemed to be promise of change for the Greek Patriarchate. On his installation the new patriarch, Ireneios, indicated he would end secret contracts, review existing arrangements, and establish open financial dealings. But his failure to receive the approval of the Israeli government for his appointment appears to have for now halted his movement toward reform.

Inevitably, the fate of the Palestinian Christians in Israel will depend very much on Israeli and Jewish public opinion. Normalization of life, in the wake of an Israeli-Palestinian final status agreement, may permit more enthusiastic implementation of the Vatican-Israel agreement and reduce the incentives for Israelis to place pressures on Christian Arabs. But, given the independence of Israeli bureaucrats and the readiness of people on the fringe to make trouble, trusting in normalization may be naive. The future of Palestinian Christianity may depend, rather, on altering general Israeli popular opinion and, therefore, energizing the local Jewish-Christian dialogue at several levels.

In the Palestinian Self-Rule Areas, Muslim-Christian dialogue may be hard to build, though it certainly must go forward. Such dialogue has a relatively short history and has yet to prove seriously productive in regard to tensions between the two communities. Thus, in Palestine, the means to secure the Christian future are more likely to be political and social. A strategy for Christian survival in Palestine may call, above all, for the maintenance of secular government and for institutional as well as religious pluralism. The Basic Agreement with the Holy See provides a legal structure for guaranteeing freedom of religion and assuring the rights of Christians governed by the Palestinian Authority. The implementation of the agreement will be more reliable, however, in a pluralistic institutional context rather than in one where it must be effected as an exception to the general style of governance. Christian communities are more likely to have room to live and thrive in a pluralistic society.

On completing an extended journey among the Christians of the Middle East, Scottish writer William Dalrymple concluded, "But if the pattern of Christian suffering was more complete than I could possibly have guessed at the beginning of this journey, it was also more desperate. In Turkey and Palestine, the extinction of the descendants of John Moschos's Byzantine Christians seemed imminent; at current emigration rates, it was unlikely that either community would be in existence in twenty years."[56] Many observers share Dalrymple's pessimistic judgment. But the record of the last fifteen years shows that the Christian communities of the Holy Land have evolved in ways that were quite unexpected. The churches have come together to defend their people and to secure the churches' common interests. They have developed their own very practical version of ecumenism, and together they have entered in an unprecedented way into public affairs. They have also worked to give their people hope with economic development programs and to prevent emigration by providing new housing.

In many ways, Palestinian Christianity is stronger and more confident than it was two decades ago. But the collapse of Christian confidence in the Galilee over the past five years, symbolized by the Nazareth mosque controversy, shows how vulnerable Christians remain to adverse social pressure, religious prejudice, and political manipulation. The impact of the second or al-Aqsa intifada on Palestinian Christians, especially those living in the "Christian triangle" of Bethlehem, Beit Jala, and Beit Sahour, has been devastating. Before September 2000, these three towns accounted for 35,000 of the 50,000 Christians living on the West Bank and in Gaza. The repeated fighting between Muslim militants and the Israel Defense Force (IDF) in this area has already led to the emigration of many, to the destruction of homes for others, and the impoverishment of all. The five-week-long occupation and siege of the Church of the Nativity in April 2002 led to increased suspicion in the Christian community of both Muslim militants and the Israeli government, and to the radicalization of a few Christians. Any relaxation of Israeli control is likely to see still further emigration of Christians from the Palestinian Territories until peace is established once and for all.

While predictions of the disappearance of Palestinian Christianity may be premature, given conflicting currents in which it finds itself, one can truly say the future of "the living Christian presence" in the Holy Land lies in the hands of God.

## NOTES

1. For a survey of Arab Christianity, see Anglican bishop Kenneth Cragg, *The Arab Christian: A History of the Middle East* (London: Mowbray, 1992).

2. The first version of this chapter was completed before the outbreak of the second or al-Aqsa intifada, but the current text has been revised to include events through summer 2003.

3. See Peter Du Brul, S. J., "The Crisis of Palestinian Christians," in *Voices from Jerusalem: Jews and Christians Reflect on the Holy Land, Studies in Judaism and Christianity,* ed. David Burrell and Yehezkel Landau (New York: Paulist, 1992), 118–58.

4. The term "Holy Land" refers in common Christian usage to what we know today as Israel, Jerusalem, and the Palestinian Self-Rule Areas. Some ecclesiastical jurisdictions, like the Latin Patriarchate and the Melkite Archdiocese of Akko, with considerable historical justification also include Jordan. The historic Holy Land also included areas of what are today Lebanon and Syria, and that wider reference is maintained by some Eastern churches.

5. For an evangelical perspective, see Don Wagner, *Anxious for Armageddon: A Call to Partnership for Middle Eastern and Western Christians* (Scottdale, Pa.: Herald Press, 1995).

6. For a summary of the history of the Jerusalem community in New Testament times, see Michael Prior, C. M., " 'You will be my witnesses in Jerusalem, in all Judaea and Samaria, and to the ends of the earth': A Christian Perspective on Jerusalem," in Anthony O'Mahony, *Palestinian Christians: Religion, Politics and Society in the Holy Land,* ed. Anthony O'Mahony (London: Melisende, 1999), 107–10. On the return of Christians to Mount Zion after the destruction of the city and the later Bar Kochba rebellion, see Karen Armstrong, *Jerusalem: One City, Three Faiths* (New York: Knopf, 1996), 154–55, 170.

7. On the ascendancy of Jerusalem and the establishment of the patriarchate, see F. E. Peters, *Jerusalem: The Holy City in the Eyes of Chroniclers, Visitors, Pilgrims and Prophets from the Days of Abraham to the Beginning of Modern Times* (Princeton, N. J.: Princeton University Press, 1985), 157–58.

8. Ibid., 291. The defining note of a patriarchate in the ancient church was that a local church had been founded by an apostle. Thus, Antioch and Rome traced their origins to the apostle Peter, and Jerusalem to Saint James. Later the nomenclature came to refer in the East to autonomous national churches, such as the Moscow Patriarchate or the Serbian Orthodox Patriarchate.

9. For more extended treatment of modern Palestinian Christian history, see Anthony O'Mahony, "Palestinian Christians: Religion, Politics and Society, c. 1800–1948," in *Palestinian Christians,* 9–55.

10. In the wake of the al-Aqsa intifada, Christians, who were generally middle class and not used to working with Palestinian welfare agencies, once again turned to the Church for assistance.

11. Naim Stifan Ateek, *Justice and Only Justice: A Palestinian Theology of Liberation* (Maryknoll, N.Y.: Orbis, 1989), 6.

12. See Naim S. Ateek, Marc H. Ellis, and Rosemary Radford Ruether, eds., *Faith and the Intifada: Palestinian Christian Voices* (Maryknoll, N.Y.: Orbis, 1992), for a variety of Christian Palestinian views on the intifada and contemporary Palestinian Christian identity. Section Five, "International Responses," offers views of international supporters of Sabeel, including Marc Ellis and Rosemary Ruether. Also, see James W. Douglass, *The Nonviolent Coming of God* (Maryknoll, N.Y.: Orbis, 1991), and Michael Prior, *The Bible and Colonialism: A Moral Critique* (Sheffield: Sheffield Academic Press, 1997) and *Western Scholarship and the History of Palestine* (London: Melisende, 1998).

13. See Elias Chacour, *Blood Brothers* (Eastbourne: Kingsway, 1985) and *We Belong to the Land* (San Francisco: Harper, 1992).

14. See especially Michel Sabbah's pastoral letter "Reading the Bible in the Land of the Bible" (Jerusalem: Latin Patriarchate, 1993).

15. For a summary and analysis of the Basic Agreement, see my "The Vatican-PLO Agreement: A Catholic Perspective," *Information Brief,* Center for Policy Analysis on Palestine, no. 28 (March 16, 2000): 1–2.

16. Archbishop Jean-Louis Tauran, "Resolving the Question of Jerusalem," *Origins* 28, no. 21 (Nov. 5, 1998): 367.

17. See "Jerusalem: Considerations of the Secretariat of State," *Origins* 26, no. 21 (Oct. 3, 1996): 250–53.

18. See "The Future of Jerusalem," *Origins* 26, no. 21, 254–59.

19. Tauran, "Resolving the Question of Jerusalem," 367.

20. Ibid.

21. Ibid., 369.

22. "On the Significance of Jerusalem for Christians: Memorandum of Their Beatitudes, the Patriarchs and the Heads of Christian Communities in Jerusalem" [Jerusalem, private printing], Nov. 14, 1994, 2 (no. 5).

23. Ibid., 5 (no. 14).

24. Ibid.

25. On housing and other forms of Israeli discrimination against Arab residents of East Jerusalem, see Amir S. Chesin, Bill Hutman, and Avi Melamed, *Separate and Unequal: The Inside Story of Israeli Rule in East Jerusalem* (Cambridge, Mass.: Harvard, 1999); on the housing issue, see especially 29–37, 50–55.

26. Untitled survey by Bernard Sabella [typescript], p. 4. Mr. Sabella, a Christian, is a leading Palestinian sociologist.

27. Ibid., 13.

28. See "As the Third Millennium Draws Near," *Origins* 24, no. 24 (Nov. 24, 1994): 401, 403–16.

29. "Service of Pardon," *Origins* 29, no. 40 (Mar. 23, 2000): 647.

30. Commission for Religious Relations with the Jews, "We Remember: A Reflection on the 'Shoah'," *Origins* 27, no. 40 (Mar. 26, 1997): 669–75.

31. Joint Communique, International Catholic-Jewish Liaison Committee, Sixteenth Meeting, Vatican City, Mar. 23–26, 1998, 3.

32. Ehud Barak, "A Nation That Remembers," *Origins* 29, no. 42 (Apr. 6, 2000): 680.

33. Pope John Paul II, "Toward a Just and Lasting Peace in the Holy Land," *Origins* 29, no. 41 (Mar. 30, 2000): 667.

34. Pope John Paul II, "The Difficult but Essential Road to Christian Unity," *Origins* 29, no. 42 (Apr. 6, 2000): 690.

35. See *Annuaire de l'Eglise Catholique au Terre Sainte* (Jerusalem: Latin Patriarchate, 1999).

36. Ibid., n. 10.

37. "'Recheche la Paix et poursuis-la': Questions et Responses sur la Justice et la Paix en Notre Terre Sainte" (Jerusalem: Latin Patriarchate, 1998).

38. Ibid., 13.

39. Ibid., 19.

40. On the role of Christians in Arab and Palestinian nationalism, see O'Mahony, *Palestinian Christians*, 41–53.

41. "Ensemble devant Dieu pour le Bien de la Personne et de la Societe: la coexistence entre musulmans et chretiens dans le monde arabe," 3eme Lettre Pastorale des Patriarches Catholiques d'Orient adressee a leurs fideles, en Orient et dans la Diaspora (Bkerke, Liban: Secretariat General du Conseil des Patriarches Catholiques d'Orient, 1994), 67.

42. Ibid., n. 10.

43. "Ensemble vers l'Avenir: 'Voici, Je Fais Toutes Choses Nouvelles.'" 6eme Lettre Pastorale des Patriarches Catholiques d'Orient adressee a leurs fideles en Orient et dans la Diaspora (Bkerke, Liban: Secretariat General du Conseil des Patriarches Catholiques d'Orient, 1999), 36 (no. 17).

44. Ibid.

45. "Ensemble devant Dieu," 10–11.

46. Ibid., 14.

47. Matthew Price and Charles Lechner with additional research by Bassam Eid, "For the Record: The 'Persecution' of Christians under the Palestinian National Authority," *The Palestinian Human Rights Monitor* 2, no. 2 (February 1998). (The report comprises the entire issue of *The Monitor.*)

48. Sabella survey, 11.

49. For an overview of the first two years of the Nazareth controversy, see Drew Christiansen, "Nazareth Journal," *America* 182, no. 4 (Feb. 7, 2000): 7–13.

50. The Scharansky Commission is discussed in "Israel halts plans for Mosque in Nazareth," *The Christian Century* 199, no. 6 (Mar. 13, 2002): 14. See also "Religious Freedom in Nazareth," *Jerusalem Post*, Mar. 5, 2002.

51. Alan Philips, "Nazareth Mosque Scheme Halted," *Daily Telegraph*, Mar. 4, 2002, p. 11.

52. Ibid. See also David Rudge, "Arab leaders call for restraint," *Jerusalem Post,* Mar. 4, 2002.

53. Sabella survey, 11.

54. Ibid.

55. More recently, after the death of Patriarch Diodoros in 2001, the Sharon government has meddled in the appointment of a successor, first blocking certain candidates from consideration in the election and then refusing to give its approval to the election of Patriarch Ireneios. (The Jordanian government and the Palestinian Authority, the two other political bodies whose jurisdiction overlaps with that of the patriarchate, had already granted their approval.)

56. William Dalrymple, *From the Holy Mountain: A Journey among the Christians of the Middle East* (New York: Henry Holt, 1997), 448.

VI

# CATHOLIC-JEWISH RELATIONS AS BACKGROUND TO THE ACCORD

# 15

## JEWS AND CATHOLICS IN
## THE LAST HALF CENTURY

*Jack Bemporad*

Whatever may have been the matters of state leading to the Fundamental Agreement establishing full diplomatic relationships between Israel and the Holy See, its overarching significance can only be understood in the context of two religions which shared a two-millennial history characterized by considerable misunderstanding and frequent conflict.

The Fundamental Agreement has to be understood in the context of the revolutionary changes that have taken place in Catholic-Jewish relations since Vatican II and as an important and essential part of the process of reconciliation emerging between these two religions.

The agreement has adumbrations and associations which are religious and theological and which can serve as a springboard for fruitful theological discussions. The preamble to the agreement states this religious character clearly, and it can also be gleaned from the statement that the pope made to the Israeli ambassador when he presented his credentials as well as from the address of the Israeli ambassador, who stated:

> What this agreement does do, in my opinion, is put to rest the view that the Jews were only a nation in exile and in no sense a universal historic religious

people. It puts to rest the view that Judaism is a nation condemned to wander not as a witness to God but as a witness to what is the fate of those who reject Christ.

Pope Innocent III succinctly summarizes this view. He states, "The Jews . . . by their own guilt are consigned to perpetual servitude because they crucified the Lord." In another bull he made the following statement. "Thus the Jews, against whom the blood of Jesus calls out, although they ought not to be killed lest the Christian people forget the Divine Law, yet as wanderers they ought to remain upon the earth until their countenance be filled with shame and they seek the name of Jesus Christ, the Lord."[1] In commenting on these statements of Pope Innocent III, Solomon Zeitlin points out that "he [Innocent III] compared the Jews to Cain who had killed his brother Abel and upon whom God had set a sign so that he should not be killed by any one who found him, but should wander from place to place until the end of the world. Like Cain the Jews also were branded so as not to be slaughtered but to be doomed to wander from place to place."[2]

The entire development of Catholic thinking from Vatican II to documents such as the Guidelines, the Notes, as well as the "We Remember" document rejects that view. The Fundamental Agreement stands most directly in this direction of a revised theology of Judaism. This is no minor matter, and unfortunately this movement toward a new theological understanding of Judaism has not been properly stressed on either side. Rather what has been noticed is specific texts and individual documents, but the cumulative character of these Church statements, including most recently the pontifical statement on the Jews and their sacred scriptures in the New Testament, has not been properly evaluated.

Now what is the task before us? The task it seems to me for Jews and Christians is to work together to develop not just a recognition of Judaism as a living entity, but to develop a theology of a living Judaism that would take the place of the theology of a dead Judaism which in one form or other has dominated Christian theology throughout the centuries.

A prerequisite for such a theology is to take to heart the injunction, which the present pope gave in his first meeting with Jewish leaders, "that a religion must be represented in terms that the adherents of that religion would recognize as a fair representation."

Because of the Shoah and the destruction of European Jewry, the land of Israel, not only as a land of refuge, but as a place for the rebirth of Jewish life, has taken on a central significance in Jewish consciousness. Vatican II has rejected the theology of a dead or fossilized Judaism, and in its subsequent documents and proclamations the Church has sought to elaborate a theology of a living Judaism. It is important to view the Fundamental Agreement in the light of that transformation.

It is true that *Nostra Aetate* quotes the apostle Paul in his Epistle to the Romans that the promises of God to the Jewish people are irrevocable. This text has been repeated by the pope and in numerous other writings, both official and unofficial. But what does Romans 11 actually entail? What does that body of scriptural text mean, that the gifts and calls of God are irrevocable? That is a very general statement. And it is my opinion that there is no settled agreement on the Catholic side on this issue.[3] I am not aware of any Catholic text that theologically explores the exact meaning of this affirmation in the context of an explanation of the status of Judaism as a religion, the status of the Jewish people as a people, and in the particular context of our discussion—the status of the nature and significance of the land of Israel for Jews.

The place of Israel, both as a people and Israel as a nation, has been and continues to be at the heart of Jewish concerns in the dialogue process.

In the many years that I have been involved in Christian-Jewish dialogue, the two overarching concerns of the Jewish representatives were anti-Semitism (which concerns the fate of the Jewish people) and the land of Israel, which throughout Jewish history has been viewed as not simply a place of refuge but also as the historic place of homecoming spoken of in Jewish sacred texts associated with messianic fulfillment.

The Hebrew Bible clearly affirms the irrevocable covenant between God and Israel, an affirmation which I believe Romans 11 builds upon. There are many passages which predict the restoration of the Jewish people to its land in connection with their ethical behavior, and especially in association with those passages which foretell the coming of the Messiah. However, there are also numerous passages which refer to the promise of God to Israel as a people and to its land which are irrevocable on God's part and are in no sense conditional upon either accepting God's teachings or fulfilling his commandments. For example, the prophet Hosea in chapter 2:19 states, "I will betroth you to me forever." And chapter 11 verses 8 and 9 says, "How can I give you up, O Ephraim! How can I hand you over, O Israel! My heart recoils within me, my compassion grows warm and tender. I will not execute my fierce anger. I will not again destroy Ephraim for I am God and not man the Holy One in your midst and I will not come to destroy."

Amos 9:13–15 tells us, "I will restore the fortunes of my people Israel and they shall never again be plucked up out of the land which I have given them."

Ezekiel 36:22–28 states, "You shall dwell in the land which I gave to your fathers and you shall be my people and I will be your God."

Further, there are passages in Jeremiah and in Isaiah which endow the covenant of God with Israel with a kind of ontological fixity that is equivalent to the laws of nature. For example, Jeremiah says, "Thus says the Lord, who gives the sun for light by day and the fixed order of the moon and the stars for light by night. If this fixed order departs from before me," says the Lord, "then shall the descendants of Israel cease from being a nation before me for ever" (Jeremiah 31:35–36).

Isaiah 54:10, making the same connection between the covenant with Israel and with the order of nature, states that "the mountains may depart and the hills be removed but my steadfast love shall not depart from you and my covenant of peace shall not be removed, says the Lord who has compassion upon you." These are non-conditional promises, and they are elaborated in rabbinic texts.

Rabbinic sources present the continuity of the self-understanding within the Jewish people of the concept of peoplehood. In commenting on the passage from Jeremiah there is a reaffirmation and elaboration of the cosmic significance of the election of Israel.

God chooses Israel, and this is prior to any act on Israel's part to take upon itself the obligations entailed in accepting the burden implicit in this choice. It is a mutual relationship, which entails not only the relationship between God and Israel but between the people of Israel as a community of faith.

The late Professor Ephraim Urbach refers in his great work *The Sages*[4] to the rabbinic view that the election of Israel was a cosmic act. He states,

> Some Tannaim regarded Israel's election as a cosmic act. The verse Exodus xiv: 15 was expounded by the Tanna R. Eleazar of Modi'im thus: "Wherefore criest thou unto Me?"—do I require an instruction where My sons are concerned? "Concerning My sons, and concerning the work of my hands, command ye Me?" (Isaiah xiv: 11). Have they not already been designated to be before Me since the six days of creation? For it is said "If these ordinances depart from before Me, saith the Lord, then the seed of Israel shall also cease from being a nation before Me for ever. (Jeremiah xxxi: 35)[5]

He continues,

> The view that the election of Israel had been planned by God when the world was created makes the election, of course, absolute and independent of any circumstances. This was the doctrine of R. Akiba, who said, "Beloved are Israel in that they are called children of the Omnipresent. Still greater is the love in that it was made known to them that they were called the children of the Omnipresent, for it is said, 'Ye are children of the Lord your God.'"[6]

Urbach stresses the mutual relationship between God and Israel. Thus,

> R. Eleazar b. Azariah expounded: "Thou hast avouched the Lord this day . . . and the Lord has avouched thee this day" (Deuteronomy xxvi: 17–18). The Holy

One, blessed be He, said to Israel: You have made Me a unique object of your love in the world, as it is written, "Hear, O Israel, the Lord our God, the Lord is one" (ibid. vi: 4); and I shall make you a unique object of My love in the world, as it is said, "Who is like unto Thy people Israel, a nation one in the earth."[7]

This was a "twofold concept of election . . . the Lord's choice was answered by Jacob's choice."

The covenant with God was seen as entailing a solidarity with the Jewish people, as Urbach states:

Rabbi said, this tells us the merit of Israel. When they all stood at Mount Sinai to receive the Torah, they all resolved, with like mind, to accept the kingdom of God with joy. Nay more, they pledged themselves for one another.[8] The election was of one entire people and the covenant was made on condition that all "Israel be sureties for one another."[9]

Henry Slonimsky, in his important essay "The Philosophy Implicit in the Midrash,"[10] refers to "the seven ideas which the Rabbis have distinguished for the high status of being primeval forms or essences present before creation." We are told of Six Things or Words (a seventh is later to follow) concerning which it is expressly said that they preceded the creation of the world. And of these six, two are reserved for a special first place within the group. These two are Torah and the Seat of Glory, but concerning both we must make a preliminary mark at once. The Torah originally stands for the whole sum of ideas, for the objectified mind of God so to speak, at least for the concentration of them all in the purpose of God, in the "final" cause of creation. Here it seems to be just one of the ideas coordinated with the others.

The Seat of Glory may be understood as the veiled designation of God himself, certainly of his prime attribute, namely, dynamic power, which was at first reserved for Torah, conceived not merely as plan but also as architect. However, something of the old balance in favor of Torah is presently restored. For the question is raised as to which of these two firsts has the further priority, and the decision is made in favor of Torah, so that in a sense Torah becomes prior to God himself. After these two absolutely primary beings, four further forms or essences are enumerated: the Patriarch, Israel, the Temple, and the Name of the Messiah. These are the constituent categories of history and of temporal events, from its beginning in the "founding fathers" of the chosen people to its culmination in the establishment of the Kingdom of God on earth. That Abraham, Isaac, and Jacob are heavenly ideas, above all, that Israel is a timeless and ideal prototype, can mean only the enormous sense of the unique role to be played by this people as the bearer of Torah from

God to the world. The Heavenly Temple is of course the ideal prototype of all earthly places of true worship. And the Name of the Messiah, in which the virtue and potency of the Messiah is concentrated, assumes the final victorious realization of the messianic kingdom. With pathos and with humor a seventh idea is singled out for the high status of pre-mundane existence or subsistence, namely, Repentance. It is chosen because it is indispensable.

Without its beneficent presence and protection men simply could not get on; it is the pathetic reminder of the incessant drama and vicissitude of man's moral life. The culminating debate as to which of the seven has the real primacy, even after the question seems to have been settled, is the most interesting part of the whole passage. With his tongue in his cheek, one rabbi urges that "the idea of Israel preceded them all." Thus, Israel takes precedence over Torah itself, as Torah had taken precedence over the Seat of Glory. And therewith the matter is allowed to rest.

The substance of the above passages, the theological reaffirmation of the promise to Abraham that it is through God's people, the seed of Abraham, the Jewish people, that all the families of the earth are to be blessed, has to be seen in its proper theological significance.

Now, it is true that it may have been perceived in the past that this blessing to Abraham is exhausted in Christ, a view incidentally which goes contrary to the biblical statement of Paul, as well as the documents issuing out of Vatican II. Since such a view is out and out supersessionism, the question of what Romans 11 could possibly mean must become the subject of theological investigations on the part of the Christian community, especially since it has been quoted so frequently.

The rejection of supersessionism and the recognition of the special place that the land of Israel and Jerusalem in particular has in Jewish consciousness is clearly understood and made explicit most emphatically and repeatedly by Pope John Paul II.

One may wonder why it took so long for the Christian community to explicitly recognize the significance of the State of Israel to Jews both as a land of refuge and as the land of promise as proclaimed in the Bible.

In spite of the many ways in which the Jewish community views and has viewed the land and the State of Israel, almost all Jews, whatever other differences they may have, affirm its significance as a land of refuge for Jews who found themselves completely vulnerable as citizens of other countries. This is true not only for those Jews singled out by Hitler for extermination, but also those from other lands as well.

Israel has also been seen as a place of refuge since the Shoah for all those Jews who choose to live there because it is the land of their fathers and a place of refuge from post-Shoah anti-Semitism. Almost a million Jews have come to Israel from Arab countries that treated them in the harshest manner. Also, hundreds of thousands of Jews from Russia and Eastern Europe came to Israel for surcease from persecution and discrimination.

Pope John Paul II explicitly recognized the connection between Israel and anti-Semitism when he first mentioned the State of Israel in a homily at Otranto, Italy, in October 1980. He stated, "[T]he terms of the Middle East drama are well known: the Jewish people, after tragic experiences connected with the extermination of so many sons and daughters, driven by the desire for security set up the state of Israel."[11]

Before this homily the pope did mention the "land" without mentioning Israel in his first meeting as pope with representatives of the Jewish community in Rome on March 12, 1979. There he stated,

I intend to foster spiritual dialogue and to do everything in my power for the peace of that land which is holy for you as it is for us, with the hope that the city of Jerusalem will be effectively guaranteed as a center of harmony for the followers of the three great monotheistic religions of Judaism, Islam and Christianity, for whom the city is a revered place of devotion.[12]

In those 1979 comments, the pope stated that the land was as holy to Jews as it is to Catholics and that all three monotheistic religions had a stake in the peace and harmony of Jerusalem. The pope also promised to do all for peace in that area. While reiterating in his Otranto homily the special place of "the Holy City, Jerusalem," the pope specifically prayed for it to be a place of "reconciliation and peace" instead of "the object of a dispute that seems without a solution."

In connecting the State of Israel with the "tragic experiences connected with the extermination of so many sons and daughters" and the "desire for security," the pope in that homily also noted that "at the same time the painful condition of the Palestinian people was created, a large part of whom are excluded from their land."[13]

While the pope does his best to impartially recognize the claims of both Jews and Palestinians to the "land," as undoubtedly he should since he was fully conscious of the many Christians in Arab countries as well as the human claims of the Palestinian people, one cannot help but detect a deep concern for the Jewish people, whom he fully recognized were singled out for extermination and therefore were "driven by the desire for security."

I think it is of utmost importance to point out that Pope John Paul II was the first pope to officially mention the State of Israel. Pope Paul VI, who traveled to Israel as pope, to the best of my knowledge never mentioned Israel, only the Holy Land or Palestine.

While visiting Auschwitz, after stopping before the inscription in Hebrew, Pope John Paul II said in a homily, "[T]his inscription awakens the memory of the people whose sons and daughters were intended for total extermination. . . . [T]he very people who received from God the commandment 'thou shalt not kill' itself experienced in a special measure what is meant by killing."[14]

It seems that in the early stages of the pope's reign he seemed to recognize the special relationship that existed between Jews and Christians and the history that indissolubly connected them.

In the pope's first meeting with representatives of the Jewish community he stated, "Our two religious communities are connected and closely related at the very level of their respective religious identities." It is this very connection that makes it incumbent on both faiths "to fulfill God's commandment of love, and to sustain a truly fruitful and fraternal dialogue that contributes to the good of each of the partners involved and to our better service of humanity."[15]

Obviously the pope reflected deeply on these questions, which he formulated in principle at the beginning of his pontificate. In later pronouncements he often returned to the significance of the city of Jerusalem for Jews, Christians, and Muslims and also felt the deep plight of the Jewish people and their concern for the land of their origins and the land of promise.

In the apostolic letter *Redemptionis Anno* for Easter, April 20, 1984, Pope John Paul II speaks at length of the place of the city of Jerusalem for the three Western monotheistic religions and its place in their understanding. He clearly states the essential significance of Jerusalem. It is the city where "Jesus offering his life has made us both one, and has broken down the dividing wall of hostility . . . bringing the hostility to an end" (Eph. 2:14,16). The pope continues, "[B]efore it was the city of Jesus the redeemer, Jerusalem was the historic site of the biblical revelation of God, the meeting place as it were, of heaven and earth, in which more than in any other place the word of God was brought to men."[16]

The pope in a short paragraph gives the essence of the Christian significance of Jerusalem, and his statement deserves to be quoted in full:

> Christians honor her with a religious and intense concern because there the words of Christ so often resounded, there the great events of the redemption were accomplished: the passion, death and resurrection of the Lord. In the city of Jerusalem the first Christian community sprang up and remained throughout the centuries a continual ecclesial presence despite difficulties.[17]

He also mentions in much more general terms the significance of Jerusalem for Muslims: "Muslims also call Jerusalem 'holy,' with a profound attachment that goes back to the origins of Islam and springs from the fact that they have there many special places of pilgrimage and for more than a thousand years have dwelt there, almost without interruption."[18]

But in dealing with the Jewish claim on Jerusalem the pope speaks much more particularly and more emotionally. He states, "Jews ardently love her and in every age venerate her memory, abundant as she is in many remains and monuments from the time of David who chose her as the capital, and of Solomon who built the Temple there. Therefore they turn their minds to her daily, one may say, and point to her as a sign of their nation."[19]

I believe that anyone reading this statement cannot help but notice the understanding Pope John Paul II has of the emotional tie between Jerusalem and the Jewish people. It is certainly a significant addition to the remarks made in the homily at Otranto. But it is even more, since the pope does not leave it there as he might well have done. Instead, after describing Jerusalem as a city of religious significance for the monotheistic faiths he continues dealing with the contemporary situation and states, "[F]or the Jewish people who live in the state of Israel and who preserve in that land such precious testimonies to their history and their faith, we must ask for the desired security and the due tranquillity that is the prerogative of every nation and condition of life and of progress for every society."[20]

Here again, as is only proper, the pope speaks of the Palestinian people, but again one cannot help but notice a certain abstract quality to his discussion of Palestinian claims. He states, "[T]he Palestinian people who find their historical roots in that land and who for decades have been dispersed, have the natural right in justice to find once more a homeland and to be able to live in peace and tranquillity with the other peoples in the area."[21]

The pope does not speak merely of a land, as he did in 1979, but rather of a nation with the legitimacy of a nation and of a state entitled to live with the prerogatives of every nation. Indeed, the pope fulfilled the promise of understanding the Jews as they saw themselves.

The very next year after *Redemptionis Anno*, on June 24, 1985, the Notes appeared. Just as the Guidelines were prepared by the then-newly constituted Vatican Commission for Religious Relations with the Jews headed by the truly extraordinary leadership of Cardinal Johannes Willebrands and signed by him and Father Pierre-Marie de Contenson, the secretary of the commission, so the Notes were written under the direction of Cardinal Willebrands also, in association with Father (now Bishop) Pierre Duprey and Monsignor (now Cardinal) Jorge Mejia. Without wishing in any way to detract from the responsibility of these outstanding and devoted individuals, nevertheless one cannot help but see the papal influence if not the papal imprint in the Notes.

While in the Guidelines no papal statement is quoted at all, the Notes begin with a quote from Pope John Paul II and his statements are quoted seven times. Furthermore, these quotes are not decorative or incidental but get to the very heart of the message of the text. The Notes embody what we have already seen to be the thinking of Pope John Paul II on the question of the state and land of Israel. The

Notes do, however, go beyond anything stated by the pope up to that point. It is unfortunate that these significant and revolutionary words have not had the hearing, or better, the understanding they deserve.

Judaism is seen here as a vital living religious tradition that did not end with the destruction of the Temple but which continued in faithfulness to God and with the bearing of witness to God in "numerous diasporas," "while preserving the memory of the land of their forefathers at the heart of their hope" (section VI of the Notes).

The Notes indicate the importance of the land of Israel for the Jews and the significance of the continuation of the land and the people for a true understanding of God's design.

In Judaism, there is hope throughout its history of a return and establishment of a presence in its land as a people. The hope has haunted the Jewish people throughout their history. Jerusalem was in the minds and prayers of Jews and in fact, as we have seen, the pope acknowledged this. But most important, the Notes speak of the permanence of Israel "as a sign which must be interpreted within God's design."

Also, let us not overlook the very significant reading from the Book of Genesis that took place at the historic 1986 visit of the pope to the main synagogue in Rome. At that epochal event the text read was Genesis 15:1–7. This text concludes with the words: "Abraham believed in the Lord and it was accounted to him for righteousness. And (God) said unto him, I am the Lord who brought you from Ur of Chaldees to give to you this land as an inheritance."

The next year, the pope affirmed that there were no theological obstacles to the establishment of full diplomatic relations between Israel and the Holy See. Bishop Krister Stendhal wrote in the Harvard Divinity Bulletin for autumn 1967 that "for Christians and Muslims that term [i.e., holy sites] is an adequate expression of what matters. Here are sacred places, hallowed by the most holy events, here are the places for pilgrimage, the very focus of highest devotion . . . but Judaism is different . . . the sites sacred to Judaism have no shrines, its religion is not tied to 'sites' but to the land, not to what happened in Jerusalem but to Jerusalem itself."[22]

The pope expressed the Christian concern very well in affirming that "Jerusalem is where Christianity was born. It is here where Jesus lived and preached and where he died and according to Christian faith was resurrected and went to heaven. The holy places are indeed holy to Christians, and indeed concern for the safety of the Christian holy places has been a major concern for the Catholic Church."

Just as it took an extraordinary amount of daring in 1986 to enter the synagogue and embrace Rabbi Toaf, it also took great courage for the pope in March 1992 to initiate discussion with the Israeli government toward the establishment of full diplomatic relations with Israel.

I believe in light of the above and as evidenced by the interview the pope granted the *Parade* magazine reporter Ted Sczulc, in which the pope was quoted as saying that a state "is their right," that the single most important factor in making the Fundamental Agreement was the determination on the part of the pope that full diplomatic relations be a reality and that such relations be established during his pontificate.

In March 1998 under the leadership of Cardinal Cassidy, the Pontifical Commission issued the "We Remember" document. This document deals with the Holocaust (Shoah) and the issue of Forgiveness (Teshuvah). The intent of "We Remember" can best be understood by the following paragraph:

> At the end of this millennium the Catholic Church desires to express her deep sorrow for the failures of her sons and daughters in every age. This is an act of repentance (*Teshuvah*), since as members of the Church we are linked to the sins as well as the merits of all her children. The Church approaches with deep respect and great compassion the experience of extermination, the Shoah suffered by the Jewish people during World War II. It is not a matter of mere words, but indeed of binding commitment. We would risk causing the victims of the most atrocious deaths to die again if we do not have an ardent desire for justice, if we do not commit ourselves to ensure that evil does not prevail over good as it did for millions of the children of the Jewish people. Humanity cannot permit all that to happen again.

In January 2000, in St. Peter's Basilica, the pope conducted an unprecedented liturgy of repentance in the name of the whole Church for sins committed by Christians over the past millennium. One of the seven categories of great historical sins specified in the liturgy was devoted to those against Jews and Judaism, including the Holocaust:

> . . . we pray because in remembering the suffering endured by the people of Israel in their history Christians know and recognize the sins committed by not a few of them against the people of the Covenant of Benedictions. . . . You have chosen Abraham and his descendants so that your name could be brought to all peoples. We are profoundly pained for the behavior of many who in the course of history have made these your children to suffer and asking forgiveness we want to commit ourselves to an authentic brotherhood.

In March 2000 Pope John Paul II made a jubilee pilgrimage to Israel and prayed at Yad VaShem, Israel's memorial to the 6 million Jews murdered during the Holocaust. During his visit the pope placed a prayer in the Western Wall. This prayer acknowledges the election of Abraham and the Jewish people. It also expresses deep sorrow over the way the Jewish people have suffered and asks God's forgiveness for such action. Finally, the pope resolves to commit the Church to genuine brotherhood with the Jewish people. No greater testimony to the revolutionary changes that have taken place in Christian-Jewish relations can be expressed than in the words of this prayer:

> God of our fathers,
> You chose Abraham and his descendants
> To bring your name to the Nations:
> We are deeply saddened
> By the behavior of those
> Who in the course of history
> Have caused these children of yours to suffer,
> And asking your forgiveness
> We wish to commit ourselves
> To genuine brotherhood
> With the people of the Covenant
> Jerusalem, 26 March 2000.

Jewish peoplehood implies that one's Jewish life must be a part of a larger Jewish community. The Jew sees himself as a part of a historical people who have a universal, world-transforming mission. However, such a life must also embody in itself a community, which enables it to live that life to the fullest in its social context. Land and nation are an expression of this latter dimension of Jewish identity. While the universal values and principles as enunciated by the prophetic heritage are the expression of its universalism, the latter is also necessary as a corrective to an overly utopian perspective. Ideals have to be grounded and expressed in actual historical and social realities.

The Enlightenment, with its ideals of the rights of man, liberated the Jews politically. Vatican II, with its recognition of the Jewish people, began to liberate the Jews religiously, and when the final accord agreed to "combat anti-Semitism wherever it existed," the religious recognition of the Jews achieved ratification. It will be complete when the proper theological understanding of the Jews becomes established in Christian and ultimately in Muslim teaching.

We can see that this theological understanding gradually has taken hold in Catholic teaching largely at the urging of Pope John Paul II with the help of many devoted cardinals and bishops.

We must underscore that in order to effectively establish Christian-Jewish relationships on a proper plane we must engage in theological discussion with our religious neighbors. We cannot help but ask, what constitutes God's design from a Catholic perspective? What is the place of Jews, Judaism, and the land of Israel in a Catholic understanding of salvation history? These questions cry out for discussion, for investigation, and for an answer. These questions cannot be dealt with except through theological discussion.

Now, what is the problem and what has been the problem with respect to theological discussion?

First of all, there is the problem of developing a language of dialogue which is a language in which we use the same words and not mean different things. We use terms like suffering, salvation, revelation, redemption—there is a whole list of terms that we use, but unless we talk to one another, unless we listen to one another, there is no way that we can be sure that we really hear each other because their connotations are different. Only theological dialogue can help us understand each other's religious language.

All religious traditions hold certain beliefs to be true and have reasons for holding them to be true. When a religious tradition asks about what it believes and why it believes it is talking theology, since theology is concerned with the meaning and truths of the claims that a religious tradition makes. To affirm, therefore, that Judaism is not theological or should not discuss theology is to affirm either that Judaism makes no doctrinal claims or if it does make such claims it has no reason of a rational character for making them. Both affirmations seem to me to be untrue.

Practically speaking, theological dialogue with the Church is critical to prevent misunderstanding of each other's beliefs and doctrines as well as to expose any misperceptions we may have. It is only through dialogue that we can learn something about the other, not as some kind of an abstract statement even in the best of writing, but in a mutual give and take between human beings, people of flesh and blood who have the same interest in doing God's will. Here, the writings and speeches of Father Remi Hoeckmann are most important. He has repeatedly expressed the fact that what dialogue is first and foremost is a dialogue between concrete individuals, individuals of faith who are searching together to find ways of reconciliation and understanding. Cardinal Cassidy in Jerusalem made a very similar statement:

> Let me make it clear that there is a real and important distinction between theological dialogue and Christian mission. When I speak of a theological dialogue with Jewish representatives, I am not speaking of unity in faith, but of a dialogue that helps with the partners to understand and accept each other as they really are in order to be what God wants them to be in their societies today despite their basic differences. I am truly amazed at times to read Catholic teaching and doctrine explained in Jewish publications in such a way that no Catholic

would recognize them as part of his or her faith. It is likely that Jews would have a similar reaction to some Catholic understandings of their faith.

Now, here I think it is very important to point out that the conditions set for theological dialogue by the late Rabbi Soloveitchik have to be seen in a somewhat different light than the way they have been perceived by many in the Jewish community. In his 1964 essay "Confrontation,"[23] which incidentally was published before *Nostra Aetate*'s epochal transformation of the Church's attitude toward the Jews, Rabbi Soloveitchik says, "[N]on-Jewish society has confronted us through the ages in the mood of defiance as if we were part of the subhuman objective order." He continues, "We shall resent any attempt on the part of the community of the many to engage us in a peculiar encounter in which our confronter will command us to take a position beneath him, while placing himself not alongside of but above us." That was Soloveitchik's position, and given the history of Catholic-Jewish relations for a thousand years he had ample warrant for making that statement. However, he also states in the very same essay, in a passage that unfortunately has not often been quoted, "It is self-evident that a confrontation of two faith communities is possible only if it is accompanied by clear assurance that both parties will enjoy equal rights and full religious freedom. Equal rights and full religious freedom is not where one is putting oneself in front or on top of the other." This requirement, it seems to me, since Vatican II and the promulgation of *Nostra Aetate,* the Guidelines, the Notes, and numerous other Vatican affirmations, not to speak of and especially the many statements of John Paul II, has fulfilled for decades the conditions that Rabbi Soloveitchik has made for fruitful dialogue. Therefore I call upon the Jewish community to recognize Rabbi Soloveitchik's position in its full context.

I can think of no better way to conclude than by quoting Rabbi Leo Baeck, survivor of Treblinka and leader of the Berlin Jewish community. In his post-Holocaust book *The People Israel*,[24] he eloquently summarizes the Jewish perspective.

Every people can be chosen for a history, for a share in the history of humanity. Each is a question which God has asked, and each people must answer. But more history has been assigned to this people than to any other people. God's question speaks stronger here.

Many peoples turned toward the commandments of idols, and, in that, they lost the history which has been promised them. The word of the One God penetrated this people from the beginning. When the commandment of God awakes in man, freedom also opens its eyes; and where freedom commences, history begins. A difficult task was assigned this people in history. It is so easy to listen to the voices of idols, and it is so hard to receive the work of the One God into oneself. It is so easy to remain a slave, and it is so difficult to become a free man.

But this people can only exist in this freedom which reaches beyond all other freedoms. Its history began when it heard the word, rising out of the mystery, and emerging into clarity: "I am the Lord thy God, who brought thee out of the land of Egypt, out of the house of bondage" (Exod. 20:2). . . .

Man lives within the universe and within history. This people understood that history and universe testify to a oneness, and reveal a totality and order. One word has dared to be the one expression for that which keeps everything together: "covenant"—"the enduring," the covenant of the One God. It is the covenant of God with the universe, and therefore with the earth; the covenant of God with humanity and therefore with this people contained in it; the covenant with history and therefore with every one within it; the covenant with the fathers and therefore with the children; the covenant with days which are to come. "As true as My covenant is"—this was the word of the Eternal One heard by the prophet when he thought about his people in a time of oppression and dark destiny, and certainly entered him. The question of all questions, that of the entrance of the eternal, the unending, the one, into the domain of the many, the terrestrial, the passing, this question in which the searching, the thinking, the hope of this people has always lived, in which it once grew and in which it was ever reborn—this question itself possesses the answer: "As true as My covenant is."

This people traveled through the history of humanity, century after century, millennium after millennium. Its very history became divine guidance for it. Once Moses and the children of Israel sang this song to the Lord, and said: "Thou in Thy love hast led the people that Thou hast redeemed" (Exod. 15:13). And confidence, whenever it looked backward or forward, then said: "Once they sang unto the Lord; so will they sing unto the Lord."

## NOTES

1. Solomon Grayzel, *The Church and the Jews in the XIIIth Century,* quoted by Solomon Zeitlin in *The Ecumenical Council Vatican II and the Jews,* reprinted from the *Jewish Quarterly Review* 56 New Series (1965): 588.

2. Ibid.

3. For a careful and important study of the historical interpretation of this text, one should consult Joseph Sievers's excellent study "God's Gifts and Calls Are Irrevocable: The Reception of Romans 11:29 through the Centuries and Christian-Jewish Relations," in *Reading Israel in Romans: Legitimacy and Plausibility of Divergent Interpretations,* ed. Christina Grenholm and Daniel Patte (Harrisburg, Pa.: Trinity Press International, 2000), 127–73.

4. Ephraim Urbach, *The Sages, Their Concepts and Beliefs* (Hebrew University, Jerusalem: Magnes Press, 1975).

5. See the discussion at ibid., 527.

6. Ibid., 528.

7. Ibid., 529.

8. Ibid., 538.

9. Ibid., 539.

10. Henry Slonimsky, *Essays* (Cincinnati: Hebrew Union College Press, 1967), 28 ff. For a further analysis of rabbinic statements on Israel and the land of Israel see Mordecai M. Kaplan, *The Greater Judaism in the Making: A Study of the Modern Evolution of Judaism* (New York: Reconstructionist Press, 1980), 40–44.

11. John Paul II, *Spiritual Pilgrimage: Texts on Jews and Judaism, 1979–1995,* ed. Eugene J. Fisher and Leon Klenicki (New York: Crossroad, 1995), 12.

12. Ibid., 6.

13. Ibid.

14. Ibid.

15. Ibid., 7.

16. Ibid., 33.

17. Ibid., 34.

18. Ibid.

19. Ibid.

20. Ibid., 36.

21. Ibid.

22. Quoted by R. J. Zwierblowsky, "The Meaning of Jerusalem to Jews, Christians, and Muslims," published by Israel Universities Study Group for Middle Eastern Affairs and originally the Charles Strong Memorial Lecture (Australia, 1972).

23. Rabbi Joseph Soloveitchik, "Confrontation," *Tradition* 6, (spring-summer, 1964): 5–29.

24. Leo Baeck, *The People Israel* (Cincinnati: U. A. H. C., 1964), 402–3.

# APPENDIX I

## Fundamental Agreement between the Holy See and the State of Israel

*(Acta Apostolicae Sedis* 86 [1994])

December 30, 1993

*Preamble*

The Holy See and the State of Israel,

Mindful of the singular character and universal significance of the Holy Land;

Aware of the unique nature of the relationship between the Catholic Church and the Jewish people, and of the historic process of reconciliation and growth in mutual understanding and friendship between Catholics and Jews;

Having decided on 29 July 1992 to establish a 'Bilateral Permanent Working Commission', in order to study and define together issues of common interest, and in view of normalizing their relations;

Recognizing that the work of the aforementioned Commission has produced sufficient material for a first and Fundamental Agreement;

Realizing that such Agreement will provide a sound and lasting basis for the continued development of their present and future relations and for the furtherance of the Commission's task,

Agree upon the following Articles:

*Article 1*

- The State of Israel, recalling its Declaration of Independence, affirms its continuing commitment to uphold and observe the human right to freedom of religion and conscience, as set forth in the Universal Declaration of Human Rights and in other international instruments to which it is a party.

- The Holy See, recalling the Declaration on Religious Freedom of the Second Vatican Ecumenical Council, 'Dignitatis humanea', affirms the Catholic Church's commitment to uphold the human right to freedom of religion and conscience, as set forth in the Universal Declaration of Human Rights and in other international instruments to which it is a party. The Holy See wishes to affirm as well the Catholic Church's respect for other religions and their followers as solemnly stated by the Second Vatican Ecumenical Council in its Declaration on the Relation of the Church to Non-Christian Religions, 'Nostra aetate'.

### Article 2

- The Holy See and the State of Israel are committed to appropriate cooperation in combatting all forms of antisemitism and all kinds of racism and of religious intolerance, and in promoting mutual understanding among nations, tolerance among communities and respect for human life and dignity.

- The Holy See takes this occasion to reiterate its condemnation of hatred, persecution and all other manifestations of antisemitism directed against the Jewish people and individual Jews anywhere, at any time and by anyone. In particular, the Holy See deplores attacks on Jews and desecration of Jewish synagogues and cemeteries, acts which offend the memory of the victims of the Holocaust, especially when they occur in the same places which witnessed it.

### Article 3

- The Holy See and the State of Israel recognize that both are free in the exercise of their respective rights and powers, and commit themselves to respect this principle in their mutual relations and in their cooperation for the good of the people.

- The State of Israel recognizes the right of the Catholic Church to carry out its religious, moral, educational and charitable functions, and to have its own institutions, and to train, appoint and deploy its own personnel in the said institutions or for the said functions to these ends. The Church recognizes the right of the State to carry out its functions, such as promoting and protecting the welfare and the safety of the people. Both the State and the Church recognize the need for dialogue and cooperation in such matters as by their nature call for it.

- Concerning Catholic legal personality at canon law the Holy See and the State of Israel will negotiate on giving it full effect in Israeli law, following a report from a joint subcommission of experts.

*Article 4*

- The State of Israel affirms its continuing commitment to maintain and respect the 'Status quo' in the Christian Holy Places to which it applies and the respective rights of the Christian communities thereunder. The Holy See affirms the Catholic Church's continuing commitment to respect the aforementioned 'Status quo' and the said rights.

- The above shall apply notwithstanding an interpretation to the contrary of any Article in this Fundamental Agreement.

- The State of Israel agrees with the Holy See on the obligation of continuing respect for and protection of the character proper to Catholic sacred places, such as churches, monasteries, convents, cemeteries and their like.

- The State of Israel agrees with the Holy See on the continuing guarantee of the freedom of Catholic worship.

*Article 5*

- The Holy See and the State of Israel recognize that both have an interest in favouring Christian pilgrimages to the Holy Land. Whenever the need for coordination arises, the proper agencies of the Church and of the State will consult and cooperate as required.

- The State of Israel and the Holy See express the hope that such pilgrimages will provide an occasion for better understanding between the pilgrims and the people and religions in Israel.

*Article 6*

The Holy See and the State of Israel jointly reaffirm the right of the Catholic Church to establish, maintain and direct schools and institutes of study at all levels; this right being exercised in harmony with the rights of the State in the field of education.

*Article 7*

The Holy See and the State of Israel recognize a common interest in promoting and encouraging cultural exchanges between Catholic institutions worldwide, and educational, cultural and research institutions in Israel, and in facilitating access to manuscripts, historical documents and similar source materials, in conformity with applicable laws and regulations.

*Article 8*

The State of Israel recognizes that the right of the Catholic Church to freedom of expression in the carrying out of its functions is exercised also through the

Church's own communications media; this right being exercised in harmony with the rights of the State in the field of communications media.

### Article 9

The Holy See and the State of Israel jointly reaffirm the right of the Catholic Church to carry out its charitable functions through its health care and social welfare institutions, this right being exercised in harmony with the rights of the State in this field.

### Article 10

- The Holy See and the State of Israel jointly reaffirm the right of the Catholic Church to property.

- Without prejudice to rights relied upon by the Parties:

  - The Holy See and the State of Israel will negotiate in good faith a comprehensive agreement, containing solutions acceptable to both Parties, on unclear, unsettled and disputed issues, concerning property, economic and fiscal matters relating to the Catholic Church generally, or to specific Catholic Communities or institutions.

  - For the purpose of the said negotiations, the Permanent Bilateral Working Commission will appoint one or more bilateral subcommissions of experts to study the issues and make proposals.

  - The Parties intend to commence the aforementioned negotiations within three months of entry into force of the present Agreement, and aim to reach agreement within two years from the beginning of the negotiations.

  - During the period of these negotiations, actions incompatible with these commitments shall be avoided.

### Article 11

- The Holy See and the State of Israel declare their respective commitment to the promotion of the peaceful resolution of conflicts among States and nations, excluding violence and terror from international life.

- The Holy See, while maintaining in every case the right to exercise its moral and spiritual teaching-office, deems it opportune to recall that, owing to its own character, it is solemnly committed to remaining a stranger to all merely temporal conflicts, which principle applies specifically to disputed territories and unsettled borders.

### Article 12

The Holy See and the State of Israel will continue to negotiate in good faith in pursuance of the Agenda agreed upon in Jerusalem, on 15 July 1992, and confirmed at the Vatican, on 29 July 1992; likewise on issues arising from Articles of the present Agreement, as well as on other issues bilaterally agreed upon as objects of negotiation.

### Article 13

- In this Agreement the Parties use these terms in the following sense:

    - The Catholic Church and the Church—including, inter alia, its Communities and institutions,

    - Communities of the Catholic Church—meaning the Catholic religious entities considered by the Holy See as Churches sui juris and by the State of Israel as Recognized Religious Communities;

    - The State of Israel and the State—including, inter alia, its authorities established by law.

- Notwithstanding the validity of this Agreement as between the Parties, and without detracting from the generality of any applicable rule of law with reference to treaties, the Parties agree that this Agreement does not prejudice rights and obligations arising from existing treaties between either Party and a State or States, which are known and in fact available to both Parties at the time of the signature of this Agreement.

### Article 14

- Upon signature of the present Fundamental Agreement and in preparation for the establishment of full diplomatic relations, the Holy See and the State of Israel exchange Special Representatives, whose rank and privileges are specified in an Additional Protocol.

- Following the entry into force and immediately upon the beginning of the implementation of the present Fundamental Agreement, the Holy See and the State of Israel will establish full diplomatic relations at the level of Apostolic Nunciature, on the part of the Holy See, and Embassy, on the part of the State of Israel.

### Article 15

This Agreement shall enter into force on the date of the latter notification of ratification by a Party.

Done in two original copies in the English and Hebrew languages, both texts being equally authentic. In case of divergency, the English text shall prevail.

Signed in Jerusalem, this thirtieth day of the month of December, in the year 1993, which corresponds to the sixteenth day of the month of Tevet, in the year 5754.

FOR THE GOVERNMENT OF THE STATE OF ISRAEL

FOR THE HOLY SEE

*Additional Protocol*

- In relation to Art. 14 (1) of the Fundamental Agreement, signed by the Holy See and the State of Israel, the 'Special Representatives' shall have, respectively, the personal rank of Apostolic Nuncio and Ambassador.

- These Special Representatives shall enjoy all the rights, privileges and immunities granted to Heads of Diplomatic Missions under international law and common usage, on the basis of reciprocity.

- The Special Representative of the State of Israel to the Holy See, while residing in Italy, shall enjoy all the rights, privileges and immunities defined by Art. 12 of the Treaty of 1929 between the Holy See and Italy, regarding Envoys of Foreign Governments to the Holy See residing in Italy. The rights, privileges and immunities extended to the personnel of a Diplomatic Mission shall likewise be granted to the personnel of the Israeli Special Representative's Mission. According to an established custom, neither the Special Representative, nor the official members of his Mission, can at the same time be members of Israel's Diplomatic Mission to Italy.

- The Special Representative of the Holy See to the State of Israel may at the same time exercise other representative functions of the Holy See and be accredited to other States. He and the personnel of his Mission shall enjoy all the rights, privileges and immunities granted by Israel to Diplomatic Agents and Missions.

- The names, rank and functions of the Special Representatives will appear, in an appropriate way, in the official lists of Foreign Missions accredited to each Party.

Signed in Jerusalem, this thirtieth day of the month of December, in the year 1993, which corresponds to the sixteenth day of the month of Tevet, in the year 5754.

FOR THE GOVERNMENT OF THE STATE OF ISRAEL

FOR THE HOLY SEE

# APPENDIX II

**Agreement between the Holy See and the State of Israel
Pursuant to Article 3§3 of the Fundamental Agreement
between the Holy See and the State of Israel**
(also referred to as the Legal Personality Agreement,
*Acta Apostolicae Sedis* 91 [1999])

### *Article 1*

This Agreement is made on the basis of the provisions of the "*Fundamental Agreement between the State of Israel and the Holy See*" which was signed on 30 December 1993, and then entered into force on 10 March 1994 (hereinafter: the "Fundamental Agreement").

### *Article 2*

Recalling that the Holy See is the Sovereign Authority of the Catholic Church, the State of Israel agrees to assure full effect in Israeli law to the legal personality of the Catholic Church itself.

### *Article 3*

1. The State of Israel agrees to assure full effect in Israeli law, in accordance with the provisions of this Agreement, to the legal personality of the following:
   a. these Eastern Catholic Patriarchates: the Greek Melkite Catholic, the Syrian Catholic, the Maronite, the Chaldean, the Armenian Catholic (hereinafter: the "Eastern Catholic Patriarchates");

b. the Latin Patriarchate of Jerusalem, id est the Latin Patriarchal Diocese of Jerusalem;

c. the present Dioceses of the Eastern Catholic Patriarchates;

d. new Dioceses, wholly in Israel, Eastern Catholic or Latin, as may exist from time to time;

e. the "Assembly of the Catholic Ordinaries of the Holy Land".

f. The Holy See states, for the avoidance of doubt, that the listing in par. 1 does not prejudice in any way the established order of precedence of the Heads of the various entities, according to their personal rank and as it is fixed by traditional usage and accepted by them.

g. For the avoidance of doubt, it is stated that the question of assuring full effect in Israeli law to the legal personality of any new cross-border Diocese is left open.

h. For the purposes of this Agreement, a Parish is an integral part of the respective Diocese, and, without affecting its status under the canon law, will not acquire a separate legal personality under Israeli law. A Diocese may, subject to the canon law, authorise its Parishes to act on its behalf, in such matters and under such terms, as it may determine.

i. In this Agreement, "Diocese" includes its synonyms or equivalents.

## Article 4

The State of Israel agrees to assure full effect in Israeli law, in accordance with the provisions of this Agreement, to the legal personality of the Custody of the Holy Land.

## Article 5

The State of Israel agrees to assure full effect in Israeli law, in accordance with the provisions of this Agreement, to the legal personality of the following, as they exist from time to time in Israel:

a. the Pontifical Institutes of Consecrated Life of the kinds that exist in the Catholic Church, and such of their Provinces or Houses as the Institute concerned may cause to be certified;

b. other official entities of the Catholic Church.

## Article 6

1. For the purposes of this Agreement the legal persons referred to in Articles 3–5 (hereinafter, in this Article: "legal person"), being established under the canon law, are deemed to have been created according to the legislation of the Holy See, being Sovereign in international law.

2.

    a. The law which governs any legal transaction or other legal acts in Israel between any legal person and any party shall be the law of the State of Israel, subject to the provisions of sub-paragraph (b).

    b. Any matter concerning the identity of the head, of the presiding officer or of any other official or functionary of a legal person, or their authority or their powers to act on behalf of the legal person, is governed by the canon law.

    c. Without derogation from the generality of sub-paragraph (b), certain kinds of transactions by a legal person concerning immovable property or certain other kinds of property, depend on a prior written permission of the Holy See in accordance with its written Decisions as issued from time to time. Public access to the aforesaid Decisions will be in accordance with the Implementation Provisions.

3.

    a. Any dispute concerning an internal ecclesiastical matter between a member, official or functionary of a legal person and any legal person, whether the member, official or functionary belongs to it or not, or between legal persons, shall be determined in accordance with the canon law, in a judicial or administrative ecclesiastical forum.

    b. For the avoidance of doubt it is stated that the provisions of 2(a) shall not apply to disputes referred to in the above sub-paragraph (a).

4. For the avoidance of doubt, it is stated:

    a. a legal person, whose legal personality is given full effect in Israel, is deemed to have consented to sue and be sued before a judicial or administrative forum in Israel, if that is the proper forum under Israeli law.

    b. Sub-paragraph (a) does not derogate from any provision in Articles 6–9.

## Article 7

The application of this Agreement to any legal person is without prejudice to any of its rights or obligations previously created.

## Article 8

1. For the avoidance of doubt, nothing in this Agreement shall be construed as supporting an argument that any of the legal persons to which this Agreement applies had not been a legal person prior to this Agreement.

2. If a party makes a claim that such a legal person had not been a legal person in Israeli law prior to this Agreement, that party shall bear the burden of proof.

*Article 9*

Should a question with regard to the canon law arise in any matter before a Court or forum other than in a forum of the Catholic Church, it shall be regarded as a question of fact.

*Article 10*

The terms "ecclesiastical" and "canon law" refer to the Catholic Church and its law.

*Article 11*

1. Without derogating from any provision, declaration or statement in the Fundamental Agreement, the ecclesiastical legal persons in existence at the time of the entry of this Agreement into force are deemed as being legal persons in accordance with the provisions of this Agreement, if listed in the ANNEXES to this Agreement, which are specified in par. 4.
2. The ANNEXES form, for all intents and purposes, an integral part of this Agreement.
3. The ANNEXES will include the official name, respective date or year of establishment in the Catholic Church, a local address and, if the head office is abroad, also its address.
4.
    a.  ANNEX I list [*not included*]

# APPENDIX III

**The Basic Agreement between the Holy See and the Palestinian Liberation Organization**
(drawn from Vol. 29 *J. of Palestinian Studies* 143–44 No. 3, Spring 2000)

*Preamble*

The Holy See, the Sovereign Authority of the Catholic Church, and the Palestine Liberation Organization (hereinafter: PLO), the Representative of the Palestinian People working for the benefit and on behalf of the Palestinian Authority:

Deeply aware of the special significance of the Holy Land, which is inter alia a privileged space for inter-religious dialogue between the followers of the three monotheistic religions;

Having reviewed the history and development of the relations between the Holy See and the Palestinian people, including the working contacts and the subsequent establishment—on October 26, 1994—of official relations between the Holy See and the PLO;

Recalling and confirming the establishment of the Bilateral Permanent Working Commission to identify, study and address issues of common interest between the two Parties;

Reaffirming the need to achieve a just and comprehensive peace in the Middle East, so that all its nations live as good neighbors and work together to achieve development and prosperity for the entire region and all its inhabitants;

Calling for a peaceful solution of the Palestinian-Israeli conflict, which would realize the inalienable national legitimate rights and aspirations of the Palestinian people, to be reached through negotiation and agreement, in order to ensure peace and security for all peoples of the region on the basis of international law, relevant United Nations and its Security Council resolutions, justice and equity;

Declaring that an equitable solution for the issue of Jerusalem, based on international resolutions, is fundamental for a just and lasting peace in the Middle East, and that unilateral decisions and actions altering the specific character and status of Jerusalem are morally and legally unacceptable;

Calling, therefore, for a special statute for Jerusalem, internationally guaranteed, which should safeguard the following: a. Freedom of religion and conscience for all; b. The equality before the law of the three monotheistic religions and their institutions and followers in the City; c. The proper identity and sacred character of the City and its universally significant, religious and cultural heritage; d. The Holy Places, the freedom of access to them and of worship in them; e. The Regime of "Status Quo" in those Holy Places where it applies;

Recognizing that Palestinians irrespective of their religious affiliation are equal members of Palestinian society;

Concluding that the achievements of the aforementioned Bilateral Permanent Working Commission now amount to appropriate matter for a first and Basic Agreement, which should provide a solid and lasting foundation for the continued development of their present and future relations, and for the furtherance of the Commission's on-going task,

Agree on the following Articles:

### Article 1

Paragraph 1:
The PLO affirms its permanent commitment to uphold and observe the human right to freedom of religion and conscience, as stated in the Universal Declaration of Human Rights and in other international instruments relative to its application.

Paragraph 2:
The Holy See affirms the commitment of the Catholic Church to support this right and states once more the respect that the Catholic Church has for the followers of other religions.

### Article 2

Paragraph 1:
The Parties are committed to appropriate cooperation in promoting respect for human rights, individual and collective, in combating all forms of discrimination and threats to human life and dignity, as well as to the promotion of understanding and harmony between nations and communities.

Paragraph 2:

The Parties will continue to encourage inter-religious dialogue for the promotion of better understanding between people of different religions.

### Article 3

The PLO will ensure and protect in Palestinian Law the equality of human and civil rights of all citizens, including specifically, inter alia, their freedom from discrimination, individually or collectively, on the ground of religious affiliation, belief or practice.

### Article 4

The regime of the "Status Quo" will be maintained and observed in those Christian Holy Places where it applies.

### Article 5

The PLO recognizes the freedom of the Catholic Church to exercise her rights to carry out, through the necessary means, her functions and traditions, such as those that are spiritual, religious, moral, charitable, educational and cultural.

### Article 6

The PLO recognizes the rights of the Catholic Church in economic, legal and fiscal matters: these rights being exercised in harmony with the rights of the Palestinian authorities in these fields.

### Article 7

Full effect will be given in Palestinian Law to the legal personality of the Catholic Church and of the canonical legal persons.

### Article 8

The provisions of this Agreement are without prejudice to any agreement hitherto in force between either Party and any other party.

### Article 9

The Bilateral Permanent Working Commission, in accordance with such instructions as may be given by the respective Authorities of the two Parties, may propose further ways to address items of this Agreement.

### Article 10

Should any controversy arise regarding the interpretation or the application of provisions of the present Agreement, the Parties will resolve it by way of mutual consultation.

*Article 11*

Done in two original copies in the English and Arabic languages, both texts being equally authentic. In case of divergency, the English text shall prevail.

*Article 12*

This Agreement shall enter into force from the moment of its signature by the two Parties.

# APPENDIX IV

### Forerunner to the Accord:
### A Personal Recollection on Issues of Pilgrimage
*Richard Mathes*

In 1979 talks were held at the Israeli Foreign Ministry on the founding of the Pontifical Institute of Notre Dame of Jerusalem Center. Since both Ambassador David Ephrati, who was in charge of religious affairs in the Foreign Ministry, and myself are German speaking, understanding was much facilitated. From time to time we met for a cup of tea and continued our dialogue, discussing much broader matters also. Over these cups of tea we explored ways to promote an eventual understanding between church and state, between the Holy See and the State of Israel. Sometimes we joked about our work, calling it "knitting around the problems," like one knits Brussels-lace. But you know, lace is sometimes quite precious.

The apostolic delegate of those days encouraged me. Indeed, I believe that Ephrati and I would have opened a good "backchannel" if the time had not been against us. On both sides other, "bigger" interests took over: in the Vatican it was the "Ostpolitik," and in Israel it was the conclusion of the Camp David Agreements, and later the beginning of the war in Lebanon. Both parties had other, "bigger" interests.

During that period, in April 1981, a big problem arose for the Church: in 1978 dispositions were made by the Israeli authorities that every group—pilgrims or others—"has to be accompanied by a licensed travel guide," or so it read in the small print of the new licence documents for travel agencies. Nobody took this very seriously—it was in the small print! In the winter of 1981, however, several pilgrim groups were harassed by organized licensed guides. The Pastoral Commission for Pilgrimage wrote letters of complaint to the Ministry of Religious Affairs, but there was never an answer. Nobody took this matter very seriously.

In the spring of 1981 a number of travel agencies that dealt with pilgrimage received from the competent authority a circular letter threatening them with immediate closure if they continued to ignore the dispositions. Two travel agencies informed the Church that priests could no longer serve as guides for pilgrims. The apostolic delegation in Jerusalem as well as the Latin Patriarchate were asked to intervene.

Internal discussions in the Church came to the conclusion that vital rights of religious pilgrimage were seriously endangered. There was, on the other hand, also a certain understanding for the need and right of the state to issue regulations for mass tourism, especially because many groups were led by incompetent foreign tour leaders in order to save the fee of a competent locally licensed guide.

### The Ensuing Negotiation

Shortly thereafter, the Pastoral Commission for Pilgrimage of the Latin Patriarchate wrote a letter to the Ministry of Religious Affairs, asking for assurance that with these new measures the millennial rights of the Church would not be touched. The letter was made public, and there was a quick response on Israel radio: "Inside the Church the priests may do what they want; outside the church the law of Israel prevails." With this, a strict division was drawn between "inside the church" and "outside the church," which was unacceptable to the Christian community. The conflict had precise contours: on one side the Church defending the millennial rights of pilgrimage to the holy shrines not being disturbed by outsiders, on the other side the sovereignty of the state regarding law and order.

A first public exchange took place that heated up into a media brawl. The Pastoral Commission created a subcommittee involving the Franciscans, the Latin Patriarchate, the Ecumenical Commission, and indirectly through the membership of the Committee in Charge of the Notre Dame of Jerusalem Center, the Holy See.

The apostolic delegation sent me to the Foreign Ministry to explore matters (using the "backchannel," if you like) and eventually finish the conflict over a cup of tea, maybe in the hope that the Ministry of Religious Affairs would write an appeasing letter to the Pastoral Commission of the Latin Patriarchate reaffirming the traditional rights of the Church. The continuing absence of such a letter induced the Church to see in the growing conflict a matter of principle: whether the State of Israel would be ready to limit its sovereignty (including its claimed sovereignty on Jerusalem) in order to respect the traditional rights of the religious communities. On this principal question it seemed both sides were digging their heels in. The situation was about to get out of hand. Then Cardinal Casaroli, the secretary of the Holy See, gave me a verbal instruction through the apostolic delegate "[t]o make peace as soon as possible, however not to sacrifice one centimeter of the essence of the Traditional Rights."

So I called for a definitive meeting in the Notre Dame Center in Jerusalem to hammer out an agreement; a lot of journalists were waiting outside the room. The result was a common press release published at the end of the meeting:

> Today, July 5th, 1981, a meeting took place between representatives of the Government of Israel—Ministry of Foreign Affairs, Ministry of Religious Affairs, Ministry of Commerce, Trade and Tourism—and Representatives of the Pastoral Commission for Pilgrimage of the Latin Patriarchate in Jerusalem. . . . [The representatives agreed] that pilgrim groups [may] be guided by tour leaders and priests in Churches, Holy Sites and every other place in the country where religious and spiritual guidance is the primary object of the visit. . . . Further meetings to work out details and improvings are foreseen.[1]

In a follow-up meeting use of the so-called "Green Card" was proposed by the Pastoral Commission (and later accepted by the Israeli government) as a means to easily identify the religious groups that fall under that protocol.

### Further Developments

There were still some ups and downs, as the Tour Guides Union did not accept this accord. However, this basic agreement—although not ratified—became a sound basis for the dealings between church and state in the Holy Land. A certain cooperation established itself, strongly visible when the Guides Union attacked both state and church at the High Court of Justice some years later. On November 9, 1987, the High Court of Justice rejected the guides' petition, reaffirming the agreement as well as the practice of the Green Card. It did so again in 1992, finding that intervention on its part would be an inappropriate political act by the judiciary.[2] The matter was also raised, unsuccessfully, in the Knesset as late as 1994.[3]

The "gentlemen's agreement" of the Notre Dame Center holds. It surely contributed in its sometimes rocky history to building up trust by its basic stability. Twelve years later, the issue of the overdue overall agreement leading to the recognition between Israel and the Holy See was settled. The endeavor on which the Vatican negotiator, Archbishop Montezemolo, had to embark was tremendous in size and in political risks. It was concluded successfully. On later occasions Ambassador David Ephrati and myself always stressed that the agreement of Notre Dame Center could be seen as a "small exploring ship testing the way for the bigger one to come."

### Conclusion

I would like to draw some modest conclusions from these informal talks and agreements between the State of Israel and the Holy See from 1979 till the early 1980s. While they were talks on a low-key level, they had a certain "confidence-building" function for the respective authorities.

From an analysis of the reconciling letter of the Ministry of Religious Affairs of July 2, 1981, and the common press release given at Notre Dame on July 5, 1981, four points are clear.

First, an unsigned, and I stress, *unsigned*, common protocol was published, but it is respected like a full treaty. It is a political gentlemen's agreement, a pragmatic accord that got its legally binding force by judgment of the High Court of Justice. I think this is unique!

Second, it was the first time that the State of Israel and the Church came to some sort of agreement on an issue of principle involving the whole Church in the Holy Land, where the Holy See was closely involved.

Third, this whole procedure has established, in spite of the ups and downs, a certain trust and good faith on both sides, facilitating partnership in other important issues.

Fourth, in fact by this agreement the State of Israel restricted its sovereignty in favor of religious needs. The Church, on her side, acknowledged the right of the state to care for the common good of its citizens, taking this into account by limiting the exercise of her ancient rights in pilgrimage by and with the use of the Green Card: not everybody, not every priest, can lead a group on pilgrimage, only the well-examined holder of the Green Card. In this way, the Pastoral Commission for Pilgrimage helps the state in its task of upholding law and order.

Thus, with the agreement on pilgrimage, the Holy See and Israel started down a path leading to more common understanding of the mutually relevant issues, which later encouraged the formal negotiations on a larger scale.

### NOTES

1. The full Press Release, in the possession of the author, reads as follows:

Today, July 5th, 1981, a meeting took place between representatives of the Government of Israel—Ministry of Foreign Affairs, Ministry of Religious Affairs, Ministry of Commerce, Trade and Tourism—and Representatives of the Pastoral Commission for Pilgrimage of the Latin Patriarchate in Jerusalem.

The Representatives of the Government and of the Pastoral Commission came to the agreement that pilgrimages are religious activities and may be freely assisted by spiritual leaders or animateurs, following the letter of Mr. Daniel Rossing, Director of the Department for Christian Affairs, July 2, 1981, in which it is said:

"The Ministry of Commerce, Trade and Tourism wholeheartedly accepts the view that pilgrim groups, because of their specific religious and spiritual needs, be guided by tour leaders and priests in Churches, Holy Sites and every other place in the country where religious and spiritual guidance is the primary object of the visit."

It is self-evident that the Ministry of Commerce, Trade and Tourism has the task of ameliorating the conditions of acceptance of pilgrims, as well as of tourists in the country.

The meeting took place in a constructive spirit. Further meetings to work out details and improvings are foreseen.

2. The court case is discussed in Evelyn Gordon, "Vatican Details Stand on 'Palestine' Guides," *Jerusalem Post,* Feb. 20, 1992.

3. Haim Shapiro, PM aide, "Sovereignty Over Christian Holy Sites Lost," *Jerusalem Post,* Dec. 15, 1994.

# INDEX

Abu Mazen-Beilin "non-paper," 8,
    20n57
Adoption of Children Law (1981),
    258, 271n77
Agreement on the Gaza Strip and
    the Jericho Area (1994), 256
Agreement on Legal Matters (Spain,
    1979), 129
Amos 9:13–15, 345
anti-Semitism, cooperation in combating,
    38–39, 43, 73–75
Arab Orthodox Church, 313
Arafat, Yasser, 8, 333
Argentina, church-state relations,
    post–Vatican II, 99–101, 144
Asia, pilgrimage rights in, 213
Assembly of Catholic Bishops of the
    Holy Land, 310, 323–24
Ateek, Naim, 313
Austria, concordats with Holy See,
    142, 144, 147
Autonomous Communities (Spain),
    125–27

Baeck, Rabbi Leo, 356
Bahai-Israeli taxation agreement, 12
Basic Agreement between the Holy See
    and the Palestinian Liberation
    Organization
    Article 1, commentary, 155
    Article 4, commentary, 157, 158
    consequence to Israel, 160–61
    Fundamental Agreement compared
        to, 147, 153–61
    Holy Places protection in the, 70–71
    overview, 8, 315–16
    preamble, comments on, 153–54
    reasons for entering into, 150–51
    text of, 369–72
    Vatican-Israel relations, effect on, 174–75
Beilin, Yossi, 34–35, 41–42
Benveniste, Abraham, 121
Berlin, Isaiah, 184
Bethlehem, 2–3, 7, 17n22
Bilateral Permanent Working
    Commission, 32, 35–43
Bosnia, pilgrimage rights in, 213

Cairo Agreement (1994), 152
campaign of exclusion, 319–20, 331–32
Camp David negotiations (2000), 8, 321
Catholic Church
    Fundamental Agreement goals, 70
    in the Holy Land, 310, 314, 323–26, 333
    Jerusalem position
    —internationalization, 2–3, 17n22, 317
    —internationally guaranteed special
        statute, 9, 316–19
    —reconciliation, 289–90
    Judaism, theological understanding of,
        1–2, 343–45, 354–56
    recognition as legal entity. *See* Legal
        Personality Agreement
    as sovereign state, 58–61, 69–70
Celli, Archbishop Claudio, 4
*Centesimus Annus* (John Paul II), 240
charitable services. *See* social welfare
China, pilgrimage rights in, 214,
        229n111
Christian churches in Israel, legislation,
        40, 46n31
Christian community
    defined, 80
    in the Holy Land, 6, 19n45, 54–55, 284
    of Jerusalem, 6–8, 19n48–49, 320,
        327–28
Christian Embassy, 330
Christian-Muslim relations. *See* Muslim-
    Christian interreligious coexistence
Church of the Annunciation, 11, 63, 173,
        328–30, 333
Church of the Holy Sepulcher, 151
    ownership dispute, 6, 8, 19n43, 322–23
    Status Quo arrangement and, 78–79,
        157, 254
Church of the Nativity, Bethlehem, 10,
        25n114, 78, 151, 157, 254
Churches for Middle East Peace
        (CMEP), 317
church-state relations. *See specific
    locations*, e.g. Israel

Colombia, church-state relations,
        99–101, 144, 145
Commission of Advisors on Religious
        Liberty (Spain), 125
Community of Saint James, 323
concordats, role in church-state relations,
        122–23, 139–47
Conference on Security and Co-operation
        in Europe (CSCE), 212
"Confrontation" (Soloveitchik), 356
conscience, freedom of. *See* religion and
        conscience, freedom of
"Considerations of the [Vatican]
        Secretariat of State on Jerusalem"
        (1996), 317
conversion. *See* religious freedom
cooperation principle, 124
Copts, Holy Places control issues, 6, 18n41
Crime of Genocide (Prevention and
        Punishment), 259
Criminal Law Ordinance (Palestine,
        1936), 255
Croatia, church-state relations, 98,
        113n29, 146–47
cultural exchanges, adoption date, 39

Dalrymple, William, 335
Declaration on the Elimination of
        All Forms of Intolerance and
        of Discrimination Based on
        Religion or Belief (1981), 74,
        185–87
Declaration on the Establishment of
        the State of Israel (1948), 250–52
Declaration of Principles, PLO-Israel
        (1992), 152
Defamation Law, 259
Deir al-Sultan monastery, 6, 18n41, 254
del Val, Cardinal Merry, 16n9
Deuteronomy
        26:17–18, 346
        6:4, 347
*dhimmi*, 54–55, 279, 284

*Dignitatis Humanae* (Vatican II), 104, 105,
142, 143, 240
diplomatic normalization, Israel–Holy See
John Paul II's visit to Israel, effect on,
175–77
negotiations process, 33, 37–38,
167–69
diplomatic relations, Israel–Holy See
beginnings, 30–33, 35
declaration of full, 42–43
goals, 29–30
Gulf War influence on, 32–33, 285–86
independence from Western powers
maintained, 280–81, 285–86
key figures, 31–33
Oslo Accords influence on, 30, 34–35,
69–70
special representatives to the
negotiations, 38–39
diplomatic relations, Jordan–Holy See,
294–95
discrimination based on religion.
*See* equality/nondiscrimination
principle

economic issues. *See also* taxation
agreement negotiations overview, 37
in Basic vs. Fundamental Agreement,
159
of property, 12, 78, 84–85, 126
subcommission purpose, 61, 62
Vatican-Israel relationship and, 11–13
ecumenism, events affecting Holy Land,
8, 310–13, 318–27
education
agreement negotiations overview, 36
in Basic vs. Fundamental Agreement,
158–59
financial obligation for, 11, 82
religious
—in Israel, 177, 262
—in Jordanian society, 294
—in Spain, 126

responsibility for
—Israel vs. Church, 75–76, 82,
106–7, 108
—in Italy, 144
Egyptian Christian Church, Holy Places
control issues, 6, 18n41
emigration
contributory factors, 286, 319–20
future of, 335
as Middle East policy failure, 286–87,
305n116
right to return provision vs. right to
entry, 210–11, 222n62, 223n65
Employment Service Law, 259
equality/nondiscrimination principle
discrimination based on religion
—Israeli legislation on, 258–60,
271n77, 272n89
—pilgrimage rights and, 209,
211–12, 216
exemptions to, 258, 259
historical issues (*dhimmi, millets*),
54–56, 279, 284
John Paul II on, 52
Recognized Religious Community
and, 56–61, 65n19, 86, 262–64
in Spanish Constitution (1978), 124
Estonia, post–Vatican II concordats, 146
Ethiopian Christians, Holy Places control
issues, 6–7, 18n41
European Convention on Human Rights
(ECHR, 1950), 125, 192–94, 227n99
European Court of Human Rights, 125,
192–93, 227n99
Evangelical entities, agreement with
Spain, 126–27
expression, freedom of, 83, 200n57.
*See also* proselytize, freedom to
Ezekiel 36:22–28, 345

Fadlallah, Sheik Mohammed Hussein,
305n99
faith, as factor in peace, 243–44

*Faithful of the Temple Mount et al. v. Commander of Police in the Jerusalem Area,* 252–53
financial matters. *See also* taxation
  charitable services, financing obligations, 83–84
  church-state agreements (Spain), 126
  ecclesiastical property, 84–85, 126
  education, financing obligations, 11, 82
  Italian Concordat of 1984 and, 144
  negotiations process, 37, 62
  Spanish agreements vs. Fundamental Agreement, 130
Financial Status Agreement, 70
Fischer-Chouvel agreement (1948), 11, 23n89
Fitzmaurice, Gerald, 223n70
France, 147, 213
Freedom of Occupation Law (Israel), 250, 251, 252
Friends of Sabeel, 313
Fundamental Agreement (1993)
  background, 69–72, 315
  Basic Agreement compared to, 147, 153–61
  basic concepts, 3–6, 69
  commentary
  —Article 1, 72–73, 81, 103–9, 185–86
  —Article 2, 71, 73–75
  —Article 3, 75–76, 107–9, 116n66
  —Article 3(3), 76–78
  —Article 4, 78–81, 158
  —Article 5, 81–82, 208–9
  —Article 6, 82
  —Article 7, 82
  —Article 8, 83
  —Article 9, 83–84
  —Article 10, 84–85
  —Article 11, 85, 154
  —Article 12, 62, 86
  —Article 13, 59–60, 86–87
  —Article 14, 87
  —Article 15, 87
  —preamble, 72

implementation delays/setbacks, 4, 63, 330–31
Israel's approval of, 65n21, 252
John Paul II, role in, 352–53
legal matters in Basic vs. Fundamental Agreement, 159
as model for conventions with non-Christian countries, 110–11, 116n74
negotiations process, 42–43, 58–60, 167–69
Netanyahu government position, 4
outcomes desired, Israel vs. Holy See, 29–30, 70, 167–69
Palestinian reaction to, 314
politics-religion distinction made in, 31
post-signing
—church-state relationship, 167–78
—results attained, Israel vs. Holy See, 43–44
Spanish agreements (1976) compared, 119–31
text of, 359–64
treaty status of, 204–8

Gabon, concordats with Holy See, 147
*Gaudium et Spes* (Second Vatican Council), 142, 143
Genesis 15:1–7, 352
Germany, concordats with Holy See, 142, 144, 147
Great Jubilee (2000), 173, 175–77, 321–22, 323, 353–54
*Greece v. Kokkinakis,* 192–93
*Greece v. Larissis,* 193–94
Greek Catholic (Melkite) community, 172, 323, 332
Greek Orthodox Church, 6, 19n45, 312–13, 334, 339n55
Gulf War (First), 32–33, 285–86, 300n45, 301n48
Gur, Shlomo, 39, 41

Haiti, post–Vatican II concordats, 144

Hajj, 213, 214, 215, 217, 228n101–6, 229n109, 231n127

Hanna, Archimandrite Atala, 331

Haram al-Sharif (Temple Mount), 256–57

Hasmonean Tunnel, 319

Herzegovina, pilgrimage rights in, 213

Herzl, Theodore, 1–2

Hirsch, Moshe, 203, 209

Holy Land
  Christian community in, 6, 19n45, 54–55, 284
  churches of the, 312–18, 323–26. *See also specific churches*
  church-state relations, history, 53–61
  defined, 336n4
  language of, interpretations, 72

Holy Places. *See also* pilgrimage, "right" to; *specific sites*
  administration of, 257
  Basic vs. Fundamental Agreement, 157–58
  control issues, 6–8, 12, 79, 150, 254–57, 269n40
  demographic concerns, 9
  desecration of, protection against, 255–57
  freedom of access and worship at, 256–57, 331–32
  international guarantees for, 2–3, 10–11, 171–72
  jurisdiction issues, 12, 256–57, 271n66
  official designation of, 80, 269n40
  Status Quo arrangement and, 19n45, 78–81, 157–58, 254–55

Holy Places Law (1967), 79

Holy See
  components constituting, 206, 219n27
  Fundamental Agreement, results derived from, 43–44
  statehood qualifications of, 205–6
  treaty-making capacity of, 205–7
  Vatican and the, juridical differences, 206

Hosea
  11:8–9, 345
  2:19, 345

Hours of Work and Rest Law (1950–1951), 258

Human Dignity and Liberty Law (1992), 127–28, 250, 251, 252, 267n20

human rights
  in Basic vs. Fundamental Agreement, 155–57
  Church teachings on, 239–40
  Fundamental Agreement guarantees, 110–11
  for Palestinians, Catholic Church on, 314
  peace, relationship to, 235–45, 325
  religious freedom, relationship to, 240–41
  right to change one's belief, 155–56

human rights law
  pilgrimage and, 81, 209–13, 216–17
  proselytism freedoms under, 184–85

Hungarian Concordat of 1964, 145, 146

Hussein, King of Jordan, 294–95

India, pilgrimage in, 212, 213

indigenous people, 214, 220n40, 230n221

Innocent III, Pope, 344

Interim Agreement on the West Bank and the Gaza Strip (Israel-Palestine, 1995), 256

International Convention on the Elimination of All Forms of Racial Discrimination, 74, 225n81, 260

International Court of Justice, on pilgrimage, 214–15

International Covenant on Civil and Political Rights (ICCPR, 1996)
  Fundamental Agreement, specifications of, 106
  Israeli amendation to, 263, 274n113
  Israel's commitment to, 252
  pilgrimage, 81

International Covenant on Civil and
Political Rights (*cont.*)
religious freedom limitations in, 253
on right to maintain and change a
religion, 155–56, 185–90, 194,
200n54
right to return provision vs. right to
entry, 211, 226n84
International Covenant on Economic,
Social and Cultural Rights, 106,
114n37
intifada (1987–1993), 310, 312–14, 318
intolerance prohibition vs. freedom of
opinion, 259
Iraq, travel-related restrictions affecting
pilgrimage, 215, 232n137
Ireneios, Patriarch, 334, 339n55
Isaiah
4:11, 346
54:10, 345–46
Islam
discrimination, historical, 54–55
Holy Places control issues, 7–8
pilgrimage regulation in, 213, 214
on right to maintain and change a
religion, 155–56, 186–88, 191
territory of, *dar-al-islam* vs. *dar-al-harb*,
53–54
Islamic fundamentalism, 284–85,
328. *See also* Nazareth Mosque
controversy
Israel. *See also* religious freedom, Israel
Basic Agreement, consequence to,
160–61
basic law of human rights in, 250
Christian churches, legislation in,
40, 46n31
Christian churches legislation, 46n31
Christian Embassy relationship, 330
covenant of God with, 345–48
discrimination, historical, 56–58
Hasmonean Tunnel opening, 319

history (1917–1946), overview
Jerusalem access denied to Palestinians,
319–20, 331–32
Jewish character of, 250–51
Legal Personality Agreement approved
by, 18n33
legal system and Jewish law, 250–51
pilgrimage regulation in, 214, 215,
231n127, 232n127
Recognized Religious Community and,
56–61, 65n19, 86, 260–63
significance to Jews, 348–52
statehood qualifications of, 205, 218n16
treaty-making capacity of, 205
Israel, Basic Law
Freedom of Occupation (1992), 250,
251, 252
Human Dignity and Liberty (1992), 127,
250, 251, 252, 267n20
Jerusalem Capital of Israel (1980), 79
the Knesset, 250–51
Law on the Foundations of Law, 251
the President of the State (1964), 258
Israel, church-state relations. *See also*
Fundamental Agreement; Legal
Personality Agreement
Basic Agreement's effect on, 174–75
education, financing obligations, 82
framework, in Fundamental
Agreement, 71
Holy Places protection and, 10–11
Holy See vs. local church triangulation,
330
Mouallem controversy, 332
Nazareth Mosque controversy, 10–11,
63, 173, 328–30, 333
post–Fundamental Agreement, 167–78
property rights, 84–85
proselytizing vs. right to freedom of
expression, 83
Recognized Religious Community,
56–61, 65n19, 262–64

religious freedom, commitment to, 104–8

social welfare, financing obligations, 83–84

Spanish system compared to, 119–20, 123, 127–31

state law–religious law interaction, 56–58

Israel–Holy See, state-state relations. *See also* Fundamental Agreement; Legal Personality Agreement

anti-Semitism, cooperation in combating, 74–75

education, responsibility for, 75–76

framework in Fundamental Agreement, 71

goals, Israel vs. Holy See, 70

Holy See's involvement with secular issues, 85

principle of distinction, 107–9

religious freedom, obligation to, 73, 185–86, 195

social welfare, responsibility for, 75–76

succession of Archbishop Saloum, 172–73

Israeli-Palestinian conflict, 287–90

Italy, church-state relations, 97–98, 142, 143–44

Jaeger, David, 35, 40, 41, 46n40

Japan, pilgrimage in, 213, 229n112

Jehovah's Witnesses, 126

Jeremiah 31:35–36, 345–46

Jerusalem

Christian community in, 6–8, 19n48–49, 320, 327–28

Christian population decline in, 7, 19n48–49, 320

church history, 311–12

internationalization of, 2–3, 17n22, 154, 317

internationally guaranteed special statute for, 9, 43–44, 316–19

John Paul II on significance of, 289–90, 350

Palestinians denied access, 319–20, 331–32

Jerusalem Capital of Israel Law (1980), 79

Jesus' Cradle, 7–8

Jewish-Catholic reconciliation

incidents of negative impact, 177–78

Jerusalem, significance to, 289–90

Jubilee pilgrimage of John Paul II (2000), 175–77, 321–22, 323, 353–54

—Yad VaShem memorial visit of John Paul II (2000), 353–54

liturgy of repentance, St. Peter's Basilica (2000), 353

post–Fundamental Agreement, 174

Jewish-Catholic relations

framework in Fundamental Agreement, 71

overview, 10

Jews/Jewish people. *See also* Zionism

covenant between God and Israel, 345–48

discrimination based on religion, 258, 259–60

Innocent III compares to Cain, 344

Israel, significance of, 348–52

Jerusalem, significance to, 350–51

pilgrimage by, 214, 230n119–20

recognition of, 1–2, 16n9

Spain and the, 120–22, 126–27

theological understanding by Catholic Church, 1–2, 31, 343–45, 354–56

John Paul II, Pope

on equality/nondiscrimination principle, 52

on freedom of religion, 52, 240–43

Gulf War comments, 285–86, 300n45, 301n48

on human rights, 239–40, 243

John Paul II, Pope (*cont.*)
influence on Fundamental Agreement,
352–53
on Israel-Shoah connection, 348–49
Jerusalem, significance of, 289–90,
350
Jubilee pilgrimage (2000), 175–77,
321–22, 353–54
liturgy of repentance, St. Peter's
Basilica (2000), 353
Middle East policy under, 283–87
on Palestinian suffering, 322
on peace, 239, 243
synagogue visit (1986), 352
Universal Declaration, response to,
239
World Peace Day message (1982), 245
World Peace Day message (1991), 243
Jordanian model of inter-religious
coexistence, 294–95
*Justice and Only Justice* (Ateek), 313
just-war concept, 285, 300n45, 301n48

Kandallaf, Ibrahim, 7
Kazakhstan, concordats with Holy See,
110–11, 147
Keeler, Cardinal William, 4
Klein, Menachem, 175
*Kokkinakis v. Greece*, 192–94
Kuwait, 297n9

laicity (secularity) principle, 124
Länder of the Weimar Republic,
concordats with, 144–45
*Larissis v. Greece*, 193–94
Latvia, post–Vatican II concordats, 146
Law on the Foundations of Law, 251
Law of the Political Reform (Spain, 1977),
122
Law of Return, 259, 272n89
Lebanon, model of mixed religious
society, 279, 290–94, 303n81, 305n99

legal matters
in Basic vs. Fundamental Agreement, 159
Bilateral Permanent Working
Commission agenda item, 36
church-state agreements, Spain, 126
Legal Personality Agreement
Bilateral Permanent Working
Commission negotiations, 40–41
Catholic Church and Holy See, legal
status of, 77–78
Fundamental Agreement Article 3(3)
and, 4–5, 76–78
immovable property, legal status, 78
implementation
—delays/setbacks, 63
—Israeli Court, influence on, 65n21
Israel approval, 18n33
juridical subcommission, 61, 170
Netanyahu government position, 4
overview, 61–62
PLO position, 6
purpose, 5
Recognized Religious Community
component, 60–61
text of, 365–68
legal personality, recognition of
in Basic vs. Fundamental Agreement, 159
church-state agreements, Spain, 126
Church vs. organizations of, 108–9
Israel, requirements for, 130
Spanish agreements vs. Fundamental
Agreement, 128–31
Leo XIII, 281
Levi, David, 170, 174
liberation theology, Palestinian, 310, 313–14
Libya, travel-related restrictions affecting
pilgrimage, 215, 233n137, 233n141
Lithuania, post–Vatican II concordats, 146

Madrid International Peace Conference
(1991), 30, 33, 34, 288
Malta, post–Vatican II concordats, 146–47

Margalit, Eitan, 29–30
Maronite Christians, 323
Melkite (Greek Catholic) community, 172,
    323, 332
Mexico, right to return provision, 226n84
Middle East policy of the Holy See
    diplomacy independent from Western
        powers, 280–81, 285–86, 301n53
    Christian-Muslim society, development
        of, 279–83, 286
    emigration as failure of, 286–87,
        305n116
    for Islamic fundamentalism, 284–85
    Israeli-Palestinian conflict and, 287–90
    John Paul II papacy, 283–87
    Lebanon model, 290–94, 303n81,
        305n99
    local churches acknowledged, 281–82
    maintain a Catholic presence in the
        Holy Land, 278–79, 305n116
    objective, 278–79
    overview, 295–96
    tri-polar model, 276–78
Middle East policy of the Holy See,
    strategy
Milk Grotto, 254
*millets*, 56–57, 279. *See also* Recognized
    Religious Community
minorities, defined, 132n7
Missionary Law (1977), 173–74
Monaco, post–Vatican II concordats, 144
Montevideo Convention, 206
Montezemolo, Monsignor Andrea
    Cordero Lanza di, 31–35, 38, 40, 41
Morocco, 101–2, 110, 113n20, 146
Mouallem, Bishop Boutros, 172–73, 332
Muslim-Christian interreligious
    coexistence. *See also* Palestinian
    Christians
    demographic tensions, 327–28
    Holy See Middle East policy strategy,
        279–83, 286

Islamic fundamentalism and, 328
Jordanian model, 294–95
Lebanon model, 290–94, 303n81,
    305n99
Middle East Christians role,
    326–27
Nazareth Mosque controversy,
    10–11, 63, 173, 328–30, 333
tensions in, causes of, 310
Zionism's effect on, 287–90
Muslim Commission (Spain),
    126–27
Muslims, pilgrimage by, 213, 215,
    217, 231n127

Nationality Law, 259
National Pact of Community Coexistence
    (1943), 290–91
Native Americans, 214, 220n40,
    230n221
Nazareth, *corpus separatum*
    recommendation, 2–3, 17n3
Nazareth Mosque controversy, 10–11,
    63, 173, 328–30, 333
Netanyahu government, 4, 170,
    172–73, 319–20, 332
Nigerians, pilgrimage by, 228n104
nondiscrimination/equality principle.
    *See* equality/nondiscrimination
    principle
normalization of diplomatic
    relations. *See* diplomatic
    normalization
*Nostra Aetate* (Paul VI), 282, 288
Notes on Correct Way . . . in the
    Roman Catholic Church, 31

"On the Significance of Jerusalem for
    Christians" (1994), 317, 319
Organization of African Unity, 147
Organization of the Islamic Conference
    (OIC), 213

Organization on Security and
Cooperation in Europe (OSCE), 212
Oslo Accords (1993–2000), 30, 34–35,
69–70, 153–54, 314–15

*Pacem in Terris* (John Paul II), 142, 239
Palestine (Holy Places) Order in Council
(1924), 12, 79, 254–55, 256, 269n40
Palestine Liberation Organization
(PLO)–Vatican agreement. *See* Basic
Agreement
Palestine mandate, 2–3, 16n13, 16n14,
17n22
Palestine Royal Commission Report,
2, 17n22
Palestinian Authority (PA), 7–8, 150,
152–53, 332–33. *See also* PLO
Palestinian Christians. *See also* Muslim-
Christian interreligious coexistence
future for, 333–36
intifada, effect on, 310, 312–13, 318
Jerusalem access denied, 319–20,
331–32
liberation theology of, 313–14
Oslo Accords effect on, 314–15
religious freedoms of, 331–32
Palestinians
Jerusalem access denied, 319–20,
331–32
John Paul II on suffering of, 322
Muslim-Christian society, effect on,
287–90
right to pilgrimage, 230n119
Paul VI, Pope, 175, 239, 283, 288
Pazner, Avi, 31–32
peace and human rights, relationship of,
235–45, 325
Peel Report, 2, 17n22
Penal Law, 259
*People Israel, The* (Baeck), 356
Peru, church-state relations, 99–101
"Philosophy Implicit in the Midrash, The"
(Slonimsky), 347

pilgrimage. *See also* religious freedom
advantages to favoring, 216–17
discrimination on basis of religion
and, 209, 211–12, 216
Fundamental Agreement on, 208–9
regulation of, 213–17, 228n101–6,
229n109, 232n127, 233n141
right to return provision vs. right to
entry, 210–11, 222n62, 223n65,
225n81, 226n82–84
travel-related restrictions affecting,
215, 233n137, 233n141
Vatican paper on, 234n153
pilgrimage, "right" to
approval date, 36
Holy See recognition of, 209
human rights law on, 81–82, 209–13
Israel, recognition of, 209, 231n127
language of, interpretations, 203–4
negotiations overview, 39
summary, 217
"Pilgrimage in the Great Jubilee of the
Year 2000," 234n153
pilgrimage legislation
future of, 217
human rights law on, 81, 216–17
international law on, 214–15
summary, 216
United States, 214, 230n121
Pius IX, Pope, 281
Pius X, Pope, 1–2
PLO (Palestine Liberation Organization).
*See also* Palestinian Authority (PA)
foreign relations capacity of,
152–53
Vatican links established, 8
Poland, church-state relations, 98,
145, 146–47
Pontifical Institute for Oriental
Studies, 281
Portugal, 144–45, 213
President of the State Law (Israel,
1964), 258

property
  ecclesiastical, 12, 84–85, 126
  immovable, 78
proselytize, freedom to. *See also* religious
    freedom
  in Basic Agreement, 153
  in Basic vs. Fundamental Agreement, 156
  freedom of expression vs., 83, 200n57
  freedom to maintain a religion without
    interference vs., 184–85, 188–91,
    195–96, 200n54
  international law and, 188–96
  in Israel, 261
  Israel vs. Holy See obligations, 195
  Missionary Law (1977) and, 173–74
Protection of the Holy Places Law, 255, 256
Protocol Concerning the Redeployment
    in Hebron (1997), 256
Prussian Concordat (1929), 142

Rabin, Yitzhak, 170
Rabin government, 32, 170
Rachel's Tomb, 254
"Reading the Bible in the Land of the
    Bible" (Sabbah), 324
Recognized Religious Community, 56–61,
    65n19, 86, 262–64. *See also millets;*
    religious community
*Redemptionis Anno* (John Paul II), 350
*Redemptor Hominis* (John Paul II), 239, 241
religion and conscience, freedom of
  approval/adoption dates, 36
  inclusion of conscience, PLO objection
    to, 155
  in Israel, 251–54
  Israel vs. Holy See obligations to, 73
  purpose of inclusion, 103–4
Religious Communities Ordinance
    (1926), 57
religious community. *See also* Recognized
    Religious Community
  Autonomous Communities, Spain,
    125–27

Muslim, discrimination via
    *millets,* 55
  religious freedom rights, 109,
    260–61
Religious Community (Change)
    Ordinance (1927), 261
religious confessions, Spain,
    128–29. *See also* Autonomous
    Communities, Spain
*Religious Entities Register Book,* 125–26,
    128–29
religious freedom. *See also* education,
    religious; pilgrimage; proselytize,
    freedom to
  in Basic vs. Fundamental Agreement,
    155–57
  defined by Vatican II, 104
  European Court of Human Rights
    contribution, 125
  Fundamental Agreement as
    model for conventions with
    non-Christian countries,
    110–11, 116n74
  human rights, as an aspect of,
    240–41
  inclusion of conscience, PLO
    objection to, 155
  individual vs.collective right to,
    105–7, 109–10, 128
  international guarantees for, 9–10
  Israel vs. Holy See obligations, 73,
    185–86, 195
  John Paul II on, 52, 240–41
  minority guarantee of, 163n37
  of Palestinian Christians, 331–32
  right to maintain or change a
    religion, 155–56, 173–74,
    184–91, 195–96, 200n54
  Second Vatican Council on, 240
  in Spanish Constitution (1978),
    123–25, 134n25–29
  worship, right to, 80–81, 254,
    256–57, 331–32

religious freedom, Israel. *See also* Israel
  commitment to, 127–28
  —access to Jerusalem denied, 331–32
  —international commitments to, 252,
    267n23
  equality/nondiscrimination principle,
    258–60, 271n77, 272n89
  jurisdiction over matters of personal
    status, 262–64
  legislation guaranteeing, 250–53
  limitations, 253–54
  proselytize, freedom to, 261
  right to change one's religion,
    260–61
  summary, 264–65
Religious Liberty Law (Spain, 1967), 122
Religious Liberty Law (Spain, 1980),
  125, 129
religious liberty principle, 124, 131
*Rerum Orientalium* (Pius XI), 281
Romans 11, 345, 348
Roosevelt, Eleanor, 224n74
Russia, pilgrimage legislation, 214

Sabbah, Michel, 310, 312, 319, 324–26, 333
Sabeel, 313
Sacred Congregation for the Oriental
  Church, 281
sacred places. *See* Holy Places
*Sages, The* (Urbach), 346–47
Saloum, Maximus, 172–73
Sanctuary of the Ascension, 78, 157, 254
San Marino, post–Vatican II concordats,
  144, 146
Saudi Arabia
  pilgrimage regulation in, 213, 214, 215,
    217, 228n101–6, 229n109
  on right to maintain and change a
    religion, 186–87
Sea of Galilee, 2–3, 17n22
secularity (laicity) principle, 124
"Seek Peace and Pursue It" (Sabbah), 325

Shamir government, 33
Sharon, Ariel, 172
Sharon government (2001–2003),
    319–20, 331–32, 339n55
Shepherd's Field, 254
Slovakia, post–Vatican II concordats, 146
social welfare
  approval date, 37
  in Basic vs. Fundamental Agreement,
    158–59
  financial obligation for, 12
  responsibility for, Church vs. state,
    75–76, 83–84, 108
Society of Saint Yves, 314
Soloveitchik, Rabbi Joseph, 356
Spain
  concordats with Holy See, 122–23, 142,
    143, 144
  human rights protection, Constitution
    of 1978, 125
  notorious settlement clause, 126
  religious affiliation statistics, 132n6,
    132n8
  religious freedom principles,
    Constitution of 1978, 123–24
  religious history, 120–22
  Second Republic hostility toward
    religion, 121–22
  transition to democracy, 122–23
Spain, church-state relations
  Autonomous Communities structure
    for, 125–27
  as European model, 125
  post–Vatican II, 97, 122
  religious minorities agreement system,
    125–31
  Spanish agreements vs. Fundamental
    Agreement, 119–20, 123, 127–31
  Spanish Constitution establishing,
    123–24
  Spanish history relevant to,
    120–22

transitional agreements,
122–23
Spanish Constitution (1978), 123–24,
134n25–29
Status Quo arrangement
British rule and the, 79, 254–55
Christian community position, 6–7
evolution of, 79, 157–58
Holy Places and the, 19n45, 78–81,
157, 254–55
Holy See desire for, 157–58
international recognition of,
254–55
interpreting the meaning of,
268n35
purpose of, 78
right to property and the, 84–85
right of worship within the, 80–81
taxation and the, 11, 85
Stendhal, Bishop Krister, 352
Succession Law, 259, 263, 274n114

Taif Agreements (1989), 292–93
Taqqanot of Valladolid (1432), 121
Tauran, Jean-Louis, 4, 316, 318
taxation. *See also* economic issues;
financial matters
church-state agreements, Spain, 126
exemption from, 85
Fischer-Chouvel agreement, 11,
23n.89, 85
Spanish agreements vs. Fundamental
Agreement, 130
Status Quo arrangement and, 85
Vatican-Israel relations, effect on,
11–13, 23n89
Taylor, Myron C., 38
Temple Mount (Haram al-Sharif),
256–57, 270n63
*Tertio Millennio Adveniente* (John Paul II),
238–39
Tiberias, Lake. *See* Sea of Galilee

"Together Before God for the Common
Good of the Person and Society"
(pastoral letter, 1994), 327
Tomb of the Virgin (Mare Nostrum),
78, 157, 164n38, 254
tourism, right to, 39, 210
treaty interpretation, bilateral vs.
multilateral, 67–69, 88n6
Treaty of Peace (Israel and Jordan,
1994), 255
Tunisia, 101–2, 110, 145
Turkey, pilgrimage rights in, 212
"Two Concepts of Liberty" (Berlin), 184

Ukraine, pilgrimage in, 230n120
UN Charter, 236
UN Convention on the Rights of the
Child (1989), 262
UN Declaration on the Elimination of
Religious Intolerance (1981), 211–12
UN Declaration on the Right to Leave
and Return (1986), 210
Universal Declaration of Human Rights
(UDHR, 1948)
basic principles of, 236–38
religious freedom
—freedom to maintain a religion
without interference, 189–91
—freedom to proselytize, 189–91,
194, 200n54
—in Israel, effect on, 252
—Israel vs. Holy See obligations,
185–86
—limitations under, 253
—pilgrimage, 81, 209–11
—right to change one's belief, 155–56,
186–88, 191, 194
right to return provision vs. right to
entry, 210–11
Roosevelt (Eleanor) on charter of,
224n74
Urbach, Ephraim, 346–47

Vagts, Detlev, 210
Vatican City, 205–8, 219n25, 220n30
Vatican–Holy See juridical differences, 206
Vatican II
    anti-Semitism, cooperation in
        combating guidelines, 73–74
    church-state relations, impact on, 142–43
    on right to freedom of religion, 240
Vatican II, church-state relations, 97–99,
    108
    Islamic countries, 101–2, 110–11
    Latin America, 99–101
    summary, 102
Vienna Convention on the Law of
    Treaties, 88n3, 204–5, 208
Vietnam, pilgrimage regulation in, 214

"We Remember" (1998), 321–22, 353
Western Wall, 79, 177, 254, 322
World Peace Day (1982), 245
World Peace Day (1991), 243
World Tourism Organization, 210
worship, right to, 80–81, 254, 256–57,
    331–32. *See also* religious freedom

Yad Veshem (Holocaust memorial
    center), 177, 322
Yemen, 297n9
Yugoslavian Concordats (1936, 1966), 145

Zeitlin, Solomon, 344
Zionism, 1–2, 55–56, 287–90. *See also*
    Jews/Jewish people